C000108583

ANTHROPOLOGY AND CLIMATE CHANGE

In this third edition of *Anthropology and Climate Change*, Susan Crate and Mark Nuttall offer a collection of chapters that examine how anthropologists work on climate change issues with their collaborators, both in academic research and practicing contexts, and discuss new developments in contributions to policy and adaptation at different scales. Building on the first edition's pioneering focus on anthropology's burgeoning contribution to climate change research, policy, and action, as well as the second edition's focus on transformations and new directions for anthropological work on climate change, this new edition reveals the extent to which anthropologists' contributions are considered to be critical by climate scientists, policymakers, affected communities, and other rights-holders. Drawing on a range of ethnographic and policy issues, this book highlights the work of anthropologists in the full range of contexts – as scholars, educators, and practitioners from academic institutions to government bodies, international science agencies and foundations, working in interdisciplinary research teams and with community research partners.

The contributions to this new edition showcase important new academic research, as well as applied and practicing approaches. They emphasize human agency in the archaeological record, the rapid development in the last decade of community-based and community-driven research and disaster research; provide rich ethnographic insight into worldmaking practices, interventions, and collaborations; and discuss how, and in what ways, anthropologists work in policy areas and engage with regional and global assessments.

This new edition is essential for established scholars and for students in anthropology and a range of other disciplines, including environmental studies, as well as for practitioners who engage with anthropological studies of climate change in their work.

Susan A. Crate is an environmental and cognitive anthropologist and Professor Emeritus of George Mason University, USA.

Mark Nuttall is Professor and Henry Marshall Tory Chair of Anthropology at the University of Alberta, Canada. He is also Adjunct Professor at Ilisimatusarfik/University of Greenland and the Greenland Climate Research Centre in Nuuk, and Fellow of the Royal Society of Canada.

"This third edition of *Anthropology and Climate Change* is an excellent assemblage of articles and case studies exploring the reorientations required for fully capturing the multiple and complexly intertwined challenges of climate change, the need to reconfigure through a process of world-making different ways (worlds) of envisioning how we relate to one another and to our environments, and finally, the problems and pitfalls that occur when global policy fails to recognize local capacities and vulnerabilities. Challenging the neoliberal logic that negates the possibility of other possible futures, essentially construing neoliberal capitalism as some ultimate stage of human evolution (Baschet 2003), the authors assert that anthropology thus must tap into the full array of resources, past, contemporary and imagined, for guides for creating alternative futures beyond the current relentless construction of risk. Framing the focus of the third edition with the subtitle "From Transformations to World-Making," Crate and Nuttall and the various authors contend that if climate change doesn't move us toward imagining other worlds (ways) than current neoliberal approaches, we never will, and the consequences will be catastrophic. The third edition of *Anthropology and Climate Change* moves that discussion significantly forward."

Anthony Oliver-Smith, *Professor Emeritus of Anthropology, University of Florida*

ANTHROPOLOGY AND CLIMATE CHANGE

From Transformations to Worldmaking

Third Edition

Edited by Susan A. Crate and Mark Nuttall

Routledge
Taylor & Francis Group

NEW YORK AND LONDON

Designed cover image: At the terminus of Iterlassuup Qinngua (the Sun Glacier), a tidal outlet glacier north of Qaanaaq in Northwest Greenland (Photograph Mark Nuttall).

Third edition published 2024
by Routledge
605 Third Avenue, New York, NY 10158

and by Routledge
4 Park Square, Milton Park, Abingdon, Oxon OX14 4RN

Routledge is an imprint of the Taylor & Francis Group, an informa business

© 2024 selection and editorial matter, Susan A. Crate and Mark Nuttall; individual chapters, the contributors

The right of Susan A. Crate and Mark Nuttall to be identified as the authors of the editorial material, and of the authors for their individual chapters, has been asserted in accordance with sections 77 and 78 of the Copyright, Designs and Patents Act 1988.

All rights reserved. No part of this book may be reprinted or reproduced or utilised in any form or by any electronic, mechanical, or other means, now known or hereafter invented, including photocopying and recording, or in any information storage or retrieval system, without permission in writing from the publishers.

Trademark notice: Product or corporate names may be trademarks or registered trademarks and are used only for identification and explanation without intent to infringe.

First edition published by Left Coast Press 2009
Second edition published by Routledge 2016

Library of Congress Cataloging-in-Publication Data
Names: Crate, Susan Alexandra, editor. | Nuttall, Mark, editor.
Title: Anthropology and climate change : from transformations to worldmaking / Edited by Susan A. Crate and Mark Nuttall.
Description: Third edition. | New York, NY : Routledge, 2024. | Includes bibliographical references and index.
Identifiers: LCCN 2023023768 | ISBN 9781032150925 (hardback) | ISBN 9781032150932 (paperback) | ISBN 9781003242499 (ebook)
Subjects: LCSH: Climatic changes. | Climatic changes–Social aspects. | Ethnology. | Anthropology.
Classification: LCC QC981.8.C5 A63 2024 | DDC 304.2/5–dc23/eng/20230524
LC record available at https://lccn.loc.gov/2023023768

ISBN: 978-1-032-15092-5 (hbk)
ISBN: 978-1-032-15093-2 (pbk)
ISBN: 978-1-003-24249-9 (ebk)

DOI: 10.4324/9781003242499

Typeset in Sabon
by Taylor & Francis Books

CONTENTS

PART II
Worldmaking Practices

ILLUSTRATIONS

Figures

Tables

CONTRIBUTORS

Astrid Oberborbeck Andersen is Associate Professor in the Department of Culture and Learning, Aalborg University. Her research centers on human–environment relations and anthropological perspectives on climate change. She is a co-editor of *Rubber Boots Methods for the Anthropocene: Doing fieldwork in multispecies worlds* (University of Minnesota Press 2023).

Beatriz Barros is an activist and PhD candidate in Anthropology at Indiana University Bloomington who is devoted to environmental and social justice.

Sydney Blume helped co-found ClimAct in 2018, drawing on her Sustainable Development degree from Appalachian State and undergraduate research on the Zapatistas. With a Master's in Food Systems, Sydney now explores climate justice through food working at Blue Ridge Women in Agriculture. Her research and work centers on food sovereignty, agroforestry, agroecology, and community organizing. She enjoys gardening and thinking about shifting subjectivities that align with a climate just world.

Eduardo Sonnewend Brondizio is Distinguished Professor of Anthropology and Director of the Center for the Analysis of Social and Ecological Landscapes and Senior Research Fellow of the Ostrom Workshop at Indiana University, Bloomington. His long-term research program connects on-the-ground research in Amazonia and international collaborative research on global environmental and climate change. He served as co-Chair of the Global Assessment Report of IPBES and is co-Editor-in-Chief of Global Environmental Change.

Brian Burke is Associate Professor in the Department of Sustainable Development at Appalachian State University and co-founder of ClimAct. His research examines how communities mobilize to address environmental and economic injustices via solidarity economies and community organizing. He feels continually and productively trapped between the violence of his bourgeois existence and the possibilities of living justice fully, and he is grateful to his students and son for always nudging him in the right direction.

Susan Alexandra Crate is Professor Emeritus of Environmental and Cognitive Anthropology at George Mason University, who since 2005 has analyzed perceptions, understandings, and responses to climate change among Sakha, Arctic Canadian, Peruvian, Welsh, I-Kiribati, Mongolian, and Chesapeake watermen communities. Her most recent book is *Once Upon the Permafrost: Knowing culture and climate change in Siberia* (Univ Arizona Press 2021). She was lead author on the IPCC Special Report on Oceans and Cryosphere and AAA's Task Force on Climate Change. She resides in Bynum, NC where she works on building resilient communities at home and afar.

Raychelle Aluaq Daniel is Yup'ik and grew up in the village of Tuntutuliak, Alaska located at the mouth of the Kuskokwim River and Bering Sea. She works to equitably bridge Indigenous knowledge and science, advance the co-production of knowledge, and identify policy priorities from an Indigenous perspective. In the Office of Science and Technology Policy, she served as Deputy Director for the Arctic Executive Steering Committee and Policy Advisor on Indigenous knowledge. She worked at the Pew Charitable Trusts US Arctic Program.

Second Chairman Donald Dardar was born and raised in Pointe-au-Chien and has served as the Tribe's Second Chairman since 1999. Donald began fishing and trapping with his father as a child. A life-long commercial fisherman, he represents the Tribe on the First People's Conservation Council of Louisiana (FPCC) and Gulf Organized Fisheries in Solidarity and Hope (GO FISH). His first language is Indian French. He is very active in cultural preservation efforts, including the maintenance and preservation of sacred sites and burial mounds.

Elder Theresa Dardar is an advocate for the Gulf of Mexico ecosystems and coastal Louisiana's tribal communities. A Pointe-au-Chien Indian Tribal Member, Elder Theresa serves as a spokesperson from local to international forums, like the UN Human Rights of Indigenous Peoples Conference. Theresa is a First People's Conservation Council of Louisiana (FPCC) leader. She was the Diocesan American Indian liaison at the Catholic Diocese of Houma-Thibodaux. Her work voices justice concerns for her tribe and greater native community.

Dennis Davis is a self-taught Inupiat photographer and has been taking pictures and videos of the western coastline of Alaska for over twenty years. He uses an Inupiat vision of the connections between land, animals, and people to create new forms of photography and video, that offer a glimpse into the subsistence lifestyle. Dennis's goal is to show others what his culture is all about; to highlight the risks that Arctic peoples face with the coming of climate change; and to give a voice to his people.

Penelope Dransart is Honorary Reader at the University of Aberdeen. Since 1986, she has worked with pastoralists of llamas and alpacas in Isluga, Chile. Her research focuses on herding practices, seasonal rituals, fleece and weaving in the context of changing weather events. She is author of *Earth, Water, Fleece and Fabric* (2002), co-author of *Textiles from the Andes* (2011), and co-editor of *Animales humanos, humanos animales.*

Relaciones y transformaciones en mundos indígenas sudamericanos (2022). In 2022 she was awarded a Janet Arnold travel grant.

A.J. Faas is Associate Professor of Anthropology at San José State University and the author of *In the Shadow of Tungurahua: Disaster politics in Highland Ecuador* (2022).

Janne Flora is Associate Professor in the Department of Anthropology, Aarhus University. Her research is concerned with human–environment relations in hunting communities in Greenland. She is author of *Wandering Spirits: Loneliness and longing in Greenland* (Chicago 2019).

Sarah Forgesson (Ngāti Whakaue) is the Climate Heritage Specialist of the International Co-Sponsored Meeting on Culture, Heritage, and Climate Change at ICOMOS. She is also working on the *Alliance for Research on Cultural Heritage in Europe* project via ICCROM, and previously worked as part of the CAAL (Central Asian Archaeological Landscapes). Sarah is currently in the process of completing doctoral research focused on Indigenous solutions to the impact of climate change of heritage landscapes, based in the South Pacific.

Donna Green is an environmental scientist and Associate Professor at the University of New South Wales, Sydney with international recognition for world-leading multidisciplinary applied research on the disproportionate health impacts of climate change, energy policy and air pollution.

Anne Stevens Henshaw is Programme Officer with Oak Foundation where she supports the rights of Indigenous Peoples in community-led conservation, food sovereignty, co-management and to engage in international governance policy forums. Before Oak, she was Visiting Professor in the Sociology and Anthropology Department at Bowdoin College 1996–2007, and Director of Bowdoin's Coastal Studies Center 2000–2007. She holds a PhD in Anthropology from Harvard University and a BA, magma cum laude, from the University of New Hampshire in Anthropology.

Grete K. Hovelsrud is Professor of Environmental Sociology, Nordland Research Institute and Nord University, Bodø, Norway. She conducts research in East and West Greenland, Svalbard, and Northern Norway, focusing on interdisciplinary studies of adaptation to climate change, adaptive capacity of coupled social-ecological systems, on transformation to a low-emission society, and how to best co-produce knowledge. She is President of the Norwegian Scientific Academy for Polar Research and International Arctic Social Sciences Association.

Jerry K. Jacka is Professor of Environmental Anthropology at the University of Colorado Boulder. His research examines the intersections of resource extraction, climate change, and societal responses to environmental disruptors.

Alessandra Jerolleman is a community resilience specialist and applied researcher at the Lowlander Center and co-founder of Hazard Resilience, a US-based consultancy providing leadership and expertise in disaster recovery, risk reduction, and hazard policy.

She is Associate Professor of Emergency Management at Jacksonville State University and expert in climate adaptation, hazard mitigation, and resilience. She works in the public, private, and nonprofit sectors, including with the Lowlander Center on coastal community resettlement.

Franz Krause is Professor of Environmental Anthropology at the University of Cologne. He has conducted research in Finnish Lapland, Southwest England, Estonia, and the Canadian Arctic. He works with Gwich'in and Inuvialuit inhabitants of the Mackenzie Delta of the Canadian Northwest Territories, with a broad approach to everyday life, struggles, and well-being. He studies the role of water in society and culture, from irrigation to flood management and from hydropower to ice roads and permafrost thaw. He is the author of *Thinking Like a River* (2023) and co-editor of *Delta Life: Exploring dynamic environments where rivers meet the sea* (Berghahn 2021).

Courtney Kurlanska is Assistant Professor of Teaching at Worcester Polytechnic Institute (WPI) in Massachusetts and co-directs the Ecuador Project Center in Cuenca, Ecuador. Before WPI, she held positions at the University of Akron, Appalachian State University, and at Rochester Institute of Technology. Kurlanska conducts research on the social and solidarity economy and alternative economies. She also examines the impact and efficacy of innovative pedagogy such as Open Educational Resources (OERs), ungrading, and cultural competency across the curriculum.

Jonella Ququngaq Larson, a lifelong Alaskan, Jonella/Ququngaq (Yupik) is committed to using her knowledge to help others meet the needs of their communities. Jonella was raised in Nome with strong family ties to Savoonga on St. Lawrence Island. She and her children are tribal citizens of the Native Village of Savoonga. She earned her Bachelor of Arts in Alaska Native and Rural Development with an emphasis in cultural documentation and community planning from University of Alaska Fairbanks and a Masters in Museum Studies from Harvard University.

Heather Lazrus was an environmental anthropologist at the National Center for Atmospheric Research (NCAR) in Boulder, Colorado. She co-founded the Rising Voices Center for Indigenous and Earth Sciences at NCAR, centering Indigenous knowledge systems in Earth sciences for innovative responses to climate change. Heather's research contributed to improving the utility of weather forecasts and warnings, reducing social vulnerability to atmospheric hazards, and understanding cultural adaptations to climate change.

Rebecca Lovingood is a retired physical oceanographer. She is sharing her past experience working with both brown and blue water oceanography and regulatory agencies to assist in mitigation of coastal erosion and restoring the dredged canals. She is assisting the First People's Conservation Council of Louisiana (FPCC) as research coordinator and administrator. She is also the team leader for the Presbytery of South Louisiana Disaster Preparation Team.

Erin Dougherty Lynch is Managing Attorney of Native American Rights Fund's (NARF) Alaska office. She has represented the Bering Sea Elders Group since 2010 and is also counsel in two federal court cases representing a Tribe, a tribal organization, and

Alaska Native individuals to protect Alaska Native subsistence rights. Erin received her JD from the University of Michigan Law School and her BA from Willamette University. She was a Fulbright Scholar at University of Tromsø and is a member of the Alaska Bar, and several United States bars.

Pamela McElwee is Professor of Human Ecology at the School of Environmental and Biological Sciences at Rutgers University. She has served as a lead author for both the Intergovernmental Panel on Climate Change (IPCC) and Intergovernmental Science-Policy Platform for Biodiversity and Ecosystem Services (IPBES), and is currently co-Chair of the upcoming IPBES "nexus" assessment on the interlinkages between biodiversity, water, food, climate, and health. She holds a joint PhD in Anthropology and Forestry from Yale University.

Elizabeth Marino is Associate Professor of Anthropology at Oregon State University-Cascades. She studies the relationships among climate change, vulnerability, slow and rapid onset disasters, human migration, and sense of place. She focuses on how historically and socially constructed vulnerabilities interact with climate change and disasters – including disaster policy, biophysical outcomes of disasters and climate change, and disaster discourses. She is also interested in how people make sense of changing environmental and social conditions; and how people interpret risk.

Julie Maldonado is Associate Director and co-founder of the Livelihoods Knowledge Exchange Network (LiKEN) and co-director of The Rising Voices Center for Indigenous and Earth Sciences. Her disciplinary background is in public anthropology, focusing on collaborations with communities experiencing repeat disasters and climate chaos, including with Tribes in coastal Louisiana to restore marsh ecosystems, reduce land loss and flood risk, and protect sacred sites; and co-initiating a network for justice-driven disaster recovery.

William Megarry is Co-Chair of the International Co-Sponsored Meeting on Culture, Heritage and Climate Change and focal point for climate change at the International Council on Monuments and Sites (ICOMOS). He is Senior Lecturer in Archaeology in the School of Natural and Built Environment at Queen's University Belfast. His research interests include the intersections between culture and climate change, island archaeologies and the use of digital technologies for heritage management.

Hana Morel is Scientific Coordinator of the International Co-Sponsored Meeting on Culture, Heritage and Climate Change at ICOMOS, and the Sustainability and Advocacy Lead for MOLA. She is also working on the Alliance for Research on Cultural Heritage in Europe project via ICCROM. Previously, she worked as Sustainability Manager for the Coastal and Intertidal Zone Archaeological Network, CITiZAN; Senior Policy Advisor (Climate Change) at Historic England (2020–21).

Mark Nuttall is Professor and Henry Marshall Tory Chair of Anthropology at the University of Alberta. He is also Adjunct Professor at Ilisimatusarfik/University of Greenland and the Greenland Climate Research Centre in Nuuk. He has carried out anthropological research in Greenland, Alaska, Canada, Finland, and Wales. His books include *Climate, Society and*

Subsurface Politics in Greenland: Under the Great Ice (Routledge 2017), and *The Shaping of Greenland's Resource Spaces: Environment, territory, geo-security* (Routledge 2023).

Ciaran O'Faircheallaigh is Professor of Politics and Public Policy at Griffith University, Brisbane. His research focuses on Indigenous governance especially as it relates to large-scale resource development on Indigenous lands. For over thirty years he has acted as a negotiator and advisor for Indigenous communities in Australia and Canada.

Mira Olson is Associate Professor in the Civil, Architectural, and Environmental Engineering Department at Drexel University, protecting source water quality, including remediation of contaminated groundwater, assessing the impact of water resources technologies and policies on source water supply, and predicting the fate and transport of both chemical and biological agents in the environment. She is Director of the newly established Peace Engineering program at Drexel, teaching impacts of technology and partnering with communities.

Jessica O'Reilly, Associate Professor of International Studies at Indiana University Bloomington, studies the science and politics of climate change in Antarctica and among international climate experts. She is author of *The Technocratic Antarctic* (2017), and co-author of *Discerning Experts* (2019). Her National Science Foundation research is an interdisciplinary analysis of knowledge production in the Intergovernmental Panel on Climate Change. She is advisor to the Antarctic and Southern Ocean Coalition (ASOC) and the US delegation to the Antarctic Treaty meetings.

Marietta Ortega Perrier is Dean of the Faculty of Social Sciences at the University of Tarapacá in Arica, Chile. She first began fieldwork in 1978 in the highlands and pre-cordillera of the far north of Chile. Her research interests focus on the use of symbolism and rituals amongst contemporary Aymara people in broader social and political processes within Chile. After graduating in Anthropology from the University of Chile, she obtained a Master of Science in Social Anthropology at the London School of Economics and a PhD at the University of Cambridge, where she was awarded a Wyse Studentship in Social Anthropology and a Newnham College Research Studentship, amongst other distinctions. Currently she is also President of an NGO, the Corporación Chinchorro Marka, which successfully nominated and administers the UNESCO World Heritage listed "Settlement and artificial mummification of the Chinchorro Culture" (2021). Fieldwork conducted jointly with Penelope Dransart (2017) received support from the Wenner Gren Foundation.

Elder Chief Shirell Parfait-Dardar is Elder Chief of the Grand Caillou/Dulac Band of Biloxi-Chitimacha-Choctaw in Louisiana and President of First People's Conservation Council of Louisiana (FPCC). She was an advisor to LA H.B.660–Act #102 establishing the Native American Commission and the first Native American Chairwoman of the Louisiana Governor's Office of Indian Affairs Native American Commission. She is an active advocate for coastal restoration and preservation, development and utilization of alternative energy sources, community resiliency, education, and human rights.

Majken Paulsen is a senior researcher at Nordland Research Institute, Bodø Norway. Majken is a social anthropologist from University of Oslo, with a PhD in Sociology from Nord University. Her research focuses on interactions between humans and other-than-humans in northern Norway. In her PhD thesis, Majken explored the enactment of humans and animals in Sámi reindeer husbandry when the reindeer are fed.

Kristina Peterson is an applied social scientist, with decades of experience leading community-centered participatory research projects in Louisiana, who garners holistic resources for program and project development to support community endurance and sustainability in the midst of complex issues and risks like climate change, disaster events, and cultural continuity. She works on large-scale and complex disasters to create local systems of justice to develop networks and response mechanisms.

Fred Phillip of Kwigillingok, Alaska, serves as Chair of the Bering Sea Elders Group (BSEG), protecting traditional ways of life and the Bering Sea since 2007. Fred is a US Navy veteran, served in the Alaska Army National Guard, and has held leadership roles at a variety of organizations in the Yukon-Kuskokwim region. For over a decade Fred has been a critical player in awareness of the importance of traditional knowledge, tribal stewardship of traditional lands and waters, and prioritizing the preservation of traditional ways of life.

Elder Rosina Philippe is an Atakapa-Ishak/Chawasha Tribal Elder and former First People's Conservation Council of Louisiana (FPCC) President. She focuses on partnering with leaders to address climate change, environmental justice, gentrification, and coastal restoration/preservation. Elder Philippe is a firm believer that people facing similar problems, through informed education and information sharing, can affect positive long-term changes and, through collaboration, take charge of their own destinies, to build a more resilient, humane, and sustainable life.

Ornella Puschiasis is Associate Professor of Geography in the Department of South Asia and Himalaya at the National Institute of Languages and Oriental Civilization (INALCO) in Paris, France. She is affiliated to the Center for Social Studies on African, American and Asian Worlds and to the Center for South Asian and Himalayan Studies in France. Her research is concerned with human-nature interactions focusing on a social approach of water and climate in Nepal. Her recent work explore the Sherpa diaspora in North America and the long distance relationship with their environment.

Katie Quail is a PhD candidate at the Climate Change Research Centre, UNSW, Sydney. Her research focuses on maximizing benefits for First Nations peoples in the context of climate change, with a specific focus on large-scale renewable energy developments on Indigenous lands. She has a background in science and education having previously worked as a high school mathematics teacher in both Australia and the UK.

Camilla Risvoll is a senior researcher (PhD, Sociology), at Nordland Research Institute, Bodø Norway. Camilla is a sociologist specializing in human–environment interactions in various settings. Her focus is on knowledge systems, co-production methods and on local adaptation in contexts related to food systems, with a particular emphasis on Sámi reindeer husbandry sheep farming and fjord fisheries in northern Norway.

Carla Roncoli is Faculty in the Departments of Anthropology and Environmental Sciences and Director of the Master's in Development Practice at Emory University. She studies how rural producers in Africa engage different knowledge systems in making agricultural and livelihood decisions under conditions of climate uncertainty. For nearly three decades, she has conducted research in Burkina Faso, and more recently, among smallholder farmers in East Africa and the southeast United States. She is contributing author for the IPCC 5th and 6th Reports (WGII).

Arlene Miller Rosen is Professor of Anthropology and Environmental Archaeology at University of Texas at Austin. She works on human–environmental relations during later prehistory and in early complex societies in the Mediterranean Levant, China, Mongolia, and New Mexico. She is the author of *Civilizing Climate* (2007), a special issue entitled *The Anthropocene in the Longue Durée* (The Holocene 2015) and numerous journal articles. She serves as Associate Editor for the journal, *The Holocene* and sits on the editorial board of *Journal of Anthropological Archaeology*.

Pasang Yangjee Sherpa is a Sharwa anthropologist from Pharak, northeastern Nepal. She is an assistant professor of lifeways in Indigenous Asia, jointly appointed in the Institute for Critical Indigenous Studies and the department of Asian Studies at the University of British Columbia. Her research areas include climate change and Indigeneity in the Himalayas, with a focus on the Sherpa.

Astrid B. Stensrud is Associate Professor at the Department of Global Development and Planning, University of Agder. She is the author of *Watershed Politics and Climate Change in Peru* (Pluto Press 2021) and co-editor of *Climate, Capitalism and Communities: An anthropology of environmental overheating* (Pluto Press 2019).

Sarah Strauss is Professor of Anthropology at Worcester Polytechnic Institute (WPI) and co-directs the Community Climate Adaptation graduate program. She taught at the University of Wyoming for 24 years, and has been visiting faculty at NCAR (US National Center for Atmospheric Research), University of Fribourg (CH), and Pondicherry University (IN), and served on the AAA's Global Climate Change Task Force. She is co-editor of *Weather, Climate, Culture* (2003) and *Cultures of Energy* (2013).

Julie Torres, a lifelong southeast Louisiana resident, has Bachelor of Science degrees in Earth and Environmental Sciences with a concentration in Coastal Science, a degree in Biology with a concentration in Ecology, and a Master of Science degree in Coastal Geomorphology from the University of New Orleans. Julie has skills in field biology, environmental monitoring, teaching, and using GIS to support technical papers, non-profits, and Jean Lafitte National Park. She is currently an Environmental Consultant with Environmental Resource Management (ERM).

Colin Thor West is a human ecologist in the Department of Anthropology at the University of North Carolina – Chapel Hill (UNC-CH). He has conducted long-term environmental fieldwork in northern Burkina Faso among Mossi smallholders. His research focuses on household adaptation to climate change, which he investigates through the lens of sustainable livelihoods.

Robert Eugene Turner is LSU Boyd Professor at Louisiana State University. His research focuses on biological oceanography, conservation, environmental management, restoration, and wetlands. He has led projects focused on hypoxia and water quality issues of the Mississippi River and adjacent wetlands and the impact of the Deepwater Horizon Oil Spill on the Louisiana coastal environments. He works with the First People's Conservation Council of Louisiana (FPCC) to restore the dredged canals surrounding their communities, mitigate present and future climate hazards, and protect their sacred sites.

Michael Z. Weiss graduated from Appalachian State in 2021 with a BS in Sustainable Development. He continues to explore the nexus of climate justice, community organizing, participatory democracy, and cooperative economics, and he has some gorgeous houseplants.

Meredith Welch-Devine is Associate Professor of Anthropology and Assistant Dean of the Graduate School at University of Georgia. She studies climate change adaptation, collective management of common-pool resources, and policy related to climate and conservation. Her interdisciplinary project in the northern Basque Country seeks to understand how to sustain pastoral systems in a changing climate. She has explored the impacts of extreme weather events on people and examined perceptions of climate change using political ecology and ethnoecology.

Richard Wilk is Distinguished Provost's Professor Emeritus at Indiana University, where he has researched and written on many anthropological topics, all concerned with culture and the environment.

INTRODUCTION

From Transformations to Worldmaking

Susan A. Crate and Mark Nuttall

The first edition of *Anthropology and Climate Change: From encounters to actions* was published in 2009 and has been considered by reviewers and colleagues in anthropology, as well as those from other disciplines in the social sciences and humanities, as a landmark volume. It was inspired by, on the one hand, the huge potential we saw within anthropology to work in climate change spheres and, on the other, by a concern with the paucity of activities to do so. We were both involved in research that was seeking to understand how climate change was affecting the people with whom we had been working in Siberia and Greenland over the previous twenty years, how they were experiencing the transformations in their surroundings, the anxieties and concerns that preoccupied them, and how they were pondering ways of responding and adapting. We were also collaborating with colleagues in the natural and physical sciences and participating in regional and global assessments of climate change. In developing that first book, we set out to bring together anthropologists who were doing similar things, or who were venturing into unknown research terrain, to write about their work and to reflect, where possible, on their experiences as well as the theoretical and methodological challenges that confronted them. The result was a volume that assessed the novel ways anthropologists were engaging with climate change in a diversity of ethnographic and policy settings, showcased important new academic research, as well as applied and practicing approaches, and issued a call to the discipline for action.

Our second edition (subtitled *from actions to transformations*), seven years later in 2016, explored some of the many directions and areas in which scholars and practitioners had taken their work to understand and address climate change. It featured both authors from the first edition and new scholars and practitioners with the aim of updating anthropological engagements with the rapidly changing field of climate-related studies. That second volume was published at a time when it had become more acceptable to refer informally (but increasingly in published work) to Earth's current geological epoch as the Anthropocene (even if this is still, at the time we were completing this book, an unofficial term), as distinct from the Holocene. This also drew more attention to anthropology as an area of enquiry concerned with, among many things, understanding

DOI: 10.4324/9781003242499-1

how the world has been transformed, modified, and impacted by human action – including those activities that have contributed to anthropogenic climate change – in a continual process of engagement between people and their surroundings, and prevalent since industrialization in more capital-intensive forms of extraction and production.

And now, another seven years later as it goes to press in late 2023, this third edition builds on the first two to update and examine anew how anthropologists work on climate change issues with their collaborators, both in academic research and practicing contexts, and to discuss new developments in contributions to policy and adaptation at different scales. In a sense, this third volume represents our discipline's fullest development within what was once a nascent field. Not only are more and more anthropologists working on some aspect of climate change research that is deeply entrenched with the discipline's many endeavors, both the nature of our work and the value of our contributions are increasingly accepted and understood as critical contributions by both social and natural scientists and by policymakers, affected communities and other rights-holders. Herein we decided that "transformations and worldmaking practices" were the appropriate descriptors for the current state of the field and to frame how our contributors crafted their respective chapters. As we did for the second edition, we have also invited contributors who have been with us since the first volume as well as others – both senior and emerging scholars, and community-based research partners – who work on climate change and are focusing on reorientations, worldmaking practices, interfaces, and interventions. This book, then, highlights the work of anthropologists in the full range of contexts – as scholars, educators, and practitioners, from academic institutions to government bodies, international science agencies and foundations, working in interdisciplinary research teams, and with community research collaborators.

But the move, seven years later, into developing our third edition, to track further the evolution of anthropology and climate change, came with at least two major global disruptions. First, at the time when our publisher contacted us about a third edition, the world was one year into the Covid-19 pandemic, a global health crisis that was unprecedented in the experience of most of us living on the planet today. Then, one year later, in February 2022, Russia invaded Ukraine and we witnessed a shutting down on a completely different level. The war in Ukraine has broken a three-decade period of East–West cooperation following the end of the Cold War. What a moment in history to be reflecting on and writing about worldmaking! In many ways, however, with the urgency of both the pandemic and the war in Ukraine, it seemed that efforts and progress made in taking action on climate change had been pushed to the back burner. Of course, these more immediate crises demanded attention, and they still do. But climate change has continued to accelerate. According to meteorologists, the last decade has been the warmest on record, with global temperatures in 2022 being the sixth highest since modern record keeping began in 1880.[1] In December 2020, at the end of the first year that had seen the devastating effects of the Covid-19 pandemic, UN Secretary-General António Guterres warned that humanity is waging war on nature and called on the world to declare a climate emergency. In October 2022, on the release of the UN Environment Programme's (UNEP) *Emissions Gap Report 2022*, which shows that Earth is heading for 2.8 degrees of warming by the end of this century, Guterres reiterated that the window is closing for taking action and, unless countries scale-up their efforts to tackle climate change, the world faces catastrophe.[2] In March 2023, the Intergovernmental Panel on

Climate Change (IPCC) released the *AR6 Synthesis Report: Climate Change 2023*, which summarizes five years of reports on global temperature rise, fossil fuel emissions and climate impacts. It acknowledged that there had been some progress in policies and legislation around climate mitigation since the previous synthesis report (AR5) was published in 2014. However, like the UNEP's report, the AR6 warned that it is likely that warming will exceed 1.5°C this century. Furthermore, it stressed that the viability of human life within planetary boundaries will depend on the action to be taken in the next seven years. Four months after the publication of the AR6 report, as scientists warned that July was likely to be the hottest month on record, Guterres declared that the era of global warming had ended and that the world had entered the "era of global boiling."[3] The question becomes *can* we not also continue to make a world that is prepared to address the existential challenge of climate change?

In framing our introductory words to this third edition in the context of these new layers of uncertainty, we emphasize that climate change has to be understood alongside multiple stressors. As the first two volumes of *Anthropology and Climate Change* show – and indeed, the work of many other anthropologists does – climate change is not always the most immediately pressing issue, concern, or preoccupation in people's lives. Rather, it magnifies and amplifies other social, economic, political, and environmental circumstances and challenges people are confronted with and which they have to deal with and negotiate on a daily basis (Nuttall et al. 2005; Crate and Nuttall 2009). Although it is recognized that societies around the world, whether urban or rural, are being affected by climate change in some way, the impacts are often disproportionate and uneven. For many communities, regions, and even nations, the impacts highlight existing socio-economic situations and inequalities. Climate change is a complex interplay of physical processes, environmental, historical, social, and economic factors. Its effects are highly variable and regionally specific and so it follows that climate change will be consequential for people and for local and regional economies in multiple and contrasting ways. Some environments and peoples are more exposed to the effects of climate change than others and, as a result of their social, political, and economic circumstances and situations, they are significantly more vulnerable to its impacts and long-term consequences. Even groups within the same environment are affected more than others due to disparities and inequities at local levels. For Indigenous peoples in Canada's Mackenzie Delta, for instance, who, like other Indigenous communities in the country are dealing with the legacies and the intergenerational trauma of profoundly disruptive social and cultural change, climate change matters, but it is a colonial echo, as Franz Krause phrases their experience in his chapter in this volume.

Both Covid-19 and the war in Ukraine amplify the complexity we wrote about in the first two books. The pandemic and later the war have and continue to alter life around the globe. Early on in the pandemic, and based on the immediate response to Covid-19 to isolate and coordinate, there was much written in the media – both mainstream and social – that stressed the opportunity the world now had: at the time it was argued that if we could organize and respond to Covid-19 effectively, then presumably we could also do so in the face of climate change. As motorways were emptied of traffic, as the skies were clear of aircraft, as smog and haze lifted, and as global air pollution declined, there was optimism that the world could head into a brighter, cleaner future once the pandemic ended.

The emergence and spread of Covid-19 also, and obviously, raised serious questions about its origins. Was it created and released accidentally, unwittingly, or on purpose, from a laboratory, many asked; or was it another case of how, as *The New York Times* put it, humanity has unleashed new diseases that have jumped from animals to humans as a result of habitat destruction and the ruination of ecosystems?[4] Either way, Covid-19 was framed as anthropogenic – if it was not manufactured, it was argued, then it was the result of our intervention into, and destruction of biodiversity and planetary boundaries (just as climate change is). While geologists look for stratigraphic markers in the world's subsurface as evidence for the Anthropocene, the human imprint is more immediately observed above ground. Early in the pandemic, stories circulated in the global media that the coronavirus was transmitted to humans from bats, or the Malayan pangolin used in traditional Chinese medicine, or from bush meat sold in Southeast Asian markets, or that factory farming played its part. In March 2023, it was reported that data being analyzed by a WHO committee appeared to show there was a likelihood that animals including racoon dogs, as well as seafood, present at the Huanan market in Wuhan, China, were potentially infected with a form of coronavirus (Crits-Christoph et al. 2023). In this way, the pandemic and climate change have been linked as manifestations of the human violation of wildlife and their habitats, the illegal trade of wild species, and the transformation of global ecosystems. And, as a number of scholars point out, the melting cryosphere also means we could face more epidemics and pandemics given that icy ground such as permafrost is considered to be a potential reservoir of microbial pathogens (e.g., Malavin et al. 2020). As permafrost thaws, the risk is that uncharacterized microorganisms and viruses could be released. Wu et al. (2022), for example, argue that so little is known about permafrost-resident microbes that the risk they pose to humans, animals, and plants is uncertain and potentially enormous.

The communication of the severity of the pandemic was then, and still is, as urgent as it is for climate change. The early encouraging thought that we could come together in a global, unified way to tackle pandemics and climate change was short-lived, however. As lockdown measures were extended by governments around the world, many people, exasperated and exhausted, clung to the idea that life would go back to normal after much of the global population was vaccinated. It is almost as if the pandemic has been seen as an intrusion into the modernity which many people regard as having made a risk-free world. While concentrations of tropospheric and ground-level pollution may have been reduced (Venter et al. 2020), for governments and businesses, lockdown prevented everything that was essential and necessary for the workings of the modern world – global economic activity, mobility, and global connectivity. It did not take long for politicians, corporate leaders, airports, and airlines to stress the urgency of getting back to business and back to normal, which meant getting people back in their cars, back to work, back to flying, and back to being global consumers. After all, economic models for nation states and the corporate world tend to be predicated on the idea and pursuit of growth.

In May 2023, the World Health Organization (WHO) downgraded the Covid-19 pandemic. It no longer defines it as the public health emergency of international concern it had declared it to be in January 2020 (the WHO characterized the outbreak as a pandemic in March 2020). However, dangerous strains of coronavirus continue to be identified and scientists warn that the risks Covid-19 presents have not gone away. Indeed, in an editorial in January 2023, *The Lancet* called the global response inadequate and fragmented.[5] Yet, following the WHO position, many governments no longer consider Covid-19 to be a public health emergency and have lifted most, if not all, of the measures they had imposed beginning in 2020. No wonder there is a public perception that the pandemic is over. What hope, then, for a coordinated global effort to limit global temperature increase to 1.5°C above pre-industrial levels, as the 2015 Paris Agreement – a legally-binding international treaty on climate change ratified (as of February 2023) by 194 states and the European Union – is committed to doing? Nevertheless, climate change will continue to affect societies and economies, and we should have some optimism that the Paris Agreement will be effective. It is also worth remembering that the WHO considers climate change to be one of the greatest public health challenges for the twenty-first century, and this is reinforced by stark warnings from the IPCC that deteriorating social and economic circumstances brought on by climate change could have significant effects on human health. But the uncertainty that the pandemic and the conflict in Ukraine bring continues to affect our lives and the work that is done to ameliorate climate change.

Anthropologists working on issues of climate change, especially in the context of other world crises like pandemics and major conflicts, must bring their work into inter-disciplinary framings and collaborations. Although there has been some progress towards interdisciplinarity in the last few decades of global change research, it remains largely a natural science endeavor. Despite calls to engage the humanities and social sciences with the natural sciences effectively in interdisciplinary research (Lahsen 2016; Castree 2014), the integration of investigations at the local scale remains underdeveloped in many instances. There is much to be done. Analyses that engage both biological and cultural complexities at local levels and their integration with larger scale natural science research are critical to facilitating community-driven adaptation appropriately. Such approaches must understand individuals and communities as *complex adaptive systems* (Crumley 2012) who perceive, understand, and respond to change at the local level but within the context of global connections (Hastrup 2013). Herein it is necessary to understand how knowledge, in its many forms (Indigenous, local, generalizable, tacit, etc.), informs humans' interactions in the context of a dynamic bio-cultural system. This, in turn, calls for an understanding of "bottom-up complexity," itself an example of interdisciplinary framing. Bottom-up-complexity exists across disciplinary fields and is used here as a hybrid of anthropological and climate science, the former conceptualized to convey the complexity of both social and cultural systems (Hastrup 2009), and the latter to describe the biophysical dynamics and consequence of climate change and other unprecedented changes (Pielke et al. 2012).

In turn, the pandemic situation and the conflict in Ukraine will usher in a new gen-eration of anthropologists working in an increasingly uncertain world who understand the need to work across disciplines as a way of examining and understanding such bottom-up complexity within a context of geopolitics. This, in turn, amplifies the need to convey that the planet is fragile and that the world is a risky place full of surprises. But has it ever been anything other? As Jeffrey Alexander (2013) writes, modernity is not progressive and liberating but masks the uncertainties and dangers inherent in the world, bringing its own fragmenting and destructive processes. This links to the discussion of knowledge systems and how our Indigenous and local collaborators know, as they always have, that there is uncertainty and danger in the world around them. Their experience in being prepared for surprises and attuned to risk further justifies engaging multiple ways of knowing in our work and daily lives. Many of these Indigenous and local communities maintain a direct and daily dependence on their environment and thereby nurture an expertise in the local with a readiness for surprises and a high capacity to be flexible and adaptable. In Northwest Greenland, for example, the world is perceived as one of constant becoming, of renewal and beginnings, in which imagination and creativity are put into daily practice. Nothing can be expected, much can be anticipated, and surprise is one thing people can be certain of (Nuttall 2009). The world is always coming into being, always being made – and worldmaking in Greenland, as Andersen and Flora show in their chapter, also arises from multispecies engagement and interaction. All of this further emphasizes the importance of the local scale which, in many ways, is the most important human scale to know and from which to proceed in addressing these issues.

This third edition also underscores where the work of anthropology and climate change has been and where it is going. When we invited the contributors, both former and new, whose chapters comprise this volume, we also asked them, where appropriate, to reflect on the trajectory of their own work since its inception. Our own stories, as we both continue ethnographic place-based work over the decades, reflect substantial change in our orientation. In the Arctic, in ever changing environments, a world of movement and surprise that challenges people and requires them to be attentive at all times, a fundamental prerequisite for survival is awareness and acknowledgement of the reality of this shifting world. Today, in the context of the Anthropocene, these inherent skills are being tested by the rapidity of the transformations being experienced. Susie recounts how over a short 12-year period, the *alaas*, Sakha's ancestral homestead areas, are literally changing under Sakha people's feet. This begs the question of what effects there are when a people see a landscape and culture-scape, once thought eternal, permanently transforming? Mark tells of the transformation people experience in northern Greenland, where ice is melting. What effect does this have on a people's sense of place, how they orient their lives/position themselves/envision their future when such changes come into their world? Beyond our field work observations and analyses, how can we communicate these sensorial experiences of change? We draw attention, for instance, to the central place of language in local experiences of climate change to the extent that there are no longer the types of ice at the times of year people expect there to be and no longer the *alaas* that people have known. Concomitantly there swells a deep sense of loss and mourning in these communities.

As Cunsolo and Ellis (2018) put it, ecological grief is a mental health response to climate change-related loss of land, animals, livelihood, and a sense of place. These kinds of changes at the local level and our capacity as anthropologists to interpret their ramifications to cultural mores and norms only verifies the continued importance of longitudinal ethnographic studies (Hoffman, Eriksen, and Mendes 2022; Sillitoe 2022). Such work has always been the hallmark of anthropology, but in the context of the Anthropocene it has evolved into a pluralistic endeavor in which we prioritize community needs, research interests, and ownership. The decolonization of research methods has been in process for decades (Smith 1999; Chilisa 2019) but its realization is happening in the local, immediate ethnographic interactions many of us find ourselves in as anthropologists.

The IPCC's 1.5 report (2018) delivered an urgent call, telling us we have only ten years to make a turnaround or we will commit to levels of temperature that will permanently transform life as we know it. Since then, the IPCC's ten-year countdown has been used to fuel many campaigns to greatly reform and even shut down the fossil fuel industry (for example, as illustrated by Greta Thunberg's campaign and by https://climateclock.world/), and it is likely that these campaigns will, now that the AR6 report has been released, stress with even more alarm that time is running out. These efforts do serve a purpose but could there be other ways to approach our predicament? As anthropologists we can consult with the diverse ancient wisdom of our collaborators and reflect on their capacity to adapt, be flexible and create new ways of being within their local and immediate worlds. In this way, such unnerving urgent calls to action can also be our path forward. Our intent in this is by no means to discount the urgency of our situation but rather to create novel approaches to it. Afterall, the ancient Greek word "apocalypse," means revelation and disclosure. So let this be a time of revelation and of full disclosure. Herein we link directly to worldmaking practices.

Worldmaking

So what kind of world(s) *are* we making? And what do we want those worlds to look like? Calls to act on climate change by scientists, activists, and by fora such as the IPCC emphasize the need for transformative social and economic change – to reflect on worldviews, rethink our ways of life, our wants, wishes, needs, and desires, our attitudes and relationships to the planet, and to envision futures that are desirable but realistic (Milkoreit 2017). As Anita Girvan (2017: 1052) puts it, "climate change challenges us to imagine the worlds we would like to inhabit through creative forward thinking." This invites interventions, manipulations, and worldmaking practices. Examples of these could be at scales that demonstrate and enact controversial programs of weather modification, such as global climate geoengineering, strategies for renewable energy such as decarbonization projects, and the rethinking and redesign of economic systems and forms of urban life. For instance, worldmaking draws our attention to techno-political practices and technofixes and how they involve knowledge and expertise in the calculation and design of future energy systems (Bridge 2015). We may see these interventions, manipulations, and practices of worldmaking as part of the envisioning of desirable futures. However, such worldmaking practices as driven by governments and corporations are often at odds with how people imagine their own futures at the level of household, community, place, and region. And technofixes, especially those that champion "green energy" initiatives, do little to tackle the very human practices and the economic and cultural values that have contributed to anthropogenic climate change in the first place. We may think that driving an electric vehicle may be better for the planet, but perhaps we need to reflect a little more deeply on the consequences that car culture has for the environment (Bohren 2009). As Jerry Jacka points out in his chapter in this volume, "green mining" for the critical minerals necessary for a post-carbon world still involves extraction. Given the pressure for increased production of renewable energy technologies, he argues that we will soon be undergoing a global imperative of extractivism. How, he asks, can we save the planet when we are turning it into a giant mine for renewable energy and the making of sustainable economies?

In his seminal book *Ways of Worldmaking*, American philosopher Nelson Goodman wrote that worldmaking consists of a process of taking apart and putting together, but that "it always starts from worlds already on hand; the making is a remaking" (Goodman 1978: 6). Goodman's concern was with asking what worlds are made of, what role words, language, and symbols have in their making, and how knowing is related to worldmaking. From this starting point, Goodman declared that his interest was in how worlds are built out of others. As such, in this process of taking apart, reassembling, and reimaging, worldmaking involves, decomposition and composition, unbecoming and becoming. But as Hilary Putnam (1979) argued, Goodman's book should be read as a defense of pluralism. There is no singular world and anthropology shows us the multiple contexts, spatial dimensions and temporalities in which people go about their daily lives.

Indeed, it can be argued that much of what anthropology does is concerned with understanding worldmaking – how people perceive and make sense of their surroundings, how they create their worlds of social relatedness, and how they nurture multispecies relations. Much of what anthropology sets out to do is about making sense of experience as well as seeking to understand the human world as a fundamentally social one that is comprised of different, yet intersecting temporal and spatial modalities. Through an anthropological lens we then can think of worldmaking, at local and regional scales, as a much more powerful response to climate change and the transformations people witness and are affected by than one that is characterized by a nervous anticipation of a future shaped by dramatic, far-reaching, and irreversible climatic, environmental, economic, political, and social change.

Worldmaking practices offer an alternative to the scientific language of tipping points and thresholds, which influences the development of narratives and policy discussions of ecological catastrophe and humanity in crisis, and which call for urgent action in the form of technofixes. A "tipping point" suggests something transformative, disruptive, decentering, and fatalistic. In climate change science it seems to point to a revival of climatic determinism that ignores human agency and the complexity of social and cultural life (Nuttall 2012). In reflecting on worldmaking, anthropologists consider agency, intentionality, and creativity, and also how people imagine themselves into the future. Such a focus brings greater clarity to understanding how people think about the world around them and the changes they notice and are affected by, how they engage with the world and move around in it, how they think ahead and imagine the future, and how they create and enact change within a world that is also undergoing a constant process of remaking and reshaping.

Because how communities perceive, respond, and adapt to change is largely based on their cultural and historical understanding of and experience in a given place, the most effective adaptation approaches are based in the Indigenous and local knowledge of that community in collaboration with scientific understandings specific to their place. Furthermore, in contexts where communities have devolved forms of government (self-governance) and territorial land claims, both enabling them to have agency in decision-making processes, such collaborative multi-science adaptation approaches will have the most success.

There are many areas where work is bringing to fruition these processes. Take, for example, Arctic Canada scientists' experience working in the last few decades with Indigenous collaborators that, in the process, are bringing about worldmaking practices:

> Evolving governance in the form of territorial devolution and Indigenous land claims have begun to transform Canada's North. We may now transition from a place

where people come from away and do things in or for the north to a future where partnerships are with the North or even led by the North. This amazing shift creates promise for a resilient northern society and a place where your contributions as permafrost scientists and engineers can increasingly be supported, understood and applied in a collaborative framework through equitable partnerships.[6]

This quote, by Steve Kokelj, Head of Permafrost Science at the Geological Survey of the Northwest Territories, reflects how scientists, who are able to offer their knowledge in a context of mutual trust and collaboration, can be agents of worldmaking via their recognition of their partners' depth of experience and understanding of their local environs. Furthermore, such collaborations, founded upon an openness to the immense diversity of not only how cultures experience and respond to change but of ecological contexts, defy the existence of any one approach to ameliorating the issues of thawing of ice-rich permafrost at local levels. Permafrost-thaw induced landscape change is heterogeneous, impacts different communities in different ways and therefore requires a wide range of adaptation strategies. Worldmaking takes on a whole new dimension. This example from Arctic Canada is one of many across the world where local and regional stakeholders are increasingly engaging with and being engaged by social and natural scientists towards more equitable and long-lasting solutions based upon worldmaking and collaboration. In turn, these processes provide deep insights for scientists of all fields to reassess and realign their own approaches to worldmaking back home and often within the context of consumer societies.

Layout of the Book

Part I: Reorientations

Here we build upon the foundational concepts and explorations of the first two volumes, bringing more sharply into light new archaeological, cultural anthropological, disaster research, interdisciplinarity, and knowledge systems research in the context of increasing changes from the local to the global. Herein contributors of the first three chapters emphasize important aspects of human agency in the archaeological record, the rapid development in the last decade of community-based and community-driven research, and a close-up view into the ethnographic underpinnings of disaster research. The final two chapters deal with anthropology's critical work within interdisciplinary research to bring all disciplines within the context of community-based projects to the fore and emphasize the importance of bringing all relevant knowledge systems into engagement with each other.

Arlene Rosen begins the section with her chapter emphasizing the importance of deep-time human–environment relationships to provide context for today's challenges. Specifically, she details how the tools of archaeology have the capacity to merge multiple deep-time histories including environmental, social/political and economic to inform the new epoch of the Anthropocene. She grounds her discussion in the history and contemporary work of environmental archaeology, showing its roots in determinism, its gradual move to recognizing human agency with the concept of Niche Construction and its further evolution to investigate issues of climate change. It is human agency that ushers in both the field's integration of concepts of adaptation, both physical and cultural, and our species' overall tendency towards subsistence intensification, advanced tool use, and social-cultural complexity. This development was not linear but worked in concert with global climatic changes, most notably the leveling off of the world's climate which began the Holocene and humans' move to settle and develop agriculture and pastoralism. The author frames her analysis using four key phases of human impact on the environment: 1) global colonization, 2) emergence and spread of agriculture and pastoralism, 3) island colonization, and 4) urbanism and the elaboration of trade networks. Much of her discussion surrounds the question of where we draw the line for the Anthropocene, considering that the archaeological record clearly shows humans as a force of environmental change and specifically atmospheric change from centuries if not millennia before present. She concludes with discussions of multispecies archaeology, which emphasizes human and non-human species mutuality and the importance of Indigenous science as both key to bringing proper context to contemporary climate change. In sum, archaeology can lend significant insights, both cautionary and prescriptive, to how humans have interacted with and altered the environment and also how they have lived in sustainable ways from deep time to present.

Meredith Welch-Devine and **Heather Lazrus** next ground us in the multitude of transformations that have taken place in the field of cultural anthropology with the advent of climate change investigations, or as they term it, climate anthropology. They begin with the disclaimer they will not be rehashing the last two decades of cultural anthropological investigations into climate change but rather draw upon that history's key messages to explore the where, how, and with whom anthropologists, both academic and "academic adjacent" *need to* do our research. The last two decades of anthropological climate enquiry clarify that anthropologists need to work with urgency, equity, and inter- and transdisciplinarity. The authors provide explicit examples, many from their own groundbreaking work, of how anthropologists can pursue these goals by detailing community-driven research, cross-scale study, team science, and engagement with science communication and policymaking. The central goal of community-driven research is for affected communities, be they Indigenous or not, to lead the research from its initial questions through to its write up, findings, and implementation. Cross-scale research provides the insight about how humans both affect the environment and are affected by it from local to global scales. Similarly, with the last decade of anthropologists actively engaged in international and regional climate policy work, it can also reveal how priorities are made and how equity can be brought into these global forums. Team science also works across scales but here it involves the many disciplines and rights- and stakeholders critical to a given context. Anthropologists need to organize such collaborations and also act as interlocuters, communicating across what can be vast divides in knowledge systems, disciplinary viewpoints and life experience. Finally, anthropologists need to engage with science communication and policymaking, specifically to be witness to this moment of decisive action and the urgency to respond. All four of these approaches work to bridge the vast differences that exist as we confront a global to local issue that is human caused and can only be human cured.

In the third foundational chapter, **A.J. Faas** takes us on an exploration of how climate change interfaces the forces of disasters and displacements in the context of a relatively long history of neoliberal colonial settlements and more recent climate change effects in several "post-disaster" resettlements in the Chimborazo Province of the Andean highlands of Ecuador. He shows how inhabitants who, pre-colonization, used forms of mobility and networks based on Ecuador's vertical archipelago that spans the microclimate, resource availabilities, and political economic interstices of the area, have since worked in increasingly horizontal directives to realize wage-labor through rural-to-urban mobility. He makes a point to differentiate mobility and itinerancy, the former being how inhabitants adapted successfully in the vertical archipelago and the latter being more of a maladaptation, an almost incessant wandering in search of opportunities that once were predictable but now are dubious due not only to the spoils of neoliberal colonial pressures but also the relatively new uncertainties of climate change. But that is not the whole story. There is also the Covid-19 pandemic that has unequally affected displaced and stateless people regarding infection, healthcare access, and discrimination. This begs the question of just how the world and anthropologists in particular, frame and work to ameliorate disasters, which can no longer be approached from the historical development standpoint of a *return to normal* but rather somehow else, perhaps in a *worldmaking* frame.

In a true ethnographic style, **Mark Nuttall** weaves the next foundational chapter focused on interdisciplinarity by first immersing readers in his field research in Northwest Greenland. His point is made thus: although most scientific assessments track the unprecedented melting of Arctic sea ice and the Greenland ice sheet based upon distant satellite imaging, the real story is on the ground, engaging with the communities who have thrived in this ecosystem for millennia and are observing these transformations in real time as they interface daily and seasonal rhythms. We see how through language inhabitants clearly articulate these changes' immediate affects by making their life "off balance," causing a "swimming, shaking, moving" head/mind and revealing the ever-present process of worldmaking as the world around them changes. These on-the-ground understandings compelled the author to enter into the interdisciplinary project ICE-ARC on the grounds that all involved sought to balance the disciplines from the beginning scoping and through to the project's end. This involved not only engaging local people but bringing them on as research partners. In the end, ICE-ARC succeeded in building a unique Arctic monitoring capacity and data record by engaging Inuit communities in the design, planning, and completion of the program. Indeed, anthropologists may have established their disciplinary approaches and methodological tools in "lone ranger" mode but today's pressing issues, founded in a world of increasing complexity, demand that our discipline redirect our skills into collaborative and multidisciplinary partnerships.

Susan Crate's chapter illustrates, pointedly, how the hegemony of (what we could call western) scientific knowledge has influenced and determined how policy decisions are made for the rest of the world. This, she argues, perpetuates a dominant neoliberal agenda. However, she does not argue that scientific knowledge is irrelevant – rather that, at present, it dominates, but fails to provide a complete understanding of global change. The world, she argues, can be more pluralistic if we understood that knowledge is a situated event, shaped and determined by its immediate biophysical and cultural context. Indigenous knowledge and local knowledge not only offer a balance to the uneven ways that science frames the climate crisis, they provide a cultural context for global change. In this way, rather that undermining scientific knowledge, the inclusion of Indigenous knowledge and local knowledge calls its sanctity into question.

Crate's chapter builds on both her long-term and extensive ethnographic fieldwork and engagement with the IPCC to reflect on the ways anthropology works hard in arguing for the inclusion of vernacular ways of knowing in climate change research, assessments, and policy. There have been positive developments. The increased understanding, and the gradual acceptance and appreciation of the critical place of knowledge systems has gone from field encounters to policy applications, including IPBES and IPCC. As such, Crate argues that this is, in many ways, akin to how anthropologists first found themselves encountering climate change in their field sites, called for action, and moved into advocacy and policy spheres.

Part II: Worldmaking Practices

From those foundational chapter insights, we next explore worldmaking practices as they emerge from anthropological encounters old and new. Herein we present some of the first two editions' authors to share how their field settings and collaborators have changed over time and to reflect on their own evolution. This section also highlights new authors, some in world areas already covered in earlier volumes and some in new places.

As we move towards a post-carbon future, the development of green, low carbon, technologies is held to be one solution to reducing greenhouse gases in the atmosphere. Numerous initiatives are underway globally to capture energy from the wind and sun and store it in batteries to electrify transportation networks and other polluting industries, and critical minerals are mined to provide the materials needed for the components for these technologies, as well as for consumer goods such as smart phones and computers. As **Jerry Jacka** points out in his chapter, the impact of extracting the minerals needed for the low carbon energy transition is often missing from discussions about the making of a cleaner future. Drawing on his extensive work on extractive industries on Papua New Guinea and Colorado, Jacka examines what the implications are for the planet from increased mining, and also considers what effects climate change may have on mines and mineral production. While Papua New Guinea is the site of several active mines, which have considerable impacts on the environment and the communities near them, in southwestern Colorado, like much of the mountainous, western United States, there are thousands of abandoned mines dotted across the landscape. Jacka draws attention to how, in both current and past mining sites, there are profound social and ecological consequences that will need to be addressed to mitigate climate change through an increase in so-called "clean energy" mineral extraction. The chapter highlights some of the paradoxes of what, in political narratives and corporate discourse and business-speak has come to be seen as a solution to climate change – that we can mine our way to a more sustainable future.

As **Katie Quail, Donna Green,** and **Ciaran O'Faircheallaigh** discuss in their chapter, Australia has an abundance of solar and wind resources and is proximate enough to Asian markets to enable the export of green electricity, and to make it profitable. The combination of these ideal conditions positions Australia to become a "renewable energy superpower." However, vast amounts of new renewable energy generation will need to be deployed if Australia is to achieve these ambitious goals and transition to net-zero emissions. Quail, Green, and O'Faircheallaigh point out, though, that much of the land that is suitable for such large-scale renewable development belongs to the Indigenous Estate, including both Aboriginal freehold title and Native Title land. This represents significant opportunities for Traditional Owners and local First Nations' communities to participate in and benefit from these developments. The reality, however, is that Australia's history with the extractive industry has shown that outcomes from land use agreements can be highly variable and do not always deliver their intended benefits to First Nations. Research shows there is no guarantee that renewable energy developments will bring beneficial outcomes unless measures are taken to ensure this. Quail, Green, and O'Faircheallaigh explore what can be learnt from Australia's history with the extractive industry, what best-practice agreement making looks like, and describe their research methods as they investigate what needs to be done to ensure First Nations' participation and benefit from large-scale renewable energy developments on Country.

Penelope Dransart and Marietta Ortega Perrier discuss how bilingual Aymara-Spanish speaking people in Isluga, a community in the highlands of northern Chile, talk about weather phenomena and their observations and experiences of the increasing unreliability of expected seasonal weather events. In doing so, Dransart and Ortega Perrier use strong winds as a case study in weather-worlding. They describe how, during the cold and dry windy season, exceptionally strong westerlies prevent rain-bearing clouds from entering Isluga territory. Softer easterlies bring in moisture-bearing clouds from Bolivia, ushering in the warmer rainy season, during which precipitation can fall as rain or snow. Sometimes the more lively, ebullient, and unruly westerlies intrude into the moist season, preventing rain from falling. Isluga residents endow winds with a sense of agency and talk about their capacity for movement. The winds are personified as cannibal brothers and people also describe wind directions in relation to the social organization of Isluga territory. From the 1920s onwards, a rain-calling ceremony was introduced as a ritual practice in Isluga in response to periods of drought during the rainy season. In recent decades, many Isluga residents have converted to an evangelical form of Protestantism, which forbids such practices. While this means the rain-calling ceremony is now no longer observed, people nonetheless use a cycle of saints' days to keep track of constancies and inconstancies in seasonally occurring weather events. The chapter provides insight into people's spatial construal of temporal weather experiences. By exploring how people consider winds as agents of change, it demonstrates how local views make important contributions to the understanding of weather patterns from the past, and how this understanding allows people to make sense of present change and helps them to prepare for those changes that are anticipated in the future.

Based on her ethnographic research in the Caylloma province of the southern Peruvian Andes, Astrid Stensrud shows how both the effects of climate change and adaptation projects can have unequal impact as well as unintended consequences. She argues that a greater understanding of these consequences cannot be achieved by only taking socio-economic factors into account. Stensrud points to the importance of understanding human–nonhuman relations and the ways that worldmaking practices are enacting diverging, yet partially connected, worlds. With a focus on water, she shows how farming in this semi-arid region has always depended upon irrigation and collaboration between people to construct and maintain irrigation systems, canals, and terraces. Humans need to work to make the water flow and make life possible. However, local customary practices stand in opposition to modern statecraft and science, and Stensrud argues that water-related worlds need to be understood as open-ended and emerging through practices and encounters, which people navigate in different ways. At the same time, neoliberal economic policies have led to a marketization of agriculture and water management, fostering individualization and commodification. These different practices are often contradictory, leading to tension, disagreement, and "disencounters." State discourses that focus on "water scarcity" and "inefficient water use," ignore the issue of inequality in allocation of water, and dismiss local ways of relating to water, and local strategies for ensuring access to it. Stensrud points to the social and economic consequences of this approach, arguing how, in addition to the pressure of climate change and economic change, people are experiencing the pressure of development programs that are presented as climate change adaptation strategies.

Worldmaking is concretely illustrated through the co-problem-solving process engaged in by **Julie Maldonado, Kristina Peterson, Theresa Dardar, Shirell Parfait-Dardar, Rosina Philippe, Donald Dardar, R. Eugene Turner, Alessandra Jerolleman, Julie Torres, Rebecca Lovingood,** and **Mira Olson.** Their project, Lagniappe for the Working Coast, brings together local Indigenous leaders, knowledge-holders, and scientists with western physical and social scientists, centering Indigenous knowledge and local knowledge, and modeling to co-produce a decision matrix to determine the optimal places for canal restoration, and then restore them. Their biogeographical context is coastal Louisiana's intricate ecosystem web of canals, both human-made and natural, which is unraveling due to hydrological, meteorological, and environmental disasters, extractive industries, river mismanagement, and climate change. The collaboration was initiated by three Tribes in coastal Louisiana – Grand Bayou, Grand Caillou/Dulac, and Pointe-au-Chien – with the objective to restore marshland in their communities in order to preserve sacred places and reduce land loss. This environmental justice- and community-driven project fills a critical role in shaping cumulative best practices for integrating coastal resilience activities and cultural heritage in all at-risk regions of the United States.

Over the last few decades, life in the Arctic has been affected by rising temperatures, extreme weather events, the transformation of the seasons, and animal migrations. In his chapter, **Franz Krause** illustrates how climate change is experienced by the Indigenous peoples of the Gwich'in and Inuvialuit Settlement Regions of Canada's Northwest Territories. However, as he shows, climate change is not a radical intrusion into a previously stable equilibrium. Life in the region has long been characterized by dramatic fluctuations in northern ecosystems, as well as by social and cultural transformations and the often awkward relations between Indigenous and settler groups. People also continue to deal with the legacy of colonization. Krause's argument follows that of Indigenous scholars who have demonstrated that current and future climate crises constitute a continuation, rather than a rupture, in their colonial histories. Climate change – the newest installment of developments produced elsewhere, with which Arctic people must contend and struggle – is experienced, perceived, and understood as a new wave of colonial violence and dispossession. Grounding his chapter on ethnographic material from the Mackenzie Delta, straddling the border of the Gwich'in and Inuvialuit Settlement Regions, Krause shifts the focus from seeing climate change as impeding collapse to understanding, on the one hand, how exploitation and marginalization make climate change a colonial echo in the delta, and on the other, how delta inhabitants are working to re-build decent lives despite the echoing challenges.

Astrid Oberborbeck Andersen and **Janne Flora** explore the reconfiguration of human–muskox relations in two Greenlandic settings: Ittoqqortoormiit on the northeast coast and Kangerlussuaq on the west coast. They show how, in both these places, humans and muskoxen came into contact and how their relations were reconfigured in disparate ways. In 1925 in Ittoqqortoormiit some 70 Iivit were relocated from Tasiilaq 1000 km northwards to the unpopulated Scoresbysound Fjord as part of a Danish sovereignty project; and in West Greenland in the 1960s 27 muskoxen were translocated from Scoresbysound to Kangerlussuaq. Andersen and Flora discuss how these relocations – of people and muskoxen – occurred in response to uncertainties in climatic, geopolitical, and economic circumstances. These uncertainties continue to inform many biological and political discussions about the management of muskoxen today. In particular, wildlife biologists struggle with the question of whether it is climate change or overhunting that poses the greatest risk to the survival of muskoxen (and, indeed, other animals that Inuit depend on). Tracing climate change and the uncertainties tied to muskoxen and other terrestrial game animals over time and space, Andersen and Flora argue that muskoxen and humans mutually reconfigure each other's worlds through worldmaking practices in a multitude of ways. The chapter shows how, by gaining new insight into climate pasts, presents and futures in Greenland, a new perspective on how an anthropology of multiple species can be practiced, begins to emerge.

Majken Paulsen, Grete K. Hovelsrud, and **Camilla Risvoll** explore the processes of worldmaking in contemporary Fennoscandian reindeer husbandry, a time-tested co-existence between reindeer and humans. The authors explain how historically herding is based upon a practice called *louthu*, in which deer maintain a free and autonomous existence – not domesticated and also not wild. *Louthu* is based upon reindeer's keen adaptation to the extreme Fennoscandian climate where, in winter they track their fodder under the snow using their keen sense of smell and in the short summer period locate in dense forage to build their reserves. *Louthu* has been the basis of the human–animal relationship of reindeer herding since time immemorial. Today various factors, including climate change, human encroachment, resource development, infrastructure, and predators threaten *louthu*. Most herders have moved to supplementary feeding of their deer in order to survive. This, however, is counterintuitive to the principle of *louthu* which inherently maintains herds as self-sufficient and independent. The authors explore three aspects of this change as it relates to worldmaking practices: time, money, and knowledge. They conclude that although supplementary feeding is necessary to keep animals alive in these times of rapid change, there need to be alternative worldmaking practices that keep the reindeer in the mountains and natural pastures and thereby perpetuate Sami reindeer herding and *louthu*.

In her second chapter in this volume, **Susan Crate** goes further to explore the relationship of Sakha, horse, and cattle pastoralists of northeastern Siberia, and *alaas*, which are the permafrost ecosystems that Sakha depend on for their subsistence and for their livelihoods. She shows that this relationship is both physical and spiritual. In a time of climate change, *alaas* are changing dramatically because the permafrost is thawing. This results in these critical pastures being unusable for Sakha people. Crate argues that we must consider and accommodate the cognizant reverberations of such change for a people who are gradually losing a recognizable landscape central to their cultural identity. These questions are highly relevant for anthropologists working with the diversity of cultures challenged by similar "dislocations" from their known places, ancestral environments, and the core sources of their cultural identities. Furthermore, such investigations are essential to effective global change research, revealing how engaging all relevant knowledge systems counters the hegemony of scientific knowledge and moves toward more equitable and just adaptation responses and policy prescriptions.

Pasang Yangee Sherpa and **Ornella Puschiasis** contribute a chapter that highlights the ever-evolving role of ethnography in a world with a changing climate and, in the process, the important worldmaking that ethnographers can do by focused, community-driven research. The team, a native Sherpa anthropologist and a French geographer, respectively, reflect on their experiences conducting over a decade of climate change research in the Mount Everest region of Nepal. Based upon their work they provide insights for other anthropologists on how to conduct more ethically sound research. The inspiration for their insights was finding each other during an international climate change event and reflecting on the dissonance between the jargon being offered and the real concerns of the local inhabitants which they had both individually experienced during their field research. They discern two types of climate change: institutionally defined and in their context synonymous with melting snow, glaciers, and GLOFs (glacial lake outburst floods) and the multiple ways that climate change effects were being experienced and observed by local communities. Although their approach is by no means new to anthropologists in terms of a focus on local perceptions, understandings, and knowledge systems, the context of their work in one of the more rapidly changing environments on the planet provides particular insights that inform other world contexts. The question is not about how communities relocate from their region that appears, at first sight, terminally doomed but rather: what are the communities' orientations towards livability? They leave us with the question: *Whose livability are we concerned about, and who gets to decide what livability is for the residents of Khumbu and Pharak?*

Part III: Interventions

In this third section we position anthropological work focused on interventions that include anthropologists working within policy contexts, climate assessments, facilitating community and social change, activism in academic institutions, training climate professionals, heritage, and critiquing world economic systems. Here we also include returning authors of the first two editions and new authors.

We begin with **Beatriz Barros** and **Richard Wilk's** insightful chapter on the insidious role of excessive wealth and inequitable resource distribution as both fuel and fodder for climate change. Not only are rich countries more responsible for climate change effects and have greater resources to buffer themselves against them, likewise wealthy individuals, most of whom originate in those wealthy countries, carry the bulk of the responsibility for climate change. The authors delve deep into details of some of the wealthiest offenders' lifestyles to illustrate not only their excessive consumption but also to provide a sense of disproportionality in comparison to the extreme poverty on the planet today. The existing efforts to curb carbon, most commonly by carbon pricing, have no effect on billionaires who can easily pay their way out of sanctions and fines. Herein anthropology can play a role. Because culture lies at the heart of economic behavior, anthropologists have a clearly defined role in addressing the issue of billionaire overconsumption via engaged social activist campaigns to bring about social, economic, and climate justice.

Mark Nuttall writes about his experience working with communities in the Welsh county of Flintshire and the English county of Cheshire whose subterranean world has been earmarked as a testing ground for a project heralded to be the future of carbon capture and renewable energy. HyNet North West is a decarbonization and hydrogen energy production initiative that promises to "unlock a low carbon future" for not only this northernmost stretch of border between Wales and England but also for other parts of the UK, Europe, and globally. He enters into the process specifically at the level of discussion about and consultation on the route of the pipeline from energy intensive industries in Cheshire and Flintshire that will carry CO_2 emissions to be stored in depleted gas reservoirs in the Irish Sea. He analyzes the ways in which the project is framed as both urgent and necessary and also supported by narratives of futuring and worldmaking. His study reveals how these high regards and intentions for HyNet North West are not prevalent in the affected communities. Contrarily, local inhabitants are not sold on the project being some sort of beacon into a carbon neutral future but rather show deep concern about the local disruption in constructing the pipeline and the ongoing environmental risk once it is in operation. Overall those participating in the community discussions felt they were in a sacrifice zone for the good of everyone else's carbon neutral future. Moreover, they understood the project's promises of solving some of the high levels of social and economic deprivation to be unfounded. In the end, by engaging with these local concerns, it is clear that a widespread support for the project's high ambitions is lacking at the local levels, replaced by deep concerns about impacts on everyday life, health, and the environment.

Dennis Davis and **Elizabeth Marino's** chapter illustrates how anthropologists can facilitate worldmaking via co-creating community representation with Indigenous collaborators. It describes how anthropologist Elizabeth Marino collaborates with Iñupiat photographer and videographer Dennis Davis to not only bring an Iñupiat perspective on community and climate change visually to the fore but, in the process, also to reify the Indigenous wisdom inherent in Iñupiat ways of being and sustainable lifeways. They do so by investigating how knowledge and communication of climate change within Shishmaref, one of many Alaska Indigenous communities experiencing erosion, storm surges, and flooding as a result of a changing Arctic climate, has changed over the last twenty years. This chapter works to upend the common discourse of Arctic and other communities most hard hit by climate change today as being victims and refugees to show how Indigenous philosophies work to open the discussion towards solutions, pluralistic discourses, and worldmaking possibilities.

Colin Thor West and **Carla Roncoli** collaborate on their chapter to provide a comprehensive and comparative picture, based on ethnographic research since 1997 combined with spatial data, that explores smallholder adaptation to climate change in two communities in the northern Central Plateau region of Burkina Faso. Once a place of severe desertification, the northern Central Plateau has recently become known as a place of renewal largely due to adopted soil and water conservation (SWC) measures in combination with appropriate intensification of traditional practices. Here we see a semblance of worldmaking in process. However, all communities are not created equal and the adoption of SWC varies. The authors chose two contrasting communities in order to highlight how adaptation to or the lack thereof results in very different outcomes. By combining their longitudinal ethnographic data with spatial information the authors highlight how householders individually and within community are agents of worldmaking depending on their propensity to adopt new technologies, in this case, SWC but also, and perhaps more importantly, with the strong institutional support necessary to sustain that adoption.

Another interface for anthropologists working on climate issues is that of international policy forums. **Pamela McElwee** writes about both the increasing engagement of anthropologists in the assessment process and also anthropologists' ethnographic analyses of these policy processes to critique how authority is produced and knowledge flows. The author speaks from personal experience as a lead author of the IPCC and upon the increasingly prolific anthropological literature analyzing the policy process and the struggle to bring qualitative scholarship, Indigenous representation, and more Global South authors into a system that is dominated by viewpoints of the Global North and founded upon quantitative, predictive work modelling future impacts and responses. Although there has been significant progress in IPCC work to engage Indigenous knowledge and local knowledge and also more qualitative ways to account for the concepts of adaptation and vulnerability, gaps remain. Overall these are about human behavior as it relates to energy use, consumption, and mitigation. Perhaps most poignantly, anthropologists make important contributions to the IPCC and other international, national, and regional climate policy assessments by acting as interlocuters between the reports and how the public receives and acts upon them. Anthropologists can deliver stories and framings that provide the emotive appeal towards more climate engagement.

Jessica O'Reilly's chapter illustrates how, when scientists and their work show up in diplomatic spaces, anthropologists have the opportunity to observe what she calls "the rough edges where climate science and policy meet." She argues that these spaces constitute powerful epistemic and discursive zones, whose boundaries or interfaces can help anthropologists learn about and understand what is at stake in the negotiations and translations that go on between science and policy. O'Reilly's chapter draws on ethnographic observations and reports from meetings of the IPCC, the Antarctic Treaty, and the United Nations Framework Convention on Climate Change, and analyzes the key tactics that scientists, diplomats, and technocrats use. As she shows, these tactics are framings, ethical or ideological interventions, or strategies for stalling or accelerating progress. They are deployed to shift conversations and decisions in specific directions, or to consolidate or challenge power dynamics, including the privileging of western science. Such challenges, O'Reilly argues, are particularly important as they highlight power relations and historical inequalities among nations. When representatives of these nations meet at the IPCC, Antarctic Treaty or COP sessions, discussions over scientific knowledge become, necessarily, tangled up with global climate politics. By considering science and policy spaces as sites of cultural production, O'Reilly's chapter also analyzes a case study of how powerful developing countries intervene in tactical ways to attempt to shift, or at least underscore, how uneven epistemic and political terrains are erased in calls for a unified, global climate policy. In this way, it shows how anthropology contributes to understanding the problems of and solutions to climate change by studying the knowledge communities and practices which form competing and contested ideas around climate concern.

Sarah Strauss and **Courtney Kurlanska** explore the interface of anthropologists training the next generation for careers in community climate adaptation. They begin by tracing the evolution of anthropologists' engagement with climate change, going from a "lone ranger" approach to increasingly collaborative work across anthropology's four fields as well as in inter- and transdisciplinary ways. Their main argument is that the combination of our discipline's holistic approach and emphasis on community context makes anthropologists prime actors in facilitating the meeting of local needs and innovative strategies for communities to adapt to a changing climate. By way of illustration, they present their work in this effort: a transdisciplinary master's program collaborating with engineers and other disciplines to train students as climate adaptation professionals. They argue for their approach as being one of the many needed efforts to facilitate the diverse range of cultural strategies to face the many challenges of a changing climate. Anthropology provides the toolkit to navigate the local particularities of places, times, and different knowledge orientations. This toolkit in concert with anthropology's collaborative approach to framing problems are foundations to our discipline's transformational capacity. The authors detail the importance of project-based learning, interdisciplinarity and local community involvement, the foundation of the theory and practice requirement for their degree and an offshoot of a required module of their institution. In the end the authors endeavor to balance the playing field of the current emphasis on technological solutions to climate change by training the next generation in applying anthropological approaches to solicit human engagement and behavioral change.

Brian Burke, Sydney Blume, and **Michael Weiss** contribute insights on their powerful anthropological intervention involving student-faculty-community organizing to cultivate university culture that "walks the walk." The trio organized a campus-wide movement in response to the 2018 publication of the *IPCC Special Report on Warming of 1.5°C*. Their intent was to mobilize the campus community to go beyond the existing Office of Sustainability and a student-funded and student-run renewable energy program to bring about the university's potential to test and model just sustainability with their campus as a microcosm. Key to bringing about real change in their campus community was to inculcate the cultural preparation necessary to bring about just transition. They practiced a type of organization that forefronted both transparency and rotating leadership in order to model an alternative to top-down and unelected leadership. They pushed the bounds of a campus environmental campaign by confronting the most powerful decisionmakers of university life, the Board of Trustees, those who make decisions behind closed doors. Based on their experience they share four main strategies: using coursework and formal trainings to build new subjectivities and skills for a sense of empowerment; revealing the inability to address vital concerns through conventional institutional approaches; building new imaginations of self-governed climate justice and institutions that (attempt to) embody those visions; and reducing the material challenges that constrain activist engagement.

In their chapter, **Fred Phillip, Raychelle Aluaq Daniel, Jonella Ququngaq Larson, Anne Stevens Henshaw**, and **Erin Dougherty Lynch** set out to reframe the climate crisis as a *aaqsunarqelriitin* (an Alaska Yupi'k word for crisis) in the frameworks and systems of today's institutions and organizations that lack the deep values-based relationships that lie at the center of Indigenous ways of knowing and being. They point out that such systems were designed at a time that did not value emergent approaches to address the complex challenges we face today – nor were they designed by taking into account values of equity or trust. These values, they argue, are prerequisites for advancing new governance and management regimes rooted more in what Yupi'k know and reflect upon as *ciungani atullruaqa* (peoples' lived experience) and that embrace multiple ways of knowing and being in a rapidly changing climate. Phillip, Daniel, Larson, Henshaw, and Lynch explore efforts underway to rebuild, repair, and renew those relationships in ways that exercise localized cultural values and governance in their own right and with allied organizations and institutions. For example, they show how this is informed, among other ways of being, by *caiyugluku*. This describes problems and problem-solving by drawing on one's strength, whether it be physical (such as the need to pull a sled or seal across the ice) or drawing from the strength of one's values that center on pulling from the generational mental, spiritual, and emotional relationships of a person's lived experience.

The contribution by **William P. Megarry, Hana Morel, Sarah Forgesson**, and **Eduardo S. Brondizio** closes Part III. Their chapter discusses how the immense value of cultural heritage as a driver and resource for climate action remains under-appreciated. This is especially the case in assessment reports from the IPCC which summarize and synthesize the state-of-the-art in climate research to produce policy relevant but not policy prescriptive guidance for state parties and other actors. Megarry, Morel, Forgesson, and Brondizio explore efforts from researchers in the cultural heritage sector to engage more meaningfully in this synthesis process. To do so requires acknowledging, respecting, and implementing a plurality of knowledge systems inherent in culture, heritage, and creative practices. They look specifically at methodology and select findings from the International Co-Sponsored Meeting on Culture, Heritage and Climate Change, a collaboration between the International Council on Monuments and Sites (ICOMOS), the United Nations Educational, Scientific and Cultural Organization (UNESCO) and the Intergovernmental Panel on Climate Change (IPCC). The meeting brought together over 100 international researchers and practitioners from diverse knowledge systems (scientific, local, Indigenous) to explore the contributions of culture and heritage for understanding and responding to climate change. The chapter shows how heritage and cultural practices act as a bridge between different ways of knowing, embody inherited knowledge accumulated over generations, and serve as entry points for climate action.

In closing this Introduction, we thank our many contributors who have worked with us to produce this volume. It has been both an honor and a pleasure to collaborate once more with those colleagues who have now been involved in all three editions of *Anthropology and Climate Change*, and equally so to work with the many other authors who agreed to be part of this new book. We dedicate this volume to our contributors, their research partners, and the people and communities who are working so hard to take action on climate change and to make a better world for us all and for future generations. At Routledge we thank Meagan Simpson, Genni Eccles, Iman Hakimi, and Fiona Hudson Gabuya for their support, patience, and encouragement in bringing this third volume to production, and our thanks also go to Ruth Bourne for her work in copyediting the manuscript.

It was with deep sadness that we heard our colleague, Heather Lazrus, passed away at the end of February 2023. Heather contributed immensely to our understanding of human–environment interactions in our time of climate change. Her broader body of writing, activities, and leadership were truly inspirational and have had a profound influence on our discipline. Her work and commitment to interdisciplinary engagement was exemplary, as was her dedication to Indigenous communities. Among her many contributions, perhaps her most significant achievement was co-founding and co-leading The Rising Voices Center for Indigenous and Earth Sciences at the National Center for Atmospheric Research in Boulder, Colorado. Heather contributed to all three editions of *Anthropology and Climate Change*. We are grateful to be able to share her insights.

Notes

1 See the Annual 2022 Global Climate Report from the National Centers for Environmental Information, available at: https://www.ncei.noaa.gov/access/monitoring/monthly-report/global/202213
2 "World headed for climate catastrophe without global action: UN Secretary-General." UNEP, 27 October 2022. https://www.unep.org/news-and-stories/story/world-headed-climate-catastrophe-without-urgent-action-un-secretary-general
3 Ajit Naranjan, "'Era of global boiling has arrived,' says UN chief as July set to be hottest month on record." *The Guardian* 27 July 2023. https://www.theguardian.com/science/2023/jul/27/scientists-july-world-hottest-month-record-climate-temperatures
4 Ferris Jabr, "How humanity unleashed a flood of new diseases." *The New York Times Magazine*, 17 June 2020, https://www.nytimes.com/2020/06/17/magazine/animal-disease-covid.html
5 "The Covid-19 pandemic in 2023: far from over." *The Lancet* 401 (10371), p. 79, 14 January 2023.
6 This is a quote from a PPT presentation by Steve Kokelj that was recorded here: https://geoscienceforum.entegyapp.com/Page/61/27 It is the first presentation at the top of the page and the words are spoken while you are viewing the title slide.

References

Alexander, Jeffrey. 2013. *The Dark Side of Modernity*. Cambridge: Polity Press.
Bohren, Lenora. 2009. "Car culture and decision-making: choice and climate change." In Susan A. Crate and Mark Nuttall (eds.) *Anthropology and Climate Change: From encounters to actions*. Walnut Creek, CA: Left Coast Press, pp. 370–379.
Bridge, Gavin. 2015. "Energy (in)security: world-making in an age of scarcity." *The Geographical Journal* 181 (4): 328–339.
Castree, Noel, et al. 2014. "Changing the intellectual climate." *Nature Climate Change* 4 (9): 763–768.
Chilisa, Bagele. 2019. *Indigenous Research Methodologies*. London: Sage.
Crate, Susan A. and Mark Nuttall. 2009. *Anthropology and Climate Change: From encounters to actions*. Walnut Creek, CA: Left Coast Press.
Crits-Christoph, Alex, Karthik Gangavarapu, Jonathan E. Pekar, Niema Moshiri, Reema Singh, Joshua I. Levy, Stephen A. Goldstein, Marc A. Suchard, Saskia Popescu, David L. Robertson, Philippe Lemey, Joel O. Wertheim, Robert F. Garry, Angela L. Rasmussen, Kristian G. Andersen, Edward C. Holmes, Andrew Rambaut, Michael Worobey, and Florence Débarre. 2023. "Genetic evidence of susceptible wildlife in SARS-CoV-2 positive samples at the Huanan Wholesale Seafood Market, Wuhan: analysis and interpretation of data released by the Chinese Center for Disease Control." *Zenodo*. https:doi.org/10.5281/zenodo.7754299. Pre-print report published online 20 March 2023. Accessed 23 March 2023.
Crumley, Carole L. 2012. "A heterarchy of knowledges: tools for the study of landscape histories and futures." In T. Plieninger and C. Bieling (eds.) *Resilience and the Cultural Landscape: Understanding and managing change in human-shaped environments*. Cambridge: Cambridge University Press, pp. 303–314.
Cunsolo, Ashlee and Neville R. Ellis. 2018. "Ecological grief as a mental health response to climate change-related loss." *Nature Climate Change* 8 (4): 275–281. https://doi.org/10.1038/s41558-018-0092-2.
Girvan, Anita. 2017. "Trickster carbon: stories, science, and postcolonial interventions for climate justice." *Journal of Political Ecology* 24 (1): 1038–1054.
Goodman, Nelson. 1978. *Ways of Worldmaking*. Indianapolis: Hackett Publishing Company.
Hastrup, Kirsten. 2013. "Anthropological contributions to the study of climate: past, present and future." *WIREs Climate Change* 4: 269–281.
Hastrup, Kirsten (ed.). 2009. *The Question of Resilience: Social responses to climate change*. Copenhagen: Royal Danish Academy of Sciences and Letters.
Hoffman, Susanna M., Thomas Hylland Eriksen, and Paulo Mendes. 2022. *Cooling Down: Local responses to global climate change*. Oxford and New York: Berghahn.

Lahsen, Myanna. 2016. "Toward a sustainable future Earth: challenges for a research agenda." *Science, Technology, & Human Values* 41 (5): 876–898.

Malavin, Stas, Lyubov Shmakova, Jean-Michel Claverie, and Elizaveta Rivkina. 2020. "Frozen Zoo: a collection of permafrost samples containing viable protists and their viruses." *Biodiversity Data Journal* 8: e51586. doi: doi:10.3897/BDJ.8.e51586.

Milkoreit, Manjana. 2017. "Imaginary politics: climate change and making the future." *Elementa* 5: 62, doi:doi:10.1525/elementa.249.

Nuttall, Mark. 2009. "Living in a world of movement: human resilience to environmental instability in Greenland." In Susan A. Crate and Mark Nuttall (eds.) *Anthropology and Climate Change: From encounters to actions*. Walnut Creek, CA: Left Coast Press, pp. 292–310.

Nuttall, Mark. 2012. "Tipping points and the human world: living with change and thinking about the future." *AMBIO* 41 (1): 96–105.

Nuttall, Mark, Fikret Berkes, Bruce Forbes, Gary Kofinas, Tatiana Vlassova and George Wenzel. 2005. "Hunting, herding, fishing and gathering: Indigenous peoples and renewable resource use in the Arctic." In ACIA. *Arctic Climate Impact Assessment: Scientific Report*. Cambridge: Cambridge University Press, pp. 649–690.

Pielke, R.A., R. Wilby, D. Niyogi, F. Hossain, K. Dairuku, J. Adegoke, G. Kallos, T. Seastedt, and K. Suding. 2012. "Dealing with complexity and extreme events using a bottom-up, resource-based vulnerability perspective." In A. Surjalal Sharma, A. Bunde, V.P. Dimri, and D. N. Baker (eds.) *Extreme Events and Natural Hazards: The complexity perspective*. Geophysical Monograph Series, 196, published online: 2 April 2013 doi:10.1029/2011GM001086.

Putnam, Hilary. 1979. "Reflections on Goodman's *Ways of Worldmaking*." *The Journal of Philosophy* 76 (11): 603–618.

Sillitoe, Paul. 2022. *The Anthroposcene of Weather and Climate: Ethnographic contributions to the climate change debate*. Oxford and New York: Berghahn.

Smith, Linda Tuhiwai. 1999. *Decolonizing Methodologies: Research and Indigenous peoples*. London and New York: Zed Books Ltd.

Venter, Zander S., Kristin Aunan, Sourangsu Chowdury, and Jos Lelieveld. 2020. "COVID-19 lockdowns cause global air pollution declines." *PNAS* 117 (32): 18984–18990.

Wu, Ruonan, Gareth Trubi, Neslihan Taş, and Janet K. Jansson. 2022. "Permafrost as a potential pathogen reservoir." *One Earth* 5 (4): 351–360.

PART I
Reorientations

1

THE ARC OF THE ANTHROPOCENE

Deep-Time Perspectives From Environmental Archaeology

Arlene Miller Rosen

Introduction

In an influential article, Dipesh Chakrabarty (2008) pointed out that we can no longer think of natural science and environmental histories as separate from human histories and the humanities, due to the widespread impact of our species on the earth through time. In order to address modern global challenges of living sustainably on this planet, urban developers, economists, politicians, agricultural scientists and other public-facing planners would benefit from the blending of Western scientific knowledge with alternative ways of knowing expressed by Traditional Ecological Knowledge and Indigenous Science (R. Kimmerer 2013). Perspectives that blend the "nature" of humans and the humanness of nature with multispecies understandings, the impacts of human niche construction, and issues of social and environmental justice can help formulate more equitable and sustainable ways of living in our modern world. It is equally important to account for the deep-time roots of these human–environmental relationships in order to truly understand and learn from the varied and variable characteristics of past human responses to similar challenges. This highlights the importance of contributions from the many sub-branches of archaeological inquiry.

Archaeology has the potential to play an influential role in addressing many of the challenges of the Anthropocene because of its tools for merging both environmental histories with social/political and economic histories in deep time. For decades, archaeologists have directly addressed some of the environmental challenges posed by the Anthropocene from the early years of the concept, onward to more recent concerns of environmental and social justice (Rockman and Hritz 2020; Boivin et al. 2016; Haldon et al. 2020; Izdebski, Haldon and Filipkowski 2022; A. Rosen 2022). These contributions are slowly coming to the attention of public awareness, and hopefully will eventually gain more influence with environmental planners.

The concept of the Anthropocene first received wide academic attention after Crutzen and Stoermer (2000) proposed it as a new geological epoch. From the time of its inception, it has been a controversial notion beginning with discussions of the "need" for a

DOI: 10.4324/9781003242499-3

new geological epoch which seemed to overlap uncomfortably with the current Holocene interglacial epoch. The discussions then moved on to the idea that if we accept it as a new epoch where do we draw the line in the geological sand (both literally and metaphorically), to allow it to conform to geological rules of stratigraphic nomenclature, and how do we reconcile the geological indications of its recognizability with its "true" beginnings in deeper time?

Along with these concerns came the questions about what the Anthropocene concept means for our interpretation of relationships between humans and nature, and indeed questions concerning the validity of the dichotomy itself (Caillon et al. 2017; Escobar 1996; Latour 2011; Toncheva 2019). The Anthropocene notion added new dimensions to these interests which had occupied anthropologists and particularly environmental archaeologists since at least the beginning of the twentieth century. Archaeologists have contributed data from both historical periods and deep time, leading to revelations about the extent and evolutionary impact of environmental manipulation at the hands of our ancestral and descendant communities (Boivin et al. 2016; Braje and Erlandson 2013; Edgeworth 2021; Smith and Zeder 2013). More recently, some have attempted to understand the interconnectedness and even absence of separation between humans and the other life forms, as well as minerals, hydrology, and atmospheric gases which form the basis of our planet's ecological systems (Campbell 2021). Many other studies have pointed to the need for understanding traditional systems of ecological knowledge (TEK) as one productive way forward (Bruchac 2014; Nicholas and Markey 2015). Researchers are also realizing the critical importance of environmental and social justice as a key to developing a more sustainable "good Anthropocene" for future generations (Boivin and Crowther 2021; Hoelle and Kawa 2020; Hornborg 2019; Simpson 2020).

Archaeology of the Anthropocene

Historical Background

Archaeologists are well-placed to address issues related to the Anthropocene, due to their long history of investigations into the relationships between humans and their landscapes and environments. They have been aware of the significance of the environment from the beginnings of controlled excavations across Eurasia. Notable early examples include projects by the Danish archaeologist Jens Jacob Asmussen Worsaae (1821–1885) who was among the earliest archaeologists to develop the concept of archaeobotany at bog sites in Denmark in the mid-nineteenth century (Rowley-Conwy 2006). Another pioneer in environmental archaeology was the American geologist/archaeologist Raphael Pumpelly who led an interdisciplinary team to Turkmenistan to excavate the Bronze Age site of Anau beginning in 1903 (Pumpelly 1908).

In later years, British archaeologist Grahame Clark of Cambridge University initiated further ground-breaking work at the Mesolithic site of Starr Carr from 1949 to 1951 (Clark 1954). In order to obtain information on the Mesolithic environment, Clark made a systematic effort to include natural scientists on his team to collect, catalogue, and analyze geological, botanical, and faunal data from the site and surrounding area.

In these early days of academic archaeology, the environment was conceived of as a backdrop for human activities and each element was compartmentalized as landforms, minerals, water sources, fauna, and plants, with each sphere studied by corresponding specialists. These specialists were tasked with the job of supplying a distinct report on the remains they studied, and these were bound together, often as appendices in volumes reporting on the artifacts, architecture, and stratigraphy of the site itself as the main purpose of the research project. There was little notion of an Anthropocene, or the profound and lasting impacts that humans could make on their surrounding environments. This "multidisciplinary" paradigm began to change in the 1950s and 1960s when forward-thinking researchers such as Robert Braidwood (1951), who excavated the Neolithic site of Jarmo, Iraq, and Karl Butzer (1964), a prominent geoarchaeologist and founder of the field of Environmental Archaeology, called for environmental studies to be integrated into the research design of archaeological projects. In particular, Butzer highlighted the distinction between the older model of "multidisciplinary" and the newer concept of an integrated, contextualized "interdisciplinary" archaeology (1982). This shift in paradigms for the practice of Environmental Archaeology set researchers on a path towards an eventual understanding of humans as indistinct from nature. This is an orientation that we now see in some of the most current themes of the Anthropocene literature.

In the late 1960s through the 1970s environmental archaeological paradigms aligned with Western social movements that highlighted Green environmental issues (Carson 1963; Leopold and Schwartz 1968). This archaeological trend followed anthropological perspectives delineated by the paradigm of "Cultural Ecology" first envisioned by Julian Steward (1955) and defined as a theoretical approach that attempts to explain similarities and differences in culture in relation to the environment (Tucker 2013: 142–147). This school of thought later gave rise to perspectives such as "political ecology" "human behavioral ecology," and "historical ecology." The latter paradigm added a deep time depth and is currently widely used as a theoretical perspective to explain archaeological transformations in societies, cultures, and landscapes (Crumley, Lennartsson, and Westin 2018; Hornborg and Crumley 2006).

With growing global concern over a warming planet and human-induced climate change in the 1980s through to the present day, an ever-increasing number of archaeologists began to tackle the role of climate change and its impact on societies worldwide. Many papers emerged as cautionary tales about the demise of a host of complex civilizations which seemingly failed to adapt to abrupt climate changes in the form of catastrophic droughts and floods (cf. H. Weiss et al. 1993; Haug et al. 2003). Most of these studies took the form of a neo-climatic determinism, but others were more nuanced analyses of social/political and economic processes which led societies to be resilient or vulnerable to changing climatic conditions, both abrupt and secular over long time frames (Butzer 2012; Butzer and Endfield 2012; Hassan 2000; McIntosh, Tainter, and McIntosh 2000; Rosen and Rivera-Collazo 2012).

The subsequent adoption of theoretical concepts such as human Niche Construction from the mid-1990s onward, brought archaeologists closer to visualizing humans as active players in shaping the natural world and buffering themselves against environmental change. Archaeologists adopted the Niche Construction paradigm from its source as a concept of Biology and Ecology (Smith 2011; Spengler 2021). It is defined by Laland and O'Brien (2010: 303) as "...a fledgling branch of evolutionary biology that places emphasis on the capacity of organisms to modify natural selection in their environment and thereby act as co-directors of their own, and other species', evolution." This occurs with other animal and plant populations, but the difference with humans is that natural selection and cultural selection are both involved because of these interspecies exchanges. This concept contrasted with previous views that societies were passive entities reacting to environmental forces beyond their control. In this role as active agents of environmental modification, humans alter the course of their own species' evolution, as well as the evolution of other life forms in their surroundings. A key element of this dual impact on human populations is that culture leaves traces in the archaeological record which researchers can use to track evolutionary changes in humans, their built environments, and the other species within their sphere of influence (Boivin et al. 2016; Spengler 2021; Stiner 2021).

Niche Construction studies in archaeology are fundamental for understanding the impact of humans on ecosystems and the history of the Anthropocene due to the conjoined elements of ecological engineering and the resulting shift of evolutionary trajectories of biological elements within these ecosystems. Although much work has been conducted on Niche Construction practices of incipient and early agriculturalists (c.f. Daru et al. 2021), hunter-gatherers have long traditions of ecological engineering at various levels of complexity. Archaeological evidence shows that hunter/gatherer societies also function within the Niche Construction model. Foragers intensify their subsistence opportunities through water manipulation, movement of plants to new habitats, and most importantly through the use of fire on landscapes to alter ecozones and increase opportunities for successful hunting (Bliege Bird et al. 2020; Feeney 2019; Field et al. 2016; Lourandos 2010; Scherjon et al. 2015).

Some archaeological evidence indicates that humans have been impacting ecological systems from early in our evolutionary history (Foley et al. 2013; Glikson 2013; Thompson, Wright, and Ivory 2021). Archaeological studies have also shown that humans impact animal populations when they move into a region. One study (Faith et al. 2020) showed that populations of African carnivores shifted during the Lower Paleolithic period when hominins likely began to compete with them for herbivore prey. Human hunters also put selective pressure on their own wild animal prey which could have altered the evolutionary trajectory of those animal populations. But the ecological footprint of early Lower Paleolithic populations was low and barely perceptible in archaeological data sets. Human impact begins to be more evident with the appearance of the early members of our genus *Homo erectus* and *Homo ergastor*. These are the hominins who displayed great capacity for innovation, adjustment to diverse environments, and adaptability. These features went hand in hand with the development of more complex tool kits and increasing socio-cultural complexity. It was also the beginning of two of the most impactful influences on natural environments that began in the later Lower Paleolithic. One was the control of fire, and the other was global expansion and colonization (Boivin et al. 2016).

One of the earliest documented and most significant implementations of ecological change was the control and use of fire on the part of our hominin ancestors (Glikson 2013; Thompson, Wright, and Ivory 2021). To identify controlled use of fire within archaeological sites, researchers use features such as hearths, reddened earth, burnt clay, and charred macrobotanical remains, bones, or shells as evidence for controlled use of fire (Albert 2015). Some claims for the early control of fire come from the Lower Paleolithic sites of Gadeb 8E in Ethiopia (Barbetti 1986), Koobi Fora FxJj East (Bellomo 1994; Rowlett

2000), and Chesowanja 1/6E in Kenya (Gowlett 2006). Many claims of early (Lower Paleolithic) fire use at open-air campsites have been controversial due to the possibilities of post-depositional disturbance, or inability to establish a human rather than natural origin (Roebroeks et al. 2021). However, compelling evidence from Fourier Transform Infrared spectrometry combined with analyses of burned and unburned artifacts at Koobi Fora FxJj20 suggest that hominins did indeed control fire for on-site purposes as far back as 1.5 million years ago at a time contemporary with Developed Oldowan tool industries (Hlubik et al. 2019). However, it is most likely that a greater ecological footprint of hominins occurred during the Middle Paleolithic. There is now much evidence for the initial spread of fire-use knowledge and traditions during the Middle Pleistocene, around 400–500 ka ago. The occurrences of fire use by hominins appears to be worldwide around that time (Albert 2015; MacDonald et al. 2021; Roebroeks et al.2021). As *Homo erectus* and *H. egastor* colonized areas across most of Eurasia, they brought with them their sophisticated tool kits and the use of fire to shape habitats and increase their own adaptability.

The control and use of fire for domestic purposes in archaeological contexts does not automatically point to the use of fire on nearby landscapes. This evidence comes from off-site contexts such as charcoal from lake cores, bogs, and alluvial sediments. There are many reasons why hunter-gatherers may benefit from igniting landscapes. This is one method of subsistence intensification. One of the more common reasons for hunter-gatherers burning the landscape is for clearing forest vegetation to allow grasslands to expand and provide attractive pastureland for grazing herbivores or to encourage pre-ferred wild food plants to grow. Other reasons can include clearing out dense vegetation to allow for easier passage along trails or to enable more favorable viewsheds (Bliege Bird et al. 2020; Kimmerer and Lake 2001; Nikulina et al. 2022; Scherjon et al. 2015).

This shift in theoretical perspectives on the relationships of past human societies to their natural environments opened new understandings of how profoundly our species could impact landscapes, environments, and climate. Archaeologists then were poised to formulate new understandings of the Anthropocene.

Key Phases of Human Impact on the Environment

Boivin and others (2016) point to four key phases of anthropogenic transformation: 1) Global Colonization, 2) Emergence and Spread of Agriculture and Pastoralism, 3) Island Colonization, and 4) Urbanism and the Elaboration of Trade Networks.

Global Expansion

The rise of anatomically modern *Homo sapiens* around 300,000 BP (Hublin et al. 2017) brought even more complex social organizations and tool types which allowed even greater ability for direct and indirect ecological engineering. *Homo sapiens* began to colonize regions throughout Eurasia systematically replacing other populations of the genus *Homo*. At some time around 60–45,000 years ago, *Homo sapiens* had reached Australia, and we now have clear evidence that by at least 18,000–16,000 years ago humans had begun to colonize the Americas, most likely traveling along a coastal route from Siberia, and spreading south and eastward across the two continents of North and South America (Allen and O'Connell 2003; Williams et al. 2018).

Pleistocene Extinctions

In many places this global expansion occurred close to the time of the extinction of vast numbers of Pleistocene mammalian species. In Northern Eurasia and Beringia 35% of megafauna went extinct in two phases, and at least two-thirds of Earth's megafauna went extinct between 50,000 and 10,000 years ago (Braje and Erlandson 2013; Boivin et al. 2016).

There has been much debate over the role of humans in these extinctions due to the profound climatic changes occurring with the retreat of the Pleistocene glacial ice in the Terminal Pleistocene, and the mismatch of some dates for the megafauna extinctions and human expansion. Some researchers implicate climate change as an overriding cause of megafauna extinctions, particularly in North America, citing the very small number of extinct megafauna kill sites in the archaeological record across the Western hemisphere in contrast to the much larger number of Clovis period kill sites of large herbivores such as bison which are still extant. Meltzer (2020) also points to the numerous other species of mammals which became extinct with no evidence of having been hunted. He puts more emphasis on a climatic change explanation, highlighting the need to learn more about the habitats and tolerance of the individual species lost, as well as more data of the types of changes to these habitats that occurred with the glacial to interglacial transition.

Although Meltzer's argument for the Americas is well grounded, numerous researchers still point to hunters entering new territories as one of a number of pressures to animal populations, rather than as a sole cause of extinctions. Some argue there are particular species which show the effects of human predation more than others including mammoths, horses, and sloths (Broughton and Weitzel 2018; Wolfe and Broughton 2020). Prates and Perez (2021), for example, show a strong correlation between the appearance of hunters bearing Fishtail Point lithic technologies and the rapid decline of megafauna in South America around 12,500 BP.

Sandom and others (2014) conducted a comprehensive study of global extinctions comparing the data of faunal loss with evidence for both climate change and human expansion. They concluded that most of the extinctions coincided more closely with human impact than with climatic change and local environmental factors. Their findings demonstrated that 177 large (10 kg or more) mammal species became extinct globally in the period between 132,000–1,000 years BP. This is broken down by species per continent: Africa 18, Australasia 26, Europe 19, North America 43, and South America 62. Focal points of extinction were southern South America, southeast North America, Western Europe, and southern Australia. Regions with notably fewer species' extinctions were sub-Saharan Africa, and southern Asia (Sandom et al. 2014).

With the later Pleistocene came the beginnings of cultivation and eventual spread of farming lifeways which resulted in the most profound impact of *Homo sapiens* on the environment. Food production led to accelerated Niche Construction behaviors and an increasing expertise in ecosystem engineering which culminated in the current effects of human impact that have influenced soil erosion, hydrology, and almost every biological taxon on the planet.

Spread of Agriculture and Pastoralism

Some of the most compelling archaeological studies of the terminal Pleistocene and early Holocene/Anthropocene address the impact of humans on landscapes with plant and animal food intensification, leading up to fully committed farming communities.

Agricultural and pastoral practices provide the most visible examples of Niche Construction leading to the Anthropocene through the propagation of plants and animals, and the altering of their genetic structures through the process of domestication. The Origins of Agriculture is a subject of much interest in archaeology. There have been numerous studies of these changing relationships between humans, plants, and animals worldwide spanning environments as diverse as deserts, grasslands, and tropical rain forests. In the past two decades, we have acquired extraordinary amounts of new data which have helped us understand the timing and processes of domestication worldwide (Fuller, Allaby, and Stevens 2010).

Much of this research shows that in the millennia preceding the advent of full agricultural lifeways, humans began to broaden their range of targeted plant and animal species in a foraging strategy known as "Broad Spectrum" (Stiner 2001; Zeder 2012). Many human groups began to intensify their food resources in the late Pleistocene and early Holocene periods by utilizing a form of low-level cultivation of wild plants. This was initially an opportunistic endeavor in which populations would sow the seeds of wild food plants to increase the foraging yield within the plants' habitats as well as within new environmental zones away from their natural habitats, to increase the availability of these preferred foods. Some researchers attribute this to the decrease in large mammals at the end of the Pleistocene, and the necessity of expanding the range of food types selected with "Broad Spectrum" foraging (Stiner 2001). This phenomenon profoundly changed the relationship between humans and other organisms, adding new forms of selective pressure on plant and animal populations. This is also a time when foragers were beginning to intensify their impact on environments primarily through burning of brush and forests, and possibly also some small-scale manipulation of water resources to enhance the habitat of favored plants and increase their propagation (Fuller and Qin 2009).

Most researchers no longer view the transition from foraging to agriculture as a direct progression from wild plant collection to cultivation and eventual domestication with a full commitment to a farming lifestyle. Nor do they regard the general process as originating from a single core locality. In the case of wheat (*Triticum* sp) and barley (*Hordeum* sp), the protracted shift from the wild to domestic species is not due to the lack of mutability of the cereal grass genome. Experimental studies involving generations of wild wheat and barley cultivated in modern fields showed that the change from fully wild to fully domesticated species could have occurred as rapidly as a couple hundred years if the farmers had purposely selected and cultivated individual plants for desirable traits. However, the archaeological data indicate much longer time frames (Hillman and Davis 1990).

In Southwest Asia for example, genetic information from aDNA on founder crops such as wheat and barley combined with macrobotanical analyses from the spikelets of ancient cereals shows that the process of domestication most likely took place over the course of thousands of years (Bogaard et al. 2021; Fuller, Allaby, and Stevens 2010; Fuller, Willcox, and Allaby 2011; Weiss, Kislev, and Hartmann 2006). Research in Southwest Asia as well as China indicates that the early stages of plant cultivation were opportunistic, combined with a heavy reliance on wild plant foods, and often abandoned in favor of reversion to full-time foraging. In Southwest Asia this long transition took place for the most part during the late Pleistocene, either beginning during the Last Glacial Maximum (LGM) at around 23,000 BP (Snir, Nadel, and Weiss 2015), or with the general warming that occurred shortly after the LGM around 15,000 BP (Fuller, Willcox, and Allaby 2011; Fuller, Asouti, and Purugganan 2012; Asouti and Fuller 2012).

As the planet warmed at the beginning of our current interglacial period from 11,700 BP onward, broad spectrum foraging and ecological engineering intensified in both Southwest Asia as well as China. Some of the world's early sedentary villages developed in these two regions, although the inhabitants were primarily foragers who practiced some low-level cultivation as a supplementary source of subsistence. This is evident at localities such as Netiv Hagdud and Dhra in the Jordan Valley (Bar-Yosef and Kislev 1989; Goring-Morris and Belfer-Cohen 2014; Kuijt and Mahasneh 1998), where wild cereals such as oats, barley, and some wheat were stored foods. This was also the case with some of the first villages in China such as Tianluoshan, Hemudu, and Jiahu, where rice (*Oryza* sp) was a component of the diet, but most foods were wild (Hu, Ambrose, and Wang 2006; Fuller and Qin 2010; Liu et al. 2007). Populations of foragers began to grow throughout this early Holocene period.

True farming villages only began to appear in Southwest Asia around 10,000 years ago. This was a period in the middle Holocene which was the wettest and warmest climatic episode in our current interglacial epoch. It is likely that the intensification of foraging and the shift to a farming lifestyle was the result of both push and pull factors. The push factor was the growing populations of foragers in the most productive and well-watered regions. This would have led to decreased sizes of home ranges for any given forager group, creating the necessity for intensifying production within the home territory to maintain an adequate level of food supply. The pull factor would have been the higher rainfall amounts, and predictability of rainy seasons that occurred at this time period, also referred to in Eurasia as the Holocene Climatic Optimum. The amount and predictability of rainfall would have decreased the risk associated with a farming lifestyle and allowed for more investment in formulating the artificial ecosystem that comes with a full-time investment in farming (Rosen and Rivera-Collazo 2012). The intensification of food production accelerated the impacts of humans on the landscape, including increased deforestation, burning of grasslands, changes in soil composition, soil erosion, and alterations of hydrological systems (Laland and O'Brien 2010). This was accompanied by a loss of biodiversity (Smith and Zeder 2013).

Throughout most of the period of research interest in the origins of agriculture, archaeologists have been concerned with showing the ways in which humans have increased their ability to mold the natural world and engineer artificial ecosystems by altering plants and animals through domestication (Bar-Yosef and Belfer-Cohen 1992; Liu et al. 2018; Zeder and Hesse 2000). However, more recently, there is an increasing trend in Anthropocene research to move away from an anthropocentric view of these new human/plant relationships and examine the process as a symbiotic interaction in which both the plants and the human populations benefit from this increase in plant propagation (Bogaard et al. 2021).

Island Colonization

Boivin and others (2016) identify Island Colonization as one of their four inflection points of global human impact on natural environments. They point out that island ecologies were often more fragile than continental ecological zones. One of the earliest examples of island colonization is the island of Flores in Southeast Asia which has evidence of early *Homo erectus* at 800,000 BP (Rick et al. 2013; Morwood et al. 2004). More substantial human expansion continued much later with the spread of *Homo sapiens* to New Guinea and Australia around 45–50,000 years ago. At the end of the Pleistocene, near-shore islands began to be colonized by foraging groups as is seen by archaeological evidence from the Channel Islands in California, and the Mediterranean (Erlandson et al. 2007; Rick et al. 2013). By the middle Holocene, early agriculturalists were settling islands in the Caribbean and the Mediterranean regions. An example was Cyprus in the Eastern Mediterranean. Here, Neolithic colonists brought an array of cereal crops, domesticated animals such as sheep, goat, cattle, pigs, dogs, and cats, and game animals such as deer and boar, and settled on Cyprus about 11,000 years ago (Lucas et al. 2011; Vigne et al. 2012).

However, the true final frontier of human settlement around the globe was the occupation of the Pacific islands by Polynesian Lapita peoples during the late Holocene, beginning around 2,800 BP. These populations performed extraordinary feats of navigation to reach the Pacific islands in sophisticated outrigger canoes. They brought with them a horticultural technology which contributed to establishing an artificial ecosystem on the islands that transformed the evolutionary paths of many island species. The Polynesians exploited wild food resources on and around the islands, cleared forests for horticulture, modified landscapes for fields and irrigation systems, and introduced a number of important economic plants and animals for food and materials. They also unintentionally introduced invasive species of plants and animals. One of the most destructive of these was the Pacific rat (*Rattus exulans*) because of its propensity for eating the eggs of nesting birds, and especially targeting palm nuts. The introduction of the rat to a number of Polynesian islands had a profound deforestation impact on palm forests, and sometimes these effects were so rapid, that deforestation signals in pollen cores detect this result hundreds of years before archaeological evidence for remains of the human settlers themselves (Rick et al. 2013; Anderson 2002; Hunt 2007; Athens 2009; Athens et al. 2002).

Archaeology of the Columbian Exchange and the Anthropocene

Another inflection point which is measurable by a combination of archaeological, historical, and geological data is the beginning of the so-called *Columbian Exchange* after 1492 when Europeans first landed in the Caribbean. From that time on, there began a flow of animals, plants, diseases, and other biotic materials, along with profound changes in ecological zones of both hemispheres (Boivin, Fuller, and Crowther 2012; Daru et al. 2021; Jones 2015). This was the start of true global trade networks (Crosby 2003). Archaeologically, we can detect the first evidence of maize phytoliths and pollen in the Eastern Hemisphere from lake and sea cores as well as evidence of crops from Europe, Asia, and Africa such as wheat, barley, sugarcane, and rice in North and South America (Lewis and Maslin 2015). Settler colonists introduced domestic animals from Eurasia to the Americas early in this trajectory. For example, the introduction of sheep, goats, cattle, pigs, and horses to the American Southwest had a profound impact on vegetation communities, landscapes, soil erosion, and hydrology (Jones 2015).

The overwhelming reduction in Indigenous human populations in the Americas that resulted from European contact and expansion, due to diseases, enslavement, war, and famine, also had an extreme impact on the natural environment of the Americas. Before European contact, there was a population of approximately 61 million Indigenous hunters, foragers, and farmers who actively managed the forests, grasslands, and woodlands.

The utter decimation of this population due to colonial policies between 1492 and 1650 to a level of only 6 million individuals, left many landscapes unmanaged across the Americas. The regeneration of forests and grasslands resulted in a massive increase in carbon sequestration leading to a measurable decline in CO_2 between 1570–1620 CE as indicated by Antarctic ice core records. It is likely that these effects contributed to the coldest period of the Little Ice Age (Lewis and Maslin 2015). Some other more nuanced studies of neotropical zones of the Americas suggest the neotropical forest regenerations occurred only in some areas, and in some cases the forest renewal might have begun before European contact (Hamilton et al. 2021).

Archaeological Contributions to Anthropocene Themes

The Question of When the Anthropocene Began

From the time of the first articles by Crutzen and Stoermer (2000) and Crutzen (2002), the question of when the Anthropocene began became a matter of primary concern for defining the period. The "Subcommission on Quaternary Stratigraphy" and the "International Commission on Stratigraphy" formulated the Anthropocene Working Group (AWG) to evaluate the need for a new formal chrono-stratigraphic unit, and to pinpoint the beginning in the chrono-stratigraphic record. Most members of the AWG voted for this new epoch and advised that the starting point (the "golden spike") be placed in the mid-twentieth century, after the explosions of the first nuclear weapons profoundly changed the atmospheric chemistry of the planet (Anthropocene Working Group 2019).

This new interest in tracing the origins, trajectory, and acceleration of the human ability to alter planetary environments, led many environmental archaeologists to the task of finding this "line in the sand" in the deep-time archaeological record. Consideration of the origins of the Anthropocene became seamlessly integrated into discussions about the ability of humans to profoundly alter their environments and became linked to the concept of "human niche construction." To muddy the waters of nomenclature further, some influential archaeological thinkers (c.f. Smith and Zeder 2013) proposed that a major acceleration in human impact on their environments began with the intensification and spread of agricultural lifestyles around 10,000 years ago. As discussed above, intensive cultivation went hand-in-hand with widespread forest clearance leading to change in the ecozonal assemblages of plants and animals, increasing soil erosion, alteration of hydrology, and the introduction of domesticated plants and animals into new habitats. However, this time period converged uncomfortably close to the beginning of our current interglacial epoch, the Holocene which began at 11,700 BP (Roberts 2014). This seemingly called in to question the need for two overlapping epochs. Recognizing this, Smith and Zeder (2013) proposed that we discard the notion of a distinct line between the Holocene and Anthropocene epochs. They suggested that it would be both more accurate, and more helpful to converge the two epochs into one and define successive phases of increased human impact within this combined epoch.

Paleoclimatologist Bill Ruddimen teamed up with archaeologists such as Dorian Fuller and published several insightful articles showing a clear and highly significant rise in atmospheric methane (CH) levels around 5,000 BP (Ruddiman et al. 2008; Ruddiman, Ellis, et al. 2015; Ruddiman, Fuller, et al. 2015). This was exactly within the time frame of the first expansion of wetlands for rice paddy farming in East and Southeast Asia. The expansion of these rice paddies would have led to more forest clearance, and an increase in decaying organics raising the level of methane emissions to globally detectable levels. This rise in methane within the middle of a Quaternary Period interglacial episode was unprecedented when compared with data from other interglacial phases throughout the Pleistocene.

Other historians and geographers have proposed we place the line at the beginning of the "Columbian Exchange", ca. 1492, with the intensified exchange of plants, animals, diseases, and goods between the Western and Eastern hemispheres. The rise of greenhouse gases in the atmosphere took a sudden and dramatic turn upwards in the early modern period beginning in the seventeenth century as the now well-known graphic called the "hockey stick" dramatically displays. This evidence was brought to the attention of the public by Michael Mann, sparking what he terms as the current "climate wars." There began the struggle for control over the public perception of modern global warming, and the extent to which humans (and for the most part industrialized nations) are responsible (Mann 2012).

In a recent paper, Gibbard and others (2022) propose a very reasonable solution that may help resolve the issue of when to place the beginning of the Anthropocene geological epoch. They point to the archaeological evidence indicating that human impact on the planet accelerates steadily over the course of the two-million-year existence of the genus *Homo* and has no clear beginning point. Therefore, they suggest that we shouldn't make the Anthropocene a geological epoch at all. Rather, they recommend that we use the term to define an ongoing geological *event* within the Holocene Epoch and record it as the Anthropocene Event.

What the Anthropocene Concept Means for Our Interpretation of Relationships Between Humans and Nature

Within the past two decades, many anthropologists have examined the relationships between humans and the natural world from a perspective that rejects anthropocentrism (Birch 2018; Haraway 2008; Hartigan 2015). There is an acknowledgement that our methods of conducting scientific inquiry, the questions we ask, and the interpretations we come up with are rooted in a Western science perception of human exceptionalism that in essence considers humans as separate from the natural world. This concept is very familiar to modern Western societies, but actually, somewhat unusual for other world traditions.

Some anthropological archaeologists recently have begun to employ this perspective as well. These scholars are beginning to explore the relationships between humans and other biological entities from a paradigm of human integration with the natural world. Some of these studies also examine the agency of the non-human biological world. In exploring new ways to understand relationships between humans and nature, particularly relating to domestication, there is a growing number of researchers who advocate moving away from the simple dichotomy of wild/domestic plant and animal life and consider the plants and animals we depend upon to have their own agency. This is especially evident in the relationships leading up to origins and expansion of agriculture and pastoralism (c. f. Birch 2018; Bogaard et al. 2021; Boyd 2017; Head 2014).

Multispecies Archaeology

The concept of the Anthropocene and increasing investigations into the impact of humans on the biological spheres of the planet are primarily driven by the paradigm of "anthropocentrism" which has been ever-present in most anthropological analyses of our relationships with the earth and other lifeforms. In recent years, anthropologists have begun to explore a multispecies perspective of the Anthropocene (c.f. Hartigan 2015; Haraway 2008). Although little of this literature relates to the ancient past (Boyd 2017), some archaeologists have investigated this new perspective, attempting to develop narratives of the human past without humans as the focal point of the research questions (Birch 2018). Boyd (2017: 308) points to work by scholars (c.f. Armstrong Oma 2010) who recommend a blending of human and animal perspectives within a context of a social contract or partnership between both entities. However, as Boyd points out, there is a lack of symmetry and equity in this relationship when the non-human animal can only function as a "tacit collaborator." Boyd (2017: 310) recommends that tracing human/animal relationships in the past requires more attention to issues of "mutualism and exclusion" including questions of nonhuman agencies such as "animal gender, embodiment, semiosis, and ways of becoming that are not necessarily tied to the human" and formulating studies encompassing a broader understanding of a more integrated human/nonhuman ecology. Frie (2021) rightly claims that the concept of a multispecies archaeology has great heuristic value as we adjust our perspectives of human/animal and human/plant relationships from deep-time hunting/gathering economies, through the transition to domestication, and onward into the present state of low species biodiversity, allowing us to learn lessons from the past that will help usher us into a more compassionate, caring, and sustainable new version of the Anthropocene going forward into the future.

Traditional Ecological Knowledge

The importance of Traditional Ecological Knowledge (TEK) and Indigenous science is evident from an early literature review by Sillitoe (1998). In this paper he highlights the need to account for traditional ways of knowing in developmental planning for a world that is increasingly challenged by the effects of climate change. Sillitoe points out that these traditions and perspectives are rooted in expert knowledge that is often more effective in managing environmental systems than methods developed by colonial and modern Western societies.

Past human societies and present Indigenous communities throughout the world have demonstrated great resilience in the wake of ecological changes through time and have developed innovative ways to live sustainably in diverse ecological settings, by employing varying levels of environmental management. They are well-placed to utilize this knowledge and techniques because they have inherited "toolkits" born from long-term memories of survival strategies. These traditions are transmitted through generations of memories, and stories assembled from deep-time information embedded in oral traditions, myths, legends, rituals, and songs (Butzer 1982; Rosen et al. 2022; Rosen and Rivera-Collazo 2012). These constitute "memory-messages" that convey information about the sustainable use of water resources, plants, and animals over the long-term. An excellent example of this is highlighted by Kimmerer and Lake (2001) who discuss the way Indigenous populations in North America traditionally used fire to manage vegetation in their home ranges. The regular controlled burns facilitated the growth of economically useful wild plant varieties and impeded uncontrolled wildfires. Kimmerer and Lake propose that such Indigenous knowledge of forest management should be a consideration for modern contemporary policy and developmental planners. Archaeologists can access this kind of Traditional Knowledge through interviews with modern descendant communities, ethnohistorical records, and archaeological data including settlement distribution, ancient tool kits, and plant and animal remains from archaeological excavations, as well as geoarchaeological paleolandscape reconstruction (Nicholas and Markey 2015; Rosen et al. 2022).

Archaeologists have long focused on ancient systems of food production and environmental management in many localities worldwide. However, now there is an increased interest and urgency in finding and perhaps adapting these traditional systems to agricultural production in our modern world. One example of this is the discovery of the vast extent of ancient Maya irrigation systems in the lowlands of Guatemala and Belize. These networks made use of lowland "bajos" (seasonal swampland) to create ridged fields, check-dams, and irrigation canals to intensify food production in neotropical environments (Dunning and Beach 2010; Krause et al. 2021). Neotropical regions are characterized by poor soils that rapidly loose fertility through leaching and erosion under modern swidden agricultural techniques, intensive logging, and ranching. The discovery of more sustainable land-use systems of the past can contribute to long-term planning of better land-use practices for future intensification and support of larger populations on those landscapes. Similar work has also been undertaken in highland Peru (Erickson 1988).

Similarly, for dryland regions of the earth, geographers and anthropologists have begun to point out that mobile pastoralists in marginal regions for the most part are stewards of the desert landscapes rather than agents for widespread devegetation and erosion. For example, in the historical past and modern present, local governments throughout Africa, the Middle East, and East Asia among other localities have restricted herder mobility, access to prime grasslands, and water sources which has forced these societies to put excess pressure on vegetation and landscapes of more restricted ranges. When unrestricted by local governments, mobile pastoralists often maintain the biodiversity and ecological sustainability in their home ranges by moving between pastures before they are overgrazed. This TEK of sustainable living in dryland regions has imparted great resilience to communities living in vulnerable dryland regions during episodes of climatic change (Davis 2005; Marshall et al. 2018; Rosen et al. 2019; Rosen 2011; Wright 2019).

Concluding Remarks: How Can Archaeology Help Design a "Good Anthropocene"?

Several recent papers point to the importance of studying the past through history, archaeology, and paleoecology for information which can aid us in developing a future Anthropocene that is more sustainable and equitable for ourselves and all other lifeforms on the planet (Boivin and Crowther 2021; Edgeworth 2021; Lane 2015; Rick and Sandweiss 2020). A number of international organizations acknowledge the benefits of studying the environmental challenges of past societies from interdisciplinary perspectives. Examples of these include PAGES, Past Global Change (PAGES, International Project 2020–2023), IHOPE, Integrated History and Future of People on Earth (IHOPE 2023), the Climate Change and History Research Initiative (CCHRI 2023), and ArchaeoGLOBE (Harvard Dataverse 2023). All of these organizations are actively assembling data from past climates and societies with the goal of addressing current and future global challenges.

Archaeology in particular can provide insights about why we as humans are compelled to alter the ecology of our surroundings and how past societies lived on their landscapes in sustainable ways. It can inspire us with new ideas for reviving ancient agricultural technologies, crops, and varieties of domestic animals that are more resilient to changes brought on by recent global warming. It can help us revive and reconstruct ancient water systems to provide renewable sources of water and reconstitute soil fertility. All of this is especially pertinent for supporting food security in modern developing nations, and some of our knowledge about the past can help us build sustainable cities which include green spaces and small-holding urban farming systems. The information we learn about past societies not only informs us about past successes of survival and continuity in the face of climate change, but also about social systems which failed to survive the challenges of ever-shifting climatic regimes. Archaeological research has shown that this is a phenomenon that impacted all environmental zones of the planet. We are not alone on this planet as a generation facing new threats and challenges caused by over-exploitation of resources, the impacts of shifting weather and climatic patterns, reduction of biodiversity, inequities in distribution of commodities, and struggles to feed growing populations living in areas with decreasing productivity and political strife. Past societies dealt with all of these issues and problems, and some had succeeded to overcome these adversities, albeit on a smaller scale than our current integrated world system. Still, if we listen to our own heritage of "memory-messages" from deep time, there is much we in the twenty-first century can learn from our ancestors that can help us work towards an equitable and sustainable future.

References

Albert, Rosa M. 2015. "Anthropocene and early human behavior." *The Holocene* 25 (10): 1542–1552. https://doi.org/10.1177/0959683615588377.

Allen, Jim and James O'Connell. 2003. "The long and the short of it: Archaeological approaches to determining when humans first colonised Australia and New Guinea." *Australian Archaeology* 57 (1): 5–19.

Anderson, A. 2002. "Faunal collapse, landscape change and settlement history in remote Oceania." *World Archaeology* 33 (3): 375–390.

Anthropocene Working Group. 2019. "Report of Activities 2019." *Newsletter of the Anthropocene Working Group* 9: 1–31. http://quaternary.stratigraphy.org/wp-content/uploads/2020/09/Anthropocene-Working-Group-Newsletter-Vol-9-final.pdf.

Armstrong Oma, Kristin. 2010. "Between trust and domination: Social contracts between humans and animals." *World Archaeology* 42 (2): 175–187.

Asouti, Eleni and Dorian Q. Fuller. 2012. "From foraging to farming in the southern Levant: The development of Epipalaeolithic and Pre-pottery Neolithic plant management strategies." *Vegetation History and Archaeobotany* 21 (2): 149–162. https://doi.org/10.1007/s00334-011-0332-0.

Athens, J. Stephen. 2009. "Rattus exulans and the catastrophic disappearance of Hawai'i's native lowland forest." *Biological Invasions* 11 (7): 1489–1501.

Athens, J. Stephen, H.D. Tuggle, J.V. Ward, and D.J. Welch. 2002. "Avifaunal extinctions, vegetation change, and Polynesian impacts in prehistoric Hawai'i." *Archaeology in Oceania* 37: 57–78.

Bar-Yosef, Ofer, and Anna Belfer-Cohen. 1992. "From foraging to farming in the Mediterranean Levant." In *Transitions to Agriculture in Prehistory*, edited by Anne Birgitte Gebauer and T. Douglas Price, in Monographs in World Archaeology, 21–48. Madison: Prehistory Press.

Bar-Yosef, Ofer and Mordechai E. Kislev. 1989. "Early farming communities in the Jordan Valley." In *Foraging and Farming: The Evolution of Plant Exploitation*, edited by David R. Harris and Gordon C. Hillman, 632–642. London: Unwin Hyman.

Barbetti, Mike. 1986. "Traces of fire in the archaeological record, before one million years ago?" *Journal of Human Evolution* 15 (8): 771–781.

Bellomo, Randy V. 1994. "Methods of determining early hominid behavioral activities associated with the controlled use of fire at FxJj 20 Main, Koobi Fora, Kenva." *Journal of Human Evolution* 27 (1–3):173–195.

Birch, Suzanne E. Pilaar, ed. 2018. *Multispecies Archaeology*. London: Routledge.

Bliege Bird, R., C. McGuire, D.W. Bird, M.H. Price, D. Zeanah, and D.G. Nimmo. 2020. "Fire mosaics and habitat choice in nomadic foragers." *Proc Natl Acad Sci U S A* 117 (23): 12904–12914. https://doi.org/10.1073/pnas.1921709117. https://www.ncbi.nlm.nih.gov/pubmed/32461375.

Bogaard, Amy, Robin Allaby, Benjamin S. Arbuckle, Robin Bendrey, Sarah Crowley, Thomas Cucchi, Tim Denham, Laurent Frantz, Dorian Fuller, Tom Gilbert, Elinor Karlsson, Aurélie Manin, Fiona Marshall, Natalie Mueller, Joris Peters, Charles Stépanoff, Alexander Weide, and Greger Larson. 2021. "Reconsidering domestication from a process archaeology perspective." *World Archaeology* 53 (1): 56–77. https://doi.org/10.1080/00438243.2021.1954990.

Boivin, N. and A. Crowther. 2021. "Mobilizing the past to shape a better Anthropocene." *Nat Ecol Evol* 5 (3): 273–284. https://doi.org/10.1038/s41559-020-01361-4. https://www.ncbi.nlm.nih.gov/pubmed/33462488.

Boivin, Nicole, Dorian Q. Fuller, and Alison Crowther. 2012. "Old World globalization and the Columbian exchange: Comparison and contrast." *World Archaeology* 44 (3): 452–469. https://doi.org/10.1080/00438243.2012.729404.

Boivin, N.L., M.A. Zeder, D.Q. Fuller, A. Crowther, G. Larson, J.M. Erlandson, T. Denham, and M.D. Petraglia. 2016. "Ecological consequences of human niche construction: Examining long-term anthropogenic shaping of global species distributions." *Proc Natl Acad Sci U S A* 113 (23): 6388–6396. https://doi.org/10.1073/pnas.1525200113. https://www.ncbi.nlm.nih.gov/pubmed/27274046.

Boyd, Brian. 2017. "Archaeology and human–animal relations: Thinking through anthropocentrism." *Annual Review of Anthropology* 46 (1): 299–316. https://doi.org/10.1146/annurev-anthro-102116-041346.

Braidwood, Robert. 1951. "From cave to village in prehistoric Iraq." *American Schools of Oriental Research* 124: 12–18.

Braje, Todd J. and Jon M. Erlandson. 2013. "Human acceleration of animal and plant extinctions: A Late Pleistocene, Holocene, and Anthropocene continuum." *Anthropocene* 4 (0): 14–23. https://doi.org/http://dx.doi.org/10.1016/j.ancene.2013.08.003. http://www.sciencedirect.com/science/article/pii/S2213305413000118.

Broughton, J.M. and E.M. Weitzel. 2018. "Population reconstructions for humans and megafauna suggest mixed causes for North American Pleistocene extinctions." *Nat Commun* 9 (1): 5441. https://doi.org/10.1038/s41467-018-07897-1. https://www.ncbi.nlm.nih.gov/pubmed/30575758.

Bruchac, Margaret M. 2014. "Indigenous knowledge and traditional knowledge." In *Encyclopedia of Global Archaeology*, edited by Claire Smith, 3814–3824. New York: Springer.

Butzer, Karl W. 1964. *Environment and Archaeology*. Aldine Chicago.

Butzer, Karl W. 1982. *Archaeology as Human Ecology: Method and Theory for a Contextual Approach*. Cambridge: Cambridge University Press.

Butzer, Karl W. 2012. "Collapse, environment, and society." *PNAS* 109 (10): 3632–3639. https://doi.org/10.1073/pnas.1114845109/-/.

Butzer, Karl W., and Georgina H. Endfield. 2012. "Critical perspectives on historical collapse." *Proceedings of the National Academy of Sciences* 109 (10): 3628–3631. https://doi.org/10.1073/pnas.1114772109. http://www.pnas.org/content/109/10/3628.abstract.

Caillon, Sophie, Georgina Cullman, Bas Verschuuren, and Eleanor J. Sterling. 2017. "Moving beyond the human–nature dichotomy through biocultural approaches: Including ecological well-being in resilience indicators." *Ecology and Society* 22 (4). https://doi.org/10.5751/es-09746-220427.

Campbell, Peter B. 2021. "The Anthropocene, hyperobjects and the archaeology of the future past." *Antiquity* 95 (383): 1315–1330. https://doi.org/10.15184/aqy.2021.116.

Carson, Rachel. 1963. *Silent Spring*. London: Hamilton.

CCHRI. 2023. *Climate Change and History Research Initiative*. Princeton University. https://climatechangeandhistory.princeton.edu/.

Chakrabarty, Dipesh. 2008. "The climate of history: Four theses." *Critical Inquiry* 35: 197–222.

Clark, Grahame. 1954. *Excavations at Star Carr: An Early Mesolithic Site at Seamer near Scarborough, Yorkshire*. CUP Archive.

Crosby, Alfred W. 2003. *The Columbian Exchange: Biological and Cultural Consequences of 1492*. Westport, Conn: Preager.

Crumley, Carole L., Tommy Lennartsson, and Anna Westin, eds. 2018. *Issues and Concepts in Historical Ecology: The Past and Future of Landscapes and Regions*. Cambridge, UK: Cambridge University Press.

Crutzen, Paul. 2002. "Geology of Mankind." *Nature* 415: 23.

Crutzen, Paul J. and Eugene F. Stoermer. 2000. "The 'Anthropocene'." *International Geosphere-Biosphere Program (IGBP) Global Change Newsletter* 41: 17–18.

Daru, B.H., T.J. Davies, C.G. Willis, E.K. Meineke, A. Ronk, M. Zobel, M. Partel, A. Antonelli, and C.C. Davis. 2021. "Widespread homogenization of plant communities in the Anthropocene." *Nat Commun* 12 (1): 6983. https://doi.org/10.1038/s41467-021-27186-8. https://www.ncbi.nlm.nih.gov/pubmed/34873159.

Davis, Diana K. 2005. "Indigenous knowledge and the desertification debate: Problematizing expert knowledge in North Africa." *Geoforum* 36 (4): 509–524. https://doi.org/10.1016/j.geoforum.2004.08.003.

Dunning, Nicholas P. and Timothy Beach. 2010. "Farms and forests: Spatial and temporal perspectives on ancient Maya landscapes." *Landscapes and Societies*: 369–389.

Edgeworth, Matt. 2021. "Transgressing time: Archaeological evidence in/of the Anthropocene." *Annual Review of Anthropology* 50 (1): 93–108. https://doi.org/10.1146/annurev-anthro-101819-110118.

Erickson, Clark L. 1988. "Raised field agriculture in the Lake Titicaca basin: Putting ancient agriculture back to work." *Expedition* 30 (3): 8–16.

Erlandson, Jon M., Michael H. Graham, Bruce J. Bourque, Debra Corbett, James A. Estes, and Robert S. Steneck. 2007. "The Kelp Highway Hypothesis: Marine ecology, the coastal migration theory, and the peopling of the Americas." *The Journal of Island and Coastal Archaeology* 2 (2): 161–174. https://doi.org/10.1080/15564890701628612.

Escobar, Arturo. 1996. "Construction nature. Elements for a poststructuralist political ecology." *Futures* 28 (4): 325–343.

Faith, J. Tyler, John Rowan, Andrew Du, and W. Andrew Barr. 2020. "The uncertain case for human-driven extinctions prior to Homo sapiens." *Quaternary Research* 96: 88–104. https://doi.org/10.1017/qua.2020.51. https://www.cambridge.org/core/article/uncertain-case-for-humandriven-extinctions-prior-to-homo-sapiens/F91F1125CC0A988E322DA9AD9564F0C5.

Feeney, John. 2019. "Hunter-gatherer land management in the human break from ecological sustainability." *The Anthropocene Review* 6 (3): 223–242. https://doi.org/10.1177/2053019619864382.

Field, Judith H., Lisa Kealhofer, Richard Cosgrove, and Adelle C. F. Coster. 2016. "Human–environment dynamics during the Holocene in the Australian Wet Tropics of NE Queensland: A starch and phytolith study." *Journal of Anthropological Archaeology* 44: 216–234. https://doi.org/10.1016/j.jaa.2016.07.007.

Foley, Stephen F., Detlef Gronenborn, Meinrat O. Andreae, Joachim W. Kadereit, Jan Esper, Denis Scholz, Ulrich Pöschl, Dorrit E. Jacob, Bernd R. Schöne, Rainer Schreg, Andreas Vött, David Jordan, Jos Lelieveld, Christine G. Weller, Kurt W. Alt, Sabine Gaudzinski-Windheuser, Kai-Christian Bruhn, Holger Tost, Frank Sirocko, and Paul J. Crutzen. 2013. "The Palaeoanthropocene – the beginnings of anthropogenic environmental change." *Anthropocene* 3 (0): 83–88. https://doi.org/http://dx.doi.org/10.1016/j.ancene.2013.11.002. http://www.sciencedirect.com/science/article/pii/S2213305413000404.

Frie, Adrienne C. 2021. "Multispecies futures." *Current Swedish Archaeology* 29 (1): 34–37.

Fuller, Dorian, Robin Allaby, and Chris Stevens. 2010. "Domestication as innovation: The entanglement of techniques, technology and chance in the domestication of cereal crops." *World Archaeology* 42 (1): 13–28. https://doi.org/10.1080/00438240903429680.

Fuller, Dorian Q., Eleni Asouti, and Michael D. Purugganan. 2012. "Cultivation as slow evolutionary entanglement: Comparative data on rate and sequence of domestication." *Vegetation History and Archaeobotany* 21 (2): 131–145. https://doi.org/10.1007/s00334-011-0329-8.

Fuller, Dorian Q. and Ling Qin. 2009. "Water management and labour in the origins and dispersal of Asian rice." *World Archaeology* 41 (1): 88–111. https://doi.org/10.1080/00438240802668321.

Fuller, Dorian Q. and Ling Qin. 2010. "Declining oaks, increasing artistry, and cultivating rice: The environmental and social context of the emergence of farming in the Lower Yangtze Region." *Environmental Archaeology* 15 (2): 139–159. https://doi.org/10.1179/146141010x12640787648531.

Fuller, D.Q., G. Willcox, and R.G. Allaby. 2011. "Early agricultural pathways: Moving outside the 'core area' hypothesis in Southwest Asia." *J Exp Bot*. https://doi.org/10.1093/jxb/err307. http://www.ncbi.nlm.nih.gov/pubmed/22058404.

Gibbard, Philip, Michael Walker, Andrew Bauer, Matthew Edgeworth, Lucy Edwards, Erle Ellis, Stanley Finney, Jacquelyn L. Gill, Mark Maslin, Dorothy Merritts, and William Ruddiman. 2022. "The Anthropocene as an event, not an epoch." *Journal of Quaternary Science* 37 (3). https://doi.org/https://doi.org/10.1002/jqs.3416. https://onlinelibrary.wiley.com/doi/abs/10.1002/jqs.3416.

Glikson, Andrew. 2013. "Fire and human evolution: The deep-time blueprints of the Anthropocene." *Anthropocene* 3 (0): 89–92. https://doi.org/http://dx.doi.org/10.1016/j.ancene.2014.02.002. http://www.sciencedirect.com/science/article/pii/S2213305414000046.

Goring-Morris, A. Nigel and A. Belfer-Cohen. 2014. "The southern Levant (Cisjordan) during the Neolithic period." In *The Oxford Handbook of the Archaeology of the Levant (ca. 8000–332 BCE)*, edited by Mary Steiner and Ann E. Killebrew, 147–169. Oxford: Oxford University Press.

Gowlett, John A.J. 2006. "The early settlement of northern Europe: Fire history in the context of climate change and the social brain." *Comptes Rendus Palevol* 5 (1–2):299–310. https://doi.org/10.1016/j.crpv.2005.10.008.

Haldon, John, Merle Eisenberg, Lee Mordechai, Adam Izdebski, and Sam White. 2020. "Lessons from the past, policies for the future: Resilience and sustainability in past crises." *Environment Systems and Decisions*. https://doi.org/10.1007/s10669-020-09778-9.

Hamilton, Rebecca, Jesse Wolfhagen, Noel Amano, Nicole Boivin, David Max Findley, José Iriarte, Jed O. Kaplan, Janelle Stevenson, and Patrick Roberts. 2021. "Non-uniform tropical forest responses to the 'Columbian Exchange' in the Neotropics and Asia-Pacific." *Nature Ecology & Evolution* 5 (8): 1174–1184. https://doi.org/10.1038/s41559-021-01474-4. https://doi.org/10.1038/s41559-021-01474-4.

Haraway, Donna J. 2008. *When Species Meet*. Minneapolis: University of Minnesota Press.

Hartigan, John. 2015. *Aesop's Anthropology: A Multispecies Approach*. Minneapolis: University of Minnesota Press.

Harvard Dataverse. 2023. *ArchaeoGLOBE*. https://dataverse.harvard.edu/dataverse/ArchaeoGLOBE.

Hassan, Fekri. 2000. "Environmental perception and human responses in history and prehistory." In *The Way the Wind Blows: Climate, History, and Human Action*, edited by Roderick J.McIntosh, Joseph A.Tainter and Susan Keech McIntosh, 121–140. New York: Columbia University Press.

Haug, G.H., D. Ganther, L.C. Peterson, D.M. Sigman, Y.R. Hughen, and B. Aeschlimann. 2003. "Climate and the collapse of Maya civilization." *Science* 299: 1731–1735.

Head, Lesley. 2014. "Contingencies of the Anthropocene: Lessons from the 'Neolithic'." *The Anthropocene Review* 1 (2): 113–125. https://doi.org/10.1177/2053019614529745.

Hillman, G.C., and M.S. Davis. 1990. "Measured domestication rates in wild wheat and barley under primitive cultivation, and their archaeological implications." *Journal of World Prehistory* 4 (2): 157–222.

Hlubik, S., R. Cutts, D.R. Braun, F. Berna, C.S. Feibel, and J.W.K. Harris. 2019. "Hominin fire use in the Okote member at Koobi Fora, Kenya: New evidence for the old debate." *J Hum Evol* 133: 214–229. https://doi.org/10.1016/j.jhevol.2019.01.010. https://www.ncbi.nlm.nih.gov/pubmed/31358181.

Hoelle, Jeffrey, and Nicholas C. Kawa. 2020. "Placing the Anthropos in Anthropocene." *Annals of the American Association of Geographers* 111 (3): 655–662.

Hornborg, Alf. 2019. "Colonialism in the Anthropocene." *Journal of Human Rights and the Environment* 10 (1): 7–21.

Hornborg, Alf and Carole L. Crumley. 2006. *The World System and the Earth System: Global Socio-environmental Change and Sustainability since the Neolithic*. Walnut Creek, CA: Left Coast Press.

Howe, Cymene. 2015. "Latin America in the Anthropocene: Energy transitions and climate change mitigations." *The Journal of Latin American and Caribbean Anthropology* 20 (2): 231–241. https://doi.org/10.1111/jlca.12146.

Hu, Yaowu, Stanley H. Ambrose, and Changsui Wang. 2006. "Stable isotopic analysis of human bones from Jiahu site, Henan, China: Implications for the transition to agriculture." *Journal of Archaeological Science* 33 (9): 1319. http://www.sciencedirect.com/science/article/B6WH8-4JWMTCS-1/2/6be1f10273fd906256070e474107cb01.

Hublin, Jean-Jacques, Abdelouahed Ben-Ncer, Shara E. Bailey, Sarah E. Freidline, Simon Neubauer, Matthew M. Skinner, Inga Bergmann, Adeline Le Cabec, Stefano Benazzi, Katerina Harvati, and Philipp Gunz. 2017. "New fossils from Jebel Irhoud, Morocco and the pan-African origin of Homo sapiens." *Nature* 546 (7657): 289–292. https://doi.org/10.1038/nature22336. https://doi.org/10.1038/nature22336.

Hunt, Terry L. 2007. "Rethinking Easter Island's ecological catastrophe." *Journal of Archaeological Science* 34 (3): 485–502. https://doi.org/10.1016/j.jas.2006.10.003.

IHOPE. 2023. "Integrated history and future of people on Earth." https://ihopenet.org/.

Izdebski, Adam, John Haldon, and Piotr Filipkowski, eds. 2022. *Perspectives on Public Policy in Societal-Environmental Crises: What the Future Needs from History, Risk, Systems and Decisions (RSD)*. New York: Springer.

Jones, Emily Lena. 2015. "The 'Columbian Exchange' and landscapes of the Middle Rio Grande Valley, USA, AD 1300–1900." *The Holocene* 25 (10): 1698–1706. https://doi.org/10.1177/0959683615588375.

Kimmerer, Robin. 2013. *Braiding Sweetgrass: Indigenous Wisdom, Scientific Knowledge and the Teachings of Plants*. Minneapolis: Milkweed editions.

Kimmerer, Robin Wall, and Frank Kanawha Lake. 2001. "The role of Indigenous burning in land management." *Journal of Forestry* (November): 36–41.

Krause, Samantha, Timothy P. Beach, Sheryl Luzzadder-Beach, Duncan Cook, Steven R. Bozarth, Fred Valdez Jr, and Thomas H. Guderjan. 2021. "Tropical wetland persistence through the Anthropocene: Multiproxy reconstruction of environmental change in a Maya agroecosystem." *Anthropocene* 34: 100284.

Kuijt, Ian and Hamzeh Mahasneh. 1998. "Dhra': An early neolithic village in the southern Jordan valley." *Journal of Field Archaeology* 25 (2): 153–161. http://links.jstor.org/sici?sici=0093-4690%28199822%2925%3A2%3C153%3ADAENVI%3E2.0.CO%3B2-O.

Laland, Kevin N. and Michael J. O'Brien. 2010. "Niche Construction theory and archaeology." *Journal of Archaeological Method and Theory* 17 (4): 303–322. https://doi.org/10.1007/s10816-010-9096-6.

Lane, Paul J. 2015. "Archaeology in the age of the Anthropocene: A critical assessment of its scope and societal contributions." *Journal of Field Archaeology* 40 (5): 485–498. https://doi.org/10.1179/2042458215y.0000000022.

Latour, Bruno. 2011. "Politics of nature: East and West perspectives." *Ethics & Global Politics* 4 (1): 71–80.

Leopold, Aldo, and Charles Walsh Schwartz. 1968. *A Sand County Almanac, and Sketches Here and There*. London: Oxford University Press.

Lewis, S.L. and M.A. Maslin. 2015. "Defining the anthropocene." *Nature* 519 (7542): 171–180. https://doi.org/10.1038/nature14258. https://www.ncbi.nlm.nih.gov/pubmed/25762280.

Liu, Li, Gyoung-Ah Lee, Leping Jiang, and Juzhong Zhang. 2007. "Evidence for the early beginning (c. 9000 cal. BP) of rice domestication in China: A response." *The Holocene* 17: 1059–1068. http://hol.sagepub.com.libproxy.ucl.ac.uk/cgi/reprint/17/8/1059.

Liu, Li, Maureece J. Levin, Michael F. Bonomo, Jiajing Wang, Jinming Shi, Xingcan Chen, Jiayi Han, and Yanhua Song. 2018. "Harvesting and processing wild cereals in the Upper Palaeolithic Yellow River Valley, China." *Antiquity* 92 (363): 603–619. https://doi.org/10.15184/aqy.2018.36.

Lourandos, Harry. 2010. "Change or stability? Hydraulics, hunter-gatherers and population in temperate Australia." *World Archaeology* 11 (3): 245–264. https://doi.org/10.1080/00438243.1980.9979765.

Lucas, Leilani, Sue Colledge, Alan Simmons, and Dorian Q. Fuller. 2011. "Crop introduction and accelerated island evolution: Archaeobotanical evidence from 'Ais Yiorkis and Pre-Pottery Neolithic Cyprus." *Vegetation History and Archaeobotany*. https://doi.org/10.1007/s00334-011-0323-1.

MacDonald, K., F. Scherjon, E. van Veen, K. Vaesen, and W. Roebroeks. 2021. "Middle Pleistocene fire use: The first signal of widespread cultural diffusion in human evolution." *Proc Natl Acad Sci U S A* 118 (31). https://doi.org/10.1073/pnas.2101108118. https://www.ncbi.nlm.nih.gov/pubmed/34301807.

McIntosh, Roderick J., Joseph A. Tainter, and Susan Keech McIntosh. 2000. "Climate, history, and human action." In *The Way the Wind Blows: Climate, History, and Human Action*, edited by Roderick J. McIntosh, Joseph A. Tainter and Susan Keech McIntosh, 1–42. New York: Columbia University Press.

Mann, Michael E. 2012. *The Hockey Stick and the Climate Wars: Dispatches from the Front Lines*. New York: Columbia University Press.

Marshall, F., R.E B. Reid, S. Goldstein, M. Storozum, A. Wreschnig, L. Hu, P. Kiura, R. Shahack-Gross, and S.H. Ambrose. 2018. "Ancient herders enriched and restructured African grasslands." *Nature* 561 (7723): 387–390. https://doi.org/10.1038/s41586-018-0456-9. https://www.ncbi.nlm.nih.gov/pubmed/30158702.

Meltzer, D.J. 2020. "Overkill, glacial history, and the extinction of North America's Ice Age megafauna." *Proc Natl Acad Sci U S A* 117 (46): 28555–28563. https://doi.org/10.1073/pnas.2015032117. https://www.ncbi.nlm.nih.gov/pubmed/33168739.

Morwood, M.J., R.P. Soejono, R.G. Roberts, T. Sutikna, C.S.M. Turney, K.E. Westaway, W.J. Rink, J. x Zhao, G.D. van den Bergh, Rokus Awe Due, D.R. Hobbs, M.W. Moore, M.I. Bird, and L.K. Fifield. 2004. "Archaeology and age of a new hominin from Flores in eastern Indonesia." *Nature* 431 (7012): 1087–1091. https://doi.org/10.1038/nature02956. https://doi.org/10.1038/nature02956.

Nicholas, George and Nola Markey. 2015. "Traditional knowledge, archaeological evidence, and other ways of knowing." In *Material Evidence: Learning from Archaeological Practice*, edited by Robert Chapman and Alison Wylie, 307–328. New York: Routledge.

Nikulina, Anastasia, Katharine MacDonald, Fulco Scherjon, Elena A. Pearce, Marco Davoli, Jens-Christian Svenning, Emily Vella, Marie-José Gaillard, Anhelina Zapolska, Frank Arthur, Alexandre Martinez, Kailin Hatlestad, Florence Mazier, Maria Antonia Serge, Karl-Johan Lindholm, Ralph Fyfe, Hans Renssen, Didier M. Roche, Sjoerd Kluiving, and Wil Roebroeks. 2022. "Tracking hunter-gatherer impact on vegetation in Last Interglacial and Holocene Europe: Proxies and challenges." *Journal of Archaeological Method and Theory*. https://doi.org/10.1007/s10816-021-09546-2.

PAGES, International Project. 2020–2023. "PAGES, past global change." https://pastglobalchanges.org/.

Prates, L., and S.I. Perez. 2021. "Late Pleistocene South American megafaunal extinctions associated with rise of Fishtail points and human population." *Nat Commun* 12 (1): 2175. https://doi.org/10.1038/s41467-021-22506-4. https://www.ncbi.nlm.nih.gov/pubmed/33846353.

Pumpelly, Raphael, ed. 1908. *Explorations in Turkestan: Expedition of 1904: Prehistoric civiliza-tions of Anau: Origins, Growth, and Influence of Environment.* Washington, D.C.: Carnegie Institution of Washington.

Rick, Torben C. and Daniel H. Sandweiss. 2020. "Archaeology, climate, and global change in the Age of Humans." *Proceedings of the National Academy of Sciences* 117 (15): 8250–8253.

Rick, Torben C., Patrick V. Kirch, Jon M. Erlandson, and Scott M. Fitzpatrick. 2013. "Archeology, deep history, and the human transformation of island ecosystems." *Anthropocene* 4 (0): 33–45. https://doi.org/http://dx.doi.org/10.1016/j.ancene.2013.08.002. http://www.sciencedirect.com/scien ce/article/pii/S2213305413000106.

Roberts, Neil. 2014. *The Holocene: An Environmental History.* John Wiley & Sons.

Rockman, Marcy and Carrie Hritz. 2020. "Expanding use of archaeology in climate change response by changing its social environment." *Proceedings of the National Academy of Sciences* 117 (15): 8295–8302. https://doi.org/10.1073/pnas.1914213117. https://www.pnas.org/content/pnas/117/15/8295.full. pdf.

Roebroeks, J.W.M., MacDonald, K., and Scherjon, F. 2021. "Establishing patterns of early fire use in human evolution." In *The Beef behind All Possible Pasts. The Tandem Festschrift in Honour of Elaine Turner and Martin Street,* edited by S. Gaudzinski-Windheuser, 29–38. Heidelberg: Propylaeum.

Rosen, Arlene. 2022. "Resilience at the edge: Strategies of small-scale societies for long-term sus-tainable living in dryland environments." In *Perspectives on Public Policy in Societal-Environ-mental Crises: What the Future Needs from History,* edited by Adam Izdebski, John Haldon, and Piotr Filipkowski, 161–176. Cham: Springer International Publishing.

Rosen, Arlene M., Thomas C. Hart, Jennifer Farquhar, Joan S. Schneider, and Tserendagva Yadmaa. 2019. "Holocene vegetation cycles, land-use, and human adaptations to desertification in the Gobi Desert of Mongolia." *Vegetation History and Archaeobotany* 28 (3): 295–309. http s://doi.org/10.1007/s00334-018-0710-y.

Rosen, A.M., L. Janz, Bukhchuluun Dashzeveg, and Davaakhuu Odsuren. 2022. "Holocene deser-tification, Traditional Ecological Knowledge, and human resilience in the Eastern Gobi Desert, Mongolia." *The Holocene* 32 (12): 1462–1476.

Rosen, Arlene Miller, and Isabel Rivera-Collazo. 2012. "Climate change, adaptive cycles, and the persistence of foraging economies during the late Pleistocene/Holocene transition in the Levant." *PNAS* 109 (10): 3640–3645. https://doi.org/10.1073/pnas.1113931109.

Rosen, Steven A. 2011. "The desert and the pastoralist: An archaeological perspective on human-landscape interaction in the Negev over the millennia." *Annals of Arid Zone* 50 (3–4): 295–309.

Rowlett, Ralph M. 2000. "Fire control by Homo erectus in East Africa and Asia." *Acta Anthropologica Sinica* 19 (Suppl): 198–208.

Rowley-Conwy, Peter. 2006. "The concept of prehistory and the invention of the terms 'prehistoric' and 'prehistorian': The Scandinavian origin, 1833–1850." *European Journal of Archaeology* 9 (1): 103–130.

Ruddiman, William F., Erle C. Ellis, Jed O. Kaplan, and Dorian Q. Fuller. 2015. "Geology: defining the epoch we live in: Is a formally designated "Anthropocene" a good idea?" *Science* 348 (6230): 38–39.

Ruddiman, W.F., D.Q. Fuller, J.E. Kutzbach, P.C. Tzedakis, J.O. Kaplan, E.C. Ellis, S.J. Vavrus, C.N. Roberts, R. Fyfe, F. He, C. Lemmen, and J. Woodbridge. 2015. "Late Holocene climate: Natural or Anthropogenic?" *Reviews of Geophysics* 54 (1): 93–118. https://doi.org/10.1002/ 2015rg000503.

Ruddiman, William F., Zhengtang Guo, Xin Zhou, Hanbin Wu, and Yanyan Yu. 2008. "Early rice farming and anomalous methane trends." *Quaternary Science Reviews* 27 (13–14): 1291–1295. http://www.sciencedirect.com/science/article/B6VBC-4SR6G06-1/1/eaca e8399d699c9f0e8071205346eb7a.

Sandom, C., S. Faurby, B. Sandel, and J.C. Svenning. 2014. "Global late Quaternary megafauna extinctions linked to humans, not climate change." *Proc Biol Sci* 281 (1787). https://doi.org/10. 1098/rspb.2013.3254. https://www.ncbi.nlm.nih.gov/pubmed/24898370.

Scherjon, Fulco, Corrie Bakels, Katharine MacDonald, and Wil Roebroeks. 2015. "Burning the land." *Current Anthropology* 56 (3): 299–326. https://doi.org/10.1086/681561.

Sillitoe, Paul. 1998. "The development of Indigenous Knowledge: A new applied anthropology." *Current Anthropology* 39 (2): 223–252. https://www.jstor.org/stable/10.1086/204722.

Simpson, Michael. 2020. "The Anthropocene as colonial discourse." *Environment and Planning D: Society and Space* 38 (1): 53–71. https://doi.org/10.1177/0263775818764679.

Smith, Bruce D. 2011. "General patterns of niche construction and the management of 'wild' plant and animal resources by small-scale pre-industrial societies." *Philosophical Transactions: Biological Sciences* 366 (1566): 836–848. https://doi.org/10.1098/rstb.2010.0253. http://rstb.royalsocietypublishing.org/royptb/366/1566/836.full.pdf.

Smith, Bruce D. and Melinda A. Zeder. 2013. "The onset of the Anthropocene." *Anthropocene* 4 (0): 8–13. https://doi.org/http://dx.doi.org/10.1016/j.ancene.2013.05.001. http://www.sciencedirect.com/science/article/pii/S2213305413000052.

Snir, Ainit, Dani Nadel, and Ehud Weiss. 2015. "Plant-food preparation on two consecutive floors at Upper Paleolithic Ohalo II, Israel." *Journal of Archaeological Science* 53: 61–71. https://doi.org/10.1016/j.jas.2014.09.023.

Spengler, Robert N. 2021. "Niche Construction theory in archaeology: A critical review." *Journal of Archaeological Method and Theory* 28 (3): 925–955. https://doi.org/10.1007/s10816-021-09528-4. https://doi.org/10.1007/s10816-021-09528-4.

Steward, Julian H. 1955. *Theory of Culture Change: The Methodology of Multilinear Evolution.* Urbana: University of Illinois Press.

Stiner, Mary C. 2001. "Thirty years on the 'Broad Spectrum Revolution' and paleolithic demography." *PNAS* 98 (13): 6993–6996.

Stiner, M.C. 2021. "The challenges of documenting coevolution and niche construction: The example of domestic spaces." *Evol Anthropol* 30 (1): 63–70. https://doi.org/10.1002/evan.21878. https://www.ncbi.nlm.nih.gov/pubmed/33382521.

Thompson, J.C., D.K. Wright, and S.J. Ivory. 2021. "The emergence and intensification of early hunter-gatherer niche construction." *Evol Anthropol* 30 (1): 17–27. https://doi.org/10.1002/evan.21877. https://www.ncbi.nlm.nih.gov/pubmed/33341104.

Toncheva, Svetoslava. 2019. "Redefining human–nature dichotomy: The voice of spiritual-ecological movements in enviromentality debate." Antropologija/Anthropology. *Journal for Sociocultural Anthropology* 6: 57–73.

Tucker, Bram. 2013. "Cultural ecology." In *Theory in Social and Cultural Anthropology: An Encyclopedia*, edited by R. Jon McGee and Richard L. Warms, 142–147. Thousand Oaks, CA: Sage.

Vigne, J.D., F. Briois, A. Zazzo, G. Willcox, T. Cucchi, S. Thiebault, I. Carrere, Y. Franel, R. Touquet, C. Martin, C. Moreau, C. Comby, and J. Guilaine. 2012. "First wave of cultivators spread to Cyprus at least 10,600 y ago." *Proc Natl Acad Sci U S A* 109 (22): 8445–8449. https://doi.org/10.1073/pnas.1201693109. https://www.ncbi.nlm.nih.gov/pubmed/22566638.

Weiss, Ehud, Mordechai E. Kislev, and Anat Hartmann. 2006. "Autonomous cultivation before domestication." *Science* 312: 1608–1610.

Weiss, Harvey, M.-A. Courty, W. Wetterstrom, F. Guichard, L. Senior, R. Meadow, and A. Curnow. 1993. "The genesis and collapse of third millennium North Mesopotamian civilization." *Science* 261: 995–1004.

Williams, Thomas J., Michael B. Collins, Kathleen Rodrigues, William Jack Rink, Nancy Velchoff, Amanda Keen-Zebert, Anastasia Gilmer, Charles D. Frederick, Sergio J. Ayala, and Elton R. Prewitt. 2018. "Evidence of an early projectile point technology in North America at the Gault Site, Texas, USA." *Science Advances* 4(7): 1–7.

Wolfe, Allison L. and Jack M. Broughton. 2020. "A foraging theory perspective on the associational critique of North American Pleistocene overkill." *Journal of Archaeological Science* 119. https://doi.org/10.1016/j.jas.2020.105162.

Wright, David K. 2019. "Long-term dynamics of pastoral ecology in northern Kenya: An old model for new resilience." *Journal of Anthropological Archaeology* 55. https://doi.org/10.1016/j.jaa. 2019.101068.

Zeder, Melinda A. 2012. "The Broad Spectrum Revolution at 40: Resource diversity, intensification, and an alternative to optimal foraging explanations." *Journal of Anthropological Archaeology* 31 (3): 241–264. https://doi.org/10.1016/j.jaa.2012.03.003.

Zeder, Melinda A. and Brian Hesse. 2000. "The initial domestication of goats (Capra hircus) in the Zagros Mountains 10,000 years ago." *Science* 287: 2254–2257. https://doi.org/10.1126/science.287. 5461.2254.

2

RE-FIELDING CLIMATE CHANGE IN CULTURAL ANTHROPOLOGY

Meredith Welch-Devine and Heather Lazrus

Introduction

Anthropology's applicability to addressing the climate crisis is clear, and there has been no shortage of pieces taking stock of the field's contributions and suggesting next steps and new directions (for example, Baer and Singer 2014; Barnes and Dove 2015; Crate and Nuttall 2016; Fiske et al. 2014; O'Reilly et al. 2020). In this chapter, we do not seek to retread that ground. Rather, we build on these efforts to consider what those calls mean both for the field of anthropology and for the "field(s)" in which we do our research. In this chapter, we distill a few key messages that are threaded through these pieces, and we explore their implications for where, how, and with whom we do our research. We use our positions as academic (Welch-Devine) and "academic-adjacent" (Lazrus) anthropologists to give concrete examples of how we, and others, have attempted to approach our research and action in ways that respond to the unique challenges of our time.

These excellent scoping articles converge on a few key messages: anthropology needs to work with urgency, to center equity, and to engage in inter- and transdisciplinary work. First, on the issue of urgency, there is no doubt that our changing climate presents very real challenges for the Earth's eco- and social systems and for all the beings that call it home. Baer and Singer are particularly pointed in their calls for anthropologists to engage in climate research, and action, to "avoid calamity" (2014: 3). As a social science that can contribute insights from the most local of contexts through to global climate politics and from individuals' perceptions, understandings, and beliefs through to production of global climate science and international decision-making, anthropology has the opportunity – and some would argue the imperative – to engage and contribute much more broadly and deeply than it has to date. Roncoli, though, provides an important reminder that our work is not just about heralding doom, but rather, it is critical that we also highlight agency and the options that remain open to us as we confront the challenge of a changing climate (Roncoli 2020).

DOI: 10.4324/9781003242499-4

Second, as we move forward, we must center equity in our work. It is well recognized that climate change is a threat multiplier; those already facing challenges of food insecurity, conflict, and other hazards will see these contexts exacerbated (Crate and Nuttall 2009; O'Reilly et al. 2020; Siddiqui et al. 2022; Shaffer 2017), and some among us will feel climate change's impacts much more keenly than others. The violence of our warming climate lies not only in the changes that are wrought but also in our responses to them (Dervieux and Belgherbi 2020; Seara et al. 2020). O'Reilly et al. (2020) argue that this calls for increased attention to the political nature of climate solutions, and both O'Reilly et al. and Barnes et al. (2013) point out that anthropologists can make sure there is rigorous attention to equity and justice in both climate research and climate action. Anthropology's paradox is that while we are, perhaps, uniquely positioned as a science to work genuinely and authentically with our partners and to ensure equitable access, processes, and outcomes, we also have a long disciplinary history of failing to do so. The urgency of the climate crisis and the very uneven impacts of changing patterns of rainfall, collapse of marine food webs, increasing severe weather, and desertification – to name only a few expected challenges arising from climate change – must compel us to do better.

Third, these contributions and others call for anthropologists to engage in more inter- and transdisciplinary climate research. As O'Reilly et al. point out, anthropologists have studied climate science and scientists, the production of knowledge, and policymaking processes, but our expertise in language, human behavior, and building relationships, along with an interest in "ontological pluralism," positions us well to work more closely with the scientists and policymakers who are often our subjects, introducing "more and varied perspectives" into our efforts to combat the climate crisis (2020: 18). Maldonado and Middleton (2022) further argue that bringing multiple worldviews and knowledges into conversation can help provide the means to address climate with a justice orientation. Indeed, concerted efforts are being made to bring Indigenous knowledges into international climate science and policymaking (IPCC 2019), both because they can help us understand change over time and because they can help inform adaptation efforts (Parry et al. 2007). Whyte argues that the value of foregrounding Indigenous climate knowledge and supporting the concomitant work of renewing relationships goes far beyond providing "useful information about the nature of ecological changes," to providing strategy and motivation for addressing climate change (2017: 158).

Reorienting How Anthropologists Approach "the Field"

Calls to act with urgency, to center equity, and to reach across disciplinary divides and outside of academe can be easy to embrace in the abstract, as it is clear that they are critical to addressing the climate crisis. Anthropology and anthropologists may be uniquely situated for uniting these threads and leading on climate, but it can be difficult to understand exactly how to do these things in practice. There are, though, excellent examples in our field that can serve as guides. We aim here to highlight some approaches to research and action that address these calls, focusing on community-driven research, cross-scale study, team science, and engagement with science communication and policymaking. Whenever possible, we use our own experiences to provide deeper insight into enabling conditions, logistics, decision-making, and the impact of different approaches.

Engaged, Community-Driven Research

Research that is both community-engaged and community-driven can help shift our work towards an equity orientation, while also broadening the perspectives included and laying the groundwork for sustained engagement and rapid responses. Maldonado and Middelton (2022) argue that centering Indigenous leadership in projects is essential in supporting Indigenous lifeways and livelihoods, fostering approaches that are innovative, holistic, and equity-focused. Community-driven work can also make the knowledge produced more reliable and the resulting action more effective, in part by improving our understanding of the ways in which climate is entangled with all of the other concerns of life (Barnes and Dove 2015; Cassidy 2012; Salick, Staver, and Hart 2020; Sourdril et al. 2020). Because people rarely experience or respond to climate-related changes in isolation, understanding how they articulate with other facets of livelihoods and community enhances our ability to respond appropriately. Similarly, deep community engagement can surface knowledges and perspectives that may be overlooked, thereby improving not only the ability of different people to be heard and influence the process but also the processes and outcomes themselves (Burke et al. 2020; Schnegg 2022; Welch-Devine et al. 2022). Furthermore, building relationships with and among community members early and for the long term poises us to act with urgency when the opportunity or need arises and can improve the effectiveness of crisis response. When working with communities, though, it is critical that we recognize and think forward to how our work is being used, by whom, and to what ends. For example, if a project exploring differential carbon storage and emissions among various farming or pastoral activities demonstrates that the "best" course of action for decarbonizing the atmosphere would be to halt efforts to sustain pastoralism, who might use that information, and what would be the consequences for the families and communities in question and for those who rely on their food provisioning?

Despite continuing calls for community involvement at the earliest stages of project development (cf. Minkler and Wallerstein 2011), in many community-engaged research projects the scientific team decides on the research questions and may simply consult with community members to determine methods to use or outputs to produce. While these efforts are valuable and certainly represent an improvement upon scientists working in isolation, there is much room to grow. Schneider and Buser (2018) lay out a continuum of modes of co-production, illustrating that the projects in which communities are most highly engaged have members participate in development of the research objectives and questions. This requires that the science team be open to potentially changing the entire frame of the research. In addition to being expensive and time consuming, co-development of research questions presents tensions as the science team may need to demonstrate to funders that they will be advancing theory and generating transferable knowledge, while local partners may need specific answers to problems that they find vexing but that will not fill gaps in knowledge or push the boundaries of our disciplines. Negotiating these decisions requires a high degree of trust among the partners, willingness to be clear and transparent about needs, and a strong desire to find common ground.

Meredith Welch-Devine's most recent work in the southwest of France illustrates the challenges and benefits of this type of approach. Meredith has worked in the region since 2005, initially seeking to understand how Basque cattle and sheep raisers were negotiating the implementation of a European Union conservation initiative and how the long-standing regime for management of the commons was adapting to new policies and pressures (Welch-Devine and Murray 2011). Since that time, she has had ongoing conversations with these same pastoralists about climate change and its likely impacts in the region. Until recently, most people there saw climate as a global problem that they would be relatively protected from, due to their mountain setting with abundant water, but recent years have brought precipitation extremes that have caused many to rethink that sense of comfort. Both the agricultural system and the climate of the northern Basque region have many parallels with that of Southern Appalachia, where Meredith has also worked in the context of the Coweeta Long Term Ecological Research project, and the time and context seemed right to propose a comparative project across the two areas.

Rather than proceed directly to a full research proposal Meredith sought out, with Anne Sourdril (CNRS, France) and Brian J. Burke (Appalachian State), seed funding from the US National Science Foundation (NSF) and the Thomas Jefferson Fund (now the Transatlantic Research Partnership), a program of the FACE Foundation and the French Embassy, to engage farmers in designing the project. The seed project proposals themselves required research questions, but without funding for international travel and meetings, and due to slow internet connections in the rural Basque Country, the scientists developed initial questions on their own. After receiving seed funding, the team held two intensive workshops with researchers and farmers, both Basque and American, in May (in France) and October (in the United States) 2019, as well as a multi-day meeting in France in September 2021. These workshops included farm tours and farmer-led discussions of production systems, major challenges, and hopes for the future. It is instructive to see how the research focus changed as a result of this engagement and the foregrounding of community priorities and needs. During our time together, farmers repeatedly posed the questions: "What will this landscape look like in 50 years? Will there still be farms here? Will there still be farmers?" Centering that concern for continuity and vibrant futures, we shifted from our initial idea of identifying approaches that can both decrease the climate impacts of food production and make farmers and their communities more resilient to the changes they will face to focus more broadly on the factors that sustain pastoral systems, with climate as one key driver among a suite of articulating pressures and supports. The NSF program Dynamics of Integrated Socio-Environmental Systems (DISES) was a good fit for translating these priorities into fundable science without losing the essence of what we wanted to accomplish, and the project was chosen for funding in late 2022.

The resulting project will better serve the needs of the community while providing multiple avenues for theoretical development and myriad options for action at multiple scales. The farmers were key not only to ensuring the outputs will be useful to them but also to improving the science, as they led the team to center the research on what they intuitively knew to be the key local-scale system drivers: farmers' willingness and ability to continue their work and maintain their lands and communities. Together, we co-developed the research problem and goals and co-designed the main elements of the project methodology, and farmers will be fully engaged in analysis and interpretation of data and the dissemination of results. One note of caution, though, is that it proved unfeasible to design a comparative, interdisciplinary, international project on the available budget. We chose to focus only on the Basque Country for this iteration, due to the availability of long-term land management data and strong relationships built over more than a decade, and we plan to expand to Southern Appalachia in a subsequent project. It is important also to note that this development process lasted for multiple years and cost nearly $30,000, for only the development of the research questions and approaches. This highlights the need for funders to make significant investments in pre-research collaborations if they truly wish to see more efforts at knowledge co-production.

Heather Lazrus's work further illustrates the need for deep relationship building. Engaged and community-driven research may emerge when anthropologists have opportunities to bring their theories and perspectives into a community of practice, or when that community of practice forms around an anthropological effort. The Center for Indigenous and Earth Sciences emerged from a conversation between Heather and Bob Gough, then a visiting scientist at the National Center for Atmospheric Research (NCAR) where Heather had begun working in 2011. NCAR is a major research facility dedicated to all things related to atmospheric research, where researchers investigate topics spanning from space weather to coastal ecosystems. A handful of social scientists, including Heather, at NCAR also examine how people understand and respond to climate, weather, and water hazards. In that early conversation, Bob told Heather about a long-standing question of his: "What have we learned from decades of work intended to integrate Indigenous and western sciences about weather and climate change? What are the barriers and the best practices?" Heather suggested a workshop on the topic, and with that first workshop, the Rising Voices Center for Indigenous and Earth Sciences (Rising Voices) at NCAR was initiated.

Now, a decade after the initial workshop (at the time of writing), Rising Voices facilitates opportunities for Indigenous and non-Indigenous scientific experts and community leaders from around the world to jointly address how extreme weather and climate events are impacting communities and to develop action plans. Rising Voices aspires to advance science through the collaborations of Indigenous and Earth (atmospheric, social, biological, ecological) sciences, along with an intercultural approach to addressing and understanding extreme weather events. Over the years, Rising Voices has evolved, now with another anthropologist, Julie Maldonado, also at the helm as co-director along with Heather. Together, Julie and Heather have created a co-governance structure that includes Indigenous leadership on the steering committee, council, and workshop planning teams. Above all else, Rising Voices is a space to establish relationships of trust, and without these, no research collaboration is possible. Relationships form the foundation of the trust that must underpin all interactions as Rising Voices works to decolonize centuries of harmful interactions with Indigenous peoples in the name of science (Lazrus et al. 2022).

In 2022 the National Science Foundation awarded a large-scale award of twenty million dollars to a consortium of Rising Voices members to address coastal hazards from the perspectives of local communities and knowledge holders, Earth scientists, and social scientists (Lenart 2022). The grant, entitled Rising Voices, Changing Coasts, grows directly from the work and trust built by the Rising Voices program. Each stream of expertise comes together in four regional hubs – communities in Puerto Rico, Louisiana, Alaska, and Hawaii. Rather than each expert simply working to address their own research questions and priorities, hub gatherings will ensure that they are interwoven to address the research questions of the project holistically, led by the knowledge, wisdom, and observations of the hub communities. In fact, the research questions at the heart of the project are derived from a decade of conversations at annual Rising Voices workshops, ensuring that they represent community concerns and observations. This framework is transformative in the Earth Sciences and represents a new way of building knowledge towards taking action against climate-driven coastal hazards.

The influence of anthropology is threaded throughout the Rising Voices program and the new Rising Voices, Changing Coasts project. Primarily, this is through centering marginalized voices in the conversation about what knowledge "counts," and for whom, for understanding and responding to climate change. While Indigenous peoples throughout the world have temporally deep knowledge and systems of practice that have facilitated survival for thousands of years, colonization has relegated that knowledge to the category of anecdote. Anthropology has a long and rich tradition of acknowledging local knowledge, but for many in the Earth sciences, the idea of non-western ways of knowing contributing meaningfully to how we know about the environment and our interactions with it is new and challenges long-held beliefs in the object truth of science – and even what science is. Rising Voices works to familiarize western-trained scientists with other ways of knowing and recognizing the ways in which science is embedded in particular political economic structures of knowledge production. To acknowledge that the production of western science is entangled with colonial legacies and present systems of inequity is a major shift in how non-anthropologists think about the primacy of objectivity. However, the fact that we are seeing these shifts, for example, at the interfaces of community-engaged research projects, in national dialogues, and in top international climate change policy-setting fora (Funes 2022) indicates an awakening and readjustment is underway. Anthropologists are suited to guide this shift through our research collaborations that extend both through our academic hallways and into communities.

Cross-Scale Research

The nature of climate change, a global phenomenon with intensely felt impacts in particular places, and its responses, with efforts both to mitigate and to adapt originating at levels from the household to the international, demands attention to interaction across scales, both spatial and temporal (Crate 2011). Kirsten Hastrup argues that anthropology is well-placed to do this because the field directs attention toward the "implicit connections" of "the local" to "other places, other times, other kinds of knowledge" (2013: 278). Anthropology's ability to untangle cross-sector interactions can help address issues of equity and urgency, while also encouraging transdisciplinary work. Barnes et al. (2013) point out that cross-scale anthropology work on policy can uncover who is influencing the policy process, how its impacts are variably felt, and which impacts are prioritized. These insights are critical for an equity approach to climate change and can help create better policy (Barnes and Dove 2015). Working across scales may also help us address calls for urgency by providing avenues for more easily translating research insights into policy and action. Furthermore, investigating climate across scales invites holistic collaboration from a range of specialties, from political and atmospheric sciences to soil chemistry and anthropology, as we seek to link cause and effect (Crate 2011).

Elizabeth Marino's (2015) ethnography of Shishmaref, Alaska provides a clear example of the value of crossing temporal scales and disciplinary fault lines in our research on climate. She shows how slow change like warming and erosion, punctuated impacts like

floods, cyclical dynamics of seasonal subsistence calendars, and historical legacies of settler colonialism all interact to shape experience. Marino illustrates how the impact of
colonial pressures has restricted mobility and foreclosed options for adaptation, transforming flooding and infrastructure damage from manageable events to catastrophic
ones. There are, similarly, examples we can turn to of work that crosses spatial scales or
scales of governance. In her 2015 chapter, Jessica Barnes examines contrasting perspectives on Egypt's water futures through fieldwork both with farmers and at international
water conferences. She uncovers vastly different ways of conceptualizing the forces that
impact water availability. At the conferences, she analyzed both the discussions taking
place in public fora and the closed-door negotiations. She found that the first neglected
human agency and political decision making, focusing on climate as the key determinant
of water availability, while the second foregrounded geopolitics and human agency. In
both cases, the discussion at the international level was focused on how much water
makes it through the river system to Egypt. In contrast, farmers focused on who gets to
use that water once it arrives, and rather than seeing water availability as being determined by climate, they view it as being controlled by those who control the dams and
weirs. A cross-scale examining of the issues reveals both the differing priorities at play
and the ways in which conceptualization of causality may differ across scales, becoming
increasingly abstract as they are distanced from local experience. Such insights may allow
for a different approach to both crafting and communicating policy.

Another example of cross-scale, interdisciplinary research comes from Lazrus' collaboration with physical scientists at NCAR who study water resources and drought
(Towler et al. 2019). Using interviews conducted with community members in southern
Oklahoma, collaborators connected people's perceptions of drought risk with different
regional drought outlooks and water management strategies to understand how water
resource management strategies could best fulfill community members' priorities –
including agriculture, recreation, cultural, and environmental conservation uses. This
work brought together the anthropological Cultural Theory of Risk, originally developed
by Mary Douglas (Douglas 1966; McNeeley and Lazrus 2014) with work on drought
indices and hydrologic projections under a changing climate. Because community members tended to consider water resources at a smaller scale than the areas covered by
broader regional climate projections, collaborators overlapped areas that interviewees
reported as important to them with downscaled regional climate information. Doing so
allowed Towler at al. to connect localized information in the area of the Arbuckle
Simpson Aquifer in southern Oklahoma with drought projections over the southern
United States.

Team Science

No one discipline or worldview holds the key to addressing our climate crisis, and to pull
together the many different insights that are needed often necessitates working in teams
(Eriksen and Mendes 2022). As Heather outlined in a 2020 piece for Anthropology News,
Margaret Mead recognized this early on and in 1975 organized a conference with atmospheric scientists to discuss "the ways to maintain [the atmospheric environment] as a
healthy place in which to live" (Kellogg and Mead 1975: xv). Since then, interest in
interdisciplinary team science has continued, and in 2016, Growing Convergence

Research was identified as one of the 10 Big Ideas for Future NSF Investments. The US National Science Foundation (NSF) characterizes convergence research as "integrating knowledge, methods, and expertise from different disciplines and forming novel frameworks to catalyze scientific discovery and innovation" (National Science Foundation 2018). The social sciences and humanities, though, must be equal partners in the endeavor lest disciplinary divisions be "reproduced rather than transformed" (Geoghegan et al. 2019: 4). Moreover, our teams must include more than just our colleagues from different scientific fields. As Heather points out, "We need intercultural collaborations for climate solutions as well as interdisciplinary ones. Anthropologists are well positioned to help people from different cultural backgrounds and knowledge systems build relationships of trust as the bedrock for these collaborations" (Lazrus 2020). Anthropologists can help serve as the interlocutors who facilitate exchange between vastly different ontologies and knowledge systems because we strive to understand those knowledges in their contexts and are attuned to issues of power and representation, and we must use our positions to ensure access for multiple ways of knowing.

At the National Center for Atmospheric Research, interdisciplinary teams are often composed of atmospheric and other Earth scientists. More and more, the value of social science team members is being recognized, following a shift at the National Science Foundation to bring in social scientists from the beginning – not as last minute additions to a project who are tasked simply with "communicating" the research results. This encouraging turn has gained momentum under the NSF's focus on convergence research. For collaborations to be truly convergent, and to yield novel results that could not otherwise be achieved by individual disciplines working alone, a great deal of work goes into making each form of expertise legible and valuable. This means continually iterating the language used to define research problems, the measures used to conduct particular methodologies, and how research goals are defined, set, and re-evaluated (Morss et al. 2018). One example is the NSF-funded Communicating Hazard Information in the Modern Environment (CHIME) research project on which Heather was a co-investigator. This project aimed to reduce harm from hurricanes and other hazards, alleviate social vulnerability, and enhance resilience by improving hazardous weather risk communication and response in the modern information environment. This includes building understanding of how evolving weather forecasts and warnings interact with societal information flow and decisions as a hurricane approaches and arrives. The project brought together concepts, methods, and expertise from computer and information sciences, atmospheric and related sciences, and social and behavioral sciences to integrate study of the real-world hazard information system with computational, physical, and social modeling. The research included analysis of data from social media streams; focus groups with more vulnerable populations; development and testing of prototype integrations of information; high-resolution ensemble hurricane and storm-surge modeling; and agent-based modeling of social actors who pursue, process, and transmit information. To enhance applicability of the research, our project also involved interactions with key stakeholder groups (Morss et al. 2017). In the CHIME project, the focus groups with more vulnerable populations provided the backbone of how we understood key ways in which people's decision-making capacities were hindered or enabled through risk communication (Lazrus et al. 2020). By understanding first-person experiences of hurricanes – including Superstorms Sandy, Matthew, Harvey, and Irma – the team could anchor the insights we gained through social media analysis, offer priorities for storm-surge modeling, and inform the agent-based modeling.

Successful team science requires careful attention to team formation, motivation, and management, and most team leaders and members would benefit from assistance and directed training. Many universities have launched programs to help connect faculty and students across campus and to better position them to undertake interdisciplinary and convergent projects. This may take the form of networking opportunities, seed funding, or training in team science. At the University of Georgia, Meredith is involved in one such program. Leading Large Integrative Research Teams (L2-IRT) is an effort to help faculty members understand team composition and dynamics, learn how to motivate teams and keep them on track, and engage with various communities and constituencies. L2-IRT offers panel discussions so that faculty members can learn from those who have been successful in team initiatives, as well as practical instruction in topics such as developing team charters. When university trainings and resources are not available, researchers who would like assistance can seek out freely available materials, such as those curated on teamscience.net (hosted by Northwestern University) or the Collaboration and Team Science field guide from the National Institutes of Health (Bennett, Gadlin, and Marchand 2018).

Engagement with Science Communication and Policy

Anthropologists, like many other scientists, have traditionally been hesitant to engage in outreach to the public or to participate in the policymaking process. Both, though, are critically important for increasing the impact of anthropology in combating the climate crisis. Addressing the changing climate with the urgency it demands requires that we use what we learn – e.g., about climate impacts in particular places, about the likely adoption and consequences of different interventions, and about inequities that actions (or inaction) will exacerbate or introduce – both to help people make sense of the changes they are experiencing (Paerregaard 2019) and to help those in positions of power to craft policy that is both more equitable and has a better chance of being accepted (Barnes et al. 2013; Fiske 2016; Pokrant and Stocker 2011; Victor 2015). Our job is not only to communicate the science but also to "communicate the transformative imperative" and the critical urgency of meeting this moment with decisive action (Moser 2019, 142). There is increasing interest in having anthropology more deeply engage with the study of environmental communication (Sjölander-Lindqvist, Murin, and Dove 2022) and strong arguments that a better analysis of how people understand the information they receive on climate change and reconcile it with their lived experiences and perceptions has the potential to "[open] up knowledge spaces for multi-directional and democratic approaches to living (with) climate change" (de Wit and Haines 2021: 13). Krause (2021) calls for anthropologists to enter the public discourse on climate change and, specifically, to move beyond simply telling people "what" is happening and why it matters (the "so what") to helping journalists and politicians understand what needs to be done next (the "now what"). We have an opportunity to draw upon our experiences and partnerships not only to integrate the varied sciences that are important to understanding and planning for climate change but also to envision "now whats" that are inspired by other perspectives and ontologies (see also Whyte 2017).

There are many options available for training in general science communication and on working with policymakers. The American Anthropological Association (AAA) hosts tools for advocacy on its website and is a member of both the National Humanities Alliance and the Consortium of Social Science Associations, both of which provide additional resources. These materials include teaching resources, primers on how to work with the United States Congress, and tips for making your research accessible. The AAA has a section of the website specifically devoted to anthropology and climate change, and it has used its United Nations NGO status to field delegations to UNFCCC Conference of the Parties (COP) meetings. Additionally, there are several options for hands-on training in this work. For example, the non-profit COMPASS, founded in 1999 and originally focused on improving public understanding of ocean science, trains scientists to hone a clear and understandable message and provides additional articles and resources on the website. The American Association for the Advancement of Science (AAAS) Center for Public Engagement with Science & Technology offers virtual trainings for individuals and will come to campuses to host group workshops. Similarly, the faculty and staff of the Alan Alda Center for Communicating Science at Stony Brook University have trainings on climate communication offered to groups, or individuals. Finally, many universities offer science communication or media training either through the Office of Research or through the Marketing and Communications divisions, and many can assist with communication with policymakers through their offices of Government Relations.

One opportunity for anthropologists to engage with policy is through the scientific assessment process. The Intergovernmental Science-Policy Platform on Biodiversity and Ecosystem Services (IPBES) and the Intergovernmental Panel on Climate Change (IPCC) periodically publish calls seeking experts to contribute to their assessment reports. Several noted anthropologists have had key roles in these assessment reports. Dr Susan Crate was a lead author for the IPCC Special Report on the Ocean and Cryosphere in a Changing Climate. She was assigned to Chapter One, which framed the rest of the report. Crate oversaw the section "Indigenous Knowledge and Local Knowledge" (Abram et al. 2019). Although she and her team, made up of the two other social scientists on the chapter, at first struggled to convince the chapter team that the topic was worthy of inclusion, by the time the report was published, the lead authors of all of its chapters enthusiastically embraced the section. The report included a cross chapter box showing how these knowledge systems are woven throughout the report. Although the IPCC had to date not included Indigenous and local knowledge holders directly as authors, the team was able to engage with several knowledge holders as contributing authors to refine the section and offer their recommendations on how to engage these knowledge systems in climate work. Crate discusses the challenges and rewards of the process in her monograph, *Once Upon the Permafrost: Knowing Culture and Climate Change in Siberia* (2021).

We spoke with Dr Pamela McElwee about her experiences with IPBES and IPCC, and she points to the publication of her 2016 book, *Forests are Gold*, as a pivotal moment in her engagement with science policy: "I'd just finished this book on Vietnam, and I thought I should scale up. I was interested in thinking about the implications of the work globally. That book was on the topic of deforestation and why it's so difficult to tackle using different tools like payments for ecosystem services (PES) and protected areas, and that has clear implications for global assessments" (personal communication, June 20, 2022). With that desire to think more broadly, she applied and was chosen to contribute to the next IPBES assessment. Also in 2016, as it became apparent that the US would be withdrawing from the Paris Climate Agreement, McElwee applied to work on the IPCC report. Ultimately, she worked on the two assessments simultaneously, and both were published in 2019. McElwee, along with several other anthropologists, is also contributing to the next US National Climate Assessment (NCA). Increasingly, anthropologists are dispersed throughout the chapters of the NCA, authoring and contributing to sections on health, transportation, and ecosystems, among others, which is critical for promoting more equitable, ethical, and holistic assessments and recommendations.

Dr McElwee encourages all scholars, even those in the early stages of their careers, to consider participating in the scientific assessment process. Contributing to a scientific assessment offers an unparalleled opportunity to understand global policymaking and connects scholars to others across the globe. The high visibility of national and global reports can also help build a scholarly profile and identity. Both IPBES and IPCC offer media and communications training to those working on their assessments, and IPBES has a Fellows program for early career scientists that includes additional professional development. Dr McElwee notes that contributing to a scientific assessment may prove challenging for social scientists: "Our tendency is to be cautious about making broad claims, and you have to get out of that. Natural scientists have no problem generalizing. You can add caveats, but you have to be a bit bolder about saying 'these are some general patterns.'" These national and global assessment exercises offer the opportunity for anthropologists to translate our insights into broader impact: "It's an amplified platform. No one is going to read my book in the Vietnamese government, but some of the messages about how hard it is to tackle deforestation without thinking about how forests figure into people's lives can get conveyed in these assessments. This can have an impact at policy levels in ways that individual research would have a hard time breaking through" (McElwee, personal communication, June 6, 2022).

Conclusion

In this chapter, we have highlighted three themes that emerge from "state of the discipline" papers on climate change: urgency, equity, and transdisciplinarity. We argue that we can address these themes by engaging in research that is community-driven and cross-scale, by working in teams that include a wide variety of knowledge systems and knowledge holders, and by directly engaging with policymakers and our publics. Our skills of deep listening, building relationships, and unraveling complex connections position us well to do these things.

Deeply-engaged, community-driven climate science, however, requires careful preparatory work and long term commitments (Krause 2021). To facilitate that work, more funders must make seed awards available, allowing flexibility for true co-development of research and co-production of knowledge. Similarly, recognizing the critically important role of the social sciences in understanding and addressing climate change, more emphasis should be placed on funding climate social science and convergence research. The US National Science Foundation's recent strides in this area are highly encouraging. Social scientists commonly complain, though, that their work in interdisciplinary teams is often secondary to that of the biophysical scientists, that the social sciences are simply seen as being in service to the physical and natural sciences, and that they do not have room to explore the questions and issues that will advance their own fields. One antidote to this problem, of course, is for more of us to step up and lead interdisciplinary teams. Doing so can be highly productive and deeply rewarding, and it gives us one more opportunity to help ensure that Indigenous and local knowledge systems have an equal place at the table.

Addressing the climate crisis requires that we come together across vast differences – in worldviews, in expertise, in methodologies, and in lived experiences – which, in turn, requires building relationships and developing trust and respect among scientists of different stripes, between scientists and policymakers, and within and between communities. Anthropologists have the training, experience, and tools to facilitate that convergence and, we would argue, the ethical imperative to do so. For many of us, this means embracing new roles, thinking differently about fieldwork, and exploring new ways of making our work available and actionable. Anthropologists have an opportunity to lead, and we must embrace it. The peril, and hope, of our current moment demands nothing less.

References

Abram, N., J.-P. Gattuso, A. Prakash, L. Cheng, M.P. Chidichimo, S. Crate, H. Enomoto, M. Garschagen, N. Gruber, S. Harper, E. Holland, R.M. Kudela, J. Rice, K. Steffen, and K. von Schuckmann. 2019. "Framing and context of the report." In IPCC *Special Report on the Ocean and Cryosphere in a Changing Climate*, edited by H.-O. Pörtner, D.C. Roberts, V. Masson-Delmotte, P. Zhai, M. Tignor, E. Poloczanska, K. Mintenbeck, A. Alegría, M. Nicolai, A. Okem, J. Petzold, B. Rama, N.M. Weyer, 73–129. Cambridge, UK and New York, NY, USA: Cambridge University Press. https://doi.org/10.1017/9781009157964.003.

Baer, H. and M. Singer. 2014. *The Anthropology of Climate Change: An integrated critical perspective*. London: Routledge.

Barnes, J.M. 2015. "Scale and agency: climate change and the future of Egypt's water." In *Climate Cultures: Anthropological perspectives on climate change*, edited by J.M. Barnes and M.R. Dove, 127–145. New Haven: Yale University Press.

Barnes, J.M. and M.R. Dove. 2015. *Climate Cultures: Anthropological perspectives on climate change*. New Haven: Yale University Press.

Barnes, J.M., M. Dove, A. Lahsen, P. Mathews, P. McElwee, R. McIntosh, F. Moore, J. O'Reilly, B. Orlove, R. Puri, H. Weiss, and K. Yager. 2013. "Contribution of anthropology to the study of climate change." *Nature Climate Change* 3 (6): 541–544. https://www.nature.com/articles/nclimate1775.

Bennett, L.M., H. Gadlin, and C. Marchand. 2018. *Collaboration and Team Science: A field guide*. Rockville, MD: US Department of Health & Human Services, National Institutes of Health, National Cancer Institute.

Burke, B.J., M. Welch-Devine, S. Rzonca, and C. Stacey. 2020. "Using local observations of climate change to identify opportunities for community conversations in Southern Appalachia." In *Changing Climate, Changing Worlds. Local knowledge and the challenges of social and ecological change*, edited by M. Welch-Devine, A. Sourdril, and B.J. Burke, 199–220. Cham, Switzerland: Springer.

Cassidy, R. 2012. "Lives with others: climate change and human-animal relations." *Annual Review of Anthropology* 41: 21–36.

Crate, S. 2021. *Once Upon the Permafrost: Knowing culture and climate change in Siberia*. Tucson: University of Arizona Press.

Crate, S. 2011. "Climate and culture: anthropology in the era of contemporary climate change." *Annual Review of Anthropology* 40: 175–194.

Crate, S. and M. Nuttall (eds). 2009. *Anthropology and Climate Change: From encounters to actions*. Walnut Creek, CA: Left Coast Press.

Crate, S. and M. Nuttall (eds). 2016. *Anthropology and Climate Change: From actions to transformations*. New York: Routledge.

Dervieux, Z. and M. Belgherbi. 2020. "'We used to go asking for the rains': local interpretations of environmental changes and implications for natural resource management in Hwange District, Zimbabwe." In *Changing Climate, Changing Worlds. Local knowledge and the challenges of social and ecological change*, edited by M. Welch-Devine, A. Sourdril, and B.J. Burke, 35–54. Cham, Switzerland: Springer.

de Wit, S. and S. Haines. 2021. "Climate change reception studies in anthropology." *WIREs Climate Change* 13 (1). https://doi.org/10.1002/wcc.742.

Douglas, M. 1966. *Purity and Danger: An analysis of concepts of taboo and pollution*. London: Routledge & K. Paul.

Fiske, S. 2016. "'Climate skepticism' inside the beltway and across the bay." In *Anthropology and Climate Change: From actions to transformations*, 2nd ed., edited by Susan A. Crate and Mark Nuttall, 319–335. New York: Routledge.

Fiske, S., S. Crate, C.L. Crumley, K. Galvin, H. Lazrus, G. Luber, L. Lucero, A. Oliver-Smith, B. Orlove, S. Strauss, and R.R. Wilk. 2014. *Changing the Atmosphere. Final report of the American Anthropological Association Global Climate Change Task Force*. Submitted to the President and Executive Board of the American Anthropological Association on May 15, 2014.

Funes, Yessenia. 2022. "Yes, colonialism caused climate change, IPCC reports." *Atmos Magazine*. https://atmos.earth/ipcc-report-colonialism-climate-change/.

Geoghegan, H., A. Arnall, and G. Feola. 2019. "Climate and culture: taking stock and moving forward." In *Climate and Culture: Multidisciplinary perspectives on a warming world*, edited by G. Feola, H. Geoghegan, and A. Arnall, 1–19. Cambridge: Cambridge University Press.

Hastrup, K. 2013. "Anthropological contributions to the study of climate: past, present, future." *WIREs Climate Change* 4: 269–281. doi:10.1002/wcc.219.

Eriksen, T.H. and P. Mendes. 2022. "Scaling down in order to cool down." In *Cooling Down: Local responses to global climate change*, edited by S.M. Hoffman, T.H. Eriksen, and P. Mendes, 1–24. New York: Berghan.

IPCC. 2019. *Climate Change and Land: An IPCC Special Report on climate change, desertification, land degradation, sustainable land management, food security, and greenhouse gas fluxes in terrestrial ecosystems* [P.R. Shukla, J. Skea, E. Calvo Buendia, V. Masson-Delmotte, H.-O. Pörtner, D.C. Roberts, P. Zhai, R. Slade, S. Connors, R. van Diemen, M. Ferrat, E. Haughey, S. Luz, S. Neogi, M. Pathak, J. Petzold, J. Portugal Pereira, P. Vyas, E. Huntley, K. Kissick, M. Belkacemi, J. Malley, (eds.)]. Cambridge University Press, Cambridge, UK and New York, NY, USA, https://doi.org/ 10.1017/9781009157988.

Kellogg, W. and M. Mead. 1975. *The Atmosphere Endangered and Endangering*. Workshop Proceedings. https://archive.org/stream/in.ernet.dli.2015.132143/2015.132143.The-Atmosphere-Endangered-And-Endangering_djvu.txt.

Krause, F. 2021. "Now what? Repositioning anthropology vis-à-vis climate change activism." *Social Anthropology* 29 (1): 229–231.

Lazrus, H. 2020. "Ten things about collaborating for climate solutions." *Anthropology News* https://www.anthropology-news.org/articles/ten-things-about-collaborating-for-climate-solutions/.

Lazrus H., J. Maldonado, P. Blanchard, M.K. Souza, B. Thomas, and D. Wildcat. 2022. "Culture change to address climate change: collaborations with Indigenous and Earth sciences for more just, equitable, and sustainable responses to our climate crisis." *PLOS Clim* 1 (2): e0000005. https://doi.org/10.1371/journal.pclm.0000005.

Lazrus, H., R. Morss, O. Wilhelmi, J. Henderson, A Dietrich. 2020. "Information as intervention: how hurricane risk communication interacted with vulnerability and capacities in superstorm Sandy." *International Journal of Mass Emergencies and Disasters* 38 (1): 89–120.

Lenart, M. 2022. "Haskell receives $20 million climate change grant." *Native Science Report*. https://nativesciencereport.org/2022/11/haskell-indian-nations-university-receives-20-million-climate-change-grant/.

Maldonado, J. and B.R. Middleton. 2022. "Climate resilience through equity and justice: holistic leadership by Tribal Nations and Indigenous Communities in the southwestern United States." In *Cooling Down: Local responses to global climate change*, edited by S.M. Hoffman, T.H. Eriksen, and P. Mendes, 269–291. New York: Berghan.

Marino, E. 2015. *Fierce Climate, Sacred Ground: An ethnography of climate change*. Fairbanks, Alaska: University of Alaska Press.

McNeeley, S.M. and H. Lazrus. 2014. "The cultural theory of risk for climate change adaptation." *Weather, Climate, and Society* 6 (4): 506–519.

Minkler, M. and N. Wallerstein, eds. 2011. *Community-based Participatory Research for Health: From process to outcomes*. John Wiley & Sons.

Morss, R.E., J.L. Demuth, H. Lazrus, L. Palen, C.M. Barton, C.A. Davis, C. Snyder, O.V. Wilhelmi, K.M. Anderson, D.A. Ahijevych, J. Anderson, M. Bica, K.R. Fossell, J. Henderson, M. Kogan, K. Stowe, and J. Watts. 2017. "Hazardous weather prediction and communication in the modern information environment." *Bulletin of the American Meteorological Society* 98: 2653–2674.

Morss, R.E., H. Lazrus, and J. Demuth. 2018. "The "inter" in interdisciplinary research: achieving integration across fields." *Risk Analysis*. https://doi.org/10.1111/risa.13246.

Moser, S. C. 2019. "Not for the faint of heart: tasks of climate change communication in the context of societal transformation." In *Climate and Culture: Multidisciplinary perspectives on a warming world*, edited by Feola, G., H. Geoghegan, and A. Arnall, 141–167. Cambridge: Cambridge University Press.

National Science Foundation. 2018. *Dear Colleague Letter: Growing Convergence Research*. NSF 18–58. Accessed June 7, 2022. https://www.nsf.gov/pubs/2018/nsf18058/nsf18058.jsp?WT.mc_id= USNSF_25&WT.mc_ev=click.

O'Reilly, J., C. Isenhour, P. McElwee, and B. Orlove. 2020. "Climate change: expanding anthropological possibilities." *Annual Review of Anthropology* 49:13–29.

Paerregaard, K. 2019. "Communicating the inevitable: climate awareness, climate discord, and climate research in Peru's highland communities." *Environmental Communication* 14 (1): 112–125.

Parry, M.L., O.F. Canziani, J.P. Palutikof, P.J. van der Linden, and C.E. Hanson, eds. 2007. *Contribution of Working Group II to the Fourth Assessment Report of the Intergovernmental Panel on Climate Change*. Cambridge University Press, Cambridge, United Kingdom and New York, NY, USA.

Pokrant, B. and L. Stocker. 2011. "Anthropology, climate change, and coastal planning." In *Environmental Anthropology Today*, edited by H. Kopnina and E. Shoreman-Ouiment, 179–194. Routledge.

Roncoli, C. 2020. "Foreword." In *Changing Climate, Changing Worlds. Local knowledge and the challenges of social and ecological change*, edited by M. Welch-Devine, A. Sourdril, and B.J. Burke, 35–54. Cham, Switzerland: Springer.

Salick, J., B. Staver, and R. Hart. 2020. "Indigenous knowledge and dynamics among Himalayan peoples, vegetation, and climate change." In *Changing Climate, Changing Worlds. Local knowledge and the challenges of social and ecological change*, edited by M. Welch-Devine, A. Sourdril, and B.J. Burke, 55–70. Cham, Switzerland: Springer.

Schnegg, M. 2022. "Environmental pluralism: knowing the Namibian Weather in times of climate change." In *Cooling Down: Local responses to global climate change*, edited by S.M. Hoffman, T.H. Eriksen, and P. Mendes, 29–48. New York: Berghan.

Schneider, F. and T. Buser. 2018. "Promising degrees of stakeholder interaction in research for sustainable development." *Sustainability Science* 13 (1): 129. https://doi.org/10.1007/S11625-017-0507-4.

Seara, T., R. Pollnac, and K. Jakubowski. 2020. "Fishers' perceptions of environmental and climate change in Puerto Rico: implications for adaptation and sustainability." In *Changing Climate, Changing Worlds. Local knowledge and the challenges of social and ecological change*, edited by M. Welch-Devine, A. Sourdril, and B.J. Burke, 15–34. Cham, Switzerland: Springer.

Shaffer, L.J. 2017. "An anthropological perspective on the climate change and violence relationship." *Current Climate Change Reports* 3: 222–232. https://doi.org/10.1007/s40641-017-0076-8.

Siddiqui, T., M.J.U. Sikder, and M.R.A. Bhuiyan. 2022. "Climate change and mitigation in Bangladesh: vulnerability in urban locations." In *Cooling Down: Local responses toglobal climate change*, edited by S.M. Hoffman, T.H. Eriksen, and P. Mendes, 113–130. New York: Berghan.

Sjölander-Lindqvist, A., I. Murin, and M. Dove. 2022. *Anthropological Perspectives on Environmental Communication*. Palgrave MacMillan.

Sourdril, A., E. Andrieu, C. Barnaud, L. Clochey, and M. Deconchat. 2020. "Observing 'weeds' to understand local perceptions of environmental change in a temperate rural area of Southwestern France." In *Changing Climate, Changing Worlds. Local knowledge and the challenges of social and ecological change*, edited by M. Welch-Devine, A. Sourdril, and B.J. Burke, 71–98. Cham, Switzerland: Springer.

Towler, E., Lazrus, H., and PaiMazumder, D. 2019. "Characterizing the potential for drought action from combined hydrological and societal perspectives." *Hydrology and Earth System Sciences* 23: 1469–1482. https://doi.org/10.5194/hess-23-1469-2019.

Victor, D. 2015. "Climate change: embed the social sciences in climate policy." *Nature* 520: 27–29. https://doi.org/10.1038/520027a.

Welch-Devine M., B.J. Burke, C. Steacy, and S. Rzonca. 2022. "Environmental change in Southern Appalachia: local ecological knowledge across residential groups." *Ambio*. 51 (1): 280–290. doi:10.1007/s13280-021-01559-1.

Welch-Devine, M. and D.S. Murray. 2011. "We're European Farmers Now": transitions and transformations in Basque agricultural practices." *Anthropological Journal of European Cultures* 20 (1): 69–88.

Whyte, K. 2017. "Indigenous climate change studies: indigenizing futures, decolonizing the Anthropocene." *English Language Notes* 55(1–2): 153–162.

3

A PICARESQUE CRITIQUE

The Anthropology of Disasters and Displacement in the Era of Global Warming and Pandemics

A.J. Faas

Itinerant Rogues

On the afternoon of Friday, September 9, 2011, I attended an Irrigation Committee meeting in Pusuca, in the Chimborazo Province of the Andean highlands of Ecuador. Then in its third year, Pusuca was one of two resettlements built in Canton Penipe for the thousands of campesinos displaced by evacuations following the 1999 and 2006 eruptions of the stratovolcano Tungurahua, who casts her shadow over Penipe's three northern parishes. Another resettlement I call "Penipe Nuevo," just five kilometers away, was constructed in the central town of Penipe by the Ecuadorian Ministry of Urban Development and Housing and the US-based Christian Evangelical disaster relief organization Samaritan's Purse with no land or economic resources for the displaced campesinos they purported to resettle. In Pusuca, campesinos had worked with the progressive Ecuadorian NGO Fundación Esquel to build the 45 houses, three communal buildings, infrastructure, and park, and were well on their way to completing the roughly ten-kilometer irrigation canal that would feed water to the hectare of land they were each granted in the resettlement. Until the water began running (it had been three years and there was nearly one more to go), campesinos in Pusuca were by and large in the same situation as those down the hill in Penipe Nuevo – commuting to the cities near and far for wage labor or taking their chances farming on their lands on the still erupting volcano. It was now four years after the last major eruption and people were still dealing with acute resource insecurity, economic precarity, and draconian rules governing their occupation of resettlement houses, participation in community affairs, and potential loss of rights and housing for failure to comply. As was common at the time, meeting participants plodded through basic updates on the progress of the construction of the canal, planned material deliveries, schedules for mandatory *minga* work parties on the canal, and the usual quarreling over the accounting of minga participation credit.

Despite the banality of the affair, the meeting quickly assumed the kind of tense atmosphere you could feel in your belly, even if you were only half aware, as I was at the time, of the relations provoking the tension. As the committee made their way through

DOI: 10.4324/9781003242499-5

the modest agenda, everyone was surprised by the attendance of Jefferson Toapanta and his wife, Neli Morocho, as neither had been present in the community for more than a year.[1] Even when they had resided there, they had a poor history of meeting community obligations; what is more, Jefferson had been accused of the theft of his neighbors' property on more than one occasion and their neighbors worried about the welfare of their five young children – all born after 1999, three since the 2006 eruptions.

After concluding the usual business, Irrigation Committee President Zandro Villacis began thanking attendees for coming and adjourned the meeting. But, just as everyone began to get up and leave, resettlement village council (*directiva*) President Angel Turushina, visibly shaken by the combination of the surprise presence of the erstwhile and much maligned community members and, as he told me moments later, the thorny responsibility of managing their case in fairness despite his strong emotions, jumped to his feet and implored everyone to remain for an additional twenty minutes to discuss an important issue. Once everyone returned to their seats, Angel addressed Jefferson and Neli, who were both seated at the back of the room. He said that they returned to the community after being away for some time; that they were heavily in arrears with community dues – somewhere around $1000 (a massive debt in local terms) – and they needed to pay soon. He even noted that they were in possession of a community-owned pickaxe they must return in haste. Jefferson and Neli looked confusedly at each other for a second, but then unscrewed their brows and quietly nodded their belated recollection. Angel explained that he really wanted to help relieve them of their bad reputations and return to good standing in the community, but they would have to begin paying soon and respect community standards.

The story being narrated in this encounter was of the politics of deservingness and the accounting of household obligations to the collective and to the state. Martha Santiago, the Fundación Esquel representative who oversaw community meetings and affairs, had stepped out midway through the meeting, only to return for the final portion of the conversation. Having heard the complaints and accounting of what was owed, she offered Jefferson and Neli an opportunity to facilitate their return to good standing. She invited the two of them to work with paid laborers on the irrigation canal, saying that the chief engineer would render half of their pay directly to the community chest (*caja comunitaria*) and half to them, so that they would have some income while paying down their debts. Speaking in a hushed tone, almost mumbling, Jefferson agreed, saying they would do it. Martha reiterated that both he and Neli could work and encouraged them to leave their children at the community childcare center, which had been established by two young mothers in the resettlement, during the day while they worked.

The story was also one of care and repairing relations with the community. Just as Martha concluded, Angel's mother, the ordinarily reserved Teresa Caicedo, rose to speak and asked Jefferson and Neli to let the community know if they had really returned to live there and intended to be members of the community again. Speaking with unmistakably sincere compassion and concern, she said they needed to make a conscious decision and to make it known. Clearly, she said, they needed help with their half dozen young children; Teresa and others could help as a community, as fellow parents, but they needed to know if they truly intended to be members of the community.

On Monday, I was happy to see Jefferson working with the paid laborers on the irrigation canal as I made my way to work on the minga labor party further down the canal.

Though the offer to work had been extended to Neli as well, I did not see her. Perhaps she had chosen to look after the children, I thought. Sadly, this was the one and only time Jefferson showed up for work. By the end of the week, they were gone from Pusuca again, and I did not know them to return in the next several years.

I cut the story of Jefferson and Neli out of my book, *In the Shadow of Tungurahua: Disaster Politics in Highland Ecuador* (2023) because I was well over the word limit, which set me on the unhappy hunt for outliers and redundancies. While I wanted to allow as many stories as I could to live on the page beyond the scoring of theoretical points, some clearly had to go. The first part of the book, where this story once appeared, is about how state-imposed legibility (e.g., forced settlement, occupation, enumeration) is a form of violence in its intolerance of adaptive subaltern mobility; the production of a comprehensible grid for governance that is openly hostile to multiplex livelihoods. I found Jefferson and Neli's story helpful for illustrating something like how individuals working through state assemblages (here configured around Fundación Esquel) and traditional institutions like village councils and minga work parties – themselves reconfigured in the encounters and shifting assemblages of the state and disaster – at times did attempt to adapt institutional forms, practices, and politics of deservingness to accommodate rogues like Jefferson and Neli, largely driven by a recognition that their "deviance" was to some degree born of vexing circumstance. But the case stood outside the main themes of the text; it could be cut, in my estimation at the time, without consequence for the reader's understanding of the (re)production and politics of disaster and resettlement. Such is the politics of ethnographic writing – lives live well beyond the first page and the last (Thornton 2009).

I realize now, however, that Jefferson and Neli's story really *is* a story of disasters, displacement, and resettlement in the era of global warming and pandemics, and a decidedly instructive one at that. As Stacey Balkan (2022) argues rather fiercely, in the era of global warming and open-ended upheavals wrought by colonialism and the unchecked excesses of extractive capitalism, *itinerancy* displaces mobility as the field and problematic of critique and inquiry as it exposes cascading contingencies of precarity *sine fine*. I have therefore, with indebtedness to Balkan, written this chapter as a variety of picaresque critique, storying the itinerancy of rogues (strange strangers) like Jefferson and Neli as they reveal and embarrass the power relations that subtend the parameters of the possible. Along the way, I examine how my interlocutors in Penipe have iterated with stories – explicitly and implicitly – to enroll actants in political projects and more-than-human assemblages to realize otherwise possibilities in times of crisis and change. And I conclude with a reflection on storying new politics of deservingness, new varieties of ecological connection, new worldings for new climates.

Ground Gives Way, or So Many Protean Archipelagos

For centuries, Indigenous peoples of the Andes practiced forms of mobility and networks of exchange that passed through the coastal, highland, and Amazonian regions – long referred to as the "vertical archipelago" (Murra 1968) – to take advantage of the many microclimates, resource niches, and social and political economic relations these regions hosted. Spanish colonization introduced new fixed settlement patterns and environmental and economic practices, all of which would be constantly modified throughout the colonial period. Society around Tungurahua took shape over the next three centuries from highly mobile communities into Indigenous and mestizo campesino settlements tied to haciendas through debt peonage and forced labor tribute. In the twentieth century, new state assemblages formed around the project of imposing legibility on the rural periphery in Penipe even as new mobility practices rooted in the conditions of previous waves of rural enclosure (e.g., land scarcity) emerged in tension with state imperatives. Neoliberal reform and land concentration added a more decidedly *horizontal* dimension to the archipelago that included rural-to-urban mobility tied in large part to wage labor. These mobility patterns and networks extended (and often complicated) village social boundaries (Faas 2023; Kingman and Bretón 2016). People moved between village and city, highland and coast, according to periodic opportunities and, at times, exigency. At the turn of the twenty-first century, these human–environmental relations, a shifting state and institutional milieu at the rural margins, and several national political and economic crises, aligned to co-produce disaster around an erupting volcano. But, by the close of the first decade of the twenty-first century, the ground – both literally and figuratively – began giving way beneath the archipelagos.

On one level, traditional institutions like village councils simply changed in important ways following displacement and resettlement. Resettlement councils, or directivas, were subsumed under the more powerful governmental and, in the case of Pusuca, nongovernmental organizations that played outsized roles in the governance of everyday life. Directivas frequently had little power beyond translating the prerogatives of the greater state assemblages. Back in the villages, traditional village councils, or *cabildos*, were more flexible and responded to the contingent needs of villagers in ways that the directivas could not. Thus, while village cabildos had almost no concern for occupation and scheduled work parties to accommodate villagers, the Pusuca resettlement directiva had strict regulations for occupying houses and even stricter rules for participation in minga labor parties. But people still needed to participate in village affairs and their ability to do so was, at least in part, still undermined by their need to meet obligations in resettlements and long commutes and migrations for wage labor. Thus, the best efforts of institutional flexibility in either context often could not bend as far as some people needed.

The problem of coming home to a fugitive familiarity after the disasters in Penipe was also complicated by the accelerated aging of the rural parishes. A movement to reanimate and story village life and agriculture known as *El Retorno* (The Return) began in 2009 and accelerated in the coming years. While many elders and most of the families joined in these efforts, younger and unmarried folks did not return at the same rate. Many found themselves completing their schooling in the nearby city of Riobamba while renting or staying with kin, and those who completed their schooling often preferred to pursue work opportunities in the city. Thus, the villages aged while the pool of available farm labor declined.

It was not long before villagers sensed the climate was changing. In July 2018, I spoke with Washington Sanchez, formerly of Pungal de Puela, who was by then one of the very few resettlers to have completely forgone farming and community life in his home village. The patterns of rain and climate had gone "weird," he said. Their soils, previously rich thanks to generous deposits of minerals from volcanic ash, required more fertilizer to sustain the crops they had been planting for several hundred years. People still attempted to maintain the same planting and harvesting cycles, but they were beset by pests and crop diseases. The rains became increasingly unpredictable and pests of all sorts, most especially the *gorgojo* (maize weevil, *sitophilus zeamais*) began plaguing staple maize crops with greater frequency and intensity. There was also a strange disease affecting potatoes and another plaguing blackberries, the latter of which had emerged as a profitable campesino cash crop in the past decade. Washington said that the increasing volumes of pesticides and fertilizers not only drove up the cost of farming, but also the risk of human illness from toxins. This, he said, was just another reason why he had sold his lands.

The Way Back for Strange Strangers?

I have come to regard Jefferson and Neli's story as a figuration of the strange stranger haunting the interstices of colonialism, the state, late-stage capitalism, subaltern communities, the naturecultural ecology of life in the shadow of Tungurahua, and a warming and weirding globe. Timothy Morton (2010: 50) invites people to reckon with the "uncanny, the strangely familiar or familiarly strange" as an actor-subjectivity-Other emergent, not from elsewhere, but from within the convergence of the quotidian and the extraordinary right at home. Due to the many factors chiseling away at the institutions, relations, and materiality of the nodes in people's mobility networks – which, often but for the draconian governance of resettlement, proved resilient and adaptable – the loops and cycles of mobility grew increasingly circuitous and gave way to open-ended itinerancy as more and more people moved about in search of scarce opportunities that loosed them from the rural margins.

Everything about Jefferson and Neli was at once known and incomprehensible. They were well known to most Pusuca resettlers prior to displacement. Their families all went back generations in their home village of Pungal de Puela. At the time of the first eruptions, they had been living with Neli's parents. They became one of the thirty or so *new* households – formed of multigenerational household fissioning during displacement – out of a total of 327 across the two resettlements. In the politics of resettlement deservingness, new households faced a sort of double bind – while the state preferred to allocate property and resources to single-generation households, locals were hypervigilant about people who appeared to benefit in ways disproportionate to their losses, which meant that when folks like Jefferson and Neli who never previously had houses of their own were suddenly granted one in resettlement, this was bound to raise eyebrows. They "benefitted" from the state and then did not do their part in the community. They had more children than any of their neighbors, but they were barely able to care for themselves. Neither of their families had sufficient land to support themselves, let alone a new generation, so when shelter and food aid ran out, Jefferson and Neli found themselves house "rich" and otherwise utterly impoverished. They were by no means alone in turning to wage labor, day labor, and odd jobs to scrape by, but they had no land or agricultural production to make ends meet. After a short while in the resettlement, while many of their neighbors were struggling, they were outright failing. Though there was never more than circumstantial evidence, it is certainly possible that their circumstances made them desperate enough to steal. They had nothing to turn back to and had found no new futures. They thus became strange strangers to their neighbors, not accommodable by any existing institutions, relations, or stories. Through little fault of their own, they no longer fit in anywhere.

What of Familiar Pasts and Futures? Troubling Disaster Timelines

Storying the historical production of disaster root causes – political, economic, sociocultural – has been one of the central contributions of the critical anthropology of disasters. Anthropologists have for some years been reckoning with the long arc of history as the source of root causes, destabilizing our sense of when disaster "begins" (Bonilla 2020; Marino 2015; Oliver-Smith 2020; Schuller 2016; García-Acosta 2018). In recent decades, one of the unsettling trends in these analyses of disasters and displacement has only become more certain and dire with the acceleration of anthropogenic climate change driven by global warming: there is no zero hour of disaster, nor any end of disaster history. Critical work in recent years has connected the production of disasters to the displacement, resettlement, and genocide of Indigenous populations by, for example, Spanish colonizers in Latin America (Faas 2023; Barrios and Batres 2020; Oliver-Smith 2020); Dutch, British, French, and American settler-colonists in North America (Ghosh 2021; Maldonado 2019; Marino 2015); the Danish, British, French, and Portuguese in Asia (Swamy 2022; Balkan 2022; Ghosh 2021; Hsu et al. 2015); and the British in Africa (Faria et al. 2021). At the broadest level of scale, global warming is fueled by capitalist extraction, production, and consumption itself set in motion by colonial economies, political domination, and resource extraction, and its direst consequences are so far felt most intensely and frequently by those who had the least to do with their causes (Ghosh 2021; Balkan 2022; Bonilla 2020; Maldonado 2019; Marino et al. 2022). The local effects of climate change have been increasingly driving displacement while contributing to the frequency and intensity of hazard event/processes. Many of the displaced hail from climate "hotspots" that are, not incidentally, postcolonial contexts known for above average rates of poverty, insecurity, and conflict (Ghosh 2021; Schuller 2021; Burkett 2018; Marino 2015).

If anthropological work troubles our sense of when disaster begins, it must also unsettle our sense of when (or even *if*) it ends. The resettlements of Penipe are what scholars often refer to as "post-disaster" resettlements, but it is absurd to consider the "post" as signaling the *end* of disaster; it is far better to consider them, like other "posts" (e.g., modernity, colonialism), as following the *beginning* of disaster. There is always a variety of mobility patterns unfolding prior to, during, and following disasters (Faas 2023; Maldonado 2019; Marino and Lazrus 2015), "some of which empower, and are even led by, local efforts, while others marginalize and disempower those resettling" (Jessee 2020, 151). The disaster experienced by Penipeños was an assemblage that included eruptions, iterative evacuations, long periods of displacement and despondency, the loss of crops and animals, and the restrictive governance of resettlements that was intolerant of their livelihoods and mobility strategies. In Penipe Nuevo, resettlers in houses built by the federal government faced regular threats of eviction if their houses were found unoccupied in the evenings by visiting agents. In Pusuca, the directiva and Fundación Esquel monitored house occupation as one of several conditions for granting housing deeds and access to community projects for economic development. In most cases, people were merely away for a few nights, either working for wages in the city or tending to lands and animals in their home villages where the commutes were longer and more cumbersome as a result of damaged roads and bridges. For them, disaster hardly came to an end with the advent of resettlements. They spent years without stable livelihoods and were beset by all sorts of new regulations on their lives and mobilities and the looming sense that they could lose what little they had at any moment.

As Carla Roncoli and colleagues (2009) explain, the era of anthropogenic climate change has thus far been characterized by interminable liminality, a weighty sense of having left an old familiar and not yet having arrived at anything approximating a new one. Important as certain departures from the past are, it is equally important to recognize how people continue to iterate with material-semiotic arrangements with deep roots in the past as they confront climatic change (Vaughn 2022). Anthropologists must attend to the characters in this trouble, to conduct the genealogical and inductive examinations of how people arrive there and how they make their way out (or not). One critical story is that of "rogues" like Jefferson and Neli cutting capers among agents of the state, elites, and the upstanding members of their communities, which is also a story that so far wants for a structuring metaphor to conjure or adapt institutions and relationalities that can accommodate these rogues. In Penipe, people began iterating with stories to make sense of their changing worlds and to enroll new characters in them and give them meaning. Their capacity to do so has me wondering at the possibility and the politics of finding new roles and meanings for the rogues like Jefferson and Neli in the story.

Ten Years On

Had I been asked to make a prediction in any of my prior fieldwork stints in 2009, 2011, or 2013, I would have ventured that Pusuca would have "succeeded" in developing a viable community where people could live and work, while I worried that things would only grow more untenable in Penipe Nuevo, mostly because Pusuca had land for animals and cultivation while Penipe Nuevo did not. However, in 2018 I not only witnessed surprising outcomes in these communities, I also came to appreciate that the standards by which I might have evaluated "success" years ago were decidedly wrongheaded.

Gone were the threats of eviction in the landless resettlement of Penipe Nuevo and so people moved much more freely between the resettlement and, somewhat paradoxically, demonstrated a greater investment in their resettlement homes with modifications ranging from simple decorations and family name plates to additions and new businesses. While at least twenty-five of the 287 houses appeared abandoned, people nevertheless came and went on buses between the cities and their home villages, and the community was genuinely lively, unlike the veritable ghost town it had been just a few years prior, now with bustling car and foot traffic passing by the many restaurants, food stalls, and shops, and the two new schools. People everywhere told me that things were much better and that they were genuinely doing well.

In the landed resettlement of Pusuca, I found myself at first struck by overwhelming evidence of abandonment. Though a mere dozen of the 45 houses were occupied, it had become, since irrigation water began running in 2013, an important space for agropastoral production and the reimagination of campesino lives and livelihoods. Juan Ortíz, who was once only barely present in Pusuca, had become a fixed resident and now he and his wife were the most successful farmers in the resettlement, regularly taking large harvests of blackberry to market. Blanca Sánchez was also farming and taking advantage of government subsidies for planting avocados. Others lived fulltime elsewhere but traveled to their lands in Pusuca to tend to extensive farming operations almost daily. Judith

Guamushi, her husband, and two daughters resided in their home village but tended to cattle and crops they planted in Pusuca. Angel Turushina, former directiva president and perennial Pusuca booster, now lived with his family in Penipe Nuevo, where they operated a convenience store, barbecue food stall, and cybercafe, but Angel was in Pusuca each day tending to his rich variety of fruit crops. Alberto Sánchez and his wife and children resided in the city of Riobamba, an hour drive away, but came each week to work their fields.

Then there were Jefferson and Neli, Jhon Jaya, Ramiro González, Walter Guerrero, and Cristobal Barragan – strange strangers all – moving about for day labor in the rural highlands, seasonal work on the coast or in the oil fields of the Amazon, and wage work in the cities, their pathways constantly changing. In 2018, it had been years since anyone saw Jefferson, Neli, or Jhon, but Ramiro, Walter, or Cristobal might appear every few months or so, though never long enough to establish themselves in the community or on their lands. I chose not to critique this as a failure of resettlement, as I might have in the past, because, especially since I saw how many more folks were cultivating there than living there, I feared judging it on standards of occupancy would be to judge it in terms of the legibility standards of the state that were fundamental to the production of disaster – and just so much suffering – in the first place.

Itinerant Rogues and Stubborn Boundaries

Jefferson, Neli, and the other Penipeños gone rogue are far from alone in their plight. They are among the many millions facing disaster and climate-related displacement across the Americas (García-Acosta 2020; Maldonado 2019; Taddei 2020; Barrios and Batres 2020; Jessee 2020; Marino 2015; Farbotko and Lazrus 2012). Often, these displacements drive Indigenous and campesino communities to urban spaces thereby enabling entrepreneurial classes who can afford the agricultural inputs and weather disruptions in production few subsistence farmers can, to consolidate their ownership of lands and control of resources in the region (Murgida and Radovich 2020; Murgida 2013). Beyond the Americas, more than 82 million people were forcibly displaced worldwide in 2020, marking an increase of more than 100 percent over the past ten years (UNHCR 2020). More than 26 million were refugees, 48 million internally displaced people, and over four million asylum seekers. Nearly 70 percent of the displaced originated from Syria (6.7 million), Venezuela (4 m), Afghanistan (2.6 m), South Sudan (2.2 m), and Myanmar (1.1 m), all former European colonies and active conflict zones. Over 30 million were internally displaced by disasters – three times the number displaced by conflict and violence – primarily associated with floods and storms, but also wildfire, heat waves, drought, and landslides (IFRC 2021). At the time of writing, the cumulative confirmed Covid-19 cases total is over 400 million and displaced and stateless people have been among the most severely affected by infection, healthcare access, and socio-political hostility (Johns Hopkins University n.d.).

Everywhere strange strangers haunt the boundaries of the world's imagined communities as states and nations enact laws to prevent the entry or movement of migrants on quests for survival and subsistence following all sorts of disasters and upheavals (Cuéllar 2021; Miller 2017; De León 2015). Communities facing displacement pressures – be they from disaster, climate, or combinations of the two – often also contend with the "lack of governance mechanisms or budgets to support the communities, which intensifies community impoverishment, negative economic and health impacts, and loss of place, social networks, and culture" (Maldonado et al. 2013: 608). This is compounded by what we might consider the limit cases of the institutions of liberal constitutional democracy, which are exclusively capable of recognizing individuals and property rights to the exclusion of collective and territorial claims (Marino et al. 2022; Maldonado 2019; Jesse 2020; Sawyer 2004).

The problem is not only the lone rogues like Jefferson and Neli or the massive scale displacements, but rather that we keep trying to "repair" disaster situations by attempting to reconstruct a fugitive familiar. Disaster management worldwide remains predicated on a bygone climate stability (Lizaralde et al. forthcoming; Marino et al. 2022; Schuller 2021; Maldonado 2019). While activists and critical disaster scholars have long advocated a reframing of the common sense of a *return to normal*, "decision-makers will soon have to confront loss of physical territory and the unviability of many places human communities currently call home" (Burkett 2018). Each day that the millions of folks like Jefferson and Neli navigate the Aeolian currents to just get by until the next move, it becomes ever more urgent to rethink and reframe human–environmental relations, juridico-legal accountability to the state (i.e., *legibility*), and humanitarian sensibilities of deservingness and belongingness.

Social Witnessing: The Politics of (Humanitarian and Mutual) Aid

All forms of aid – from governmental to NGO to community-based mutual aid – rely on varieties of social witnessing to story deservingness, to sort the deserving from the undeserving. When the Ecuadorian government assessed the need for resettlement in Penipe, they sent representatives to census the evacuated villages. Surveyors, of course, found people absent more often than not. Only a few neighbors could usually be found milling about their lands, salvaging what they could, repairing structures, tending to animals. They therefore regularly spoke to neighbors about the living situations and needs of those who were absent. In a time before widespread cellphone use in the villages, information was especially fragmentary. But people's disparate experiences with displacement had also yet to accumulate into any thematic storytelling that would infuse these themes with any overt collective politics. People who had found their own housing elsewhere were deemed undeserving of houses in the planned resettlements, so a comment to the effect of "they're living in Riobamba" could (and did) result in a household being removed from the rolls, even if they were sleeping five to a room in a relative's apartment. Often, village leaders had to reach out to government officials to correct the resettlement rolls and ensure that people previously excluded were granted "dossiers" indicating the deservingness for resettlement. During the prolonged displacement, officials and volunteers asked those in queues for food rations to publicly verify the eligibility of others who joined the line. And during the worst throes of the Covid-19 pandemic when the inter-village bus system was suspended, it was village leaders and the very few who owned vehicles who shuttled shut-in villagers to the city to collect their government aid and pension checks.

Minga is perhaps the most pervasive and historically significant institution and structuring metaphor of pan-Andean culture since long before the Spanish colonization that transformed it for centuries into an instrument of extraction, domination, and governance. In late 2020 I interviewed my old friend Bernardo Huerta, long-serving cabildo president in Manzano, who reminded me of how they were able to return to their devastated village after the 2006 evacuations and had endured incredible scarcity in the resource-barren resettlements. "The time in which you first came was lamentably a very sad time. At the time we returned, we asked God for the strength to move forward. And secondly, we organized ourselves to work in the community. And that has given us the strength we have in our community." The story he told with greater fervor in each retelling was that they built back with community organized minga cooperative work parties. Village leaders like Bernardo operationalized the story of *El Retorno* by organizing minga work parties to repair damaged buildings – one of my first mingas involved helping repair a schoolhouse – roads, irrigation canals, potable water systems, and to rotate from household to household to salvage, harvest, and, later, plant. Minga has long served campesinos as a simultaneously pastoral project meant to recover idealized pasts and a prescriptive project meant to prefigure a more perfect future.

Just as villagers had begun to feel like they were moving on, they felt the environmental impacts of climate change, and "now we're facing this epidemic," Bernardo said as he turned to the topic of the Covid-19 pandemic then raging in Ecuador and around the world. He said that he and the villagers of Manzano were

> happy with what little we have...although now the chemicals and fertilizers are expensive and the markets, because of this epidemic, have completely reduced, and the sale of animals is no longer as it was. Before, you could sell a 300lb pig for $500. Now we're getting $200. It's because of [the Covid-19 pandemic] that we're in that situation.

When Bernardo raised the precipitous drop in prices for animals, he was consciously storying a parallel with the same phenomenon in 1999 following the eruptions. Everyone who evacuated had nowhere to take their animals in 1999, so they flooded the market and the prices tanked. "But, however, with prayers to God, we must keep moving forward, brother." He went on,

> We have organized the community, the group. Now with this epidemic in which we find ourselves, thanks to God we are working in the community in whatever way we can...[W]e ourselves must take care of ourselves; in one way or another, we have to take care of ourselves and, whatever happens in our community...if there are problems, we protect ourselves and take care of ourselves.

Coming together often proved challenging when keeping social distance was the order of the day during the pandemic, but minga remained an abiding institution and ethic.

Minga practice is imbued with state and colonial power and even when enrolled in projects of resistance it retains an often-rigid ethic of deservingness. When organized by the state, there is a strict accounting of attendance, task completion, and the varieties of deservingness (e.g., water, housing) they unlock. When organized by villagers, participation is still strictly accounted, though no individual tasks are assigned or assessed, and the spaces and times of minga practice are far more in sync with the quotidian temporal regimes of campesino livelihoods. State-run mingas are exacting and often challenging for campesino households to satisfy, while participating in village-level mingas is simply easier. Ironically, however, the discourse of minga ethics – all for one, one for all, and equal participation as a condition for equal deservingness – is driven above all by campesinos and even more passionately when working with the state. At times it veritably reeks of colonialist panopticism. But this reveals something about the contested coloniality of institutions of governance that accumulate into assemblages that enroll actors (human, nonhuman, landscape) into state projects, and also how these institutions and assemblages are, on occasion, enrolled in subaltern practices of mutual aid and care. What often appears as neighbors policing neighbors in a jealous politics of deservingness frequently obtains as a "diagnostic social process" (James 2010) that exerts pressure on the state to align its practices with local ethics. Local politics of deservingness is often riddled with personal or household concerns about material and political precariousness. This means that the human economies and institutional rules of village mingas only flex so far because there are real boundaries to be defended. Can local politics of deservingness better accommodate Jefferson and Neli? Perhaps, but this is not guaranteed because the politics of deservingness remains decidedly partial to model "victims" with unassailable reputations.

Storying (the Politics of) Co-Living

Villagers from Penipe's northern parishes have iterated several metaphors for going home. While people no doubt reflected on the notion of "home" and what it meant to them in their years-long displacement from 1999 to 2008, the first phase of going home was perhaps the least reflexive. People wanted to be home, where things were familiar, where they could live as they had always learned. In 2009 people started storying the return home under the theme of El Retorno, a movement to reanimate village life, which was promoted with posters and loosely coordinated speeches by village leaders, and which coincided with the first parish saints' festivals since 1999. El Retorno was inhibited by public and private sector divestment in the area due to its official political storying as a "high risk" zone, meaning that roads, bridges, and hydraulic infrastructure remained destroyed or in disrepair. It was also impeded by the intolerant policing of housing occupancy in the resettlements.

Convivir, or "co-living," emerged after 2015 as a way of storying changing environments and institutions, reframing relations with Tungurahua, leading state assemblages according to local logics of the good, and motivating and inspiring campesinos to reclaim their roots and revitalize their culture. Convivir is invoked in everyday speech about living, cultivating, and building community in the villages around the volcano; printed on pamphlets and signs advertising agricultural extension programs, parish fiestas, and projects supporting risk management and emergency response programs; and inscribed on a mosaic in the tourist town of Baños along with the phrase, "We will never leave our lands because we have always co-lived with the volcano." That phrase neatly captures one of the core political objectives of convivir – defending people's right to live there as they please. Convivir is not *solely* about Tungurahua. The term almost always accompanies claims about cooperation among the community of humans, animals, and crops and forests. It's also the structuring idiom of volcanic monitoring training with the Geophysics Institute, evacuation drills with the Secretariat of Risk Management, and various emergency preparedness projects organized in the parishes. Convivir has become at once a story about historical relations, a sort of mnemonic for indexing varieties of knowledge, and a social and *very* political argument for the future of life in the shadow of the volcano. It is a story that informs and guides the state assemblage in Penipe's northern parishes, including Jefferson and Neli's home village. Truly dangerous discourse that challenges the figures of the thinkable may be exceedingly rare and virtually impossible, but convivir comes about as close as I've seen.

I see crafting metaphors to story human pathways to otherwise possibilities as necessary to politics, science, and the good life, and especially necessary to the future of multispecies life on earth in the time of climate change and pandemics. Convivir collects new arrangements and old within a vision of what could be, of what could be good, of response-ability (Haraway 2016), a direct engagement with people's capacity to *affect* and *be affected* (Butler 2016). It is a vitalist storying of more-than-human assemblages, of connecting to the environment as something more than inert stuff for manipulation and consumption. Villages rebuilding in the name of convivir have found ways to be flexible with minga practice and local standards of belonging, but people have yet to write the rogues like Jefferson and Neli into this new story.

Several scholars have identified the promise of working with more-than-human collectives and Indigenous ontologies to craft otherwise possibilities in the climate crisis (Chao and Enari 2021). And, to anticipate a facile critique, longing for stories signals neither a turn to romanticism nor idealism. Humankind requires art, religion, and dreams to enroll our increasingly specialized knowledge into larger moral-ethical visions, absent which rationality is "necessarily pathogenic and destructive of life" (Bateson 2000 [1972], 146). Amitav Ghosh (2021) expresses a concern that one dismal legacy of colonialism is that it devastated vitalist ontological commitments sustained by people all over the world and imposed mechanistic worldviews and the notion that scientific mastery has conquered Nature. The value of scientific knowledge notwithstanding, as a figure of discourse in the public square it meets with four well-documented onto-epistemological limitations: 1) advanced scientific work is so esoteric as to be virtually incomprehensible to non-specialists; 2) naïve techno-optimism abets environmental degradation; 3) the distribution of inputs and outputs in the capitalist world system leaves unfathomable chasms between most (but not all) people's immediate spheres and their entanglements far afield; and 4) there is a tendency to represent and regard science as a "view from nowhere," when all knowledge is, in fact, quite situated. This is, ironically, what brings otherwise secular thinkers to explore possibilities for storying the entanglement of the near and the far and fostering transspecies kinship and accountability that recognizes an at once transcendental and earth-bound life force around which to build ethical futures (Ghosh 2021; Liboiron 2021; Haraway 2016; Tsing 2015). I would argue also that a new vitalism can provide opportunities to make space for the rogues like Jefferson and Neli, to challenge state politics of deservingness with a subaltern politics of care.

Exit, in Pursuit of a Bear

Months after I last saw Jefferson at his final minga in 2011, I tracked down Neli's brother Ramon in Baños, where he and his wife were living for the time-being with their three young daughters in a small motel room they paid for by the week. Ramon worked as a day laborer, but their expenses consumed basically all his earnings, and his work, he said,

made it impossible for him to return to Pusuca and cancel his debts of community obligations. At that point, it had been nearly two years since they had returned. Once you fell far
enough behind, as Jefferson and Ramon had, the way back became insurmountable, as they
found themselves venturing further and further afield to earn what they could and provide
for their families. Subaltern politics of deservingness does contest state power and vitalist
metaphors like *convivir* enroll more-than-human assemblages in new, often expressly political, projects. And I have witnessed a more flexible and tolerant politics in natal villages
than in resettlements mostly because local leaders must be more responsive to their neighbors
than resettlement agency personnel. But the unconscious bias in favor of the model victim
persists and discourses of deservingness tend to leave little room for itinerant rogues like
Jefferson and Neli, much as they leave little room for migrants and refugees elsewhere.

Alas, the Global North wants for new metaphors as much as anyone. As I write, my
mind wanders to Allen Ginsberg's *Howl*, "while you are not safe I am not safe, and now
you're really in the total animal soup of time." The centers in which the warming that
drives anthropogenic climate change is produced may not yet experience (or choose to
acknowledge) its worst effects as do those at the margins of global capitalism and empire.
If the production of this devastation is not arrested by stories which connect the far
consequences of near actions to effect radical transformations of practice, it is no hyper-
bole to say that devastation awaits. The Covid-19 pandemic has revealed that science
alone is insufficient for organizing and enrolling human practices and communities.

The search for new stories cannot be an extractivist appropriation of Indigenous metaphors. Often, following talks about Penipe, I'm asked how we can "do" minga or convivir in
the USA. This, to my mind, is the wrong question. Though anthropology in the modern (and
largely American) sense has always to some degree been about the otherwise, the questioning
I would like to encourage is how to story and enact our *own* naturecultural entanglements in
an affective register. That things are otherwise elsewhere indicates that we can learn to see
and do things differently at home. Convivir is the concept metaphor of the assemblage and
politics in the shadow of Tungurahua. Anywhere else, people must craft stories rooted in
their own entanglements. Since the very beginnings of the modern and rather fraught
American anthropology in which I was trained, the otherwise – say, of Samoan adoles-
cence – was never itself intended for export. Rather, it was taken as compelling evidence that
other worlds and futures are possible.

Note

1 All names are pseudonyms.

References

Balkan, Stacey. 2022. *Rogues in the Postcolony: Narrating extraction and itinerancy in India.* Morgantown: West Virginia University Press.
Barrios, Roberto E. and Carlos Batres. 2020. "The anthropology of disasters that has yet to be: The case of Central America." In *The Anthropology of Disasters in Latin America: State of the art,* edited by Virginia García-Acosta, 63–81. New York: Routledge.
Bateson, Gregory. 2000 [1972]. *Steps to an Ecology of Mind.* Chicago: University of Chicago Press.
Bonilla, Yarimar. 2020. "The coloniality of disaster: race, empire, and the temporal logics of emergency in Puerto Rico, USA." *Political Geography* 78: 102181.

Burkett, Maxine. 2018. "Behind the veil: climate migration, regime shift, and a new theory of justice." *Harvard Civil Rights-Civil Liberties Law Review* 53: 445–493.

Butler, Judith. 2016. "Rethinking vulnerability and resistance." In *Vulnerability in Resistance*, edited by Judith Butler, Zeynep Gambetti, and Leticia Sabsay, 12–27. Durham: Duke University Press.

Chao, Sophie and Dion Enari. 2021. "Decolonising climate change: a call for beyond-human imaginaries and knowledge generation." *eTropic* 20 (2): 32–54. http://dx.doi.org/10.25120/etropic.20.2.2021.3796.

Cuéllar, Jorge E. 2021. "Waterproofing the state: migration, river-borders, and ecologies of control." *Comparative American Studies* 18 (1): 59–74.

De León, Jason. 2015. *The Land of Open Graves: Living and dying on the migrant trail.* Oakland: University of California Press.

Faas, A.J. 2023. *In the Shadow of Tungurahua: Disaster politics in Highland Ecuador.* New Brunswick: Rutgers University Press.

Farbotko, Carol and Heather Lazrus. 2012. "The first climate refugees? Contesting global narratives of climate change in Tuvalu." *Global Environmental Change* 22 (2): 382–390.

Faria, Caroline, Jovah Katushabe, Catherine Kyotowadde, and Dominica Whitesell. 2021. "'You rise up…they burn you again': market fires and the urban intimacies of disaster colonialism." *Transactions of the Institute of British Geographers* 46: 87–101. https://doi.org/10.1111/tran.12404.

García-Acosta, Virginia (ed.). 2020. *Anthropology and Disasters in Latin America and the Caribbean: The state of the art.* New York: Routledge.

—2018. "Vulnerabilidad y desastres: génesis y alcances de una visión alternativa." In *Pobreza y Vulnerabilidad: Debates y estudios contemporáneos en México*, edited by Mercedes González de la Rocha and Gonzalo AndrésSaraví, 212–239. Mexico City: CIESAS.

Ghosh, Amitav. 2021. *The Nutmeg's Curse: Parables for a planet in crisis.* Chicago: University of Chicago Press.

Ginsberg, Allen. 2002 [1956]. *Howl and Other Poems.* San Francisco: City Lights Books.

Haraway, Donna J. 2016. *Staying with the Trouble: Making kin in the Chthulucene.* Durham: Duke University Press.

Hsu, Minna, Ritchie Howitt, and Fiona Miller. 2015. "Procedural vulnerability and institutional capacity deficits in post-disaster recovery and reconstruction: insights from Wutai Rukai experiences of Typhoon Morakot." *Human Organization* 74(4), 308–318.

International Federation of Red Cross and Red Crescent Societies (IFRC). 2021. *Displacement in a Changing Climate: Localized humanitarian action at the forefront of the climate crisis.* Geneva: IFRC.

James, Erica Caple. 2010. *Democratic Insecurities: Violence, trauma, and intervention in Haiti.* Oakland: University of California Press.

Jessee, Nathan. 2020. "Community resettlement in Louisiana: learning from histories of horror and hope." In *Louisiana's Response to Extreme Weather*, edited by Shirley Laska, 147–184. New York: Springer.

Johns Hopkins University. N.d. *COVID-19 Data Repository by the Center for Systems Science and Engineering (CSSE).* Available at https://github.com/CSSEGISandData/COVID-19. Accessed on February 11, 2022.

Kingman Garcés, Eduardo and Víctor Bretón Solo de Zaldívar. 2016. "Las fronteras arbitrarias y difusas entre lo urbano-moderno y lo rural-tradicional en los Andes." *The Journal of Latin American and Caribbean Anthropology* 22 (2): 235–253.

Liboiron, Max. 2021. *Pollution is Colonialism.* Durham: Duke University Press.

Lizarralde, Gonzalo, Lisa Bornstein, Tapan Dhar, and the Disaster Resilience and Sustainable Reconstruction Research Alliance, editors. Forthcoming. *Shelter in the Storm: Ethical debates in responses to disasters and climate change.* New York: Columbia University Press.

Maldonado, Julie. 2019. *Seeking Justice in an Energy Sacrifice Zone: Standing on vanishing land in coastal Louisiana.* New York: Routledge.

Maldonado, Julie, Christine Scherer, Robin Bronen, Kristina Petereson, and Heather Lazrus. 2013. "The impact of climate change on tribal communities in the US: displacement, relocation, and human rights." *Climatic Change* 12: 601–614.

Marino, Elizabeth. 2015. *Fierce Climate, Sacred Ground: An ethnography of climate change in Shishmaref, Alaska*. Fairbanks: University of Alaska Press.

Marino, Elizabeth, Alessandra Jerolleman, Eli Keene, Sigvana Topkok, Annie Weyiouanna, Nathan Jessee, and Simon Manda. 2022. "Is the longue durée a legal argument? Understanding takings doctrine in climate change and settler colonial contexts in the US." *Human Organization* 81(4): 348-357.

Marino, Elizabeth, and Heather Lazrus. 2015. "Migration or forced displacement? The complex choices of climate change and disaster migrants in Shishmaref, Alaska, and Nanumea, Tuvalu." *Human Organization* 74 (4): 341–350.

Miller, Todd. 2017. *Storming the Wall: Climate change, migration, and homeland security*. San Francisco: City Lights Press.

Morton, Timothy. 2010. *The Ecological Thought*. Cambridge: Harvard University Press.

Murgida, Ana. 2013. "Cambios socio-ambientales: desplazamientos de las poblaciones históricamente postergadas en el Chaco-Salteño." *Cuadernos de Antropología 9*: 35–63.

Murgida, Ana María, and Juan Carlos Radovich. 2020. "Risk and uncertainty in Argentinian social anthropology." In *The Anthropology of Disasters in Latin America: State of the art*, edited by Virginia García-Acosta, 22–44. New York: Routledge.

Murra, John V. 1968. "An Aymara Kingdom in 1567." *Ethnohistory* 15 (2): 115–151.

Oliver-Smith, Anthony. 2020 [1999]. "What is a Disaster? Anthropological Perspectives on a Persistent Question." In *The Angry Earth: Disaster in Anthropological Perspective*, Second Edition, edited by Anthony Oliver-Smith and Susanna Hoffman, 29–44. New York: Routledge.

Roncoli, Carla, Todd Crane, and Ben Orlove. 2009. "Fielding climate change in cultural anthropology." In *Anthropology and Climate Change: From encounters to actions*, edited by Susan A. Crate and Mark Nuttall, 87–115. Walnut Creek, CA: Left Coast Press.

Sawyer, Suzanna. 2004. *Crude Chronicles: Indigenous politics, multinational oil, and neoliberalism in Ecuador*. Durham: Duke University Press.

Schuller, Mark. 2021. *Humanity's Last Stand: Confronting global catastrophe*. New Brunswick: Rutgers University Press.

Schuller, Mark. 2016. *Humanitarian Aftershocks in Haiti*. New Brunswick: Rutgers University Press.

Swamy, Raja. 2022. "Tranquebar—The tsunami, heritage tourism, power, and memory in a South Indian fisher village." *Dialectical Anthropology*, early view. https://doi.org/10.1007/s10624-021-09641-6.

Taddei, Renzo. 2020. "The field of anthropology of disasters in Brazil: challenges and perspectives." In *The Anthropology of Disasters in Latin America: State of the art*, edited by Virginia García-Acosta, 45–62. New York: Routledge.

Thornton, Robert. 2009. "The rhetoric of ethnographic holism." *Cultural Anthropology* 3 (3): 285–303.

Tsing, Anna Lowenhaupt. 2015. *The Mushroom at the End of the World: On the possibility of life in capitalist ruins*. Princeton: Princeton University Press.

United Nations High Commissioner for Refugees (UNHCR). 2020. *Global Trends: Forced displacement in 2020*. Copenhagen: UNHCR Global Data Service.

Vaughn, Sarah E. 2022. *Engineering Vulnerability: In pursuit of climate adaptation*. Durham: Duke University Press.

4

UNDERSTANDING ARCTIC MELT

Reflections on Collaborative Interdisciplinary Research

Mark Nuttall

It is a Saturday in mid-July 2014, and I am marvelling at the calm water and the early evening shimmer in the Upernavik Icefjord in Northwest Greenland. I am travelling deep into the fjord – known as Ikeq in Kalaallisut (Greenlandic) – by open boat with two friends from Aappilattoq, a settlement of around 149 people in the southern part of the Upernavik Archipelago. Aappilattoq is located on an island of the same name, and one of a chain of several islands that bounds Ikeq from the south. We are spending several days fishing for Greenland halibut, and are based at a camp that we have established on an island that lies on the northern side of the fjord. Ikeq, which means a bay, sound, or fjord that is crossed to get from one point to another, is about 70 km long and its head is at the front of the Upernavik Glacier. I have been here many times. Ikeq is one of the two most important fishing grounds in the Upernavik district – the other is Giesecke Icefjord, the official Kalaallisut name of which is Kangerlussuaq (meaning "great fjord"); locally it is known as Gulteqarffik ("the place of gold") on account of its richness as a resource space for halibut fishing. We are going as far as we can into Ikeq, sailing around the enormous icebergs that calve from the glacier and gather and float in this deep, narrow channel, and we are discussing the likelihood of which stretches of water before us contain the essence of halibut before we settle on a spot to bait and set the longlines.

Our conversation on this evening has also turned to what we can see of the Upernavik Glacier, and I comment on how I am now in parts of the fjord where I had not been before. Indeed, much of the land we see ahead of us was recently covered by glacial ice. Until the early 1980s, the glacier had a single terminus. Now it has four separate and distinct main calving termini and, over the last twenty-five years, its retreat has revealed new islands and has uncovered coastal land at the head of the fjord, while large stretches of glacier bed have been exposed and nunataks have emerged from *sermersuaq* (the inland ice), the enormous ice sheet that covers 80% of Greenland (Box and Decker 2011; Larsen et al. 2016).

For scientists who monitor Arctic climate change, this topographical reshaping of the world's high latitudes is revealed through their observing systems as a view looking down from above the Earth through Landsat satellite images. However, on the ground, on the

DOI: 10.4324/9781003242499-6

ice and on the water, people who live in Northwest Greenland observe and experience these transformations in ways that are immediate and embodied. *Sila*, for example, which is the Greenlandic word for weather, has many other meanings: the air, the outside, the world, a person's mind, consciousness, and sense. A changing climate affects not only a person's surroundings, it can be experienced as disorientation. To say "the weather is bad" (*sila ajorpoq*) is also to describe how one's own sense of being in and moving around the world is disrupted. And, when the weather is bad, I have heard people say "*silaga aalavoq*," which means "my head/my mind is swimming, shaking, moving." When the weather improves, it is said not just to get better, but to return to its senses (*silattorpoq*), just as a person does who has suffered a momentary loss of perspective and balance (Nuttall 2018).

On this Saturday in July – which, as I write about this now, was almost ten years ago – we get close to some of these new islands and see the shapes and peaks of the nunataks ahead. My companions remark on this as troubling, as indicative of changes in climate, but nonetheless they reflect on the appearance of this terrain and the disappearance of the ice as entirely consistent with how people in Northwest Greenland think of, and relate to their surroundings, as always emergent and coming into being (Nuttall 2009). They say that, of course, they are concerned about the changes in climate, but the appearance of land and water as the glacier retreats also means possibilities for exploring new places to hunt and fish. They tell me that each time they head into the fjord, they feel as if they are engaging in an experimental fishery, looking for new places where Greenland halibut can be found. As such, they say they feel a direct connection to earlier generations of hunters and fishers in the region who were regarded and admired as pioneers, always exploring areas that could provide opportunities for exploiting resources.

The history of Inuit resource use, occupancy, and dwelling in Northwest Greenland has been one of seeking out places to hunt, fish and settle in, whether this has been because of fluctuations in animal populations, poor weather, or rumours, stories, and ideas about good hunting opportunities, or to avoid competition from other hunters (Hansen 2008; Petersen 2003). The Kalaallisut word for something in the distance, *asi*, is the same word for a dwelling place. There is no word for wilderness in the sense of it as referring to a space that is empty, wild, forlorn. Everywhere has potential to be a lived in place and a rich resource space, to become part of one's surroundings rather than something to be excluded or designated as not useful. The word that is often translated into English to refer to "nature" or "environment" is *pinngortitaq*, but in Kalaallisut it means "becoming," "to unfold," "to come into existence." It refers to how the world is in a continual process of formation, shaping, and transformation. In short, through Greenlandic eyes, *pinngortitaq* is worldmaking. Understood in this context, climate change can be a revelation in how it leads to the uncovering of land through glacial melt and retreat and the appearance of new bays, and in the way it allows accessibility to places where there could be animals and fish to catch, even if it is deeply unsettling.

Earlier in the same month when I was fishing with my friends in Ikeq, I had been further north, in Qimusseriarsuaq (Melville Bay), where I had listened to hunters from the settlements of Savissivik and Kullorsuaq talk about similar transformations in their cryospheric surroundings. I was a few months into a new research project, a large-scale multidisciplinary effort funded by the European Union called ICE-ARC (Ice, Climate and Economics – Arctic Research on Change). Over the next four years I worked with people from several communities in the Upernavik and Avanersuaq districts of Northwest Greenland and, on occasion, with colleagues in the physical and natural sciences, to understand the local, regional, and global effects and consequences of melting ice. While maintaining a focus on the broader global impacts of Arctic climate change was key to the scientific work within and across all the work packages that made up the ICE-ARC program, my task was also to delve deeper into what these transformations mean to people and their livelihoods in Northwest Greenland, how their anticipatory knowledge is challenged by climate change (cf. Hastrup 2016; Nuttall 2022), and how they engage in a process of worldmaking with the non-human. In this chapter, I reflect on this collaborative process with communities and scientists by discussing what emerged from one of the work packages in which I was involved.

ICE-ARC and Understanding Arctic Melt

The high latitudes of the world – the Arctic and Subarctic regions that make up the circumpolar North – are warming rapidly. The effects of this are often dramatic and are increasingly apparent through the diminishing extent and mass loss of glacial ice, the pronounced retreat and thinning of sea ice during winter as well as summer, the thawing of permafrost, coastal erosion, an intensification of stormy and more extreme weather, and changes to the migration routes, distribution, and population sizes of a number of animal and fish species. These transformations not only have considerable effects on northern environments and animals, they impact Indigenous and local livelihoods and wider northern economies (AMAP 2017; Meredith et al. 2019). In Greenland, where I have done much of my research as a social anthropologist over the last few decades, the social, economic, personal, and emotional effects of a changing climate are especially pronounced for those people who depend on fishing and hunting for their livelihoods (Hastrup 2016; Nuttall 2017, 2019a). And while the impacts of climate change have a stark immediacy in the Arctic, and bring greater elements of risk, they extend far beyond the circumpolar North as melting ice sheets affect global ocean circulation, accelerate the rise of global sea level, and affect global weather patterns (e.g., Muilwijk et al. 2022).

The small coastal settlements of the Upernavik and Avanersuaq districts of Northwest Greenland (and many household economies in the towns of Upernavik and Qaanaaq) are based largely on hunting and fishing. Until the 1930s, and even into the 1940s and 1950s, many families continued to lead what, in a sense, could still be called a mainly nomadic way of life, especially in Avanersuaq and the northern part of Upernavik. Larger hunting settlements grew around the institutions of school and church and a shop/trading post operated by the Royal Greenland Trade Company, to which hunters sold sealskins, fox furs, whale blubber, fish, and narwhal tusks, but the seasonal round meant that people would still move around their resource spaces spending several months of the year in hunting and fishing camps (Hansen 2008). This pattern of mobility and movement continues to a considerable extent today and life in the northwest remains dependent on the living resources of sea and land. People seek out marine mammals such as seals, walrus, polar bears, narwhal, beluga, fin, and minke whales, and fish such as Greenland halibut, cod, salmon, Arctic char, Atlantic wolfish, and capelin. They also depend at times on land animals such as musk-oxen and reindeer – and on some full, part-time, or seasonal work.

Kalaalimernit – Greenlandic foods that are produced and processed from what people procure from sea and land – enter and sustain an informal economy of sharing and reciprocity in the coastal settlements. Many of the catch shares – from seals, walrus, and Greenland halibut, for instance – circulate within and around families, households, and communities, but people sell some of the things they hunt and fish. They keep what they need for their own consumption and for sharing, but meat and fish products also find their way into and around local distribution channels and provide the basis for a formal economy (alongside the informal one based on customary procurement) which gives people the opportunity to earn some of the money necessary for maintaining a hunting and fishing way of life. And it is the inshore fishery for Greenland halibut, carried out by using longlines from small boats in summer and snowmobiles on the ice during winter and spring, that is the most important commercial fishing activity for the mixed economy. Selling the halibut catch provides the vital cash that is needed for the materials and equipment that make hunting and fishing possible in the first place – rifles, bullets, nets, hooks, outboard engines, fuel, snowmobiles, and other equipment – as well as for covering the cost of daily living (Delaney et al. 2012; Nuttall 1992).

In summer 2012 I was approached by a team of scientists – oceanographers who study sea ice and the warming of Arctic seas – and was asked if I would be willing to join them in an application to the EU's 7th Framework Programme to get significant funding for research that would seek to understand and quantify the multiple stresses involved in the changes occurring in the Arctic marine environment. It was an ambitious project that would examine the rapid retreat and collapse of Arctic sea ice cover and assess the climatic (ice, ocean, atmosphere and ecosystem), economic, and social impacts of these stresses at local, regional, and global scales. We discussed how, in framing the project, collaboration between the social and physical/natural sciences should enhance understanding of the complex interactions between human societies and the environment, and how the value of this cooperation would also be underscored by its relevance for policy-making and decisive action on climate change.

At the time, I was leading the Climate and Society program at the Greenland Climate Research Centre (GCRC) and Ilisimatusarfik/University of Greenland in Nuuk and this seemed a good fit with our themes and priorities, especially as we were developing community-based research in several parts of Greenland, including projects on the changing nature of sea ice in the northwest of the country. At GCRC, we also worked according to the principle that collaboration between the natural sciences and social sciences is an essential step for improved communication and collaboration between researchers, communities, stakeholders and policymakers. Still, I was a little cautious. It had been my experience that many large scientific projects on Arctic change, especially those involving numerous researchers from several institutions, tend to proceed from a disciplinary perspective rather than interdisciplinary one, despite claims to the contrary and nods in the direction of interdisciplinarity and the inclusion of the social sciences. Far too often, I've found myself involved in projects (as well as climate assessments) that professed to be multidisciplinary and interdisciplinary yet were framed by a predominantly physical and natural sciences approach which, in the end, only diminished the role of social scientists, considering them (and myself) as little more than an "add on." This, as Miller et al. (2008), put it, is one way in which multidisciplinary research proceeds – multiple researchers from several disciplines investigate a problem, but work within their own disciplinary methodological and theoretical contexts. They may all consider a common set of issues, and have a common goal, but do not necessarily feel the need to (or know how to, for that matter) cross their disciplinary boundaries. Miller et al. consider this kind of multidisciplinary research to be done within "epistemological silos." Individual researchers, and the teams they are a part of, work from the perspective of their own epistemologies without recognizing the value of other ways of acquiring and validating knowledge. Integration, Miller and his colleagues argue, is then achieved by "stapling together" the various aspects of a project into the research product.

I was determined this application for funding to work on understanding changes to Arctic sea ice would be different and agreed to join the team. Interdisciplinarity, I argued, had to be at the heart of what we did and it had to incorporate a greater degree of integration than multidisciplinary research (Miller et al. ibid.). Importantly, our work together needed to involve community members as research partners and integrate Indigenous knowledge. This was generally agreed upon by the core proposal writing team. However, I was also concerned that, despite good intentions on the part of everyone involved, even interdisciplinary projects can end up privileging a single discipline or epistemology, and marginalize Indigenous and local ways of knowing, what Miller and colleagues refer to as "epistemological sovereignty." Typically, this is where a project is framed initially by a particular theoretical or methodological approach – say that of sea ice physics – and researchers from other disciplines are invited to come on board later. The project thus proceeds within this framework, limiting the contribution others can make and restricting the influence of different theories, methods, and perspectives. Thinking we had an opportunity to avoid this by scoping out the research in a way that did not entitle one discipline to dominate the project, I agreed to be part of it. We worked on the proposal, were successful in receiving funding, and we began our research in January 2014. Led by sea ice physicist Jeremy Wilkinson from the British Antarctic Survey, ICE-ARC was awarded €11.5 million and brought together physicists, chemists, biologists, economists, and anthropologists from 24 institutions located in twelve countries across Europe.

With research carried out in many parts of the Arctic marine environment – in Greenland, Canada, the Barents Sea, the Beaufort and Chukchi Seas, and the Arctic Ocean – the programmatic activities were clustered in and around four work packages: 1) Observations, 2) Modelling, 3) Communities, and 4) Economics. Together with Naja Mikkelsen, a marine geologist from the Copenhagen-based Geological Survey of Denmark and Greenland (GEUS), I led the work package focused on communities. It had an interdisciplinary focus and we called it "Communities, Ice, and Living Resources in Northwest Greenland." Its main concern was with understanding current and future changes in Arctic sea ice and the broader environment in Upernavik and Avanersuaq – both from changing atmospheric and oceanic conditions – and the social and economic consequences of these changes. Along with my team at GCRC (which comprised myself, Greenlandic social scientist Lene Kielsen Holm,[1] and several Greenlandic graduate students), and Naja's group at GEUS, we were joined by colleagues from the Danish Meteorological Institute (DMI), which is also based in Copenhagen. Our research aimed to be collaborative across the social and physical and natural sciences, which made it unique within the overall ICE-ARC project in terms of disciplinary integration. Importantly, it was also participatory and community-based, and we worked with local research partners to anchor the research in the communities and to discuss and generate the kinds of questions they wanted answers to. Key to this work was understanding the changing nature of sea ice and obtaining sea ice thickness data that was not only needed urgently by scientists and policymakers, but would, we hoped, empower Inuit communities to take a lead in the climate change debate. As a result, much of the work we did during the first few months was dedicated to building community relationships and initiating place-based research partnerships. It was a matter of taking our time to have conversations about what mattered most to all of us – from gathering data to plugging gaps in the scientific knowledge of sea ice, to having reliable information that would help inform local decision-making about weather forecasting, travel safety, risk, and about the best places to hunt and fish. Many of these conversations took place in people's homes, but also in hunting and fishing camps at the ice edge. In the next section, I provide some necessary background and discussion about the project before turning to some reflections on what we achieved and, indeed, whether interdisciplinarity was realized. First, though, a brief note on the changing nature of sea ice is necessary.

In Northwest Greenland, sea ice (which is called *siku* in Kalaallisut; and *hiku* in the Inuktun spoken in the Avanersuaq region) is central to people's lives for several months of the year. Yet considerable changes to its nature, consistency, thickness, and extent are being observed and experienced. The sea ice now tends to form later and break up earlier than many people have known it during their lifetimes, and how they have known it to be through the generational transmission of environmental knowledge. By way of example, the length of the period of travel by dog sledge on good, solid sea ice is around three months during winter and spring (when perhaps twenty or so years ago, the dog sledging period could last five or even six months in some parts of the region, especially in the Avanersuaq district), with decent, but somewhat fluctuating conditions for another month or so. And there are now more periods during the winter and spring when people encounter headland cracks and wide leads in the ice as well as stretches of open water. In Savissivik and Kullorsuaq, for instance, hunters concur that the ice conditions now tend to only be the best in March and April, which reduces significantly the amount of time hunters are able to hunt and fish without putting themselves and their dogs at risk. At the same time, around Kullorsuaq, hunters have, in recent years, been hunting by boat during some periods when there is open water during winter and spring. There is also an increasing level of danger when travelling far out on the ice (Nuttall 2019a, 2022).

The absence of sea ice, or its increasingly weakened structure, restricts the ability of people to move around their localities and alternative routes over glaciers are being explored. Even then, access to those routes is becoming difficult because of both the shifting sea ice regime and changes to glacial ice. Overall, the experiences and comments of hunters and fishers in the Upernavik and Qaanaaq areas point to how extreme weather events have become increasingly common and, in addition to their observations about ice, they remark on the shifting currents, more powerful waves, far stronger winds, the fiercer storms, the changes in precipitation, and the accompanying uncertainties in local weather forecasting that have become a part of daily life. Extreme weather adds to the time, effort, and cost involved in hunting animals and fishing, as well as bringing greater uncertainty and precarity.

Monitoring Sea Ice Thickness and Understanding Climate Change, Past, Present, and Future: A Community-Placed Project

Local observations and experiences, then, indicate that sea ice in the Upernavik and Qaanaaq areas is transforming in ways that scientific research and monitoring confirm.

The ice edge near Qaanaaq, for instance, is a place of constant shifts and movement, uncertainty, and increasing risk for travel, hunting and fishing in winter and spring. Local adaptive strategies include spending less time hunting marine mammals at the ice edge and exploring potential fishing grounds, seeking alternative sources of income, and increased reliance on boats during the increasingly ice-free water periods in winter. Climate change and shifting sea ice mean economic opportunities for Qaanaaq in the form of a new fishery for Greenland halibut, while at the same time having an impact on the customary practices that define the hunting culture and guide social relations – a focus on fishing means people sell more of what they procure, rather than consuming, as well as sharing, much of what they catch, which is not the case with marine mammal hunting. With a changing climate and economic transitions, households are changing, they receive more income from fishing (which is a good thing, people tend to agree) and gender roles are transformed with implications for the generational transmission of knowledge. Our work contributed to understanding the nature of community vulnerability and resilience to climate change in Northwest Greenland. It also provided insight into local experiences of how change affects local livelihoods and communities, how climate change and socio-economic change influences, shapes or hinders local adaptive capacities (as well as the ways communities are proactive in responding to change), and how it reduces or increases vulnerability and resilience. Community vulnerability and resilience, however, are influenced not just by climate change but by rapid social, economic, and political change, as well as by contemporary exploratory activities by extractive industries (Nuttall 2017), and so we set out to understand how northern communities have been affected historically, how they are situated within contemporary Greenland, especially given political aspirations for greater autonomy from Denmark, and how they are affected by a range of global processes.

The later formation and earlier melt of the sea ice in Northwest Greenland is not only due to warmer temperature, but is influenced by changes in storm patterns which can weaken and disperse the young ice. As a result, its formation and growth in late autumn and early winter is delayed, and these shifting storm patterns also contribute to an earlier ice break up in spring. This means that the dangerous period of travelling on thin unstable and unreliable ice is prolonged. As an example of our collaborative ICE-ARC work, we set about working with hunters from Qaanaaq to observe ocean and sea ice changes in the major Avanersuaq fjord system of Kangerlussuaq (Inglefield Bredning). Oceanographer and climatologist Steffen Olsen and his team from DMI identified an important gap in the scientific understanding of sea ice thickness. It is hard to detect from satellite imagery and, when we began our work, the scientific modelling of the fjord ice in the Avanersuaq area was still in its infancy, and the understanding of the processes and feedback mechanisms that influence sea ice formation and glacier–ocean interactions in the region's fjord systems was incomplete. Steffen and his colleagues engaged the community of Qaanaaq in developing ways for collecting sea ice thickness data. However, the community – and particularly the hunters and fishers in Qaanaaq – also wanted this information to be readily available to them so they could use it in their daily decision-making about travelling on the increasingly unpredictable sea ice and for their discussions about weather forecasting.

The DMI team installed instruments at various locations around the fjord to measure the short-term variability in ocean currents and sea ice surface properties. They deployed a weather station and three oceanographic moorings on the sea ice across Kangerlussuaq to monitor the currents and surface water stratification during winter and spring. This deployment was done in collaboration with local hunters, who maintained the instruments and the equipment when they journeyed out on to the ice, given that the scientists only ventured to Qaanaaq for a week or two during the winter. And Steffen and his colleagues mounted autonomous instruments on several hunters' sledges to measure the thickness of the sea ice. This meant that each time a sledge was used to travel on the ice, especially during hunting and fishing trips to the ice floe edge or deeper into the fjord, valuable scientific data were collected. This contributed to the building of a temporal and spatial database of key scientific variables. The data were transferred in real time to DMI in Copenhagen for the production of its weekly sea ice thickness charts that are available on the internet. DMI also set up an operational service which made near-real-time ice information (such as the nature of the ice edge and other ice characteristics) from the Qaanaaq area available online. Additional information and archived data are delivered on a separate, frequently visited site: http://ocean.dmi.dk/arctic/qaanaaq.php. This ice information is also posted daily at the local shop in Qaanaaq. All this work relied on community engagement and participation. Significant to these efforts, though, is DMI's Geophysical Observatory in Qaanaaq. Established in the 1950s, its presence illustrates how participatory ocean and cryosphere monitoring programs require infrastructure, field stations, and dedicated long-term funding.

Our work also sought to understand how past changes in climate affected Inuit societies and their adaptive capacities and livelihood strategies. Using a multiproxy approach, Naja Mikkelsen and her team at GEUS reconstructed seasonal sea ice and primary productivity dynamics spanning the past ca. 4000 years in the North Water polynya (Pikialasorsuaq) region, a key ecosystem for Arctic species and for the livelihoods of people in the Avanersuaq area, as well as in Melville Bay and further south. They identified periods of reduced sea ice cover coeval with warming episodes during the Holocene, whereas neoglacial cooling after ca. 2000 BP resulted in unstable ocean conditions, with a negative impact on the primary productivity of the polynya. They also produced a detailed historical sea ice reconstruction of the past ca. 150 years in Kangerlussuaq, which was based on archival data, marine sediment core records that stretch back 120 years, and high-resolution optical satellite imagery from the previous 40 years. Their findings show that the period spanning the last 15-20 years has the most reduced sea ice in the context of the past 150.

Furthermore, ICE-ARC initiated an analysis of hunting and fishing trips using high-resolution satellite images and by mapping those journeys with hunters themselves. Local partnerships and networks were established that allowed ICE-ARC researchers to communicate operational information on sea ice conditions to the community, to adapt and time the scientific information continuously to fit community needs, and to engage in a dialogue on climate change and its impacts and effects. An important outcome of this dialogue was an increased focus on delivering satellite information in particular during the early winter period, when darkness and dynamic sea ice conditions are challenging for safety when hunting and fishing on the ice.

Reflecting on the work we did as part of ICE-ARC, we were successful in building a unique Arctic monitoring capacity and data record on the interplay between sea ice and oceanographic conditions in Northwest Greenland. This was achieved by engaging Inuit communities in the design, planning, and completion of the program. People rely on good winter sea ice for travelling and hunting, so it was natural that they should have had a strong interest in the observations and in the results of the project; for their daily planning of hunting trips and journeys on the ice, and for understanding the nature and implications of the climate-related changes they are witnessing in their surroundings. Experiences from this engagement of the community were valuable in order to reach an integrated understanding of sea ice, resources, and livelihoods in Northwest Greenland. Through this collaboration and community engagement, our team at GCRC and our colleagues from GEUS and DMI were able to contribute to the development of novel Arctic monitoring systems, including proving them fit-for-purpose as essential components in future community-based climate observatories or participatory monitoring programs. And the project's results have not only been published in a number of reports and peer-reviewed journal articles, they have been disseminated to communities and highlighted in policy contexts, including COP meetings of the UNFCC and at the World Economic Forum gatherings in Davos in Switzerland.

The ICE-ARC project worked across the Arctic Ocean, at other sites beyond Greenland, and researchers collected data from satellite and airborne sensors, as well as systems deployed on the ice, on the surface of the sea, and underwater. The mobilization of this technology was essential to the climate scientists in the project, but so too was the development of a community-based observing network that provided information derived from a lifelong engagement and intimacy with land, water, and ice. While ICE-ARC and projects like it are vital in the way they help understand the consequences of a changing Arctic for the rest of the globe, they also contribute to community strategies for adapting to the changes people experience and have to negotiate on a daily basis.

Reflections on Multidisciplinary, Interdisciplinary, and Multi-Sited Research

During this new epoch we are getting used to calling the Anthropocene, the need to think and work across the boundaries of the respective academic disciplines in which we are trained is an urgent responsibility. The dichotomy between the social and natural sciences, which may be useful and convenient when allocating research funds to projects, and knowing where to place people's academic articles in disciplinary journals, becomes problematic when confronting the climate crisis. We need to move out of "epistemological silos" and work across disciplinary boundaries to achieve integration (Miller et al. ibid.). In their contribution to this volume, Sarah Strauss and Courtney Kurlanska point out that much of the pioneering work by anthropologists on climate change, especially that done in the 1980s, 1990s, and early 2000s, tended to be framed within the more usual anthropological context of the lone researcher, whether operating in "applied" or more theoretical areas. Their writing was based on what they witnessed, experienced, and learned through long-term fieldwork, participant observation, archival research, or by drawing on methods from archaeology and historical ecology. Indeed, this is represented by much of the work done by many of the contributors to all three editions of *Anthropology and Climate Change*. However, Strauss and Kurlanska point out that, building on this early work, much anthropological research has become more collaborative as well as multi-sited, as it engages more directly with communities as research partners and with scientists from a diverse range of disciplines – again, as illustrated by several chapters in this present volume.

This has certainly been true of my own career trajectory. I have long been committed to forging dialogue about multidisciplinary and interdisciplinary research and, in particular, I have been concerned with how social scientists and physical/natural scientists can develop methodological and locally and regionally situated approaches to understanding environmental change in the Arctic (e.g., Nuttall and Callaghan 2000). In the northern latitudes and elsewhere in the world, the contemporary realities of social, cultural, economic, and environmental change make demands of us to transcend rather than be constrained by established scholarly and disciplinary boundaries. These contemporary realities and this breaking down of dichotomies between the social sciences and the natural/physical sciences may have significant consequences and implications for entire disciplines, which may be a good thing if it leads to new perspectives on understanding human–environment relations, results in work that informs policymakers of the most appropriate ways to act, and can be of use to communities. Believing that we can move towards integration and can develop interdisciplinary – and even transdisciplinary – research activities that have a practical orientation and applied relevance is one reason why I engage in projects such as ICE-ARC. Transdisciplinarity, however, is something else. It should aspire to develop research that transcends categories that are entrenched and often resistant to other ways of thinking and knowing. In doing so, collaborators in a transdisciplinary effort would seek not only to redraw, and perhaps dismantle boundaries that exclude other epistemologies, but endeavor to fashion an epistemological perspective that would be recognized as unique to the task at hand (Miller et al. ibid.).

Multidisciplinarity, interdisciplinarity, and transdisciplinarity efforts all require, though, at their most basic level, a willingness to become conversant with the theories, methods, practices, and epistemologies of other disciplines, as well as with understanding Indigenous and local knowledge. My training as both a sociologist and anthropologist, and my experiences of working with colleagues from different scientific backgrounds, however, has often made me ponder the difficulties of breaking down disciplinary boundaries between natural sciences and social sciences in practice. I have never felt constrained by these disciplinary boundaries, but I have often been frustrated by them. It can be hard for many researchers – anthropologists included – to move out of their epistemological silos. Leaving aside the differences or relations between the natural and the social sciences for the time being, it can be difficult enough for some social scientists to even break down the boundaries and barriers that divide their own disciplines and often drive a wedge between people working in the same university departments. I am sure this is the case for many scientists – biologists, zoologists, chemists, physicists, and so on – who have different ideas about the nature of their respective disciplines and their various sub-fields.

It is vital that the results of scientific research, climate data and forecasts are of use to the people who live in the communities where that work is done. Our work in ICE-ARC was underpinned by this imperative – as indeed my continuing research in Greenland is. No matter how well-meaning researchers are, however, getting scientific data and project results to communities can be a difficult process, with many logistical, technical and financial barriers in the way. Brondizio and Moran (2008), for example, reflect on some of the challenges in the Brazilian Amazon, where they found that disseminating climate data was frustrated by the lack of extension services to translate large-scale forecasts to local needs. Chisadza et al. (2013) carried out research on local indicators used to forecast drought in Zimbabwe and assessed the possibility of integrating traditional rainfall forecasting techniques with scientific meteorological methods. They found that meteorological rainfall forecasts were not readily available to rural communities and when they were, people did not think them to be reliable at the local level, preferring instead to draw on traditional knowledge for producing weather forecasts.

Pennesi, Arokium, and McBean (2012) discuss how, in Canada's Nunavut territory, weather-related risk assessment can be improved by integrating local and scientific knowledge about weather and making it available to residents. Based on research in Iqaluit, they found that various barriers, such as cultural and linguistic differences, a lack of land-based experience, and an absence of social networks prevented many people from being able to access the information they needed to make informed decisions about the risks associated with travelling on land, ice, and sea in a changing climate. While experienced hunters are considered a source of reliable weather-related information, residents felt that scientific knowledge is not always as accessible or as informative as it could be. Pennesi and her colleagues argue that by increasing the potential use of traditional and scientific weather knowledge, and by making both more universally accessible to residents in Nunavut, then strategies for adapting to climate change in the Arctic would be enhanced. The establishment and continued activities of community-based monitoring networks is costly, however, and requires significant and sustained funding and capacity-building. And elsewhere in Northwest Greenland, for example, particularly in the Upernavik district, there are no geophysical observatories or research facilities such as DMI operates in Qaanaaq that can provide an infrastructural base for establishing such monitoring networks. Beyond this, though, concerns are expressed by some anthropologists as to how far Indigenous and local knowledge can be integrated with science, and whether climate science really does benefit communities, especially if the dominant methodologies and language ideologies of mainstream science silence Indigenous and local voices (Taddei 2020).

While I have discussed the multidisciplinary and interdisciplinary engagement attempted by ICE-ARC, the bringing together of different ways of knowing, and the bridging of temporal and spatial scales – and while I am confident that the work package Naja Mikkelsen and I led was interdisciplinary (as far as it could be) and community-engaged – I am not so sure that the entire program, across all work packages, could be described as such. Multidisciplinary, yes, but not interdisciplinary, and certainly not transdisciplinary, as it did not proceed from, nor did it nurture a different epistemological approach. It was a large program, involving many different disciplines, and not everyone who participated in it worried too much about staying put in an epistemological silo. And many of the scientists involved – the meteorologists, oceanographers, and physicists – did not travel for fieldwork in the Arctic, but were based in labs, where they analysed data and produced scenarios. For the most part – and this was especially evident when we all gathered for the annual ICE-ARC general assemblies, or participated in other program meetings – epistemological sovereignty was all too apparent. Interdisciplinarity also requires an attentiveness to other disciplinary literature – in the course of my own work, I try to read as much as I can of the scientific literature on sea ice and changing glaciers, but I am not so sure if my colleagues in oceanography, or marine geology, and other natural and physical disciplines, read much anthropology. I make this statement based on what I know of those with whom I collaborate. It is not a criticism of their reading preferences – it is difficult enough to keep up with the literature in our own fields.

I agree with Strauss and Kurlanska about the vital importance of collaborative, multi-sited research. But I also argue that there is still room for the "lone" anthropologist in continuing to work on long-term, in-depth ethnographic studies in collaboration with their interlocutors and place-based research partners. As I have discussed above, one major component of the ICE-ARC work was carrying out sea ice measurements and conducting ocean temperature studies, drawing upon satellite images and historical ice charts, and deriving data from marine sediment cores. We also worked with communities to learn about Indigenous knowledge of the nature of sea ice and glacial ice. All this allowed us a greater understanding of changes in drift ice and fast ice extent, freeze-up and break-up patterns, changes to glacier fronts, and iceberg calving processes, which facilitates both the formation and stability of the fast ice cover. It brought two ways of knowing and understanding ice and the wider environment together.

However, just as Michael Schnegg (2019) discusses in the case of climate change research in the arid regions of northwestern Namibia, such a scientific encounter with the world is enframed and mediated by technology, whereas Indigenous experiences are enmeshed with daily activities in surroundings that are comprised of human and non-human entities. Alessa et al. (2016) write that the people who participate in community-based observing networks are akin to sensors that make it possible for those networks to monitor environmental change and shifting ecological conditions (e.g., the weather, the state of the sea, sea ice, the health of wildlife populations), as well as activities such as ship traffic and oil and mineral exploration. They argue, though, that humans are better at detecting patterns of change than fixed instruments. Through the inclusion of Indigenous science and local knowledge with academic/government science-based work, a process of knowledge co-production can result that has potential to improve the way environmental change is monitored for the purpose of successful strategies for responding and adapting.

Schnegg (ibid.) emphasizes a concern however that, while there are good examples of agreement between Indigenous and local observations and scientific measurements, disagreement often arises when Indigenous people and scientists try to make their experiences understandable to the other. Illustrating this with reference to how Damara pastoralists and scientists both explain the arrival of rain in northwestern Namibia in terms of their understanding of the interplay between two winds, Schnegg describes how Damara talk of the relationship between loving and caring winds, while scientists account for rain as a consequence of the Intertropical Convergence Zone. Schnegg argues that the Damara understanding of the processes that bring rain to the arid lands conforms to meteorological measurements to a considerable degree. Meteorologists, though, represent their understandings in terms of the result of atmospheric processes, and specifically the movement of the Intertropical Convergence Zone, which affects sunlight, high- and low-pressure systems, the accumulation of moisture, and the winds. Schnegg's ethnography reveals two understandings of why it rains in northwestern Namibia. The scientific account is mediated through technology, whereas the Damara account arises through their involvement in a relational world of human and non-human agents. It doesn't matter, says Schnegg, if the meteorologist is sitting in front of a computer screen in Windhoek, Beijing, or Berlin – there is no direct encounter with the rain to make it intelligible. Damara, by contrast, experience rain as it falls on the ground, providing drinking water for them and their cattle, goats, and sheep, and nourishing the trees and land. Such encounters in a relational world comprised of people, animals, worms, trees, and caring and loving winds and rain have no place in a scientific and technological representation.

Similarly, much of what scientists know about the changing nature of Arctic sea ice also comes from an engagement with satellite images and data that have been relayed from autonomous instruments that measure ice thickness or water temperature. Of course, there are field-based scientists who travel to the Arctic on ships, in aircraft, and helicopters, and who spend anywhere from a few days to several weeks deploying equipment and carrying out measurements, but the data are relayed to university departments, research institutes and government agencies for computation and analysis. Just as Schnegg describes for Namibia, in Northwest Greenland the weather is enmeshed, experienced, and known through everyday skilled activity for hunters and fishers, but is enframed by technology for scientists. The world of ice, melt, and a warming ocean is understood to be a different place for each. Ways of knowing the environment and the environment can be multiple and varied, but this does not mean they are mutually exclusive (Schnegg ibid.).

Indigenous observations of the changing climate and the consistency of ice were key to the work we did in the ICE-ARC program. And in learning about these observations, and how people talk about them, it was crucial to do all this research through Kalaallisut. Sometimes, there is no better way to do this than through the deep and intensive ethnographic fieldwork that requires us to be with people in everyday contexts, living and working with them, such as in the kinds of situations in Ikeq I described at the beginning of this chapter. In this way, we aim for a more nuanced understanding of ice as something that is not just vulnerable and increasingly brittle. While the scientific monitoring of sea ice, glacial ice loss, and surface melt on the inland ice in the Upernavik region is well established, little attention has been given to what these changes to ice and water mean for people and for human and non-human relational ontologies. My own work there has been concerned with a deeper appreciation of people's experiences and sense-making of the changes happening to them and to their surroundings. In particular, as an anthropologist I am interested in how and why the words people use to describe the weather and the ice matter. They convey how climate change is experienced in ways that are sensorial and embodied, such as how the weather feels, for instance, or how some patches of snow on the ice are slimy rather than soft because of more seaweed oozing though cracks in winter, or how the runners of a sled zigzag across a slippery stretch of ice following freezing rain. Vital for understanding these changing surroundings, they not only provide insight into how people are being affected by climate change, they are becoming critical as part of a wider system of knowledge that is necessary for how people move around in and navigate a world in which daily life plays out in surroundings of movement, emergence, transformation, and becoming (Nuttall 2018).

Some words and expressions have become particularly significant as climate change makes itself increasingly felt in Northwest Greenland. On my recent field trips there, I am struck by how people are using words for thinking and talking about the weather, but also for watching and feeling it, that would only be used at certain times of the year, or which would be rarely used at all. Taqqalluk, for instance, describes slush on the ice, but is commonly a winter word; putsineq is a word used to describe how the ice is slushy at the end of spring when the weather warms and the sea ice begins to break up. Now, putsineq is heard more often in January and February, in the depths of winter, when the ice should be firm and strong. Other words are rarely being uttered. For example, sikunnaq, weather which promises a cover of ice, seems an increasingly rare occurrence in late autumn and early winter; correspondingly, *sikunnaq* also becomes a word people hear less of. Yet here, if I am honest about it, is one area in which we struggled in our ICE-ARC project discussions about the integration of different ways of thinking about and measuring ice thickness and consistency. Measurements acquired through instruments were readily accepted as data, but words that expressed the experience of the everyday entanglement of people and ice and climate were not regarded as such by my science colleagues.

No matter how visually compelling an observation or statement a satellite image makes about the decline of Arctic sea ice cover or temperature rise, or what the data that emerge from measurements taken from sledge journeys tell us, they cannot communicate how it feels when travelling on sea ice that is no longer thick and firm, or how wetter, slushier, and more slippery it is, or when rain falls in January when one expects snow, and when the winter air feels damp when it should be dry. Nor can remote sensing provide us with images of the effects of climate change on human bodies and community memories. Observing climate change from monitoring stations in a fjord or sensing it remotely from space are critical to advancing our understanding of how the Arctic is being reshaped as ice recedes and shrinks, but this cannot possibly tell us anything at all about how flow, melt, and saturation are sensed and experienced by those who live in surroundings that are increasingly liquescent and undergoing transformation (Nuttall 2019b).

This reinforces Taddei's (ibid.) point about the importance of a dialogue that engages the perspectives and experiences of Indigenous lives and Indigenous and local knowledge of the world and those of science. Astrid Ulloa (2019) stresses that while global climate change and processes of adaptation and mitigation transcend local contexts and bring together diverse forms of knowledge, global action against climate change continues to be backed by a single type of knowledge. Global policies are informed by IPCC reports that interpret climate through scientific constructions, understandings, and interpretations. The problem, she argues, is that "this global knowledge not only has political implications but has a local impact because it is implemented via a global policy that does not include local worldviews and knowledges" (Ulloa ibid.: 68). In Northwest Greenland, scientists may worry about how vulnerable an ecosystem is to climate change, while hunters and fishers may also be similarly concerned, but at the same time marvel at the world emerging and taking shape – and being re-made – around them. Like Taddei and Ulloa, Schnegg (ibid.) too argues that it is vital to take into account these multiple ways of knowing weather and climate, without privileging one over the other, but recognizing that they arise from specific encounters that produce coherent explanations. Such dialogue is a necessary step for collaborative efforts toward the co-production of the knowledge needed to address and deal with climate change.

Note

1 Lene was originally from South Greenland and she passed away in January 2021 – a tremendous loss to her family, friends, and colleagues, but also to Indigenous-led research in Greenland and the Arctic more generally. A champion of community-based research, Lene's work was always guided by a collaborative approach to the production of knowledge, and she had participated in a number of projects that contributed greatly to our understanding of climate change, human–environment relations, and Indigenous use of resources. I was privileged to work with Lene in developing the Climate and Society program at GCRC, and we carried out field research together in the Nuuk Fjord and in Avanersuaq.

Acknowledgements

This chapter is based on research funded by the Climate and Society Research Programme (Project 6400) at the Greenland Climate Research Centre in Nuuk, which ran from 2012–2019, and by the EU FP7 ICE-ARC project (Ice Climate and Economics – Arctic Research on Change), under Grant Agreement 603887, which ran between 2014 and 2017.

References

Alessa, Lilian, Andrew Kliskey, James Gamble, Maryann Fidel, Grace Beaujean and James Gosz. 2016. "The role of Indigenous science and local knowledge in integrated observing systems: moving toward adaptive capacity indices and early warning systems." *Sustainability Science* 11: 91–102.

AMAP. 2017. *Snow, Water, Ice and Permafrost in the Arctic: Summary for policy-makers* Oslo: Arctic Monitoring and Assessment Programme.

Box, Jason E. and David T. Decker. 2011. "Greenland marine-terminating glacier area changes: 2000–2010." *Annals of Glaciology* 52 (59): 91–98.

Brondizio, Eduardo S. and Emilio F. Moran. 2008. "Human dimensions of climate change: the vulnerability of small farmers in the Amazon." *Philos Trans R Soc Lond B Biol Sci.* 363 (1498):1803–1809. doi:10.1098/rstb.2007.0025.

Chisadza, Bright, Mike J. Tumbare, Innocence Nhapi, and Washington Nyabeze. 2013. "Useful traditional knowledge indicators for drought forecasting in the Mzingwane Catchment area of Zimbabwe." *Disaster Prevention and Management* 22 (4): 312–325.

Delaney, Alyne E., Rikke Becker Jakobsen, and Kåre Hendriksen. 2012. *Greenland Halibut in Upernavik: A preliminary study of the importance of the stock for the fishing populace.* A study undertaken under the Greenland Climate Research Centre. Aalborg University: Innovative Fisheries Management.

Hansen, Keld. 2008. *Nuussuarmiut: Hunting families on the big headland.* Meddelelser om Grønland 35. Copenhagen: Commission for Scientific Research in Greenland.

Hastrup, Kirsten. 2016. "Climate knowledge: assemblage, anticipation, action." In Susan A. Crate and Mark Nuttall (eds.) *Anthropology and Climate Change: From actions to transformations.* London and New York: Routledge, pp. 35–57.

Larsen, Signe Hillerup, Shfaqat Abbas Khan, Andreas Peter Ahlstrøm, Christine Schøtt Hvidberg, Michale John Wills, and Signe Bech Andersen. 2016. "Increased mass loss and asynchronous behavior of marine-terminating outlet glaciers at Upernavik Isstrøm, NW Greenland." *JGR: Earth Surface* 121 (2): 241–256.

Meredith, M. et al. 2019. "Chapter 3: Polar Regions." In H.-O. Pörtner et al. (eds.) *IPCC Special Report on the Ocean and Cryosphere in a Changing Climate.* Cambridge: Cambridge University Press.

Miller, Thaddeus R., Timothy D. Baird, Caitlin M. Littlefield, Gary Kofinas, F. Stuart Chapin, III, and Charles L. Redman. 2008. "Epistemological pluralism: reorganizing interdisciplinary research." *Ecology and Society* 13 (2), [online] URL: http://www.ecologyandsociety.org/vol13/iss2/art46/.

Muilwijk, Moven, Fiamma Straneo, Donald A. Slater, Lars A. Smedsrud, James Holte, Michael Wood, Camilla S. Andresen, and Ben Harden. 2022. "Export of ice sheet meltwater from Upernavik Fjord, West Greenland." *Journal of Physical Oceanography* 52 (3): 363–382.

Nuttall, Mark. 1992. *Arctic Homeland: Kinship, community and development in Northwest Greenland.* Toronto: University of Toronto Press.

Nuttall, Mark. 2009. "Living in a world of movement: human resilience to environmental instability in Greenland." In Susan A. Crate and Mark Nuttall (eds.) *Anthropology and Climate Change: From encounters to actions.* Walnut Creek, CA: Left Coast Press, pp. 292–310.

Nuttall, Mark. 2017. *Climate, Society and Subsurface Politics in Greenland: Under the Great Ice.* London and New York: Routledge.

Nuttall, Mark. 2018. "Arctic weather words." *Anthropology News* 59 (2): 37–43.

Nuttall, Mark. 2019a. "Sea ice, climate and resources: the changing nature of hunting along Northwest Greenland's coast." In Astrid B. Stensrud and Thomas Hylland Eriksen (eds.) *Climate, Capitalism and Communities: An anthropology of environmental overheating.* London: Pluto Press, pp. 57–75.

Nuttall, Mark. 2019b. "Icy, watery, liquescent: sensing and feeling climate change on Northwest Greenland's coast." *Journal of Northern Studies* 14 (2): 71–91.

Nuttall, Mark. 2022. "Places of memory, anticipation, and agitation in Northwest Greenland." In Kenneth L. Pratt and Scott A. Heyes (eds.) *Memory and Landscape: Indigenous responses to a changing North.* Athabasca: Athabasca University Press, pp. 157–177.

Nuttall, Mark and Terry V. Callaghan. 2000. *The Arctic: Environment, people, policy.* Amsterdam: Harwood Academic Publishers.

Pennesi, Karen, Jadah Arokium, and Gordon McBean. 2012. "Integrating local and scientific weather knowledge as a strategy for adaptation to climate change in the Arctic." *Mitigation and Adaptation Strategies for Global Change* 17 (8): 897–922.

Petersen, Robert. 2003. *Settlements, Kinship and Hunting Grounds in Traditional Greenland.* Meddelelser om Grønland 27. Copenhagen: Danish Polar Centre.

Schnegg, Michael. 2019. "The life of winds: knowing the Namibian weather from someplace and from noplace." *American Anthropologist* 121 (4): 830–844.

Taddei, Renzo R. 2020. "Anthropology and the pragmatics of climate knowledge in Brazil." *American Anthropologist* 122 (4): 944–947.

Ulloa, Astrid. 2019. "Indigenous knowledge regarding climate in Colombia: articulations and complementarities among different knowledges." In Giuseppe Feola, Hilary Geoghegan and Alex Arnall (eds.) *Climate and Culture: Multidisciplinary perspectives on a warming world.* Cambridge: Cambridge University Press, pp. 68–92.

5

'KNOWING' CLIMATE

Engaging Vernacular Narratives of Change

Susan A. Crate

Introduction

Mainstream knowledge-making of climate change, or how the general public has been informed about the issue, has, for the past 30 years, remained largely a quantitative, natural science-focused endeavor. We have been shown via charts, graphs, and models where we are in terms of planetary health, where we are headed and the various alternative scenarios and their consequences. The effort to maintain "control" of the Earth and its resources by the minority without engaging the majority only continues the colonial project and perpetuates a neoliberal agenda. This leaves little hope of moving towards an equitable, regenerative future. How can this hegemony be undone so that the rest of the inhabitants of the planet, be they human and non-human animals, plants, and other life forms, can come along? We need ways to usher in and hold council with these vernacular ways of knowing at the same level as western scientific knowledge,[1] to properly represent the issue and its manifold solutions via more holistic, interdependent, relational understandings. Anthropologists are taking up this provocation and calling for a "broadening of perspective...[to] collectively confront the urgency of climate change and the failure of narrow, technocratic, human-centric ecomodernist solutions that have dominated climate mitigation efforts to date" (O'Reilly et al. 2020: 15).

It is, in fact, Indigenous peoples and other locale-based communities who have the long, often millennial history of responding to a changing climate that makes these efforts to bring Indigenous knowledge and local knowledge into climate science inverted. It should be the other way. *They* are the experts that scientists need to listen to. My argument is not that scientific knowledge is irrelevant but that, at present, it dominates and fails to provide a complete understanding of global change. Indigenous knowledge and local knowledge offer the balance via their embodied nature to ground-truth and provide cultural context for global change. Critical to leveling this playing field is to challenge the sanctity of scientific knowledge and to repatriate the status of Indigenous knowledge and local knowledge.

DOI: 10.4324/9781003242499-7

This chapter focuses on anthropological engagement with the multiplicity of world-making practices encapsulated within other ways of knowing, specifically Indigenous knowledge and local knowledge systems.[2] Before diving into that discussion I make a caveat about the chapter and also a recognition. As anthropologists, we know we are not the only academics involved in research, writing, and interventions that focus in part or completely upon bringing vernacular knowledge systems to the fore in climate change research and policy. The best example I know of this is Robin Bronen and the work of the Alaska Institute for Justice (Bronen et al. 2020). In fact, a majority of anthropologists working in this area is engaged in interdisciplinary community-based collaboration. Both interdisciplinarity and transdisciplinarity are key to building knowledge and finding rights-based, equitable, community-focused solutions in our complex world today. That said, this chapter intentionally focuses on the tool sets and the work of anthropologists to make a difference in the policy realm.

A Personal Testimony

Anthropologists are prime interlocutors of these other ways of knowing and are well positioned to bring these critical pieces of the climate puzzle to bear. We are trained as interpreters of a given culture's way of knowing. We understand that our collaborators, be they inhabitants of a rural settlement or of an urban metropolis, don't run around trying to disprove hypotheses to go about their daily activities. Rather they use the vernacular knowledge that they have developed by living in a place, be it a small area where their ancestors have lived for millennia or the expanse of our global "home." Because we as anthropologists are trained in this sensitivity, the fact that people have different ways of understanding how the world works is plain for us to see. This is our training and it is often not familiar to others. I directly encountered others' unfamiliarity with diverse knowledge systems while working on international climate change protocols.

I served as a lead author for the Intergovernmental Panel on Climate Change's (IPCC's) Special Report on Ocean and Cryosphere in a Changing Climate (SROCC) from 2017–2019. I knew that the IPCC had functioned since 1990 with the aspiration of generating Assessment Reports (AR) to gauge the level and complexity of planetary changes due to anthropogenic climate change. The IPCC AR process has always been a highly vetted one, involving several hundred scientists from around the world to write a report collectively over the course of two or more years. Between the 5th and 6th AR, the IPCC developed three special reports on global systems that needed more in-depth analysis than the AR could provide space for. The first was "Global Warming at 1.5° C," the second, "Special Report on Climate Change and Land," and ours, "Special Report on Ocean and Cryosphere in a Changing Climate." I collaborated on Chapter 1, the framing for the rest of the report. We met for one week-long intensive writing workshop four times over two years. My main task was the framing of other knowledge systems, specifically Indigenous knowledge and local knowledge.[3]

Although I was excited to take part in this, what I considered, long overdue framing, my heart sank during our chapter team's first meeting. As we went around the table, sharing our expertise, I introduced myself as an anthropologist who conducted longitudinal ethnographic research in northeastern Siberia. Before my introduction others had explained their work in oceanography or satellite data or cryosphere science. My specialty was met with blank faces. Was I from Mars? My worry was soon abated. Two others on the chapter team looked at me assuredly. The first shared that they worked on community health issues with Indigenous populations in the Arctic. The second that they focused on socio-environmental issues with communities in South Asia. Sensing our commonalities, the three of us huddled during the first coffee break. We shared ideas on how to educate the rest of our chapter authors on exactly what Indigenous knowledge and local knowledge are and why they are important. Over the course of the week, we each proposed to the group different ways to bring the relevance of knowledge systems other than science into the report's framing. It was a hard sell. Many of our colleagues were polite. Others were outspoken, doubting that our contribution was necessary. Nevertheless, by the end of the week we had been assigned a place in the chapter outline, "Knowledge Systems for Understanding and Responding to Change." Our next task was to draft it.

By the second team meeting something amazing had happened. Everyone on the chapter team had bought into our section. Perhaps this was due to the process of group editing and feedback on the Google doc for six months. Interactions with our chapter team were qualitatively different compared with six months prior. Instead of considering our section on knowledge systems at arm's length, many engaged directly in our discussions, commenting on how they were seeing the importance of knowledge systems in their own work and the report overall. When the one scientist who originally had expressed the most hesitance in our first meeting actually vouched for the importance of including knowledge systems in the report during a larger plenary session, we knew we had made our case. Our next challenge was making the case for the "knowledge systems" section to the lead authors of the report's other five chapters. Like the six-month process of interactions and editing worked with our chapter team, over time these others also came around.

We next invited Indigenous knowledge and local knowledge holders to be contributing authors. At the time the IPCC had not included Indigenous knowledge and local knowledge holders as lead authors. We had knowledge holders reviewing and editing the knowledge section over the process of our writing it, collaborating in creating the glossary definitions for both systems and contributing written sections to the report detailing their opinions of how IPCC could best utilize Indigenous knowledge and local knowledge in the AR (Abram et al. 2019: section 1.8.2).

One of our biggest challenges was how to name these knowledge systems. We critiqued the term "scientific knowledge" first. The Indigenous knowledge holders objected to using "scientific knowledge" for what we know as "science" arguing that, "Indigenous knowledge has developed over generations, is time tested and empirical. It is also science."[4] We explored different ways to differentiate scientific knowledge from Indigenous knowledge and local knowledge, suggesting terms such as "western scientific knowledge" or "elite scientific knowledge." None of these provided an accurate descriptor. We decided to use the term "scientific knowledge" with the disclaimer that the other knowledge systems were also empirically derived.

When we got to labeling the other knowledge systems, we found ourselves in acronym soup (e.g., Reid-Shaw et al. 2021: 632). Interest in knowledge systems spans the academic disciplines (for example: ethnoecology, anthropology, geography, biodiversity, development studies, etc.), and the applied areas of NGO and policy work. Terms to signify these systems include: traditional knowledge (TK), ecological knowledge (EK), traditional ecological knowledge (TEK), Indigenous knowledge (IK), local knowledge (LK), and perhaps more. In an attempt to streamline this milieu of terminology for this and future IPCC publications, we decided the main qualitative difference was best represented by differentiating Indigenous knowledge and local knowledge. We created the following definitions,

> Indigenous knowledge (IK) refers to the understandings, skills and philosophies developed by societies with long histories of interaction with their natural surroundings. It is passed on from generation to generation, flexible and adaptive in changing conditions and increasingly challenged in the context of contemporary climate change.
>
> *(IPCC 2019: 689)*

> Local knowledge (LK) is what non-indigenous communities, both rural and urban, use on a daily and lifelong basis. It is multi-generational, embedded in community practices and cultures, and adaptive to changing conditions.
>
> *(IPCC 2019: 690)*

Another aspect of framing these knowledge systems in Chapter 1 was making a cross-chapter box to draw examples that highlighted how Indigenous knowledge and local knowledge were relevant in each of the remaining five chapters. This included creating a figure to depict our main argument visually, that climate change understandings and actions are incomplete unless they engage all relevant knowledge systems of a given context. The peer-review feedback we received early on encouraged us to depict Indigenous knowledge and local knowledge as complementary, as an add-on, to scientific knowledge. In our continued effort to educate others, we explained that each knowledge system had standing in its own right. As social scientists have emphasized already, the task of considering all knowledge systems is not to quantify other ontologies to fit into prescribed scientific categories to make generalizable arguments (e.g., Gearheard et al. 2010; Tengö et al. 2017; Reyes-Garcia et al. 2016; Makondo and Thomas 2018), but rather to let each contribute its unique elements. This makes many scientists uncomfortable. Yes it is "messy" but only so much as a quantitative assessment is concerned. Furthermore, engaging the qualitative with the quantitative can render many of the prescribed technocratic frameworks of climate science (e.g. adaptation, resilience, and vulnerability or ARV) useless (Goldman et al. 2018). But that is the point here. Including the diversity of ways to understand and act in the world cannot be understood by scientifically determined frameworks. How could an ARV frame account for the cosmological and spiritual importance of *alaas* [5] and its central place in Sakha cultural identification? This work of engaging all knowledge systems requires new inclusive frames of reference. In the end, we represented the three knowledge systems for the final IPCC figure, Indigenous knowledge, local knowledge, and scientific knowledge, as equals, each along their individual trajectories of development and change over time, and each coming into contact to intermingle and coproduce knowledge with the others in specific contexts (Abram et al. 2019: CB4.1 p. 104).

Despite the rocky beginnings of our IPCC work, we did achieve the goal to frame the knowledge systems, to present them each as empirically derived and to emphasize the use of all available knowledge systems as critical to comprehensive understandings of climate change and policy approaches. In the process, we substantiated Indigenous knowledge and local knowledge in this and all proceeding IPCC reports and also brought knowledge holders closer to being involved in the IPCC process. Case in point, the newly released

AR6 not only has a significant increase in references to Indigenous knowledge and local knowledge compared to AR5 (IPCC 2022a) but also emphasizes their importance in the Summary for Policymakers (IPCC 2022b).

Sakha Research that Communicates the Importance of Knowledge Systems

One of the critiques of qualitative information, aka testimonies from the people who live where anthropologists do their work, is that it is "anecdotal evidence" and therefore not reliable/verifiable/generalizable (Taddei 2020). The problem with this argument is that it is exactly site-specific information that is needed to "fill in/fill out" the finer details of global climate change. One way to address this is to try and corroborate regional data with inhabitants' observations. There is an unexpected benefit to this process in that what can be assumed is conflicting information can actually reveal an important aspect of cultural observation in contrast to instrumental recording.

Take an example from my fieldwork of seemingly contradictory findings. Since 2006 I have collaborated with Alexander Fedorov, a permafrost scientist at the Melnikov Permafrost Institute in Yakutsk, Russia. We conducted knowledge exchanges, community meetings inviting residents to share their observations of change, their vernacular knowledge, and Alexander to show his regional scientific findings (Crate and Fedorov 2013). We held eight knowledge exchanges in Viliui Sakha settlements in the summer of 2010. Afterwards Alexander and I tried to corroborate the nine main changes inhabitants reported with the instrumental data. When we compared what people observed as "too much rain" with the precipitation data of the last 20 years, we found conflicting results. The data showed no significant increase. Rather than outright disregarding inhabitants' observations of "too much rain" in sanctimony of the instrumental data, we pondered the possibility that both the people and the instruments were "right." As an anthropologist who, at that time, had spent two decades interacting with Viliui Sakha as an observant participant in seasonal activities, I knew there were seasonal rhythms of rain that made Sakhas' subsistence successful. I also knew that the hay seasons had been unusually rainy for the last several summers. With this insight, we looked at the seasonal precipitation data. In fact, it was the past several summers of nearly constant rain in July and August and the fact that these changes interfered with Viliui Sakhas' subsistence practices that prompted inhabitants to perceive 'too much rain.' In this way we were able to show how these seemingly contradicting forms of knowledge could instead work to complement each other.

An understanding of cultural context is critical when interpreting what is occurring due to the local effects of climate change and how affected communities are perceiving it. Such corroborating of perceptions and instrumental data provide clear examples of how on-the-ground observations, elicited by respecting and using the ways of knowing relevant to a people, are critical to understanding global change and also can show ways that qualitative and quantitative information can complement and explain each other.

A second example from my fieldwork that illustrates the importance of engaging all relevant knowledge systems goes much deeper by showing how vernacular knowledge is often entangled with cultural meanings, values, and importance. In the homeland of the Viliui Sakha there is a unique feature known to them as *alaas*. Generally speaking, an *alaas* is a cryogenic lake surrounded by fields that are bordered by taiga or boreal forest. They were the original settlement areas of Sakha's Turkic ancestors half a millennium ago, due to their rich resource base. An *alaas* is a physical phenomenon but, more and more, I understand it as a cultural concept and symbol of Sakha's core identity. For example, here are two responses from inhabitants of my two main research villages when I asked about the meaning of *alaas*:

> *Alaas* are close to a Sakha person...we hold them close...before we lived spread out by the *alaas* and in any case there is still something there...there is a good sense about the *alaas* for us...birthland – the *alaas* idea is in our minds and consciousness.
> *(Valerian Yegorovich Afanaseyev, interview, June 13, 2018)*

Sakha depended on *alaas* for their physical and spiritual sustenance,

> Sakha are children of the *alaas*...every Sakha has an *alaas* in their spirit – and we carry that *alaas* with us all our lives...the *alaas* is connected to our roots...our beginnings...the birthplace...the homeland...why is that? Because Sakha lived by the *alaas* long ago...they had *alaas*...they protected it and lived from it.
> *(Margarita Ilyinichna Zabolotskaya, interview, July 2, 2018)*

In contrast, here is how scientists in the capital city Yakutsk articulate the meaning of *alaas*:

> *Alaas* are a landscape feature unique to northeastern Siberia that form from the combination of thermokarst process and its abundant moisture in the context of the extreme dry climate of the Sakha area (Troeva et al. 2010: 13). *Alaas* cycle approximately every 150–180 years, from a maximum rise of lake water, to its minimal, then to lake area desiccation and finally to complete disappearance of water from the *alaas* basin (Bosikov et al. 2012: 56). The area is then a base for vegetation and the gradual decline of the land surface as the thermokarst process begins anew and a new lake forms (Troeva et al. 2010: 13).

These understandings of *alaas* reflect two very different ways of knowing *alaas*. These two knowledge systems assign importance to different aspects of the *alaas*, one as a cultural and spiritual landscape used by a people for centuries versus a technically defined landscape. The former is rich in cultural history, depth, and meaning, while the other is focused on specific physical technicalities. It has been only through the process of long-term ethnography complemented by the analysis of archival documents, peer-reviewed publications, and the popular press, that I have cobbled together Sakha's cultural understanding of *alaas*. In sharp contrast, I was able to gather information about scientifically defined *alaas* more easily since it can be accessed through internet searches, and it is also prominent in the contemporary parlance of climate change and permafrost science. Despite these differences in the quality of the two knowledges of *alaas* and the accessibility to them, it remains that not including Sakha's cultural meaning and place attachment to *alaas* in adaptation or policy measures would render the measures not only insufficient but also unjust. On the other hand, what would it look like to take both into consideration? I would argue here that it is not some product we are after in our pursuit to consider all knowledges but rather a process. Bringing together ways of understanding the world is made up of many acts of engagement. It is not a deliverable that will render the output from bringing the knowledges together. More on this topic later.

What Anthropologists[6] are Doing

Few people would claim to know as much about how to catch fish as a good full-time fisherman. When it comes to understanding fish behavior and the many environmental factors that help determine and predict it, marine biologists must often take a back seat. This is hardly surprising. There are hundreds as times as many fishermen today as there are marine biologists, and their forebears were plying their trade and passing on their accumulated knowledge tens of centuries before anyone heard of marine biology.

(Johannes 1981: vii)

It is one manifestation of the elitism and ethnocentrism that run deep in much of the Western scientific community. If unpublished notebooks containing the detailed observations of a long line of biologists and oceanographers were destroyed, we would be outraged. But when specialized knowledge won from the sea over centuries by formally unschooled but uniquely qualified observers – fishermen – is allowed to disappear as the westernization of their cultures proceeds, hardly anyone seems to care.

(ibid: ix)

An anthropologist may read these lines above and assume a disciplinary colleague had written them. However, they were written by a marine biologist over four decades ago. Such insight about other ways of knowing from a scholar, in this case, Robert Earle Johannes, trained in quantitative western science was at the time the exception and not the rule. It is also sobering to learn in Johannes's book his caution about the extent to which these knowledge systems are disappearing due to disinterested youth, increasing dependence upon store-bought foods and the other forces of our collective "modernity." On a positive note and as witnessed by the academic and NGO advancements focused on Indigenous and local communities challenged by these forces in the last half century since Johannes's book, there has been a substantial increase in awareness of other ways of knowing. My earlier IPCC testimonial suggests that, once others have an opportunity to consider how important vernacular knowledge systems are to planetary balance, they can often get on board.

So what *are* anthropologists actually doing in the world of vernacular knowledge systems, climate change research and its interventions? There is a lot going on in terms of the practice of identifying and working with the knowledge of on the ground collaborators, whether that ground is in a rural settlement or an urban metropolis. An overview of all the work that anthropologists are doing is not feasible here. My intent is to overview the work of anthropologists fore fronting the critical place of Indigenous knowledge and/or local knowledge within larger interdisciplinary and policy contexts. Anthropologists have been increasingly articulating the importance of our contributions in the recent decades,

Anthropological contributions [therefore] complement research from other disciplines and further global dialogue on the science and policy of climate change. As discussions on climate change expand to include not only physical descriptions of the phenomenon but also questions of different groups' receptivity to the science, policy response, and characterization of impacts, these contributions are becoming increasingly critical to a productive debate.

(Barnes et al. 2013: 541)

And it appears that we may be making some headway. The 2020 multi-authored review surveying recent developments in the ways that anthropologists are engaging with climate change has a strong thread throughout of how these various efforts feed or can feed into policy prescriptions (O'Reilly et al. 2020).

To make the case in interdisciplinary and policy contexts, anthropologists need to frame what we are talking about when we say that knowledge is more than description but also about relationships, a sense of caring for place and a language to assist the act of being. Herein anthropologists can facilitate a "dialogue between Indigenous worlds and those of science, and also [contribute] through helping science understand the performative dimensions of the knowledge it produces and the multidisciplinary collaborations they often invite and entail" (Taddei 2020: 3). Anthropologists can also work to counter the policy world's tendency to label affected communities as "victims," due to the challenge of climate change and the imminent threat to their continued habitation of their lands, to show how inhabitants are responding as agents of change and developing innovative ways to not only survive but thrive (e.g., Hermann and Kempf 2017).

Anthropologists are also integrating Indigenous mitigation and adaptation strategies into policy-led responses. Local communities often have developed ways to address changes in climate that are time-tested and involve rituals and ceremonies based in their understanding of how their world works. One example shows anthropologists bringing these adaptation approaches to the policy table through their careful documentation, analysis, and validation which, in turn, is critical for effective policy responses (Hiwasaki et al. 2015).

Another area of anthropological engagement is directly in the policy realm demonstrating the efficacy of Indigenous knowledge and local knowledge. Here we find anthropologists ground truthing climate models using Indigenous and local knowledge (e.g., Reyes-Garcia et al. 2016; Roscoe 2014). Several projects focus on clarifying how scientific frameworks used to assess policy needs can be more just, equitable, and long-lasting by integrating Indigenous narratives with scientific understandings in order to inform science and make more accessible relevant scientific information for communities (Zanotti et al. 2020; Reid et al. 2021; Alexander et al. 2011). Another approach is to frame Indigenous knowledge and local knowledge within an entire suite of ways of being by which peoples manage and maintain relationships with nature (Brondizio et al. 2021). Additionally, an increasing number of anthropologists are working as lead authors on global assessments such as IPBES, The Convention on Biodiversity and the IPCC (McElwee et al. 2020; Reyes-Garcia et al. 2022; IPCC 2019: 99–105). Globally relevant organizations, such as UNESCO, have also started to sponsored publications on the topic (Nakashima et al. 2018). Finally, anthropologists are joining with a diversity of other academics to warn about the dire consequences of losing these important ways of knowing (Fernández-Llamazares et al. 2021).

However, even if vernacular knowledge systems enter the lingua franca of global assessments, more often than not, the important work of removing the institutional barriers to make a difference in policy prescriptions and the dead-end act of pursuing knowledge "integration" as an end in itself both keep the actual process of engaging vernacular knowledge systems a stalled one (Shawoo and Thornton 2019: 2).

Which leads to my final point in this section and a continuation of my argument from earlier. Even if we can make the case, in fine articulations or not, and convince others of the importance of vernacular knowledge systems, how do we actually bring those knowledge systems into research and policy to deliver results? It is, as I mentioned earlier, messy. Those who are seeking a "deliverable" from such an endeavor may not be satisfied. I say this because I believe what is actually our goal in this effort is engagement. Our "deliverable," if we need to call it that, is the coproduction of knowledge. But again, not on a piece of paper but in living, active interactions with all rights holders. Anthropological work in this area already exists (e.g. Maldonado et al. 2016; Shaffer 2014; Crate and Fedorov 2013). This should come as no surprise since both engagement and knowledge coproduction are longtime foundational tools in the practice of anthropology.

Closing Thoughts

Contemporary humans have "known" anthropogenic climate change largely through the narrow lens of quantitative natural science for far too long. This "knowing" was formalized in response to a few brave individuals who spoke out over thirty years ago. For example, in 1988 this was a headline story,

> today Dr. James E. Hansen of the National Aeronautics and Space Administration told a Congressional committee that it was 99 percent certain that the warming trend was not a natural variation but was caused by a buildup of carbon dioxide and other artificial gases in the atmosphere.[7]

This sparked a cascade of one scientific report after another. It also triggered several formal international organizations and initiatives. In the same year as Hansen's testimony, the World Meteorological Organization (WMO) and the United Nations Environment Programme established the Intergovernmental Panel on Climate Change (IPCC), whose sole objective was to provide governments at all levels with scientific information that they can use to develop climate policies. The United Nations Framework Convention on Climate Change (UNFCCC) entered into force in 1994 and, among other things, established the Conference of the Parties (COP) that met for the first time in 1995. COP 28 is on the horizon as I write. There has been great progress, of course in both the depth of understanding in both the IPCC reports and the COP gatherings. However, they can also be critiqued for substantiating a colonial hegemonic approach to the problem of climate change. In short, we have enough science, in the western way of knowing.

Globally, scientific knowledge takes precedence over other ways of knowing global change and its effects and also determines how a privileged few think about and make decisions for the rest of the world. This reifies the neoliberal agenda, which substantiates and perpetuates global inequalities and increased poverty through the privatization of resources and the accumulation of wealth by a few. Our understanding of the world would be less hegemonic and more pluralistic if we took to heart that "All knowledge is 'local' and culturally/socially contextual, which means that scientific knowledge is situated (cultural) practice" (Goldman et al. 2011: 14). Furthermore, if we strove for "right" relations in all our immediate interactions and within all the systems and at all the levels upon which we have built the larger global sphere. Calls for this are coming from many disciplines. For example, from this art historian,

Relationality presupposes a post-human mode of being in the world, a mode of equivalence with nature that dissociates it from being an object of man and thus, a representational trope for the future. It insists instead on a radically different form of becoming with both human and non-human beings through relationships of reciprocity.

(Garzon 2020)

Seeking to preserve our multiple and heterogeneous ecosystems while also deterring growing climate violence, the notion of futurity that is being suggested here emerges from the perspective of indigenous futures. Although this notion of futurity does not refer to a specific idea or vision of the future, this has as its horizon the repositioning of our ways of relating to the environment and each other.

(ibid)

Anthropology clearly has a central role herein and, as this chapter shows, anthropologists are taking up this work. But there needs to be more. Hopefully these ideas and insights can multiply within our field and across our multiple sub-disciplines and become anthropology's contribution towards an equitable and abundant future.

Notes

1 I acknowledge up front that naming these knowledge systems (this comment refers to next footnote also) is problematic. All of them are scientific in that they are based on empirical information that is tested over time. Furthermore, here the qualifier 'western' is used to further differentiate it from the others.
2 As per the recent IPCC SROCC report, I am using Indigenous knowledge and local knowledge to speak about other ways of knowing besides western scientific. See our IPCC definition later in the chapter.
3 Although the SROCC uses the acronyms 'IK' and 'LK' for Indigenous knowledge and local knowledge respectively, and I had them here originally, my colleague, Julie Cruikshank, made an important critique about the use of those acronyms that changed my use of them, specifically, "When I was more actively working on similar issues in the North, I sometimes felt that even some scientists who grasped the *principles* of Indigenous or local knowledge were sometimes using the acronym in a way that made it more appear more 'technical' (in a bureaucratic sense) and less complex than 'knowledge' as we understand it – whether categorized as 'Indigenous knowledge' or 'local knowledge'…especially when routinely referred to as 'TEK' or 'IK' in conversations or policy documents. It's a kind of 'flattening' that sometimes seems to occur and may actually undercut the more serious issues about how various professionals and agencies think about or evaluate local understandings."
4 Personal communication Joanna Petrasek MacDonald, ICC Canada Climate Change Officer, October 16, 2018.
5 See discussion of *alaas* and Sakha towards the end of the next section in this chapter and Chapter 14, *Sakha* and *alaas*.
6 Please note: there is a lot of work being done involving vernacular knowledge systems and climate change research and a lot of it is not being conducted by anthropologists. It goes without say that the approach to this challenge must be interdisciplinary and therefore most work engages an interdisciplinary team. My discussion of 'what anthropologists are doing' is focused specifically on our discipline, hence the focus of our edited volume. That said, there are certainly more anthropological contributions than I am covering here.
7 https://www.nytimes.com/1988/06/24/us/global-warming-has-begun-expert-tells-senate.html

References

Abram, N., J.-P. Gattuso, A. Prakash, L. Cheng, M.P. Chidichimo, S. Crate, H. Enomoto, M. Garschagen, N. Gruber, S. Harper, E. Holland, R.M. Kudela, J. Rice, K. Steffen, and K. von Schuckmann. 2019. Framing and context of the report. In: IPCC *Special Report on the Ocean and Cryosphere in a Changing Climate*. [H.-O. Pörtner, D.C. Roberts, V. Masson-Delmotte, P. Zhai, M. Tignor, E. Poloczanska, K. Mintenbeck, A. Alegría, M. Nicolai, A. Okem, J. Petzold, B. Rama, N.M. Weyer (eds.)]

Alexander, C., Bynum, N., Johnson, E., King, U., Mustonen, T., Neofotis, P., Oettlé, N., Rosenzweig, C., Sakakibara, C., Shadrin, V. and Vicarelli, M., 2011. Linking indigenous and scientific knowledge of climate change. *BioScience* 61 (6): 477–484.

Barnes, J., Dove, M., Lahsen, M., Mathews, A., McElwee, P., McIntosh, R., Moore, F., O'reilly, J., Orlove, B., Puri, R., and Weiss, H., 2013. Contribution of anthropology to the study of climate change. *Nature Climate Change*, 3 (6): 541–544.

Bosikov, N.P., Isaev, A.P., Iva-Nova, E. Zakharova, V.I., Sivtseva, L.V., Ivanova, A.P., Semyonova, S.G., Ammosova, V.N., Poriadina, L.N. and Isakova, V.G. 2012. Ritmy razvitiia alasnykh ekosistem v Tsentral'noi Iakutii (Rhythms of development of forest ecosystems in Central Yakutia). *Prirodnye resursy Arktiki I Subarktiki*, 2.

Brondizio, E.S., Aumeeruddy-Thomas, Y., Bates, P., Carino, J., Fernández-Llamazares, Á., Ferrari, M.F., Galvin, K., Reyes-García, V., McElwee, P., Molnár, Z., and Samakov, A., 2021. Locally based, regionally manifested, and globally relevant: Indigenous and local knowledge, values, and practices for nature. *Annual Review of Environment and Resources*, 46: 481–509.

Bronen, R., Pollock, D., Overbeck, J., Stevens, D., Natali, S. and Maio, C., 2020. Usteq: integrating indigenous knowledge and social and physical sciences to coproduce knowledge and support community-based adaptation. *Polar Geography*, 43 (2–3):188–205.

Crate, S. and A. Fedorov. 2013. A methodological model for exchanging local and scientific climate change knowledge in Northeastern Siberia. *Arctic*, 66 (3): 338–350.

Fernández-Llamazares, Á., Lepofsky, D., Lertzman, K., Armstrong, C.G., Brondizio, E.S., Gavin, M.C., Lyver, P.O.B., Nicholas, G.P., Reo, N.J., Reyes-García, V., and Turner, N.J. 2021. Scientists' warning to humanity on threats to Indigenous and local knowledge systems. *Journal of Ethnobiology*, 41 (2): 144–169.

Garzon, S. 2020. Notes for a horizon-tality: toward the possibility of becoming together as an assemblage. https://wayback.archive-it.org/4472/20220302060407/https://www.coleccioncisneros. org/editorial/featured/notes-horizon-tality. Accessed January 20, 2023.

Gearheard, S., Pocernich, M., Stewart, R., Sanguya, J., and Huntington, H.P. 2010. Linking Inuit knowledge and meteorological station observations to understand changing wind patterns at Clyde River, Nunavut. *Climatic Change*, 100: 267–294.

Goldman, M.J., Nadasdy, P. and Turner, M.D. eds., 2011. *Knowing Nature: Conversations at the intersection of political ecology and science studies*. Chicago: University of Chicago Press.

Goldman, M. J., Turner, M.D., and Daly, M., 2018. A critical political ecology of human dimensions of climate change: epistemology, ontology, and ethics. *Wiley Interdisciplinary Reviews: Climate Change*, 9 (4): e526.

Hermann, E. and Kempf, W. 2017. Climate change and the imagining of migration: emerging discourses on Kiribati's land purchase in Fiji. *The Contemporary Pacific*, pp. 231–263.

Hiwasaki, L., Luna, E. and Marçal, J.A. 2015. Local and indigenous knowledge on climate-related hazards of coastal and small island communities in Southeast Asia. *Climatic Change*, 128 (1–2): 35–56.

IPCC. 2019. Annex I: Glossary [Weyer, N.M. (ed.)]. In IPCC *Special Report on the Ocean and Cryosphere in a Changing Climate* [H.-O. Pörtner, D.C. Roberts, V. Masson-Delmotte, P. Zhai, M. Tignor, E. Poloczanska, K. Mintenbeck, A. Alegría, M. Nicolai, A. Okem, J. Petzold, B. Rama, N.M. Weyer (eds.)].

IPCC. 2022a. *Climate Change 2022: Impacts, adaptation, and vulnerability*. Contribution of Working Group II to the Sixth Assessment Report of the Intergovernmental Panel on Climate

Change [H.-O. Pörtner, D.C. Roberts, M. Tignor, E.S. Poloczanska, K. Mintenbeck, A. Alegría, M. Craig, S. Langsdorf, S. Löschke, V. Möller, A. Okem, B. Rama (eds.)]. Cambridge University Press.

IPCC. 2022b. Summary for Policymakers. In *Climate Change 2022: Impacts, adaptation, and vulnerability*. Contribution of Working Group II to the Sixth Assessment Report of the Intergovernmental Panel on Climate Change [H.-O. Pörtner, D.C. Roberts, M. Tignor, E.S. Poloczanska, K. Mintenbeck, A. Alegría, M. Craig, S. Langsdorf, S. Löschke, V. Möller, A. Okem, B. Rama (eds.)]. Cambridge University Press.

Johannes, R.E. 1981. *Words of the Lagoon: Fishing and marine lore in the Palau district of Micronesia*. Univ of California Press.

Makondo, C.C. and Thomas, D.S. 2018. Climate change adaptation: linking indigenous knowledge with western science for effective adaptation. *Environmental Science & Policy*, 88: 83–91.

Maldonado, J., Bennett, T.M., Chief, K., Cochran, P., Cozzetto, K., Gough, B., Redsteer, M.H., Lynn, K., Maynard, N., and Voggesser, G., 2016. Engagement with indigenous peoples and honoring traditional knowledge systems. In *The US National Climate Assessment*. Cham: Springer, pp. 111–126.

McElwee, P., Fernández-Llamazares, Á., Aumeeruddy-Thomas, Y., Babai, D., Bates, P., Galvin, K., Guèze, M., Liu, J., Molnár, Z., Ngo, H.T., and Reyes-García, V. 2020. Working with Indigenous and local knowledge (ILK) in large-scale ecological assessments: reviewing the experience of the IPBES Global Assessment. *Journal of Applied Ecology*, 57 (9): 1666–1676.

Nakashima, Douglas, Krupnik, Igor, and Rubis, Jennifer T. eds. 2018. *Indigenous Knowledge for Climate Change Assessment and Adaptation*. Cambridge: Cambridge University Press.

O'Reilly, J., Isenhour, C., McElwee, P. and Orlove, B., 2020. Climate change: expanding anthropological possibilities. *Annual Review of Anthropology*, 49, pp.13–29.

Reid, R.S., Fernández-Giménez, M.E., Wilmer, H., Pickering, T., Kassam, K.A.S., Yasin, A., Porensky, L.M., Derner, J.D., Nkedianye, D., Jamsranjav, C., and Jamiyansharav, K., 2021. Using research to support transformative impacts on complex, "wicked problems" with pastoral peoples in rangelands. *Frontiers in Sustainable Food Systems*, 4: 600689.

Reid-Shaw, I., Jargalsaihan, A., Reid, R.S., Jamsranjav, C., and Fernández-Giménez, M.E. 2021. Social-ecological change on the Mongolian Steppe: herder perceptions of causes, impacts, and adaptive strategies. *Hum Ecol*. https://doi-org.oca.ucsc.edu/10.1007/s10745-021-00256-7.

Reyes-García, V., Fernández-Llamazares, A., Aumeeruddy-Thomas, Y., Benyei, P., Bussmann, R. W., Diamond, S.K., García-del-Amo, D., Guadilla-Sáez, S., Hanazaki, N., Kosoy, N. and Lavides, M. 2022. Recognizing Indigenous peoples' and local communities' rights and agency in the post-2020 Biodiversity Agenda. *Ambio*, 51 (1): 84–92.

Reyes-García, V., Fernández-Llamazares, Á., Guèze, M., Garcés, A., Mallo, M., Vila-Gómez, M., and Vilaseca, M., 2016. Local indicators of climate change: the potential contribution of local knowledge to climate research. *Wiley Interdisciplinary Reviews: Climate Change*, 7 (1): 109–124.

Roscoe P. 2014. A changing climate for anthropological and archaeological research? Improving the climate change models. *Am. Anthropol.* 116 (3): 535–548.

Shaffer, L.J. 2014. Making sense of local climate change in rural Tanzania through knowledge co-production. *Journal of Ethnobiology*, 34 (3): 315–334.

Shawoo, Z. and Thornton, T.F. 2019. The UN local communities and Indigenous peoples' platform: a traditional ecological knowledge-based evaluation. *WIREs Climate Change* 10 (3): e575.

Taddei, R. 2020. Anthropology and the Pragmatics of Climate Knowledge in Brazil. *American Anthropologist*, 122 (4): 944–947.

Tengö, M., Hill, R., Malmer, P., Raymond, C.M., Spierenburg, M., Danielsen, F., Elmqvist, T., and Folke, C. 2017. Weaving knowledge systems in IPBES, CBD and beyond – lessons learned for sustainability. *Current Opinion in Environmental Sustainability*, 26: 17–25.

Troeva, E.I., Isaev, A.P., Cherosov, M.M. and Karpov, N.S., eds., 2010. *The Far North: Plant biodiversity and ecology of Yakutia* (3). Dordrecht: Springer Science & Business Media.

Zanotti, L., Carothers, C., Apok, C.A., Huang, S., Coleman, J., and Ambrozek, C. 2020. Political ecology and decolonial research: co-production with the Iñupiat in Utqiaġvik. *Journal of Political Ecology*, 27 (1): 43–66.

PART II
Worldmaking Practices

6

"DON'T LOOK DOWN"

Green Technologies, Climate Change, and Mining

Jerry K. Jacka

Climate Change and "Clean Energy" Minerals

In the 2021 film, *Don't Look Up*, written and directed by Adam McKay, a planet-destroying comet is hurtling towards Earth on a devastating collision course. While the United States government has a plan to stop the comet and save the planet, the mission is aborted at the last minute when a tech-billionaire notifies the president that the comet contains over $130 trillion of critical mineral elements. Rather than save the planet, those in power decide to try to mine the comet. Spoiler alert: Earth gets destroyed and the minerals are never mined due to the comet mining technology drastically failing. One of the many messages in the film is clear: Let's not put our trust in tech billionaires and their technology and capitalist intentions when the future of our planet is at stake. In many ways, the satire in this film captures the same sorts of approaches that are being undertaken in the pursuit of green, low-carbon energy sources that offer a panacea for the reduction of greenhouse gases in the atmosphere. Namely, the increasing reliance on technologies dependent upon mineral extraction for their deployment, i.e., so-called "clean energy" minerals like lithium and rare earth elements used in battery production. As part of the 2016 Paris Climate Accords, the shift from fossil fuels to wind, solar, and other renewable resources is a cornerstone of many national governments' commitments to lowering the amounts of carbon they are pumping into the atmosphere. In the US, for instance, the current presidential administration recently announced a goal of having 50% of all new cars sold in America be electric cars by 2030 (*New York Times*, August 5, 2021).

In this same year, 2021, both the Intergovernmental Panel on Climate Change (IPCC) and the World Meteorological Organization (WMO) issued reports detailing the dire consequences of the global climate trajectory. The IPCC report stressed that humans need to stop burning fossil fuels immediately to prevent a two-degree Celsius rise in average global temperature by 2040 (IPCC 2021). The WMO's report highlighted that four of the world's seven climate indicators recorded their highest levels ever: ocean heat, ocean acidification, sea-level rise, and atmospheric carbon dioxide, and that surface temperatures, glaciers, and polar ice extent were of critical concern (WMO 2022). This prompted

DOI: 10.4324/9781003242499-9

United Nations' Secretary-General António Guterres to issue a call for a five-point plan for global efforts to initiate transitions to renewable energy: 1) treat renewable energy technologies as essential global public goods; 2) increase supply chains and raw materials used in renewable energy technologies; 3) fast track and streamline renewable energy projects; 4) reduce the $500 billion in subsidies that go to fossil fuel production; and 5) triple the investments in renewable energy (Guterres 2022).

While reducing atmospheric levels of carbon dioxide is critically necessary and important for humanity's future, what initiatives such as these often fail to engage with comprehensively is the consideration of what "increasing raw materials" means for the planet. As the pro-mining bumper sticker, "If it can't be grown, it must be mined!" notes, increases in the investment, production, and processing of the raw materials for renewable energy technologies is going to entail a massive commitment to mineral resource extraction on a global scale. A 2020 World Bank report noted that production for minerals used in batteries (graphite, lithium, and cobalt) would need to increase by 500% to meet renewable energy demands in the near future (World Bank 2020). While an understanding of the need for lithium production and rare-earth elements is increasingly becoming more common in public circles, there are a host of other minerals that will also need to be mined to support charging stations and the other subsidiary industries needed for battery production. An Ouray Silver, Inc. mining executive, reported at the 2021 San Juan Mining and Reclamation Conference in Telluride, Colorado that ten times as much silver as is currently being mined globally would need to be extracted from the environment in order to meet the goal of half of all new cars sold in the USA to be electric. In fact, the World Bank estimates that over 3 billion tons of minerals will need to be mined for renewables to prevent an increase greater that 2° Celsius in the average global temperature (World Bank 2020).

In 2018, in an *Annual Review of Anthropology* article on mining (Jacka 2018), I argued that one of the ubiquitous aspects of current mineral extraction was an extractive imperative ("extractivism," see Acosta 2013; Arsel et al. 2016; Chagnon et al. 2022) pursued even by left-leaning, developing countries in Latin America. The concept of extractivism was developed by Latin American scholars to explain significant increases in mining production in areas that were purportedly pursuing more sustainable economic growth. Today I would expand my argument to note that, given the global focus of the purported need for the increased production of renewable energy technologies, we will soon be undergoing a global imperative of extractivism, based on these minerals being perceived as "essential, global public goods" (see Nuttall 2013). The question I then have is, what are the implications of trying to save our planet while, at the same time, turning it into an enormous mine?

To examine this question, I use two cases from my research: one around mining extraction in several communities in Papua New Guinea and the other about the aftereffects of mining in southwestern Colorado. I also explore how the climatic changes of today (floods from heavy precipitation events, mega-droughts, etc.) will potentially affect mining sites in the future. I then discuss the ways that communities are pursuing remediation in post-mining sites. I conclude by discussing the paradox of the capitalist intensification of mining to meet clean energy needs, what I call the paradox of mining our way to sustainability.

A (Very) Partial Planetary History of Mining

The nineteenth century witnessed several gold rushes in which the lands of Indigenous peoples were violently invaded, appropriated, and "developed" by Euro-American wealth seekers. While Latin America had long been exploited for minerals since the European invasion of the New World, the nineteenth century rushes were unique in that they involved tens of thousands of Euro-Americans destroying rivers and forests in incredibly short amounts of time in their quest for gold. California, the intermountain west of the United States, Australia, the Yukon, and South Africa were all sites of rushes wherein massive amounts of land moved out of the possession of Indigenous peoples and into the hands of outsiders, resulting in the establishment of new political systems and regimes. At the heart of this process was a re-valuing of the importance of land from Indigenous systems based on resource stewardship to capitalist systems of exploitation and destruction (Carroll 2015).

For example, in Colorado, the 1858 discovery of gold eventuated in an 1859 gold rush in which close to 100,000 prospectors invaded the lands of the Arapaho, Cheyenne, and Ute. Within ten years, the Arapaho and Cheyenne had been forcibly removed to the Indian Territory (modern-day Oklahoma) and the Ute homelands had been reduced to a tiny fraction of what they were. Within twenty years of the discovery of gold, Colorado received statehood and the majority of the Ute had been forcibly removed to Utah. Mining played a significant role in Colorado state economics and determined patterns of land use as based on resource extraction and the violent desecration of the land base. A mineral belt stretching from Boulder, in the north-central part of the state, to Durango in the southwest provided rich deposits of gold, silver, lead, and zinc. As in many locations, these mineral producing areas were located in sites of tectonic instability, such as the Rocky Mountains. Their high elevations and fractured landscapes proved challenging to mining production in the early years, and complicate remediation efforts in the present. While many of the mining districts generated incredible wealth in the early years, few provided long-term wealth (Smith 2009). Overall, Colorado mining has experienced one long slow decline from the early 1900s to the present (Fell and Twitty 2008).

The last century and a half of mining has left over 25,000 abandoned, or legacy, mines in Colorado. Many of the sites haven't been worked in over 100 years, in others their owners have either gone out of business or been bankrupted and many release acid mine drainage into the waterways, impacting almost 1800 miles of Colorado's river systems. Additionally, piles of waste rock and tailings contribute to toxic metal loading as acid mine drainage and water runoff flow across the piles into surrounding rivers. Due to their status as legacy mines, their cleanup is the responsibility of community, state, and federal efforts and coalitions.

The 1960s environmental movement included a vociferous criticism of the impacts of mining on the societies and ecologies of the Global North. In turn, both the neoliberal economic policies around foreign investment and the easing of environmental regulations in the mining sector in the Global South led to massive increases in mining there (Haselip and Hilson 2005). Consequently, many of the world's dirtiest mining operations were outsourced to the less developed nations of the world (Kirsch 2014). Although I am being overly brief in this account of mining on a planetary basis, I have outlined the general patterns to explore further in this chapter – the legacy of environmentally destructive mining in the southwestern United States, the shift to mining in the Global South, and the current return to mining in the Global North for "clean energy" minerals. Within that context, I highlight the parallels between the nineteenth century disregard by miners for the land in the southwestern United States and the contemporary attitudes of mining companies in the Global South.

The Porgera Gold Mine

Some of the most environmentally devastating mines in the world can be found in the southwestern Pacific Ocean on the island of New Guinea. The Grasberg mine in West Papua, and the Panguna, Ok Tedi, and Porgera mines in Papua New Guinea (PNG) have all disposed of mine tailings in the adjacent rivers throughout their operational lives. Entire downstream landscapes and ecosystems have been ravaged for mineral resource extraction. In 1989, the Panguna mine was shut down by local landowners due to concerns over ecological damage and social disruption (May and Spriggs 1990). Landowners around the Ok Tedi mine sued the mine's owners and operators, receiving over $25 million in an out-of-court settlement (Kirsch 2014). The Grasberg mine relies upon the Indonesian military to quell any discontent with its mining operations and has been subjected to a range of complaints over human rights violations (Ballard and Banks 2009). The Porgera mine has been the subject of my research since the late 1990s.

The Porgera gold mine opened in 1990. It has produced, on average, 900,000 ounces of gold annually. During mine development, the mining company avoided the building of a tailings dam, arguing to the PNG government that it would be cost prohibitive and likely to fail given the geological instability in the region. As a result, over 17,000 metric tons of waste rock and tailings are dumped into the Porgera River system daily. (In this regard, the Porgera mine is rather moderate, as the Panguna mine is estimated to have expelled over 160,000 metric tons of waste rock daily during its 17-year life span (Doherty 2021).) After 30-plus years of mining, the waste rock pile looks (and acts) like a massive rock glacier, burying downstream forests and gardens. The Porgera River, blood-red from iron oxides released from the tailings mill, flows across the moonscape of the rock glacier. For approximately 150 kilometers downstream of the mine is what is euphemistically called "the mixing zone," an area in which the PNG government requires no environmental compliance. Additionally, one of the processes needed to extract the gold ore involves cyanide leaching, which inevitably spills to the surrounding environment and has detrimentally impacted the area.

The Porgera mine is ecologically devastating but the social consequences are perhaps more profound. In PNG nearly all of the country's land is controlled by customary social groups, called "clans" in the relevant literature. All development in the country relies upon attempts to demarcate which clans surrounding a development project are entitled to benefits from that project. This process is bedeviled by the informal nature of property rights in the country. Rights depend upon kinship linkages to the clans, long-term use of the land, the ability to argue one's case in land courts, and most often, some combination of the three. Claims to development benefits are thus very open-ended and changeable – at least from the perspective of local people.

The perspectives of the state and mining company, on the other hand, are composed of bureaucratic, formal processes that rely upon lists of official "landowners" to whom quarterly royalty checks can be issued, along with other benefits. These bureaucratic processes are systems of simplification (Scott 1998) that allow the corporations and the state to avoid any attempts at reconciling the complexities of land ownership and land management. This process in Porgera enriched just a few clans at the expense of most others in the valley (Golub 2014). The tensions between the informal–formal nexus of "landownership" associated with mining benefits have generated severe inequalities and grievances that have resulted in almost two decades of violent conflict in the area (see Jacka 2015, 2016, 2019, 2022). Over the years, hundreds of people have died, thousands of structures have been burned or razed, and entire villages dislocated. In addition to the outright violence of warfare, there is also the daily violence perpetrated against women in resource frontiers (Wardlow 2019) and the slow violence of social disruption and ecological destruction from development processes in the Global South (Nixon 2011).

Legacy Mines in Colorado

In early August 2015, a picture of three kayakers floating down a neon orange Animas River in southwestern Colorado made the headlines of international and national newspapers. The river's radical transformation in color was due to a spill from the Gold King mine outside Silverton, Colorado, during which three million gallons of contaminated mine waste was accidentally released by a contractor working for the Environmental Protection Agency (EPA) at the mine. The impounded sludge in the mine poured through a breach in the mine adit (the technical term for the horizontal entrance to a mine) turning the Animas and San Juan Rivers orange for hundreds of miles downstream.

In the six-plus years since the spill, I have worked with several communities in Colorado documenting the efforts that have gone into cleaning up Gold King and other legacy mining sites. These sites no longer have defined ownership because either the mines were developed in the late nineteenth century and then abandoned or they had twentieth century owners who have used bankruptcy as a mechanism to avoid cleanup. Many of these abandoned mines produce acid mine drainage which mobilizes toxic heavy metals (such as zinc, cadmium, and lead).

Water from precipitation percolates through the mines and mixes with sulfides and oxygen to form sulfuric acid. This acidic water carries higher loads of mobilized metals, and often runs across waste rock piles and tailings piles, freeing even more toxic metals. The combined effects of acidic waters laden with heavy metals kills macro-invertebrates which fish feed on, the fish themselves, and has deleterious effects up the food chain for miles and miles downstream. Acid mine drainage is a problem that will plague society for millennia. Roman mines in Spain from over 2000 years ago are still producing acid drainage. Spain's Rio Tinto River was so named due to the red-orange tint that the acid mine drainage contributes to the river. As the source of many of the United States' major rivers, including the Colorado, the Rio Grande, the Arkansas, and the South Platte, Colorado spreads acid mine drainage throughout a vast region of the United States.

Several communities in Colorado have formed watershed conservation groups to work on cleaning up waste rock piles, tailings piles, and other mining-based hazards to human health and ecosystem ecology. But these organizations are unable to tackle the complexities of draining mining adits because of the way liability is articulated in the Clean Water Act (see May 2004). In essence, water quality standards have to be brought up to

100% of whatever the standard is for that body of water if they try to clean up the adit. Incremental improvements in water quality standards open organizations to being sued under the Clean Water Act. Paradoxically, if a remediation effort greatly improved the quality of water coming out of a draining adit, but it was not at 100% of the water quality standards, then whoever undertook the remediation could be sued. These concerns are sufficient to prohibit citizen-led cleanup groups to attempt cleanup on their own, leading the groups to focus on cleaning up tailings piles, waste rocks, and other mining hazards that do not have acid mine drainage associated with them. In fact, Silverton's citizen-led cleanup group, the Animas River Stakeholders Group, disbanded in 2019 after 25 years of cleanup efforts as the only sites left were acid mine drainage sites. Consequently, the US government's EPA Superfund program (for an overview, see Hird 1994) undertakes cleanups in communities that prove too complicated for local management due to Clean Water Act liabilities. Yet, this is often a contentious process due to community fears of government overreach, a legacy of toxic environments, fluctuating property values, and the rise of tourism as an economic replacement industry.

To better understand what communities undergo after being placed on the National Priorities List for cleanup, I have interviewed and worked with watershed conservation organizations, EPA regulators and other government officials, mining companies, and impacted citizens in Colorado for the last six years. I focus on three communities in or near Superfund sites in Colorado: Leadville, Creede, and Silverton. The California Gulch Superfund site in Leadville was first designated in 1983, shortly after the Superfund program started. For years, the upper Arkansas River had been seriously polluted by acid mine drainage from the Yak Tunnel in California Gulch. The town itself had high levels of lead in the soil from the several dozen smelters that operated in the area in the late 1800s. The second community is near the Nelson Tunnel/Commodore Waste Rock Superfund site outside Creede that was listed in 2008 to begin cleanup operations on acid mine drainage from the Nelson Tunnel along Willow Creek, which eventually runs into the Rio Grande River. Lastly, the Bonita Peak Superfund site outside Silverton was designated in 2016 following the Gold King Mine spill. It includes numerous tunnels and mine adits which all drain acid into tributaries of the Animas River which feeds into the San Juan and, ultimately, the Colorado River.

Not only are there challenges around the politics of the litigation for cleanup, but the efforts themselves pose significant challenges to communities. The Leadville community has been undergoing almost four decades of cleanup with efforts still ongoing. The Gold King spill, however, transformed the government's slowness in dealing with abandoned mine lands. The Nelson Tunnel, outside Creede, has languished in terms of government efforts to clean up the mining waste. Inventories were conducted of the worst mines and already listed sites like Creede received redirected attention as the EPA shifted their priorities from cleaning up the Nelson Tunnel to ensuring that it wouldn't accidentally release millions of gallons of backed up mine waste (such as happened at Gold King). In the meantime, the Nelson Tunnel discharges approximately 200 pounds of zinc daily into Willow Creek, preventing trout populations from surviving in the creek. The biggest challenge for cleanup is dealing with acid mine drainage because the drainage needs to be treated in perpetuity and the technologies to address the by-products of treatment are ineffective. To this day, as mentioned, the two-thousand-year-old legacy mines in Spain are still discharging acidic waters.

An example of the challenges of acid mine drainage is the Summitville mine, also in southwestern Colorado. Summitville was initially the site of a late nineteenth century gold rush. In 1986, the Summitville Consolidated Mining Company began developing an open-pit gold mine using cyanide leaching to extract the gold. The mine, located at 11,500 feet above sea level, always posed engineering challenges to mine the ore. Shortly after the cyanide pad was poured it cracked, due to the concrete not having time to properly cure. From 1989 to 1991, copper-, zinc-, and cyanide-laced waters leaked into streams running into the Alamosa River, a major tributary of the Rio Grande (Smith 2009: 238). In 1992, the mining company declared bankruptcy, leaving 150 million gallons of cyanide-laced waste behind, along with two adits draining acidic wastes. The EPA declared the site a Superfund site and began cleanup. Twenty years and $250 million later, the site has been cleaned up. However, after 10 years, all Superfund cleanup costs are turned over to the state. The cost of running the treatment plant is approximately $10 million annually, in perpetuity, paid for by Colorado's taxpayers.

Even where and when permanent water treatment plants can be built, figuring out where to store the sludge left over from cleanup can be difficult. In 2019, I toured the interim treatment plant treating the wastes from the Gold King mine outside of Silverton. Once the water is brought into the plant, it is mixed with a polymer that settles the metals out of the water, mixed with lime to raise the pH of the acidic water, then the treated water is released back into the stream. The sludge left over in the settlement tanks is stored in massive water permeable bags that dry out the sludge so it can be permanently stored in a waste repository. The challenges are the sheer amounts of sludge (5000 to 6000 cubic yards annually) that are produced in the process. While there are multiple mines around the Gold King draining acid mine waters, their combined volume is too great for the treatment plant to handle. As a result, the plant only treats the Gold King wastes. Furthermore, the valley where the plant is located is too narrow for the long-term storage of the wastes and so the dried sludge is trucked to another location in the area and stored on top of old tailings piles from a mill that is now closed. At community meetings with the EPA in Silverton, many frustrated citizens asked why the metals couldn't be removed from the sludge and repurposed. Equally frustrated EPA regulators replied that: 1) it wasn't their job to do so, and 2) there wasn't the available technology to do so at the scale required.

Climate Change and Mining our Way to Sustainability

Above I have detailed some of the social and environmental consequences of mining. All of these are and will continue to be exacerbated further with climate change (Odell et al. 2018). We are currently seeing the effects of climate change on the extremes of our weather. Globally, more intense floods, droughts, and fires fill the headlines of the media. Extremes of precipitation will impact mining in multiple ways. Heavy rainfall events can cause surges of acid mine drainage to emit from mines. More significantly, tailings dams can become overloaded causing millions of gallons of tailings to spill into the environment. This recently occurred in British Columbia at the Mount Polley mine (Amnesty International 2017) and in Brazil at the Córrego do Feijão mine (Porsani et al. 2019). Adversely, the lack of precipitation can also impact both mining operations and legacy mines. For example, low river levels prevent mills from operating. In Porgera, the mine has shut down several times in its 32-year history during severe droughts in Papua New Guinea coincident with El Niño. For legacy mines, long-term droughts (megadroughts of two-plus decades) also increase the acidity of mine drainage (Ren et al. 2021), allowing higher concentrations of metals to be mobilized and more damage to fish and invertebrates once rainfall occurs.

I argue that this is the paradox which we face today. To mitigate the effects of climate change by reducing the amount of carbon dioxide we put into the atmosphere from burning fossil fuels, we are pursuing a path of having to mine more "clean energy" minerals. Yet, mining, as I have shown, is a highly disruptive industry both socially and ecologically. Few people willingly want mines in the communities they live in. Nevertheless, in southwestern Colorado, in Ouray, the Revenue-Virginius mine, and in Creede, the Bulldog mine, are both under consideration for development to reopen for silver mining in the near future.

Given the rise of global extractivism, more communities are going to have to pursue serious discussions about what level of mining they want to happen around them. But it is not only adjacent community areas we should be concerned about. In the United States, for example, how bad would the impacts of climate change have to get before we begin mining in protected areas? Would we be willing to mine in our national parks if critical energy minerals were discovered within them? And, of course, what is lost in this vision of the future are non-extractive alternatives (behavior change that leads to, for example, driving less) to the technological "promise" that more mining will bring by allowing us all to drive around in electric cars.

Having studied the impact of mining in communities for over 25 years, I put very little faith in the idea that mining companies are in the business of saving our planet through the extraction of "clean energy" minerals. Luckily, mining companies (in the Global North, and increasingly in the Global South) are now operating in a new era of environmental consciousness, and many require a "social license to operate" (Prno and Slocombe 2012) wherein they rely upon the public acceptance of their activities to extract resources. As well, more communities are relying upon "good neighbor agreements" (Lewis and Henkels 1996) to outline the expectations that mining corporations will be expected to follow during resource extraction. While the social license to operate is a non-formal method of pursuing corporate accountability and good neighbor agreements can be legally binding, they both remain effective tools for social and environmental justice.

And, finally, there is the very real danger of corporations using the "clean energy" transition to justify a return to increased mining to the Global North and having carte blanche to do so in environmentally devastating ways for the benefit of humanity. It is almost as if by just undertaking the extraction of these minerals, we are solving the climate crisis. However, I argue that it is impossible to mine our way to climate sustainability. We, as citizens of the planet, have to come to grips with the challenge of dealing with future climate change. Given our current technologically focused green energy transition, it is not a matter of *if* mining will increasingly impact our planet, but *when* and *how* significantly. We must ensure that it is done in the least harmful ways to our societies and our planet.

Acknowledgements

Funding for this research in 1) Papua New Guinea came from the National Science Foundation and the Wenner-Gren Foundation, and 2) Colorado came from the Institute of Behavioral Science at the University of Colorado Boulder. My greatest thanks goes to the people in the communities that I have worked with in Papua New Guinea and Colorado. All of the ideas in this paper have come from long discussions with my brilliant wife, Heather Greenwolf, who served as an Executive Director of a watershed conservation organization. I thank her for serving as co-thinker, sounding board, and critical editor in the writing of this chapter.

References

Acosta, A. 2013. Extractivism and neoextractivism: two sides of the same curse. In M. Lang and D. Mocrani (eds.) *Beyond Development: Alternative visions from Latin America*. Amsterdam: Transnational Institute, pp. 61–86.

Amnesty International. 2017. *A Breach of Human Rights: The human rights impacts of the Mount Polley mine disaster, British Columbia, Canada*. Hazelton Creek: Amnesty International. https://live-amnesty-canada-wp.pantheonsite.io/wp-content/uploads/2020/04/FINAL_May-24_Mount-Pol ley-briefing.pdf.

Arsel, M., B. Hogenboom, and L. Pellegrini. 2016. The extractive imperative in Latin America. *Extractive Industries and Society* 3: 880–887.

Ballard, Chris and Glenn Banks. 2009. Between a rock and a hard place: corporate strategy at the Freeport mine in Papua, 2001–2006. In B. Resosudarmo and F. Jotzo (eds.) *Working with Nature against Poverty: Development, resources and the environment in Eastern Indonesia*. Singapore: Institute of Southeast Asian Studies, pp. 147–177.

Carroll, Clint. 2015. *Roots of Our Renewal: Ethnobotany and Cherokee environmental governance*. Minneapolis: University of Minnesota Press.

Chagnon, Christopher W., Francesco Durante, Barry K. Gills, Sophia E. Hagolani-Albov, Saana Hokkanen, Sohvi M.J. Kangasluoma, Heidi Konttinen, Markus Kröger, William LaFleur, Ossi Ollinaho, and Marketta P.S. Vuola. 2022. From extractivism to global extractivism: the evolution of an organizing concept. *The Journal of Peasant Studies* 49 (4): 760–792.

Doherty, Ben. 2021. After 32 years, Rio Tinto to fund study of environmental damage caused by Panguna mine. *The Guardian*. July 21, 2021.

Fell, James and Eric Twitty. 2008. *The Mining Industry in Colorado*. https://www.historycolorado.org/sites/default/files/media/document/2017/651.pdf (Accessed September 22, 2022.)

Golub, Alex. 2014. *Leviathans at the Gold Mine: Creating Indigenous and corporate actors in Papua New Guinea*. Durham: Duke University Press.

Guterres, António. 2022. UN chief announces renewable energy initiative at WMO climate report launch. https://public.wmo.int/en/media/news/un-chief-announces-renewable-energy-initiative-wm o-climate-report-launch. (Accessed September 19, 2022).

Haselip, James and Gavin Hilson. 2005. Winners and losers from industry reforms in the developing world: experiences from the electricity and mining sectors. *Resources Policy* 30 (2): 87–100.

Hird, John A. 1994. *Superfund: The political economy of environmental risk*. Baltimore: Johns Hopkins University Press.

IPCC. 2021. *Climate Change, 2021: The physical science basis*. Cambridge: Cambridge University Press.

Jacka, Jerry K. 2015. *Alchemy in the Rain Forest: Politics, ecology, and resilience in a New Guinea mining area*. Durham: Duke University Press.

Jacka, Jerry K. 2016. Development conflicts and changing mortuary practices in a New Guinea mining area. *Journal of the Polynesian Society* 125 (2): 133–147.

Jacka, Jerry K. 2018. The anthropology of mining: the social and environmental impacts of resource extraction in the mineral age. *Annual Review of Anthropology* 47: 61–77.

Jacka, Jerry K. 2019. Resource conflicts and the anthropology of the dark and good in highlands Papua New Guinea. *The Australian Journal of Anthropology* 30 (1): 35–52.

Jacka, Jerry K. 2022. Place, time, and affect: changing landscapes around a New Guinea mining area. *Cultural Anthropology* 37 (3): 549–571.

Kirsch, Stuart. 2014. *Mining Capitalism: The relationship between corporations and their critics.* Berkeley: University of California Press.

Lewis, Sanford and Diane Henkels. 1996. Good neighbor agreements: a tool for environmental and social justice. *Environmental Victims* 23 (4): 134–151.

May, James R. 2004. Discharges from historic mining properties: asserting and defending citizen suits under the Clean Water Act. In *Proceedings of the Rocky Mountain Mineral Law Fiftieth Annual Institute.* Westminster, CO: Rocky Mountain Mineral Law Foundation, pp. 23. 1–23. 38.

May, R.J. and Matthew Spriggs. 1990. *The Bougainville Crisis.* Bathurst, NSW: Crawford House Press.

Nixon, Robert. 2011. *Slow Violence and the Environmentalism of the Poor.* Cambridge: Harvard University Press.

Nuttall, Mark. 2013. Zero-tolerance, uranium and Greenland's mining future. *The Polar Journal* 3 (2): 368–383.

Odell, Scott D., Anthony Bebbington, and Karen E. Frey. 2018. Mining and climate change: a review and framework for analysis. *The Extractive Industries and Society* 5: 201–214.

Porsani, Jorge Luís, Felipe A.N. de Jesus and Marcelo César Stangari. 2019. GPR survey on an iron mining area after the collapse of the tailings dam at the Córrego do Feijão mine in Brumadinho-MG, Brazil. *Remote Sensing* 11 (7): 860. http://dx.doi.org/10.3390/rs11070860.

Prno, Jason and D. Scott Slocombe. 2012. Exploring the origins of "social license to operate" in the mining sector: perspectives from governance and sustainability theories. *Resources Policy* 37 (3): 346–357.

Ren, Kun, Jie Zeng, Jiapeng Liang, Daoxian Yuan, Youjun Jiao, Cong Peng and Xiaodong Pan. 2021. Impacts of acid mine drainage on karst aquifers: evidence from hydrogeochemistry, stable sulfur and oxygen isotopes. *Science of the Total Environment* 761. https://doi.org/10.1016/j.scitotenv.2020.143223.

Scott, James. 1998. *Seeing Like a State: How certain schemes to improve the human condition have failed.* New Haven: Yale University Press.

Smith, Duane. 2009. *The Trail of Gold and Silver: Mining in Colorado, 1859–2009.* Boulder: University Press of Colorado.

Wardlow, Holly. 2019. With AIDS I am happier than I ever have been before. *The Australian Journal of Anthropology* 30 (1): 53–67.

WMO. 2022. *State of the Global Climate, 2021.* https://library.wmo.int/doc_num.php?explnum_id=11178 (Accessed September 18, 2022).

World Bank. 2020. *Minerals for Climate Action: The mineral intensity of the clean energy transition.* Washington, DC: World Bank.

7

GETTING IT RIGHT

What Needs to be Done to Ensure First Nations' Participation and Benefit from Large-Scale Renewable Energy Developments on Country?

Katie Quail, Donna Green, and Ciaran O'Faircheallaigh

Background

Australia's First Nations peoples are suffering from ongoing disadvantage. Since the arrival of European colonizers in 1788, Aboriginal and Torres Strait Islander people have suffered a history of dispossession and removal from Country. In this context, Country refers to the lands, waterways, and seas to which Aboriginal and Torres Strait Islander peoples are connected. The term Country encompasses all living things as well as spiritual beliefs, culture, language, family, and identity (AIATSIS 2022). Still today, Indigenous Australians remain disadvantaged when compared to Australia's non-Indigenous population and are suffering from significant gaps in health, income, and standards of living (Commonwealth of Australia 2020).

Climate change is entrenching this disadvantage, with Indigenous and other vulnerable populations being disproportionally affected. In Northern Australia, the impacts of climate change are exacerbating the already stressed social and economic situations for the majority of communities (Green et al. 2010; Hoicka et al. 2021; IPCC 2022a; Krupa 2013; Lipp and Bale 2018). As the global community looks to develop climate resilience, the IPCC recommends that governments, civil society, and the private sector must make inclusive development choices that prioritise equity and justice, including for Indigenous peoples (IPCC 2022a).

Australia has made commitments under the Paris Agreement to reduce its carbon emissions by 2030 to 43% of the 2005 levels and to achieve net zero by 2050 (DISER 2022). The IPCC Sixth Assessment Report makes it clear that more is needed if we want to avoid worsening impacts and irreversible change. Mitigating the impacts of climate change and increasing our chances of a sustainable future requires immediate action, including the urgent need to move away from the use and export of fossil fuels and transition towards renewable forms of energy (IPCC 2022b).

The clean energy transition, if done well, presents an opportunity to address both climate change and Indigenous disadvantage. With much of the land in Australia belonging to the Indigenous Estate (see Figure 7.1), there could be significant opportunities for First

DOI: 10.4324/9781003242499-10

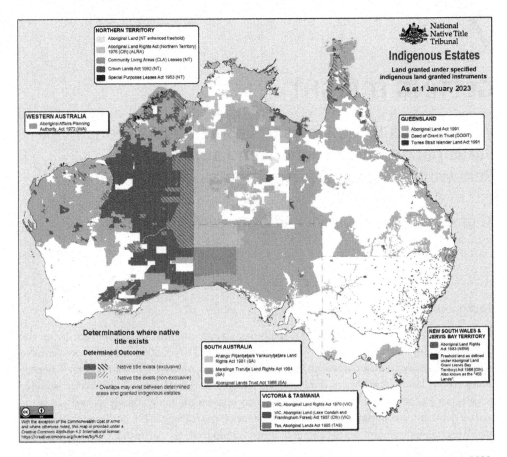

FIGURE 7.1 The National Native Title Tribunal's Map of the Indigenous Estate as at January 1, 2023. Source: National Native Title Tribunal http://www.nntt.gov.au/Maps/Indigenous_Estates_and_Determinations_A1L.pdf

Nations people to benefit from large-scale renewable energy developments on Country. First Nations communities could see benefits in the form of increased economic independence, greater employment opportunities, equity and ownership of projects, and ultimately, the right to determine how their land and its resources are used and developed by others. However, Australia's history with the extractive industry indicates that negotiating and implementing agreements is a complex issue and agreement outcomes can be highly variable (O'Faircheallaigh 2004, 2015, 2021). Researchers have warned that "there are no guarantees that inclusive Indigenous development will be achieved as this new renewable energy industry takes off unless measures are taken to ensure this" (Hunt et al. 2021: 4). As we move forward with the renewable energy industry, new approaches are needed that are built upon the foundations of Indigenous self-determination and climate justice so that the clean energy transition can also be a just transition for Australia's First Nations peoples.

In this chapter we describe the journey of the research team as we collaborate across disciplines and work with communities in adapting to both the challenges and opportunities posed by climate change. We explore what can be learnt from experiences with the extractive industry, how legal regimes shape agreement-making opportunities and what the current normative rules are for best practice in Australia. Finally, we outline our plan going forward as we work towards our goal of empowering First Nations peoples to ensure maximum benefit from future large-scale renewable energy agreements on Country.

Who are We and How Did We Get Here?

We are a group of non-Indigenous researchers with cross-disciplinary research expertise and differing career stages but with a shared interest in the goals of this research project. Donna Green, an interdisciplinary environmental scientist, has over 20 years' experience working at the intersection of energy policy, climate impacts, and Indigenous research. Ciaran O'Faircheallaigh is a political scientist whose research and professional practice focuses on the inter-relationship between First Peoples and large-scale extractive industry. Katie Quail has a background in science and education and is a PhD candidate whose research focuses on large-scale renewable energy developments on Indigenous lands.

After some initial research to scope out the topic for this chapter, we engaged with the Indigenous Land and Sea Corporation (ILSC), a corporate Commonwealth entity whose primary purpose is to assist Aboriginal and Torres Strait Islander people to enjoy opportunities and benefits associated with the return and management of Country. The ILSC shared our vision and we co-hosted a hybrid in-person/online workshop with the ILSC in Melbourne during March 2022 to discuss opportunities and creative new approaches to ensure First Nations' participation and benefit from large-scale renewable energy developments on Country. In attendance at the workshop were First Nations stakeholders, renewable energy experts, legal experts, and other academics from anthropology, law, policy, energy, and earth and environmental science backgrounds. The workshop ran over the course of two days and featured keynote presentations as well as opportunities for round table and whole group discussions. It was a lively event, full of new and enriching ideas and a collective sense of purpose and drive.

Following the workshop, we officially partnered with both the ILSC and the First Nations Clean Energy Network (FNCEN). The FNCEN is a network of First Nations peoples and organizations working in partnership with industry groups, unions, academics, technical advisors, legal experts, renewables companies and others to ensure that First Nations communities can participate in and share in the benefits of the clean energy boom. The role of the ILSC and the FNCEN has been to provide steering and feedback on the project from an Indigenous perspective, to help connect us to key stakeholders and to ensure the project aligns with the goals and aspirations of First Nations peoples.

The following sections outline the renewable energy opportunity in more detail, what we have learnt so far about agreement-making and what constitutes best practice from our review of the current literature.

Understanding the Opportunity

Australia has some of the highest solar radiation in the world, and in some locations this is matched with excellent night-time wind resources (Thorburn et al. 2019). Northern Australia is also close enough to Asian markets to enable the export of this "green" electricity. With the International Energy Agency predicting that energy demand in the

Southeast Asian region is set to rise at twice the global average in the coming decades (IEA 2019; Riley 2021), the combination of these "ideal" factors makes Australia a desirable location for large-scale renewable energy developments, positioning the country to become a "renewable energy superpower" (Chambers et al. 2018; Chandrashekeran 2021: 380; Garnaut 2019; O'Neill et al. 2019).

Taking advantage of these conditions, there have already been several major proposals for Gigawatt-scale renewable energy projects in Australia. The Western Green Energy Hub, the largest and most recent proposal with a capacity of up to 50 GW of combined wind and solar, is to be located on the lands of the Mirning People in southern Western Australia. The project intends to produce green hydrogen and ammonia[1] to be exported to Asia and when built, would be the largest renewable energy development in the world (InterContinental Energy 2022).

Similarly, the Australia-Asia PowerLink Project (AAPowerLink) being developed by SunCable would be the world's largest solar farm and battery. With a proposed capacity of up to 20 GW of solar and approximately 40 GWh of battery storage, AAPowerLink will supply 15% of Singapore's electricity needs (SunCable 2022). It will transmit electricity from Powell Creek in the Northern Territory via overhead cable to Darwin and submarine cable to Singapore. The solar arrays will be located on the Nurrdalinji Native Title Area, which is jointly shared with an existing pastoral lease (Dyer 2020).

Other notable gigawatt-scale projects that have been proposed include the Australian Renewable Energy Hub (AREH) located on the lands of the Nyangumarta People in the East Pilbara region of Western Australia and Desert Bloom, a renewable hydrogen project to be located in Tennant Creek in the Northern Territory.

In addition to these giga-projects, there are many more large-scale renewable energy developments of 10 MW or greater being developed and proposed all over Australia (see for example Renew Economy 2022a; Renew Economy 2022b). As much of this land belongs to the Indigenous Estate, there could be significant opportunities for Traditional Owners and communities to help protect Country while providing a pathway towards economic independence and the enhanced well-being that such independence will bring (Thorburn et al. 2019). In the words of Ms Karrina Nolan, Yorta Yorta woman, executive director of Original Power and steering group member of the FNCEN, "we believe we must treat the crisis of climate change as an opportunity for our people to be part of the economic transition to clean and sustainable energies" (O'Neill et al. 2021a: 2).

Through our collaboration with the ILSC and the FNCEN, we are investigating measures that could be put in place to ensure that Aboriginal and Torres Strait Islander peoples receive equitable benefits from large-scale renewable energy developments on their lands. If such measures are widely adopted, this opportunity could help to empower First Nations people and contribute to the alleviation of Indigenous disadvantage in Australia.

Lessons from the Extractive Industry

There is no literature analyzing agreements made between Indigenous parties and the renewable energy industry. There is, however, an extensive body of research analyzing agreements made with the extractive industry and on the impacts and benefits of mining on local Indigenous communities. While there are several obvious differences between the two industries, there is still much that can be learnt from these past experiences.

Important factors determining the success of benefits from agreements are the specific legal, policy, and institutional setting (O'Faircheallaigh 2018). However, even where agreements have been conducted within similar contexts, agreement outcomes can still be highly variable (O'Faircheallaigh 2004, 2015, 2021). Moreover, even when "good" agreements are negotiated, the anticipated benefits from these agreements have not always been realised (Altman 2009; Scambary 2009; Thorburn et al. 2019). This raises the question, why is this occurring? Are we able to explain these differences in outcomes? It is important that as the renewable energy industry expands, we learn from these experiences and identify the key factors associated with success to ensure maximum benefit from future agreements.

One of the challenges associated with achieving an equitable and beneficial agreement is the power imbalance that exists between Traditional Owners and companies in the negotiation of agreements. "Traditional Owners are almost always at a legal, economic, informational and political disadvantage to the companies they negotiate with" (O'Neill et al. 2021b: 6). Often, Traditional Owners are up against large multinational corporations with significant financial capability, in marked contrast to the Traditional Owners themselves (Altman 2009; O'Faircheallaigh 2017a). Negotiations typically occur according to the timelines of the developers (O'Neill et al. 2021b), and involve processes established by western law that Traditional Owners may find culturally alien (Howard-Wagner and Maguire 2010). The same situation applies in other settler states such as Canada (see for example Bielawski 2003). There are also significant cultural and language barriers potentially impeding the ability of Traditional Owners to fully understand the implications of the agreements they are signing up to (Howard-Wagner and Maguire 2010). The literature makes it abundantly clear that Traditional Owners "do not negotiate on a level playing field" (Hunt et al. 2021: 4). The role of the state can further alter these power imbalances, in both positive and negative ways. Existing asymmetries in power relations are sometimes worsened as shared interests in mining have driven governments to support companies to override Aboriginal opposition (Altman 2009; Chandrashekeran 2021; Scambary 2009). The case of the Western Australian government in the Browse Basin Liquified Natural Gas agreements provides a counter example where the state government acted to increase the negotiating power of Traditional Owners (O'Neill 2015).

Poor implementation and management of agreements is another issue that helps to explain why anticipated benefits have not always eventuated. Part of the problem is that implementation issues are often poorly dealt with or forgotten within the agreements themselves, with a lack of clarity and precision regarding objectives and responsibilities widely recognised as a major barrier to successful implementation (O'Faircheallaigh 2002). In order to achieve successful implementation, "a key finding of almost every study involves the need to allocate adequate and appropriate resources, financial and human, specifically for implementation functions" (O'Faircheallaigh 2002: 14) and to ensure that structures are put in place to oversee the implementation process (see also Martin 2005; O'Faircheallaigh 2012). These institutional arrangements should be established before benefit payments begin to flow into communities (O'Faircheallaigh ibid.). In addition, the effective use of money flowing from agreements requires considerable capacity to design management structures that ensure transparency and accountability to recipient communities, combined with an ability to identify and utilise specialist financial skills and to develop a level of financial literacy among Traditional Owner beneficiaries (O'Faircheallaigh 2012). These requirements are not easy to achieve, but are not impossible. The Argyle Diamond Ltd Agreement is an example where Traditional Owners invested time and resources into the prior development of revenue management structures with successful outcomes (O'Faircheallaigh ibid.) and the Ely Trust and Port Curtis Coral Coast Trust are examples where good implementation and management have resulted in positive outcomes from limited revenue (O'Faircheallaigh 2017b).

Difficulties also frequently arise concerning the distribution of benefits amongst Traditional Owners and affected community members. In part due to the dislocation suffered by nearly all Aboriginal groups during colonisation, many Aboriginal people no longer reside on their traditional lands (O'Faircheallaigh 2010). This can cause significant tensions around the distribution of benefits between Aboriginal people for whom the development is located on their ancestral lands and therefore feel entitled to share in the benefits regardless of where they currently reside, and other Aboriginal people residing in nearby communities who are likely to be impacted by the development (Martin et al. 2014; O'Faircheallaigh ibid.). As Martin (2005) describes, western notions of fairness in relation to the wider common good do not necessarily apply within Aboriginal groups who typically have intense loyalties and obligations to close kin and family.

The question of the equity of benefit distribution between Indigenous communities also comes into play. Some nearby communities may be more disadvantaged than others and suffer from a range of health, education, and substance abuse issues that may inhibit their ability to be employed on the project, and thus feel as though despite being the most disadvantaged, they are receiving the least of the benefits (Martin 2005; Martin et al. 2014). Positive examples where these issues have been managed well include the Western Cape Communities Coexistence Agreement and the Argyle Diamonds Agreement (O'Faircheallaigh ibid.). If structures are not put in place to manage conflicting interests and disputes such as in these examples, these issues surrounding the distribution of benefits can lead to negative impacts and an escalation of conflict between and within the affected Indigenous communities that the agreements are intended to benefit (O'Faircheallaigh 2018).

Indigenous autonomy is central to self-determination and an important consideration in the agreement making process. When decisions are made by non-Indigenous parties, they are often resisted by the Aboriginal people whom they affect (O'Faircheallaigh 2012). In some cases, past agreements have curtailed, rather than fostered, Indigenous autonomy around decisions about the use of agreement funds in accordance with local aspirations (Altman 2009). Meaningful involvement of Indigenous leaders and community actors in decision-making roles, along with a high degree of transparency, are required for agreements to have the greatest chance of success (Hunt et al. 2021; O'Faircheallaigh ibid.; Stefanelli et al. 2019). It is also important for agreements to support diverse development aspirations, and it cannot be assumed that all Indigenous groups aspire to mainstream economic participation as is often assumed by the state (Altman 2009; Martin 2005; Scambary 2009).

Finally, some would argue that agreements alone are not enough to generate economic and developmental outcomes for disadvantaged Indigenous communities (Altman ibid.; Scambary ibid.). These researchers argue that government support and policies that promote economic empowerment are needed alongside agreements to effect significant mainstream economic outcomes. According to O'Neill et al. (2021b), the state plays a key role in determining the success of benefits from agreements by creating policies and legal frameworks that act to either enable or inhibit Indigenous rights and aspirations. Other researchers, such as Langton (2013: 33), have argued that "the *Native Title Act* and engagement with the mining industry have [...] catapulted Aboriginal people engaged in the mining industry into the mainstream economy." However, even Langton concedes that "more needs to be done" (ibid.: 21) to create policies that will further enable economic development for Aboriginal people.

While the prevailing legislative regime and the influence of the state have been found to affect agreement outcomes, research from the extractive industry shows that differences in outcomes can best be explained by the relative political and organizational capacity of Traditional Owners. Those Traditional Owners with strong political and organizational capacity are best able to provide the necessary financial and technical resources to support their negotiations and to insist that companies meet their demands and exceed minimum requirements (O'Faircheallaigh 2021; O'Neill et al. 2019; O'Neill et al. 2021b). Comprehensive community engagement strategies and Indigenous involvement in decision-making, along with local capacity building to support effective decision-making, are also key to successful negotiations (Altman 2009; O'Faircheallaigh ibid.; Riley 2021). Also crucial is the need to set aside resources and develop appropriate structures specifically for the implementation and governance of agreements (Martin 2005; O'Faircheallaigh 2002, 2012, 2018).

The renewable energy industry will no doubt present its own unique challenges for agreement making and equitable benefit sharing. However, by taking on board these valuable lessons from Australia's long history of mining on Country, we can aim to learn from the successes and mistakes of the past to have the best chance of achieving desired outcomes from future agreements.

The Law of the Land

Research has pointed to landownership and native title rights as being the key to leveraging negotiations and unlocking potential benefits and opportunities for Traditional Owners and their communities (Altman 2009; Chandrashekeran 2021; O'Neill et al. 2021b; Riley 2021). The legal context in which agreements with Indigenous peoples take place provides the foundations for negotiation and implementation, and as such, "directly impacts the extent and enjoyment of benefits that flow to Indigenous parties" (Tehan and Godden 2012: 111; Gibson and O'Faircheallaigh 2015). In Australia, there are two main forms of legal regimes governing Indigenous Peoples' rights and interests in land, namely; the Native Title Act 1993 (Cth[2]), and various state or territory-based forms of land rights, most notably the Aboriginal Land Rights Act (Northern Territory) Act 1976 (Cth) (the "Land Rights Act").

While agreement outcomes depend on a multitude of factors, and as such can be highly variable (Altman 2009; O'Faircheallaigh 2004, 2021), the legal context dictates the minimum standards that must be followed particularly during the negotiation phase. In this respect, the Land Rights Act provides stronger legal rights for Traditional Owners than Native Title (Chandrashekeran 2021; O'Neill et al. 2019). Under the Land Rights Act, the land is Aboriginal freehold land and resource developers must obtain the free, prior and informed consent (FPIC) of Traditional Owners for any proposed developments. This legislation empowers Traditional Owners by giving them the right to veto unwanted development on their lands.

The Native Title Act 1993 (Cth) represents a recognition under Australian law of title that pre-existed the declaration of British sovereignty. In order for Traditional Owners to achieve a determination of Native Title, they must be able to demonstrate a continuing connection to the land from before the time sovereignty was claimed by the British until the present day. They must also prove that Native Title has not been extinguished by a valid grant of title by the Crown. This is problematic in two ways: it has trapped Indigenous Australians in a western legal definition of authenticity, requiring them to prove entitlement to their ancestral lands (Altman 2009; Howard-Wagner and Maguire 2010), and it means that Indigenous Australians who suffered the earliest and most severe forms of dispossession are least likely to be recognised under Native Title (Chandrashekeran 2021).

Determinations of Native Title can be either non-exclusive or exclusive. If at the time when a Native Title claim is determined there are other interests in the land, for example a pastoral lease, then Native Title will be determined to be non-exclusive, and Traditional Owners must share their rights in land with the other parties. Whatever its form, the right to veto that applies under the Land Rights Act does not apply to Native Title. Rather, Traditional Owners with a Native Title determination or registered claim are entitled to a six month right to negotiate. If an agreement has not been reached by the end of this period, either party may refer the case to the National Native Title Tribunal (NNTT) for a determination. It should be noted, however, that as of March 2022, 98% (137 out of 140) of these rulings have been in favour of the developer (NNTT 2022). As O'Neill et al. (2019: 9) put it, the Native Title Act was "written to allow 'future acts' to occur." It is widely recognised within the literature that the Native Title framework is skewed in favour of developers (Altman 2009; Chandrashekeran 2021; Howard-Wagner and Maguire 2010; O'Neill et al. 2021b; Riley 2021).

When the Native Title Act was legislated in 1993, it was hard to imagine at the time that wind, solar, and other renewable energy projects would be developed on the scale that we are seeing today. As a result, the Act does not specifically refer to such projects, leaving it open to interpretation as to how the law will be applied.

Section s24KA of the Native Title "future acts" division deals with facilities for services to the public and is the most relevant section of the future act division for large-scale renewable energy developments. The division contains a list of covered facilities, including any other thing that is similar to the listed facilities, for which the subdivision should apply. Depending on whether large-scale renewable energy developments are considered to be similar to the facilities listed in the act, s24KA may or may not apply. Arguments for both cases are presented in the literature (O'Neill et al. 2021b; Chandrashekeran 2021).

If s24KA is found to apply, it is possible that Native Title holders may not have the right to negotiate or object to renewable energy developments on their land, which would be a weakening of their rights compared to those afforded to mining proposals. However, O'Neill et al. (2021b: 4) argue that the more persuasive view is that the subdivision would not apply, in which case "renewable energy developers, unlike mineral extraction proponents, likely require native title holders to consent to the grant of any interests required for any renewables development – unless a government moves to compulsorily acquire the land."

With the uptake of large-scale renewable energy developments being relatively recent in comparison to the long history of extractive projects, and the lack of transparency shrouding agreements related to renewable energy projects, it is difficult to determine which interpretation of s24KA is guiding agreement making in practice (O'Neill et al. 2021b). Uncertainty remains as to whether the right to negotiate that exists for extractive projects will continue to apply to renewable energy developments, and if not, what the new procedures will be. If the second, "more persuasive" view presented by O'Neill et al. (ibid.) is in fact correct, there is, however, the potential for the leverage of Traditional Owners in the negotiation of agreements to increase with the transition to renewable energy developments.

Normative Rules for Best Practice in Australia

In writing on renewable energy development on the Indigenous Estate and best practice agreement making in Australia, O'Neill et al. (ibid.: 7) propose the following best practice principles based on their review of agreement making experiences predominantly involving the extractive industry in Australia and Canada over the past two decades.

Best practice is:
- Adhering to a robust interpretation of "free, prior and informed consent" when seeking to access and use land on the Indigenous Estate.
- Paying attention to the priorities of the local community.
- Ensuring that the land holding group are resourced to obtain qualified independent legal, scientific, business, accounting and other advice for the negotiation.
- Having all parties develop the agenda, nature and timelines of the negotiation, rather than these being determined by a company alone.
- Negotiating in a respectful manner and in good faith, while recognising the need for a robust negotiation.
- Quantifying benefits based on a "sharing the benefit" methodology for the proposed activity.
- Ensuring a whole-of-company and whole-of-lifecycle commitment to these principles, including by future owners of the project should company structure or ownership change, and that arrangements for eventual land rehabilitation are made.
- Considering paying benefits to more First Nations people than just the Traditional Owners, including, for example, neighbouring Traditional Owners or other First Nations peoples in the region.
- Adhering to the agreement fully at the implementation stage, and regularly monitoring, evaluating and reviewing whether the agreement is being fully adhered to.
- Recognising that First Nations people retain sovereignty over all land in Australia, whether they have legal rights or not.
- Recognising that a company must obtain a "social licence to operate" that may be well above what is legally required.
- Recognising that a social licence to operate, particularly for multi-generational projects, may need to allow for review and renegotiation of certain clauses from time to time.

At an international level, the United Nations Declaration on the Rights of Indigenous Peoples (UNDRIP) stipulates the rights of Indigenous Peoples and the role of the state when it comes to resource development on Indigenous lands. Article 32 is of particular relevance, and is shown in full below:

1. Indigenous peoples have the right to determine and develop priorities and strategies for the development or use of their lands or territories and other resources.
2. States shall consult and cooperate in good faith with the Indigenous Peoples concerned through their own representative institutions in order to obtain their free and informed consent prior to the approval of any project affecting their lands or territories and other resources, particularly in connection with the development, utilisation or exploitation of mineral, water or other resources.
3. States shall provide effective mechanisms for just and fair redress for any such activities, and appropriate measures shall be taken to mitigate adverse environmental, economic, social, cultural or spiritual impact (UNDRIP 2007).

UNDRIP advocates for Indigenous self-determination and free, prior, and informed consent (FPIC), both of which are recognised pillars of best practice agreement making (O'Neill et al. ibid.). Although Australia is a signatory of UNDRIP, these principles are yet to be enshrined within domestic law (O'Neill et al. ibid.). The legal rights afforded to Traditional Owners within the Native Title framework in particular are far from that of FPIC and do not represent best practice (O'Neill et al. ibid.). This is despite the fact that, as Riley (2021) notes, implementing FPIC can be beneficial not just for Traditional Owners but for companies and their investors as well, by reducing their financial, legal, operational and reputational risk. In the absence of a nationally recognised cogent policy framework on best practice agreement making, several other organizations, industry groups and state-level government institutions have developed their own best practice standards and guides for benefit sharing (see for example CEC 2019, 2021; DELWP 2019 2021; O'Neill et al. 2021a).

The literature shows that where companies engage in genuine partnerships with Indigenous Peoples and are themselves committed to best practice principles, Traditional Owners are empowered to create agreements tailored to their specific goals and aspirations which go beyond economic development to include recognition of title to the land, Caring for Country, autonomy and the choice between traditional and mainstream livelihoods (Altman 2009; Chandrashekeran 2021; Hoicka et al. 2021; Riley 2021; Scambary 2009; Stefanelli et al. 2019). Not only this, but when renewable energy policies and processes are in alignment with the UNDRIP and adhere to FPIC, they have the potential to support reconciliation and healing efforts in settler-colonial states such as Australia (Stefanelli et al. ibid.).

Where to from Here?

Our analysis of the literature and the discussions from the workshop have provided us with a useful starting point from which to go forward. Following the workshop, we obtained ethical approval to conduct a series of one-on-one interviews to further discuss these ideas in depth. Beginning with the participants of the workshop, we used snowball sampling to increase the diversity and range of participants. Interview questions were developed based on the ideas and themes that came out of the workshop discussions and literature review. At the time of writing this chapter, these interviews are currently underway and we hope that they will shed light on what is needed to ensure First Nations benefit from large-scale renewable energy developments on Country.

Conclusion

Climate change is occurring at a rapid and unprecedented rate, with irreversible damage and catastrophic impacts becoming increasingly more likely for every additional degree of warming (IPCC 2021). In every region of the world, it is those populations that are most vulnerable that are likely to experience the worst of these impacts (IPCC 2022a). For Australia, this means the potential for climate change to further entrench the ongoing disadvantage faced by Aboriginal and Torres Strait Islander peoples.

Transitioning to renewable forms of energy will be crucial for limiting greenhouse gas emissions and the mitigation of climate change. Large-scale renewable energy developments on Indigenous owned land represent a unique opportunity for reconciliation and the empowerment of First Nations Australians through equitable benefit sharing and First Nations' ownership of projects while at the same time taking much needed action on climate change.

However, the issues associated with agreement making are complex, multi-dimensional, and intertwined. With no guarantee of a just transition unless measures are taken to ensure this, we have been working with the ILSC and FNCEN to explore what such measures could be. By drawing on valuable research from past experiences with the extractive industry and engaging in cross-disciplinary research incorporating the views of a range of different actors from community, government, and industry, we attempt to tackle some of these issues to better understand how to overcome the barriers associated with effective agreement making and identify what measures can be taken to empower Aboriginal and Torres Strait Islander peoples as we urgently transition towards a clean energy future.

Notes

1 The synthetic production of hydrogen through the electrolysis of water and similarly of ammonia by combining nitrogen with hydrogen requires large amounts of energy. When the energy used for this process comes from renewable energy sources such as solar and wind, it is considered to be "green" hydrogen or ammonia. This is in contrast to "grey" hydrogen or ammonia in which fossil fuels are used as the source of energy, or "blue" hydrogen or ammonia in which fossil fuels are used but the emissions from these fossil fuels are captured through various methods of carbon capture and storage.
2 In Australian jurisdictions, Cth refers to the Commonwealth of Australia.

References

AIATSIS. 2022. What is Country? *AIATSIS*. May 25, 2022. https://aiatsis.gov.au/explore/welcome-country#toc-what-is-country-.

Altman, Jon. 2009. Benefit sharing is no solution to development: experiences from mining on Aboriginal land in Australia. In *Indigenous Peoples, Consent and Benefit Sharing*, edited by

R. Wynberg, D. Schroeder, and R. Chennells. Dordrecht: Springer Netherlands. https://doi.org/10.1007/978-90-481-3123-5_15.

CEC. 2019. *A Guide to Benefit Sharing Options for Renewable Energy Projects.* https://assets.cleanenergycouncil.org.au/documents/advocacy-initiatives/community-engagement/guide-to-benefit-sharing-options-for-renewable-energy-projects.pdf.

CEC. 2021. *Best Practice Charter for Renewable Energy Projects.* https://www.cleanenergycouncil.org.au/advocacy-initiatives/community-engagement/best-practice-charter.

Chambers, Ian, Jeremy Russell-Smith, Robert Costanza, Julian Cribb, Sean Kerins, Melissa George, Glenn James, et al. 2018. Australia's North, Australia's future: a vision and strategies for sustainable economic, ecological and social prosperity in Northern Australia. *Asia and the Pacific Policy Studies* 5 (3): 615–640. https://doi.org/10.1002/app5.259.

Chandrashekeran, Sangeetha. 2021. Rent and reparation: how the law shapes Indigenous opportunities from large renewable energy projects. *Local Environment* 26 (3): 379–396. https://doi.org/10.1080/13549839.2020.1861590.

Commonwealth of Australia. 2020. *Closing the Gap Report 2020.* https://ctgreport.niaa.gov.au/sites/default/files/pdf/closing-the-gap-report-2020.pdf.

DELWP. 2019. *Pupangarli Marnmarnepu "Owning Our Future": Aboriginal Self-Determination Reform Strategy 2020–2025.* https://www.delwp.vic.gov.au/__data/assets/pdf_file/0038/483887/Pupangarli-Marnmarnepu-Owning-Our-Future-Aboriginal-Self-Determination-Reform-Strategy-2020-2025.pdf.

DELWP. 2021. *Community Engagement and Benefit Sharing in Renewable Energy Development in Victoria: A guide for renewable energy developers.* https://www.energy.vic.gov.au/__data/assets/pdf_file/0036/536787/Community-Engagement-and-Benefit-Sharing-Guide.pdf.

DISER. 2022. *"International Climate Change Commitments."* June 17, 2022. https://www.industry.gov.au/policies-and-initiatives/international-climate-change-commitments.

Dyer, Blake. 2020. *Submission by Nurrdalinji Native Title Aboriginal Corporation Regarding Australia-ASEAN PowerLink.*

Garnaut, Ross. 2019. *Superpower.* Melbourne: La Trobe University Press.

Green, Donna, Jack Billy, and Alo Tapim. 2010. Indigenous Australians' knowledge of weather and climate. *Climatic Change* 100 (2): 337–354. https://doi.org/10.1007/s10584-010-9803-z.

Hoicka, Christina E., Katarina Savic, and Alicia Campney. 2021. Reconciliation through renewable energy? A survey of Indigenous communities, involvement, and Peoples in Canada. *Energy Research and Social Science* 74 (April). https://doi.org/10.1016/j.erss.2020.101897.

Howard-Wagner, Deirdre and Amy Maguire. 2010. "The Holy Grail" or #2The Good, the Bad and the Ugly"?: A qualitative exploration of the ILUAs agreement-making process and the relationship between ILUAs and Native Title. *Australian Indigenous Law Review* 14 (1): 71–85. https://doi.org/10.3316/ielapa.587125905959902.

Hunt, J., B. Riley, L. O'Neill, and G. Maynard. 2021. Transition to renewable energy and Indigenous People in Northern Australia: enhancing or inhibiting capabilities? *Journal of Human Development and Capabilities.* https://doi.org/10.1080/19452829.2021.1901670.

IEA. 2019. *Southeast Asia Energy Outlook 2019.* Paris. https://www.iea.org/reports/southeast-asia-energy-outlook-2019.

InterContinental Energy. 2022. *Western Green Energy Hub.* https://intercontinentalenergy.com/western-green-energy-hub.

IPCC. 2021. *Climate Change 2021: The Physical Science Basis: Summary for policymakers.* Contribution of Working Group I to the Sixth Assessment Report of the Intergovernmental Panel on Climate Change. Cambridge and New York: Cambridge University Press. https://www.ipcc.ch/report/ar6/wg1/downloads/report/IPCC_AR6_WGI_SPM.pdf.

IPCC. 2022a. *Climate Change 2022: Impacts, Adaptation and Vulnerability: Summary for policymakers.* Contribution of Working Group II to the Sixth Assessment Report of the Intergovernmental Panel on Climate Change. Cambridge and New York: Cambridge University Press. https://www.ipcc.ch/report/ar6/wg2/downloads/report/IPCC_AR6_WGII_SummaryForPolicymakers.pdf.

IPCC. 2022b. *Climate Change 2022: Mitigation of Climate Change: Summary for policymakers.* Contribution of Working Group III to the Sixth Assessment Report of the Intergovernmental Panel on Climate Change. Cambridge and New York: Cambridge University Press. https://report.ipcc.ch/ar6wg3/pdf/IPCC_AR6_WGIII_SummaryForPolicymakers.pdf.

Langton, Marcia. 2013. *Boyer Lectures 2012: The Quiet Revolution: Indigenous people and the resources boom.* Sydney: ABC Books.

Martin, David. 2005. Enhancing and measuring social sustainability by the minerals industry: a case study of Australian Aboriginal People. In *Sustainable Development Indicators in the Minerals Industry*, proceedings of the Aachen International Mining Symposia, RWTH Aachen University, Institute of Mining Engineering, Aachen University, Germany, 663–679.

Martin, David, David Trigger, and Joni Parmenter. 2014. Mining in Aboriginal Australia: economic impacts, sustainable livelihoods and cultural difference at Century Mine, Northwest Queensland. In *Natural Resource Extraction and Indigenous Livelihoods: Development challenges in an era of globalisation*, edited by Emma Gilberthorpe and Gavin Hilson, 37–56. Ashgate.

NNTT. 2022. *Register of Future Act Decisions.* http://www.nntt.gov.au/searchRegApps/FutureActs/Pages/default.aspx.

O'Faircheallaigh, Ciaran. 2002. Implementation: the forgotten dimension of agreement making in Australia and Canada. *Indigenous Law Bulletin* 5 (20): 14–17. https://doi.org/10.3316/agispt.20034683.

O'Faircheallaigh, Ciaran. 2004. Evaluating Agreements between Indigenous Peoples and Resource Developers. In *Honour Among Nations? Treaties and Agreements with Indigenous People*, edited by Marcia Langton, Maureen Tehan, Lisa Palmer, and Kathryn Shain, 303–328. Melbourne: Melbourne University Press. https://doi.org/10.3316/informit.837370821281146.

O'Faircheallaigh, Ciaran. 2010. Aboriginal investment funds in Australia. In *The Political Economy of Sovereign Wealth Funds*, edited by Xu Yi-chong and Gawdat Bahgat, 157–176. London: Palgrave Macmillan UK. https://doi.org/10.1057/9780230290648_9.

O'Faircheallaigh, Ciaran. 2012. Curse or opportunity? Mineral revenues, rent seeking and development in Aboriginal Australia. In *Community Futures, Legal Architecture: Foundations for Indigenous Peoples in the global mining boom*, edited by Marcia Langton and Judy Longbottom, 45–58. Routledge.

O'Faircheallaigh, Ciaran. 2015. *Negotiations in the Indigenous World: Aboriginal Peoples and the extractive industry in Australia and Canada.* 1st ed. New York: Routledge. https://doi.org/10.4324/9781315717951.

O'Faircheallaigh, Ciaran. 2017a. Shaping projects, shaping impacts: community-controlled impact assessments and negotiated agreements. *Third World Quarterly* 38 (5): 1181–1197. https://doi.org/10.1080/01436597.2017.1279539.

O'Faircheallaigh, Ciaran. 2017b. Mining royalty payments and the governance of Aboriginal Australia: Distinguished Lecture 2017. https://concernedaustralians.com.au/media/distinguished-lecture-paper-2017.pdf.

O'Faircheallaigh, Ciaran. 2018. Using revenues from Indigenous impact and benefit agreements: building theoretical insights." *Canadian Journal of Development Studies* 39 (1): 101–118. https://doi.org/10.1080/02255189.2017.1391068.

O'Faircheallaigh, Ciaran. 2021. Explaining outcomes from negotiated agreements in Australia and Canada. *Resources Policy* 70 (March). https://doi.org/10.1016/j.resourpol.2020.101922.

O'Neill, Lily. 2015. The role of state governments in Native Title negotiations: a tale of two agreements. *Australian Indigenous Law Review* 18 (2): 29–42. https://doi.org/10.3316/ielapa.886840396984099.

O'Neill, L., B. Riley, J. Hunt, and G. Maynard. 2021a. Clean energy agreement making on First Nations land: what do strong agreements contain?https://doi.org/10.25911/VHH3-F498.

O'Neill, L., K. Thorburn, and J. Hunt. 2019. Ensuring Indigenous benefit from large-scale renewable energy projects: drawing on experience from extractive industry agreement making. https://doi.org/10.25911/5c8236f43e159.

O'Neill, Lily, Kathryn Thorburn, Bradley Riley, Ganur Maynard, Esmé Shirlow, and Janet Hunt. 2021b. Renewable energy development on the Indigenous Estate: free, prior and informed consent and best practice in agreement-making in Australia. *Energy Research and Social Science* 81 (November). https://doi.org/10.1016/j.erss.2021.102252.

Renew Economy. 2022a. Large scale solar farm map of Australia. https://reneweconomy.com.au/large-scale-solar-farm-map-of-australia/.

Renew Economy. 2022b. Large scale wind farm map of Australia. 2022. https://reneweconomy.com.au/large-scale-wind-farm-map-of-australia/.

Riley, Brad. 2021. Scaling up: renewable energy on Aboriginal lands in North West Australia. https://doi.org/10.32613/nrp/2021.6.

Scambary, Benedict. 2009. Mining agreements, development, aspirations, and livelihoods." In *Power, Culture, Economy: Indigenous Australians and mining*, edited by Jon Altman and David Martin, 1st ed., 171–201. ANU Press.

Stefanelli, Robert D., Chad Walker, Derek Kornelsen, Diana Lewis, Debbie H. Martin, Jeff Masuda, Chantelle A.M. Richmond, Emily Root, Hannah Tait Neufeld, and Heather Castleden. 2019. Renewable energy and energy autonomy: how Indigenous peoples in Canada are shaping an energy future. *Environmental Reviews*. Canadian Science Publishing. https://doi.org/10.1139/er-2018-0024.

SunCable. 2022. *SunCable - The World's Largest Solar Energy Infrastructure Project*. 2022. https://suncable.sg.

Tehan, Maureen and Lee Godden. 2012. Legal forms and their implications for long-term relationships and economic, cultural and social empowerment. In *Community Futures, Legal Architecture: Foundations for Indigenous Peoples in the global mining boom*, edited by Marcia Langton and J. Longbottom, 1st ed., 111–132. Routledge.

Thorburn, K, L. O'Neill, and B. Riley. 2019. Renewable energy projects on the Indigenous Estate: identifying risks and opportunities of utility-scale and dispersed models. https://doi.org/10.25911/5dbaaa5c47c6a.

UNDRIP. 2007. *United Nations Declaration on the Rights of Indigenous Peoples*. GA Res 61/295, 61st Sess, 107th Pen Mtg, Supp No 49, UN Doc A/RES/61/295. September 13, 2007.

8

WHITHER THE WINDS OF CHANGE? WORLDMAKING WINDS AND SEASONAL DISRUPTIONS IN THE NORTHERN CHILEAN ANDES

Penelope Dransart and Marietta Ortega Perrier

Isluga is a community located in the highlands of northern Chile, next to the frontier with Bolivia. Its people are well acquainted with the regime of ferocious winds which buffet the area. Hence our question "whither the winds of change?" is paired by another: "from whence the winds of change?" These questions are inspired by the periods of time we have spent in conversation with the community's bilingual Aymara-Spanish speakers since the late 1970s and 1980s. Frequently, on returning to Isluga, we exchange greetings with residents, who then quickly tell us how strongly the wind has whipped the arid volcanic soils in the surrounding steppe-like environment. When the wind blows without rain it is *"puro viento corriendo"* ("only wind running") or *"tierra así corriendo viento"* ("earth running so with wind"). People often use the Spanish verb *correr* – to run – to characterize the activities of winds and breezes. That winds are "runners" conveys an idea of the winds' persistence, intruding into people's daily activities. The strongly felt presence of winds goes beyond that of simply making air and clouds move.

Water and winds are both examples of what Frank Salomon (2018: 159) termed a "circulating element of the cosmos." In our conversations in Isluga, people talk about winds as though they possess a capacity for movement, endowing them with a sense of agency. Two main seasons of the year are recognized. *Jallu pacha* is the time of rains and it ought to start in November or December, ushering in a period of summer warmth. Barbara Göbel (2008) cogently draws attention to the equivalent period in northwestern Argentina by calling it "the potential rainy season." By March, the rains become more infrequent and, from May onwards, boisterous winds start to evict rain-bearing clouds from Isluga airspace.[1] The other main season, *Thaya pacha*, is the arid windy season, which dominates until a cyclical regeneration occurs with the return of the rains sometime after the feast of All Souls on November 1.

In conversations emerging from visits we made to Isluga in January and July 2017, people voiced concerns about increasing inconstancy in the seasonal occurrence of atmospheric events. Their perceptions lead us to consider what has been changing: can local residents distinguish in their daily lives between temporal variations and longer processes of change?

DOI: 10.4324/9781003242499-11

From a meteorologist's perspective, one must have access to statistical analyses of observations in series, regularly recorded over time, to detect possible symptoms of disruption in the sequencing of seasons (Lamb 2011: xxx). Longer periods over which records have been made are far more useful than short timescales to compare weather observations with those of the past and to make forecasts for the future. Unlike France, however, which from 1775 established the daily keeping of records, such as temperature, barometric pressure, and rainfall, on a country-wide basis (Lamb 2011: xxv), weather recording in northern Chile presents a much shorter series. The earliest weather records from Colchane, on the Chilean frontier with Bolivia, run from the second half of the 1980s, soon after our first visits to Isluga (Figure 8.1). Our conversations with community elders concern memories reaching back further in time. Such recall by people in the present is nevertheless a short-term perspective in terms of meteorological time depth.

Local people's understanding of weather conditions coincide in important respects with meteorologically collected data (Dransart and Ortega Perrier 2021: 107). In this chapter, we consider how people talk about the seasons in relation to spatial and temporal awareness of Isluga terrain, including the atmosphere accompanying that terrain. Instead of offering a meteorological approach, our focus is more similar to that of Esther Katz and Annamária Lammel (2008), in their consideration of human intersections with weathers in Mesoamerica, where people regard water and wind as having capacities to "feel" or to "be annoyed" by certain human actions. They explain that air, water, and the warmth of the sun enter and leave our bodies; weather is "in us and we are in the weather" (*"El clima está en nosotros y estamos en el clima,"* – Katz and Lammel 2008). Further north in the Americas, Mark Nuttall (2009: 299) observes that Greenlanders know weather, or climate, as *sila*, which they understand "as the breath of life, the reason things move or change."

Previous studies have drawn attention to the importance of water in concepts of worldmaking (for example, Hastrup 2009; Orlove and Caton 2010; Crate 2011; Hastrup and Rubow 2014; Rasmussen 2015). In some of our earlier publications, we have drawn

FIGURE 8.1 Mean wind speed at 100 m in the Province of Tarapaca, Chile. Map generated by Global Wind Atlas online application website (v3.1), owned by the Technical University of Denmark, with place names added relevant to this chapter.

attention to the cycling of water/blood through the land in relation to the souls of the dead in Isluga (Ortega Perrier 2001) and the circulation of air through living bodies and hand-woven textiles (Dransart 2002: 122–123; Dransart 2010: 91–92). This chapter develops our study of winds and airs in what we call weather-worlding, taking into account seasonal relationships between airs and waters.[2] Tim Ingold has also considered the "commingling" of human bodies in air, in what he characterises as a "weather-world" (Ingold 2007: S29). What we offer here is a study of not only how people relate to the airs within and surrounding human and other bodies, but how winds shape physical and conceptual worlds using the case of Isluga (Figure 8.2) to illustrate.

Residents in Isluga characterize the bitterly cold and aggressive winds of *thaya pacha* as older and younger brothers in a form of weather-worlding in which airs, land, waters, and seasons constitute each other in a relational manner. People are attentive to the timing of seasonal periodicities. What intrigues us is how, in a society not used to relying on written records such as diaries or calendars, people track seasons and seasonal variation.

How the alternating drought of one season and the rains of another behave through time in Mesoamerica is one of the concerns addressed by Katz and Lammel (2008). Ancient Maya people devised an ephemeris, a tabulation of future positions of celestial bodies such as planets or comets, in order to track weather cycles. Such devices might not always exist in documentary form and, in our concluding section, we consider calendrical record keeping in the Andes in relation to the seasons. Without establishing sequences of what happens when, it is difficult to be certain how weather patterns are changing, or whether observed changes fit within a range of more or less normal variations.

FIGURE 8.2 Moist pasture grounds called *bofedal* in Araxsaya, Isluga, northern Chile. A standing stone called *abuelo* ("grandfather") in the foreground is eroded by winds. Kawaraya, a mountain range in Bolivia, is in the background. Photograph by P. Dransart taken on July 22, 2017.

Winds from Above and from Within

Rain-bearing clouds arrive in Isluga during *Jallu pacha* by convection from the Atlantic Ocean and Amazon River basin. Present-day precipitation over the Andean plateau is strongly associated with upper-level easterlies, which influence air circulation at low levels between November and March (Garreaud 2009: 6; Insel et al. 2010: 1486). Isluga people use the term *qinaya* for a cumulus cloud (plural *qinayanaka*). They say that such clouds arrive with Manqhathaya, which are winds from the east, perceived as from "within" or "below." The community's territory is spatially divided into two moieties, one located north of the central town of Islug Marka and the other on its south and southeast. Araxsaya is the more mountainous or northernmost "upper" division, while Manqhasaya is the "inner" or "lower" part next to the international frontier with Bolivia, facing "inwards" towards the high Andean plateau. This social organization of territory forms the basis that residents use to describe the directions from where the winds and rains come, as well as the seasons when these directions prevail. During *Thaya pacha*, strong westerlies sweep into Isluga airspace, blocking circulation from the east. In Isluga, these fierce westerlies are called Araxthaya ("winds from above"). Rain or snow fall in *Jallu pacha* when the softer Manqhathaya winds arrive from "below."

Qinayanaka do not release their moisture in the form of precipitation on their own. People associate rain-producing clouds when a mist they call *kamañchaka* or *urpu* carries moisture from the Pacific and joins with *qinaya*. Mama Macrina described the event as an encounter: "*Se encuentra con kamañchaka con qinaya y llueve*" ("*Kamañchaka* meets with *qinaya* and it rains"). These now saturated cumulonimbus clouds have a flat underbelly which has turned black (Figure 8.3). Mama Soria called them *urpu* or *ch'iju*

FIGURE 8.3 Cumulonimbus clouds known as *ch'iju jallu* in the sky above the volcano hill in Araxsaya, Isluga, northern Chile. Mama Soria and her son Roberto are earthing up potatoes. Photograph taken by M. Ortega Perrier on January 26, 2017.

jallu, a term for rain-bearing clouds often used in ritual contexts. She described them as *ch'iyara* ("black") and seated over the hills. This use of the Aymara term for "black" featured in a phrase listed by the Jesuit Ludovico Bertonio, an early European student of the language, along with an approximate rendition in Spanish:

> Hallu quenaya cchaara pachaqui huayujascana: Esta va sobre el monte vna nube muy cargada de agua [Jallu qinaya ch'iyara pachaki wayujaskana: This goes over the hill, a cloud very charged with water].
>
> *(Bertonio 1612: 100)*

In the original Aymara, the cloud is "black," which equals "saturated" or, in the Spanish gloss, "charged with water." It is "seated" (*pachaki*) over the hill while it drops its contents on the earth.

Tata Andrés observed that, in his youth, the rains usually arrived by December 4. This date is significant because it was the day when people used to celebrate the fiesta of Santa Bárbara, a saint popularly associated with thunderbolts. It marked the beginning of a month of fiestas during which people from various parts of Isluga congregated in Islug marka (Dransart 2002: 53–56). The period culminated in the fiesta of Santo Tomás, the patron of Isluga, coinciding with the summer solstice on December 21. Tata Andrés described *qinaya* as being "*más blanquecino*" ("whiter") than *ch'iju jallu*, which "*más negro sale, medio negro*" ("come out more black, half black").

During *Thaya pacha*, the fierce westerlies strip the clouds from Isluga airspace. Visible clouds during this cold season include wispy cirrus formations, called *siñawaya*, and halo phenomena. People associate particularly strong winds, called Thaya Santiago, with the fiesta of St James the Greater on July 25. According to the Global Wind Atlas, the months with the least variable wind speeds in Isluga are March and April.[3] Wind speeds increase rapidly by June and are highest during July. These speeds drop slightly in August but are reinvigorated in September. With the onset of *Jallu pacha*, wind speed variability lessens between October and December, dropping further in January and February.

During *Thaya pacha*, people share stories of the cannibal westerlies. They tell how a mother, wishing to feed her sons, served them meat she had cut from her leg and cooked. The brothers ate the meat and transformed themselves into winds; the elder brother became Araxthaya and the younger, Manqhathaya. In Mama Felisa's retelling, Araxthaya left Isluga territory at Rincón Apachita, a pile of stones on the western edge of Isluga territory, a place associated with strong westerlies.[4]

At times, the cannibal brothers thrust themselves into the rainy season, herding rain-bearing clouds beyond the confines of Isluga airspace. If, in the past, the rains failed to arrive in December, Isluga people organized a territory-wide rain ceremony in January with the purpose of summoning the *ch'iju jallu* clouds. Annually elected husband-and-wife teams, known as *caciques* or "stewards," one pair representing Araxsaya and the other Manqhasaya, organized the ceremony. In Araxsaya, the upper moiety, the cacique and his wife led community members to a shrine dedicated to Saint James the Greater on the top of Q'urawani, a hill located next to the hamlet of Caraguano (Figure 8.4). The people of Manqhasaya, the lower moiety, held the equivalent ceremony on low rising ground in the hamlet of Jach'a Uta (Martínez 1976: 301, 307). Previously, the caciques of the respective *saya* had collected sea water from the Pacific. Mama Soria's late husband

FIGURE 8.4 Cumulus clouds known as *qinayanaka* above the hill of Q'urawani in Araxsaya, Isluga, northern Chile. These clouds will not produce precipitation. Photograph taken by P. Dransart on January 22, 2017.

Tata Felipe served as cacique in Araxsaya, and they went to Iquique for the sea water. During the night time ceremony they carried it in a white basin to the top of Q'urawani, covered with white cotton, fluffy as the clouds (Dransart 2002: 56). The caciques then ground shells and starfish to suspend in the sea water as a liquid offering to the earth (Ortega Perrier 1999: 107), alongside another vessel containing local spring water (Martínez 1976: 301, note 25).

Four boys, two chosen from Araxsaya and two from Manqhasaya, were instructed to lie in beds prepared for them in the respective *saya* and to sleep until dawn. When Tata Andrés and his wife Mama Luisa were caciques in Araxsaya, the rainfall was good in January and they did not have to organize a rain calling ceremony. Tata Andrés, however, has vivid recollections of being one of the selected boys, when he and his brother were about twelve and fourteen years of age. Here is his account:

> On the hill we were made to sleep. I went with my brother, the two of us. Then the ritual specialist told us. "You know what? Now, you are not going to make a sound, nothing, and very quiet." And he knocked us to the ground. I faced below. The other, my brother, faced above, like this. So the bed was ready there; there was a *paskana* [shelter] there on the top of the hill – this is called a *jarra*, what we call a narrow bed. To wake us they make a signal with the foot. We stay asleep, asleep. Later, after a while, I wake up at around four or five in the morning, I wake up when hail has fallen, snow, covered with it, then! I didn't realise.[5]

The *ch'iju jallu* ceremony also included the sacrifice of one or two llamas and a cockerel, whose flesh was cooked and shared among the participants, and dancing to music, before the people returned to their homes (Ortega Perrier 1999: 107). Here we draw attention to some of the salient spatial and temporal dimensions of the event. During the darkness of night, the sleeping boys were made to face the directions of "above" and "below," the elder brother facing the direction of the cannibal winds from the west and the younger brother the direction from which the rain-bearing clouds were to be called into Isluga airspace. The winds tend to be at their strongest by late afternoon, and again during the night. According to Tata Andrés, Araxthaya leaves the sea and enters Isluga through the air, rushing past Rincón Apacheta. It would go on to Tata Sabaya, a mountain peak in Bolivia, visible from parts of Isluga, unless the sleeping boys can persuade it to rest.

Mama Soria's explanation that "*quta um[a] apsunini Ikikita*" ("from the lake, water is to be taken from Iquique"), emphasizes what she saw as distinctive about the rain calling ceremony; it explicitly enables the cycling of moisture from the Pacific, in the form of *kamañchaka*, to make its encounter with rain-bearing *qinayanaka* entering Isluga airspace from Bolivia. She described how the winds had to be calmed during the ceremony and the rain clouds awakened. Her use of the term "lake" in reference to the Pacific as a body of water is paralleled in our conversation with Mama Simona, a native of Pisiga Centro in Manqhasaya, now resident in Colchane. She named the sea in Iquique as "the Great River," saying

> Wind is running. Wind down below; from out of the Great River [the Pacific Ocean] then it leaves. This cloud comes out...Wind runs with a lot of air.[6]

What has been Changing?

Phrases such as "climate change" have little currency among people in Isluga. "Climate change" might not feature in daily talk because people lack familiarity with the sorts of terms used by climate scientists. More fundamental reasons, however, are likely to influence the acceptance or rejection of phrases from external sources. Because climate events take place in time and through space, the spatial construal of those temporal experiences will be different for Aymara speakers than for speakers of European languages because Aymara speakers regard the past as being in front of one's body and the future as coming from behind (Miracle and Yapita Moya 1981; Núñez and Cooperrider 2013: 224). In the Aymara language, moreover, speakers distinguish between sources of information, whether they speak from personal knowledge or from non-personal knowledge (Miracle and Yapita Moya 1981: 34). Isluga people speak from their own personal knowledge of the weather events they have experienced. They might be reluctant to invoke notions of climate change because the phrase also seems to encompass events in other people's airspaces, of which they do not have direct personal knowledge.

Isluga people do, however, recognise that the seasons are behaving differently, especially when Araxthaya winds expel rain-bearing clouds during November and December. Mama Simona explained:

> Now it is changing. There isn't rain. Wind from above [Araxsaya] is falling. Thaya pacha, from there rain arrives late. After Santiago [July 25], summer. For more rain, who knows? For four, five years it doesn't arrive.[7]

People living in the highlands of northern Chile and the western part of highland Bolivia depend on rainfall. Due to the prevailing aridity, there is a gap in glaciers and permanent snow patches on Andean mountains at latitudes of about 19° south, where Isluga is situated (Dransart and Ortega Perrier 2001: 103). Glacial meltwaters do not contribute to the hydrography of the region. When rain arrives late, the moist pastures of the *bofedales* cannot regenerate properly before the onset of *Thaya pacha*, at a time when female llamas and alpacas are still lactating after the birth of their young during *Jallu pacha*. Gaps in cloud cover allow frost to fall preventing people from planting quinoa and potatoes, the main crops cultivable at high altitude. In the words of Mama Simona:

> Without rain it's not possible to plant. Dry is this sand. No more than a little water arrives.[8]

The four or five years which Mama Simona mentioned could fit within the cycles of what Tata Apolinario called *"siete años malo, siete años bien"* (seven years bad, seven years good). During the times we have been in Isluga, we have often heard people make reference to them. These cycles might be Biblically inspired in reference to the dreams of Pharaoh in Genesis 41, in which there was an alternation between years with well-fed cattle accompanied by good-yielding grain and with emaciated cattle accompanied by wind-blasted grain (Lawrence-Mathers 2020: 7). Alternatively, they might refer to periodic El Niño events, which are repeated every two to seven years, causing ocean warmth to be redistributed in the eastern Pacific. In a preliminary report on precipitation in Isluga prepared by Paulina Ponce Philimon (n.d.), the author noted that between the second half of the 1980s and 2016, precipitation varied greatly during *Jallu pacha*, with Decembers tending to experience little rainfall. There is increasing uncertainty over which will be the driest months during the potential rainy season, although she observed that Februaries with the most rainfall tend to be associated with years of oceanic cooling during La Niña events, which intervene between El Niño oscillations.

Just as Isluga people do not use the term "climate change," they also do not refer to these cyclical events as El Niño and La Niña oscillations. In commenting on the inconstancies of rainfall in November and December, they add that February tends to be a relatively wet month of the year. Precipitation occurring during the days close to February 2, coinciding with the Catholic fiesta of Candelaria, the Virgin of Candlestick, receives the epithet of *Umaphukhullu jallu* ("downpour water rain") (Dransart and Ortega 2021: 107).

In our conversations, Isluga residents have tended to volunteer the term "change" in relation to religious observation. From the 1980s and earlier, many families in highland Chile have converted from Catholicism to Evangelical Pentecostalism. Dancing and the taking of alcohol is no longer permitted and festivities tolerated under Catholicism have ceased to be observed. In the words of Tata Andrés, *"no es como antes"* ("it is not like before"). The rain calling ceremony is a casualty of this change, because there are too few Catholic families to take on the task of coordinating the event in both Araxsaya and Manqhasaya. Yet members of Evangelical families continue to mention significant fiestas, including Santiago and Candelaria, as reference points in order to correlate weather events with the seasons of the year. A wall-painting in the Evangelical church in Enquelga of the Last Judgement depicts the volcano hill of the local landscape and the Lord appearing from *ch'iju jallu* clouds. La Candelaria is absent in the imagery, but her unspoken presence is evoked by the black base of the clouds (Figure 8.5).

FIGURE 8.5 Wall painting in an Evangelical Pentecostal Church in Araxsaya, Isluga. It depicts the second coming of Christ in a nimbus of *ch'iju jallu* clouds above the volcano hill in Isluga territory. Photograph taken by M. Ortega Perrier on January 24, 2017.

Although there are pre-Hispanic antecedents for rain petitions in the Americas (Katz and Lammel 2008), we caution against regarding all rain-calling rituals in the Americas as ancient. In reviewing the literature on rain-calling in the Andes, Francisco Gil García (2012: 146) commented that many researchers suggest that such rituals survived the extirpation of idolatry during the Colonial Period. Yet elder community members in Isluga did not consider the form of the rain-calling ceremony we described in the previous section to have Inka origins, which they sometimes attribute to other ritual practices. In conversation with Tata Paulino who, with his wife, had led a rain ceremony in 1955, Ortega Perrier (1999: 108–109) found that rain-calling in the form we report here probably dated back to no earlier than the 1920s. Prior to that, the caciques led a different ritual around the boundaries of Isluga territory.

William Bollaert wrote an account of visiting Isluga with George Smith, while fulfilling a commission in 1827 from the Peruvian government to survey the Province of Tarapaca (Bollaert 1860). They ascended the Quebrada de Pisagua to Camiña and proceeded to the altiplano through a pass in the mountains called Abra de Pichuta. Describing Isluga marka as the largest "village" in the area, he regarded other human settlements as no more than "many solitary spots" (Bollaert 1860: 164). The two surveyors visited Isluga when it still formed part of Peruvian national territory, well before the War of the Pacific (1879–83), and the loss of territory to Chile. During the first few decades of the twentieth century, Aymara-speaking families settled in Isluga from communities in Carangas, Bolivia, and from western valleys in the Province of Tarapaca (Ortega Perrier 1999: 62–64). The reorganization of Isluga and the institution of the rain-calling ceremony, as remembered by people late in the twentieth century, dates from a period of demographic increase.

Another important point to make is that this *ch'iju jallu* ritual was devised to take into account the rainfall regimes of the period experienced by the generation of Tata Paulino's grandparents and parents. When Bollaert and Smith ascended a rocky track through the Abra de Pichuta, the former described a "piercing gale of wind from the S.E." and Isluga volcano as covered "with snow to its base" (Bollaert 1860: 164). At the risk of accepting Bollaert's observations somewhat uncritically – despite the advice of Lamb (2011: xxix) not to accept traveller's tales at face value – it would seem that Bollaert experienced conditions favouring the fall of precipitation already in November 1827. His observations imply that in 1827 the winds of *Thaya pacha* did not impede the onset of *Jallu pacha*.

Whither the Winds of Change?

Meteorologically trained specialists and lay observers of weather cycles alike make use of comparisons between past events and future possibilities. In this final section we briefly reflect on some methods used in the past to correlate weather events to the seasons of the year, in order to ask how this knowledge might be relevant for understanding seasonal changes in the future. As we have demonstrated above, in Isluga, people adopt a pragmatic approach. They have borrowed from the liturgical cycle of saints' days, long established by Christian practice, in order to track constancies and inconstancies in seasonally occurring weather events. To regard their borrowing as a folkloristic survival would be to ignore their lived experience of the spatial and temporal dimensions of change and its relevance for future understandings.

Long before the use of barometers to measure atmospheric pressure (starting from the seventeenth century), attempts to forecast the weather in Europe between ca. AD 700 and ca. 1600 relied on what has been called astro-meteorology. It was based on the role of planets and stars in an interplay of "constantly modulating phenomena experienced on Earth as weather" (Lawrence-Mathers 2020: 2). Prognostication tended to be treated as superstition by medieval church leaders and weather forecasting often met with suspicion. By the fourteenth century, nevertheless, there was an established science of astro-meteorology, the practice of which was undertaken by individuals possessing high levels of technical skill and who wrote texts intended for astrologers and physicians (Lawrence-Mathers 2020: 168–9). The skills they used depended on identifying the earth's position in relation to other celestial bodies.

In Mesoamerica, the pre-Hispanic Maya Dresden Codex incorporated an ephemeris for charting future positions of the planet Venus, set in a larger document focusing on the interpretation of omens (Aldana y Villalobos 2014: 89). Venus was of particular importance to Mesoamericans because its appearance in the evening sky at its northern extremes occurred between April and June and at its southern extremes between October and December, approximately coinciding with the onset and cessation of the rainy season (Sprajc 2008). Ancient Mesoamericans were aware of an eight-year cycle of variation in these extremes, but there was more regularity in the movement of astral bodies than in seasonal weather patterns on earth.

It seems too that, in the Andes, the Inkas used zenith passage dates as well as solstices and equinoxes to partition the year. These dates were detected by observing shadows cast by a gnomon or by the angle of sunlight passing through the window of an observatory (Dearborn and Schreiber 1989: 50–53). Early in the seventeenth century, Felipe Guaman Poma de Ayala commented that native Andean specialists knew the cycles of the sun and moon, as well as the timing of eclipses and risings of the stars and comets, in addition to "*los cuatro vientos del mundo*" ("the four winds of the world") (Guaman Poma de Ayala 1615: 883 [897]). In particular, he named an elderly philosopher, Juan Yunpa of Uchuc Mara in Lucanas (Peru), who used the position of the sun on the Christian calendrical date of the Beheading of John the Baptist (29 August) to announce the season for "opening" the land prior to planting (Guaman Poma de Ayala 1615: 884 [898], 1154 [1164]). This commentary provides an early account combining Indigenous methods of recording the annual cycle with dates chosen from the Catholic *santorale* relevant to subsistence activities in the local area.

Our study of weather-worlding has focused particularly on winds in relation to the seasons in shaping the existence of human beings, herd animals, and plants. We recognize the need for longer series of meteorological records; the Global Wind Atlas we consulted produced results from 2010 to 2017 and Bollaert's description of 1827 only represented November of that year. The unifying theme in our study comes from the observations made by Isluga people themselves and how what they tell us can be related to observations made in the past, such as Bertonio's description in Aymara of rain-bearing clouds and Guaman Poma's account of calendrical time keeping. In a study of water resources in Recuay, Peru, Mattias Rasmussen (2015: 164) comments that other than as a potential medium of pollution, air is neglected in place-based politics focusing on water. This chapter offers a view of winds as agents of change and it demonstrates how local views make important contributions to the understanding of weather patterns from the past. It also highlights the importance of listening to how local consultants explain changes by taking into account their spatial and temporal construals of weather events to help prepare for changes anticipated in the future.

Notes

1 "Airspace" is a term for the atmosphere above the earth or "above a certain area of land or water." More specifically, it refers to "the space lying above a nation and coming under its jurisdiction" (Merriam-Webster.com Dictionary, https://www.merriam-webster.com/dictionary/airspace, accessed December 5, 2022). We use the term as shorthand to convey the idea that the local atmosphere forms part of Isluga territory, not just the extent of the land itself.

2 The plural form of "airs" is used under the influence of the Spanish "*aires*" (as in Buenos Aires). Additionally, it has to do with the different personalities of winds and breezes in Isluga.

3 This information was obtained from Global Wind Atlas on March 28, 2022. It defines itself as a "free, web-based application developed, owned, and operated by the Technical University of Denmark (DTU). The Global Wind Atlas 3.0 is released in partnership with the World Bank Group, utilizing data provided by Vortex, using funding provided by the Energy Sector Management Assistance Program (ESMAP). For additional information: see https://globalwindatlas.info"

4 Mama Nati first told this story to P. Dransart in May 1987; Mama Felisa told her version of it to her in July 1995. Tata Apolinario gave his version to both authors in July 2017. Variants of the story exist in other parts of the Andes and we suggest that, in Isluga, it dates from at least the nineteenth century (Dransart and Ortega Perrier 2021: 107–109).

5 "En el cerro nos hacen dormir. Yo fui con mi hermano, los dos. Entonces, el qullandiri nos dijo "¿Saben qué? ya, ustedes no van a hacer bulla, nada y calladito". Y nos tiró al suelo. Yo miraba para abajo. El otro, mi hermano, miraba para arriba, así. Entonces la cama estaba listo [sic] allá; había una paskana ahí en el cerro arriba —esto se llama jarra, cama estrecho [sic] para nosotros. Para levantarse lo hacen un señal de pie. Nos quedamos dormidos, dormidos. Después, al rato despierto como a las cuatro o cinco de la mañana, me despierto cuando ese ha caído granizo, nevado, tapado de este pu! No me di cuento."

6 "Viento está corriendo. Viento pa' abajo. Este grande río pues ahí sale. Este nube sale . . . Viento, mucho aire corre."

7 "Ahora está cambiando. No hay lluvia. Viento pa' arriba está lloviendo. Thaya pacha; de ahí viene lluvia atrasa'o. Pasado Santiago verano. Más pa' lluvia ¿quién sabe? Cuatro, cinco años no viene."
8 "Sin lluvia no se puede sembrar. Seco son [sic] este arena. Agua llega poco no más."

Acknowledgements

We thank the people of Isluga for the times we have been able to spend together and their willingness to converse with us. We wish to thank the Wenner-Gren Foundation for Anthropological Research in supporting our visits in January and July 2017 and the editors for their helpful comments and questions.

References

Aldana y Villalobos, Gerardo. "An oracular hypothesis: the Dresden Codex Venus Table and the cultural translation of science." *Archaeoastronomy and the Maya*, edited by Gerardo Aldana y Villalobos and Edwin L. Barnhart, 77–96. Oxford: Oxbow Books, 2014.

Bertonio, Ludovico. "Algvnas phrases de la lengva aymara, y romance." In *Arte de la lengua aymara, con vna silva de phrases dela misma lengua y su declaracion en romance*. Juli, Peru: Impresso en la casa de la Compañia de Iesus de Iuli enla Prouincia de Chucuyto. Por Francisco del Canto, 1612.

Bollaert, William. *Antiquarian, Ethnological and Other Researches in New Granada, Equador, Peru and Chile: With observations on the Pre-Incarial, Incarial, and other monuments of Peruvian nations*. London: Trübner, 1860.

Crate, Susan. "A political ecology of 'water in mind': attributing perceptions in the era of global climate change." *Weather, Climate, and Society* 3, no. 3 (2011): 148–164.

Dearborn, David S.P. and Katharina J. Schreiber. "Houses of the rising sun." In *Time and Calendars in the Inka Empire*, edited by Mariusz S. Ziółkowski and Robert M. Sadowski, 49–74. Oxford: BAR International Series 479, 1989.

Dransart, Penelope Z. *Earth, Water, Fleece and Fabric: An ethnography and archaeology of Andean camelid herding*. London: Routledge, 2002.

Dransart, Penelope Z. "Animals and their possessions: properties of herd animals in the Andes and Europe." In *Animals and Science: From colonial encounters to the biotech industry*, edited by Maggie Bolton and Cathrine Degnen, 84–104. Newcastle: Cambridge Scholars Publishing, 2010.

Dransart, Penelope and Marietta Ortega Perrier. "When the winds run with the Earth: cannibal winds and climate disruption in Isluga, Northern Chile." *Current Anthropology* 62, no. 1 (2021): 101–109.

Garreaud, R.D. "The Andes climate and weather." *Advances in Geosciences* 22 (2009): 3–11.

Gil García, Francisco M. "Lloren las ranas, casen las aguas, conténganse los vientos: rituales para llamar la lluvia en el centro y el sur andino." *Revista Española de Antropología Americana* 45, no. 1 (2012): 145–168.

Göbel, Barbara. "Dangers, experience, and luck: handling uncertainty in the Andes." In *Culture and the Changing Environment: Uncertainty, cognition, and risk management in cross-cultural perspective*, edited by Michael J. Casimir, 221–250. Oxford: Berghahn, 2008.

Guaman Poma de Ayala, Felipe. *Nueva Corónica y Buen Gobierno*. Royal Danish Library, 1615. GKS 2232 4° http://www5.kb.dk/permalink/2006/poma/info/en/frontpage.htm.

Hastrup, Kirsten, ed. *The Question of Resilience: Social responses to climate change*. Copenhagen: Det Kongelige Danske Videnskabernes Selskab, 2009.

Hastrup, Kirsten and Cecilie Rubow, eds. *Living with Environmental Change: Waterworlds*. London: Routledge, 2014.

Ingold, Tim. "Earth, sky, wind, and weather." *Journal of the Royal Anthropological Institute* 13 (2007): S19–S38. (Special Issue *Wind, Life, Health: Anthropological and Historical Perspectives*).

Insel, Nadja, Christopher J. Poulsen, and Todd A. Ehlers. "Influence of the Andes mountains on South American moisture transport, convection, and precipitation." *Climate Dynamics* 35 (2010): 1477–1492.

Katz, Esther and Annamária Lammel. "Introducción. Elementos para una antropología del clima." In *Aires y Lluvias. Antropología del clima en México*, edited by Annamária Lammel, Marina Goloumbinoff, and Esther Katz, 27–50. México: Centro de Estudios Mexicanos y Centroamericanos, 2008.

Lamb, Hubert Horace. *Climate: Present, past and future.* Vol. 1: Fundamentals and Climate Now. Abingdon: Routledge Revivals, 2011.

Lawrence-Mathers, Anne. *Medieval Meteorology: Forecasting the weather from Aristotle to the Almanac.* Cambridge: Cambridge University Press, 2020.

Martínez, Gabriel. "El sistema de los *uywiris* en Isluga." *Anales de la Universidad del Norte (Chile)* 10 (1976): 255–327.

Miracle, Andrew W. and Juan de Dios Yapita Moya. "Time and space in Aymara." In *The Aymara Language in its Social and Cultural Context*, edited by Martha J. Hardman, 33–56. Gainesville, Florida: University of Florida, 1981.

Núñez, Rafael, and Kensy Cooperrider. "The tangle of space and time in human cognition." *Trends in Cognitive Sciences* 17 no. 5 (2013): 220–229.

Nuttall, Mark. "Living in a world of movement: human resilience to environmental instability in Greenland." In *Anthropology and Climate Change: From encounters to action*, edited by Susan Crate and Mark Nuttall, 292–310. Walnut Creek, CA: Left Coast, 2009.

Orlove, Ben and Steven C. Caton. "Water sustainability: anthropological approaches and prospects." *Annual Review of Anthropology* 39 (2010): 401–415.

Ortega Perrier, Marietta. *By Reason or Force: Islugueño identity and Chilean nationalism.* PhD thesis, University of Cambridge, 1999.

Ortega Perrier, Marietta. 2001. "Escatología andina: metáforas del alma." *Chungara* 33 no. 2 (2001): 253–258.

Ponce Philimon, Paulina. "*Informe tentativo de precipitaciones: sector localidad de Isluga período 1966–2017.*" Unpublished report, 2017.

Rasmussen, Mattias Borg. *Andean Waterways: Resource politics in Highland Peru.* Seattle: University of Washington Press, 2015.

Salomon, Frank. *At the Mountains' Altar: Anthropology of religion in an Andean community.* London: Routledge, 2018.

Sprăjc, Ivan. "Observación de los extremos de Venus en Mesoamérica: astronomía, clima y cosmovisión." In *Aires y Lluvias. Antropología del clima en México*, edited by Annamária Lammel, Marina Goloumbinoff, and Esther Katz, 91–120. México: Centro de Estudios Mexicanos y Centroamericanos, 2008.

9

THE WATER OBLIGES

Climate Change and Worldmaking Practices in Peru

Astrid B. Stensrud

As part of a research project on climate change and water in Colca Valley in the southern Peruvian Andes, I got to know many peasant farmers who I interviewed about their water-related practices and organizations. In Yanque district, a farmer who was elected leader of one of the irrigation associations (officially called "commission of water users") for a four-year period, explained to me how farmers and water are interdependent:

> The commission is the only solid organization here, because the water unites us. The water is the reason [*motivo*], because we cannot live without water. So, everyone attends the meetings, and everyone participates in the collective work [*faena*], because the water obliges us [to do so].

Being a semi-arid valley, farming in Colca has always depended upon irrigation and collaboration between people to construct and maintain irrigation systems, canals, and terraces. During my stay in Colca, I learned through listening, observing, and participating in various activities, how humans need to work to make the water flow and make life possible. Irrigation is an inherently collective activity, where success is achieved through cooperation both among farmers and in their relation to the water as a sentient being. I also learned how the impacts of climate change have in the past few decades exacerbated the need to care for water sources and collaborate to get ready access to water. Climate change has become real in the twenty-first century, not only as discourse but as a reality which farmers navigate in different ways. In the same period, neoliberal economic policies have led to a marketization of agriculture and water management, fostering individualization and commodification. In addition to the pressure of climate change and economic change, development projects and state programs meant to improve productivity and profitability in agriculture have been framed in the context of climate change, water scarcity and adaptation, and have in turn been pushing the implementation of more efficient and modern technology. Development programs presented as climate change adaptation, together with climate changes and economic change, can hence be understood as not only a problem of double exposure of global warming and economic globalization (O'Brien and Leichenko

DOI: 10.4324/9781003242499-12

2000), but as triple exposure. Wilhite and Salinas (2019) have argued that people living in forests in the Global South suffer a triple burden brought on by extractive capitalism, climate change, and "market-based global environmental regimes established in the name of climate mitigation" (Wilhite and Salinas 2019: 151).

Climate change has indeed most intensively impacted "climate sensitive" areas: high altitude (i.e., Andes, Himalayas), high latitude (i.e., Arctic, Antarctic), and near sea level (i.e., Pacific islands), which are often inhabited by "place-based people," human populations depending directly and daily upon their local environment (Crate 2011: 149). As affirmed by Susan Crate and Mark Nuttall in the first edition of *Anthropology and Climate Change* (2009), the effects of climate change produce new uncertainties for local populations and add to existing vulnerabilities and challenges regarding adaptation to a harsh environment and economic inequalities. I suggest that the effects of the multiple exposures of global neoliberal capitalism, global warming and market-based adaptation programs are mutually reinforcing each other and exacerbating the pressure on small-scale farmers. Furthermore, the various impacts of climate change in the Peruvian Andes are entangled with the effects of colonial legacies, especially racialized and gendered socio-economic inequalities.

The responses made by farmers in Colca, however, show us that practices of collaboration and care involve more than technology and markets. To better understand the human condition in the face of climate change, we (researchers, scholars, development workers, activists) should also pay attention to other practices as well as relations to nonhuman sentient beings and entities. These practices and relations are often not seen because they are deemed inefficient and unproductive, and therefore made irrelevant. They often go under the radar as "culture," since their immediate goal is not to directly enhance efficiency, productivity, and profitability. However, as argued elsewhere (Stensrud 2021), I suggest that so-called unproductive and inefficient wateractivities can often be seen as *worldmaking practices*, and as such they are productive of projects and worlds emerging from particular human–nonhuman assemblages. Worldmaking practices are inherently entangled with peoples' relationships with water, earth, and mountains. Multiple worlds emerge from diverse worldmaking practices, and as they are enacted in the practices of peasants, farmers, engineers, bureaucrats, politicians, NGO workers and activists, these worlds are not existing side by side, but are partially connected in everyday life.

Hence, my argument in this chapter is twofold. First, not only does climate change have an unequal impact on different people and places, but I also argue that projects for adaptation and sustainability can have unequal impact and unintended consequences. Second, to gain a more complete understanding of these consequences we should not only take socio-economic factors into account, but also human–nonhuman relations and the ways that worldmaking practices are enacting diverging, yet partially connected, worlds.

The arguments presented in this chapter are based on ethnographic research in Caylloma province in Arequipa Region in the southern Peruvian Andes, where I spent thirteen months doing fieldwork during the period 2011–14. The fieldwork mainly took place in Colca valley, which is part of the Majes-Colca watershed, where the water flows from the high mountains and down to the Pacific Ocean. The majority of the people living here are peasant farmers who speak the Indigenous language Quechua in addition to Spanish.[1]

Responding to Climate Change

Colca valley is a semi-arid area, where the landscape is marked by cultivated terraces and a network of small irrigation canals. Water comes from various sources, like meltwater from snow on the mountaintops, springs, and streams. Although the permanent glaciers are gone, and several mountain springs have dried up because they are no longer fed by glacial melt water, the mountains continue to be important sources of water. Some of the largest mountains provide water for several villages. Mountains are also powerful sentient beings with a notable presence in the landscape and in the everyday lives of people. What I learned in Colca was that the mountain-beings have different personalities and abilities, some are more powerful than others and they can be capricious if they are not met with respect and proper gifts from humans. The earth, river, lakes, and springs are also seen as living beings that should be treated respectfully (see also Allen 1988; de la Cadena 2015; Salas Carreño 2019; Stensrud 2016a).

In the past decades, farmers in Colca – as in the rest of the Andes – have experienced changing weather patterns, irregular rain, seasonal instability, extreme temperatures, and dwindling water supplies. The environmental changes observed in Colca correspond with the changes in temperature, precipitation, seasonality, glacier retreat, and water supply that have been reported by farmers and scientists all over the Andes, and which are seen as the result of global warming (see for example Bates et al. 2008; Bolin 2009; Carey 2010; Vuille et al. 2008, 2018). Peasant farmers, however, do not experience climate change as an isolated phenomenon, but as one of many issues that smallholders have to deal with (see e.g., Rasmussen 2015). Since my first fieldwork in Colca in 2011, there have been reports of ruined harvests due to irregular frost, drought, and hailstorms in the rain season. Many smallholders have been left with little but debt, because of the increasing dependency on loans and credits from micro-finance agencies.

The less secure water supply makes farmers even more dependent on irrigation systems and makes the cooperation between districts that share water sources and irrigation canals critical. Irrigation in Colca is an inherently collective and social activity, where success is achieved through cooperation among farmers. All water users are obliged to participate in the collective work, where they clean and repair the canals in order to have the right to access water. This work is organized by local irrigation associations (formally called commissions and committees of water users).

The commissions elect water allocators for each irrigation sector once a year, and these allocators (*regidores de agua*) are responsible for distributing water on a daily basis and for maintaining good relations among farmers. In addition, they are also responsible for maintaining good relations with water beings and for performing offering ceremonies (*pagos*) twice a year. With climate change, disappearing glaciers and dwindling water supplies, these pagos have gained new importance and interest. One example is the annual celebration and pago made by the villagers in Pinchollo to Mount Hualca Hualca, a 6000-meter-high peak that supplies several villages with water. Farmers in Pinchollo receive irrigation water for 60% of their cultivated fields from Hualca Hualca. Having abandoned the custom for several years, the villagers started again after increasingly worrying about the disappearance of the permanent ice, and they were supported by NGO workers who highlighted the cultural importance of the custom. I suggest that these responses to climate change that emerge from Indigenous and "other-than-modern" life-projects in particular places are not only "cultural," a view that hinges on a separation between nature as objective and singular reality, and culture as subjective construction of meaning. Instead, responses emerge from and are entangled with practices that make worlds in which "nature" and "culture" as separate spheres do not make sense (Kohn 2013; de la Cadena 2015).

Water Worlding

To better understand the various responses to climate change and changes in water supplies, I sought inspiration from scholars in Science and Technology Studies and decolonial thinking. Annemarie Mol (2002) and John Law (2004) argue against the assumption that reality is a determinate set of entities, ready to be discovered. On the contrary, they say, there is no singular reality that precedes practice, and reality is multiple and messy. Particular realities are constantly enacted by, and shaped in, particular mundane practices (Mol 1999, 2002; Law 2004). Inspired by Annemarie Mol's (2002) study of how the practices of doctors, patients, and laboratory scientists in a Dutch hospital enact multiple, but overlapping, versions of a body and of the illness arthrosclerosis, I decided to look ethnographically at how particular water practices enact different versions of water and water bodies in the Majes-Colca watershed.

I have argued elsewhere (Stensrud 2021) that the realities made through water practices can be understood as different water-worlds. Hence, I suggest that they can be called *worldmaking practices*. However, this does not mean that the different realities are separate and disconnected units. Instead, worlds are continuously emerging and partially connected, meaning that they are overlapping, but not completely. Hence, I do not see Andean water governance as an unchanging body of knowledge, customs, and traditions standing in opposition to modern statecraft and science, but rather an emerging world made in multiple, often contradictory, practices and in translocal encounters, similar to what Zhan (2009) has argued is the case for "Chinese medicine." Anna Tsing (2015) suggests that worldmaking projects emerge from practical activities of making lives in the ruins of capitalism, and in the process these projects alter our planet.[2] Thinking with her interlocutors in Pacchanta in Southern Peru, Marisol de la Cadena (2015) argues that practices that enact earth-beings and humans as related to each other are continuously making worlds in the Andes. Hydrosocial relations are also part of a mutual composition of place, as in the concept of "in-ayllu," in which "humans and other-than-humans are inherently connected and compose the ayllu" (de la Cadena 2015: 101), and that their relationship is also part of them. "Being in-ayllu" means that humans and earth-beings "emerge *within* ayllu as relationship, and from this condition they, literally, take-place" (de la Cadena 2015: 102). The Andean collective called *ayllu* is thus neither just a place nor just a kinship group: "It is a dynamic space where the whole community of beings that exist in the world lives; this includes humans, plants, animals, the mountains, the rivers, the rain, etc. All are related like a family" (Oxa 2004 in de la Cadena 2015: 102). In other words, people, land, and water co-constitute each other. This perspective is also a critique of dominant dichotomies such as traditional–modern, local–global and cultural–scientific. I propose to understand water-related worlds as open-ended and emerging through practices and encounters. Different practices enact different worlds; these worlds are fragmented, overlapping, and changing, and they can all co-exist as part of each other through negotiation.

In the words of Arturo Escobar (2018), people's ontological design of land- and waterscapes – as heterogeneous assemblages of life – enact non-dualist, relational worlds (Escobar 2018: 66). A world of many worlds is what Escobar (2018) and Blaser and de la Cadena (2018) call a pluriverse: "heterogeneous worldings coming together as a political ecology of practices, negotiating their difficult being together in heterogeneity" (Blaser and de la Cadena 2018: 4). Hence, the absence of singularity does not imply that we live in a fragmented world composed of an indefinite number of disconnected water bodies and water management institutions. When multiple worlds coexist, they are neither completely separate nor completely equivalent, but what Marilyn Strathern has called "partially connected" because they are "neither singular nor plural, neither one nor many" (Strathern 2004 [1991]: 54), but always overlapping in different degrees.

In Colca valley, humans engage in different kinds of relationships with multiple entities: offering gifts in relations of reciprocity, constructing and maintaining infrastructure, organizing distribution, regulating access and sharing food and drink with humans and other-than-human beings, paying tariffs and taxes to water user organizations and state authorities, formalizing licenses for the right to use water, and participating in development projects aiming to enhance water use through modern technology and efficiency (Stensrud 2016a, 2021). I suggest that the different water practices enact multiple versions of water, and partially connected worlds that cannot be disentangled and separated into pure and bounded units; they exist together. This dual reality is perhaps best described by the Aymara concept of "*ch'ixi*," which Silvia Rivera Cusicanqui (2012) uses to describe how Indigenous and mestizo worlds can be combined without being mixed. *Ch'ixi* has many connotations and reflects the idea of something that is and is not at the same time. Hence, the notion of *ch'ixi* can illuminate the "motley" [*abigarrada*] quality of Andean society, expressing the parallel coexistence of multiple differences that do not extinguish, but instead both antagonize and complement each other (Rivera Cusicanqui 2012:105).

Rivera's use of *ch'ixi* as analytical concept is also part of her critique of the neoliberal multiculturalism that has been dominant in Latin America, where national authorities have emphasized Mestizaje as the ideal hybridization; a multi-cultural melting pot where all become "the same." As Rivera argues, however, multiculturalism is concealing new forms of colonization and subalternization (2012: 99). It does not imply any real change beyond the rhetorical recognition and subordinates the Indigenous to purely symbolic functions (2012: 101). Hence, multiculturalism and the idea of hybridity makes difference invisible without erasing it. Instead, Indigenous ways of life are excluded from national identities, and the Spanish/European social forms are reproduced as the dominant mode of being. As will be discussed in the next section, difference often creates tensions, although not always open conflicts, and in everyday life there are pragmatic ways of navigating difference and creating points of connection.

Ontological (Dis)encounters and Partially Connected Worlds

Since climate change was introduced as a mainstream explanatory discourse, adaptation increasingly became a priority for research and policy (Crate and Nuttall 2009), and development programs have been re-phrased in terms of climate adaptation. In such programs and projects, the main issue at hand is often pre-defined and reduced to a single problem that is manageable, for example "water scarcity" and "inefficient water use."

This definition completely ignores the issue of inequality in allocation of water in the watershed. The discourse of water scarcity also tends to be followed by discourses of efficiency, leading to so-called techno-fix solutions.

In 2011, a program sponsored by the Peruvian state and the World Bank sent engineers to teach the farmers in Colca how to irrigate more efficiently by using modern technology. This irrigation modernization program was called PSI (*Programa Subsectorial de Irrigaciones*), and the goal was to achieve higher productivity and profitability through modern technology. The PSI was legitimized by the need for climate change adaptation and efficient water use. Since efficiency is premised on the discourse of scarcity of resources, the coming water scarcity crisis, caused by global warming, was repeated in speeches and workshops. However, although most farmers had observed changes in the weather and water supply, they did not necessarily agree that water scarcity was the one and only problem. Most peasant farmers experience other problems that are more pressing, like the uncertainties connected to price volatility, debt, and out-migration. Many young people give up farming and move to the city because of the difficulties of sustaining a viable livelihood on small farms. Hence, most farmers were not easily convinced, and the PSI engineers had a hard time recruiting enough participants. Some of the engineers interpreted this as lack of knowledge, consciousness, and motivation among the peasants.

What I observed was an apparent mismatch between priorities, possibilities, and power to define problem issues. I have analyzed this as "disencounters" between the modernization program and the farmers (see Stensrud 2019; 2021). This concept is taken from the Spanish *desencuentros*, which would mean failed meetings, or disagreements. By disencounters, I mean the encounters between different modes of knowledge and practice that often lack mutual resonance and a shared understanding of what is at stake. The workshops were supposed to be a space of mutual learning and dialogue, but they were embedded in structures of inequality and hierarchies of knowledge, embodied both by the engineers and the farmers. Within the program, there was only one right answer to all questions: the need to invest in modern technology.

This paradox was exacerbated by the existence of the Majes Irrigation Project (MIP) further down the watershed; a prestigious state-sponsored project created in the 1970s and 1980s to foster economic development in the region. The former desert areas of Majes Pampa are irrigated by water from the Colca highlands and by using modern technology sponsored by foreign aid agencies (see Stensrud 2016b; 2021). To put it bluntly, Indigenous peasants were told to implement expensive modern technology to use water more efficiently to adapt to current climate change and future water scarcity, and at the same time water was transported to the desert to create economic growth in the export-oriented agribusiness industry, which is increasingly dominated by large-scale companies, exporting crops like avocados, artichokes, and red peppers to markets in the US and Europe.

Furthermore, a shift from collective and collaborative irrigation methods to modern technology would have many direct and indirect consequences, some of them probably unintended, including increased individuality and inequality, less communal work and collaboration between groups and districts, and less reciprocity in relations with fellow humans and with nonhuman beings. The last point brings back the importance of including landscapes and nonhuman sociality in the analysis of collectives and world-making practices. Since farming in Colca depends on access to water, the farmers must maintain good relations with the water sources and water-beings, and make the appropriate *pagos*, which can be translated as payments, gifts or offerings (Figure 9.1). The *pagos* are given to the mountains and springs, ponds, and canals. Twice a year, the irrigation committees send representatives to the mountains to make *pagos* to the springs. The *pago* rituals are performed by an expert (*paqu*), often accompanied by a small group of farmers, who knows how to compose the *pagos* with the right ingredients, like herbs, llama fat, maize, sweets, coca leaves, and alcohol. The *pagos* are burnt in a fire beside the springs, and the springs are also given *chicha*, sweet wine, and holy water, served in tiny goblets. When farmers explained this practice to me, they talked about the springs as living beings that can be thirsty. Springs, lakes, mountains and other water-beings and earth-beings are called by names, they have personal characteristics, they are related, and they can feel hunger and respond to human action. These beings are not inherently good or evil, but they are powerful and can be quite capricious and dangerous. They demand proper respect and gifts of food and alcohol in return for water, fertility, and well-being (Stensrud 2016a; see also Salas Carreño 2019). Hence, water practices are based on reciprocal relations of mutual care and nurture, which has also been documented by ethnographic research in other parts of the Peruvian Andes (see e.g., Ramírez González 2020).

FIGURE 9.1 August 2011: A group of farmers – one of them a ritual expert (*paqu*) – preparing offerings to water sources nearby Chivay in Colca Valley. Photo: Astrid Stensrud.

On one occasion, I got the chance to observe a ritual technique that, until then, I had only heard about. I was accompanying Aurelio, a farmer who was also a ritual expert, to make *pagos* to the mountain springs that gave water to the fields in his irrigation sector. After the *pago*, Aurelio took a bottle full of seawater that had been brought all the way from the Pacific Ocean. He poured this seawater into a small plastic container, covering it with a piece of cotton. After libations and invocations, he placed these items – together with a starfish from the ocean – into the spring. In my attempt to understand, I started by asking Aurelio why he put seawater into the spring. He told me that the seawater "will call for more water." He also explained that the cotton was "clouds, so that there will be rain." When offering this explanation to me, he translated the relations with which this practice had meaning into a theory that he thought I could conceive. Accepting that knowledge is generated in translations between practices, experiences, and meaning, it is also important to remember that the translations depend on the perspective and the social position of the persons involved. The dominant discourses about society and nature, both in academia and society at large, do not challenge the Modern Constitution, as identified by Bruno Latour (1993), which make a division between the real and material world which can be studied and known by natural science on one hand, and the symbolic representations, expressed through social systems of religion and culture, that can be studied by social scientists on the other hand. In Peru, these discourses are also informed by hierarchies of knowledge, which again are informed by "coloniality of power" and hierarchies of gender, class, and ideas of race.[3] In the dominant discourse of modernization, Indigenous practices are stigmatized and ridiculed as "absurd pantheistic ideologies" and "primitive forms of religion" that should be eradicated because they are hindering progress and economic growth, as was publicly expressed by former president García (García Pérez 2007; Los Andes 2011).

The NGOs and development workers I met in Colca Valley had another perspective, which was sympathetic and supportive, but still did not consider contemporary Indigenous practices as real. They tended to emphasize that rituals and ceremonies are so-called "ancient" customs that are part of a millenarian culture and heritage that should be celebrated and remembered. This message is also repeated by the municipality and the tourist agencies and guides, who want to promote the valley as a tourist destination that is rich not only in natural beauty, but also in colorful cultural diversity. The echo from the multi-culturalism criticized by Rivera Cusicanqui (2012) is evident.

However, from what Aurelio said, we can see that the practice of calling for water had a specific purpose, which was concrete, material, and pragmatic: to enable the springs to generate more water. In this sense, it is more a technique than a custom. He didn't do it just to make a performance for a public, he did it in an interaction with each of the springs before burning the *pagos*. "To summon the water" is a specific technique to call or attract the water from the ocean and make clouds and rain. It is also a specific practice that contributes to enact a particular world. This perspective supports the ideas presented by scholars in Material Semiotics. Arguing that reality does not exist a priori of our practice, but rather is produced in, through, and by our practices, we can say that different practices enact different realities (Mol 2002; Law 2004). These realities are not best understood as separate and disconnected (Indigenous, Spanish, Mestizo) cultural units that interact. On the contrary, we can see how worlds are connected and continuously emerging (de la Cadena 2015).

One of the persons who helped me understand water practices in Colca, by translating and explaining, was Miguel, who had grown up in Colca, and had studied engineering at the university in the city. In 2011, he was working as technical manager in a water organization in Colca Valley. He told me the following:

> In the time of the Incas, it is told that the *chasquis* (runners) went down from the mountains to the ocean, where they did a *pago* to the ocean. Afterwards, they took seawater in pitchers, and they put one pitcher on each mountaintop, from the ocean to the highlands. And then rain clouds were formed, and the clouds followed the seawater to the highlands, where it rained. Today, when they make *pagos* to the water springs, they put seawater in [the spring]. They bring water from the sea in bottles. There must be a scientific reason; we should look for a scientific explanation. For example, when the clouds follow the seawater, it could be that the seawater contains ions.

By suggesting that there are ions in the seawater that attract the rainclouds, Miguel made an attempt to explain why it works in a way that science could accept. As an engineer who was constantly seeking to understand how the world worked, he tried to find scientific evidence for why "calling the water" and other practices seemed to work. When Miguel grew up in Colca, he learned that all sentient beings are connected, and how to relate to them with respect and care. As a university student of engineering, he learned abstraction and the importance of measurement and standardization. It is crucial to see that when he translates between these two worlds, he translates from the relational world and into the language of science, not the other way around. This illustrates that different knowledge systems and worlds are not symmetrical in terms of power, they are organized in a hierarchy where some ways of knowing are more legitimate and are recognized as "true." Persons living with this kind of constant tension in everyday life, I suggest, will continuously attempt to make coherence, for example by trying to find a scientific explanation to why the calling of rainwater works.

Miguel mediated between the state and the farmers, and between science and Indigenous forms of knowledge. However, he does not move from one world and back, and he is never in-between: he lives in both simultaneously, yet it is always partially. This reminds us again of the Aymara word *ch'ixi*, which according to Rivera Cusicanqui (2012) is also the name of a grey color that comes from the imperceptible mixing of black and white spots, which are confused by perception, without ever being completely mixed. A *ch'ixi* color is white but is not white at the same time; it is both white and its opposite, black. This notion, then, reflects the Aymara idea of something that is and is not at the same time. Thinking through *ch'ixi* may nurture an understanding of both-and, instead of neither-nor, like the notion "not only" (de la Cadena 2019). For example, water in Colca is a resource for producing food and generating money, but *not only*; it is also a vital source of life and a living being that responds to human actions.

In my ethnographically grounded critique of the modernization program, I do not mean to say that technology itself is incompatible with relational water practices; on the contrary, technological devices can be part of a human–nonhuman collective. Farmers in Colca are not *against* technology and change. But they want to be in charge of defining their priorities and making the design of their landscape and their future (see also Paredes and Li 2019). A more relevant critique would be to point out how the technology is embedded in the discourse of "efficiency," and hence how this excludes practices that are deemed "inefficient," making them irrelevant and invisible. Communal and relational practices that maintain webs of relationships and strengthen collective well-being, are often deemed as hinders to efficiency. In this way, it is the imposition and demand of "efficiency," and not the technology itself, which creates gaps and dissonance between worlds. The main concern in the idea of efficiency is to put every drop of water into productive use, to generate economic value, without letting water get lost or seep into other unproductive uses. However, seen from other perspectives, the so-called unproductive and inefficient uses may have other kinds of value. One example is the building of new and modern water pipes, enclosing water and not losing a drop from the source to the prioritized use, e.g. safe drinking water and irrigation of crops. However, when looking more closely at the consequences of the enclosure, there are often beings losing out from accessing the water flow, like for examples animals grazing on pastures that are green thanks to the water leaking from the water canals (see Verzijl 2020).

Conclusion: The Challenges of Urgency and Slowing Down

I often heard farmers and engineers talk about the "good use" of water, and I suggest that when they say "good use," it can refer to at least two different, but overlapping meanings. It could be "efficient use" as defined in the water resources law, and it could also mean "careful use" according to a relational logic where attending to and maintaining relations among humans and nonhumans is of key importance. I am inclined to thinking that it can have both meanings at the same time. However, misunderstandings may often happen – whether it is in a research project or development project – if you use the same word and are not aware of the diverging understandings of how the world works; of what water *is*, or what land and mountains are (cf. Viveiros de Castro 2004). Just imagine how challenging it would be to agree with someone on what sustainability means in a project, if you disagree on what water is, or what land is (see Blaser 2009).[4]

Instead of locking analysis and action to particular concepts and narratives, and the realities produced by these, an alternative way would be to follow the lead of Isabelle Stengers (2005) in her proposal to "slow down reasoning," and not take for granted that we know the meaning of the things we observe and the concepts we use. I suggest that terms such as crisis, change, efficiency, and sustainability, or even the meaning of water and land, could blind us and hinder understanding when taken for granted. As proposed by Andrea Ballestero (2019), instead of focusing on climate change and water in terms of crisis, we could aim to slow down and use hesitation and wonder to think generatively about the everyday politics of water and water rights.

Furthermore, difference should be acknowledged and made productive instead of ignored or hidden, as proposed by Helen Verran (2013).[5] Taking ontological disjunctures and disruptions into account, and at the same time seeing the partial encounters and entanglement, would make us better equipped to appreciate the complexity of the world as it is emerging. This approach would undoubtedly raise several issues and challenges – both ethical and practical – for researchers working with communities affected by climate change. Approaching human–nonhuman relations and worldmaking practices in the context of global warming with an attitude based on wonder and hesitation would seem counterintuitive for many. The main challenge consists of combining a sense of urgency and need of urgent action with a need to slow down thinking and not jump to conclusions and quick-fix solutions that may have unforeseen long-term consequences.

Notes

1 My ethnographic fieldwork consisted of participant observation, interviews, interactions, and conversations with various actors in Peru. This was primarily done in two periods (2011 and 2013–14), as part of two research projects; the first one at the University of Copenhagen (funded by The Danish Research Council for Culture and Communication), and the second at the University of Oslo (funded by the Research Council of Norway, project no. 222783, and the European Research Council, grant agreement no. 295843). In this chapter, I aim to synthesize some of the arguments presented in my monograph *Watershed Politics and Climate Change in Peru* (Pluto Press, 2021).
2 Tsing has explored the worlds emerging from the multiple encounters and practices taking place in the supply chain of the matsutake mushroom (picking, exporting, consuming), and she argues that following these practices shows us the "possibilities of coexistence within environmental disturbance" (2015: 4).
3 "Coloniality of power" is a term coined by the Peruvian sociologist Aníbal Quijano and refers to a matrix of power between the colonizers and the "others," established on the idea of "race" as the fundament of all social classification in the Americas (Quijano, 2000).
4 This point is made by Mario Blaser (2009) in an article about a sustainability project among the Yshiro in Paraguay, where he introduces the term "political ontology" to analyze the ontological disagreements about worlds.
5 Viveiros de Castro has made a related argument about controlling the "equivocation," which is not just a failure to understand, but: "a failure to understand that understandings are necessarily not the same, and that they are not related to imaginary ways of 'seeing the world' but to the real worlds that are being seen" (Viveiros de Castro 2004: 11). What he proposes is that these equivocations can be controlled so that we can learn from them. So, instead of unmaking the equivocation, we should emphasize it.

References

Allen, Catherine J. 1988. *The Hold Life Has: Coca and cultural identity in an Andean community.* Washington, DC: Smithsonian Institution Press.

Ballestero, Andrea. 2019. *A Future History of Water.* Durham, NC: Duke University Press.

Bates, B.C., Z.W. Kundzewicz, S. Wu, and J.P. Palutikof (eds). 2008. *Climate Change and Water.* Technical Paper of the Intergovernmental Panel on Climate Change, IPCC Secretariat, Geneva, 210 pp.

Blaser, Mario. 2009. "The threat of the Yrmo: the political ontology of a sustainable hunting program." *American Anthropologist* 111 (1): 10–20.

Blaser, Mario and Marisol de la Cadena. 2018. "Introduction. pluriverse: proposals for a world of many worlds." In Marisol de la Cadena and Mario Blaser (eds.) *A World of Many Worlds.* Durham, NC: Duke University Press, pp. 1–22.

Bolin, Inge. 2009. "The glaciers of the Andes are melting: Indigenous and anthropological knowledge merge in restoring water resources." In Susan A. Crate and Mark Nuttall (eds.) *Anthropology and Climate Change: From encounters to actions.* Walnut Creek, CA: Left Coast Press, pp. 228–239.

Carey, Mark. 2010. *In the Shadow of Melting Glaciers: Climate change and Andean society.* New York: Oxford University Press.

Crate, Susan A. 2011. "Climate and culture: anthropology in the era of contemporary climate change." *Annual Review of Anthropology* 40: 175–194.

Crate, Susan A. and Mark Nuttall (eds). 2009. *Anthropology and Climate Change: From encounters to actions.* Walnut Creek, CA: Left Coast Press.

de la Cadena, Marisol. 2015. *Earth-beings: Ecologies of practice across Andean worlds.* Durham, NC: Duke University Press.

de la Cadena, Marisol. 2019. "Earth-beings: Andean Indigenous religion, but not only." In Keiichi Omura, Grant Jun Otsuki, Shiho Satsuka, and Atsuro Morita (eds.) *World Multiple: The quotidian politics of knowing and generating entangled worlds.* London: Routledge.

Escobar, Arturo. 2018. *Designs for the Pluriverse: Radical interdependence, autonomy, and the making of worlds.* Durham, NC: Duke University Press.

García Pérez, Alan. 2007. "El síndrome del perro del hortelano." *El Comercio*, October 28: http://elcomercio.pe/edicionimpresa/html/2007-10 28/el_sindrome_del_perro_del_hort.html.

Kohn, Eduardo. 2013. *How Forests Think: Toward an anthropology beyond the human.* Berkeley: University of California Press.

Latour, Bruno. 1993. *We Have Never Been Modern.* New York: Harvester Wheatsheaf.

Law, John. 2004. *After Method: Mess in social science research.* London: Routledge.

Los Andes. 2011. *Ignorancia de García Pérez Califica de Absurdas Creencias Andinas.* Video, June 17: http://www.losandes.com.pe/Nacional/20110617/51373.html, accessed May 5, 2017.

Mol, Annemarie. 1999. "Ontological politics. A word and some questions." In John Law and John Hassard (eds.) *Actor Network Theory and After.* Oxford: Blackwell.

Mol, Annemarie. 2002. *The Body Multiple: Ontology in medical practice.* Durham, NC: Duke University Press.

O'Brien, K. and R. Leichenko. 2000. "Double exposure: assessing the impacts of climate change within the context of economic globalization." *Global Environmental Change* 10: 221–232.

Paredes Peñafiel, Adriana Paola and Fabiana Li. 2019. Nourishing relations: controversy over the Conga mining project in northern Peru. *Ethnos* 84(2): 301–322.

Quijano, Aníbal. 2000. "Coloniality of power, Eurocentrism, and Latin America." *Nepantla. Views from South*, 1 (3): 533–580.

Ramírez González, María Elena. 2020. "Criando agua y humanos en el Ande: la experiencia de la comunidad Fortaleza Sacsayhuaman en Cusco, Perú." *Anthropologica* 38 (45): 109–132.

Rasmussen, Mattias Borg. 2015. *Andean Waterways: Resource politics in Highland Peru.* Seattle, WA: University of Washington Press.

Rivera Cusicanqui, Silvia. 2012. "Ch'ixinakax utxiwa: a reflection on the practices and discourses of decolonization." *The South Atlantic Quarterly* 111 (1): 95–109.

Salas Carreño, Guillermo. 2019. *Lugares parientes: Comida, cohabitación y mundos andinos.* Lima: Pontificia Universidad Católica del Perú, Fondo Editorial.

Stengers, Isabelle. 2005. "The cosmopolitical proposal." In Bruno Latour and Peter Weibel (eds.) *Making Things Public: Atmospheres of democracy.* Cambridge, MA: MIT Press.

Stensrud, Astrid B. 2016a. "Climate change, water practices and relational worlds in the Andes." *Ethnos: Journal of Anthropology*, 81 (1): 75–98 (First published online in 2014).

Stensrud, Astrid B. 2016b. "Dreams of growth and fear of water crisis: the ambivalence of 'progress' in the Majes-Siguas irrigation project, Peru." *History and Anthropology Journal*, 27 (5): 569–584.

Stensrud, Astrid B. 2019. "'You cannot contradict the engineer': Disencounters of modern technology, climate change and power in the Peruvian Andes." *Critique of Anthropology* 39 (4): 420–438.

Stensrud, Astrid B. 2021. *Watershed Politics and Climate Change in Peru.* London: Pluto Press.

Strathern, Marilyn. 2004 [1991]. *Partial Connections.* Walnut Creek, CA: AltaMira Press.

Tsing, Anna L. 2015. *The Mushroom at the End of the World: On the possibility of life in capitalist ruins.* Princeton, NJ: Princeton University Press.

Verran, Helen. 2013. "Engagements between disparate knowledge traditions: toward doing difference generatively and in good faith." In Lesley Green (ed.) *Contested Ecologies: Dialogues in the South on nature and knowledge.* Cape Town: HSRC Press.

Verzijl, Andres. 2020. *Water Movements: Fluidity and visibility among Andean worlds.* PhD thesis. Wageningen University, The Netherlands.

Viveiros de Castro, Eduardo. 2004. "Perspectival anthropology and the method of controlled equivocation." *Tipití: Journal of the Society for the Anthropology of Lowland South America* 2 (1): 3–22.

Vuille, Mathias, Bernard Francou, Patrick Wagnon, Irmgard Juen, Georg Kaser, Bryan G. Mark,
and Raymond S. Bradley. 2008. "Climate change and tropical Andean glaciers: past, present and
future." *Earth-Science Reviews* 89: 79–96.

Vuille, Mathias et al. 2018. "Rapid decline of snow and ice in the tropical Andes – impacts,
uncertainties and challenges ahead." *Earth Science Reviews* 176: 195–213.

Wilhite, Harold and Cecilia G. Salinas. 2019. Expansive capitalism, climate change and global climate
mitigation regimes: a triple burden on forest peoples in the global South, in Stensrud, A.B. and
Eriksen, T. H., eds, *Climate, Capitalism and Communities*. London: Pluto Press, pp. 151–170.

Zhan, Mei. 2009. *Other-worldly: Making Chinese medicine through transnational frames*. Durham,
NC: Duke University Press.

10

CLIMATE ACTION WITH A LAGNIAPPE

Coastal Restoration, Flood Risk Reduction, Sacred Site Protection and Tribal Communities' Resilience

Julie Maldonado, Kristina Peterson, R. Eugene Turner, Theresa Dardar, Shirell Parfait-Dardar, Rosina Philippe, Donald Dardar, Alessandra Jerolleman, Julie Torres, Rebecca Lovingood and Mira Olson

> Because of the resilience and the determination of our ancestors, we are still here. I can break down all of these things that I tell you that I do and it adds up to one word. Love. Our saying is that we live for the next seven generations. Everything we do and everything we don't do is going to impact them….Because of the challenges that we're facing, we have an opportunity with the time that we've been given to do something good for the next generations.
>
> *(Chief Shirell Parfait-Dardar, Grand Caillou/Dulac Band of Biloxi-Chitimacha-Choctaw Indians, National Geographic 2021)*

The first edition of this volume, published in 2009, included a chapter about a participatory action research approach informed by Grand Bayou tribal members, in partnership with social and physical scientists. Weaving together Indigenous ecological knowledge and elements of western earth sciences to map climate change impacts and support adaptation planning (Button and Peterson 2009; Bethel et al. 2011), it has expanded and grown to include more communities and contexts (Bethel et al. 2022). That writing was followed by a chapter in the volume's second edition seven years later. It focused on the tribal and historied communities along the coast of southeast Louisiana and the process between the "now and then" of community-led adaptation and the spectrum of actions from protecting-in-place to community-led resettlement, to maintain cultural integrity and preserve traditional lifeways (Peterson and Maldonado 2016).

Since those writings, coastal Louisiana Tribes have experienced a multitude of layered disasters and their cascading effects, as well as a groundswell of engagement with and participation in policy and action forums ranging from the local to international scales. They have furthered their existing collaborations and partnerships together with new allies, working together in the space of Tribal citizen activism to restore the coast for the betterment of all communities. While the previous chapter iteration (Peterson and Maldonado 2016) grappled with the challenges facing climate-forced displacement and relocation, the crisis has since hit a socio-ecological tipping point (Walker and Salt 2006) and now calls for immediate reimagined action. As was attributed to Chief Si'ahl in 1854,

DOI: 10.4324/9781003242499-13

"Man did not weave the web of life – he is merely a strand in it. Whatever he does to the web, he does to himself."

This chapter focuses on peeling back the layers of socio-political complexities and impacts of successive disasters and exposes the root causes of harm upon those who carry the burden of risks – the risk-bearers. We share some locally driven, culturally appropriate, and effective pathways and solutions for reducing risks from extreme weather events and the climate crisis. The need for expedience and immediacy of actions is profound. Yet actions taken should not be for what is commonly referred to as "the greater common good" – not sacrificing one community over another – at the detriment of those who first called this land home, and whose ancient wisdom carries critical tools and applications to help guide the way to not only survive the current overlapping crises, but to thrive. The communities are putting their deep place-based knowledge and wisdom into action, weaving additional expertise and knowledge to address violent obstacles, in order to protect and restore sacred homelands, to preserve culture and livelihoods, and to continue their lifeways into future generations. This chapter is a testament to their actions and the lessons held for coastal communities around the world for community activism, coastal restoration, and climate action.

The Structural Violence Embedded in Agency Disaster Responses

> It's tough. It's like we're at the end of the world, and we're treated that way too. We're always last for everything.
>
> *(Elder Theresa Dardar, Pointe-au-Chien Indian Tribe, Chavez 2021)*

Disasters reveal multiple layers of systemic social and environmental injustices, violence, and racism (Jerolleman and Waugh Jr. 2022; Tierney 2010). Socially constructed vulnerability is often attributed to the risk bearers instead of the inequitable and violent systems (Blaikie et al. 1994). Communities and population groups that have been made most at-risk to extreme weather and climate events endure disproportionate hardships and have historically often suffered harm from external decisions benefiting others at the expense of "expendable populations" (Maldonado and Peterson 2021).

There are a multitude of policies, programs, and institutional practices, and their resulting processes that perpetuate systemic barriers to communities placed increasingly in harm's way to hazards. Examples include benefit–cost analysis, gentrification, development of plans to address the impacts, and funding mechanisms. They disadvantage populations and neighborhoods made marginalized, exacerbate injustices and disaster risk, and hinder community actions and implementation (Marino et al. 2019).

Benefit–cost analysis (BCA) processes can perpetuate systemic barriers to hazard risk-bearing communities in various ways. One way is that what counts as a cost and benefit can leave out critical assets for some communities, including subsistence fishing, trapping, hunting, and gathering rights and cultural assets. In short, a BCA does not include the social, psychological, cultural, health, and spiritual costs borne by communities bearing the risks. A second way is that a BCA perpetuates the disadvantages that historically exploited communities have which have been neglected by government and infrastructure investments. These economic-driven decisions, which are legitimized by government authorities, dictate and determine who and what is being sacrificed for "the greater common good" (Roy 1999), with the concept of "good" determined by economic measures (Oliver-Smith 2010). Such decisions discount the non-material, social, spiritual, and cultural components empowering communities to function, survive, and thrive (Maldonado 2019; Comardelle 2020; Jessee 2022). A question rarely asked is who benefits and who pays the cost?

Gentrification has become a predictable outcome following disasters, resulting in further harm and displacement of under-resourced and historically overburdened populations, in both urban and rural contexts. For example, intensive rural gentrification followed Hurricanes Katrina and Rita in Louisiana in 2005 and had severe impacts on agricultural and fishing economies (Solet 2006). Since then, and following each hurricane, gentrification has increased and exacerbated this harm and displacement.

People's lives and entire ecological systems depend greatly on which stakeholders develop plans that address anticipated large-scale, climate-driven disaster impacts and how those plans are implemented. These impacts are particularly critical for coastal tribal settlements that have historically suffered from the decisions made by stakeholders – but not the risk-bearers – outside their communities; the community rightsholders most often endure a disproportionate share of the hardships from climate and environmental risks, as well as the ecological systems already degraded by unsustainable development and extractive practices (Maldonado and Peterson 2021). Decisions about hurricane disaster recovery, for example, are based on "master plans" and regional economic models created by stakeholders who stand to gain economically, and which often negatively impact Black, Indigenous, and people of color (BIPOC) communities (Sand-Fleischman 2019).

There are also significant systemic barriers to being able to implement mitigation actions to stem further disaster impacts. For example, the current requirement to supply a FEMA-approved Hazard Mitigation Plan in order to receive FEMA hazard mitigation funds is a barrier for the smaller, under-resourced, and overburdened communities that are most at risk of hazards. These communities will have difficulties finding personnel assistance for planning, accessing data, and meeting match requirements. Although slow-onset events are increasingly resulting in cumulative impacts, the disaster declaration process has yet to be expanded to include slow-onset events (Jerolleman et al. 2021). Further, the 18-month period for official financial assistance following a disaster declaration is too short due to the layered issues. In sum, the prevailing governance is often ineffectual and structural violence continues to render the long oppressed, overburdened, and overlooked communities as invisible and dispensable. At the same time, rural and coastal territories are becoming more precarious. What then, can be done?

Place Context

When I was growing up, my family would take the boat down the bayou and I could pull the grass on either side of the boat with my hands. Now it is just wide-open canals. It was pretty here before. Now all we have are skeletons.

Our community is made up of my people. We are all family. Everybody knows everybody. You can stop at the first house and ask where so and so lives. We don't lock our doors. We trust everyone here. Before the oil spill, you could go in front of your house and catch fish or crabs for supper or throw a cast net and catch shrimp.

You need your people and you need your land. But our land is slowly washing away. Without the land, our community will be separated. Our younger generation is leaving. Pretty soon we're going to be just an elderly community. The land, at least what's left, is what keeps our community together. If we scatter into other communities, we will lose our Indian bloodline. We want our children to be able to stay in the community to keep the Tribe going...

Our people have always lived off the water and land. We're bayou people. After a storm, sometimes there's still water on the road, but we come back. People here come back. It's like nowhere else.

(Elder Theresa Dardar, Pointe-au-Chien Indian Tribe describing her homeland, an excerpt from "I Came and I Stayed", Maldonado 2019: 96–98).

Coastal Louisiana's intricate web of natural ecosystem diversity is unraveling. Hydrological, meteorological, and environmental disasters, extractive industries' effects, river mismanagement, and climate change are drastically transforming the coastal near-shore landscape and waterscape. Tribal perseverance in-place has become more tenuous this century as sea level rise accelerated, storm frequency and intensity increased, and with it, the loss of coastal wetlands. The eustatic sea level rise in the Gulf is about twice the global average (Sweet et al. 2017, 2022) and approaching the "tipping point" in places where wetlands in low tidal amplitude environments cannot survive (Turner et al. 2018; Turner and Mo 2021; Kirwan et al. 2010).

In the twentieth century, ten thousand miles of dredged canals were cut through Louisiana's coastal wetlands to create passageways for pipelines and navigation and to drill for oil and gas. Local and Indigenous knowledges and observations explain that the dominant cause of contemporary land loss are the canals, primarily constructed for oil and gas extraction, in and around the Tribal communities, particularly from the 1950s–1970s (Bethel et al. 2011). These anthropogenic influences, and others, have resulted in Louisiana having among the highest land loss rates in the world (Carter et al. 2018). Complicating matters further is that the requirement for oil and gas companies to close off pipeline canal entrances and fill in unproductive canals is not enforced.

The Tribe's homes have been damaged by hurricanes, storm flooding, and wind speeds that have increased in recent years (Burkett and Davidson 2012; Peterson 2020). Hurricane Ida (2021) caused catastrophic damage to the Tribal communities in southeast Louisiana. Sixty of sixty-eight homes of the Pointe-au-Chien Indian Tribe were unlivable after Hurricane Ida – a Category 4 storm that passed over them in August 2021. The communities face increasing flood risks and the vitally important sacred sites (mounds) that have great significance to the Tribes will disappear due to erosion if immediate action is not taken. The Tribes' livelihoods are based on receiving harvests dependent on these wetlands. Wildlife co-existing in these places, such as the monarch butterflies and birds using the region as a fly-zone, as well as the coastal terrestrial and freshwater ecosystems, are at-risk from increasing inundation and salinity (Carter et al. 2018).

Satellite imagery taken soon after Hurricane Ida in 2021 is no longer relevant a few months later because the land shown in this imagery is no longer there. This begs the question: How can coastal land restoration processes be expedited to save what's save-able now, especially considering the increasingly active hurricane seasons, potentially destructive damage, and the very real potential of the whole landscape changing with more land loss?

Community-Driven Actions

Our ancestors made these mounds, so we won't just stand by while they are washed away.

(Second Chairman Donald Dardar, Pointe-au-Chien Indian Tribe, CRCL 2019)

Modern government systems in the US are not adequately equipped or prepared to address compound, multiple disasters from the increasingly extreme weather and climate impacts, historical and continued environmental racism, aging and collapsing infra-structure, social inequalities and limited access to resources, and the failure of agencies to respond effectively. Yet to address immediate needs, reduce inequities, and work towards healthier, sustained outcomes (Romanello et al. 2021), many communities are already making bottom-up adaptation decisions. They are taking preparedness and risk-reduction actions to mitigate and reduce their risk to climate and extreme weather impacts, share capacity, and enhance healing and resilience in the face of historical traumas and con-tinued uncertainties (Maldonado et al. 2021).

Within this context, and in response to the rapidly increasing climate crisis, three Tribes in coastal Louisiana – the Grand Bayou Atakapa-Ishak/Chawasha Tribe, Grand Caillou/Dulac Band of Biloxi-Chitimacha-Choctaw Tribe, and Pointe-au-Chien Indian Tribe – initiated a project to restore marshland in their communities in order to preserve sacred places and reduce land loss. The Tribes are all unique and culturally diverse and have always lived as stewards and "in sync" with the lands and waters as fishers, farmers, and hunters. The Tribes have been resilient and are now working to maintain their sub-sistence lifeways.

Today, the coastal Tribes, among other communities in Louisiana, are in existential crisis because of the rapidly changing environment. The water is rising and the wetlands are quickly disappearing. They have watched their lands wash away into the Gulf of Mexico or become inundated with floodwaters and drastic changes in salinity impacting plants, animals, and lands, because of the increasing effects of hurricanes, storm surges, erosion, and relative sea level rise, and the effects of canals cut through the marsh to build pipelines to carry the oil drilled from along the Louisiana coast or beneath the wetlands. There are distinct risks to the Tribes' cultural continuity into the future as their lands and sacred sites quickly erode, along with their knowledge of land, identities, and cultural connections between generations. Yet, the Tribes are taking proactive measures to preserve historical sites and preserve and restore medicinal plants and refurbish the marshlands. The real solution, we believe, is to work with the natural environment for solutions to both mitigate and adapt to increasing sea level rise, storm-surges, erosion, and flooding, while restoring the wetlands and simultaneously, the tribal interests and cultures.

This will be done by filling in the canals dredged in Louisiana's wetlands, whose dredged materials create continuous levees, or spoil banks, that are aligned perpendicular to the canal. Canals are created in the marsh and the dredged material is placed in continuous levees aligned parallel on both sides (aka, "spoil banks") to recover oil and gas thousands of meters below the wetland. The spoil bank height may be multiple times the tidal range and the spoil bank weight compresses soils beneath it. These hydrologic changes inhibit both overland and below-ground water flows. Twenty-seven thousand canals in the Louisiana coastal parishes' wetlands are plugged and abandoned but continue to erode (Turner and McClenachan 2018; Figure 10.1).

Filling in canals with the spoil bank is called "backfilling" and is intended to restore marsh on the spoil bank and in the canal and prevent further marsh loss. Backfilling

FIGURE 10.1 Abandoned and plugged wells on land, 2017. From Turner and McClenachan 2018 (open access journal article; https://doi.org/10.1371/journal.pone.0207717).

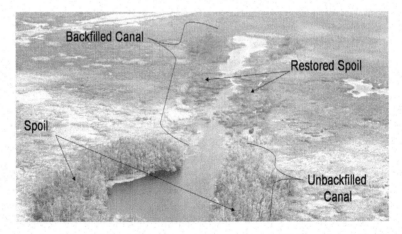

FIGURE 10.2 A canal backfilled in Cameron Parish, Louisiana visible at the top half of the picture extending from an unfilled canal with elevated, tree lined spoil banks. Notice marsh reestablishment on the former spoil banks and in portions of the canal. From Turner and McClenachan 2018 (open access journal article; https://doi.org/10.1371/journal.pone.0207717).

canals and spoil banks quickly and inexpensively restores wetlands by moving the dredged materials forming levees back into the canals (Figure 10.2). No sediments need be added. The potential co-benefits are: improved resiliency for subsistence living, reduced erosion rates, protecting sacred sites, and as an example from which others can learn.

The core of the project team are the three Tribes who bring together Indigenous leaders, knowledge-holders, and scientists with western physical and social sciences. The group includes experts in: Indigenous and local knowledges and community science, environmental, cultural, and public anthropology and sociology on disaster resilience, hazard policy, human migration, coastal ecology and biological oceanography, GIS, water resources engineering, and planning and legal studies of hazard mitigation and emergency management. Subject matter experts are giving in-kind expertise. Project outcomes are critical for the future health and well-being of the Tribes and of the coast. The team is working to document, analyze, and assess relationships between cultural and Indigenous heritage, coastal restoration, and community resilience, and bridge gaps between the knowledge and experience held by community knowledge-holders, and other scientists, while enhancing community resilience across generations. We are creating new knowledge by weaving Indigenous knowledges and local knowledges with additional science data and expertise to determine the optimal places for canal restoration, and then to restore them. This is being done first by identifying the many abandoned canals threatening sacred places and discerning places that can be restored or conserved.

Chief Parfait-Dardar shared the view that:

> This will ultimately save tribal communities along the coast. Indigenous community sites have been lost to coastal erosion in Louisiana, and many families have been forced to relocate from sacred lands due to coastal land loss. The implementation of this project will help restore much of what's been lost throughout the years.
>
> *(Lowlander Center 2021b)*

The project offers a distinct opportunity – transferable to at-risk communities throughout the United States and US territories – to put into action how local knowledge and Indigenous knowledge can be paired with additional scientific expertise creating knowledge to determine the most optimal places for mitigation work and co-create a nature-based restoration process that enhances both community and ecosystem resilience. In restoring canals in the Louisiana delta, vegetation almost immediately begins to grow on the former spoil bank and then the canal gradually fills in over decades. Backfilling increases wetland habitat, reduces the indirect effects of the spoil bank on nearby marshes, improves coastal marsh quality, provides for various storm water protection values and protects nearby sacred mounds and habitat.

This Tribal-driven project reflects coastal Louisiana's Tribes' decisions to apply nature-based solutions to climate-related hazards such as sea level rise and flooding. It tests innovative and replicable strategies to increase community resilience capacity and protect irreplaceable cultural landscapes and sacred sites. It fills a critical role in shaping cumulative actions for integrating coastal resilience activities and cultural heritage across Louisiana and other at-risk coastal communities with strong traditional practices and cultural and heritage connections to place. The project addresses mitigating, but not eliminating, existing and future challenges from sea level rise, flood protection, and wetland loss for

Louisiana's coastal tribes. It will simultaneously reinvigorate commitment to the sacred, cultural heritage sites and critical human dimensions – a holistic approach to the integral connections between the human community and natural environment. Without this project, these vital sacred sites will disappear due to erosion from the surrounding canals and spoil banks, and with them their legacy and significance for the Tribes (Figure 10.3).

Community Resilience and Adaptive Capacity through Trusted Collaborations

> Join us in the fight to fill Louisiana's empty canals and to protect the coastline now and into the future.
>
> *(Chief Shirell Parfait-Dardar, Grand Caillou/Dulac Band of Biloxi-Chitimacha-Choctaw Indians, Lowlander Center 2021a)*

All communities – Indigenous and non-Indigenous – have the potential to inform and benefit from the very tangible outcomes of this work. Building community resilience and adaptive capacity for healing and regeneration will be a critical, practical, and innovative approach to ensure the protection and relevance of these important, irreplaceable, and sacred places and cultures in the twenty-first century and for future generations.

Multiple other restoration approaches are currently in place to help manage Louisiana's coastal lands including barrier island restoration and sediment slurry depositions. But some barriers to effective restoration are that much useful information is trapped in disciplinary or issue siloes, or that communities and scientists often lack time to distill research findings into action plans, education, or scalable lessons learned. Building collaborative research requires time to develop trust and translate between diverse (ecological, social, Indigenous) sciences. One aim of this project is to address these very problems by working across these boundaries to lower barriers to

FIGURE 10.3 The canals backfilling project highlights the importance and connections of people, place, livelihoods, sacred sites, and all living relatives.

collaboration and to produce usable and actionable science. This includes working to ensure that diverse knowledges are equally valued, credited, and respected in scientific research collaborations. The effect will be to safeguard the culturally irreplaceable landscape to support the communities' well-being and contribute to a thriving eco-cultural system.

This project's collaboration is able to function because of the long-established partnership, based on trust, mutual respect, and reciprocity, between the Lowlander Center, which "supports lowland communities and places, both inland and coastal, for the benefit of both people and environment" (Lowlander Center n.d.) and the First Peoples' Conservation Council of Louisiana (FPCC). The FPCC was formed through a partnership with the US Department of Agriculture's Natural Resources Conservation Service (USDA-NRCS), and is a non-profit formed to provide a forum for Native American Tribes in Coastal Louisiana "to identify and solve natural resource issues on their Tribal lands" (FPCC n.d.). The FPCC member tribes include the Atakapa-Ishak/Chawasha Tribe, Grand Bayou Indian Village; Grand Caillou/Dulac Band of Biloxi-Chitimacha-Choctaw Tribe; Pointe-au-Chien Indian Tribe; Jean Charles Choctaw Nation; Avoyel-Taensa Tribe; and the Bayou Lafourche Band of Biloxi-Chitimacha-Choctaw Tribe, who work together to increase capacity to protect their homelands and sacred places from the rising waters, industrial contamination, and gentrification, for the sake of their tribes and for the future generations of all that reside in the region. They have worked together as a coalition for more than a decade, to support the needs of individual Tribes and for joint goals that are pertinent to all the Tribal families.

This work is certainly not isolated to only refilling the dredged canals in the wetlands (Baniewicz 2020). It also includes a petition to the UN Special Rapporteur (UUSC 2020), preparing and responding to major disasters (including educating and data collection on the BP Deepwater Horizon oil disaster and many named hurricanes), contributing to the US National Climate Assessment, re-establishing and reinvigorating the Louisiana Governor's Commission on Native American Affairs, and more. The FPCC does this together as family because no one Tribe or entity can do it alone. The work includes a vision for a just and sustainable world, and for the love of home and generations yet to come. Settler mentality, racism, economic oppression, storms, and loss of land do not deter from this vision, nor do the powers and principalities of extractive violence pull them apart. They are family, human and more-than-human, and are coming together in the fight of their lives, living on among the fastest disappearing landmass on Earth (Marshall 2014; Kolbert 2019). The coastal tribes that collaborate together through the FPCC are the original stewards of these sacred, religious, spiritual places, lands, waters. Their acumen and foresight for knowing how to live with their human and more than-human relatives and ecologies, what Native scholar Dr Daniel Wildcat calls "indigenuity" (2009, 2013), should be better understood to translate to modern conditions.

The spiral of partnerships and collaborations only expands out from the established core, weaving in partners of networks of mutual aid such as the Disaster Justice Network, university partners such as Louisiana State University, Drexel University, and University of South Alabama, other non-profit organizations such as the Livelihoods Knowledge Exchange Network and Healthy Gulf, other networks such as the Rising Voices Center for Indigenous and Earth Sciences, faith-based organizations such as the Unitarian Universalist Service Committee and the Presbyterian Church (PCUSA), and communities facing similar challenges and shared experiences such as in Alaska and the Pacific Islands.

Critical to this work is cross-boundary organizing, which includes multiple disciplines, communities, and ideas that can help link programs with projects that reduce natural hazards while emphasizing community benefits. Boundary organizations can act as facilitators, interpreters, and resource advocates (Peterson 2020), fostering collaborative work and serving as connectors of organizational resources, while working across communities of research and practice, epistemologies, and generations to coordinate complementary expertise (Maldonado et al. 2016). We share this web of connections in this project here, and it is much bigger and deeper than what is included in this short writing, to demonstrate the deep and broad complexity of the issues and that it is through such a networked web of connections and relations that capacity, actions, and solutions emerge and are implemented.

Actions with a Lagniappe (Extra Value) – A Broad and Inclusive Look

It's not just 'land' that we're restoring. We are restoring habitat…There's a plethora of life besides human life that's dependent on these places – the microscopic life, the insect populations, the mammals, birds, *nesting* birds, the marine population – all of these are dependent on the land that we restore.

(*Elder Rosina Philippe, Grand Bayou Atakapa/Ishak Chawasha Tribe,*
as quoted in Baniewicz 2020)

Increasing extreme weather events and climate crisis necessitate urgent, innovative, justice- and eco-centered sustainable actions. This existential threat also creates – and requires – an opening to look to a diversity of knowledge systems, such as Indigenous knowledge systems based on time- and on-the-ground tested, holistic, place- and experience-based observations, witnessing, hypothesizing, monitoring, and evaluation developed and reimagined over millennia, for regenerative and sustainable solutions (Lazrus et al. 2022). This includes "flipping the script" on who is considered an "expert" and whose voice "counts" in disaster and emergency management policies and practices. The intent is to democratize the planning process, so that the risk bearers, those most impacted by the decision-making, are included. By involving those who are most likely to bear the consequences of extreme events, then visions of the future can be inclusive, and the quality of the planning will benefit from a variety of knowledge, backgrounds, and experiences. Experiencing climate-driven disaster impacts first and foremost, communities forced onto the frontlines of the climate crisis are facing further key human rights concerns and implications, such as access to and loss of food, water, sanitation, life, property, health, housing, work, self-determination, education, and sovereignty (Moulton et al. 2017). The dual threats from increasing climate-related hazards and impacts, and key human rights concerns and implications (Moulton et al. 2017), require proactive planning to meet residents' priorities.

The project described in this chapter honors the Indigenous knowledge and wisdom of the Tribes and leaders guiding the work and brings together diverse ways of knowing with best principles and scientific insights on disaster resilience to inform nature-based solutions determined by Louisiana's Tribal communities, leading the way as stewards of the lands and waters and voices that champion climate-resilient futures. This work provides a lagniappe, the extra value gained from simultaneously restoring marshes, reducing land loss, and protecting sacred sites. These actions enable a sustainable and justice-centered adaptation process and a regenerative future that is based on human and environmental rights with full participation in the well-being of community.

Acknowledgments

We thank the National Estuary Program and the National Fish and Wildlife Foundation for funding some of the planning work for the canals backfilling project and for the Barataria-Terrebonne National Estuary Program (BTNEP) for implementation support. We are fortunate to have an abundance of partners, collaborators, and co-conspirators that are too vast to list individually in this limited space, but please know our love and gratitude for all you do, and the limitless value that you bring, is appreciated far beyond these pages.

References

Baniewicz, T. 2020. Coastal Louisiana tribes team up with biologist to protect sacred sites from rising seas. *Southerly*, September 2, https://southerlymag.org/2020/09/02/coastal-louisiana-tribes-team-up-with-biologist-to-protect-sacred-sites-from-rising-seas/.

Bethel, M.B., Braud, D.H., Lambeth, T., Dardar, O.S., and Ferguson-Bohnee, P. 2022. Mapping risk factors to climate change impacts using traditional ecological knowledge to support adaptation planning with a Native American Tribe in Louisiana. *J Environmental Management* 301 (Jan): 113801. doi:10.1016/j.jenvman.2021.113801. Epub 2021Sep 30. PMID: 34600422.

Bethel, M.B., Brien, L.F., Danielson, E.J., Laska, S.B., Troutman J.P., Boshart W.M., Giardino, M. J., and Phillips M.A. 2011. Blending geospatial technology and traditional ecological knowledge to enhance restoration decision-support processes in coastal Louisiana. *CHART Publications*. Paper 23: 555–571. https://scholarworks.uno.edu/ chart_pubs/23

Blaikie, P., Cannon, T., Davis, I., and Wisner, B. 1994. *At Risk: Natural hazards, people's vulnerability, and disasters*. London: Routledge.

Burkett, V., Davidson, M., eds. 2012. *Coastal Impacts, Adaptation and Vulnerability: A technical input to the 2012 National Climate Assessment*. Cooperative Report to the 2013 National Climate Assessment.

Button, G., and Peterson K.J. 2009. Participatory action research: community partnership with 327 social and physical scientists. In *Anthropology and Climate Change*, 1st edition. S. Crate and M. Nuttall, eds. Walnut Creek, CA: Left Coast Press, pp. 327–340.

Carter, L., et al. 2018. Southeast. In *Impacts, Risks, and Adaptation in the United States: Fourth National Climate Assessment*, Volume II. [Reidmiller D.R., et al. (eds.)]. Washington, DC: US Global Change Research Program.

Chavez, R. 2021. Why some Indigenous tribes are being left behind in Louisiana's Ida recovery. *PBS Newshour*, 20 October, https://www.pbs.org/newshour/nation/why-some-indigenous-tribes-are re-being-left-behind-in-louisianas-ida-recovery.

Comardelle, C. 2020. Preserving our place: Isle de Jean Charles. *Non-Profit Quarterly* October 19. https://nonprofitquarterly.org/preserving-our-place-isle-de-jean-charles/.

CRCL (Coalition to Restore Coastal Louisiana). 2019. The coalition to restore coastal Louisiana builds second living shoreline from recycled oyster shells. Press release, April 17, https://www. crcl.org/_files/ugd/1f121e_5c01a572d7e4479fa664a199a2030eba.pdf.

FPCC (First People's Conservation Council of Louisiana). n.d. *Our History*. https://fpcclouisiana. org/about-usour-history/our-history/.

Jerolleman, A., Maldonado, J.K., Marino, E. 2021. *Public Comment*. FEMA's Call for Public Comments on Climate Change and Underserved Populations. July 19.

Jerolleman, A. and Waugh, W. Jr., eds. 2022. *Justice, Equity, and Emergency Management*, Community, Environment, and Disaster Risk Management, Volume 25.

Jessee, N. 2022. Reshaping Louisiana's coastal frontier: managed retreat as colonial decontextualization. *Journal of Political Ecology* 29 (1): 277–301.

Kirwan, M.L., Guntenspergen, G.R., D'Alpaos, A., Morris, J.T., Mudd, S.M., Temmerman, S. 2010. Limits on the adaptability of coastal marshes to rising sea level. *Geophysical Research Letters* 37: L23401.

Kolbert, E. 2019. Louisiana's disappearing coast. *The New Yorker Magazine*, March 25, https://www.newyorker.com/magazine/2019/04/01/louisianas-disappearing-coast.

Lazrus, H., Maldonado, J.K., Blanchard, P., Souza, M.K., Thomas, B., and Wildcat, D. 2022. Culture change to address climate change: collaborations with Indigenous and Earth sciences for more just, equitable, and sustainable responses to our climate crisis. *PLOS Climate* (2): e0000005.

Lowlander Center. n.d. Mission, https://www.lowlandercenter.org/mission.

Lowlander Center. 2021a. *Canals Project Video*. https://www.lowlandercenter.org/projects.

Lowlander Center. 2021b. Restoring Louisiana Marshes: protecting sacred sites, increasing tribal resilience, and reducing flood risk. Press release, American Geophysical Union Annual Fall Meeting,December 13.

Maldonado, J.K. 2019. *Seeking Justice in an Energy Sacrifice Zone: Standing on vanishing land in coastal Louisiana*. London/New York: Routledge.

Maldonado, J.K., Lazrus, H., Gough, B., Bennett, S.K., Chief, K., Dhillon, C., Kruger, L., Morisette, J., Petrovic, S., and Whyte, K. 2016. The story of rising voices: facilitating collaboration between Indigenous and western ways of knowing. In *Responses to Disasters and Climate Change: Understanding vulnerability and fostering resilience*. M. Companion and M. Chaiken, eds. CRC Press.

Maldonado, J.K., and Peterson, K.J. 2021. *Justice-Driven Disaster Recovery: Baseline data to support safe communities, healthy ecosystems, and a rejuvenated future*. Natural Hazards Center. https://hazards.colorado.edu/quick-response-report/justice-driven-disaster-recovery.

Maldonado, J.K., Wang I.F.C., Eningowuk, F., Iaukea, L., Lascurain, A., Lazrus, H., Naquin, A., Naquin, J.R., Nogueras Vidal, K.M., Peterson, K.J., Rivera-Collazo, I., Souza, M.K., Stege, M., and Thomas, B. 2021. Addressing the challenges of climate-driven community-led resettlement and site expansion: knowledge sharing, storytelling, healing, and collaborative coalition building. *Journal of Environmental Studies and Sciences* 11 (3): 294–304.

Marino, E., Jerolleman, A., and Maldonado, J.K. 2019. *Law and Policy for Adaptation and Relocation Meeting*. Summary report of the meeting of the National Center for Atmospheric Research, Boulder, Colorado. https://risingvoices.ucar.edu/sites/default/files/2021-08/law-and-p olicy-adaptation-and-relocation-meeting-2019.pdf.

Marshall, B. 2014. Losing ground: Southeast Louisiana is disappearing, quickly. *The Lens, ProPublica*, August 28.https://www.scientificamerican.com/article/losing-ground-southeast-louisiana-is-di sappearing-quickly/.

Moulton, A., Soqo, S., and Ferreira, K. 2017. *Community-led, Human Rights-based Solutions to Climate-forced Displacement: A guide for funders*. Unitarian Universalist Service Committee, https://www.uusc.org/wp-content/uploads/2017/12/UUSCGuideforFunders_W.pdf.

National Geographic. 2021. *Impact with Gal Gadot: Killer red fox*. https://www.nationalgeographic.com/tv/shows/impact-with-gal-gadot/episode-guide/season-01/episode-05-killer-red-fox/vdka23399798.

Oliver-Smith, A. 2010. *Defying Displacement: Grassroots resistance and the critique of development*. Austin: University of Texas Press.

Peterson, K.J. 2020. Sojourners in a new land: hope and adaptive traditions. In *Louisiana's Response to Extreme Weather: A coastal state' s adaptation challenges and successes*. S. Laska, ed., pp. 185–214. Springer Open.

Peterson, K.J., and Maldonado, J.K. 2016. When adaptation is not enough: between now and then of community-led resettlement. In *Anthropology and Climate Change*, 2nd edition. S. Crate and M. Nuttall, eds. London/New York: Routledge Press.

Romanello, M., et al. 2021. The 2021 report of the Lancet Countdown on health and climate change: code red for a healthy future. *Lancet* 398 (10311): 1619–1662. doi:10.1016/50140-6736(21) 01787-6.

Roy, A. 1999. *The Cost of Living*. New York: The Modern Library.

Sand-Fleischman, M. 2019. *Circumventing the Next Trail of Tears: Re-approaching planning and policy for the climatologically displaced Indigenous communities of coastal Louisiana*. Doctoral dissertation, City and Regional Planning, Cornell University.

Solet, K. 2006. *Thirty Years of Change: How subdivisions on stilts have altered a southeast Louisiana parish's coast*, Landscape and People. Master's thesis, Department of Urban Studies, University of New Orleans.

Sweet, W.V., Kopp, R.E., Weaver, C.P., Obeysekera, J., Horton, R.M., Thieler, E.R., and Zervas, C. 2017. *Global and Regional Sea Level Rise Scenarios for the United States*. Washington, DC: NOAA.

Sweet, W.V., et al. 2022. *Global and Regional Sea Level Rise Scenarios for the United States: Updated mean projections and extreme water level probabilities along US Coastlines*. NOAA Technical Report NOS 01. National Oceanic and Atmospheric Administration, National Ocean Service.

Tierney K. 2010. Growth machine politics and the social production of risk. *Contemporary Sociology*, 39 (6): 660–663. https://doi.org/10.1177/0094306110386715b.

Turner, R.E., Kearney, M.S., and Parkinson, R.W. 2018. Sea level rise tipping point of delta survival. *Journal of Coastal Research* 34: 470–474.

Turner, R.E., and McClenachan, G. 2018. Reversing wetland death from 35,000 cuts: opportunities to restore Louisiana's dredged canals. *PLOS ONE* 13 (12): e0207717.

Turner, R.E., and Mo, Y. 2021. Salt marsh elevation limit determined after subsidence from hydrologic change and hydrocarbon extraction. *Remote Sensing* 13: 49.

UUSC [Unitarian Universalist Service Committee]. 2020. US Tribes facing climate crisis unite to address human rights violations, https://www.uusc.org/initiatives/climate-justice/special-rapp orteur-letter/.

Walker, B., and Salt, D. 2006. *Resilience Thinking: Sustaining ecosystems and people in a changing world*. Island Press.

Wildcat D. 2009. *Red Alert! Saving the planet with Indigenous knowledge*. Fulcrum.

Wildcat D. 2013. Introduction: climate change and Indigenous peoples of the USA, *Climatic Change* 120 (3): 509–515.

11

CLIMATE CHANGE AS COLONIAL ECHO IN THE CANADIAN ARCTIC

Franz Krause

Encountering Collapse

The image of the dilapidated house below, poised on the crumbling edge of an eroding riverbank, may appear like the epitome of climate change in the Circumpolar North. It shows the house – the material manifestation of family, shelter, and stability – literally undermined by a climatic regime that destabilizes land and water, ice and permafrost, and displaces lives and livelihoods. But is this really what is happening here?

I snapped the photo in May 2018, on a boat trip through the Mackenzie Delta with three young hunters. They were mainly out on the water to hunt beavers, an animal that had recently become extremely abundant in the delta, after decades of near extirpation.

FIGURE 11.1 Old house of the late George White, Aklavik River, Gwich'in Settlement Region, May 2018. Photo: Franz Krause.

DOI: 10.4324/9781003242499-14

Now, the main season for hunting beaver for its warm fur was over, and the government program that bought furs at fixed rates was closed until the coming winter. But hunters who had personal use for the fur, or would consume the meat, continued to hunt beaver. They also continued to hunt to benefit from an ongoing research project that bought samples from beaver carcasses for the handsome sum of $100 CAN, more than twice the money that a stretched beaver skin could fetch during the season.

The young hunters had also brought a grizzly bear tag, which is a license to hunt one of a limited number of grizzlies in the Gwich'in Settlement Region, along on the trip. This was the time of year when the bears had emerged from their wintertime dens and roamed the delta and adjacent areas. Grizzly bear skins can fetch upwards of $1000 CAN, but the hunt is strictly regulated with a limited number of tags for the area. When we did come across a grizzly, however, my companions did not make any effort at shooting it. They explained that it was only a cub, probably around two years old and only just separated from its mother. After the cub ran along the riverbank next to our boat, it swam through the channel and disappeared in the willows on the opposite bank.

We continued towards the main branch of the Mackenzie River. Some of the watercourses in the delta were still frozen over. Only six days earlier, the river channels around Aklavik – the delta settlement where we had begun our trip a few hours ago – had shed their ice crust and opened the boating season. It is a tradition in Aklavik to place bets on when exactly this happens: experience, stories, as well as high-tech meteorological and hydrological data and weather forecasts help form an idea of when the ice will break up around Aklavik; nevertheless, the actual moment this happens is always anticipated, but never determined. In many springs, the main Mackenzie branch piles up huge masses of broken river ice along its banks and across the river, but this year, the heaps were rather small and there was no major ice dam. My companions were not surprised: the snow pack in the catchment had been rather low, and the ice in the delta rather thin, so there was neither a major spring flood nor a particularly recalcitrant ice cover.

But there were still large flocks of geese in the flooded delta, resting on open water bodies and mudflats during their annual migration north. As long as the ice still held, hunters from many settlements in the region had been spending as much time as possible in their blinds at popular goose resting spots throughout the delta. Now, after a period of waiting for the unstable ice to disintegrate, my companions were keen on hunting geese again, but it was very difficult to get into shooting range with the noisy, motorized boat. We passed various camps, some apparently still in use recently, others abandoned. One of the abandoned camps belonged to the grandfather of one of my companions. His family had used it until a few years ago. But the building had become old and the location was increasingly subject to flooding. So my companion, alongside his father and a family friend, had set up a new camp on a high bank two kilometers downstream, where they had cleared the willows and built three new buildings. This was where we went next to have some food and warm up; open boat rides just after break-up are chilly!

By the time we continued the hunting trip after the break, it was early morning. At that time of the year it stayed light all night. The hunters shot a few more beaver, some ducks, seven muskrats and even a goose. Muskrats used to be very abundant in the delta during the twentieth century. In fact, hunting and selling their pelts had contributed to an economic boom in the region and the establishment of Aklavik as a trading post, settlement, and administrative hub in the first half of the twentieth century. The muskrat adorns Aklavik's coat of arms, and people say not without pride that this small place used to be known as "the muskrat capital of the world." From a trip like ours, hunters would expect to return with several dozens of muskrats in those days.

Today, muskrats are rare (Turner, Lantz, and Gwich'in Tribal Council Department of Cultural Heritage 2018), and Aklavik people provide several explanations: perhaps there had been so many of them that they depleted their favorite food sources in the delta; or they were pushed out by other animals that have been moving north with a warming climate; or maybe if people would hunt and trap them more, their numbers would surge again? Be this as it may, even if there were many more muskrats around, it would still not restore the glory of the old days.[1] Their pelts only fetch five dollars apiece, which hardly justifies the effort and cost to hunt, trap, skin, and prepare them. "Ratting," as people call muskrat hunting in the delta, is a cherished activity, but it is no longer financially lucrative work.

Afterwards, I learned that the old house on the collapsing riverbank had belonged to the late George White, an Aklavik elder who had passed away two months before. His father, who had come to the delta as a fur trapper, had built the house and used it frequently. George had worked as a guard for the Aklavik police detachment and was not known to be as enthusiastic about the delta house as his father. Once his father had passed away, he visited the house infrequently and had not used it at all for a few years before his death. And because George did not have any children to take over the house, it was left to lapse. In fact, abandoned and decaying buildings, whether collapsing down an eroding bank or rotting away on higher ground, are common sights in the delta. Delta inhabitants are not bothered by them. In fact, alongside the abandoned buildings, there are plenty of new houses, some in the immediate vicinity of the old cabins, others at new spots, as in my companion's family's case.

Spending time in the delta and building and maintaining camps continue to be cherished activities (Wishart and Loovers 2013). Indeed, young families interested in establishing their own camps in and around the delta are today in a much better position to choose a suitable spot than a few decades ago, when there were so many camps that it was impossible not to infringe on already used areas. Perhaps the catastrophic scenario that we may easily read into the picture of the collapsing house is more of a projection of our specific expectations of stability and particular anxieties about transience, impermanence, and renewal than an understanding of climate change in the Arctic.

Arctic and Other Crashes

Other dynamics in the delta have been much more significant than old cabins sliding down eroding riverbanks. Take, for example, the aforementioned population dynamics of beaver and muskrat. As a wide range of studies brought together by Igor Krupnik and Aron Crowell (2020) have recently made clear, radical ecological fluctuations have long been the rule in the Arctic, rather than a recent doomsday scenario. Rising temperatures and declining sea ice are certainly affecting peaks and crashes in animal populations, but this does not happen in a linear and generalized manner. Most often, regionally specific combinations of factors, including extreme weather events but also, as Indigenous participants in these studies have emphasized, sustained hunting efforts, help some animal populations thrive while causing others to collapse. And while decreasing ice cover and thawing permafrost do pose major challenges in the Arctic, Mark Nuttall (2019) has argued that the common focus on liquefaction as a linear process of melting or thawing is misleading. Yes, there is a clear trend in the reduction of ice and the increase in thermokarst. However, the way this matters to many Arctic inhabitants is less as a continual process and more as an extension of uncertainties and sudden events, phenomena that many know from the annual periods of freeze-up and break-up. Climate change proliferates these periods and the unstable processes of "liquescence," in Nuttall's words, where ice might hold or break, and ground might be solid or fluid (Krause 2021b).

The instabilities, collapses, and fluctuations that characterize life in the Arctic are not limited to ecological dynamics (Veldhuis et al. 2019). In fact, it is a common limitation for climate change narratives to focus on ice, erosion, and animals and then assess their impacts on human lives (Cameron 2012). In the Mackenzie Delta, fluctuating prices, and other economic booms and busts have been at least as volatile as climate and ecology. Some of the most striking economic surges and crashes in and around the delta included the baleen whaling boom and the Yukon gold rush at the turn of the twentieth century, the large-scale construction of military infrastructure during the Cold War, and the hydrocarbon-exploration waves of the 1960s/70s and 2000s (Krause 2021a).

The infrastructure-construction and hydrocarbon-exploration booms and busts provided wage labor opportunities, mostly in menial, low-paying, and easily replaceable positions, for the Indigenous inhabitants of the Mackenzie Delta. Hunters and trappers who neglected their subsistence activities for employment in these short-lived booms were sometimes able to make up for the declining income from the fur trade, but also risked getting out of touch with the skills, relations, and routines through which they had thrived before. Nevertheless, many Mackenzie Delta inhabitants skillfully managed to integrate these fluctuating economic opportunities into existing pursuits like subsistence hunting and fishing and other valuable activities (Krause 2022). Other economic fluctuations have not served inhabitants well, most notably the plummeting fur prices with a simultaneous rise in the costs of equipment like snowmobiles and gasoline. While in midcentury, successful trappers were able to buy new snowmobiles and outboard engines from their income from selling fur, today, a trapper needs income from other sources to be able to trap successfully (Wenzel 2009).

Current instabilities in relation to melting ice, thawing permafrost, and erratic animal presence therefore occur in a context where many other phenomena, too, have been unstable for a long time, such as price ratios and employment opportunities. Instability is not only, and not even primarily, a natural or hydrological process, but climate-induced volatility intersects with many other volatile dynamics. In the Mackenzie Delta, these also include colonial history and politics. Located in a far periphery relative to the Canadian state, the region came into direct contact with the colonial administration only in the late nineteenth century, when whaling, gold mining, and the fur trade brought settlers and their institutions, including missionary stations, trading posts, and police detachments (Alunik, Kolausok, and Morrison 2003; Loovers 2019). Their presence and influence led to shifts in inhabitants' mobile land-use patterns, reducing the flexibility through which they had previously been able to respond to economic and ecological shifts (Krech 1978). They also led to rampant epidemics that all but exterminated many communities in and around the delta (Piper 2019). In 1920, the Canadian government realized the area's potential for hydrocarbon exploitation and rushed to sign Treaty 11 the next summer with the First Nations in the region, intending to secure legal dominion over its resources by making band leaders sign pre-fabricated documents (Fumoleau 2004). Although Treaty 11 territory extends throughout most of what is today the continental Northwest Territories, Inuvialuit representatives of the communities living in the lower delta and along the coast did not sign the treaty.

Both Inuit and First Nation children, however, were forced to attend so-called Indian residential schools for most of the twentieth century, a system that a recent Canada-wide investigation has come to summarize as "cultural genocide" (Truth and Reconciliation Commission of Canada 2015: 3). These government-mandated and church-run institutions forced Indigenous children into boarding school where, alongside a long list of racist atrocities, they were taught to abandon their traditional languages, practices, and knowledges, and to reposition themselves at the social and economic bottom of settler society (Di Mascio and Hortop-Di Mascio 2011). Furthermore, the schools were located in fixed mission centers, often far away from the children's homes, fish camps, and hunting grounds. On the one hand, mandatory attendance meant that some children were unable to see their relatives for months or years, and on the other hand, the need to remain close to their children and protect them from harm meant that more families came to live in the settlements for ever-longer periods. The terrible consequences of this social engineering project are felt to this day, for example through the process of "intergenerational trauma" (Bombay, Matheson, and Anisman 2014), where suffering accumulates in families and manifests in current generations who have not themselves attended residential school.

During the second half of the twentieth century, the traumatizing of the Indigenous population was paralleled only by the simultaneous exploitation of the land. Large hydrocarbon companies looking for oil and gas in and around the delta bulldozed a tight network of straight lines through the landscape, where they detonated explosives for seismic exploration. In some places in the delta and offshore, they drilled oil and gas wells. These activities displaced animals, polluted water courses, and interfered with people's trails and traplines, all in the hopes that the Makenzie Delta would prove to be a second Niger Delta in terms of hydrocarbon wealth (Berger 1977). As a rule, no benefits or compensations were paid to the delta's Indigenous inhabitants, because the colonial government and the hydrocarbon companies claimed that these people had foregone their land ownership when their elders signed Treaty 11.

But the Indigenous Peoples of Treaty 11 territory saw this differently and learned to resist the continual processes of exploitation on the settlers' own terms. The Committee for Original Peoples' Entitlement (COPE) and the Indian Brotherhood of the Northwest Territories were established in 1970, fueled by a long history of colonial infringements and violence, and alarmed by the impact of hydrocarbon explorations and impending projects like the gargantuan 1200 km pipeline that was to link gas fields around the Mackenzie Delta to the national pipeline network in the province of Alberta to the south (Nuttall 2010). These organizations explicitly formulated that ecological problems – such as overhunting and oil pollution – were, at their core, political and cultural issues, as they impinged on ways of life and territorial sovereignty. This spawned the processes that led to the signing of the Inuvialuit Final Agreement in 1984 and the Gwich'in Comprehensive Land Claim Agreement in 1992. Indigenous fieldworkers and negotiators managed to, on the one hand, garner inputs and support for the land claims from the Inuvialuit and

Gwich'in people, and on the other hand, formulate their concerns and assertions in terms that were legally binding for the settler government.

Echoes of Collapse and Renewal

Uncertain and radical transformations with intersecting ecological, political, and cultural dimensions characterize life in the Mackenzie Delta today, as they have for over a century (Usher 1971). Nevertheless, Mackenzie Delta life is characterized also by the remarkably resilient ways in which its inhabitants selectively appropriate, adapt to, and resist these transformations. Despite collapses in animal populations, economic busts, deadly epidemics, and concerted efforts of assimilation, Gwich'in and Inuvialuit still inhabit the delta. Even Aklavik, the settlement that the Canadian government already declared obsolete due to flooding and erosion in the mid-twentieth century, is still there (Gruppuso and Krause, forthcoming). What does this imply for current and future impacts of climate change?

Potawatomi scholar and activist Kyle Whyte (2017a) argues that North American Indigenous Peoples experience climate change in a fundamentally different way than North American settler societies. Economically, culturally, and territorially marginalized people may already feel the impacts of a changing climate much more saliently than those at the economic and political centers, occupying the more secure lands appropriated through colonial dispossession. But for Indigenous Peoples, climate change is an echo rather than something fundamentally new. Whyte observes that climate change, in mainstream settler discourse, figures in apocalyptic terms, as the end of the known world. This is a world that has, by and large, been characterized by stability, progress, and growth, always improving and turning more comfortable. While he does not deny the fundamental scope of impending changes, Whyte points out that for Indigenous Peoples, the world of today is not the pinnacle of a steady story of progress. Instead, Indigenous Peoples' worlds have already been upended, often multiple times, through colonial violence, dispossession, and displacement. Their apocalypse has already happened.

This paints a fundamentally different picture of current predicaments of Indigenous Peoples around the world. For example, some Iñupiat communities in Alaska, close relatives of the Inuvialuit in Canada, may have to be relocated, as the permafrost on which their buildings sit is thawing and eroding into the sea (e.g. Marino 2015). This threat is therefore no less dramatic, but it manifests only as the most recent wave of relocation forced by industrial settler society. Earlier waves include the displacement of Indigenous communities to reservations on marginal land and the coercing of Indigenous children into Indian residential schools (Wildcat 2009). In Whyte's words, this means that "some indigenous peoples already inhabit what our ancestors would have likely characterized as a dystopian future. So we consider the future from what we believe is already a dystopia" (2017b: 207).

Whyte elaborates that this Indigenous, post-apocalyptic view to the future is neither nostalgic nor fatalist, but rather pragmatic. With examples citing Anishinaabe inhabitants of the North American Great Lakes region, he shows that Indigenous Peoples have long been engaged in practices of social and ecological restoration, re-growing relations among more-than-human communities after their violent destruction. This implies that while settler populations are bracing themselves for a coming climate apocalypse, Indigenous

Peoples have already been working on restoring livable worlds for a long time. This restoration, too, is not a linear process, but has had numerous setbacks; climate-change related shifts are likely to be among them, another echo of externally induced, unprecedented change, just like previous colonial terraforming violence (Ghosh 2021).

Already in their introduction to the first edition of *Anthropology and Climate Change*, Susan Crate and Mark Nuttall observed that "climate change is environmental colonialism at its fullest development" (2009: 13). They summarized that, in many cases, climate change in itself is less of an issue compared to its role as a threat multiplier, amplifying other and often more pressing problems, like social and economic concerns. Therefore, climate change is a justice issue as much as a problem of carbon dioxide concentrations. And social, political, and economic issues might be much more pressing than climate change on its own. Today, this view is widespread among social science and humanities researchers (e.g. Whyte 2017a; Huntington et al. 2019; Ready and Collings 2021). These studies also point out that this relationship works both ways: not only does climate change exacerbate social and economic issues, but prevailing social and economic issues also make climate change more problematic. Colonial dispossession and marginalization greatly increase Indigenous Peoples' vulnerability to climate change impacts; and other issues like sedentarization, economic dependence, substance abuse and colonial laws and regulations decrease their ability to creatively adjust to an always dynamic environment (Nuttall 2009).

Understanding climate change from the perspective of Indigenous Peoples as an echo of ongoing colonial violence points not only to the close relationships between physical and socio-economic issues, but also to the fact that these interwoven issues are part of a longer history (Davis and Todd 2017). This is a history of multiple assaults on Indigenous lifeworlds, but also a history of continued resistance to the colonial project, including in the form of caring for the land with its more-than-human relations and of continuing to build livable worlds in the ruins of destruction.

Echoes and Expectations

The late George White's house, about to collapse into the Aklavik River, remains a symbol of decline. It is not just an icon of accelerated erosion, but also an index of a family line that ended its presence in this place. It can be seen as a sign of a changed lifestyle and of broken economic opportunities. Mackenzie Delta inhabitants now reside in the settlement, with their camps as secondary and optional homes, and many rely on cash income in order to be able to afford to hunt, fish, trap, and travel in the delta, instead of the latter activities providing the cash. But this snapshot picture is, indeed, just that: a snapshot. It says nothing about the longer histories of colonial dispossession that have contributed to undercutting the house and the lifestyle that went with it. And it equally says nothing about the continued and often successful efforts of Inuvialuit and Gwich'in people to re-build their post-apocalyptic worlds.

The photograph is blind, for example, to the fact that this house stood on Gwich'in land, which has been affirmed as such by the 1992 Land Claim Agreement. It also cannot show that the involvement in the fur trade, which likely played a role in the establishment of this camp in the delta, was already a re-invention of a world after a previous one had been eradicated. The demise of this particular camp does not indicate the popularity of new camps in other places and among other families. And the way I framed this picture does not show that while I was photographing, my companions were refueling the boat and preparing the next leg of our journey in search of beavers, muskrats, geese, and perhaps a more mature grizzly bear. My companions were the unmistakable proof that despite collapses induced by colonial structures, climate change, and other destabilizing dynamics, delta inhabitants were re-growing new worlds. Muskrat numbers and prices made working with these animals difficult, but beavers were plentiful and the current research project made them lucrative. This allowed my companions to be out and about in the delta, travelling its channels, visiting its camps, and connecting with its animals – very old pleasures, just under new conditions.

The collapsing house also invokes the popular image of the "tipping point" in climate change discussions. It is often asked at what tipping point, for example in global temperature or carbon dioxide concentration, our climate changes beyond recognition. When will the house tip down the bank, or is it already beyond redemption? This concern, as Nuttall (2012) has pointed out, is rooted in a simplistic, mechanistic understanding of human behavior, which ignores people's anticipation and agency, reducing human lives to adaptations to a determining, physical world. Whyte (2020) adds that it would be myopic to discuss ecological tipping points without considering simultaneously what he calls "relational tipping points." The latter refer to continued breaches in trust, respect, consent, accountability, and reciprocity that have characterized the relations between settlers and Indigenous Peoples for centuries. These must be addressed alongside ecological issues, lest climate change adaptation measures turn into another form of colonialism, no different from climate change in the first place. While ecological tipping points may be ahead, relational tipping points have already been crossed.

Where tipping points have upended previous worlds, Indigenous worldmaking practices grow new worlds. This is not a facile process; lost worlds, places, species, and tasks are real losses, and starting anew is cumbersome. Nevertheless, Gwich'in and Inuvialuit inhabitants of the Mackenzie Delta confront current collapses from a perspective of having survived previous collapses, not as glorious heroes but as practitioners engaged in re-growing relationships. The unease that some observers may feel when contemplating the photo of the late George White's house on the riverbank may be fueled by a projection of their own expectations of stability and their anxieties about transformations of physical features onto a different world where "crashes" occur regularly and the "apocalypse" has already happened. Here, people take physical and biological transformation for granted. Material objects like buildings are not expected to last forever. The focus is less on reproducing things as they used to be, and more on forging viable ways forward, informed and motivated by time-tested ethics and wisdom (Krause 2022).

Seeing only impending collapse means overlooking the real problems and their causes, including the exploitation and marginalization that make climate change a colonial echo in the Mackenzie Delta. It also means overlooking how delta inhabitants are re-building decent lives despite the echoing challenges.

Note

1 Indigenous ontologies from this region hold that animal populations prosper when people treat them respectfully. Spencer (1959, cited in Ingold 1986: 271) has reported this for the Iñupiat of

Northern Alaska, and Brightman (1993) for the Asinskâwôiniwak, or Rock Crees, of Northern Manitoba. Respectful treatment, however, does not mean leaving the animals alone, but includes hunting and killing them.

Acknowledgements

This research has been developed in collaboration with the Gwich'in Tribal Council's Department of Cultural Heritage and the Aklavik Hunters and Trappers Committee. Fieldwork was conducted with the NWT Scientific Research Licenses No 16098 and 16219. I am grateful to the people of the Mackenzie Delta for sharing their time and teachings with me. Special thanks are due to Freddie Furlong, Kaonak Gordon, and Bobby Kasook. This text has been improved thanks to constructive comments by Kristi Benson, Susan Crate and Mark Nuttall. The research was supported by the Deutsche Forschungsgemeinschaft (DFG), project number 276392588, and by an Aurora Research Institute Research Fellowship.

References

Alunik, Ishmael, Eddie D. Kolausok, and David Morrison. 2003. *Across Time and Tundra: The Inuvialuit of the Western Arctic*. Vancouver: Raincoast Books.

Berger, Thomas R. 1977. *Northern Frontier, Northern Homeland: The Report of the Mackenzie Valley Pipeline Inquiry*. Vol. 1. Ottawa: Minister of Supply and Services Canada.

Bombay, Amy, Kimberly Matheson, and Hymie Anisman. 2014. "The intergenerational effects of Indian residential schools: implications for the concept of historical trauma." *Transcultural Psychiatry* 51 (3): 320–338. https://doi.org/10.1177/1363461513503380.

Brightman, Robert Alain. 1993. *Grateful Prey: Rock Cree Human-Animal Relationships*. Berkeley: University of California Press.

Cameron, Emilie S. 2012. "Securing Indigenous politics: a critique of the vulnerability and adaptation approach to the human dimensions of climate change in the Canadian Arctic." *Global Environmental Change* 22 (1): 103–114.

Crate, Susan A. and Mark Nuttall. 2009. "Introduction: anthropology and climate change." In Susan A. Crate and Mark Nuttall (eds) *Anthropology and Climate Change: From Encounters to Actions*. Walnut Creek, CA: Left Coast Press, pp. 9–36.

Davis, Heather and Zoe Todd. 2017. "On the importance of a date, or, decolonizing the Anthropocene." *ACME: An International Journal for Critical Geographies* 16 (4): 761–780.

Di Mascio, Anthony and Leigh Hortop-Di Mascio. 2011. "Residential schooling in the Arctic: a historical case study and perspective." *Native Studies Review* 20 (2): 31–49.

Fumoleau, René. 2004. *As Long as This Land Shall Last: A History of Treaty 8 and Treaty 11, 1870–1939*. Calgary: University of Calgary Press.

Ghosh, Amitav. 2021. *The Nutmeg's Curse: Parables for a Planet in Crisis*. Chicago: University of Chicago Press.

Gruppuso, Paolo and Franz Krause. forthcoming. "Displacing the in-between: wetlands, urbanity and the colonial logics of separation." In Peter Loovers and Caroline Gatt (eds) *Beyond Perception: Correspondences with the Work of Tim Ingold*. London: Routledge.

Huntington, Henry P., Mark Carey, Charlene Apok, Bruce C. Forbes, Shari Fox, Lene K. Holm, Aitalina Ivanova, Jacob Jaypoody, George Noongwook and Florian Stammler. 2019. "Climate change in context: putting people first in the Arctic." *Regional Environmental Change* 19 (4): 1217–1223. https://doi.org/10.1007/s10113-019-01478-8.

Ingold, Tim. 1986. *The Appropriation of Nature: Essays on Human Ecology and Social Relations*. Themes in Social Anthropology. Manchester: Manchester University Press.

Krause, Franz. 2021a. "Economy, identity and hydrology: toward a holistic approach to intersecting volatilities in the Mackenzie Delta, Canada." In Franz Krause and Mark Harris (eds) *Delta Life: Exploring Dynamic Environments Where Rivers Met the Sea*. Oxford: Berghahn, pp. 102–125.

Krause, Franz. 2021b. "The tempo of solid fluids: on river ice, permafrost, and other melting matter in the Mackenzie Delta." *Theory, Culture & Society* 39 (2): 31–52. https://doi.org/10.1177/02632764211030996.

Krause, Franz. 2022. "Inhabiting a transforming delta: volatility and improvisation in the Canadian Arctic." *American Ethnologist* 49 (1): 7–19.

Krech, Shepard III. 1978. "Disease, starvation, and Northern Athapaskan social organization." *American Ethnologist* 5 (4): 710–732.

Krupnik, Igor and Aron Crowell (eds). 2020. *Arctic Crashes: People and Animals in the Changing North*. Washington, DC: Smithsonian Institution Scholarly Press.

Loovers, Jan Peter Laurens. 2019. *Reading Life with Gwich'in: An Educational Approach*. London: Routledge.

Marino, Elizabeth K. 2015. *Fierce Climate, Sacred Ground: An Ethnography of Climate Change in Shishmaref, Alaska*. Fairbanks: University of Alaska Press.

Nuttall, Mark. 2009. "Living in a world of movement: human resilience to environmental instability in Greenland." In Susan A. Crate and Mark Nuttall (eds) *Anthropology and Climate Change: From Encounters to Actions*. Walnut Creek, CA: Left Coast Press, pp. 292–310.

Nuttall, Mark. 2010. *Pipeline Dreams: People, Environment, and the Arctic Energy Frontier*. Copenhagen: IWGIA.

Nuttall, Mark. 2012. "Tipping points and the human world: living with change and thinking about the future." *AMBIO* 41 (1): 96–105. https://doi.org/10.1007/s13280-011-0228-3.

Nuttall, Mark. 2019. "Icy, watery, liquescent: sensing and feeling climate change on northwest Greenland's coast." *Journal of Northern Studies* 13 (2): 71–91.

Piper, Liza. 2019. "Freeze-up, break-up, and colonial circulation." *Journal of Northern Studies* 13 (2): 17–41.

Ready, Elspeth and Peter Collings. 2021. "'All the problems in the community are multifaceted and related to each other': Inuit concerns in an era of climate change." *American Journal of Human Biology* 33 (4). https://doi.org/10.1002/ajhb.23516.

Truth and Reconciliation Commission of Canada. 2015. *Honouring the Truth, Reconciling for the Future: Summary of the Final Report of the Truth and Reconciliation Commission of Canada*. www.trc.ca.

Turner, C.K., T.C. Lantz, and Gwich'in Tribal Council Department of Cultural Heritage. 2018. "Springtime in the delta: the socio-cultural importance of muskrats to Gwich'in and Inuvialuit trappers through periods of ecological and socioeconomic change." *Human Ecology* 46 (4): 601–611. https://doi.org/10.1007/s10745-018-0014-y.

Usher, Peter. 1971. "The Canadian Western Arctic: A Century of Change." *Anthropologica* 13 (1/2): 169–183. https://doi.org/10.2307/25604848.

Veldhuis, Djuke, Pelle Tejsner, Felix Riede, Toke T. Høye and Rane Willerslev. 2019. "Arctic disequilibrium: shifting human-environmental systems." *Cross-Cultural Research* 53 (3): 243–251. https://doi.org/10.1177/1069397118815132.

Wenzel, George W. 2009. "Canadian Inuit subsistence and ecological instability: if the climate changes, must the Inuit?" *Polar Research* 28 (1): 89–99.

Whyte, Kyle. 2017a. "Indigenous climate change studies: Indigenizing futures, decolonizing the Anthropocene." *English Language Notes* 55 (1): 153–162.

Whyte, Kyle. 2017b. "Our ancestors' dystopia now: Indigenous conservation and the Anthropocene." In Ursula Heise, Michelle Niemann, and Jon Christensen (eds) *The Routledge Companion to the Environmental Humanities*. London: Routledge, pp. 206–215.

Whyte, Kyle. 2020. "Too late for Indigenous climate justice: ecological and relational tipping points." *WIREs Climate Change* 11 (1): e603. https://doi.org/10.1002/wcc.603.

Wildcat, Daniel R. 2009. *Red Alert! Saving the Planet with Indigenous Knowledge.* Speaker's Corner. Golden, CO: Fulcrum.

Wishart, Robert P. and Jan Peter Laurens Loovers. 2013. "Building log cabins in Teetł'it Gwichin Country: vernacular architecture and articulations of presence." In David G. Anderson, Robert P. Wishart, and Virginie Vaté (eds) *About the Hearth: Perspectives on the Home, Hearth and Household in the Circumpolar North.* Oxford: Berghahn, pp. 54–68.

12

ON NEW GROUND

Tracing Human–Muskox Reconfigurations in Greenland

Astrid Oberborbeck Andersen and Janne Flora

Introduction

In Greenland, climatic changes and critical ecosystem transitions are manifested in several ways. Polar amplification, the phenomenon that surface warming in the polar regions happens at an intensified rate compared to the rest of the globe (Holland and Bitz 2003) and the changes in the immense Inland Ice that holds climate memory, has resulted in Greenland, as also in the Arctic more broadly, becoming a hot spot for climate science (Crate and Nuttall 2016). Changing patterns of different forms of ice – the thinning of sea ice, the thawing of permafrost, the movements and melt-run off from the Inland Ice and glaciers – lend themselves to natural science studies that produce knowledge of the severity of climate presents and futures, relating these to past climates and changes. The different bodies of ice and their thinning, melting, and thawing have become indicators for how fast the climate is changing and for how severe the effects will be for ecosystems and communities worldwide. Across Greenland, communities are impacted by the changes happening in their environments, and these are experienced in or out of sync with socio-economic and political transformations. The changes felt most harshly are those in sea ice dynamics, and the resulting change in patterns of availability of and access to animals for hunting and fishing (see Nuttall 2009; Nuttall et al. 2005; Hastrup 2009; Holm 2010; Andersen and Flora 2019; Sejersen 2015).

This chapter performs an anthropology of climatic fluctuations and changes by zooming in on interspecies relations in the Arctic. More specifically, the focus is on how muskoxen and humans shape each other's worlds in Greenland, and how this mutual shaping – or worldmaking - changes over time due to climatic and other changes. Muskoxen have ruminated their ways through geological epochs, climatic eras, continents, and ecosystems; across historical and prehistoric periods and geographic regions, humans and muskoxen have shaped each other's environments – or worlds (Flora and Andersen 2022; Hastrup 2022). Honing in on this particular interspecies relation thus makes an interesting case to study how worldmaking practices take place between species in wider ecologies, and how changes in such ecologies are effects of different forces and dynamics – of climatic changes,

DOI: 10.4324/9781003242499-15

geopolitical interests and processes, and local and global economies – tangling up. Human–muskox worldmaking always unfolds within broader contexts of environmental and multispecies dynamics.

Anthropological scholarship on climate change and environmental crises shows how detailed and context-specific perspectives play a significant role when it comes to understanding climate change as a phenomenon that is simultaneously one (singular and global) and multiple – with many disparate local manifestations and effects (multiple and plural). Anthropology has been strong in describing and analyzing how climate change is experienced, understood, and responded to in local settings, and how it becomes a mobiliser of political and other forms of collective action. The climate crisis and its manifold local manifestations is in many ways a world-changing – or worldmaking – phenomenon.

We explore the effects of climate change anthropologically by studying the reconfigurations of human–muskox relations in Greenland at two different historical moments and geographic settings: Ittoqqortoormiit in East Greenland, and Kangerlussuaq in West Greenland, occasionally extending our perspective and ethnographic view to other locations and time periods. Common for these places and moments is that humans and muskoxen came into contact and were reconfigured, not in similar, but dissimilar ways – in 1925 in Ittoqqortoormiit, when ca. 70 Iivit (East Greenlandic Inuit) were relocated from Tasiilaq 1000 kilometers northwards to the then unpopulated Scoresby Sound Fjord; and in West Greenland in the 1960s when 27 muskox calves were translocated from Northeast Greenland to West Greenland. These relocations were not directly effects of climate change as experienced at their time, but – as we shall see – knowledge of climatic fluctuations played a central role. Both relocations were responses to uncertainties in climatic, geopolitical, and economic environments – uncertainties that continue to inform many scientific and political discussions about the management of muskoxen today and the persistent question of whether it is climatic changes or over-hunting that poses the greatest risk to the survival of wildlife.

We trace climatic changes and the uncertainties tied to muskoxen over time and space and argue that muskoxen and humans mutually reconfigure each other's worlds through worldmaking practices in a multitude of ways. By displaying this insight into climate pasts, presents, and futures in Greenland, we provide a new perspective on how an anthropology of interspecies relations can be practiced.

First, we outline the different ways in which climate, humans, and muskoxen have made each other's worlds at different times in their common history in Greenland, and we clarify what we mean by worldmaking practices conceptually. We then zoom in on the specific muskox–human worldmaking practices in Ittoqqotoormiit and Kangerlussuaq in two respective sections. Finally, we discuss how the tracing of the mutual reconfiguration of humans and muskoxen in environments, contexts, and fields also reconfigures anthropological practices.

Muskoxen, Humans, and their Mutual Worldmaking Practices in Greenland

Humans and muskoxen are not just part of each other's worlds. They have also participated in making those worlds in various regions and moments in history throughout Greenland. The brief human experimentation with muskoxen around Independence Fjord in North Greenland 4000 years ago, how it gave name to an entire "culture"

(Independence I) and to the theory of the "Muskox Way" (Steensby 1916; Jensen and Gotfredsen 2022) as an example of worldmaking. So too are various pre-historical and historical human engagements with muskoxen across the Arctic region, which bring into view a world of multiple kinds of muskoxen (Hastrup 2022).

Worldmaking is also found in the cohabitation of muskoxen with other species such as the little auk, itself a High Arctic worldmaker in a very literal sense (Davidson et al. 2018; Mosbech et al. 2018). The nesting little auks in Qoororsuaq in Northwest Greenland transport nutrients from sea to land where muskoxen trample and graze, and so causing a favorable transformation of mosses to grasses, thus co-making its own food, or what biologists call a "vegetation hotspot" (Mosbech et al. 2018: 234). This ecological worldmaking sustains a muskox population of some 300 today – a population that began with the translocation of 7 muskoxen to the area in 1986 (Vibe 1986) in a move to reintroduce muskoxen to the southern parts of Northwest Greenland after they had become extirpated. Today, these 300 muskoxen are hunted for meat, skins, and as trophies. Biological concerns that underpin efforts and actions in conservation thus also contribute to the worldmaking of Greenlandic environments, ecosystems, and multispecies livelihoods.

Almost since the moment of the European German Koldewey expedition in 1869 "discovering" muskoxen in Northeast Greenland, zoologists have been concerned that human engagement – or, as they mean by this, exploitation – of the muskox has put the muskox in danger of local extinction. Muskoxen literally fed and fueled the movement of polar expeditions in Northeast Greenland, while Danish and Norwegian trappers in the region would hunt muskoxen to feed themselves, their dogs, and to lay them as bait in their fox traps. Trappers would also trade muskox calves to zoos and nature parks throughout Europe, having captured the calves by the only method they knew how – by exterminating entire herds (Madsen 1900; Pedersen 1934). This concern led to the Greenlandic Society (Det Grønlandske Selskab) in Denmark finding in favor in 1913 of a proposal to extend the territory of muskoxen by introducing a small herd to West Greenland (Vibe 1954: 402).

Zoologist Christian Vibe devoted years of his professional life to studying muskoxen, carrying out several scientific expeditions to Northeast Greenland in the 1950s and 1960s, which eventually resulted in the translocation of 27 muskoxen to Kangerlussuaq in West Greenland. He observed muskoxen and counted them wherever he went, paying attention to their herd structure and especially the number of females and calves in the herd, since these were telling about the prospects of the overall population. He also studied muskox bones and skulls wherever he happened upon them, to assess the migrations and distribution of the muskox prior to their "discovery," and the degree to which an earlier Inuit population in the Scoresby Sound area had depended on muskoxen to the extent that they had driven muskoxen away (Vibe 1967: 162).

Having secured funding and assembled a small team, Vibe arrived in Northeast Greenland in 1954 intending to enact his idea to extend the area of muskoxen, by capturing and translocating some calves to West Greenland. He had even secured the assistance of the US airbases in Greenland to help with transportation. Upon arriving to Mestersvig however, he found only two lone bulls, and fifteen dead muskoxen: ten bulls, three cows, and two calves (Vibe 1954: 407). This picture was much the same throughout the 500 km surveyed between Mestersvig and Danmarkshavn: hardly any calves, and "many hundreds or some thousands" (Vibe ibid.: 410) of muskoxen that appeared to have starved to death. After a desperate attempt to capture a cow on Ymer Ø, which broke its leg and was put down, they abandoned the mission (Vibe ibid.: 408).

The expedition revealed some rather troubling causes for the enormous muskox death count. First, they cited the unusually large amount of precipitation during the previous winter, including large areas along the coast where there was as much as four meters of snow. Additionally, there had been a warming in the climate in November causing a layer of ice atop the snow. This repeated in February, making it impossible for the muskox to reach their food beneath the deep layers of ice and snow. The most vulnerable animals, especially the calves, were unable to survive. Connecting his findings to studies of the southward flowing pack ice, Vibe suggested these were the result of extreme climatic fluctuations, caused by the irregular changing temperatures in the Polar Sea, and subsequent variations in patterns of the pack ice:

> It is not the Arctic cold that makes Greenland a fateful country to live in for animals and humans – it is the country's ever-changing climate – nature's whimsical instability, which is not so much felt at temperate latitudes, but which creates insecure conditions both in the tropics and in Arctic regions – and in particular in Greenland – on whose midst the eternal ice sheet rests, cold and mighty.
>
> *(Vibe 1959: 201)*

Vibe feared that the Northeast Greenlandic climate was slowly becoming too mild for the muskox, and that we might well expect similar catastrophes in the future. He identified contingencies between climatic fluctuations, population dynamics in plants and wildlife, and human well-being. Because caribou had extirpated in Northeast Greenland due to such climatic changes around the year 1900, he feared the same could happen to muskoxen, and therefore called for a complete ban on muskox hunting, and for additional funding to be secured for a thorough scientific study of the Northeast Greenlandic muskox.

This brief history of various early muskox–human interactions in Greenland exemplifies several ways in which muskoxen and humans take part in shaping, even making, each other's worlds of partially shared ecological, social, and livelihood conditions. The account also shows situations in which different humans – sometimes individuals – and different kinds of muskoxen – sometimes individuals – have played dissimilar and dynamic roles in their shared histories and trajectories. Muskoxen and humans are thus relational beings within wider ecologies that are neither purely natural nor societal, but always simultaneously both, in dynamic configurations. Climatic fluctuations and uncertainties about future catastrophes in earlier days also intervened in the making of today's muskox worlds.

The focus on several species was not there when "worldmaking" as a concept first made its way into anthropology through the Amazon and Joanna Overing (1990). Her article "The shaman as a maker of worlds" draws on philosopher Nelson Goodman's work that questions and theorizes whether there is one or many worlds – not necessarily multispecies – and how worlds come into being (Goodman 1978). Overing (1990) shows how religious leaders among the Piaroa in the Amazon construct different versions of the world through their chants, and that new versions of the world sometimes replace preexisting realities. Worldmaking, here, may be seen as a concept in the analytical order of social constructivism, and the emphasis is on the capacity of humans to create worlds. Later, anthropologists of environments and multispecies relations have used the concept of worldmaking (instead of culture-making), to highlight how other species and nonhuman elements (organic or material, such as toxins, waste, plastic, or immaterial, such as spiritual beings) actively participate in making environments that are neither entirely social nor natural (Ingold 2000; Tsing 2013, 2014, 2015; Tsing and Bubandt 2020).

Two dimensions to worldmaking are important in our use of the concept. Firstly, by focusing on human muskox relations as mutual worldmakers, we highlight that humans always live in and are dependent on larger ecologies. Worldmaking is making the world *with* others, both humans and other-than-human beings (Haraway 2008). Their relations – their making – unfold in movements (Flora 2022). Secondly, a focus on worldmaking highlights that the world is always unfinished and in continuous becoming (Kirksey and Helmreich 2010). Worldmaking practices of humans – with others – at one point in time continue to cause effects and unfold in multi-layered pathways and temporalities. This dimension has ethical and political implications, in that it matters how we contribute to making our shared world. The "we" of this sentence must necessarily be open-ended and complex (see de la Cadena 2019), and situationally specified. The making of complex "we's" and "they's" is inherently a part of worldmaking; a claim to which we will return.

Our aim is not a post-human anthropology. There is already a problem with the way climate science generally excludes human perspectives from their accounts. Therefore, we suggest focusing on inter- and multispecies relations in order to keep sight of the importance of human communities, of the well-being and development of ecosystems, and the importance of ecosystems and other than human species in the life and well-being of human communities. Interspecies relations is a term that we here use to refer to the specific dynamics between humans and muskoxen, while multispecies refers to relations between more than two species. Anna Tsing writes that "world-making occurs as organisms find niches within which they live with others" (Tsing 2014: 224). The making of worlds, of course, also implies their continuous unmaking. Climate change and environmental crises can also be seen as world unmaking processes, at times disastrous and violent in form and at other times unfolding as a "mild apocalypse" (Brichet and Hastrup 2019). The muskox–human worldmaking practices of this chapter more than finding and settling in niches disrupt these and result in slippages and the unmaking of worlds that unfold continuously in disparate temporalities. We now turn to Ittoqqortoormiit and Kangerlussuaq to show how the human–muskox reconfigurations continue and take new forms. Climate, in these contexts and processes, appears, and acts in various forms.

Ittoqqortoormiit: Endangerments, Relocations, and Layers of Uncertainty

For the 70 or so Iivit who arrived to the newly established Scoresbysund colony (later Ittoqqortoormiit) in 1925, the landscape was completely unknown. There were no humans to share with them their knowledge or practices, since those Indigenous to that area had disappeared around 100 years earlier (Clavering 1830: 20–24; Sørensen and Gulløv 2012). Everything they came to know about the land, its places, its toponyms, its history, animals, ice, weather, winds, and currents had so to speak to be discovered and invented through their own engagement. They had been relocated from Ammassalik (later

Tasiilaq) nearly 1000 km south of their new home by the Scoresby Sound (later Kangertitti-vaq) fjord, due to a looming geopolitical conflict between Denmark and Norway who both had claimed Northeast Greenland as their own (Mikkelsen 1934: 119–122; Rud 2017: 251).

The new landscape offered many new conditions with which to become accustomed – or to make worlds with: muskoxen especially, but fewer species of fish, fewer cetaceans, and a vast fjord that was covered with land fast ice for most of the year all presented new conditions. The hunters learned to catch seals in nets suspended beneath the sea ice, and they taught themselves to hunt by the polynya ice edge along the 30-kilometre-wide mouth of the fjord. Only a few decades after settling here, most hunters abandoned using the kayak, favoring instead a small plywood dinghy to fetch animals they shot directly from the ice edge.

They were not initially allowed to hunt muskoxen, since zoologists, including the founder of the colony, the explorer Ejnar Mikkelsen believed the muskox was in serious danger of extirpation, owed partly to their low reproduction rate, and especially to overhunting by Danish and Norwegian trappers who roamed the vast area north of the colony. Having not been accustomed to large land mammals in the Tasiilaq area at all however, the Iivit did not themselves have any immediate desire to eat the muskox. Nor did they bring with them knowledge or traditions for hunting, flensing, or for sharing muskoxen. However, hunting was not always stable, and periods of starvation ensued, such as during the winter of 1934–35, when the sea ice never properly set, and made it difficult for hunters to set seal-nets (Petersen et al. 1957: 146). During such times they were to request permission by the colony manager to hunt a single muskox to feed their families and dogs. But as desperation set in, and hunters and their families discovered the use and versatility of muskox meat, illegal muskox hunting would increasingly occur, resulting in the issuing of fines and meat being confiscated. Today, people in Ittoqqor-toormiit recount stories from their grandparents of hardship and of a time when, after having been denied to hunt a muskox, desperation pushed one family to boil the soles of boots that were made of thick harp-seal skin, in order to find some kind of nutrition for their children. Hunters also sometimes asserted that they had killed muskoxen in self-defense, since muskoxen occasionally charged through the settlements, trampling humans and dogs who happened to stand in their way. They also reported how they were both-ered by aggressive muskoxen when out on the land to check their fox-traps. Some colony managers were more lenient than others, fining the hunters, but allowing them to keep the meat and pelt, thus giving the fine an air of transaction rather than penalty. One hunter stated that he would rather pay the fine than see his family go hungry or his dogs starve to death (ibid.: 146).

Though humans and muskoxen in Ittoqqortoormiit were thereby legislatively kept apart, we can nevertheless talk of a worldmaking in which humans and muskoxen, hitherto beings that scarcely knew of each other, came to inhabit and make a world together – initially in separation and enmity, but also as vital food resource in times of need. In time, as hunters became familiar with the fact that muskoxen were not out of bounds to European and American expeditions that travelled to the area nor to Scandi-navian trappers, it became increasingly difficult for the administration to defend why muskoxen should then be out of bounds to the Iivit. By 1958, when communal hunts were instated, allowing families to organize themselves around the hunt and share of one muskox, many had already begun using the warm muskox wool (*qivii*) as stuffing for sleeping pillows, and some hunters had started making sleeping bags out of muskox hides and using these during long hunting trips in winter. When Vibe made a second failed attempt to capture a muskox calf for translocation in 1956, hunters, who by then had become so accustomed to dealing with muskoxen, helped him capture a calf. Vibe described the hunters' competence and bravery with much admiration, (Vibe diary, 1956: August 16), all of which suggests that the human-muskox worldmaking is multi layered, littered with uncertainties, and continually taking form in new directions.

Muskox hunting has now been legal for decades, and the muskox has grown to become one of the most cherished animals, for its meat, its wool, its charm, and its economic potential. Yet these economic potentials remain largely unfulfilled, since the municipality's decade-old promise of a procurement facility that would allow hunters to trade muskox meat and create new employment in town, remains unfinished. Minimum counts of muskoxen over the past decades suggest that the muskox population is large enough to carry such a venture, and inhabitants in town continue to hope that it might one day be established. Meanwhile especially dexterous women experiment with new ways of securing the muskox wool from the hides, spinning, and knitting it, while struggling to produce enough to sell to cruise-ship tourists during the brief ice-free period during summer. Against this optimism for the human–muskox future worldmaking, other inhabitants in Ittoqqortoormiit are concerned that such ventures are hopeless. Some envision the more frequently occurring winter rains will drive the muskox northwards and away from Jameson Land, where most muskoxen are hunted. Others fear that the polar bears, which are being pushed closer to land due to the thinning of sea ice, eventually will abandon their search for seals and turn their attention to muskoxen instead.

We may then talk of a human–muskox worldmaking within a context where the uncertainties of climate change, survival, death, economic opportunities, and creativity coexist in many forms and formations. The uncertainties about future muskox existence transpiring from early zoologists' concerns of muskox extinction, may on some level seem to correspond to those in Ittoqqortoormiit today where muskoxen are regarded integral to the economic viability of the town or those who are concerned by its direct or indirect impact by climate change. Yet, the concerns and uncertainties about climate fluctuations that drove Vibe to make several attempts to save muskoxen by translocating them to West Greenland, is not the same kind of concern, or uncertainty about climate change, that causes some Ittoqqortoormiit inhabitants today to worry about muskoxen drawing northwards, or polar bears drawing closer to land to feed on muskoxen. Nor are the opportunities, endangerments, motivations, or dreams of Scandinavian trappers the same as starving Iivit in the early years of the colony. Nor indeed those of today who labor to keep Ittoqqortoormiit as a viable home for themselves, muskoxen, and their future descendants. The uncertainties here are not wholly of one long winding human–muskox worldmaking, but of several layered kinds of uncertainty that share parts and similarities in their disparate worldmakings, ultimately rendering not just the worldmakings themselves, but also humans and muskoxen complex and in flux.

Kangerlussuaq: Muskoxen and Humans on New Grounds

For the 27 young muskoxen that were translocated to West Greenland and released in Angujaartorfiup Nunaa, in the Kangerlussuaq area in the 1960s, the landscape was in many ways unknown and had to be discovered and taken in. As argued by Christian Vibe and colleagues, the climate of the area was more stable than the homelands of the muskoxen in East Greenland. The stability of the weather and climate in this area was also the reason why the US Air Force had established their Bluie West-8 Air Base in Sondrestrom (Søndre Strømfjord in Danish) at the bottom of the long Kangerlussuaq Fjord in 1941, during World War II.

More than 100 km from the coast, this inland climate, with little precipitation year-round, resulted in good conditions for calves to forage and grow without the risk of getting wet during summertime, and during wintertime free of the lethal trouble of sudden thaws and freezes. The young muskoxen were released into the tundra landscape, after being kept safely inside a corral where they ate willow and drank water fetched for them by Vibe and his companions. They appeared to adapt to their new home without complications. Winter and summer climates in their new habitat were relatively stable, with annual temperatures ranging between -45° C in wintertime and +22° C during summer. The melting of the Inland Ice and snowbanks during summer irrigated the vegetation, and, Vibe mused, had likely contributed to the surge in the caribou population some 100 years earlier (Vibe 1961: May 4). Arctic willows and the graminoids on which the muskoxen forage abound in this landscape, especially in the valleys, and the introduced flock of muskoxen soon started reproducing, and multiplied with a speed not previously observed in any muskox population (Olesen 1993). The latest official count, carried out by biologists and wildlife authorities in 2018, estimated the population to exceed 20,000 individuals (Marques 2018). With this growth in numbers the population has spread in the area and migrated south and northwards, as far as ecology and landscape conditions permit them.

The Angujaartorfiup Nunaa area, to which the 27 muskoxen were translocated, is an ancient caribou hunting ground during summer and autumn. For millennia, families and hunting parties from the coast, of different archaeological epochs (so called Saqqaq and Thule cultures), travelled inland during summertime to hunt for caribou, fish Arctic char, and to exchange goods, socialize, and share stories with Inuit from north and south Greenland (Meldgaard 1983; Grønnow 1986). The intensity of this activity has changed over the years, along with socio-economic transformations but also with the size of the caribou population, which is known to fluctuate dramatically in cycles of 60–120 years of population growth followed by near collapse (Meldgaard 1983; Pasda 2014). The crucial point here is that caribou, different humans, as well as other animal and plant species inhabited and frequented the Kangerlussuaq area when the muskoxen were introduced in the 1960s. Before their arrival, politicians and hunters' associations had welcomed the overall plans of introducing muskoxen to create a new hunting resource and source of meat in West Greenland. Yet, they had hoped for the muskoxen to be introduced to areas further north, where the newcomers would not put an already existing hunting culture at risk. They feared that muskoxen would outcompete their treasured caribou, just like they had, so they argued, in East Greenland some 150 years earlier. Thus, local politicians from neighboring Sisimiut voiced their concern and lobbied against the introduction of muskoxen to this particular area (Nielsen and Küter 2000). Vibe's concern of the endangerment of one species, the muskox, based on zoological assessments and reasoning, and the subsequent efforts of conservation, resulted in concerns of endangerments of another species, caribou, along with the hunting and traditions that came with them, in another register of engagement with the environment. Interspecies relations, in this case human–

muskox relations, and worldmaking, thus, unfold within larger ecologies of natural, social, and political forces that also entail colliding interests and worldviews. And interspecies relations are thus always embedded in multispecies networks.

During their first years in Angujaartorfiup Nunaa, the muskoxen were fully protected. Muskox hunting was prohibited. This meant that the muskoxen could freely roam the landscape that in summertime was inhabited by Inuit families hunting for caribou, and by US soldiers and personnel working at the US airbase traveling the land for spare time activities. In the 1960s the airstrip started serving as a hub for international commercial flights to and from Greenland, augmenting the population of Søndre Strømfjord, later Kangerlussuaq, to include Greenlandic and Danish professionals. This mixed and multilayered ecology resulted in awkward, sometimes violent encounters between muskoxen and humans, in a landscape that was simultaneously one of ancient hunting traditions and one of a variety of newcomers (Dzik 2014; Andersen 2022). The families that today spend their summers inland hunting for caribou, a hunt that now also includes muskoxen, tell stories of how hunters, when first encountering a muskox during caribou hunting, were frightened by the strange and hairy animals with horns, and for the first time ever found themselves running away from an animal, instead of towards it. Back then, the muskoxen had not yet discovered that humans could be a threat and were not at all frightened by human presence. In 1988, the first quotas for muskox hunting in the area were issued by the Greenlandic hunting authorities. Hunting muskox and preparing and eating the meat was unfamiliar to people in the area, and many relay that it took them several years to get used to the smell and taste of muskox meat. Some even suggest that the muskoxen gradually came to acquire the flavor of caribou, since the muskoxen and caribou ruminated on the same land. How the muskox was slowly culturally adapted or adopted into a hunting ecology dominated by caribou traditions and flavors, can be seen as a process of mutual worldmaking. To some degree muskoxen, caribou, and new hunting activities found a niche in which to live together (Tsing 2014). The muskoxen, however, while making their niche, also attracted new kinds of activities and actors, introducing slippages in that niche, and in the worldmaking itself.

With the growth of the muskox population came new business dreams: export of meat, trophy hunting, and the production of exclusive wool (*qiviut*) products; a process we have elsewhere analyzed as "biosocial multiplication" and as resource-making (Andersen 2022). The US Air Force left Kangerlussuaq in 1992, and the airport and most base facilities were handed over to the Greenlandic home rule authorities. A settlement developed around the airport and new businesses emerged, attracting people from coastal towns to Kangerlussuaq for temporary or permanent settlement. Since then, tourism, subsistence and occupational hunting for meat, trophy hunting, and a small industry related to the production of wool are some of the commercial activities that the muskox population sustains. How much hunting pressure the muskoxen can sustain while still thriving as a population is a much-debated concern. Especially among the handful of occupational hunters who have moved to Kangerlussuaq to build their families' lives around the different kinds of economies that muskoxen enable: hunting for meat for the local and national market, providing the raw material (hides) for the muskox wool industry, or serving as outfitters and guides for international trophy hunters. The winter hunt on muskoxen is particularly intensive. Up to 80 occupational and spare time hunters travel to the area from neighboring towns and settlements in late January to participate in the hunt during February. The meat during winter is by many considered to be tastier, and thus the meat coming out of Kangerlussuaq supplies hotels, restaurants, and supermarkets in major towns along the Greenlandic west coast. The hides are traded for a favorable price for wool production, and all together, occupational hunters make good money on this hunt. From August to October, muskoxen attract spare time and occupational hunters from different parts of Greenland, and trophy hunters from different parts of the world. This expansion in types of hunting and traffic has caused a rupture in the summer hunting practices of some families that traditionally inhabited the inland during summertime as a "free-space." Altogether, the introduction of muskoxen has augmented the hunting opportunities, but simultaneously altered the seasonal rhythms for different kinds of hunting in the area. Introducing the muskoxen to the Kangerlussuaq area was a worldmaking practice of one order that has since triggered and enabled multilayered worldmaking processes that keep unfolding, causing new relations to emerge and others to disrupt.

Although all hunting for muskox is regulated by quotas, and although the abundance surveys result in numbers higher than the carrying capacity of the area around Kanger-lussuaq, hunters are concerned that the many kinds of hunting result in too much pressure on the muskox population. They experience a population that is more scattered; living in smaller groups than earlier and higher in the mountains where the vegetation is less nutritious. It is not only hunting, however, that is endangering the sustainability of muskoxen near Kangerlussuaq. Hunters and other residents observe increased precipitation during summer and winter, and sudden high temperatures in wintertime do occur, creating fears for ice layers preventing muskoxen from foraging. Parasites and larvae that are normally seen to attack only caribou are now also being observed on muskoxen, a phenomenon that is foreseen to increase with global warming (Raundrup et al. 2012). Zoonotic pathogens are another phenomenon of concern that may change dynamics with global warming (Berg et al. 2021). Even in Kangerlussuaq, known by many to be climatically stable, things are changing. One could worry that Vibe's concerns regarding the climate in East Greenland are starting to haunt Kangerlussuaq: is the climate slowly becoming too mild and fluctuating? That is, too wet, variable, and unsuitable for the muskox?

Grounds and Slippages: Human–Muskox Uncertainties in Climate Pasts, Presents, and Futures

Our concern in this chapter is twofold. The first is with human–muskox worldmakings during different moments in history and across different locations in Greenland. We have attempted to show how human–muskox worldmakings seem to continuously reconfigure and are always in flux. We may think of this as slippages – worlds and worldmakings that seem to slip apart as soon as they are established. Neither humans, nor muskoxen seem to ever settle in their niches before these morph. This has occurred through the translocations of muskoxen from East to West Greenland, which were embedded in dynamics related to climatic fluctuations and uncertainties about future livability; but also within the sites of worldmaking themselves, where layers of uncertainties, interests, and concerns with climate, economy, survival, and future are more than mere contexts and come to underpin the worldmakings themselves.

The muskox–human worldmaking practices described in this chapter thus show how climatic changes beyond predictable patterns trigger uncertain presents and futures, for humans as well as animals and their shared ecosystems, and that past climate uncertainties and the worldmaking events in which they culminated, keep producing relations and effects across species. Climatic changes are understood and responded to differently in different times and places, and such responses keep generating effects, unfolding in complex temporalities.

Our second concern in this chapter is about how anthropology itself necessarily changes when the object of study is one focusing on human–animal relations within larger ecosystems, and when these relations are in continuous transformation – even potential collapse. If humans and muskoxen make each other's worlds over time and climatic changes interfere with (and thus co-create) such worldmaking, then what are the implications for how anthropology is practiced?

In our study of human–muskox relations we focus on "muskox pathways": the ways and processes through which muskoxen and humans mutually shape each other's worlds. This focus on mutual human and muskox histories asks, among other things, for a revised delimitation of "the field" of ethnographic fieldwork. Not only from single-sited to multi-sited, one extending across locations, but also across times and scales. We work across geographical locations – sites in which we do fieldwork, but also stretch our gazes to historic and prehistoric times, and to ecological relations. This implies that anthropological theories and methods alone cannot cover all there is to know or to explore about human–muskox relations. We therefore invite archaeologists, zoo archaeologists, biologists, and the expertise of hunters and professionals in wildlife management into our spaces of knowledge-making, to add to the multiplicity of voices that always shape the way we, anthropologists, learn and know about the world. The boundaries between research object and subject, between "informant" and "researcher" are sometimes blurred, resulting in new formations of researcher "we's" and informant "they's." Worldmaking practices take place between species and in wider ecosystems while the world is in its simultaneous making and unmaking, and it is difficult to discern a clear "we" and "they." We call for a re-making of "we's" and "they's"; new constellations that can embrace communities of muskoxen-with-humans in multispecies complexities and uncertainties.

Acknowledgements

Research for this chapter was carried out between 2019 and 2023. The authors would like to thank the respective populations of Ittoqqortoormiit and Kangerlussuaq for their hospitality as well as their astute observations and conversations about muskox-related matters. We also thank our fellow researchers on the project *Muskox Pathways: Resources and Ecologies in Greenland*, and the editors of this book. The Muskox Pathways project is funded by The Independent Research Fund Denmark, grant number 9037–00140B.

References

Andersen, Astrid Oberborbeck. 2022. "Muskox multiplications: the becoming of a resource, relations and place in Kangerlussuaq, West Greenland." *Acta Borealia* 39 (1): 75–94, doi:10.1080/08003831.2022.2060619.

Andersen, Astrid Oberborbeck and Janne Flora. 2019. "Puzzling pieces and situated urgencies of climate change and globalisation in the High Arctic: three stories from Qaanaaq." In Astrid B. Stensrud and Thomas Hylland Eriksen (eds.) *Climate, Capitalism and Communities: An anthropology of environmental overheating*. London: Pluto Press, pp. 115–132.

Berg, Rebecca P.K.D., C. Rune Stensvold, Pikka Jokelainen, Anna K. Grønlund, Henrik V. Nielsen, Susan Kutz, and Christian M.O. Kapel. 2021. "Zoonotic pathogens in wild muskoxen (Ovibos moschatus) and domestic sheep (Ovis aries) from Greenland." *Veterinary Medicine and Science* 7 (6): 2290–2302. DOI: doi:10.1002/vms3.599.

Brichet, Nathalia and Frida Hastrup. 2019. "Curating a mild apocalypse: researching Anthropocene ecologies through analytical figures." In Malene Vest Hansen, Anne Folke Henningsen and Anne Gregersen (eds.) *Curatorial Challenges. Interdisciplinary perspectives on contemporary curating*. London/New York: Routledge, pp. 120–132.

Clavering, Douglas C. 1830. "Journal of a voyage to Spitzbergen and the east coast of Greenland, in his Majesty's Ship Griper. Communicated by James Smith, Esq." In Robert Jameson (ed.) *The Edinburgh New Philosophical Journal, Exhibiting a View of the Progressive Discoveries and Improvements in the Sciences and the Arts*, 1–30. Edinburgh: Printed for Adam Black, North Bridge, Edinburgh and Longman, Rees, Orme, Brown & Green, London.

Crate, Susan A. and Mark Nuttall. 2016. "Introduction: anthropology and climate change." In Susan A. Crate and Mark Nuttall (eds.) *Anthropology and Climate Change: From actions to transformations*. London: Routledge, pp. 11–34.

Davidson, Thomas A., Sebastian Wetterich, Kasper L. Johansen, Bjarne Grønnow, Torben Windirsch, Erik Jeppesen, Jari Syva¨ranta, Jesper Olsen, Ivan Gonza´lez-Bergonzoni, Astrid Strunk, Nicolaj K. Larsen, Hanno Meyer, Jens Søndergaard, Rune Dietz, Igor Eulears, Anders Mosbech. 2018. "The history of seabird colonies and the North Water ecosystem: contributions from palaeoecological and archaeological evidence." *AMBIO* 47 (Suppl. 2): 175–192. https://doi.org/10.1007/s13280-018-1031-1.

de la Cadena, Marisol. 2019. "An invitation to live together. making the 'complex we.'" *Environmental Humanities* 11 (2): 477–484. doi:10.1215/22011919-7754589.

Dzik, Anthony J. 2014. "Kangerlussuaq: evolution and maturation of a cultural landscape in Greenland." *Bulletin of Geography. Socio-economic Series* 24: 57–69. DOI: http://dx.doi.org/10.2478/bog-2014-0014.

Flora, Janne. 2022. "Muskox movements: human–animal entanglements in Northeast Greenland." *Acta Borealia* 39 (1): 53–74. https://doi.org/10.1080/08003831.2022.2060577.

Flora, Janne and Astrid Oberborbeck Andersen. 2022. "Introduction: human–muskox pathways through millennia." *Acta Borealia* 39 (1): 1–5. https://doi.org/10.1080/08003831.2022.2061129.

Goodman, Nelson. 1978. *Ways of Worldmaking*. Indianapolis: Hackett Publishing Company.

Grønnow, Bjarne. 1986. "Recent archaeological investigations of West Greenland caribou hunting." *Arctic Anthropology* 23(1/2): 57–80.

Haraway, Donna. 2008. *When Species Meet*. Minneapolis: University of Minnesota Press.

Hastrup, Kirsten. 2009. "Waterworlds: framing the question of resilience." In K. Hastrup (ed.) *The Question of Resilience: Social responses to climate change*. Copenhagen: Det Kongelige Danske Videnskabernes Selskab, pp. 11–30.

Hastrup, Kirsten. 2022. "The muskox world: human–animal histories in the Arctic." *Acta Borealia* 39 (1): 6–23.

Holland, Marika M. and Cecilia M.Bitz. 2003. "Polar amplification of climate change in coupled models." *Climate Dynamics* 21: 221–232. https://doi.org/10.1007/s00382-003-0332-6.

Holm, Lene Kielsen. 2010. "Sila-Inuk: study of the impacts of climate change in Greenland." In Igor Krupnik, Claudio Aporta, Shari Gearheard, Gita J. Laidler, Lene Kielsen Holm (eds.) *SIKU: Knowing our ice*. Dordrecht: Springer Netherlands, pp. 145–160.

Ingold, Tim. 2000. *The Perception of the Environment. Essays on livelihood, dwelling and skill*. London/New York: Routledge.

Jensen, Jens Fog and Anne Birgitte Gotfredsen. 2022. "First people and muskox hunting in north-ernmost Greenland." *Acta Borealia* 39 (1): 24–52. https://doi.org/10.1080/08003831.2022.2061763.

Kirksey, Eben and Stefan Helmreich. 2010. "The emergence of multispecies ethnography." *Cultural Anthropology*, 25 (4): 545–576.

Klein, David R. 1992. *"Comparative ecological and behavioral adaptations of Ovibos moschatus and Rangifer tarandus." Rangifer*, 12 (2): 47–55.

Klein, David R. 2003. "Moskusokser og pil i Peay Land." In Gunnar Martens, Jens Fog Jensen, Morten Meldgaard, and Hans Meltofte (eds.) *Peary Land. At tænke sig til Peary Land – og komme der.* Nuuk: Atuagkat, pp. 283–295.

Koldewey, Karl. 1874. *The German Arctic Expedition of 1869–1870, and Narrative of the Wreck of the "Hansa" in the Ice.* London: Sampson Low, Marston, Low & Searle.

Madsen, Johannes. 1900. "Polarjagt. Moskusoxer og Bjørne." *Illustreret Tidende* 3: 39–42.

Marques, Tiago A. 2018. *Estimating Caribou Abundance for GINR's 2018 West Greenland Caribou Survey.* CREEM Report 2018. Report produced for GINR under a research contract between CREEM and Greenland Institute of Natural Resources.

Meldgaard, Morten. 1983. "Resource fluctuations and human subsistence: a zoo-archaeological and ethnographical investigation of a West Greenland caribou hunting camp." In Juliet Clutton-Brock and Caroline Grigson (eds.) *Animals and Archaeology 1: Hunters and their prey.* Oxford: British Archaeological Reports International Series 163: 259–272.

Mikkelsen, Ejnar. 1934. *De Østgrønlandske Eskimoers Historie.* Copenhagen: Gyldendalske Boghandel – Nordisk Boghandel.

Mosbech, Anders, Kasper Lambert Johansen, Thomas A. Davidson, Martin Appelt, Bjarne Grønnow, Christine Cuyler, Peter Lyngs, Janne Flora. 2018. "On the crucial importance of a small bird: the ecosystem services of the little auk (*Alle alle*) population in Northwest Greenland in a long-term perspective." *AMBIO* 47 (Suppl. 2): S226–S243.

Nielsen, Anne Marie and Lothar Küter. 2000. "Flytningen af moskusokser fra Øst- til Vest-grønland." *Tidsskriftet Grønland* 48(3/4): 111–134.

Nuttall, Mark. 2009. "Living in a world of movement: human resilience to environmental instability in Greenland." In Susan A. Crate and Mark Nuttall (eds.) *Anthropology and Climate Change: From encounters to actions.* Walnut Creek, CA: Left Coast Press, Inc., pp. 292–310.

Nuttall, Mark, Fikret Berkes, Bruce Forbes, Gary Kofinas, Tatiana Vlassova, and George Wenzel. 2005. "Hunting, herding, fishing, and gathering." In *ACIA, Scientific Report.* Cambridge: Cambridge University Press, pp. 650–690.

Olesen, Carsten Riis. 1993. "Rapid population increase in an introduced muskox population, West Greenland." *Rangifer* 13 (1): 27–32.

Overing, Joanna. 1990. "The shaman as a maker of worlds: Nelson Gooodman in the Amazon." *Man* 25 (4): 602–619.

Pasda, Clemens. 2014. "Regional variation in Thule and colonial caribou hunting in West Greenland." *Arctic Anthropology* 51 (1): 41–76.

Pedersen, Alwin. 1934. *Polardyr.* København: Gyldendalske Boghandel – Nordisk Forlag.

Petersen, Johan, Bent Rosenkilde Nielsen, Gustav Holm, and William Thalbitzer. 1957. *Ujuâts dagbøger fra Østgrønland 1894–1935 – Østgrønlændernes Sagn og Fortællinger: Johan Petersens (Ujuâts) danske Oversættelser.* Det grønlandske Selskabs skrifter 19. Charlottenlund: Det Grønlandske Selskab.

Raundrup, Katrine, Mohammad Nafi Solaiman Al-Sabib, Christian Moliin Outzen Kapel. 2012. "First record of Taenia ovis krabbei muscle cysts in muskoxen from Greenland." *Veterinary Parasitology* 184: 356–358.

Rud, Søren. 2017. "Kapitel 5: Grønland til Debat 1905–39." In Hans Christian Gulløv (ed.) *Grønland: den Arktiske Koloni.* København: Gads Forlag, pp. 238–276.

Sejersen, Frank. 2015. *Rethinking Greenland and the Arctic in the Era of Climate Change: New northern horizons.* London: Routledge.

Sørensen, Mikkel, and Hans Christian Gulløv. 2012. "The prehistory of Inuit in Northeast Greenland." *Arctic Anthropology* 49 (1): 88–104.

Steensby, Hans Peter. 1916. "An anthropogeographical study of the origin of the Eskimo culture." *Meddelelser om Grønland* 53 (2): Copenhagen: Bianco Lunos Bogtrykkeri.

Tsing, Anna Lowenhaupt. 2013. "More-than-human sociality: a call for critical description." In Kirsten Hastrup (ed.) *Anthropology and Nature*. New York: Routledge, pp. 27–42.

Tsing, Anna Lowenhaupt. 2014. "Strathern beyond the human: testimony of a spore." *Theory, Culture & Society* 31 (2/3): 221–241. doi:10.1177/0263276413509114.

Tsing, Anna Lowenhaupt. 2015. *The Mushroom at the End of the World: On the possibility of life in capitalist ruins*. Princeton and Oxford: Princeton University Press.

Tsing, Anna and Nils Bubandt. 2020. "Swimming with crocodiles: nature is avenged by prehistoric animal." *Orion* 39 (1): 35–42. https://orionmagazine.org/article/swimming-with-crocodiles/.

Vibe, Christian. 1954. "Problemerne omkring Grønlands moskusokser (Danish: Problems concerning the Greenlandic muskoxen)." *Tidsskriftet Grønland*, 11: 401–414.

Vibe, Christian. 1959. "Grønlands Vildtbestand som Reserve for Grønlands Fremtid (Danish: Greenland's wildlife population as surplus for Greenland's future)." *Tidsskriftet Grønland* 6: 201–208.

Vibe, Christian. 1967. "Arctic animals in relation to climatic fluctuations." *Meddelelser om Grønland* 170 (5). Københaven: C.A. Reitzels Forlag.

Vibe, Christian. 1986. "Tilbage til de gamle græsgange." *Uagut*: 6–7. (In Danish).

Unpublished sources

Vibe, Christian. 1956. Muskox Expedition diaries, all accessed at Danish Arctic Institute, Copenhagen, Denmark: Arktisk Institut, A407, lb.nr. 20.

Vibe, Christian. 1961. Muskox Expedition diaries, all accessed at Danish Arctic Institute, Copenhagen, Denmark. Arktisk Institut, A407, lb.nr. 24.

13

THE DISAPPEARING FREE REINDEER

Unexpected Consequences of Climate Change for Fennoscandian Reindeer Herding

Majken Paulsen, Grete K. Hovelsrud, and Camilla Risvoll

Introduction

Inspired by scholars such as Lien (2015), Law and Mol (2008), and Mol (2002), we explore supplementary feeding of reindeer as a worldmaking practice that has consequences for Sámi reindeer herding in Norway and across Fennoscandia (Paulsen 2021; Risvoll, Hovelsrud, and Riseth 2022; Hortskotte et al. 2020). Supplementary feeding is an adaptive response to the cumulative effects of climate change, pasture encroachments, national management regimes and large carnivores. We are inspired by Mol's depiction of realities as products of the practices that constitute them, and that the ontology of the world is shaped, maintained, degraded, or abandoned through socio-material practices (Mol 2002). When these practices change, she argues, so do the realities they produce (ibid.). In this chapter we discuss how the increased use of supplementary feeding affects Sámi reindeer husbandry in Norway, but this is currently occurring across Sápmi – the Sámi homeland covering the northern parts of Norway, Finland, Sweden, and Russia – as more herders find themselves in situations where natural pastures are increasingly inaccessible, where feeding the herds becomes the only option. This change is emphasized by Norwegian legislation that promotes feeding as the most important measure to increase the animal welfare in reindeer husbandry (Forskningråd 2005; Norwegian Ministry of Agriculture and Food 2017; Stenevik and Mejdell 2011) .

Reindeer inhabit the severe environmental conditions of Fennoscandia and reindeer husbandry is based upon the use of natural pastures as food supply for reindeer. Nevertheless, in some winters and under certain conditions, herders need to support the reindeer to prevent starvation (Horstkotte et al. 2020). To be able to feed the herd is a solution to starvation that is as old as reindeer husbandry itself (Skjenneberg, Lyftingsmo, and Poulsson 1965). But such feeding does more than alleviate hunger. It introduces new practices into the reindeer assemblage creating new pathways and trajectories (Paulsen 2021). We argue that this has the potential to significantly change the worldmaking practices that constitute Sámi reindeer husbandry in Norway. This is the background for our reflections on supplementary feeding as a strategy to handle the cumulative effects of climate change and interlinked stressors.

DOI: 10.4324/9781003242499-16

We draw extensively on fieldwork and collaboration with Sámi reindeer herders, but we are fully aware that we cannot do justice to all the particularities among all reindeer herders or reindeer. This is an important caveat for our chapter. While we fully respect that the empirical information belongs to the herders, the analysis we present is our, the researchers' responsibility.

Below we start with outlining the context of reindeer herding as a backdrop for discussing how the multiple factors converge in supplementary feeding and finally how this affects reindeer herding as a worldmaking practice, the freedom of the reindeer, and the Sámi herders.

Context

Meet the Reindeer and Reindeer Husbandry

Reindeer are an herbivore ungulate and a key species in Arctic, subarctic, and alpine ecosystems. Reindeer are herded and hunted by humans and are a key prey species for large predators. Reindeer can utilize marginal pasture resources typically covered in snow during long winters (Pedersen 2019: 60). During the short (Arctic) summer the reindeer must build enough reserves to get through the winter (Grøndahl and Mejdell 2012). During the winter they utilize their well-developed sense of smell to locate vegetation in ice-free micro habitats and to separate between good and poor pastures under the snow (Pedersen 2019).

In Norway reindeer husbandry is predominantly a vocation and a cultural practice reserved for the Sámi, an Indigenous people. Like other Indigenous peoples, Sámi have been exposed to aggressive colonial practices that have led to assimilation, loss of land, language, and culture. Although assimilation of Sámi was abolished as an official policy in Norway after World War II, colonization continued through informal structures, affecting Sámi lives and practices, including reindeer husbandry. This is reflected in the lack of recognition of Indigenous knowledge (Benjaminsen et al. 2016; Dankertsen 2016; Johnsen et al. 2015; Kuokkanen 2007; Marin and Bjørklund 2016; Nergård 2011).

The mutual dependencies between the reindeer, the landscape, and the herders are at the core of Sámi reindeer husbandry (Beach and Stammler 2006; Istomin and Dwyer 2010; Reinert 2014; Stammler 2010). In general, the Sámi separate animals into three categories, placing the reindeer in its own specific category of *luothu*, which means free (Magga, Oskal, and Sara 2001). Reindeer are thereby taxonomically positioned somewhere in between animals who depend on human care for their well-being such as the dog or the cow, and the wild wolf. Indeed, the free reindeer are according to the Sámi ethical system entitled to freedom – luohtu – and the reindeer is considered to do best when free in luohtu (ibid). The reindeer in luohtu exemplifies a more than human undertaking, dating back thousands of years, where collaboration rather than control is at the core.

In Norway most reindeer are owned by someone, typically a Sámi reindeer herder who has some control over the reindeer, but without compromising the autonomy of the animals (Sara 2001; Magga, Oskal, and Sara 2001). Under ideal circumstances the herder should follow the reindeer and protect them, but not disturb their natural behavior. The reindeer follows the wind (Sara 2009, 2001) and it cannot and should not be controlled (Oskal 1995). Unlike other human-non-human-animal relationships in which starvation is predominantly associated with neglect, "hunger" is an inherent part of reindeer husbandry (Åhman and White 2019; Kalstad 2010; Paulsen 2021).

Although owned, the reindeer live most of their lives in a free state, autonomously migrating with the seasons, from east to west from coast to inland. This freedom comes with both opportunities and challenges. Reindeer, unlike other production animals on farms, traditionally live an autonomous life throughout all seasons in a habitat they are well adapted to. The downside is that the reindeer are exposed to risks and threats such as unpredictable weather conditions, food shortage, predators, fragmented pastures and avalanches, falls and traffic incidents (Grøndahl and Mejdell 2012). The owned reindeer have a similar life to what we consider to be "wild" ungulates (e.g., moose, deer), and the animal welfare challenges in reindeer husbandry are therefore different from those of farmed animals.

Multiple Stressors: Climate Change, Encroachments from Human Activities and Infrastructure, and Predators

We argue in this chapter that the ideal state of reindeer in luohtu is becoming increasingly difficult to maintain for the herders. This is related to a set of interlinked and multiple drivers of change, including climate change, encroachments from human activities and infrastructure such as roads, rails, cabins, trails, windmills and mines, predator losses, emergent diseases, and institutional constraints. Frequent freeze–thaw cycles in pastures due to climate change, increases in the presence of predators lynx (*Lynx lynx*), wolverines (*Gulo gulo*), golden eagles (*Aquila chrysaetis*), bear (*Ursus arctos*), rapid land use change, and changing human presence all result in fragmented pastures and an increasing pressure on land resources that impact herders disproportionately (Horstkotte et al. 2022; Horstkotte, Lépy, and Risvoll 2020; Hovelsrud et al. 2021; Landauer, Rasmus, and Forbes 2021; Pape and Löffler 2012; Paulsen 2021; Risvoll et al. 2022; Skarin and Åhman 2014; Tyler et al. 2021; Vikhamar-Shuler et al. 2016).

Snow, combined with more precipitation falling as rain increase the frequency and intensity of freeze–thaw and rain on snow events, creating hard layers of snow and ice (locked pastures) that are difficult or impossible for reindeer to dig through. The changes in weather and climate increase the frequency of "locked pastures," creating more challenging winter grazing conditions (Rasmus et al. 2022; Risvoll and Hovelsrud 2016). The combined and cascading effects of changes in climatic, environmental, and societal conditions put pressure on access to pastures that have been used and managed by Sámi reindeer herders for millennia. Increasingly, herders must defend their rights and adapt to these multiple and interacting drivers of change (Risvoll et al. 2022).

Supplementary Feeding

The outlined multiple stressors are fragmenting the grazing land rendering it partially or fully inaccessible. This is forcing Fennoscandian reindeer herders to increasingly provide fodder for their animals. This means that the herder supplements the natural diet of the reindeer with store bought feed, ensilaged grass, or reindeer lichen (*Cladonia rangiferina*) picked by the herders. Supplementary feeding is typically an agrarian practice, with complex, more-than human entanglements (Paulsen 2021). This practice comes with positive and negative implications; it contributes to reducing hunger but also to restricting the freedom of the reindeer. For reindeer herders supplementary feeding is therefore an adaptive strategy that solves some problems while creating others, aptly described by John Law as a "messy practice" (Law 2004).

Extensive supplementary feeding as a practice is relatively new to the Sámi reindeer husbandry assemblage and differs considerably both within and between the Fennoscandian countries. Although extensive feeding of large reindeer herds is relatively new, herders have historically fed valuable animals and/or smaller groups such as female reindeer kept close to the settlements for milking (Riseth, Tømmervik, and Tryland 2020). The need for supplementary feeding was in the past not critical because the traditional Sámi organization, the *siida*, allowed for greater flexibility and tolerance for the reindeer's inclination to spread over large areas if a pasture crisis occurred (Solem 1933).

Unlike their grandparents, herders today can to a greater degree mitigate hunger. Many have access to store bought feed concentrate, and they have the knowledge that allows them to feed with minimal risk. The reindeer metabolism is sensitive to changes in diet and requires approximately three weeks of adaptation to be able to digest a new type of feed, such as concentrates (Åhman 2000). To prevent fatal outcomes, the reindeer must be in good health when feeding is initiated. When the herd has weakened, it is often too late to start feeding. Furthermore, feeding-related infrastructure such as feed trays and feed hangers are sold in farm shops. Still, herders prefer natural pastures over feeding, even in cases where feeding has obvious benefits such as increased slaughter weight (Paulsen 2021; Horstkotte et al. 2020; Åhman et al. 2022). This skepticism is rooted in Sámi reindeer herders' experience and worldview that feeding threatens the reindeer's ability to survive on their own and thereby reduces their ability to live in luohtu, the ideal free state (Magga, Oskal, and Sara 2001).

Supplementary Feeding as a New Worldmaking Practice: Discussion and Analysis

The "free reindeer" – luohtu – is the archetype in traditional reindeer husbandry: the autonomous, mobile, and independent reindeer, the one who can manage on their own (Magga et al. 2001). To be free is a prerequisite for animal welfare in reindeer husbandry. Luohtu is the original state for the reindeer, and human interventions in the life of the free reindeer are and should be limited (ibid: 3). To make the reindeer totally dependent on humans is, according to Magga et al. (2001), unethical because it weakens the reindeer's ability to manage and adapt to life in luohtu. At the same time the consequences of climate change, pasture fragmentation, predators, and the cumulative effects make it increasingly harder for reindeer to live in luohtu.

As explained above, herders in Sápmi have increasingly turned to supplementary feeding as an adaptive strategy to handle these stressors. The herders explain that feeding the reindeer allow them to "sleep well at night, knowing that the herd is ok," and that they have no other options but to provide fodder. On the other hand, this practice is counterintuitive for herders who hold natural grazing as the best and most sustainable practice for the reindeer.

With this dilemma in mind, we continue with a critical examination of whether and how supplementary feeding changes the reindeer husbandry assemblages and the herding practices that constitute them. We unpack the material semiotic networks of supplementary feeding and highlight three salient aspects of feeding as a worldmaking practice: time, money, and knowledge. We pay particular attention to how these dimensions affect the reindeer's ability to live free in luohtu, the essential element in the Sámi understanding of animal welfare.

Time

Supplementary feeding is time-consuming and hard work. The herders we have talked to explain that the practice of feeding – the doing – quickly becomes a new daily task that competes with and marginalizes other husbandry tasks. One herder explains that he, for long periods of time, has hardly seen his family. To be able to do all the chores within the limited hours of daylight, he has to live in a cabin in the mountains. In general, herders state that feeding leads to a situation where other tasks, including herding, searching, and protecting the herd from predators, responding to accidents when an animal has been hit by a car – all imperative for the free reindeer – are not carried out. To manage the additional workload, some herders have had to hire help, and/or rely on help from family and friends. This is affecting the herders' physical and psychological well-being.

The new tasks associated with feeding include transporting the fodder from storage to the herd, distributing the fodder *in situ*, and cleaning and maintaining feed trays, vehicles, and corrals. The reindeer does not reside behind a barn, and there are great distances between the feed storage and the herd. In most cases, a truck is not an option for transporting the fodder to the herd, instead herders typically use snow mobiles or even in some cases helicopters. How often the herders must transport feed depends on the capacity of the snowmobile, the sled, the travel conditions, and the size of the herd. While herders traditionally often check on and tend the herd, the daily feeding witnessed today is a new practice.

The metabolism of a grazing reindeer slows down in the winter – it goes into a saving mode, but research shows that this does not equally apply to reindeer who are fed (Marin et al. 2020). When the metabolism is not naturally slowed down, fed reindeer will require more food than those grazing on natural pastures. Starting to feed is thus a commitment to continue to feed, even in situations where natural pastures are sufficient. The concentrates herders have access to are unfit in a crisis because of the sensitive reindeer metabolism, instead they turn feeding into a long-term process to be maintained throughout the fall and winter. This is so because herders find themselves in situations where the herd must be ready, if and when a pasture crisis arises. Having access to store-bought fodder that even a weak herd could eat without adjustment would solve at least parts of this problem, but this is currently unavailable to herders.

When a herd is accustomed to being fed, a new dependency develops between the herder and the herd. This is particularly relevant if the herd is fed in corrals, but it also applies to herds fed in the terrain. This compromises the autonomy and freedom of the reindeer. Instead of managing on its own in luohtu the reindeer are becoming increasingly dependent on the herder. Instead of moving through the landscape, searching for the best available pasture, new, material bindings are created between the reindeer and the place of feeding. This can be witnessed in older and dominant female reindeer who claim the feed trays, refusing access to other reindeer.

Money

Feeding is expensive. The cost of labor is added to that of concentrates, grass and/or reindeer lichen. Concentrates are frequently used as they cover all the reindeer's nutritional needs but are costly. Only one specialized reindeer concentrate is available at the agricultural cooperative (Felleskjøpet). While most herders are content with the available concentrates, others prefer to purchase feed from Sweden or Finland where the availability and prices are better, but with grain toll fees and customs this is often not an option.

Reindeer lichen is the preferred winter diet for reindeer. Until 2017 many herders would gather lichen in southern Norway for backup fodder for poor pasture conditions and to feed under particular practices such as under migrations and corral work. After chronic wasting disease (CWD) was detected in wild reindeer further south in Nordfjella, this practice was forbidden. Although this ban is accepted, the affected herders lost access to an important food source. This further reduces their ability to prepare for pasture decline. Lichen is not commonly available for purchase, but some herders note that they can buy it from Finland, at "extreme prices."

Feeding also requires new and expensive equipment. In general, until the 1970s, herders in the company of their families would move between different seasonal settlements. Such practice is less common today, and the herders increasingly commute to the herds from their permanent homes (Reinert 2009). The mobility of traditional reindeer husbandry called for light, packable, and portable infrastructure. This is reflected in traditional tools that herders still use today. The knife is a versatile tool that also makes it possible to euthanize an injured or sick reindeer on site if necessary. The lasso is used to catch the reindeer. High-quality binoculars are critical for monitoring and checking the herd without disturbing them unnecessarily. This is particularly important in the spring when the calves are born, and the herd is sensitive to disturbances.

In contrast, the herders who have contributed to our research have all emphasized that supplementary feeding requires investments in new expensive equipment and vehicles. Although herders use snowmobiles to follow the herd, the heavy weight of the feed requires stronger and larger machines and sleds. This is because of the vast geographical distances between herds and the feed storage, and the herds are spread across large areas in the highlands and mountains. Some fly out the feed with helicopters because the distance is too great, or when the topography does not allow for snowmobiles. The weight of the fodder increases fuel costs, and the wear and tear of the technical equipment (e.g., snow mobile and sled) require more frequent replacement adding to the costs.

For most herders, this means that they work more for less. As one herder said, "if I am to feed the herd from November to the spring, to be on the safe side, then I'll be bankrupt by March." On the other hand, feeding increases the weight of the reindeer and more animals survive. The herders we have talked to do not agree on how feeding affects the quality of the calves. Some note that they are in better condition because of feeding, others the opposite. What they do agree upon is that feeding allows for the survival of animals who would not have survived on their own. In the long term, this may be a concern. If feeding increases the survival of weak animals, it potentially threatens the future generations of reindeer, by reducing the natural resilience in the species. Further, the increased cost associated with feeding challenges the resilience of reindeer husbandry itself. We surmise that the increased costs may reduce the herder's willingness to take economic risks and their ability to wait and see if the reindeer find their own way.

Reindeer herders in Sápmi have relied on natural pastures to which they hold legal rights. Now they have to pay the added cost of fodder and infrastructure. One way to afford this is to increase the production (meat) and the profit (reduce loss). Waiting to see whether the pastures will improve or trusting the herds to find their own way becomes risky. As explained by one herder "if the animals are in poor condition, it is possible to feed them, and then they will survive. Even those who should have died naturally. In that way, feeding also changes the structure of the herd." Herein lies a dilemma: by increasing the control over the herd, through feeding, the herder secures the survival of the whole herd which on the one hand, potentially weakens the gene pool of the animals, but on the other hand, maintains a time tested cultural and traditional practice.

Knowledge

Herding and feeding are executed in parallel yet overlapping knowledge systems. Traditional reindeer husbandry is rooted in Sámi Indigenous knowledge about reindeer, seasonal variations, weather conditions, and pasture. Reindeer husbandry knowledge is also place-specific, and a combination of skills and knowledge is necessary to practice reindeer husbandry within a particular geographical area (Sara 2009). In contrast, knowledge on supplementary feeding stems from a different knowledge system rooted in western science and management principles. We have seen how feeding activates a new language and terminology through feed units, second harvests, feed concentrates, and "adapting the reindeer stomach."

One herder explained that there is no Indigenous knowledge about feeding. Instead, he applies Indigenous knowledge as an indicator for when to feed, and as a tool to be able to feed, in a better way. The herders are worried that the reindeer will become lazy when fed. They are also worried that the reindeer migratory pattern will change and that their behaviour become irrational (Paulsen 2021). One herder noted that some animals find refuge in the shade behind buildings instead of moving towards the snowy and cooler mountains. They are concerned that the reindeer eventually will lose essential instinctive knowledge about the landscape and how to find food on their own; knowledge that is transferred from the mother to her calf.

Supplementary feeding of reindeer is a complicated practice. Timing is crucial, as is fodder quality and weather conditions. Mild periods can lead to snow-free and wet ground, which condenses soil and manure where the reindeer walk, stand, and eat. This can potentially increase the risk of bacteria and disease outbreaks (Riseth, Tømmervik, and Tryland 2020). This is a new situation, requiring new knowledge for the herders and a new kind of preparedness, which materializes in a herd that is adjusted to feeding (Risvoll et al. 2022). This creates a significant dilemma and a double bind for the herders. They wish to be able to feed, but not on a permanent basis. But having a herd ready to digest concentrate demands that they prepare the herd early in the fall to allow the herder to intervene on short notice to avoid starvation. Feeding is both enacted as a long-term practice and is resisted.

Concluding Reflections: The Ongoing Worldmaking of Sámi Reindeer Herding

In this chapter we have shown that the ideal state of the reindeer in luothu (free and autonomous) is becoming increasingly difficult to maintain for Sámi herders. The same applies for their ability to prioritize husbandry practices in line with Sámi traditions, experiences, values, and ethics of reindeer husbandry and in accordance with a good reindeer life.

For thousands of years, humans and reindeer have co-existed and collaborated. In Sámi reindeer husbandry, the reindeer is inherently free, and not because it is an unsuccessful domestication project. It is an analytical challenge to balance perceived and established categories such as wild and tame because the reindeer is neither. The scientific literature has solved this conundrum by applying the term "'semi-domesticated" to describe the degree of domestication in reindeer husbandry (Skarin and Åhman 2014). Semi-domestication designates that the reindeer is placed on a continuum between wild and fully domesticated. We argue that this is an unprecise designation that fails to capture the core of what reindeer is the to Sámi – they are in luohtu.

We argue that the emic concept of luohtu better reflects the reality of reindeer husbandry than the notion of reindeer being semi-domesticated. Luohtu requires trust and collaboration between the herder and the reindeer rather than the exertion of control. In the recognition of the free reindeer lies a potential for expanding our perspectives on how we as researchers approach domestication of animals (Lien, Swanson, and Ween 2017; Paulsen 2021). The free reindeer is equal to the herder and transcends established categories of wild and tame. Luohtu exemplifies a promise that humans and other-than-human animals can engage in mutually beneficial relationships, where both parties remain autonomous. This has consequences for how broader society understands the effects of climate change and other multiple stressors on the practices of reindeer husbandry, and how we are to manage and address such challenges.

We suggest that instead of making the free reindeer into an animal welfare problem because of the threat of starvation (Kalstad 2010), this autonomy should be encouraged. The free reindeer require space. They require access to good pasture, also in winter. They require to move freely searching for pasture, also underneath the snow. Supplementary feeding, with the new demands on time and money, turns this logic upside down by increasing the reindeer's dependency on the herders and thereby binding them to agricultural practices and infrastructures. Structurally this is only treating the symptoms of greater challenges such as the loss of pastures and does not address the underlying causes; the cumulative effects of climate change, infrastructural encroachments, and predators, which bit by bit reduce and degrade the continuous pastures that reindeer need. Rather than accepting feeding as the solution, we argue that alternative pathways should be explored, for which more knowledge is needed about the resources needed for reindeer herders to feed when required, while at the same time allowing the reindeer to be free.

We are going down a path in which supplementary feeding as a solution to an immediate problem is creating worldmaking practices with unforeseen and possibly dire consequences for both reindeer and herders. Supplementary feeding to avoid starvation resonates well with greater society and is an accepted and even encouraged practice. But we suggest that this also carries colonial overtones with unforeseen long-term consequences; practically, culturally, and materially. In this, Sámi reindeer husbandry is at risk of becoming yet another agrarian practice. This occurs as the constituting practices change, as they do when reindeer are fed concentrates. Feeding is a complex assemblage of time, money, and knowledge that has become an Anglo-European blind-spot. It is not acknowledged that when the herding resources are channeled into feeding, other traditional husbandry practices suffer. Herein lie the colonial undercurrents. And this is the dilemma: we are exposing a practice that on the surface appears inevitable and beneficial for the reindeer, while at the same time may move the reindeer away from the mountains and natural pastures. Our findings in this chapter show that hindering natural pastures for reindeer is not an option if we are to perpetuate Sámi reindeer herding practices and the important state of luohtu.

With this in mind, we are inspired to continue our research into alternative trajectories for reindeer husbandry and to better understand the transformative powers of supplementary feeding as a worldmaking practice partially driven by climate change.

Acknowledgements

We thank the participants of this study for sharing their knowledge and time. The research was conducted with financial support from the Nordic Center of Excellence Project: Climate Change Effects on the Epidemiology of Infectious Disease – CLINF grant number 76413, and the Norwegian Research Council Project: Animal Welfare, Behavior, Health and Sustainability –the Effects of Feeding on Reindeer and Reindeer Herding – WELFED grant number 325968. We are also grateful for the comments on the text by the editors.

References

Åhman, Birgitta, Minna Turunen, Jouko Kumpula, Camilla Risvoll, Tim Horstkotte, ÉliseLépy, and Svein Morten Eilertsen. 2022. "Role of supplementary feeding in reindeer husbandry." In *Reindeer Husbandry and Global Environmental Change*, 232–248. Routledge.

Åhman, Birgitta and R.G. White. 2019. "Rangifer diet and nutritional needs." In *Reindeer and Caribou Health and Disease* edited by Morten Tryland and Susan Kutz, 107–134. CRC Press.

Åhman, B. 2000. *Utfodring av Renar*. Umeå: Svenske Samers Riksforbund Sámiid Riikkasearvi.

Beach, Hugh and Florian Stammler. 2006. "Human–animal relations in pastoralism." *Nomadic Peoples* 10 (2): 6–30. https://doi.org/10.3167/np.2006.100202. http://ezproxy.uin.no:2048/login.

Benjaminsen, Tor Arve, Inger Marie Gaup Eira, Erik Reinert, Hugo Reinert, Mikkel Nils Sara, and Hanne Svarstad. 2016. "Reindrift, makt og myter." In *Samisk Reindrift, Norske Myter* edited by T.A. Benjaminsen, Inger Marie Gaup Eira, and Mikkel Nils Sara, 9–24.

Dankertsen, Astri. 2016. *Fragments of the Future. Decolonization in Sami everyday life*. Forskningråd, Norges 2005.

Forskningsbehov, *Innen Dyrevelferd i Norge*. Norwegian Research Council (www.forskningsraadet.no). https://www.forskningsradet.no/siteassets/publikasjoner/1108644079320.pdf.

Grøndahl, Ann Margaret and Cecilie Marie Mejdell. 2012. "Beiteforhold og tap i reindriften sett fra et dyrevelferdsperspektiv." *Norsk Veterinærtidsskrift* 9: 631–639.

Horstkotte, Tim, Jouko Kumpula, Per Sandström, Hans Tømmervik, Sonja Kivinen, Anna Skarin, Jon Moen, and Stefan Sandström. 2022. "Pastures under pressure: effects of other land users and the environment." In *Reindeer Husbandry and Global Environmental Change*, 76–98. Routledge.

Horstkotte, Tim, Élise Lépy, and Camilla Risvoll. 2020. *Supplementary Feeding in Reindeer Husbandry: Results from a workshop with reindeer herders and researchers from Norway, Sweden and Finland*. Umeå University.

Hovelsrud, Grete K., Camilla Risvoll, Jan Åge Riseth, Hans Tømmervik, Anna Omazic, and Ann Albihn. 2021. "Reindeer herding and coastal pastures: adaptation to multiple stressors and cumulative effects." In *Nordic Perspectives on the Responsible Development of the Arctic: Pathways to action*, 113–134. Springer.

Istomin, Kirill Vladimirovich, and Mark James Dwyer. 2010. "Dynamic mutual adaptation: human–animal interaction in reindeer herding pastoralism." *Human Ecology* 38 (5): 613–623.

Johnsen, Kathrine Ivsett, Tor A. Benjaminsen, and Inger Marie Gaup Eira. 2015. "Seeing like the state or like pastoralists? Conflicting narratives on the governance of Sámi reindeer husbandry in Finnmark, Norway." *Norsk Geografisk Tidsskrift - Norwegian Journal of Geography* 69 (4): 230–241. https://doi.org/10.1080/00291951.2015.1033747. http://dx.doi.org/10.1080/00291951.2015.1033747.

Kalstad, André Stener. 2010. "Grensen for lovstridig avmagring av rein." *Lov og Rett* 49 (9): 539–549.

Kuokkanen, Rauna Johanna. 2007. "Myths and realities of Sami women: a post-colonial feminist analysis for the decolonialization and transformation of Sami society." In *Making Space for Indigenous Feminism*, 72–92. Fernwood Publishing.

Landauer, Mia, Sirpa Rasmus, and Bruce C. Forbes. 2021. "What drives reindeer management in Finland towards social and ecological tipping points?" *Regional Environmental Change* 21 (2): 1–16.

Law, John. 2004. *After Method: Mess in social science research*. International library of sociology. London: Routledge.

Law, John and Annemarie Mol. 2008. "The actor-enacted: Cumbrian sheep in 2001." In *Material Agency*, 57–77. Springer.

Lien, Marianne Elisabeth. 2015. *Becoming salmon: aquaculture and the domestication of a fish*. Vol. v. 55. California Studies in Food and Culture Ser.Berkeley: University of California Press.

Lien, Marianne Elisabeth, Heather Anne Swanson, and Gro B. Ween. 2017. "Naming the beast – exploring the otherwise." In *Decentering Domestication*, 4–44. Duke University Press.

Magga, Ole Henrik, Nils Oskal, and Mikkel Nils Sara. 2001. "Dyrevelferd i samisk kultur." Report published in collaboration with Samisk Høgskole. www.regjeringen. no/upload/kilde/ld/rap/// ddd/pdfv/151133-utredning_dyrevelferd_samisk. pdf

Marin, Andrei and Ivar Bjørklund. 2016. "6. Er Finnmarksvidda en allmenning?" In *Samisk Reindrift, Norske Myter*, edited by T..A Benjaminsen, I.M. Gaup Eira, and Mikkel Nils Sara. Fagbokforlaget.

Marin, Andrei, Espen Sjaastad, Tor A. Benjaminsen, Mikkel Nils M. Sara, and Erik Johan Langfeldt Borgenvik. 2020. "Productivity beyond density: a critique of management models for reindeer pastoralism in Norway." *Pastoralism: Research, Policy and Practice* 10 (1): 1–18. https://doi. org/10.1186/s13570-020-00164-3.

Mol, Annemarie. 2002. *The Body Multiple: Ontology in medical practice. Science and cultural theory*. Durham: Duke University Press.

Nergård, Jens-Ivar. 2011. "Når slutter en koloniprosess?" In *Hvor går Nord-Norge? Tidsbilder Fra en Landsdel i Forandring* edited by Svein Jentoft, Jens-Ivar Nergård and Kjell Arne Røvik, 119–128. Stamsund: Orkana akademisk.

Norwegian Ministry of Agriculture and Food 2017. Meld. St. 32 (2016–2017) *Samisk Reindrift – Lange Tradisjoner –Unike Muligheter* White Paper nr. 32 (2016–2017) Reindeer Husbandry – Long traditions – Unique Possibilities www.regjeringen.no (Norway). https://www.regjeringen. no/contentassets/ffb8837d1f32425b962ceb23e5ccfc8e/no/pdfs/stm201620170032000dddpdfs.pdf.

Oskal, Nils. 1995. *Det Rette, det Gode og Reinlykken*. Universitetet i Tromsø, Institutt for samfunnsvitenskap, Filosofiseksjonen.

Pape, Roland and Jörg Löffler. 2012. "Climate change, land use conflicts, predation and ecological degradation as challenges for reindeer husbandry in Northern Europe: what do we really know after half a century of research?" *Ambio* 41 (5): 421–434. https://doi.org/10.1007/s13280-012-0257-6.

Paulsen, Majken. 2021. *Dilemmaet Tilleggsfôring: En nymaterialistisk studie av tilleggsfôring av rein*. no. 53–2021. Fakultet for samfunnsvitenskap, Nord universitet.

Pedersen, Å.Ø. 2019. "Rangifer biology and adaptation." In *Reindeer and Caribou Health and Disease* Vol. 1, edited by Morten Tryland and Susan Kutz. CRC Press.

Rasmus, S., Horstkotte, T., Turunen, M., Landauer, M., Löf, A., Lehtonen, I., Rosqvist, G., and Holand, Ø. (2022). "Reindeer husbandry and climate change." In *Reindeer Husbandry and*

Global Environmental Change: Pastoralism in Fennoscandia, edited by T. Horstkotte, Ø. Holand, J. Kumpala, and J.Moen. Routledge.

Reinert, Hugo. 2009. *The Corral and the Slaughterhouse: Knowledge, tradition and the modernization of indigenous reindeer slaughtering practice in the Norwegian Arctic*. University of Cambridge.

Reinert, Hugo. 2014. "Entanglements – intimacy and nonhuman ethics." *Society & Animals* 22 (1): 42–56. https://doi.org/10.1163/15685306-12341318. http://ezproxy.uin.no:2048/login.

Research Council of Norway Norges forskningsråd 2005: Forskningsbehov innen dyrevelferd i Norge http://www.forskningsradet.no/siteassets/publikasjoner/1108644079320

Riseth, Jan Åge, Hans Tømmervik, and Morten Tryland. 2020. "Spreading or gathering? Can traditional knowledge be a resource to tackle reindeer diseases associated with climate change?" *International Journal of Environmental Research and Public Health* 17 (16): 6002.

Risvoll, C., G.K. Hovelsrud, and J.Å. Riseth (2022) "Falling between the cracks of the governing system: risk and uncertainty in pastoralism in northern Norway." *Weather, Climate, and Society* 14 (1): 191–204. doi:10.1175/WCAS-D-21-0052.1.

Risvoll, Camilla and Grete Kaare Hovelsrud. 2016. "Pasture access and adaptive capacity in reindeer herding districts in Nordland, Northern Norway." *The Polar Journal* 6 (1): 87–111. https://doi.org/10.1080/2154896X.2016.1173796.

Risvoll, Camilla, Jan Åge Riseth, Mats Pavall, and Svein Morten Eilertsen. 2022. *Reindriftas Tradisjons – Og Erfaringsbaserte Kunnskap – Hvordan Synliggjøres den og Hvilken Gjennomslagskraft har den? Erfaringer fra Utbyggingsprosesser i Nordland*.

Sara, Mikkel Nils. 2001. *Reinen-et Gode fra Vinden: Reindriftens Tilpasningsformer i Kautokeino*. Davvi Girji.

Sara, Mikkel Nils. 2009. "Siida and traditional Sámi reindeer herding knowledge." *Northern Review* (30): 153–178.

Skarin, Anna and Birgitta Åhman. 2014. "Do human activity and infrastructure disturb domesticated reindeer? The need for the reindeer's perspective." *Polar biology* 37 (7): 1041–1054. https://doi.org/10.1007/s00300-014-1499-5.

Skjenneberg, Sven, Erling Lyftingsmo, and Jens A. Poulsson. 1965. *Rein og Reindrift*. Lesjaskog: Fjell-Nytt.

Solem, Erik. 1933. *Lappiske Rettsstudier*. Vol. 24. Instituttet for sammenlignende kulturforskning. Oslo: Aschehoug.

Stammler, Florian. 2010. "Animal diversity and its social significance among Arctic pastoralists." In *Good to Eat, Good to Live With: Nomads and animals in northern Eurasia and Africa*, edited by Hiroki Takakura and Florian Stammler. Sendai: Center for Northeast Asian Studies, Tohoku University.

Stenevik, Inger Helen and Cecilie Marie Mejdell. 2011. *Dyrevelferdsloven: Kommentarutgave*. Oslo: Universitetsforl.

Tyler, Nicholas J.C., Inger Hanssen-Bauer, Eirik J. Førland, and Christian Nellemann. 2021. "The shrinking resource base of pastoralism: Saami reindeer husbandry in a climate of change." *Frontiers in Sustainable Food Systems*: 274.

Vikhamar-Schuler, Dagrun, Ketil Isaksen, Jan Erik Haugen, Hans Tømmervik, Bartlomiej Luks, Thomas Vikhamar Schuler, and Jarle W. Bjerke. 2016. "Changes in winter warming events in the Nordic Arctic Region." *Journal of Climate* 29 (17): 6223–6244.

14

SAKHA AND *ALAAS*

Place Attachment and Cultural Identity in a Time of Climate Change[1]

Susan A. Crate

In 2019 the international press began reporting the distinct challenges climate change brings to inhabitants of the Sakha Republic (Troianovski, Mooney, and Robinson Chavez 2019; MacFarquhar and Ducke 2019). Most dramatically, warming was thawing the ice-rich permafrost that underlay *alaas*, an ecosystem unique to the area that includes a circular lake surrounded by hayfields that transition to boreal forest. These reports visually and textually communicate the physical challenges caused by the thawing of permafrost overall and *alaas* specifically. Longitudinal ethnographic research adds to these physical descriptions to reveal the cultural underpinnings of *alaas* landscapes, and, in the process, how much more is at stake due to thawing permafrost. As Margarita Ilyinichna Zabolotskaya told me during a July 2018 interview,

> Sakha are children of the *alaas*. Every Sakha has an *alaas* in their spirit – and we carry that *alaas* with us all our lives. The *alaas* is connected to our roots, our beginnings, the birthplace, the homeland. Why is that? Because Sakha lived by the *alaas* long ago. They had *alaas* which they protected and lived from.

I have heard testimonies of *alaas* similar to Margarita's over the course of my thirty-year research relationship with Viliui Sakha. But in 2018 I began to hear depictions of *alaas* that were qualitatively different. Most memorable was from Yegor Yegorovich Treytiyakov in a 2019 interview:

> In almost all the *alaas* areas, where ötökh (flat area on *alaas* where homesteads were) were always very flat, the land surface is now rolling and wavy...we Sakha have started to call it *abaahy üngküüleebit* (where evil spirits have danced).

I knew from permafrost scientist Alexander Fedorov, my collaborator since 2006, that not all permafrost contained ice. But *alaas*, where Sakha have historically practiced horse and cattle subsistence, are underlain with ice-rich permafrost. I had an epiphany with the understanding of how climate change drove thawing to transform the *alaas* landscapes,

DOI: 10.4324/9781003242499-17

much like I had in 2005 when elders commented on how *Jyl Oghuha* (the Bull of Winter) was no longer arriving (Crate 2008). *Jyl Oghuha* is Sakha's emic understanding of the three months of bitter, snowless, windless winter. Its absence prompted me to ponder the cultural implications of climate change, specifically that an explanatory story for how the world worked was now a story of how the world worked *before*. By 2018, it was not just *Jyl Oghuha* that was absent; the landscapes that made up Sakha's main homeland were also visibly changing. Because I knew the place of *alaas* in Sakha's emic perception and cultural world, my new questions were about cultural identity and even the very roots of a people's ethnicity. For although the "evil spirits are dancing" on *alaas*, Sakha inhabitants retain a more profound understanding far beyond *alaas's* physical existence. Nadyezhda Yegorovna Savvinova explained in 2018,

> Even if the *alaas* disappear they will not change. *Alaas* is the most important and dear connection that Sakha have to nature. It is connected with everything. *Alaas* are like our mother and that connection will never change.

In this chapter I show that Sakha's relationship with *alaas* is something far beyond a physical one, perhaps bordering on the metaphysical. I invite the reader to understand this inductively, chronicling the relationship of Sakha with *alaas* via historical changes and personal testimonies. Through this on-the-ground witness, I show how longitudinal ethnography can reveal a culture's vernacular knowledge of human–environment interactions, in this case, Sakha and *alaas*. Herein I illustrate the centrality of place attachment, cultural identity, and the overall sentience of the world in the context of unprecedented climate change. Following, I discuss other anthropologists' and social scientists' research engaging vernacular understandings of change to bring my work of the loss of culturally significant landscapes due to climate change into the larger literature. I argue that such cultural information can contribute to more comprehensive, ethical, and right-holder-focused policy prescriptions.

"Being There" with Sakha in the Anthropocene

Sakha are a horse- and cattle-breeding people who make their present-day homeland in the Sakha Republic, Russia (Figure 14.1), a massive area that makes up one-fifth of the Russian Federation. Sakha's Turkic ancestors migrated from southern Siberia circa 1400, using lush *alaas* for their herds (Ksenofontov 1992). Although not considered "Indigenous people" according to Russian legislation, I consider them Indigenous because they have been inhabitants of their homeland since before colonization (ILO n.d). The Sakha Republic has continuous ice-rich permafrost, which underlays *alaas*. Across northern Russia, the Republic has the highest increase in mean air and ground temperatures, one of the results of which is thawing *alaas* (Varlamov, Skachkov, and Skryabin 2020).

I know the central place of *alaas* for Sakha from conducting longitudinal ethnography since 1991, from "being there," which allows for "a slower accumulation of evidence and understanding and for key insights to arise unexpectedly, during experiences that allow glimpses of how the world is perceived and experienced by local peoples" (Roncoli, Crane, and Orlove 2009: 88). Beyond the formal methodologies of interviews, focus groups and oral histories, I have participated in daily life for a total of seventy-six months and I am fluent in Sakha.

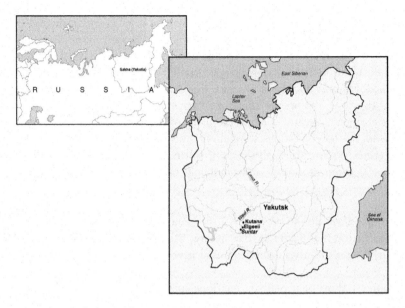

FIGURE 14.1 Location of the Sakha Republic within the Russian Federation and of the two main research villages, Elgeeii and Kutana. Artwork (Adobe Illustrator) by Susan A. Crate.

Since 2005, my focus has been climate ethnography: critical, multi-sited ethnography in collaboration with affected communities (Marino 2015; Crate 2011). I have co-created research foci and field plans, mentored research assistants, collectively written community materials, and collaborated with Sakha scientists. I have also conducted comparative climate research in Canada, Mongolia, Wales, Peru, Kiribati, and the US. Foundational to my work is discerning the multiple drivers of change and how cultures understand based on their vernacular knowledge (Huntington 2000).

Within this longer history of fieldwork with Sakha inhabitants, here I focus on recent life histories and interviews conducted in 2018–19. I analyze narratives to contextualize *what people say* within their cognitive frame and their knowledge system from which they shape, understand, give meaning to, and reference their world (Agrawal 1995). During that period, I spent three months each summer interviewing the sample of householders with whom I have worked since 1999, in Elgeeii and Kutana (see Figure 14.1), both men and women and all over the age of forty. In 2019, I also completed fifteen life histories, unstructured interviews with those who possessed particular knowledge about change in their lives.

Alaas and their Meaning

In 1991 I was en route to the International Jew's Harp Conference, my first trip to northeastern Siberia. My flight took off from the dramatic mountainous area around Lake Baikal in southern Siberia. Halfway through the trip, I looked out of the plane window to see endless flatlands dotted with circular lakes. After staring out the window for some time, I felt a tap on my shoulder. My seatmate explained that the multiple circular lakes surrounded by hayfields were called *alaas*. She went on to tell me, "Sakha say there are as many *alaas* as there are stars in the winter night sky." In that moment, the seed was planted of my future research trajectory.

E.K. Pekarski (1958: 67) defined *alaas* as "a meadow or spacious field, surrounded by woods; a piedmont valley; a long, clear glade among the forest; a field or meadow, surrounded by forest." Pekarski was a Polish ethnographer and dissident, exiled to Siberia, who mastered the Sakha language and wrote Sakha's first dictionary. The three-tome dictionary includes intricate details of word usages, proverbs, and understandings. His definition of *alaas* extends into various explanations of the many variants on the word, reflecting different environmental characteristics, naming traditions, and other traits of *alaas*. This linguistic diversity exemplifies the importance of *alaas* to Sakha life (Kempton 2002).

Sakha's Turkic ancestors settled in *alaas* to use their plentiful hay forage and fodder areas, both critical to get Sakha's herds through the summer and winter (Gogolev 1993). They were also rich with other forage, including fish, wild herbs, berries, grasses, and grains, waterfowl, wood fowl, squirrels, hare, reindeer, deer, moose, and bear. But *alaas's* importance went beyond the utilitarian. *Alaas* held a profoundly spiritual quality for Sakha, predicated upon Sakha's cosmology that recognized the sentience of all things, animate and inanimate. *Alaas* were alive, and therefore required Sakha's respect and offerings in exchange for what they provided (Gogolev 1994).

One example of these practices was a ritual for Sakha's move from their winter to their summer dwelling, the latter located near the important *alaas* resources necessary for winter preparation. In 1992, Nikolai Ignatiev explained to me in great detail how Sakha conducted *salama yiaahyna* (hanging of the *salama*), involving the offering of a braided horsehair rope (the salama) adorned with birchbark figures and colored cloth strips as gifts for the deities of the *alaas*.

Russian colonization in the mid-1600s meant that Sakha were now subjects of the Russian Empire and had to pay a fur tax and convert to Russian Orthodoxy (Forsyth 1994). Most were nominal converts, adopting the faith only superficially in order to lessen their taxes. Although some lands were annexed by the colonizers, Sakha's essential relationship with *alaas* did not significantly change. It was in the Soviet period that Sakha were physically removed, willingly or forcibly, from their ancestral *alaas* to collective farms (Basharin 1956). Nevertheless, many continued to pay homage to their ancestors at their birth *alaas* at least annually. In the early post-Soviet period, many inhabitants aspired to return to their pre-Soviet ancestral life. However, after three generations of living in villages with resource access, electricity, schools, and medical care, this aspiration soon faded (Crate 2006a). Today some use their birth *alaas* for haying, others make a pilgrimage in summer, while others have physical limitations that prevent such visits. But in any case, all Sakha I have worked with *know* their *alaas*, either in a direct physical relationship with their ancestral birth *alaas* or via an innate cultural knowledge of being Sakha.

Sacred Encounters

After that first acquaintance with *alaas* from the airplane window, my knowledge of them continued to grow. For example, I now understand why, in 1991, the Minister of Culture insisted on walking the entire circumference of his birth *alaas* before boarding the helicopter back to the regional center. I can also now fathom the profound symbolic significance of four swans who, out of nowhere, flew overhead during the 1992 *yhyakh* (Sakha's summer festival) at Ugut Küöl outside of Elgeeii village. Attendees looked up in reverence and awe. I was told later that the swans had arrived because they were the totem spirit ancestors of the pre-Soviet *agha uuha* (patrilineal clan) who inhabited the Ugut Küöl *alaas* for centuries before. There are many more of these retrospective understandings that come to me now.

In 1992 I returned to the flatlands of northeastern Siberia to study *yhyakh* for my Master's research. *Yhyakh* marks the critical time for Sakha, just before they move into the intense activities of their short summer: haying, foraging, hunting, building, and performing other outdoor tasks in preparation for the long winter. *Yhyakh* is Sakha's spiritual prostration enacted to honor and appeal to the sky deities for a bountiful and productive season. According to Sakha's historical narrative of arrival from southern Siberia to the northern climes, Sakha's ancestors Omoghoi and Ellei organized the first *yhyakh* (Alekseev, Emel'ianov, and Petrov 1995). They chose the wide-open area of the *alaas* because it was, "the center of the universe with its geo-architectural structures: the tree of life, *Aal Luuk Mas* and the horse-hitching post, *serge*" (Romanova 2015: 94).

In the pre-Soviet period, *yhyakh* was the single time of year when people gathered in one place: again, the *alaas*. The rest of the year, they lived in their extended clan homesteads on separate *alaas*, making a semi-annual move between summer and winter homes. I gained further insight about *alaas* when I documented how Elgeeii inhabitants divvied their lands to use for their household-level food production, which was the way most fed their families in the immediate post-Soviet period after the state farm disbanded overnight in 1992 (Crate 2003).

But perhaps the most profound descriptions of *alaas* came from the fifty-five elder oral histories I conducted during my dissertation research in 1999–2000 (Crate 2006a). Back then, there were still elders who had spent part of their youth living on their ancestral *alaas* where they were born, before their parents either willingly or forcibly relocated to the collective farm. One elder, for example, described how they lived far from each other, recounting the quiet and the stillness of winters. "I would go outside for wood or ice and my ears rang from the silence until I heard the bells on our neighbor's horses on the next *alaas* over. They were a full kilometer away!"

At the time I thought these depictions of life on the *alaas* would leave Sakha consciousness when these elders passed. But I was wrong. In a set of questions that I used in 2018 to gauge inhabitants' perceptions of change over time, I asked what the word *alaas* meant to them. Without hesitation, all twenty-seven interviewees in Elgeeii and all twenty-two in the village of *Kutana* shared descriptions similar to Agrafina Vasiliyevna Nazarova's in a 2018 interview:

> Our ancestors lived by the *alaas*, the round fields with forests shaped like an *alaaji* (small round pancake) with a lake. The Sakha person is born on the *alaas* and lives on the *alaas* and makes their life there and from there, it is the birthland, the *alaas*, our birth soil, where you are born and raised and connected. You can keep animals and all the rest you need to live is there, a small world in and of itself, the lake has fish and there is pasture and hay for the animals and the forest has berries and hunting animals.

Some of those I interviewed in 2018 had been to their ancestral *alaas* many times to make an annual pilgrimage to "feed the ancestors." Those who never or rarely went back to their birth *alaas* explained that it was at a great distance from their present village. Those who had never been explained that the details of their birth *alaas* were never passed down to them by their kin but that they nonetheless felt a connection with it through their identification as Sakha. The break in ancestral knowledge resulted from the Soviet state's "forced forgetting" policies, the deliberate effort to muddle and erase pre-Soviet recollections and memories before they could be passed down (Buyandelger 2013). In the post-Soviet period, many individuals and family clans actively researched their ancestral lineages and inhabitance areas using elder knowledge and archival research in an effort to "intentionally remember."

Local examples include the tireless work of two enthusiasts, Ivan Gerasimovich Ivanov and Nikolai Innokentiyevich Ivanov. In Elgeeii, it was the celebrated Soviet period Sakha writer, Ivan Gerasimovich Ivanov, pen name Ivan Nolar, who published both short and novel-length stories, featuring Sakha working and living "by the *alaas*." The publication *Sakha and Alaas* documents testimonies of a 2004 conference celebrating his seventy-fifth birthday and life works (Gerasimova 2008). The book offers many examples of Sakha's sacred association with *alaas*:

> Sakha people will never break from their identification with the *alaas*.
>
> *(ibid.: 7)*
>
> The words "Sakha" and "*alaas*" are from one source of our bloodline.
>
> *(ibid.: 20)*
>
> The meaning of *alaas* for Sakha is deep and wide. It is not just some symbol but rather a deeper philosophy of what it means to be Sakha. It is Sakha's essential identity, character, and source of origin with a mysterious primordial power for all who call themselves Sakha.
>
> *(ibid.: 67)*
>
> *Alaas*, for the Sakha person, is their original homeplace. Our ancestors made us this original bounty in nature and from it we began as a people. It is our original cradle where we each began and come from.
>
> *(ibid.: 68)*

In Kutana, Nikolai Innokentiyevich Ivanov, nicknamed *Kuola Uchuutal* (Teacher Kolya), left a legacy of teaching and promoting the cultural identification with and ancestral linkages to *alaas* within his community. He was a renowned geography teacher who practiced "experiential learning," by leading field trips with school students to study their ancestral *alaas* in both physical and historical aspects. Over his many-decade career he compiled multiple notebooks containing detailed maps and information about the historical occupants for one hundred *alaas* in the greater Kutana area. In 2015, his daughter transcribed his notes and published it in the book, *Suntaar Kutana 100 Alaas* (Pavlova 2015). The preface of the book begins with Innokentiyevich's words:

> Every person has a birthplace. We, who are now older, think often of our birth *alaas* and are happy only when we can see it. When we think of it, we remember our

childhood, all the people around us, these memories come to us clearly. I separated from my *alaas* a long time ago and I think and say to you that you are but my one and only, that which raised me, I will never forget you and every year I visit you.

(ibid.: 7)

Both Elgeeii and Kutana residents told me how they have benefited from these local historians' work of "intentional remembering."

This remembering included specific acts like an annual visit to the birth *alaas*. Vasili Mikhailovich Lvov told me in 2018 of his commitment, "I hay there every year because if I don't, the ancestral spirits will get angry at me. Why didn't our boy come and cut hay?" Some, like Anatoli Petrovich Fyodorov in 2019, shared the Sakha ways to succumb to the spirits, should a person wish to visit after a long time.

Valentina had not been to her birthland for ten years and went last year. Before she did, she found a stone with a hole in it. The first thing she did upon arrival was look at her birth *alaas* through the hole, saying words to appease the spirits. If you have not been regularly, you need to go to the river and find a stone with a hole in it and do this.

The literature cites this practice but refers to placing the stone with a hole into the hearth and feeding the fire with a sacrificial prayer (Nikolaev 1996).

In 1993, I experienced another way that Sakha make peace with their ancestors after a long time being away. That year, I helped the Yegorov clan with the hay cutting at Kuchakanga, the ancestral *alaas* of their father's lineage. My hosts hadn't hayed there for years because it is normally a boggy area and the preceding years had been especially wet. But with a new dry period, they decided to go. Several of them had been there a few days prior to cut the hay areas. Our task was to rake up the dried hay and transport it back to the village. As we were raking, suddenly I saw a *bugul* (a small pile of hay), lift off the ground and swirl up into the sky. I was shocked and looked about at my companions to see them all gazing up in reverence. After it dissipated, they explained it was a *kholoruk*, a small whirlwind that Sakha understand to be a visit by an ancestral spirit. They went on to explain that it was a benevolent one, since the hay cutters had performed the apropos rituals, namely feeding the ancestors, when they hayed three days prior.

Another documented practice that several interviewees detailed is that of taking a pouch of soil from the birth *alaas* before a long journey. "When travelling, Sakha often bring the spirit of their birth *alaas* with them by taking a handful of soil from their birth *alaas*, to smell, to speak words to, to calm themselves and to comfort their soul" (D'iachkovski and Popova 2014: 61). Even if they know the location of their birth *alaas* and it is relatively close, some have a physical constraint preventing them from traveling there. In 2018, Nadyezhda Ivanovna Zakharova, who was not able to visit due to her inability to walk, described her understanding of *alaas* thus:

It is a hay land, the main meaning a wide field. To the extent it has good conditions, then the hay will grow. If the *alaas* is good, there will be abundance and there will be cows and food and riches and all will be well. It has a huge meaning to Sakha – *Törööbüt Alaaskyn En Taptaa* (Love Your Birth *Alaas*) is a song. We are *alaas* children, which means that we clothe ourselves and eat from the *alaas*.

FIGURE 14.2 Aal Luuk Mas (Tree of Life) shown with the goddess, spirit mother of the Earth, Aan Alakhchin khotun. From: The Sakha Heroic Epos Olonkho Series. Artist: Timofei Stepanov, 1982. Used by artist's permission.

Although the majority of my research is with rural Sakha, Nadyezhda's reference to songs about *alaas* is also relevant for the relationship that Sakha urbanites have to *alaas*. One might think that urban Sakha would not share the same sentiments for *alaas* as rural Sakha, due to their physical separation and city lifestyle. However, urban Sakha maintain a robust understanding of *alaas* as their cultural identifier via the ubiquity of visual and expressive art forms that focus on it. For example, Timofei Stepanov's contemporary depiction of *Aan Alakhchin khotun* shows the tree of life by an ancestral *alaas* (Figure 14.2).

But perhaps the strongest representation of *alaas* in urban culture are in songs, including songs of nostalgia for their birth *alaas*. Some are written by the generation of Sakha who spent their early years on the *alaas* before relocating to the city. Consider Anastasia Varlamova's "*Agham Alaaha*" (My Father's *Alaas*),

> Golden autumn, summer's end
> One mysterious feeling from the season changing
> Fills my spirit with longing
> I miss my homeland more strongly everyday
>> My father's *alaas*
>> At the *Lebiie* lake
>> In the shadow of the great birch tree
>> I see it and rejoice

On the *alaas* edge there is a birch grove
By the camp tent and the fire pit
Scythes tapping, tobacco smoking
And slowly we gather the *buguls*

For as many as we are, we grow up and go our way
With our own fates, becoming people of our own
Nevertheless, in my spirit, in my heart it is always there
The unforgettable memory of my father's *alaas*
                                        (*Varlamova 1993: 56*)

Varlamova (b. 1948) of the *Baatara* village in the Menge-Khangalaas *uluus* (region), like other lyricists of her generation, wrote about her birth *alaas*, reflecting on a youth immersed in her village life and engaged in the summer work of haying, herding, gardening, berrying, hunting, and fishing. But younger songwriters who have lived most of their lives in the city with little if any direct *alaas* relationship also express a profound relationship with their *alaas*. Long-time Yakutsk resident, Pavel Semenov or Baibal, born in 1974 in the *Timpii* village, of the Viliuisk region, weaves images and other sensory qualities of his birth *alaas* into his songs.

The green field spreads out before me
A cool, light wind brushes my face
The stillness of my birth *alaas*
Makes my thoughts learn to fly.
          It's true, it's certain
          The memory does not leave
          Does not fade away, does not cool
          To you, my life's loves
          To my birthland, my mother, my father
          To all my people.
The scent of new larch needles fills the air
I wait in excitement for it every spring
And for the sun's bright, radiant rays
That spread across grandmother lake's surface

In the crowded city among other people
Trying to get used to the shallow existence
I can't sleep day or night
Constantly thinking of my birth *alaas*
                                        (*Semenov 2005*)

These songs and other artistic representations of *alaas* in urban areas maintain a sense of connection to the birth *alaas* for urban dwellers. Most Sakha urbanites have extended kin in the rural areas with whom they spend their summers, either as a family or sending their children there to *saiylyyk* (summer home) to breath the clean air and eat the *ürüng as* (literally "white foods" referring to all Sakha dairy products). Be it the contemporary songs that echo in urban and rural areas alike, or inhabitants' individual testimonies, *alaas* continue to be a central source of cultural grounding and spiritual sustenance for Sakha.

The Social Science Understanding

Within Sakha social science research, there are other clues to the status of *alaas* as a uniquely Sakha cultural symbol. One example is the publication, *Alaas: The Sakha People's Cradle* (Savvinov and Makarov 2015). The comparison of the Sakha and Russian front matter testifies to the powerful cultural meaning that *alaas* have for Sakha and the lack thereof for ethnic Russians.

Sakha:

> Every culture has a unique landscape that is revered as the one associated with their ancestral beginnings. For Sakha, without question, their original cradle is the *alaas*. *Alaas* – a land form made by the upper gods especially for Sakha to live and thrive. Our *alaas*, no matter the time of year, never lose their beauty as they are the true creative glory of our middle world. In them the Sakha person keeps their herds, makes their living, hunts, and fishes, raises their children and the next generation, in this unique nature base with the green fields, the different plants and trees, the carpet of flowers, the animals of the dark forest, the birds of the field and lakes... For the Sakha person it is their source of all life, their cradle of beginning, their original grandmother.
>
> *(ibid.: 4)*

Russian:

> A truly nature-created ecosystem, that strikes humankind with its unrepeatable natural beauty, rich animal populations, and diverse botanical wealth. It is an independent natural system with a picturesque blue lake, bordered by moist meadows and stately eastern Siberian taiga, which surrounds it with the bright green cover and plays the central ecological role in the life of the northern person.
>
> *(ibid.: 5)*

A second example of *alaas* as a uniquely Sakha cultural symbol is from linguist Sardana Savitskaia's comparison of terms that express the concepts of "homeland" and "birthplace" in both Russian and Sakha. All the concepts had parallel associations except for the term *alaas*, which was determined to be unique to Sakha (2017).

Finally, the unique place of *alaas* is clear in how Sakha frame it as a "cultural landscape," with ties to a settled subsistence:

> *Alaas*, as the native land, acts as a component of life and social space. As a study of the structure of living space in the Sakha tradition, the natural landscape determined not only the economical-social activities of an ethnicity, but all of that ethnicity's essence. Sakha pastoralists, *alaas jono* (people of the *alaas*) represented the upper level of social structure and had a broad and social nature; they were called "people from the center."
>
> *(Danilova 2011: 104)*

Overall, in the Sakha academic social science context, *alaas* are Sakha's spiritual core, a key symbol and "a cultural landscape perceived and observed through the prism of signs and symbols, coupled with a rational and emotional experience of space" (Romanova 2015: 94).

Non-Sakha social scientists are also investigating Sakha and *alaas*. Their work looks at Sakha's understanding of the possible dangers when a Sakha person fails to treat their *alaas* spirit with reverence or to regularly visit (Takakura 2010) and the unique interdependent relationship Sakha have with *alaas* as compared to other landscapes (Mészáros 2012).

> Sakha mental maps (referring to maps individuals make of their surrounding territory) are not just pathfinding exercises but rather show how travel through the boreal forest is about social relations via a series of social encounters from *alaas* to *alaas*.
>
> *(Mészáros 2021)*

A final project in *alaas* and change engages both Sakha and non-Sakha natural and social scientists in international collaboration to develop an interdisciplinary understanding of global climate change in the context of an ecosystem that humans have manipulated for centuries (Crate et al. 2017).

By allowing *alaas* to exist in both the physical and the cosmological worlds, these framings by both Sakha and non-Sakha academics provide a sustained source of cultural identification in the midst of historical relocations and urbanization: *alaas* as Sakha's cradle; *alaas* as a center; *alaas* as *the* center of social, economic and spiritual interactions and meaning.

Alaas within Natural Science Understandings

The physical, or natural, scientific understanding of *alaas* differs greatly from Sakha's vernacular understanding. The scientific "knowing" of *alaas* was initiated in the last century for economic reasons, either to extract from beneath or to build on top of *alaas*. At first *alaas* were broadly defined, much like Pekarski's definition to include all areas where Sakha practiced horse and cattle pastoralism (Desiatkin 2008). As the scientific understanding evolved, and especially as the effects of climate change became more imminent, scientists confined *alaas* to areas with highly specific geomorphological parameters. This confined their range to a relatively small area in the Central regions (Solovyev 1973), where today there is the most severe landscape transformation due to climate change (Balobaev, Gavrilova, and Fedorov 1996). During winter 2018 fieldwork with Alexander Fedorov, some Central region inhabitants provided a local perspective. For example, Valeri Ivanovich Danilov said,

> We had lots of fields of grains here. Our region was known for the amount of grain that we grew. We grew the most per hectare than any place in the Sakha Republic. Now we don't grow because our fields are useless. They are thawing and falling in. Now all our food is brought to us.

Granted, this testimony implies a sense of urgency that inhabitants of the Viliui regions to date have not dealt with. But considering that their areas are underlain by the same ice-filled permafrost, it might be only a matter of time before they do.

A second central region inhabitant, Lidiya Nikolayevna Fillipova, conveyed *alaas* as cultural identifier:

> All Sakha have *alaas*. I know my birth *alaas* and when I go there my spirit feels lighter, and I think about how my grandmother and grandfather lived there. There are small trails from one *alaas* to another and when I walk there, I think about how, as a child, my father probably ran along that path to the other *alaas*.

Testimonies of Sakha from the Viliui regions echoed these. Those I spoke with explained how the once-flat *ötökh* are now wavy from climate change, using their hands to signal a roller coaster-like line as they spoke. Some Viliui inhabitants, like Izabella Nikolayevna Treytiyakova in 2019, acknowledged these two understandings of *alaas*.

> I know that many people say that we don't have "real" *alaas* in the Viliui regions. They need to understand that we have a different understanding of *alaas* from the central regions. *Alaas* is a not necessarily a big round place. Here we understand it as an area where people can live and where they have all they need to live. We call that *alaas*. Others think of *alaas* as a huge area with specific contours. Here we have big fields and such that we understand as *alaas*, many of which are smaller places, the *ötökh* and there is always a lake.

The dissonance of these two understandings is a result of different ways of knowing *alaas*. Sakha's is a centuries-old knowledge of *alaas* that came about via their historical use of them for sustenance and survival. The other is a recent understanding, a technically defined landscape, used to economic ends. One knowledge system is rich in cultural history, depth and meaning while the other is focused on specific physical technicalities. To understand one system requires longitudinal ethnographic analysis and corroboration with secondary sources. The other is available in the contemporary parlance of climate change and permafrost science. To date, most global change research and resulting policy prescriptions are based on scientific understandings. In the process, a great deal of meaning and cultural importance is absent. One way that social scientists have found to bring Indigenous knowledge into a scientific knowledge framework is the designation of a cultural keystone species.

Alaas as Sakha's Cultural Keystone

The inherent value in assigning *alaas* as Sakha's cultural identifier is to open pathways to understanding the association between Sakha culture, their environment, and their Indigenous knowledge system. In ethnobiological parlance, *alaas* can be considered Sakha's "cultural keystone."

> All around the globe, humans identify themselves and each other by their cultural and economic affiliations with particular species of plants and animals. …These are the species that become embedded in a people's cultural traditions and narratives, their ceremonies, dances, songs, and discourse. …[W]e propose to identify them as "cultural keystone species," a metaphorical parallel with ecological keystone species.
> *(Garibaldi and Turner 2004: 1)*

Such a designation is verified by the cultural understanding of *alaas* so central to Sakha identity, bringing an immersion of memories and understandings, fragrances, and panoramas. Be it when one of the many contemporary *alaas* songs plays in an urban apartment, the many rich descriptions of contemporary Sakha's relationship with *alaas*, or the specific birth *alaas* where a person makes an annual pilgrimage or spends their *saiylyk* time, pasturing their animals and haying. The cultural keystone concept also engages the inherent interdependencies of the physical and the cultural.

> A cultural keystone is in no case directly equivalent to a biological species. Even if based around a single species, a cultural keystone is a complex, whose contribution to system structure also depends upon a range of other factors, including other biological species, artefacts, knowledge, and social practices. More importantly, it also depends upon a range of purely subjective factors: beliefs, ideas, norms and values concerning social identity and its enactment through culturally appropriate practices.
>
> *(Platten and Henfrey 2009: 498)*

The meaning of *alaas* for Sakha integrates this entire complex of physical, social, cultural, and cosmological attributes. Sakha's relationship with *alaas* further designates them as a cultural keystone place,

> A given site or location with high cultural salience…which plays, or has played in the past, an exceptional role in a people's cultural identity, as reflected in their day-to-day living, food production and other resource-based activities, land and resource management, language, stories, history, and social and ceremonial practices.
>
> *(Cuerrier et al. 2015: 431)*

Alaas are threatened ecologically due to climate change, and this limits Sakha's continued physical use of them. In a time of rapid physical changes to the *alaas*, they represent an entire annual cycle of ritual practices, an assemblage of cultural meaning, and a historical legacy.

Anthropology and Global Change Research in the Anthropocene

The long history of the hegemony of scientific knowledge has resulted in a relatively small group thinking about and making decisions based on a limited knowledge. Some of these decisions are far-reaching, often implicating the rest of the world. Historical policy pathways to date favor the formally educated and economically advantaged groups involved in the scientific assessment processes. These, in turn, bolster a neoliberal agenda, with scientific knowledge as its handmaiden. There could be a less hegemonic and more pluralistic world if we took to heart that "all knowledge is 'local' and culturally/socially contextual, which means that scientific knowledge is [also a] situated (cultural) practice" (Goldman, Nadasdy, and Turner 2011: 14). Furthermore, "Science is not a heartless pursuit of objective information. It is a creative human activity, its geniuses acting more as artists than as information processors" (Gould 1979: 201). By acknowledging and engaging all relevant knowledge systems, a more equitable understanding and way forward is possible.

Local knowledge and Indigenous knowledge deliver depth and place-specific cultural context to understandings of change (cf. Lee et al. 2015; O'Neill and Graham 2016; Nunn and Reid 2016). They represent "the nonlinear and pluralistic perspectives that increasingly are being called for to provide a socially relevant context" (Klubnikin et al. 2000: 1304). They offer the necessary elements via their capacity to ground truth and provide cultural context. Engaging them within interdisciplinary global change research is by no means a simple process, but it is vital. Only if we assign priority status to affected communities' understandings of vulnerability and risk will we avoid perpetuating the colonial project, "moving people out of the way of environmental risks as they are conceived within colonial traditions, while moving them into the way of risks as conceived through the eyes of remote Indigenous communities" (Veland et al. 2013: 314). We must engage a culture's vernacular knowledge and accommodate its cultural underpinning to achieve "a deeper understanding of the epistemology of knowledge within a culture" (Walshe and Argumedo 2016: 166). Without these measures, research and policy directives will continue to glean only what is "(arte)factual" evidence (Briggs 2005: 7). In this pursuit, anthropologists can not only contribute such perspectives but can also contextualize the cultural background and institutional foundations that these knowledge systems embody (Scott 1996) and provide the critical inroads to understanding how a culture perceives, understands, responds, and adapts to change (Tengö et al. 2014).

Some work is in progress by anthropologists and social scientists in the pursuit of bringing Indigenous knowledge and local knowledge "to the table" in interdisciplinary global change research efforts. Furthermore, some are demonstrating the efficacy of Indigenous knowledge and local knowledge to global assessments (Ford et al. 2016; IPCC 2019: 99–105) while others are adapting frameworks to integrate Indigenous narratives into those assessments (Alexander et al. 2011). Efforts within the modeling community include engaging the on-the-ground rich and fine-grained knowledge in order to ostensibly ground truth climate models (Reyes-García et al. 2016). Others are integrating Indigenous mitigation and adaptation strategies into policy-led adaptation responses (Nyong, Adesina and Elasha 2007; Orlove et al. 2020).

Within all these efforts emerges an oxymoron. Namely, the reality that Indigenous peoples and many local knowledge holders have a long, often millennial history of responding to a changing climate. The engagement of these knowledge systems into global change research should be a foregone conclusion. Indigenous and local knowledge holders are the experts that natural and physical scientists need to listen to. Indeed, scientific knowledge remains highly relevant but, taken alone, it cannot provide a comprehensive understanding that can effectively address global change.

The case of Sakha and *alaas* underscores the importance of engaging all available knowledge systems in global change research. This includes how Sakha are also challenged by other drivers of change. For example, the ubiquity of cell phones in rural Sakha villages is beginning to show a direct relationship to Sakha language loss (Crate 2019). Children access mostly Russian cartoons and other material online. As a result, many enter first-grade speaking only Russian. These patterns are in sharp contrast to how, just a few years before, the rural Sakha areas were considered safe havens for the language as compared to the urban context (Ferguson 2015). Half of all respondents to our 2019 language questions expressed the sentiment that using Russian in the place of Sakha is much more than switching out for another language. Like Osip Dmitriyevich Andreyev told me in 2019, they claimed it has implications for a person's ability to "be" Sakha:

If it's a Sakha person, they definitely ought to be able to speak Sakha. Their thoughts and dreams should all be in Sakha. How they think and solve problems and what they decide...all in Sakha. Only then will they understand other Sakha people. They'll be in a Sakha mindset.

In Sakha belief, words have their own *ichchi* (spirit), referred to as *tyl ichchite* (spirits of words): "Spoken words turn into a prophetic bird that flies according to the meaning of the words uttered and retells the original words" (Kulakovski 1979: 45). The very act of speaking words gives them the power to fulfill their meaning (Crate 2006b). In this context, the Sakha language is critical to enacting all the cultural practices, including the beckoning of the sentient beings, with which a Sakha person maintains their relationship to *alaas*.

Closing Words

Designating *alaas* as Sakha's cultural keystone and cultural keystone place provides agency, "specific to practices and activities situated in a historically contingent, socially enacted, culturally constructed 'world'" (Holland et al. 2001: 7). *Alaas* are Sakha's central cultural identifier, from their beginnings, through the tumultuous changes of the Soviet period and, perhaps more so, in the last thirty years of the post-Soviet period, reclaiming and reviving their cultural identity within an uncertain political environment and an increasingly coercive regime (Sommer 2006). In this time when Sakha, and other non-Slavic peoples, confront increasing economic and geopolitical pressures from the Russian state, *alaas* serve Sakha as a viable form of cultural resilience, "the ability to hold on to traditional [historical] beliefs and practices in the face of constant pressures to assimilate exerted by a dominant society" (Fortier 2009: 2).

Considering the Sakha case, it can be said that as the permafrost goes, so go the *alaas*. Furthermore, to the extent that climate change can be considered neo-colonialism driven by continued exploitation of lands, peoples, and resources (Whyte 2017), Sakha's language loss, due to the globalizing forces of rural life, is directly linked to permafrost degradation. In this case, both the Indigenous knowledge and scientific knowledge of *alaas*, taken together, gives the most comprehensive understanding how *alaas* are central to Sakha identity, and provides a pathway to policy prescriptions that are more comprehensive, ethical, and right-holder focused.

Note

1   This chapter was first published in *Anthropology and Humanism*: Crate, Susan Alexandra. 2022. Sakha and Alaas: Place Attachment and Cultural Identity in a Time of Climate Change. *Anthropology and Humanism* 47 (1): 20–38. It is included here with permission.

Acknowledgments

First I acknowledge my Sakha collaborators, inhabitants of Elgeeii and Kutana villages, who are too many to name individually here. I also thank Alexander Nikolaevich Fedorov, permafrost expert at the Melnikov Permafrost Institute, Yakutsk. For the funding to support my research in 2018–2019, I thank the Royal Anthropological Institute/British Museum Urgent Anthropology Fellowship.

References

Agrawal, Arun. 1995. Dismantling the divide between indigenous and scientific knowledge. *Development and Change* 26 (3): 413–439.

Alekseev, N.A., N.V. Emel'ianov, and V.T. Petrov, eds. 1995. *Predaniia, Legendy i Mify Sakha* [Traditions, Legends and Myths of the Sakha]. Novosibirsk: Science Publishers.

Alexander, Clarence, Nora Bynum, Elizabeth Johnson, Ursula King, Tero Mustonen, Peter Neofotis, Noel Oettlé, et al. 2011. Linking indigenous and scientific knowledge of climate change. *BioScience* 61 (6): 477–484.

Balobaev, T., M.K. Gavrilova, and A.N. Fedorov, eds. 1996 *Climate Influence on Permafrost Landscapes of Central Yakutia*. Yakutsk: Melnikov Permafrost Institute.

Basharin, G. 1956. *The Agrarian History of Yakutia*. Moscow: Akademiia Nauk.

Briggs, John. 2005. The use of indigenous knowledge in development: problems and challenges. *Progress in Development Studies* 5 (2): 99–114.

Buyandelger, Manduhai. 2013. *Tragic Spirits*. Chicago: University of Chicago Press.

Crate, Susan Alexandra. 2003. The great divide: contested issues of post-Soviet Viliui Sakha land use. *Europe-Asia Studies* 55 (6): 869–888.

Crate, Susan Alexandra. 2006a. *Cows, Kin, and Globalization: An ethnography of sustainability*. Vol. 4. Rowman Altamira.

Crate, Susan Alexandra. 2006b. Ohuokhai: Sakhas' unique integration of social meaning and movement. *Journal of American Folklore* 119 (472): 161–183.

Crate, Susan Alexandra. 2008. Gone the Bull of Winter? Grappling with the cultural implications of and anthropology's role(s) in global climate change. *Current Anthropology* 49 (4): 569–595.

Crate, Susan Alexandra. 2011. Climate and culture: anthropology in the era of contemporary climate change. *Annual Review of Anthropology* 40: 175–194.

Crate, Susan Alexandra. 2019. Ohuokhai: transmitter of biocultural heritage for Sakha of northeastern Siberia. *Journal of Ethnobiology* 39 (3): 409–424.

Crate, Susan A., Mathias Ulrich, J. Otto Habeck, Aleksey R. Desyatkin, Roman V. Desyatkin, Aleksander N. Fedorov, and Tetsuya Hiyama. 2017. Permafrost livelihoods: a transdisciplinary review and analysis of thermokarst-based systems of Indigenous land use. *Anthropocene* 18: 89–104.

Cuerrier, Alain, Nancy J. Turner, Thiago C. Gomes, Ann Garibaldi, and Ashleigh Downing. 2015. Cultural keystone places: conservation and restoration in cultural landscapes. *Journal of Ethnobiology* 35 (3): 427–448.

Danilova, Natalia K. 2011. *Traditsionnoye Zhilishche Naroda Sakha: Prostranstvo. Dom. Ritual.* [Traditional Housing of the Sakha People: Space, Home, Ritual]. Novosibirsk: Academic Publisher "GEO."

Desiatkin, Roman V. 2008. *Pochvoobrazovanie v Termokarstovykh Kotlovinakh – Alasakh Kriolitozony* [Soil Formation in Thermokarst Basins – Alaas of the cryolithozone]. Novosibirsk: Nauka.

D'iachkovskii, F.N. and N.I. Popova. 2014. Alaas kak kontsept yakutskoy lingvokul'tury [Alaas as a concept of the Yakut (Sakha) linguoculture]. *Uralo-altayskie Issledovaniya [Ural-Altaic Studies]* 1: 58–66.

Ferguson, Jenanne. 2015. Is it bad that we try to speak two languages? Language ideologies and choices among urban Sakha bilingual families. *Sibirica* 14 (1): 1–27.

Ford, James D., Laura Cameron, Jennifer Rubis, Michelle Maillet, Douglas Nakashima, Ashlee Cunsolo Willox, and Tristan Pearce. 2016. Including Indigenous knowledge and experience in IPCC assessment reports. *Nature Climate Change* 6 (4): 349–353.

Forsyth, James. 1994. *A History of the Peoples of Siberia: Russia's North Asian colony 1581–1990*. Cambridge University Press.

Fortier, Jana. 2009. *Kings of the Forest: The cultural resilience of Himalayan hunter-gatherers*. University of Hawaii Press.

Garibaldi, Ann and Nancy Turner. 2004. Cultural keystone species: implications for ecological conservation and restoration. *Ecology and Society* 9 (3). [online] URL: http://www.ecologyandsociety.org/vol9/iss3/art1.

Gerasimova, L.P., ed. 2008. *Sakha uonna Alaas (Sakha and Alaas)*. Yakutsk: Bichik.

Gogolev, Anatoli I. 1993. *Iakuti: Problemy etnogeneza i formirovaniia kul'tury* [The Yakut: Problems of ethnogenesis and cultural formation]. Yakutsk: Yakutsk State University Press.

Gogolev, Anatoli I. 1994. *Mifologicheskii mir Iakutov: Bozhestvo i dukhi-pokroviteli* [The Mythological World Of The Yakut: Gods and spirit-protectors]. Yakutsk: Center of Culture and Art.

Goldman, Mara J., Paul Nadasdy, and Matthew D. Turner, eds. 2011. *Knowing Nature: Conversations at the intersection of political ecology and science studies*. University of Chicago Press.

Gould, Stephen Jay. 1979. *Ever Since Darwin: Reflections in natural history*. WW Norton & Company.

Holland, Dorothy, William S. Lachicotte Jr, Debra Skinner, and Carole Cain. 2001. *Identity and Agency in Cultural Worlds*. Harvard University Press.

Huntington, Henry P. 2000. Using traditional ecological knowledge in science: methods and applications. *Ecological applications* 10 (5): 1270–1274.

ILO. n.d. Who are the Indigenous and tribal peoples? Accessed February 17, 2023. https://www.ilo.org/global/topics/indigenous-tribal/WCMS_503321/lang–en/index.htm.

IPCC. 2019. *Special Report on the Ocean and Cryosphere in a Changing Climate* [H.-O. Pörtner, D.C. Roberts, V. Masson-Delmotte, P. Zhai, M. Tignor, E. Poloczanska, K. Mintenbeck, A. Alegría, M. Nicolai, A. Okem, J. Petzold, B. Rama, N.M. Weyer (eds.)]. Cambridge University Press, Cambridge, UK and New York, NY, USA, https://doi.org/10.1017/9781009157964.

Kempton, Willet. 2002. Cognitive anthropology and the environment. In *New Directions in Anthropology and Environment*, edited by Carole L. Crumley. Walnut Creek: AltaMira Press, pp. 49–71.

Klubnikin, Kheryn, Cynthia Annett, Maria Cherkasova, Michail Shishin, and Irina Fotieva. 2000, The sacred and the scientific: traditional ecological knowledge in Siberian river conservation. *Ecological Applications* 10 (5): 1296–1306.

Ksenofontov, G.V. 1992(1937). *Uraangkhai Sakhalaar* [Points in ancient history of the Yakut (Sakha)], 2nd ed., vol. 2. Yakutsk: National Publishing House.

Kulakovski, Aleksei. 1979. *Nauchnye Trudy* [Scientific works]. *Yakutsk: Yakutsk Book Publishers*.

Lee, Tien Ming, Ezra M. Markowitz, Peter D. Howe, Chia-Ying Ko, and Anthony A. Leiserowitz. 2015. Predictors of public climate change awareness and risk perception around the world. *Nature Climate Change* 5 (11): 1014–1020.

MacFarquhar, Neil and Emile Ducke. 2019. Russian land of permafrost and mammoths is thawing. *New York Times*. Accessed 17 February 2023. https://www.nytimes.com/2019/08/04/world/europe/russia-siberia-yakutia-permafrost-global-warming.html.

Marino, Elizabeth. 2015. *Fierce Climate, Sacred Ground: An ethnography of climate change in Shishmaref, Alaska*. University of Alaska Press.

Mészáros, Csaba, 2021. A Siberian archipelago: of plants, places, and humans in the boreal forest. Paper presented at the 10th International Congress of Arctic Social Sciences (ICASS X)Arkhangelsk and online, June 15–20, 2021.

Mészáros, Csaba. 2012. The *alaas*: cattle economy and environmental perception of sedentary Sakhas in central Yakuti. *Sibirica* 11 (2): 1–34.

Nikolaev, S.I. 1996. *Customs of the Sakha People*. Yakutsk: Sakha Poligrafizdat.

Nunn, Patrick D., and Nicholas J. Reid. 2016. Aboriginal memories of inundation of the Australian coast dating from more than 7000 years ago. *Australian Geographer* 47 (1): 11–47.

Nyong, Anthony, Francis Adesina, and Balgis Osman Elasha. 2007. The value of indigenous knowledge in climate change mitigation and adaptation strategies in the African Sahel. *Mitigation and Adaptation Strategies for Global Change* 12: 787–797.

O'Neill, Saffron J. and Sonia Graham. 2016. (En)visioning place-based adaptation to sea-level rise. *Geo: Geography and Environment* 3 (2): e00028.

Orlove, Ben, Rachael Shwom, Ezra Markowitz, and So-Min Cheong. 2020. Climate decision-making. *Annual Review of Environment and Resources* 45: 271–303.

Pavlova, Matrona N. 2015. Suntaar Kutanatyn 100 alaastara / N. I. Ivanov-Kuola Uchuutal. [Suntaar's Kutana 100 alaas/ N. I. Nikolaev-Kolya Teacher]. Yakutsk: Dani-Almas.

Pekarski, E.K. 1958 [1899]. *Slovar Iakutskogo iazyka* [Dictionary of the Sakha language], Vol 1. St Petersburg: Academy of Science.

Platten, Simon and Thomas Henfrey. 2009. The cultural keystone concept: insights from ecological anthropology. *Human Ecology* 37: 491–500.

Reyes-García, Victoria, Álvaro Fernández-Llamazares, Maximilien Guèze, Ariadna Garcés, Miguel Mallo, Margarita Vila-Gómez, and Marina Vilaseca. 2016. Local indicators of climate change: the potential contribution of local knowledge to climate research. *Wiley Interdisciplinary Reviews: Climate Change* 7 (1): 109–124.

Romanova, Ekaterina N. 2015. Lanshaft v kul'ture pamiati [Landscapes in cultural memory]. *Arctic in the 21st Century Humanitarian Science* 2 (5): 93–98.

Roncoli, Carla, Todd Crane, and Ben Orlove. 2009. Fielding climate change in cultural anthropology. In *Anthropology and Climate Change: From encounters to actions*, edited by Susan Crate and Mark Nuttall. Walnut Creek: Left Coast Press: 87–115.

Savitskaia, S.V. 2017. Sopostavitel'noe issledovanie iazykovogo soznaniia Russkikh i Iakutov (na premere obraza rodiny) [Comparative study of the language consciousness of Russians and Yakuts (on the example of the image of the motherland]. *Questions of Psycholinguistics* 1 (31): 203–216.

Savvinov, G.N. and V.S. Makarov. 2015. *Alaas: Sakha noruotun bihige* [Alaas: Sakha people's cradle]. Yakutsk: Bichik.

Scott, Colin. 1996. Science for the west, myth for the rest. In *Naked Science: Anthropological inquiry into boundaries, power, and knowledge*, edited by Laura Nader, New York: Routledge, pp. 69–86.

Semenov, Pavel. 2005. *Baibal*. Duoraan Records, compact disc.

Solovyev, P.A. 1973. Thermokarst phenomena and landforms due to frost heaving in Central Yakutia. *Periglacialny Biuletyn* 23: 135–155.

Sommer, Doris. 2006. Wiggle room. In *Cultural Agency in the Americas*, edited by Jesus Martin Barbero, Diana Taylor, and Néstor Garcia Canclini. Duke University Press, pp. 1–28.

Takakura, Hiroki. 2010. The social and symbolic construction of alaas landscapes in the Siberian forest. *Acta Slavica Iaponica* 28: 51–69.

Tengö, Maria, Eduardo S. Brondizio, Thomas Elmqvist, Pernilla Malmer, and Marja Spierenburg. 2014. Connecting diverse knowledge systems for enhanced ecosystem governance: the multiple evidence base approach. *Ambio* 43: 579–591.

Troianovski, Anton, Chris Mooney, and Michael Robinson Chavez. 2019. Radical warming in Siberia leaves millions on unstable ground. *Washington Post* 3 (10). Accessed February 17, 2023. https://www.washingtonpost.com/graphics/2019/national/climate-environment/climate-change-siberia/.

Varlamova, Anastasia. 1993. Agham Alaaha. In *Ikki Surekh*, edited by A.N. Semenov, 56. Yakutsk: Sitim.

Varlamov, Stepan P., Yuri B. Skachkov, and Pavel N. Skryabin. 2020. Influence of climate change on the thermal condition of Yakutia's permafrost landscapes (Chabyda Station). *Land* 9 (5): 132.

Veland, Siri, Richard Howitt, Dale Dominey-Howes, Frank Thomalla, and Donna Houston. 2013. Procedural vulnerability: understanding environmental change in a remote indigenous community. *Global Environmental Change* 23 (1): 314–326.

Walshe, Rory and Alejandro Argumedo. 2016. Ayni, Ayllu, Yanantin and Chanincha: the cultural values enabling adaptation to climate change in communities of the potato park, in the Peruvian Andes. *GAIA-Ecological Perspectives for Science and Society* 25 (3): 166–173.

Whyte, Kyle. 2017. Indigenous climate change studies: Indigenizing futures, decolonizing the Anthropocene. *English Language Notes* 55 (1): 153–162.

15

A REFLEXIVE APPROACH TO CLIMATE CHANGE ENGAGEMENT WITH SHERPAS FROM KHUMBU AND PHARAK IN NORTHEASTERN NEPAL (MOUNT EVEREST REGION)

Pasang Yangjee Sherpa and Ornella Puschiasis

Introduction

Ornella and Pasang met one sunny morning in 2010 in the village of Khumjung. Each of us had come to the village to participate in and observe the second "Beat the GLOF Action Run." The event was organized to underscore that even the fastest runner will not be able to outrun the Imja glacial lake outburst flood (GLOF). Scientists had previously declared Imja Tsho (glacial lake), south of Mount Everest as one of the most critical glacial lakes in the Himalayas (Watanabe et al. 2009). There were food stalls, music, and people from different Khumbu villages at the event. The mood was festive. During our solitary fieldwork that involved hours and days of walking in the mountain landscape, countless conversations, and lots of note-taking, we both found this event refreshing. It was a much-needed escape from our daily routine.

Our meeting was auspicious. An unspoken bond was instantly established. It felt as if we had known each other for a long time even though it was only our first meeting. We watched the event together and danced through the night. This event could have been any other social event by the looks of it. But it was different. There was more to it. We were partaking in an NGO-sponsored climate change adaptation event. During the day, rows of special guests, who had traveled from Kathmandu and from overseas sat in front of a makeshift stage and delivered their speeches one-by-one. They had come to tell the Sherpas from Khumbu (Mount Everest region) about the risks of climate change. Media personnel, invited by the event organizers, were ready to take photographs and interview a selected few for news about prepackaged climate change stories from this beautiful tourist destination. We sat with our group of female relatives and mutual friends on the outside of the barred seating area, soaking in the incredible community mobilization happening under the banner of climate change in front of our eyes.

That serendipitous connection made it possible for us to exchange our findings with each other along the way to better understand how climate change was unfolding among Sherpas of Khumbu and Pharak (both areas are part of Solukhumbu district, Pharak means literally "in between," and is located south of Khumbu, see Figure 15.1). In the

DOI: 10.4324/9781003242499-18

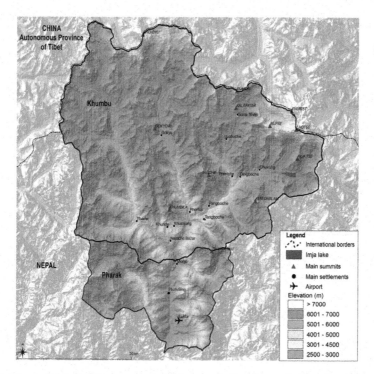

FIGURE 15.1 Map of Mount Everest region showing Khumbu and Pharak villages including Imja Tsho (glacial lake).

Source: Ornella Puschiasis

course of our long-term, place-based observations independently of one another, we continued to be struck by how the prevailing climate change narratives at the local level were fed by alarmist rhetoric generated elsewhere. We both found that the global phenomenon of climate change as institutions and researchers were using it in the Sherpa villages was not part of the everyday concerns for the villagers. The villagers were concerned about successful tourism seasons because their livelihoods depended on them. We found that the prevailing climate change narratives focused largely on potential Imja GLOF and the impending disaster for settlements downstream. The institutional and scientific ways the phrase climate change was deployed rarely mirrored the complex ways climate change impacts were observed and experienced by Khumbu-Pharak villagers (Puschiasis 2015; Sherpa, P. 2012). Over the next ten years, through our various research projects, we continued to observe lived experiences of climate change and the many ways Sherpa people have been responding to their new climatic realities in their homeland and the diaspora. We continued to pay attention to rising climate change induced uncertainties, and how climate science and policies are failing to adequately address the multitude of challenges Sherpa people are facing. We continue to witness an over reliance on institutional, techno-managerial approach and bias towards biophysical science at the expense of the reflexive, transdisciplinary, collaborative, co-produced, and plural climate knowledge of the Mount Everest region.

A decade later, we find ourselves seating outside a barred space once again and having a similar experience to the one in Khumjung. We are once again watching the dominant techno-managerial, biophysical, reductive, market-driven, popular narratives take the center stage to inform multi-level climate policies at the expense of the communities' knowledges, experiences, and capacities. This has led to a limited understanding of climate change impacts on Sherpa people and the growing ethnically diverse population that call Khumbu and Pharak their home. Whereas the population in Khumbu is predominantly Sherpa, Pharak has a mixed population of mostly Sherpa, followed by Rai, Magar, and Tamang. Our seats outside the barred space today are not entirely metaphorical. They are literal in the sense that our ethnographic work among the Sherpas continues to be treated as being on the outskirts of climate change research. The exclusion is clearly noticeable in the citational practices of climate change research coming out of the region.

The Place, its Climate, and its People

Khumbu and Pharak are Sherpa names for what is popularly known in English as the Mount Everest region located in the northeastern part of Nepal. Khumbu is also commonly used to refer to the entire Mount Everest region, including what we specify as Pharak. In geophysical terms, the region could be seen as two distinct zones. Khumbu, with villages above 3500 m, is the northern part of the Dudh Koshi (Milky River) basin. It is considered the most densely glaciated region in Nepal (Bajracharya et al. 2007). Villages in Pharak are lower in altitude (around 2600 m) with diverse and abundant vegetation and are included in the Sagarmatha National Park (SNP) Buffer Zone.

Climate in the region is strongly patterned by a South Asian subtropical monsoon climate with rainfall concentrated in the summer. Typically, more than 80% of annual precipitation falls during approximately four months between June and September (Byers 2005). Average annual precipitation is about 650 mm in Khumbu and 2050 mm in Pharak (Smadja et al. 2015).

Winter precipitations (January–March) are swept to the west by high-altitude jet streams (Bookhagen and Burbank 2010) leading to a cold and fairly dry season. Spring and autumn are typically mild (Thapa and Shakya 2008). In addition to inter-seasonal rainfall variations, precipitation also experiences strong spatial variations, characteristic of mountain areas (Bookhagen and Burbank 2010). As we show below, uncertainties and unpredictability of weather patterns have become more common with every passing year.

Khumbu-Pharak is home of the Tibeto-Burman language speaking, Nyingma Buddhism following Sherpa people (Skog 2017; Spoon and Sherpa, L. 2008). The traditional agro-pastoral and trading economy is now dominated by a tourism industry that began in the 1950s, when Nepal opened its borders to foreigners. By 1990s, every household in the region was directly or indirectly involved in the tourism industry (Brower 1991b). It was reported that just before the pandemic, in the year 2018–2019, more than 57,000 tourists visited the region (Bhatta et al. 2022). According to the 2011 census, there are 968 households with an estimated population of 3709 in Pharak, and 1031 households with 3452 people in Khumbu (Central Bureau of Statistics 2012). Many Sherpas spend winter and rainy summer in Kathmandu, and only part of the year in their ancestral villages (Spoon 2011). Migrants from neighboring regions have settled in Khumbu and Pharak in search for work in the tourism industry, making the region ethnically diverse today.

Our Approach

Ornella is a French geographer based at the National Institute of Oriental Languages and Civilizations (INALCO) in Paris. Pasang is a native Sherpa anthropologist, based at the University of British Columbia in Vancouver. Our approaches to climate change research were initially shaped by the academic disciplines in which we were trained. On the surface, our climate change research seemed divergent. Pasang was conducting an ethnographic study that centered on people and was examining multi-scalar institutional climate change practices. Ornella was part of a large-scale multidisciplinary research project involving glaciologists, hydrologists, atmospheric chemists, modelers, agronomists, and geographers from France working on the impact of climate change on water availability in Eastern Nepal (Aubriot et al. 2012). As a social geographer she was studying the uses of water and the local perception of climate change.

Despite these differences, at the core of our individual work, we were both attempting to understand how climate change was impacting the people of this place. We figured out early on that there were two types of "climate change" we were dealing with. The first one was the institutionally introduced phrase "climate change" that had become synonymous with melting snow, glaciers, and GLOFs. The term was gaining currency globally but was not part of the common Sherpa parlance at that point. There were no equivalent of "climate change" in the Sherpa language and the few who mentioned the Nepali equivalent *Jalvayu Parivartan* were people who had direct contact with governmental and non-governmental institutions working on climate change issues. The second one was the multiple ways climate change effects were being experienced and observed by the people living there, which did not always get discussed as "climate change." Therefore, each of us had made the methodological choice to investigate climate change without explicitly talking about it (Smadja et al. 2015). We instead talked about specific climatic elements (seasonal markers, snow, rain, temperature) and discussed various environmental changes. Furthermore, we were dealing with meteorological changes, trying to get a clear picture of "human sensitivity to the weather patterns" and the perceived changes. We were collecting snapshots, and feelings anchored in the daily life as experienced by Sherpas in relation to their environment (Puschiasis 2019).

We found ourselves in the Khumbu region studying climate change at the same time due to similar reasons. Our research projects were designed at a time when scientists were raising alarm about the impact of global warming on Himalayan glaciers. The increased consciousness about the planet's third pole between 2007 and 2009 had influenced like-minded scientists in France and a native scholar in the United States. Subsequently, our paths crossed in the villages conducting long-term, field-based research among the Sherpa people.

Ornella spent 15 months conducting fieldwork between March 2010 and December 2011, surviving brutally cold winters and rainy summers in Khumbu. She learned both the Sherpa and Nepali languages and worked with a Sherpa research assistant to conduct approximately 200 interviews primarily with Sherpa respondents (65%) and the rest with members of other ethnic communities (Rai, Tamang, Bahun, Chetri). The village of Pangboche (3940 m) served as her "base camp" and interviews were carried out throughout the region often walking to satellite hamlets and pastures, up to 5000 m in elevation. Her fieldwork was physically strenuous as she had to walk long distances with significant change in altitude to cover sparsely populated scattered settlements. This was supplemented by participant observation of the seasonal migration of her Sherpa inter-locutors to the capital city Kathmandu. In her research, she explored: 1) the extent to which the local population was aware of environmental changes, specifically the atmospheric and meteorological phenomena; 2) the markers of these changes; and 3) the potential impact on water resource management strategies.

Pasang's multi-sited ethnographic research was carried out over a period of 15 months between 2010 and 2011. She conducted her interviews in Nepali and Sherpa, which were then translated into English. In Pharak, she conducted participant observation of village life and explored how institutions were responding to climate change effects. She recorded formal interviews accompanied by observations during casual interactions. Since most of the institutional climate change activities occurred in Khumbu villages, her fieldwork also took her north of Pharak. In Kathmandu, she studied national level climate change institutional programming to better understand how climate change effects at the local level were identified and responded to.

Speaking of Climate Change Effects

Villagers in Khumbu and Pharak talked about the winter seasons becoming shorter and warmer. In both places, villagers recalled that there used to be plenty of snow before, from mid-December to mid-February. A local villager from Pangboche said,

> Before, we could only get out from the window sometimes because we would get so much snow during winter that our main doors [on the first floor] would get blocked. Now, time has changed, the winters are shorter, and snow does not stay for months anymore...we used to sled around our village during winter vacations, when school was closed. But we don't see that much snow anymore.

Villagers also talked about the surrounding mountains becoming darker. In order to find out when the snowfall had started to decrease, we asked the villagers for a timeframe. Most of them referred to special cultural and religious events such as *Losar*, the Sherpa New Year to mark the end of winter (mid-February) and the beginning of the planting season. Ornella also documented that infrequent and unpredictable snowfall episodes were noticed until later in the spring as far as April. In a recent publication (Puschiasis et al. 2022), she showed how the work of cross-referencing data from different disciplines (such as hydrology and geography) is useful for mountain areas where meteorological data are incomplete, and where the knowledge of the population is rich, but insufficiently considered. Along with her co-authors, she pointed out the uncertainties inherent in both qualitative and quantitative data, which requires collaboration across disciplines to meet with the challenge of understanding snow variations. For example, they shared that while it may seem to the villagers in Khumbu that there has been no snow in some years, measured data shows that this is not the case. Quantitative data about snowfall thus makes it possible to establish temporal framework of perceptions that are sometimes difficult to evaluate and judge solely based on interviews with villagers. As for qualitative data, they enrich quantitative data due to the precise knowledge villagers have of their environment. For example, villagers are able to recall facts that date back to fifty years or so, whereas measured and spatialized quantitative data, dependent on weather stations and satellite sensors, have been available only in recent decades.

Many villagers we spoke to, who were primarily farmers, paid close attention to climatic variations and how it impacted their crops. They had noticed irregular and unpredictable rainfall during monsoon season. In Khumbu, farmers were particularly concerned about the less predictable rainfall pattern describing damages to their potato production for some years when interviewed in 2010. They noted too much rain in September causing the potatoes to rot in the fields. This unpredictable rainfall pattern had also impacted the cattle herders. The grass and hay that needed cutting and drying in the September sun for winter fodder were getting spoiled by the unexpected rain. As a result, the hayfield cutting time had to be shifted. In Pharak, villagers noted that 2009 was a dry year. Many crops withered, and farmers suffered huge economic loss. The following year, villagers were initially pleased with more rain but soon became concerned by the heavy downpour later that summer.

We both noticed that the greater variability in rainfall pattern also disrupted the arrival of tourists. In the fall tourist seasons of 2010 and 2011, many travelers were stranded at the Lukla airport due to bad weather conditions, which was unusual for that time of the year. The disruption of flights also disturbed the supply of food and other household items from neighboring urban centers to this roadless region. A Khumbu woman complained to Ornella: "now we cannot trust the seasons anymore, when it is supposed to rain, it does not and when it is not supposed to, we have rain. I just don't understand the weather today."

When asked about the winter season getting warmer, villagers usually talked about the snow on the mountain tops. Villagers told Pasang that they could predict times of changing season by looking at the snow on summits when they were younger, without specifying exact time in their childhood. Pharak Sherpas described a sense of relief in 2011 when they saw snow on Kongde and Thamserku peaks. Similarly, Sherpas from Pangboche were looking at snow on Ama Dablam and Tauche peaks surrounding their village. These mountains were described as being "black," and the villagers linked the color with less snow and excessive heat. Herders in Pharak and Khumbu had also noticed, while moving vertically to and from higher grounds with their cattle, that the flowering times for crops in the villages below had changed. Furthermore, villagers told Pasang that the timing of migratory birds' arrival in their villages seemed to have changed, and that they were noticing unfamiliar insects like mosquitoes and other pests, usually associated with a warmer climate, in their villages.

In the past, growing leafy vegetables was not possible in Khumbu because of the cold weather conditions. This was documented in the first ethnography of the Sherpa in Khumbu by Christoph von Fürer-Haimendorf (1964). By the 2000s, a large variety of vegetables could be grown in lower elevation of Pharak and even in higher elevation of Khumbu villages with the use of plastic greenhouses. This change in the diversification of food production was linked to warming temperature and also to the growing demand for vegetables in tourists' meals. When observing climatic change, villagers were also quick to point out other factors that contributed to the changes in their traditional agro-pastoral lives. The tourism economy was always on the forefront of our conversations about environmental change.

Extreme events are deeply anchored in the memory of the villagers. The 1995 Panga avalanche in the upper Dudh Koshi Valley, which killed thirteen persons and damaged many houses, bridges, and fields served as a historical time marker for many villagers

(Puschiasis 2019; Puschiasis et al. 2022). A local lodge owner of Gokyo interviewed in 2011 remembered, "The Gokyo area was completely covered by snow from the avalanche. We could only see the rooftops. Since then, we have not received much snow."

In 2011, Pharak and Khumbu villagers experienced heavy rainfall, severe windstorm, and an earthquake. A middle-aged Sherpa woman described holding onto her fellow villagers in her open camping ground to avoid being blown off her feet or being hit by flying objects during the windstorm. She was relieved when the storm stopped, only to experience a similarly powerful one a few months later. Floods in August and the earthquake in September of 2011 added dread to the Khumbu and Pharak villagers. The heavy rain and subsequent flooding destroyed houses and trails in at least one village. The villagers then came together to make offerings to appease the local deities in a Pharak village. Prayer flags were hung to protect the place and its people from future harm, in keeping with Buddhist Sherpa beliefs. Several protection rituals were also organized in Khumbu in 2011. A Sherpa man in his late 60s from Khumbu mentioned the burial of a "sacred box" (Sherpa/Tibetan: sa gzhi bum pa) previously blessed by the abbot of the Tengboche monastery to appease the deities of the ground.

After the earthquake that destroyed several houses, trails, and bridges, a woman in Pharak speculated during a conversation with Pasang that the earthquake must have been related to glacial lake outburst flood and climate change, because it happened following a visit by thirty international scientists to the Imja Lake in Khumbu. The woman claimed, "If there was no threat from GLOF, why else would they come here?"

A Decade of Climate Change Studies

Research in physical science dominates the field of climate change studies in the Mount Everest region. Comparatively, there are only a handful of researchers studying human dimensions of climate change, and even fewer who conduct ethnographic studies. On the following pages, we describe our research experience followed by a discussion of three specific studies on human dimensions of climate change.

In the early 2010s, we were the only ones conducting long-term ethnographic studies of climate change in the region. Our theoretical, methodological, and analytical frameworks were influenced by the first edition of *Anthropology and Climate Change* (Crate and Nuttall 2009), the study of perceptions among apple farmers in the Western Himalayas of India (Vedwan and Rhoades 2001), and contemporary studies conducted in Tibet (Salick et al. 2012) and the Marshall Islands (Rudiak-Gould 2012). In order to situate our work within the local climate change literature, we were reading numerous institutional climate change adaptation activity reports, glaciology research articles, scientific climate change reports, and media reports on climate change covering the region. In this context of a dearth of academic literature on climate change, we found McDowell et al. (2013) and Jha and Khanal (2010) anthology, *Contemporary Research in Sagarmatha (Mt. Everest) Region, Nepal*, to be particularly useful while analyzing our data. McDowell et al. (2013) had adopted a vulnerability approach to assess human susceptibility to hydrological change in four Khumbu communities. This further encouraged us to think about climate change vulnerability from a socio-economic perspective. Pasang's research had shown that Sherpa villagers were differently vulnerable to climate change depending on their gender, age, occupation (farmers, herders, lodge owners etc.), and residence (if they lived on or off the main tourist trail) (Sherpa, P. 2012). Jha and Khanal (2010) on the other hand provided several studies that covered wide-ranging research topics from ecosystem monitoring, to medical research, and biological resources, conducted in the Mount Everest region. This provided a scientific baseline to consider the changing ecological conditions and a synopsis of what contemporary research in the region looked like. The studies included in this anthology cited Sherpa ethnographies to describe the socio-cultural and religious features of the people. Beyond that, engagement with Sherpa ethnographies was limited. It did, however, include a section dedicated to "ethnography" that contained a preliminary analysis of Y-chromosome Haplotypes, a study of altitude sickness, and a study on the "genetic adaptation of natives to hypoxia." More than an ethnographic portrayal of the place and the people, this section problematically categorized outlier studies as ethnography in turn exposing the marginalization of ethnography in Himalayan environmental studies.

In developing our understanding of climate change and its impacts on the Sherpas of Khumbu and Pharak, we relied on the rich literature on Sherpas of Khumbu (Fürer-Haimendorf 1964, 1984: Ortner 1978: Brower 1990, 1991a, 1991b, 1996; Brower and Denis 1998; Sherpa, Y. and Kayastha 2009; Skog 2010; Spoon 2011, 2012, 2014; Spoon and Sherpa, L. 2008; Stevens 1996). Over the years, our bibliography expanded to include Sherpas from other parts of the Himalayas and beyond, and also other ethnic communities that now live in the region. This was a result of more literature becoming available and widening of our respective frameworks to encompass multi-sited lived experiences of Sherpa people and recent settlers in Khumbu and Pharak. Our subsequent publications reflect these changes (Aubriot et al. 2012; Aubriot et al. 2019; Chakraborty et al. 2021; Chakraborty and Sherpa, P. 2021; Chevallier et al. 2020; Puschiasis 2015, 2019; Puschiasis et al. 2022; Smadja et al. 2015; Sherpa, P. 2012, 2014, 2015, 2021).

One of the findings we have both discussed in our separate publications is the sheer number of climate change adaptation activities that have been organized in the region involving the Sherpa people (Puschiasis 2015; Sherpa, P. 2015). Since 2004, different governmental and non-governmental institutions, and for-profit businesses have organized activities aimed at responding to climate change effects (See Table 15.1).

These activities are usually accompanied by media personnel and are showcased in various news platforms. They are often held in the name of raising awareness of climate change without substantial engagement with climate change. For example, a fashion show was organized in front of Mount Everest in January of 2020 as an awareness raising activity by a Kathmandu-based clothing company. This publicity stunt was widely covered in national media, and the event was recognized as the highest fashion show by the Guinness World Records. The media coverage regularly misses the nuances of how climate change is unfolding in Khumbu and Pharak. Instead, what we find is a circulation and further reinforcement of narrow, alarmist climate change narratives through institutional adaptation activities (Sherpa, P. 2015).

By the time we were conducting fieldwork, climate change had already appeared as a new crisis scenario in the Himalayas, reminiscent of the Theory of Himalayan Environmental Degradation (THED). The parallels between alarmist climate change narratives and THED were hard to miss. In 1989, Jack D. Ives and Bruno Messerli challenged the Theory, which was based on overly simplistic generalization of the Himalayas, and its anticipated eco-disaster. THED, first articulated by E. Eckholm (1975), had predicted

TABLE 15.1 Institutional climate change activities organized in the Mount Everest region between 2004 and 2013.

Institutions	Year	Climate Change Themed Programs	Activity Sites
World Wildlife Fund (WWF) Nepal	2001	Climate Change Program Initiated	Kathmandu
	2004	Climate Wellness Project	Khumbu
	2005	Research on Himalayan glacier project and river project	
	2008–09	Climate for Life campaign	
Hindu Kush Karakoram Himalaya (HKKH) Partnership:	2006	HKKH Regional Partnership Project Initiated	Kathmandu
Ev-K2-CNR	2007	Scenarios Planning Workshops	
CESVI	2007	Participatory 3D Model of Sagarmatha National Park (SNP)	Khumbu
IUCN	2007–08	Visitor Survey in SNP	
International Center for Integrated Mountain Development (ICIMOD) (2007–2009)	2008	Ev-K2-CNR Installed Water Purification Systems	
	2008	CKNP Team Visit to SNP	
	2008	First Mt. Everest Day Celebration	
	2008	Documents Handover to SNP and Communities	
	2008	SNP Team Visit to CKNP	
	2008	Third Sagarmatha Tourism Coordination Forum (STCF) Meeting	Kathmandu
	2008	SNP Land Cover Mapping Handover to Department of National Park and Wildlife Conservation (DNPWC)	
	2008	Training Workshop on the SNP Management Plan	Khumbu
	2009	Training for Local Stakeholders	
United Nations Development Program (UNDP) Bureau for Crisis Prevention and Recovery (BCPR)	2007–09	Regional Glacial Lake Outburst Floods (GLOFs) Risk Reduction in the Himalayas Initiative (Workshops organized)	Khumbu
ICIMOD, Asian Trekking Pvt. Ltd	2008	Eco Everest Expedition	Khumbu and Kathmandu
WWF Climate Initiative, Asian Trekking Pvt. Ltd.	2009	Eco Everest Expedition	
Asian Trekking Pvt. Ltd., The North Face	2010	Eco Everest Expedition	
	2011	Eco Everest Expedition	

Institutions	Year	Climate Change Themed Programs	Activity Sites
ICIMOD and SNP Buffer Zone (SNPBZ)	2008	Adaptation to CC and Increasing Resilience of Local People in Khumbu	Khumbu
Government of Nepal	2009	Cabinet Meeting	Khumbu
ICIMOD, iDEAS, a Kathmandu based non-governmental organization	2009	Climate Change Briefing for Sherpa Students	Kathmandu
ICIMOD, iDEAS and Sherwi Yondhen Tshokpa (SYT)	2009	Imja Tsho Action Event: Beat the GLOF Action Run Inter-school Art and Letter Writing Competition	Khumbu
iDEAS and SYT; UNDP, The North Face	2010	Beat the GLOF Action Run and Khumbu Festival	
	2011	Beat the GLOF Action Run and Khumbu Festival	
European Union (CESVI, an Italian humanitarian organization and Mountain Spirit (MS), a Nepal based community organization)	2009–12	Community-based Land and Forest Management in the Sagarmatha (Everest), National Park Nepal	Khumbu
The Mountain Institute (TMI), United States Agency for International Development (USAID), National Science Foundation (NSF), Adaptation Partnership, Univ. of Texas (Austin), ICIMOD, UNDP	2010	Meeting "Vulnerability and adaptation on Imja Glacial Lake research"	Khumbu and Kathmandu
	2011	Promoting South–South Knowledge Exchange and Collaboration between Experts and Practitioners from the Hindu Kush-Himalaya, Andes, and Central Asian Mountains for Improved Adaptation and Resilient Livelihoods	
	2012–13	Khumbu Local Adaptation Plan of Action (LAPA)	
Khumbu Alpine Conservation Council (KACC)	2011	Meeting in Dingboche: Adaptation and vulnerability to climate change	Khumbu

Himalayan environmental collapse within decades. THED as a dominating paradigm persists in providing a rational basis for development and conservation interventions (Metz 2009). Watanabe, Lamsal, and Ives (2009) addressed the climate change crisis scenario-in-the-making that zeroed in on the potential Imja GLOF without sufficient scientific backing. They explained the need to do so because of a series of alarmist mass media and scholarly prognostications about potential GLOF in Khumbu. They explained that

> [t]he imminence of catastrophic [GLOFs] accompanied by large losses of life and property in the Himalaya and on the lowlands to the south has been linked with similar dire predictions that global warming will eliminate all glaciers and snow from the mountains within a few years.
>
> *(Watanabe, Lamsal, and Ives 2009)*

The authors stressed that they had no intention to imply that rising temperatures are not affecting Himalayan glaciers and snow cover, nor that GLOFs will not increase in frequency, with associated threats to life and property. But they argued there is an urgent need for accurate appraisal of the situation, "preferably based upon a combination of sound scientific research and incorporation of traditional knowledge of the local people likely to be affected" (Watanabe, Lamsal, and Ives 2009: 255).

In 2019, a team of environmental scholars published a study which included a native Khumbu glaciologist (Sherpa, S. et al. 2019). Findings from their household survey data combined with ethnography analyzed people's perceptions of GLOF risks and the socioeconomic and cultural factors influencing their perceptions. Using a statistical logit model of household data, they showed a significant positive correlation between the perceptions of GLOF risks and livelihood sources, mainly tourism. This finding supports what both Ornella and Pasang had found earlier in Khumbu and Pharak, where residents were concerned about the effects of climate change including unpredictable weather patterns and potential disasters, particularly their impacts pertaining to tourism industry and other livelihood options. Sherpa, S. et al. (2019) additionally found that risk perceptions were influenced by spatial proximity to glacial lakes and potential flood zone. The geographical context is indeed a significant factor to understanding vulnerability in the region (Sherpa, P. 2014, 2015; Puschiasis 2015). Furthermore, the authors attributed uncertainty and confusion related to GLOF risks among locals to a disconnect between how scientific information is communicated to the local communities and how government climate change policies have been limited to awareness campaigns and emergency remediation efforts. They argue,

> a sustainable partnership of scientists, policymakers, and local communities is urgently needed to build a science-driven, community-based initiative that focuses not just on addressing a single GLOF threat but on a comprehensive cryospheric risk management plan that considers opportunities and challenges of tourism in the local climate adaptation policies.
>
> *(Sherpa, S. et al. 2019: 607)*

However, we are unclear on how the authors envision a sustained partnership of scientists, policymakers, and local communities, which they advocate with a sense of urgency, considering the exclusion of both Ornella's and Pasang's long-term research on human dimensions of climate change among Sherpas in the region even though there are many parallels with our work in the kinds of questions the authors pose and what they have found.

Two years later, another household survey of selected Khumbu villages to assess local residents' experience-based perception, perceived risk, and attitudes towards climate issues was published (Poudyal et al. 2021). In this study, the authors used multivariate cluster analysis of residents' climate change beliefs, and identified three groups of people: "cautious," "disengaged," and "alarmed." Since half of the respondents were found to be cautious or disengaged and not "alarmed" about climate change, they argued that there is a critical need for outreach on climate education in the region. The study does not address the fact that there have been numerous climate-change-specific outreach activities conducted in the region for almost two decades, something both Ornella and Pasang have written about. One such activity was the event we start this paper with.

Furthermore, the unintended negative consequences of previous climate education outreach flagged in Pasang's research remain unaddressed (Sherpa, P. 2015). Of particular concern are the cultural sensitivities around discussing risks or hazards (Sherpa, P. 2014) that may result in exhibiting what the authors identify as an "alarmed" state. They mention that alarmed residents revealed a higher perception of the severity of climate change and vulnerability to climate risk and expressed higher self-efficacy and lower response cost. They concluded that personal experience and access to informed external sources for climate information leads to higher risk perception, which in turn may help improve their understanding of vulnerability and response efficacy bolstering their confidence when taking mitigation actions. This recommendation is in contrast to what Khadka (2012) had previously reported, and what we had also discovered (Chakraborty and Sherpa, P. 2021; Puschiasis 2015; Sherpa, P. 2015). Ang Chhiri Sherpa, chairman of an association of tourism entrepreneurs in Pangboche and Dingboche, villages next to the critical Imja *Tsho* (Sherpa: glacial lake), told Khadka (2012) that:

> Every time we begin to forget about the threats from glacial lake outburst, then comes news of yet another study through the radio and television, and this has been happening over and over again for more than 15 years now...Instead of having to fear death like that again and again, we would rather die once if the lake really bursts out one day.

Poudyal et al. (2021) build on Tse-ring et al. (2010), Chaudhary and Bawa (2011), National Research Council (2012), Shrestha et al. (2012), and Devkota et al. (2013) to conclude that the overall livability in the Khumbu region may be in peril because of the melting of glaciers, warming winters, extended periods of drought, more erratic rainfall patterns, and reduced biodiversity. Whereas the authors point out real ecological concerns, and the risks climate change has brought to the residents, meaningful inclusion of local residents in order to understand how they are living with the concerns and how they understand livability in the Khumbu region is glaringly lacking. As such, it remains unclear how the authors deem livability in the Khumbu region to be in peril, and more importantly, who this information serves.

The third, and most recent, study concerning climate change and the Sherpa people in the Mount Everest region was published this year (Bhatta et al. 2022) in an edited volume exploring the last "fifty years of World Heritage Convention through shared responsibility, conflict and reconciliation" framework. The authors conducted a survey over a one-month period in the fall of 2020, during a global pandemic. It is not stated how or if the pandemic circumstances affected the responses of the residents. They do, however, mention that the respondents had been freed from their regular workload due to the absence of tourists. The study cites Khumbu native Ang Rita Sherpa's (2021) climate change manual to support their research findings. It does not engage with either Ornella's or Pasang's research.

Bhatta et al. (2022) focus on the impacts of tourism and climate change as interlinked issues in the Mount Everest region, a World Heritage Site (WHS), and identify their research problem as follows:

> Even if the Sherpa people in the Khumbu region cannot be held responsible for climate change in general, it must be their concern to get negative impacts under control as much as possible. These impacts are exacerbated by tourism, which contributes to the environmental burden. Therefore, we concentrate on the impacts of climate change and tourism that can be countered by measures at the local level. Our research asks, are the multi-stakeholder linkages between SNP management and Sherpa residents sufficient protection against current challenges, and could they be used more effectively?
>
> *(Bhatta et al. 2022: 284)*

The study identifies the Sherpa people, the SNP management, and the Nepali state as three key stakeholders in the SNP UNESCO WHS. The authors rightly point out the environmental burden from unregulated tourism, namely the lack of infrastructure for proper waste management. There are, however, two clear problems with the framing of the research question. Firstly, it is unclear how the authors see climate change and tourism as interlinked beyond the statement that tourism is the dominant industry in the region. Secondly, the treatment of the Sherpa people as one who are not already taking measures to address the negative impacts of climate change locally, including curbing negative impacts of unregulated tourism, and who must be educated or managed with support from the State party is highly problematic. Their recommendation is that in order to reduce pressures related to tourism and climate change, "the SNP-cum-World Heritage Management Plan must be stringently implemented within a multi-stakeholder governance system and engage residents in sustainable development." Furthermore, they end with the statement welcoming science and development projects with international backing that support multi-stakeholder engagement involving the residents, national, and local authorities.

Throughout this study, the Sherpa people appear as sites of research for data collection. The authors symbolically recognize that the world's highest flora and fauna is a sacred landscape of the resident Sherpa communities. The sacredness of this landscape, the relationship with the local environment, including its preservation, protection, and management by the Sherpas since time immemorial, and the burden of co-existing with the national park, ever-increasing tourism industry, and ever-expanding state presence are some of the key issues that remain disregarded.

A New Beginning

In light of the Intergovernmental Panel on Climate Change (IPCC) Assessment Reports (AR6) and Regional Assessment Report (Wester et al. 2019), which have shown that warming in the Himalayas has occurred at a rate and scale more intense than what had been previously predicted, there is no question that sustainability of Indigenous peoples in the Himalayas is at stake. The global pandemic has further exposed the socio-economic vulnerabilities throughout the Himalayas. This is also the case of the residents in the Mount Everest region. We conclude this chapter by drawing attention to the issue of livability as introduced by Poudyal et al. (2021) and Bhatta et al. (2022) for a new beginning of climate change research among ethnically diverse residents of the Sherpa homeland in northeastern Nepal. We pose the following questions to anyone invested in the topic to reflect upon: *Whose livability are we concerned about, and who gets to decide what livability is for the residents of Khumbu and Pharak?*

Our decade-long collective climate change studies have not sufficiently equipped the researchers in adequately addressing climate change effects, or the communities with reliable and useful resources, or the policymakers with ethical pathways for a livable future. The scope and gravity of the climate change reality require us to break the cycle of what Chakraborty et al. (2021) calls "disciplinary chauvinism" in the Himalayan context, and what Ojha et al. (2016) calls "technocratic control of climate change adaptation policy making in Nepal." Our research will continue to fall short in its aspirational impact on the field of study and importantly for the communities on the frontlines of climate change if we continue to ignore the contributions of various epistemologies to our understanding of climate change and if we do not take the time to collaborate with knowledge producers from different ontological traditions as equal partners.

We acknowledge this not to deter us, but to readjust our focus on ethical pathways communities are already navigating through networks of care and what Kyle Whyte (2021) calls "epistemology of coordination." Our ethnographic long-term studies (Puschiasis 2016; Sherpa, P. 2019) in the multiple places that Sherpas call home have reaffirmed how communities can come together to support each other in times of need (Sherpa, P. 2017), and how relationships with each other in the human and non-human forms make sustainability possible (Sherpa, P. 2021).

It has taken more than a decade for us to see this chapter finally come to life. Although we started working on this joint-authored piece immediately following our meeting in 2010, we were not able to see it in its complete form until now. During its initial stage, geographer Barbara Brower offered her mentorship as we navigated the challenges of making sense of what we discovered in the field without falling in the trap of reproducing climate change narratives that did not reflect the situation on the ground. Her publications, particularly the *Sherpa of Khumbu* (1991b) and "Crisis and Conservation in Sagarmatha National Park, Nepal" (1991a), were foundational to our understanding of the uneven park–people relationships that resulted from hasty planning, establishment, and ongoing management of the National Park. In 2016, our paths crossed again in Queens, New York, where we were independently studying Sherpa diasporic experiences. We connected again in Paris in 2019 when Pasang was invited to participate in a roundtable session, hosted at Ornella's institute, to discuss climate change in the Himalayas. And more recently, we contributed to a roundtable discussion "envisioning a just and plural climate change science for the Himalaya," discussing the importance of decolonizing the production of climate science for environmental justice at the Himalayan Studies Conference (2022). This long journey to co-writing was further enriched by motherhood nourishing each of us personally to reflect more deeply on our entangled engagement with climate change and Sherpas from Khumbu and Pharak in various places around the world, and a renewed sense of responsibilities as scholar-mothers for the sake of our next generation. We thus find ourselves calling for an ethical approach that seeks intentional collaborations, informed by sound, inclusive research, for a just and sustainable future.

Bibliography

Aubriot, O., Faulon, M., Sacareau, I., Puschiasis, O., Jacquemet, E., Smadja, J., André-Lamat, V., Abadia, C., and Muller, A. 2019. "Reconfiguration of the water–energy–food nexus in the Everest tourist region of Solukhumbu, Nepal." *Mountain Research and Development*, 39 (1): R47–R59.

Aubriot, O., Smadja, J., Chevallier, P., Delclaux, F., Laj, P., Neppel, L., Puschiasis, O., Savéan, M., and Seidel, J.L. 2012. "The impact of climate change on water availability in Eastern Nepal: a presentation of the project methodology taking into account the various origins of water." *Hydro Nepal: Journal of Water, Energy and Environment*, 11 (special issue): 12–17.

Bajracharya, S.R., Mool, P.K., and Shrestha, B.R. 2007. *Impact of Climate Change on Himalayan Glaciers and Glacial Lakes: Case studies on GLOF and associated hazards in Nepal and Bhutan*. Kathmandu: International Centre for Integrated Mountain Development (ICIMOD).

Bhatta, S., Boustead, R., and Luger, K. 2022. "The highest mountain in the shadow of climate change: managing tourism and conservation in a World Heritage Site: Sagarmatha National Park, Nepal." In *50 Years World Heritage Convention: Shared responsibility – conflict & reconciliation*. Cham: Springer International Publishing, pp. 281–294.

Bookhagen, Bodo and Burbank, Douglas W. 2010. "Toward a complete Himalayan hydrological budget: spatiotemporal distribution of snowmelt and rainfall and their impact on river discharge." *Journal of Geophysical Research: Earth Surface* 115 (F3).

Brower, Barbara. 1991a. "Crisis and conservation in Sagarmatha National Park, Nepal." *Society & Natural Resources* 4 (2): 151–163.

Brower, Barbara. 1991b. *Sherpa of Khumbu: People, livestock, and landscape*. Vol. 1. Oxford University Press.

Brower, Barbara. 1996. "Geography and history in the Solukhumbu landscape, Nepal." *Mountain Research and Development* 16 (3): 249–255.

Brower, Barbara. 1990. "Range conservation and Sherpa livestock management in Khumbu, Nepal." *Mountain Research and Development*, 34–42.

Brower, Barbara and Dennis, Ann. 1998. "Grazing the forest, shaping the landscape. Continuing the debate about forest dynamics in Sagarmatha National Park, Nepal." In Karl S. Zimmerer and Kenneth R. Young (eds.) *Nature's Geography: New lessons for conservation in developing countries*. Madison: University of Wisconsin Press, pp. 184–208.

Byers, Alton. 2005. "Contemporary human impacts on Alpine ecosystems in the Sagarmatha (Mt. Everest) National Park, Khumbu, Nepal." *Annals of the Association of American Geographers* 95 (1): 112–140.

Central Bureau of Statistics (CBS). 2012. *National Population and Housing Census 2011*. Kathmandu: Government of Nepal.

Chakraborty, R., Gergan, M.D., Sherpa, P.Y., and Rampini, C., 2021. "A plural climate studies framework for the Himalayas." *Current Opinion in Environmental Sustainability*, 51: 42–54. https://doi.org/10.1016/j.cosust.2021.02.005.

Chakraborty, Rithodi, and Sherpa, Pasang Y. 2021. "From climate adaptation to climate justice: critical reflections on the IPCC and Himalayan climate knowledges." *Climatic Change* 167 (3–4): 1–14. https://doi.org/10.1007/s10584-021-03158-1.

Chaudhary, Pashupati and Bawa, Kamaljit S. 2011. "Local perceptions of climate change validated by scientific evidence in the Himalayas." *Biology Letters* 7 (5): 767–770. https://doi.org/10.1098/rsbl. 2011.0269.

Chevallier, P., Seidel, J.L., Taupin, J.D., and Puschiasis, O. 2020. "Headwater flow geochemistry of Mount Everest (Upper Dudh Koshi River, Nepal)." *Frontiers in Earth Science* 8: 351. https://doi. org/10.3389/feart.2020.00351.

Crate, Susan A. and Nuttall, Mark. 2009. *Anthropology and Climate Change: From encounters to actions*. London: Routledge. https://doi.org/10.4324/9781315434773.

Devkota, R.P., Maraseni, T.N., Cockfield, G., and Devkota, L.P., 2013. "Flood vulnerability through the eyes of vulnerable people in mid-western Terai of Nepal." *Journal of Earth Science and Climactic Change*, 4 (1): 1–7.

Eckholm, Erik P. 1975. "The deterioration of mountain environments: ecological stress in the highlands of Asia, Latin America, and Africa takes a mounting social toll." *Science* 189 (4205): 764–770. https://doi.org/10.1126/science.189.4205.764.

Fürer-Haimendorf, Christoph von. 1964. *The Sherpas of Nepal: Buddhist highlanders*. Berkeley: University of California Press.

Fürer-Haimendorf, Christoph von. 1984. *The Sherpas Transformed. Social change in a Buddhist society of Nepal*. New Delhi: Sterling.

Ives, Jack D. and Messerli, Bruno. 1989. *The Himalayan Dilemma: Reconciling development and conservation*. London: Routledge.

Jha, Pramod K. and Khanal, Indra P. 2010. *Contemporary Research in Sagarmatha (Mt. Everest) Region, Nepal: An anthology*. Kathmandu: Nepal Academy of Science and Technology (NAST).

Khadka, Navin S. 2012. "Everest Sherpas in glacial lake study warning." *BBC News*, September 12, https://www.bbc.com/news/science-environment-19569256.

McDowell, G., Ford, J.D., Lehner, B., Berrang-Ford, L., and Sherpa, A., 2013. "Climate-related hydro-logical change and human vulnerability in remote mountain regions: a case study from Khumbu, Nepal." *Regional Environmental Change* 13: 299–310. https://doi.org/10.1007/s10113-012-0333-2.

Metz, John J. 2009. "Downward spiral? Interrogating narratives of environmental change in the Himalaya." In Arjun Guneratne (ed.) *Culture and the Environment in the Himalaya*. London: Routledge, pp. 35–57. https://doi.org/10.4324/9780203864364-9.

National Research Council. 2012. *Himalayan Glaciers: Climate change, water resources, and water security*. Washington, DC: The National Academic Press. https://doi.org/10.17226/13449.

Ojha, H.R., Ghimire, S., Pain, A., Nightingale, A., Khatri, D.B., and Dhungana, H. 2016. "Policy without politics: technocratic control of climate change adaptation policy making in Nepal." *Climate Policy*, 16 (4): 415–433. https://doi.org/10.1080/14693062.2014.1003775.

Ortner, Sherry B. 1978. *Sherpas Through Their Rituals*. New York: Cambridge University Press,.

Poudyal, N.C., Joshi, O., Hodges, D.G., Bhandari, H., and Bhattarai, P. 2021. "Climate change, risk perception, and protection motivation among high-altitude residents of the Mt. Everest region in Nepal." *Ambio*, 50: 505–518. https://doi.org/10.1007/s13280-020-01369-x.

Puschiasis, Ornella. 2015. *Des Enjeux Planétaires Aux Perceptions Locales Du Changement Clima-tique: Pratiques et Discours Au Fil de l'eau Chez Les Sherpa Du Khumbu (Région de l'Everest, Népal)*. PhD thesis, Université Paris Nanterre. https://www.theses.fr/2015PA100157.

Puschiasis, Ornella. 2016. "De 'Yak-Driver' à 'Taxi Driver': Les pratiques de mobilité des Sherpa du Khumbu (Népal) à New York." In *Geo Café*. Chambéry, France.

Puschiasis, Ornella. 2019. "Un vent de changements souffle Sur l'Everest. Multiples facettes de la perception de la météorologie et du climat chez les Sherpa." *Ethnographiques.Org* 38: 1–17.

Puschiasis, O., Savéan, M., Chevallier, P., Smadja, J., Aubriot, O., and Delclaux, F., 2022. "Improving knowledge about snow by crossing qualitative and quantitative data from the Everest region (Nepal)." *Journal of Alpine Research| Revue de géographie alpine*, (4). https://doi.org/10.4000/rga.9826.

Rudiak-Gould, Peter. 2012. "Promiscuous corroboration and climate change translation: a case study from the Marshall Islands." *Global Environmental Change* 22 (1): 46–54. https://doi.org/10.1016/j.gloenvcha.2011.09.011.

Salick, J., Byg, A., and Bauer, K., 2012. "Contemporary Tibetan cosmology of climate change." *Journal for the Study of Religion, Nature & Culture*, 6 (4). https://doi.org/10.1558/jsrnc.v6i4.447.

Sherpa, Ang R. 2021. *Climate Change in the Himalayas: A case from Solu Khumbu*. Kathmandu: The Partners Nepal.

Sherpa, Pasang Y. 2012. *Sherpa Perceptions of Climate Change and Institutional Responses in the Everest Region of Nepal*. Doctoral dissertation, Washington State University. https://rex.libraries.wsu.edu/esploro/outputs/99900581748201842.

Sherpa, Pasang Y. 2014. "Climate change impacts among Sherpas: an anthropological study in the Everest region, Nepal." *Habitat Himalaya* 18 (1).

Sherpa, Pasang Y. 2015. "Institutional climate change adaptation efforts among the sherpas of the Mount Everest region, Nepal." *Climate Change, Culture, and Economics: Anthropological Investigations (Research in Economic Anthropology)*, 35. Bingley: Emerald Publishing Limited, pp. 1–23. https://doi.org/10.1108/S0190-1281201535.

Sherpa, Pasang Y. 2017. "Community and resilience among Sherpas in the post-earthquake Everest region." *HIMALAYA, the Journal of the Association for Nepal and Himalayan Studies* 37 (2): 103–112.

Sherpa, Pasang Y. 2019. "Sustaining Sherpa Language and Culture in New York." *Book 2.0* 9, pp. 19–29. https://doi.org/10.1386/btwo_00003_1.

Sherpa, Pasang Y. 2021. "Nepal's climate-change cultural world." In *The Anthropocene of Weather and Climate: Ethnographic contributions to the climate change debate*, edited by Paul Sillitoe, 220–246. Berghahn Books.

Sherpa, S.F., Shrestha, M., Eakin, H., and Boone, C.G., 2019. "Cryospheric hazards and risk perceptions in the Sagarmatha (Mt. Everest) National Park and Buffer Zone, Nepal." *Natural Hazards*, 96: 607–626. https://doi.org/10.1007/s11069-018-3560-0.

Sherpa, Yangji D. and Kayastha, Rijan B. 2009. "A study of livestock management patterns in Sagarmatha National Park, Khumbu region: trends as affected by socio-economic factors and climate change." *Kathmandu University Journal of Science, Engineering and Technology* 5 (2): 110–120.

Shrestha, U.B., Gautam, S., and Bawa, K.S., 2012. "Widespread climate change in the Himalayas and associated changes in local ecosystems." *PloS One*, 7 (5): e36741. https://doi.org/10.1371/journal.pone.0036741.

Skog, Lindsay A. 2010. *Beyul Khumbu: Sherpa constructions of a sacred landscape*. Master's Thesis, Portland State University. https://doi.org/10.15760/etd.2180.

Skog, Lindsay A. 2017. "Khumbi Yullha and the Beyul: sacred space and the cultural politics of religion in Khumbu, Nepal." *Annals of the American Association of Geographers* 107 (2): 546–554. https://doi.org/10.1080/24694452.2016.1210498.

Smadja, J., Aubriot, O., Puschiasis, O., Duplan, T., Grimaldi, J., Hugonnet, M., and Buchheit, P., 2015. "Climate change and water resources in the Himalayas. Field study in four geographic units of the Koshi basin, Nepal." *Journal of Alpine Research| Revue de géographie alpine*, 103 (2). https://doi.org/10.4000/rga.2910.

Spoon, Jeremy. 2011. "The heterogeneity of Khumbu Sherpa ecological knowledge and understanding in Sagarmatha (Mount Everest) National Park and Buffer Zone, Nepal." *Human Ecology* 39 (5): 657–672. https://doi.org/10.5038/2162-4593.15.1.3.

Spoon, Jeremy. 2012. "Tourism, persistence, and change: Sherpa spirituality and place in Sagarmatha (Mount Everest) National Park and Buffer Zone, Nepal." *Journal of Ecological Anthropology* 15 (1): 41–57. https://doi.org/10.5038/2162-4593.15.1.3.

Spoon, Jeremy. 2014. "Everyday Buddhism and environmental decisions in the world's highest ecosystem." *Journal for the Study of Religion, Nature & Culture* 8 (4): 429–459. https://doi.org/10.1558/jsrnc.v8i4.19062.

Spoon, Jeremy and Sherpa, Lakpa N. 2008. "Beyul Khumbu: the Sherpa and Sagarmatha (Mount Everest) National Park and Buffer Zone, Nepal." In Josep-Maria Mallarach (ed.) *Protected Landscapes and Cultural and Spiritual Values* 2, 68–79. Heidelberg: The International Union for Conservation of Nature (IUCN).

Stevens, Stanley F. 1996. *Claiming the High Ground: Sherpas, subsistence, and environmental change in the highest Himalaya.* University of California Press. http://ark.cdlib.org/ark:/13030/ft8b69p1t6/.

Thapa, Keshab B., and Shakya, Binod. 2008. *Integrated Study on Hydrology and Meteorology of Khumbu Region with Climate Change Perspectives.* Kathmandu: WWF Nepal.

Tse-Ring, K., Sharma, E., Chettri, N., and Shrestha, A.B. 2010. *Climate Change Vulnerability of Mountain Ecosystems in the Eastern Himalayas.* Kathmandu: International Centre for Integrated Mountain Development (ICIMOD).

Vedwan, Neeraj and Robert E. Rhoades. 2001. "Climate change in the Western Himalayas of India: a study of local perception and response." *Climate Research* 19 (2): 109–117. https://doi.org/10.3354/cr019109.

Watanabe, Teiji, Damodar Lamsal, and Jack D. Ives. 2009. "Evaluating the growth characteristics of a glacial lake and its degree of danger of outburst flooding: Imja Glacier, Khumbu Himal, Nepal." *Norsk Geografisk Tidsskrift* 63 (4): 255–267. https://doi.org/10.1080/00291950903368367.

Wester, P., Mishra, A., Mukherji, A., and Shrestha, A.B. 2019. *The Hindu Kush Himalaya Assessment: Mountains, climate change, sustainability and people.* Cham: Springer Nature. https://doi.org/10.1007/978-3-319-92288-1.

Whyte, Kyle. 2021. "Against crisis epistemology." In Brendan Hokowhitu, Aileen Moreton-Robinson, Linda Tuhiwai-Smith, Chris Andersen, and Steve Larkin (eds.) *Routledge Handbook of Critical Indigenous Studies.* New York: Routledge, pp. 52–64.

PART III

Interventions

16

WHY WE NEED TO PAY ATTENTION TO WEALTH AND INEQUALITY IN LOWERING CARBON EMISSIONS

Beatriz Barros and Richard Wilk

Introduction

The gap between the rich and the poor is getting wider, and this has direct effects on the planetary environment. This inequality is being driven by the extreme accumulation of wealth by a few individuals and families. The super-rich have never been as wealthy as they are today, and there is little room for the very poor to get even poorer. This inequality has many environmental consequences. According to our research, billionaires are directly responsible for the emission of thousands of tons of CO_2 and other greenhouse gases into the atmosphere, far more than the average person, even in comparatively rich countries. Wealth and status have allowed the super-rich to avoid the consequences of climate change, while concealing many of their damaging practices. Even though some billionaires have taken pro-environmental personas in public, their lifestyles, and their competition to have the largest yachts and the most luxurious private aircraft, have turned them into what we call "carbon aristocrats." They live at a level of comfort and convenience that exceeds even that of historical royalty and nobility. And their wealth gives them outsized clout in influencing governments' economic and environmental policies. It is indisputable that everyone needs to make changes to their lifestyle if we want to avoid a climate catastrophe. But billionaires also need to be held accountable and reduce their personal carbon emissions.

We think that anthropology can play an important role by contributing with examples of how other societies have controlled inequality and redistributed wealth more equally. Public shaming has been used across time and cultures as a way of curbing antisocial behaviors. We suggest that carbon-shaming billionaires can apply pressure to their reputations and lead them to make changes in their lifestyles that would reduce their greenhouse gas emissions and set a better example for society.

Inequality on the Rise

Currently, 3.5% of all global wealth is in the hands of billionaires, whereas the bottom half of the world's population collectively owns only 2%. Billionaires' wealth has been

DOI: 10.4324/9781003242499-20

increasing since the 1990s and it hit unprecedented heights in 2020 and 2021 during the COVID-19 pandemic, when global inequality had terrible consequences for the poor (Chancel et al. 2022; Dauderstädt 2022; Fiske et al. 2022). As the wealth of the few grew, death rates were much higher among the poor and many ethnic minorities, and the portion of the world population living in extreme poverty grew from about 8% to 9.3%, reversing a longtime trend (United Nations 2021).

In 2021, while the pandemic was wreaking havoc, a record 493 people joined Forbes magazine's billionaires list, making a record total of 2755 billionaires (Forbes 2022). Together, the Forbes 2021 billionaires were worth around $13.1 trillion, a $5 trillion increase from 2020, mainly because the value of their investments and companies increased. Elon Musk's fortune, for example, increased from $24.6 billion in 2020 to $151 billion in 2021 and $219 billion in 2022 (Forbes 2022). The United States has the largest number of billionaires of any country – 745 in 2021, and their combined wealth was far greater than that held by the poorer half of all US households (Collins 2021). Just imagine what it means for less than 800 individuals to own so much of a vast country of more than 330 million people. Even the "robber barons" of the nineteenth century never came close to holding such a large portion of the country's total wealth.

Anthropologists have used comparative ethnology and the archaeological study of the past to compare societies that had varying degrees of inequality. While all societies have some degree of inequality, anthropologists have found that societies with high levels of inequality tend to be more unstable and less adaptable to changing environments and circumstances (Price and Feinman 1995). Extremes of inequality have only developed in situations where wealth has become hereditary, and where class and cultural differences restrict or eliminate marriages between rich and poor (Mattison et al. 2016). The advent of corporate capitalism in Europe in the eighteenth and nineteenth centuries made it possible for the very rich to consolidate their power and indirectly control governments, but countries with strong egalitarian values have been able to limit inequality through taxation of the wealthy, and by laws which prohibit salaries above a certain level. Yet anthropologists are only beginning to study wealthy people to understand how they rationalize and maintain their riches, build alliances with other rich families and how they understand their role in society (e.g. Osburg 2013).

Defining Climate Change in the Context of Inequality

Climate change has also become an anthropological issue over the last decades, with a particular focus on how it is affecting marginal and poor communities, and the lessons on resilience that we can learn from past societies (Fiske et al. 2014). The changing climate is projected to have much more serious effects on poorer people, and it may push the poorest into migration, deprivation, and early death. This is because the impacts of anthropogenic climate change and global warming are multilayered and far-reaching (Howard 2014). Anthropogenic climate change is the release and concentration of greenhouse gases in Earth's atmosphere, mostly through burning fossil fuels. These greenhouse gases (carbon dioxide, methane, nitrous dioxide, and fluorinated hydrocarbons) trap heat in the atmosphere and increasingly warm the planet (EPA 2022). Different greenhouse gases absorb different quantities of heat and remain in the atmosphere for different periods of time, meaning that each one of these gases has a different warming potential. To simplify, we utilize carbon dioxide equivalent (CO_2e), which translates all greenhouse gases and their global warming potential to the same unit (IPCC 2007).

One of the many consequences of global warming and climate change is the escalation of extreme weather events, for example, cold and heat waves, droughts, landslides, floods, storms, and fires. These events, in turn, can precipitate further problems, such as increased poverty, food shortages, and the displacement of people. Climate change also affects human health, causing high rates of premature mortality (Kovats et al. 2005). For instance, in 2019 approximately 4.5 million people died due to causes related to outdoor air pollution, and by 2030 an estimated 60,000 people will die prematurely every year just because of changes in air pollution attributable to climate change (Ritchie and Roser 2022; Silva et al. 2017). Regardless of the specific consequences of climate change, it is clear that the poor majority of people are paying most of the cost of climate change, while the super-rich continue to profit from it (Ritchie et al. 2022). This is why we need to pay attention to the environmental impact of wealth and to social and economic inequality when debating climate change and strategies to curb it.

Carbon Emissions and Wealth

Together, the world's population emits around 50 billion metric tons of CO_2e each year (Ritchie and Roser 2020). Among different countries, the amount of CO_2e released into the atmosphere varies widely. In 2018, China was the largest total CO_2e emitter, with 11.7 billion metric tons, and Tuvalu the smallest, with 30,000 metric tons. However, when we take into account population and income, this scenario changes considerably. One average person in a high-income country is responsible for much more CO_2e emissions than an average person in a low-income country. For example, in Luxembourg, one of the richest countries in the world, one person emits an average of 15 metric tons of CO_2e per year, and the United States is not far behind at 14.5 metric tons. In the desert country of Qatar, the figure is close to 32 metric tons (Ritchie and Roser 2020). In contrast, in Somalia, one of the poorest countries, one person averages 1.2 metric tons of CO_2e in a year, mostly from food production and burning fossil fuels for power and transportation; in Mali the yearly average is 0.3 metric tons (Ritchie and Roser 2020). This makes the point that physical geography and the way each country generates power do affect average emissions, but overall wealth differences have much larger effects, both positive and negative. Rich countries like Norway and Switzerland can afford to build giant hydroelectric dams which produce low-carbon electricity, and France depends on a large network of hugely expensive nuclear power plants.

Breaking down emissions by country and giving averages can be very deceptive, because within every country there are rich and poor, so averages don't tell the whole story. A rich person in a big city in Madagascar is probably consuming at about the same level as a well-off middle-class citizen of the USA or Japan. The country average is low because there are fewer rich and many more poor, and the poor are so much poorer, with no vehicles, no electricity, no gas or running water. This is why it is important to focus on the rich; they are everywhere responsible for an outsized proportion of carbon emissions, so they are the ones who are going to have to make major changes in their lifestyles if we are going to stabilize the atmosphere. We need to stop admiring and emulating them, and their celebrity-filled lives of luxury. We have to ask why average individuals should make sacrifices for the sake of sustainability, while the super-rich continue to enjoy their super yachts.

We also need to be concerned with distributive justice – the fundamental unfairness of obscene amounts of wealth of a chosen few juxtaposed with huge numbers of people suffering from starvation and the hard work of bare survival, due largely to the simple accident of where people are born. We need to find ways to provide the necessities of life and opportunities for everyone, rich and poor, in a more sustainable way.

The Environmental Impact of Wealth

We decided to study billionaires because they provide such a clear example of how we all pay the environmental price of the extravagant consumption of a very thin upper crust. Their business investments and companies, even their charities, often have high CO_2e emissions. Billionaires' CO_2e emissions are even higher when we count their entourages, the family and friends who cluster around them and share their luxurious lifestyle, the servants, drivers, pilots, and the crews of their superyachts.

To illustrate these problems, we took a sample of 20 billionaires and set out to calculate their personal CO_2e emissions (Table 16.1). We selected some of the world's most famous billionaires, people we are used to reading about in the press and who publicly display their palatial houses, collections of cars and aircrafts, and the biggest yachts in the world. They are not a representative or random sample, simply because most billionaires are very private and use their wealth to stay out of public view, but we believe our sample paints a clear picture of the range and causes of CO_2e emissions from billionaires' lifestyles and consumption (Barros and Wilk 2021).

Almost every human action has some amount of carbon impact, but few agree on how to calculate them. In practice, calculating CO_2e emissions is a complex task that requires many assumptions, and a level of detail that is difficult to examine unless you can follow someone around every day. There are many carbon footprint calculators online, but they will give different results. This is because calculators have different levels of detail and use different databases. For example, they can't account for the kinds of insulation in your walls, or the efficiency of individual appliances or vehicles. If you are a renter, who is responsible for the emissions from heating and cooling, you or the landlord? Imagine driving to the grocery store. Should we just count the emissions of burning fuel? What about the emissions associated with the construction, distribution, and eventual disposal of the vehicle's whole life cycle (often called the embodied carbon)? What about the fossil fuels burned to get each package of food to the store? Online carbon calculators make assumptions based on averages and tend to be oriented to middle class lifestyles in developed countries.

To figure out the emissions of billionaires we had to develop our own methods and formulas, and we had to make simplifying assumptions. For example, we could judge the size of palatial houses from publications or directly using satellite photography, but that usually left us uncertain of how many floors the house had, its method of construction, and the type of heating and cooling. For that we had to use the average energy use per square meter for the largest 10% of houses in a particular locality, and then standardize that to kilowatt hours per year, and then look at the CO_2e emissions of the power plants producing that energy. We had to do extensive research on the fuel efficiency of different

TABLE 16.1 Estimates of 2018 emissions for twenty billionaires in metric tons of CO_2e and their 2018 wealth.

	Dwellings	Transportation	Yachts	Total	Estimated wealth in 2018
				(metric tons of CO_2e)	(billions of dollars)
Roman Abramovich – steel magnate	274.1	8484.7	22,440	31,198.8	10.8
Sheldon Adelson – casinos	201.6	4381.9	7344	11,927.5	35.5
Giorgio Armani – fashion designer	298.0	10.3	3672	3980.3	8.9
Bernard Arnault – owner of Louis Vuitton	180.9	1264.4	8976	10,421.3	72.0
Ernesto Bertarelli – pharmaceutical and real estate	69.4	1860.3	8160	10,089.7	8.9
Jeff Bezos – founder of Amazon	171.0	2053.2		2224.2	112.0
Michael Bloomberg – mass media	330.6	1450.9		1781.5	50.0
Sergey Brin – co-founder of Google	18.5	1968.4	4896	6882.9	47.5
Michael Dell – founder of Dell Technologies	523.8	6529.2		7053	22.7
Larry Ellison – co-founder of Oracle	241.6	1988.3	6936	9165.9	58.5
Tilman Fertitta – food service, sports	233.7	2890.1	2040	5163.8	4.3
Bill Gates – co-founder of Microsoft	85.5	7407.6		7493.1	90.0
David Geffen – co-founder of DreamWorks	71.5	1988.3	16,320	18,379.8	8.0
Laurene Powell Jobs – widow of Steve Jobs (co-founder of Apple)	215.8	1988.3	5304	7508.1	18.8
Ann Walton Kroenke – heiress of Bud Walton (co-founder of Walmart)	424.2	3090.6	6528	10,042.8	6.6
Elon Musk – CEO of Tesla Motors and SpaceX	115.6	1968.4		2084	19.9
Larry Page – co-founder of Google	16.5	1968.4	3264	5248.9	48.8
Ron Perelman – owner of MacAndrew & Forbes	186.9	2053.2	5304	7544.1	9.8
Eric Schmidt – former CEO of Google	69.2	1484.4	1632	3185.6	13.4
Carlos Slim – telecommunications	56.8	5.8	2448	2510.6	67.1
TOTAL	3785.2	54,836.7	105,264	163,885.9	713.5

sizes of ships to arrive at an estimate for different size superyachts, and emissions from private jets and helicopters also required simplifying assumptions, since we did not know precisely how many hours each one was used. We had to settle for figures from 2018 because those were the most up-to-date available at the time. We could not include life-cycle emissions, the exact distances each billionaire flew in their jets, the kinds of fuels used to warm or cool their houses, the amount of CO_2e emissions from the companies they own, the things they bought for friends and family, the food they ate or the clothes they wore. Therefore, our figures are minimum estimates, in most cases far below their actual emissions (Barros and Wilk 2021).

If we were to account for the environmental impact of billionaires' businesses and investments, their carbon footprint would skyrocket. Consider, for example, Bill Gates, Microsoft's co-founder. In 2022, Gates ranked fourth in Forbes' billionaires list, with a net worth of $134 billion (Forbes 2022). Although Gates has stepped down from leadership of Microsoft, he still owns about 1.4% of the company's shares, worth about $24 billion in December of 2022 (Forbes 2022). According to Microsoft's environmental sustainability report, the company emitted 11.6 million metric tons of CO_2e in 2020 (Microsoft 2021). Gates' share of Microsoft emissions would therefore be 162,400 metric tons (1.4% of 11.6 million metric tons of CO_2e). Unfortunately, lacking an account of all of his stock holdings, and those of our other billionaires, we had to leave this off the balance sheets (though Oxfam has recently produced good estimates for some of our billionaires, see Dabi et al. 2022). We also have no way to account for the many assets of billionaires that are hidden in offshore tax havens and shell companies.

Green Facades

Bill Gates, together with Jeff Bezos and Elon Musk, are three billionaires in our sample of 20 who have taken very public environmentalist positions. In 2021 Gates published *How to Avoid a Climate Disaster*, where he advocates for the need to reach net zero CO_2e emissions by 2050, mostly through the development of new technology, including geoengineering to capture CO_2 from the atmosphere (Gates 2021). But while he was writing the book in 2017, Gates travelled 343,500 kilometers in 59 flights on his private jets (Gössling 2019), and he has not substantially cut down his traveling since then. Gates recognizes in his book that he has a carbon-intensive lifestyle and says that he compensates for it through the buying of carbon offset credits (Gates 2021). The problem of carbon offsets has itself generated much critical literature, and many doubt that they live up to their promise (Bachram 2004; Lovell et al. 2009).

Amazon's founder Jeff Bezos, usually in the top three on Forbes' billionaires list, shows his devotion to environmental causes through his $10 billion Bezos Earth Fund, to be distributed as grants to environmentalist projects with goals like "Decarbonizing the Economy" (Bezos Earth Fund 2022). In other words, he is paying other people to figure out how to solve the problems he has had a large hand in creating. In 2021, Amazon reported 71.54 million tons of CO_2e emissions (Amazon 2022).

Another example of carbon hypocrisy is Elon Musk's claim that he has reduced his own carbon emissions, sold all of his properties and owns no private jets. The most visible of his environmental projects is the XPRIZE for Carbon Removal, that will give $100 million to the team that can present the best carbon capture and sequestration solution (XPRIZE 2022). Many environmentalists see carbon removal as a long-term solution to an immediate problem, and a distraction from the need to cut carbon emissions now. Yet Musk hides a lot of his personal carbon emissions in his companies; for example, he travels in jets owned by his companies (for both business and pleasure), adding up to more than 240,000 kilometers in 2018 (Harwell 2019). This translates into around 2638 metric tons of CO_2e, and the rockets launched by his company SpaceX are hardly carbon neutral.

The full atmospheric effects of the Billionaire Space Race are yet to be calculated. Musk competes with fellow billionaires Richard Branson's Virgin Galactic and Bezos' Blue Origin to explore the cosmos, colonize Mars, and develop space tourism. While they enjoy the publicity and benefits, we all pay the price when it comes to their rockets' exhaust accumulating in the atmosphere (Ross and Toohey 2019).

Gates, Bezos, and Musk have a lot in common, besides their wealth. The three of them have publicized their commitment to environmental causes while personally maintaining highly carbon-intensive lifestyles. They all support technology-oriented carbon sequestration (pumping it into the ground or ocean, still an impractical technology) and carbon offsetting to control greenhouse emissions. In doing so, they push our current CO_2e emissions-driven climate crisis into an unknown future of unproven technologies and bargains that allows them to continue their own lifestyle, instead of reducing today's CO_2e emissions while lifting billions of people out of poverty (D'Alisa et al. 2015; Dyke et al. 2021).

Reducing Carbon Emissions and Inequality

The Earth's atmosphere is a common-pool resource which belongs to all of us. It is not the private property of a few billionaires. Anthropologists have been studying the management of common property for many years. They have demonstrated how holding important resources as public goods that are accessible to everyone can reduce inequality and provide broad benefits to all of society instead of a few owners (e.g. Acheson 1988; Netting 1981; Mollona 2021). Common property theory tells us that "free riders," those who enjoy the benefits without paying the price, reduce everyone's motivation to properly manage a resource pool (Ostrom 2009). Billionaires are not only responsible for disproportional CO_2e emissions, but they also negatively affect everyone else's motivation to reduce their own carbon footprint. Moreover, many billionaires have very public lives, being followed by thousands or even millions through social media, where they display accounts of their glamourized and carbon-intensive lifestyles (Gössling 2019).

Governments have historically tried to reduce economic inequality through taxes and subsidies, moving some wealth from rich to poor. Progressive income taxation and death taxes are examples of leveling policies, but in the long run they have proved insufficient to reduce inequality (Roser and Ortiz-Ospina 2016). Although it has been debated more than implemented, a Universal Basic Income (UBI) would reduce inequality by making transfer payments to the poor. UBI has been criticized by those who argue funds would be better spent on universal public services such as education, health, and transportation (Coote and Yazici 2019). Most recently, several governments have floated the idea of taxing wealth – assets and property – instead of focusing on income taxes, but so far there has been little public debate on the matter (Piketty 2013; OECD 2018). In thinking about solutions, we need to recognize that increasing the carbon emissions of the poor has to be accompanied by a substantial cut in the emissions of the rich. Whatever the chosen method, it is clear that structural change is crucial to curb not only social and economic inequality but also CO_2e emissions.

Despite having the political and institutional capacity to enact the kind of structural change necessary to curb inequality, in practice most governments shy away from making changes. The wealthy have too much power over politics in most countries, and the super-rich can often evade the law (Page et al. 2019). Many see extreme inequality as a threat to democracy, and a cause of increasingly authoritarian systems of governance (Kelly and Howard 2019). On the contrary, if the majority of people are outraged at the profligate behavior of billionaires, and they vote to restrict the privileges of wealth, that is an exercise in basic democracy. We saw something like this in the summer of 2022 when in the midst of an unprecedented drought, public outrage about private jets led the French government to debate banning them from French airspace (Ledsom 2022).

Carbon-Shaming and Activism

Considering the unprecedented climate emergency through which we are living, we think that the carbon-intensive lifestyles of billionaires are both antisocial and anti-democratic. Anthropology has many useful things to say about the way societies can control and limit inequality, and the potential for social activism to address these issues. Shaming is the basic means of controlling antisocial behavior in most egalitarian societies, particularly among hunter-gatherers. But public shaming, or its threat, is a very important part of everyday life in every society, and with the advent of social media it has become even more prevalent (Aitchison and Meckled-Garcia 2021; Bloomfield 2014; Jacquet 2016; Ronson 2015). It may be an effective way of changing the public image of billionaires, who after all are used to being admired and flattered.

Despite concerns about the ethics of public shaming of individuals on social media, we think the problem of climate change is serious enough to justify extreme measures. One example of successful public shaming is the 2017 Swedish "Flygskam" (flight shame) campaign, in which environmental groups sought to reduce business and personal flying, with its high carbon emissions (Becken et al. 2021). Flygskam has reportedly contributed to the decrease of flights and increase of train journeys in Sweden and Germany (Gössling et al. 2020; Timperley 2019). "Drought shaming" was also a successful campaign during the 2014–15 California droughts, when websites and newspapers printed the names and addresses of people who continued to water their lawns and wash their cars (Lovett 2014).

Anthropology tells us that while climate change is an economic issue, it is also deeply embedded in culture, social organization, and everyday ideology (Wilk 2010). Economic anthropologists have been arguing that culture lies at the heart of economic behavior for almost a century (Wilk and Cliggett 2007). Many economists now admit that culture makes a huge difference in basic economic activities like saving, standards of living, investing, and finance, topics anthropologists are increasingly turning to (e.g. Alexander and Sosna 2022).

Carbon as a Commodity

Public debate about CO_2e emission policy has traditionally been dominated by economists who look at cost/benefit ratios and market-based approaches, particularly carbon pricing. Carbon pricing can take many forms, including a carbon tax, emissions trading schemes, and carbon offsets, all of which have been tried in different settings, all under the assumption that if carbon emissions cost more, people will have an incentive to cut them.

There is a lot of disparity in carbon pricing. For example, in 2021 Sweden charged $137 per metric ton of CO_2e, whereas Poland had a rate of less than $1 per metric ton (Statista Research Department 2021). At present, there is no institution with the power to establish an internationally recognized price for carbon and, more importantly, to enforce it. Recently, the concept of the Social Cost of Carbon (SCC) has been used by policy-makers when considering mitigation measures and establishing carbon prices. The SCC is a monetized value for the damages produced by the release of an extra metric ton of CO_2 to the atmosphere, or the cost to society of an additional ton of CO_2 emissions. The calculations of the SCC depend on many variables, which has given rise to intense debates about how it should be calculated and how costs and benefits should be measured (Heal and Millner 2014). For example, the calculations of the US Environmental Protection Agency for the SCC in 2015 ranged from $11 to $105 per metric ton of CO_2, depending on the discount rate applied and the size of impacts considered (Fleurbaey et al. 2019). The problem of setting a price on carbon emissions in the future (called "discounting") has prompted heated debated because of its ethical implications. The effects of climate change will be felt by many generations to come, but a high discount rate suggests that the well-being of people today is worth more than that of future generations, while a zero discount rate would mean that the future is as valuable as the present. In addition, climate change is caused by an interaction of many activities and markets, and there are many effects of climate change that completely escape the monetization and calculations of SCC and carbon pricing (Bressler 2021; Howard 2014). This process of monetization is yet another argument in favor of bringing anthropology, culture, and human behavior into the discussion for a more thorough understanding of how markets affect people's behavior.

The commodification of carbon makes it easy for the wealthy to keep on having carbon-intensive lifestyles by just paying costs that are relatively insignificant for billionaires. Their lifestyle makes the consequences of their choices invisible, since they never do something as basic as driving themselves from place to place or shopping for food. However, in our unprecedented climate emergency, everyone needs to cooperate and reduce their CO_2e emissions, even billionaires, royalty, and celebrities. Sanctions and fines will not make billionaires compliant, but perhaps engaged social activist campaigns targeting their wasteful and harmful behaviors can succeed. Moreover, given the importance of structural change to successfully address social, economic, and carbon inequality, it is crucial to show public support for more ambitious social and climate legislation. In order to succeed, the fight against climate change must become a fight for social, economic, and climate justice.

References

Acheson, James M. 1988. *The Lobster Gangs of Maine.* Hanover: University Press of New England.

Aitchison, Guy and Saladin Meckled-Garcia. 2021. "Against online public shaming: ethical problems with mass social media." *Social Theory and Practice* 47 (1): 1–31. https://doi.org/10.5840/soctheorpract20201117109.

Alexander, Catherine and Daniel Sosna, eds. 2022. *Thrift and Its Paradoxes: From domestic to political economy*. Max Planck Studies in Anthropology and Economy, volume 10. New York: Berghahn Books.

Amazon. 2022. "Our carbon footprint." Accessed November 19, 2022. https://sustainability.abou tamazon.com/environment/carbon-footprint.

Bachram, Heidi. 2004. "Climate fraud and carbon colonialism: the new trade in greenhouse gases." *Capitalism Nature Socialism* 15 (4): 5–20. https://doi.org/10.1080/1045575042000287299.

Barros, Beatriz and Richard Wilk. 2021. "The outsized carbon footprints of the super-rich." *Sustainability: Science, Practice and Policy* 17 (1): 316–322. https://doi.org/10.1080/15487733.2021.1949847.

Becken, Susanne, Harald Friedl, Bela Stantic, Rod M. Connolly, and Jinyan Chen. 2021. "Climate crisis and flying: social media analysis traces the rise of 'Flightshame.'" *Journal of Sustainable Tourism* 29 (9): 1450–1469. https://doi.org/10.1080/09669582.2020.1851699.

Bezos Earth Fund. 2022. "Bezos Earth Fund." Accessed November 19, 2022. https://www.bezosea rthfund.org/.

Bloomfield, Michael John. 2014. "Shame campaigns and environmental justice: corporate shaming as activist strategy." *Environmental Politics* 23 (2): 263–281. https://doi.org/10.1080/09644016.2013.821824.

Bressler, R. Daniel. 2021. "The mortality cost of carbon." *Nature Communications* 12 (1): 4467. https://doi.org/10.1038/s41467-021-24487-w.

Chancel, Lucas, Thomas Piketty, Emmanuel Saez, and Gabriel Zucman, eds. 2022. *World Inequality Report 2022*. World Inequality Lab. https://wir2022.wid.world/.

Collins, Chuck. 2021. "Updates: billionaire wealth, US job losses and pandemic profiteers." Inequality.org. Accessed November 19, 2022. https://inequality.org/great-divide/updates-billiona ire-pandemic/.

Coote, Anna and Edanur Yazici. 2019. *Universal Basic Income: Full report*. Public Services International. http://www.world-psi.org/sites/default/files/documents/research/en_ubi_full_report_2019.pdf.

Dabi, Nafkote, Alex Maitland, Max Lawson, Hilde Stroot, Alexandre Poidatz, and Ashfaq Khalfan. 2022. "Carbon billionaires: the investment emissions of the world's richest people." Oxfam International. https://doi.org/10.21201/2022.9684.

D'Alisa, Giacomo, Federico Demaria, and Giorgos Kallis, eds. 2015. *Degrowth: A vocabulary for a new era*. New York: Routledge.

Dauderstädt, Michael. 2022. "International inequality and the COVID-19 pandemic." *Intereconomics* 57 (1): 40–46. https://doi.org/10.1007/s10272-022-1026-9.

Dyke, James, Robert Watson, and Wolfgang Knorr. 2021. "Climate scientists: concept of net zero is a dangerous trap." The Conversation. April 22, 2021. http://theconversation.com/climate-scien tists-concept-of-net-zero-is-a-dangerous-trap-157368.

EPA. 2022. "Overview of greenhouse gases." Overviews and Factsheets. United States Environmental Protection Agency. Accessed November 19, 2022. https://www.epa.gov/ghgemissions/overview-greenhouse-gases.

Fiske, Shirley, Susan Crate, Carole Crumley, Kathleen Galvin, Heather Lazarus, George Luber, Lisa Lucero, Anthony Oliver-Smith, Ben Orlove, Sarah Strauss, and Richard Wilk. 2014. *Changing the Atmosphere: Anthropology and climate change*. Arlington, VA: American Anthropological Association.

Fiske, Amelia, Ilaria Galasso, Johanna Eichinger, Stuart McLennan, Isabella Radhuber, Bettina Zimmermann, and Barbara Prainsack. 2022. "The second pandemic: examining structural inequality through reverberations of Covid-19 in Europe." *Social Science & Medicine* 292 (January): 114634. https://doi.org/10.1016/j.socscimed.2021.114634.

Fleurbaey, Marc, Maddalena Ferranna, Mark Budolfson, Francis Dennig, Kian Mintz-Woo, Robert Socolow, Dean Spears, and Stéphane Zuber. 2019. "The social cost of carbon: valuing inequality, risk, and population for climate policy." *The Monist* 102 (1): 84–109. https://doi.org/10.1093/monist/ony023.

Forbes. 2022. "Forbes Billionaires 2022: The Richest People In The World." Accessed November 19, 2022. https://www.forbes.com/billionaires/.

Gates, Bill. 2021. *How to Avoid a Climate Disaster: The solutions we have and the breakthroughs we need.* New York: Alfred A. Knopf.

Gössling, Stefan. 2019. "Celebrities, Air Travel, and Social Norms." *Annals of Tourism Research* 79 (November): 102775. https://doi.org/10.1016/j.annals.2019.102775.

Gössling, Stefan, Andreas Humpe, and Thomas Bausch. 2020. "Does 'Flight Shame' affect social norms? Changing perspectives on the desirability of air travel in Germany." *Journal of Cleaner Production* 266 (September): 122015. https://doi.org/10.1016/j.jclepro.2020.122015.

Harwell, Drew. 2019. "Elon Musk's highflying 2018: what 150,000 miles in a private jet reveal about his 'excruciating' year." Washington Post. February 4, 2019. https://www.washingtonpost.com/business/economy/elon-musks-highflying-2018-what-150000-miles-in-a-private-jet-reveal-about-his-excruciating-year/2019/01/29/83b5604e-20ee-11e9-8b59-0a28f2191131_story.html.

Heal, Geoffrey M. and Antony Millner. 2014. "Agreeing to disagree on climate policy." *Proceedings of the National Academy of Sciences* 111 (10): 3695–3698. https://doi.org/10.1073/pnas.1315987111.

Howard, Peter. 2014. *Omitted Damages: What's missing from the social cost of carbon?* Institute for Policy Integrity. https://costofcarbon.org/files/Omitted_Damages_Whats_Missing_From_the_Social_Cost_of_Carbon.pdf.

IPCC. 2007. *IPCC Fourth Assessment Report: Climate change.* Intergovernmental Panel on Climate Change. New York: Cambridge University Press.

Jacquet, Jennifer. 2016. *Is Shame Necessary? New uses for an old tool.* New York: Vintage Books.

Kelly, Marjorie and Ted Howard. 2019. *The Making of a Democratic Economy: Building prosperity for the many, not just the few.* Oakland: BK Berrett-Koehler Publishers, Inc.

Kovats, R. Sari, Diarmid Campbell-Lendrum, and Franziska Matthies. 2005. "Climate change and human health: estimating avoidable deaths and disease." *Risk Analysis* 25 (6): 1409–1418. https://doi.org/10.1111/j.1539-6924.2005.00688.x.

Ledsom, Alex. 2022 "France, Europe eyes heavy taxes or bans on private jets." Forbes. September 4, 2022. https://www.forbes.com/sites/alexledsom/2022/09/04/france-europe-eyes-heavy-taxes-or-bans-on-private-jets/.

Lovell, Heather, Harriet Bulkeley, and Diana Liverman. 2009. "Carbon offsetting: sustaining consumption?" *Environment and Planning A: Economy and Space* 41 (10): 2357–2379. https://doi.org/10.1068/a40345.

Lovett, Ian. 2014. "Californians keep up with Joneses' water use." The New York Times. July 5, 2014. https://www.nytimes.com/2014/07/05/us/californians-keep-up-with-joneses-water-use.html.

Mattison, Siobhán M., Eric A. Smith, Mary K. Shenk, and Ethan E. Cochrane. 2016. "The evolution of inequality." *Evolutionary Anthropology: Issues, News, and Reviews* 25 (4): 184–199. https://doi.org/10.1002/evan.21491.

Microsoft. 2021. *Environmental Sustainability Report.* Microsoft. https://query.prod.cms.rt.microsoft.com/cms/api/am/binary/RE4RwfV.

Mollona, Massimiliano. 2021. *Art-Commons: Anthropology beyond capitalism.* London: Zed Books.

Netting, Robert McC. 1981. *Balancing on an Alp: Ecological change and continuity in a Swiss mountain community.* New York: Cambridge University Press.

OECD. 2018. *The Role and Design of Net Wealth Taxes in the OECD.* OECD. https://doi.org/10.1787/9789264290303-8-en.

Osburg, John. 2013. *Anxious Wealth: Money and morality among China's new rich.* Stanford: Stanford University Press.

Ostrom, Elinor. 2009. "A polycentric approach for coping with climate change." World Bank Policy Research Working Paper No. 5095. SSRN Scholarly Paper. https://papers.ssrn.com/abstract=1494833.

Page, Benjamin I., Jason Seawright, and Matthew J. Lacombe. 2019. *Billionaires and Stealth Politics.* Chicago: The University of Chicago Press.

Piketty, Thomas. 2013. *Le Capital Au XXIe Siècle.* Paris: Éditions du Seuil.

Price, T. Douglas, and Gary M. Feinman, eds. 1995. *Foundations of Social Inequality*. New York: Plenum Press.

Ritchie, Hannah, Pablo Rosado, and Max Roser. 2022. "Natural disasters." Our World in Data. Accessed November 19, 2022. https://ourworldindata.org/natural-disasters.

Ritchie, Hannah and Max Roser. 2020. "CO_2 and greenhouse gas emissions." Our World in Data. https://ourworldindata.org/greenhouse-gas-emissions.

Ritchie, Hannah and Max Roser. 2022. "Outdoor air pollution." Our World in Data. Accessed November 19, 2022. https://ourworldindata.org/outdoor-air-pollution.

Ronson, Jon. 2015. *So You've Been Publicly Shamed*. New York: Riverhead Books.

Roser, Max and Esteban Ortiz-Ospina. 2016. "Income inequality." Our World in Data. Accessed November 19, 2022. https://ourworldindata.org/income-inequality.

Ross, Martin N. and Darin W. Toohey. 2019. "The coming surge of rocket emissions." Eos American Geophysical Union. September 24, 2019. http://eos.org/features/the-coming-surge-of-rocket-emissions.

Silva, Raquel A., J. Jason West, Jean-François Lamarque, Drew T. Shindell, William J. Collins, Greg Faluvegi, Gerd A. Folberth, et al. 2017. "Future global mortality from changes in air pollution attributable to climate change." *Nature Climate Change* 7 (9): 647–651. https://doi.org/10.1038/nclimate3354.

Statista Research Department. 2021. "Prices of implemented carbon taxes worldwide 2021, by select country." https://www.statista.com/statistics/483590/prices-of-implemented-carbon-pricing-instruments-worldwide-by-select-country/.

Timperley, Jocelyn. 2019. "Why 'flight shame' is making people swap planes for trains." BBC. September 9, 2019. https://www.bbc.com/future/article/20190909-why-flight-shame-is-making-people-swap-planes-for-trains.

United Nations. 2021. "Sustainable Development Goals. 1 No poverty. End poverty in all its forms everywhere." Accessed November 19, 2022. https://unstats.un.org/sdgs/report/2021/goal-01/.

Wilk, Richard. 2010. "Consumption embedded in culture and language: implications for finding sustainability." *Sustainability: Science, Practice and Policy* 6 (2): 38–48. https://doi.org/10.1080/15487733.2010.11908048.

Wilk, Richard and Lisa Cliggett. 2007. *Economies and Cultures: Foundations of economic anthropology*. New York: Routledge.

XPRIZE. 2022. "XPRIZE Carbon Removal." Accessed November 19, 2022. https://www.xprize.org/prizes/carbonremoval.

17

DECARBONIZATION AND MAKING THE ENERGY FUTURE IN THE WELSH UNDERLANDS

Mark Nuttall

Introduction

As we grapple with the reality of an overheating world and ask what we can do about our reliance on fossil fuels, we may feel some hope now that an increasing number of national and regional governments have set themselves the ambitious challenge to meet targets for net zero emissions. In discussions about shaping the energy future and finding solutions to the climate change crisis, decarbonization features as a key policy objective for many countries. For example, Denmark plans to cut greenhouse gas emissions by 70% by 2030 and achieve carbon neutrality by 2050 (Barker et al. 2022). Similarly, New Zealand has committed to becoming carbon neutral by the same year, while China has a strategy for carbon neutrality by 2060 (Zhao et al. 2022). Toward the end of 2020, the UK government published then-Prime Minister Boris Johnson's 10 Point Plan for a Green Revolution and an Energy White Paper, called *Powering our Net Zero Future*, from the Department for Business, Energy and Industrial Strategy (BEIS).[1] Both documents place considerable emphasis on the production of hydrogen and its potential to decarbonize the UK's industrial clusters, heavy transport, and domestic heating.

The goal of decarbonization is the reduction and eventual elimination of carbon dioxide (CO_2) emissions from the atmosphere that result from human activity – particularly from the burning of fossil fuels by industry. Responding to the challenge of becoming carbon neutral, cities, regions, industries (including extractive industries), manufacturers, and businesses are engaging in a process of how to develop decarbonization strategies that commit them to making a fundamental contribution to realising a net zero future in the next two to three decades. San Francisco, for instance, has a climate action plan which is intended as a roadmap to achieve the city's goal of net zero greenhouse gas emissions by 2040,[2] combatting not just climate change, but addressing racial and social equity, and promoting resilience and economic recovery along the way, while Airbus has an ambition to develop the world's first zero emission aircraft by 2035, calling it "a seismic shift for the aviation industry."[3]

DOI: 10.4324/9781003242499-21

But how hopeful can we be that decarbonization will be one major solution to the climate crisis? Having a strategy is one thing, implementing it is quite another. Decarbonization also has economic, environmental, and social costs. As John Urry (2013) has written, developing low carbon systems, let alone achieving decarbonization, is hard given that it depends on a transformed cluster of technological, economic, social, infrastructure, and governance systems across many scales. An OECD Nuclear Energy Agency (NEA) report points out that "decarbonization will require a radical restructuring of the electric power sectors of each OECD country and a truly massive deployment of low-carbon technologies, in particular nuclear energy and renewable energies such as wind and solar PV" (NEA 2019: 14). Commenting on whether it is possible for the US to achieve a goal of net zero CO_2 emissions by 2050, John Deutch argues that a transition to an essentially all electric economy is needed, but warns this cannot be done by taking incremental steps. He maintains that:

> Fundamental change is necessary in executive branch agency organization, in the private sector where investment decisions between competing firms are based on price signals, as well as congressional oversight. The extent and pace of change is comparable to what is required in wartime...
>
> *(Deutch 2020: 2239)*

A US net zero initiative is, Deutch asserts, dependent on a massive commitment of resources, with the effective mobilization of all levels of government, the energy sector, businesses, and energy consumers. But as an International Energy Agency (IEA) report claims, the pledges governments have made to date fall short of what is required to bring global energy-related carbon dioxide emissions to net zero by 2050 and give the world an even chance of limiting global temperature rise to 1.5 °C (IEA 2021). It also requires a massive shift in public opinion and action.

Carbon capture and storage (CCS) is a controversial technology for finding ways to mitigate climate change. Carbon dioxide is collected from industries that produce it and is then deposited, often by way of pipelines, in underground locations, such as depleted oil and gas reservoirs (e.g., see Bandilla 2020). Rocks, which are themselves fundamental to the carbon cycle – most carbon is stored in sedimentary rocks such as coal, limestone, chalk and shale – have come to be seen as providing ways in which climate change can be reduced or mitigated, as deep repositories for carbon dioxide (Stephenson 2018). The physical geographies and the geological structures and sedimentary layers of the Earth that have been laid down in deep time have been placed at the centre of narratives that offer hope for the planet's future. Reporting on research done in the Swedish city of Malmö, Stripple and Bulkeley (2019) recast decarbonization, though, as a matter of political geography. They argue for thinking critically about its socio-spatial configurations, its indeterminate nature, and how decarbonization politics are socio-materially constituted. They show how decarbonization in Malmö is enacted through practices of legibility, demonstration and agreement, all of which form new socio-material connections and realignments between carbon, capital, and infrastructure. Stripple and Bulkeley suggest that there is no linear blueprint for creating any pathway toward decarbonization. Instead, decarbonization is enabled through processes that realign and reorder socio-material relations in new sites and domains.

In this chapter, I take the notion of the remaking and reorientation of socio-material relations as a starting point to reflect on the early stages of what is being promoted as the UK's leading industrial decarbonization project. As part of current anthropological research on the making and ruination of industrial and post-industrial landscapes in North Wales (e.g., Nuttall 2020, 2021), I have been following the progress of HyNet North West, a decarbonization and hydrogen energy production initiative. This, its background information literature, planning documents, non-technical summaries, and website claim, will "unlock a low carbon future" while "creating and protecting local jobs."[4] The project will stretch across – and also, beneath – parts of the Welsh county of Flintshire and the English county of Cheshire. Presented as a necessary solution to climate change – and an urgent project – it is framed and supported by narratives of futuring and worldmaking in the ways the proponents claim HyNet North West will not only reshape and remake a region and its economy, but will lead the way for similar initiatives elsewhere in the UK, in Europe, and globally.

I consider one element of this project: discussion about and consultation on the route of a pipeline that will carry CO_2 emissions from energy intensive industries in Cheshire and Flintshire to storage in depleted gas reservoirs in the Irish Sea. In particular, I explore how the project as a proposed solution to climate change and the pipeline and its route were presented for public comment by the proponents during the initial non-statutory and the follow-up statutory consultation processes. I examine some of the responses that people have made about the project. In the way they plan and talk about the pipeline and its route, I also show how the proponents look to the underground as a space that is essential for worldmaking. Indeed, the underground is integral to the making of a carbon neutral future, in which a buried pipeline will transport the greenhouse gas that is the largest contributor to climate change to a subsea burial ground. In this spatial imaginary, the subsurface, then, is one domain which makes possible the realignment and reordering of socio-material relations that are necessary to enable decarbonization.

HyNet North West

The northernmost stretch of the border region between Wales and England comprises the Welsh county of Flintshire and the English county of Cheshire. Even if much of it remains rural, with rich farmland and upland hill areas, it was among the first areas in Britain to have been industrialized (Stobart 2004). In this chapter, I focus mainly on research I am doing in the part of Flintshire (Welsh: Sir y Fflint) which includes Deeside and its environs (Glannau Dyfrdwy). This is a predominantly industrialized conurbation that also encompasses towns, villages, farms, and edgelands in Cheshire across the border. Deeside is named for its proximity to the River Dee (Afon Dyfrdwy) and the Dee Estuary (Aber Dyfrdwy). The River Dee rises at a height of 884 m on the slopes of Dduallt in the North Wales mountain region of Eryri (which, since late 2022, is now the official name of Snowdonia). It then flows, meanders and twists through North Wales for some 113 km to Chester, which is Cheshire's county town, marking something of a border between England and Wales along parts of its eastern course, especially in the estuary, before entering the Irish Sea in Liverpool Bay. The Dee Estuary also acts as a national border between England and Wales, yet its very nature and substance is uncertain and permeable. A fixed national boundary has been imposed on something shifting and difficult to map.

The Dee Estuary is one of the largest estuaries in the United Kingdom. It looms large in Flintshire's history and in its contemporary social and economic settings, as does its importance for the English–Welsh border city of Chester. Broad, funnel-shaped, hyper-tidal and unpredictable, the estuary is filled with shifting sand, sediment, and silt. It has been silting up since the eleventh century, with the widespread development of salt marsh, and has been subject to dredging and land reclamation schemes ever since (Marker 1967). It extends some 30 km along a northwest trajectory from the tide limit at Chester Weir on the River Dee. At its widest point before opening out into Liverpool Bay, the Dee Estuary stretches for about 8 km between Point of Ayr in Flintshire to Hilbre Point on England's Wirral peninsula in the metropolitan county of Merseyside.

Flintshire has a long history of large industrial ventures as well as industrial decline. Lead mining, coal mining, quarrying, brickmaking, potteries, copper smelting, textiles, steel manufacturing and shipbuilding (the latter at several former ports of the Dee Estuary shoreline) were major industries in the county in the nineteenth and twentieth centuries. People were attracted by employment opportunities in the mines, brickworks, factories and shipyards to relocate there seasonally or permanently from other parts of Wales and elsewhere in the British Isles. Distinct communities, often defined by occupation, labour, class and religion, grew around these activities, while more recently the petrochemical industry, paper production, the aerospace industry, other manufacturing ventures, and the development of an industrial park have provided employment and contributed to the region's growth. That said, many communities in Flintshire, especially along the coast of the Dee Estuary, and along the proposed route of the carbon emissions pipeline, experience high levels of social and economic deprivation, especially when it comes to employment, income, housing, education, and community safety (WIMD 2019).

The decarbonization project is promoted by the proponents, a consortium called HyNet North West, as a major initiative that will help the UK meet its net zero targets by 2050. HyNet North West calls itself the UK's first hydrogen and carbon capture cluster that will place the region at the heart of leading the low carbon energy transition, transform the economy, resulting in growth, jobs, and prosperity, and contribute to climate change solutions. It has considerable UK government support, as well as the backing of local governments, and is promoted as a project that will make northwest England and northeast Wales the first global hub of its kind. The project is touted, and described in publicity material and on its website, as "an innovative low carbon and hydrogen energy project that will unlock a low carbon economy for the North West and North Wales and put the region at the forefront of the UK's drive to net zero." Reports and updates on its progress often appear in the media, as UK and Welsh government ministers and local councillors make frequent visits to regional industries and consortium partners to learn about decarbonization and innovation in hydrogen technologies.

HyNet North West will build, 1) a low-carbon hydrogen production plant and network of pipelines, with the hydrogen used in the region's industry, transport, and business, and eventually in people's homes 2) infrastructure to capture CO_2 emissions from energy-intensive industries in the area and from the hydrogen plant, and 3) a pipeline to transport and store these emissions underground. By 2030, HyNet North West claims it will reduce carbon dioxide emissions by 10 million tonnes every year. In April 2022, the consortium issued a press release that announced a further 28 companies and organizations (including Kellogs, PepsiCo, and Jaguar Land Rover) had joined it and were committed to switching to low carbon hydrogen.[5] Since then, many more organizations and industries have expressed their support and new partnerships have been formed, including one between the project proponents and Manchester Airport.

The pipeline will take away CO_2 emissions from industry, such as petrochemical and cement producers, as well as from the hydrogen plant. For example, one of the UK's largest cement works, which is operated by Hanson Cement, is located at Padeswood in Flintshire and will be one major node for the project. The emissions will be carried through parts of the Cheshire and Flintshire underlands for permanent storage in depleted gas reservoirs and abandoned gas production facilities in Liverpool Bay in the Irish Sea off the northern Welsh coast. Hydrogen will also be produced at existing industrial complexes, centred on the Stanlow oil refinery site – a major complex near Ellesmere Port – and moved by pipeline to storage in salt caverns elsewhere in Cheshire. Although the hydrogen will be used initially by industry and business, the proponents forecast that it will eventually feed into the domestic energy system. Cadent, which is the UK's largest gas distribution network, and British Gas, an energy and home services provider, had until recently been developing ideas for a "hydrogen village" in Cheshire that would form part of the wider HyNet North West initiative. Centred on the village of Whitby in the constituency of Ellesmere Port, it was argued that this would support around 2000 properties in transitioning from natural gas to using hydrogen for heating and cooking, and would be a pilot project for the wider transformation of domestic energy supply and use. It is important to note here, though, that a recent report argues that hydrogen will be ineffective for home heating (Rosenow 2022), and local opposition in Whitby was strong, with campaigns organized by a group called HyNot which has also distributed the findings of such scientific studies via social media. In early summer 2023, Cadent announced it would not be moving forward with the trials in Whitby, as the UK government's Department of Energy Security and Net Zero appeared to favor Redcar, a town on the Yorkshire coast of northeast England. Citing local protests in Whitby, the government said trials would not go ahead there without strong support, but even in Redcar there is considerable local concern about the town being selected and, at the time of writing this chapter, a decision by the regulator Ofgem (Office of Gas and Electricity Markets) was pending.

The HyNet North West project will be developed in different stages, the first of which will be the CO_2 emissions pipeline – the focus of the initial consultation. The proposals for the carbon dioxide pipeline were submitted to the UK government for consideration in autumn 2023, with a decision expected around autumn 2024. If approved, construction will begin on the pipeline in 2025. The hydrogen plant and pipeline network will be developed by Cadent and are being consulted on separately. While I have been following that consultation process as well, the hydrogen pipeline is beyond the scope of this chapter, although I will refer briefly to the place of salt caverns in worldmaking narratives towards the end.

I began to follow the discussion about HyNet North West when the project was going through the planning stages just before the first lockdown because of the Covid-19 pandemic in March 2020 and imposed by the UK government and Llywodraeth Cymru (the devolved Welsh government that was established in 1999). I have since participated in both online events and in-person consultation sessions in various locations in Flintshire, and have had a number of conversations with local residents. The project first came to my attention because of both scholarly and personal reasons. Recently, I have cast my anthropological gaze on the Welsh–English borderlands, a region where I grew up. As a social anthropologist, I have always been interested in what makes communities, how people make livelihoods, and how they live in, relate to, and interact with their surroundings. In research I am currently doing in Flintshire, I am exploring how communities and the landscapes in which they have taken root and grown, and in which they have endured times of crisis and decay, have been formed and shaped in relation to the development of industry, especially by lead mining and brickmaking, and also by the extraction of coal.

This is also something of an anthropological adventure in discovering more about my own family connections and involvement in these industries, which I plan to write about in due course. A blend of ethnography and historical and archival work, my larger research project has an element of personal, social, economic, and landscape history. The lives of many of my forebears in nineteenth and early twentieth century Flintshire were bound up with lead mines, brickworks, collieries, smelters, and shipyards – with limestone, fireclay, smoke, dust, copper, steel, mud, and a silty river. In the 1980s, high levels of unemployment in the region following redundancies at a major steelworks in Deeside and the end of the brickmaking and coal communities were some of the reasons that led me to sociology and, eventually, to anthropology. The proposed pipeline will also pass through and beneath my parents' village and surrounding farmland and woods in Flintshire, although I must make an important declaration that, in this chapter, I am neither expressing opposition to the pipeline, nor am I positioning myself as an advocate for the larger decarbonization project.

The Carbon Dioxide Emissions Pipeline Route

In summer 2021 HyNet North West organized an initial non-statutory consultation process structured around webinars, information sessions, online submission of views about the project ambitions, carbon emissions, and hydrogen production, and people were invited to enter comments on an interactive map showing the proposed pipeline routes. The project went through environmental impact assessment and consideration of the technical challenges in 2021 and 2022. In February and March 2022, a series of in-person events held in towns and villages near the pipeline route in Cheshire and Flintshire constituted the statutory consultation stage, although as I suggest below, these were mainly information sessions rather than an opportunity to provide a forum for debate, for the interrogation of the technical reports, and deep discussion of the social, economic, and environmental aspects of the project. Some of the key consultation documents (in both English and Welsh), such as non-technical summaries of the environmental impact assessment, fact sheets, videos, and maps showing the pipeline route, are available for download from the HyNet North West website (https://hynet.co.uk/), although one must look a little harder, such as on the website of the UK government's planning inspectorate, for the full environmental impact assessment scoping reports and other technical documents.

Both the non-statutory and statutory consultations focused on plans for the construction and operation of the CO_2 emissions pipeline. As I have already mentioned, these emissions, which are produced by industries in Cheshire and Flintshire, will be stored in depleted gas reservoirs in Liverpool Bay. This is a shallow-water sedimentary marine ecosystem in the eastern part of the Irish Sea. Liverpool Bay was the UK's first significant near-shore area in which commercial supplies of oil and gas were located, following exploration activities carried out by BHP Billington Petroleum in 1990. The oil produced is processed, blended, and then sent by pipeline to an offshore storage installation where it is loaded into tankers for worldwide markets. The gas that is extracted is transported via a 34 km pipeline to a terminal at Point of Ayr near Talacre, which is the northern-most point of the Welsh mainland. In the last few years, as oil and gas extraction has declined, Liverpool Bay (and a long stretch of the North Wales coast) has been developed as one of the world's largest offshore wind turbine areas.

The planned pipeline will run southwest through Cheshire into Flintshire and connect to an existing gas pipeline (which will be repurposed for CO_2) near Connah's Quay and Flint, which are both towns on the Welsh shore of the Dee Estuary. From there, the emissions will continue to the Point of Ayr terminal, connecting to a new subsea pipeline that will extend to a platform some 30 km offshore in Liverpool Bay. The CO_2 will then be injected into the depleted gas reservoirs of hydrocarbon fields owned by Eni UK. The offshore pipeline, which will be regulated by the UK's Oil and Gas Authority (OGA), and constructed by Eni, is subject to a separate consultation process and was not considered for public discussion when the carbon emissions pipeline meetings were held, even though many local residents had questions and concerns about it. They considered it vital to know about how it would be constructed and how safe it would be, but were told it was not within the purview of the CO_2 pipeline consultation.

At the start of each webinar and in-person meeting, the proponents set out an overview of the larger HyNet North West project, its rationale, and the pipeline proposals. Initi-ally, these proposals included three different pipeline routes that had been identified fol-lowing baseline studies of local geographies, cities, towns and villages, land use, roads, and railways. Essentially, these were desk studies that drew on maps, local council sur-veys, planning documents, and demographic data, rather than being based on detailed field research to understand local terrain and the built environment or involving thorough social impact assessment. The routes differed slightly because there were some variations to consider, such as alternative crossings of the River Dee and the routing through built up areas. The pipeline will be buried underground at a depth of 1.2 metres or lower. A number of above ground installations will be constructed for its maintenance and operation, including sites where the pipeline will connect to existing industries. The consultations were held so the proponents could hear people's views about the pipeline route options. In October and November 2022, I participated in the pre-application phase of consultations for some of the above ground infrastructure in the form of block valve stations and the laying of new cabling from the Point of Ayr gas terminal to the foreshore alongside the existing gas pipeline.

Listening to and reading through the comments and responses people have made does not reveal much – at least in these early stages of the project – about the public under-standing of decarbonization and, by extension, public anxieties about climate change and the urgency of responding to it. To be fair, the proponents did not wish to have such comment as a primary objective of the consultation process. Indeed, while decarboniza-tion, and the importance of achieving it because of the climate crisis, was introduced briefly at the beginning of each session as the reason behind the project, discussion was moved quickly to the subject of the pipeline route. Again, this has much to do with the fact that it was the pipeline route, not the larger project or even its rationale, that was subject to initial consultation, even if the proponents began each session with a statement about the global climate emergency and the urgency to deal with it. At this stage, the proponents just wanted the views of local residents on the pipeline's route. Not even the pipeline itself as critical infrastructure to support decarbonization efforts was under review – that, they said, would be discussed at a later stage once the actual route had been decided upon (something that may appear to be a backwards strategy).

But, in fact, people did want to talk about both the route and the pipeline itself, as well as the wider project's aims and its cumulative impacts. They also wanted a clearer understanding of the nature, properties, and materiality of carbon dioxide and what happens when it is transported by pipeline and stored underground. Commenting on the route, people expressed concern with what they considered to be a poorly-informed understanding on the part of the proponents of the social and economic nature of the region and its surface and subterranean geographies. Some comments were also critical of how carbon dioxide – the very reason for which the pipeline is to be constructed – was deftly avoided as a topic for discussion. There were concerns over the pipeline, once placed below ground, affecting homes, schools, farms and businesses, property prices, wildlife habitat and environmentally-sensitive areas, worries over the instability and volatility of strata, and anxieties about carbon emissions leaking to the surface.

A criticism from several people in Flintshire, when I asked them their views on the project both at the sessions I attended and during other conversations, was that they had not heard anything at all about HyNet North West nor the pipeline and were not aware of the consultation process, the online sessions and the in-person events. Some said they attended the events because a neighbor or a friend had told them about it. When I mentioned this to project staff at one consultation session, I was told that it was likely explained, in part, because while HyNet North West sent out almost 10,000 letters with information about the project and encouraging participation in the consultation, the letters were only sent to residents and businesses within 500 metres of the pipeline route options and in the vicinity of the existing gas pipeline. They emphasized, however, that HyNet also used social media – mainly Facebook, Twitter and LinkedIn – to raise awareness of the consultation process and to inform people that participation in the online webinars could be booked through Eventbrite. However, as one man in his early 50s said to me about the non-statutory consultation: "I think they've used Covid and lockdown as a way of launching this quietly, knowing they won't get too much opposition if people can only participate online."

In both the online webinars that constituted the non-statutory consultation, and the online sessions and in-person events that made up the statutory element, the pipeline was presented as one crucial element of a larger project that will not only decarbonize industry, but will produce hydrogen for a new ecological modernity – which made it even more curious that this worldmaking venture was not up for discussion. Each session began with a statement about the climate emergency and went on to emphasize that not only will hydrogen be used as a transition fuel for heating, electricity, and transport, as part of the UK's zero-emissions target for 2050, the project will have positive effects for local communities, creating new job opportunities and supporting the region's economic development.

PowerPoint slides supported the technocentric overview of the project, but in the form of a simplified representation for public consumption of a vast network of installations and pipelines. Diagrams and maps showed the locations of industrial CO_2 capture, transportation and storage (including the pipeline and subsea gas reservoirs), low carbon production facilities, hydrogen production and underground storage, industrial hydrogen users, places where hydrogen will be blended for businesses and homes, and where hydrogen would be produced from offshore wind facilities. This style of presentation illustrates what Nicole Starosielski (2015) has termed a strategy of interconnection, by which she means the way projects are described and developed in terms of fixed architectures and spatial practices through which activities and transfers between the various nodes of a network and its surrounding environments can occur.

However, despite this contextualization of the project as a response to the climate crisis, and the representation of HyNet North West as being developed in friction-free, smooth spaces, the larger decarbonization project itself, while explained and visualised, was presented as something that was not up for consultation. It was pointed out that this process would be underway once the government had reviewed the proposals for development – so, to date, there has been no opportunity for public comment on it. Local residents and other stakeholders, as I have already indicated, have only been invited to comment on the pipeline route.

Local Views about the Pipeline

The early public consultation revealed that many people living near the pipeline route in Flintshire appear less immediately concerned about the pipeline as part of a solution to climate change than they are about the local disruption to be caused by its construction and, once operating, about it being an ever-present, hidden environmental risk. Not many appeared to respond to the project's ambition to chart a practical path to an energy transition, and decarbonize the economy, although some did demonstrate understanding and support for the need for decarbonization, while others asked about the environmental impact assessment. There was also criticism of the science and engineering aspects of the project. At one meeting in Connah's Quay, heated discussions took place with the project representatives when a group of attendees expressed their worries and concerns about the pipeline passing close to their homes. One couple, who were farmers, were especially angry that the pipeline would pass through part of their land and that they had been informed that some farm buildings may need to be demolished. Another dairy farmer was concerned that he would be driven out of business because the construction would mean the digging up of his fields – "You may as well write me out a cheque for my house and land now," he told the HyNet staff. Others focused on the danger of leaks from the pipeline. I asked one of the senior project engineers whether many people were asking questions to the proponents about the project as a solution to climate change. He told me no, they weren't, and that he thought they (i.e. the proponents) needed to be clearer on the *why* of the project, and then, he suggested, perhaps people would not be asking too many questions at the public events about the effect on property prices and disruption to their daily lives.

The pipeline also, many people feel, reinforces an attitude the proponents have about northeast Wales, and Flintshire in particular, as a dumping ground for CO_2 emissions. For many people who have so far contributed comments, or expressed an opinion on the pipeline route, climate change does not appear to be the most immediately troubling issue they think about or face. Instead, anxieties over digging up land, the inconvenience of several months of construction along each stretch of pipeline, the effect on property prices, and carbon moving underground near houses, schools, under farms, and resting under the seabed, highlight concerns that the project will have negative social and environmental impacts and will do little to address some of the high levels of social and economic deprivation in the area.

During the consultation phase, people were invited to submit comments on an interactive map of the region on the project website showing the options for the pipeline route. Given the scale of the project, there was not a great response. As of the end of August 2021, 58 people had submitted comments, of which the following, which focus on concerns over construction, noise, the loss of land and wildlife habitat, are representative:

"There are houses and a church at this location. How will these be affected?"

"Planning permission for a new housing development has been granted on this site – how would the pipeline affect this?"

"How much destruction of trees and habit will there be for this new pipeline? What will the land look like afterwards?"

"What impact is this going to have to land now and in the future? What will be the impact of the building work? How will the land look like afterwards? Will this make it more or less appealing to housing developments in the future?"

"Will you confirm that the pipeline will be below the surface so that it can't be seen?"

"Construction impacts on adjacent farmland need to be considered."

"The pipeline in this proposed route runs adjacent to my property and across greenfield land. I am concerned about what surface infrastructure will be needed to support the pipeline, maintenance, disaster recovery, disturbance to local wildlife, flora and fauna and diminished prospects of critical greenbelt land in a historical Cheshire village."

"The pipeline is running through an environment which is full of wildlife, trees and close to very rural housing communities. There is a concern about the impact in the environment and potential for damage to trees, hedgerows and wildlife."

"In this proposed route the pipeline will run adjacent to my property: I am concerned about the level of disruption to the vast number of nesting birds and other wildlife we have in our garden and in the surrounding fields. I oppose this particular route."

"The potential for any noise from the pipeline is also of concern to local residents, for example any hissing sounds which may spoil the quiet of the area."

These comments and responses, as well as the concerns expressed at both in-person and online consultation sessions illustrate what Patrick Devine-Wright (2022) highlights in his research: that the re-making of places by industrial decarbonization projects has profound impacts on the lived experiences and on the sense of belonging, community, and identities of people who live and work in those places.

Worldmaking and the Underground

In the public consultations, people were invited to think themselves into a post-carbon future and how getting there requires their participation in transforming the economy, as well as jobs and homes. However, this was not a process that, so far, has asked them to think critically about, and offer suggestions for amending the scenarios for the kind of post-fossil fuel future that UK government policy and the HyNet North West project is focused on heading towards (cf. Raven and Stripple 2021). The subsurface that the pipeline will be laid through was also presented as a friction-free passage, a deterritorialized space beyond the everyday experience of those living and moving above it. At the in-person consultation sessions held in both Flintshire and Cheshire in March 2022, HyNet North West staff repeated that the disruption will only be minimal during construction, and that "Once the pipeline is in the ground, no-one will notice it is there."

Running through Flintshire's subsurface, the pipeline will carry the harmful, dangerous, atmosphere-clogging, world-destroying emissions of industry away to a deep site of disposal in offshore geological structures. Yet the pipeline will be constructed in a region that is densely populated and industrialized. The section running into and through Flintshire will be in an area that has, as I have described above, a history of heavy industry, from shipbuilding to steelworks, coal mining, brickmaking, lead mining, smelting, and petrochemicals. This history reveals how the subsurface and the surface have been visualised and abstracted in ways that have enabled the development of projects ranging from mines and quarries, and the networks of drainage tunnels that have allowed for the expansion of extractive industry (e.g., Nuttall 2021). Much of the area had seen significant decline in recent decades, despite the development of new industries and enterprise zones. As I mentioned above, the lead mines, collieries, brickworks, rayon mills, and shipyards are long gone, but the industrial ruins, some of which are turned into heritage sites, are experienced by some people I know (relatives included) as haunted workplaces in which memories of labour, toil, class-struggle, and loss persist (see also, Meier 2012). The Airbus aircraft wing factory at Broughton close to the Cheshire border is a major employer and recent investment in the Deeside area has focused on the aerospace sector. But while the project is taking shape in a major industrial region of the UK, it also characterized by industrial decline and environmental ruin in many parts, with significantly large pockets of low-income housing and deprived areas, especially in Flintshire. Many of the skilled jobs in the aerospace sector as well as in the cement works go to people who move to the area or who commute there daily from other parts of North Wales, Cheshire, and Merseyside.

As the pipeline route will have to go largely through built up areas, mainly towns and villages, I was interested during this initial consultation phase in getting a sense of people's understanding of what is presented as a technological entity (made up of the various facilities, infrastructure, and pipeline), the scientific description of carbon and hydrogen, and how they think and talk about carbon and hydrogen as embodied in their communities and indeed their homes. I heard many people make comments, for example, about "having to live with the pipeline," "CO_2 emissions seeping to the surface and affecting our health," the "effect on property prices," and "the pipeline ruining the countryside," while one person asked: "Is there a chance that CO_2 could leak into the surrounding ground?"

As one person commented on one of the route options that would be near their home,

"This route is unacceptable and passes directly through residential gardens and close to both a pre-school and a primary school. I am concerned about the presence of a high pressure pipeline so close to houses and schools and do not support this route."

Others expressed similar concerns, for example:

"In this proposed route the pipeline will run adjacent to or very close to the local village primary school. I am concerned about risks of gradual or catastrophic leaks of CO_2, which can have harmful effects on human health. A gradual leakage would compromise the initial objective of removing CO_2 from the atmosphere. I am concerned about the decreased level of surface structure, maintenance and general disruption to this otherwise peaceful school and preschool setting. I would suggest changing the route to avoid running the pipeline close to the school."

"Very concerned that pressure caused putting this back underground can cause earthquakes as off Spain's failed gas storage."

And responding to discussion on the hydrogen pipeline, one person made this comment:

"This is near to the estate I live in. I'm really concerned about the safety of hydrogen pipelines, particularly the impact of an adverse incident such as the release of hydrogen which could result in a fire or an explosion. Academic research on the subject suggests it is absolutely necessary to conduct a risk analysis and determine the range of zones of potential hazards. I'd like to see the map updated to show risk zones and some thought given to whether overall current routing near habitation is a good idea."

During one of the online sessions in November 2022 for the pre-application phase of the above ground infrastructure in the form of block valve stations, one participant asked if an independent assessment had been made of "the geological ability and stability of CCS." The question was dealt with swiftly and neatly by referring participants to the environmental impact assessment materials that are available online.

For the proponents of the HyNet North West project the underground is as Kearnes and Rikhards (2017) put it, a site for the realization of a hoped-for environmental future. It is viewed as a space for unmaking and becoming, where major industrial complexes can dispose of CO_2 emissions and enable the distribution of hydrogen that will allow for the development of renewable energy systems that are needed for the post-carbon world. Both CO_2 and hydrogen will need to be transported by pipelines, but for different reasons. While CO_2 will be extracted, transported, and buried in depleted gas reservoirs and will be disposed of deep within the earth, hydrogen will be transported and stored in salt caverns for future use, re-emerging from these subterranean spaces as a hopeful solution when needed. Salt caverns are currently considered by electrochemical engineers and geologists to offer a safe underground storage option – rock salt, they contend, has a large sealing capacity and salt structures are inert, which prevents contamination of the stored hydrogen (Caglayan et al. 2020).

In this way, the subterranean is "presented as a tantalizingly straight-forward 'future solution' to a contemporary problem" (Kearnes and Rikhards ibid.: 51) – even if, as some research suggests, storing hydrogen in salt caverns does actually pose some significant risk and there are uncertainties as to whether the composition of salt structures can, inevitably, be altered by the presence and action of hydrogen (e.g., Portarapillo et al. 2021). Yet contrary to this positioning of the underground as a solution to the problem of the transport and disposal of CO_2 emissions, many who have expressed views about the pipeline and its route think that Flintshire's subsurface and the seabed have been designated as sacrifice zones (cf. Kuletz 1998), while voicing an opinion that northeast Wales will not benefit from the economic growth and job creation opportunities the project promises. In February 2023, I had several conversations with people in the Deeside area who expressed their frustration about this. Their general opinion is that the offshore gas reservoirs would be waste repositories for the by-products of industrial activity, with the emissions pipeline running through areas of environmental ruin and social deprivation. Both the consultation process and the discussions I have had with local people reveal concerns and anxieties that Flintshire, again as many expressed it, is only considered useful to the project as a space for subsurface transit and as a dumping ground for CO_2.

Conclusions

Climate change makes demands of us to think of ourselves as agents of planetary transformation. In doing so, we are called upon to identify those human activities and actions that can be defined as contemporary problems, and which need to be managed with particular urgency. Anthropologists and other social scientists have examined how carbon becomes central to this process of reflection and to environmental policy and governance. They have written about carbon offsetting and sequestration, carbon trading initiatives, economic transitions, and conservation (Leach and Scoones 2015; Lyons and Westoby 2014; Paladino and Fiske 2017; Urry 2013), but they also call for understanding carbon as an ethnographic object and stress the need to identify, trace, and follow its many forms (e.g., Whitington 2016a, 2016b).

Carbon is abundant. It flows through all living organisms and moves between the atmosphere and the deep ocean by way of the carbon cycle. Most of it is stored below ground in the Earth's crust, but it permeates the human world. It is not only to be defined and understood in terms of physical processes, but as something implicated firmly and deeply in social, economic, and political life. This includes paying attention to its vitality and liveliness, or its vibrant matter (cf. Bennett 2010). Jane Bennett's argument is that vitality is "the capacity of things– edibles, commodities, storms, metals – not only to impede or block the will and designs of humans but also to act as quasi agents or forces with trajectories, propensities, or tendencies of their own" (ibid.: viii). Anthropology has a contribution to make in understanding the materialities and flows of carbon, as well as its vibrant and dangerous encounters with human and non-human entities. And we also need to be attentive to the materialities and flows of carbon emissions. Gökçe Günel (2016) has written about how some CCS professionals do not think about carbon dioxide as a waste product or dangerous material, but as a neutral gas which has tremendous possibilities as a commodity or as a drilling additive in the oil and gas industry. Anna Pasek (2021) calls an element of this way of thinking "carbon vitalism," which she argues is a strain of climate denial that casts carbon dioxide as the stuff of life itself rather than pollution.

Industrial decarbonization is presented not just as a solution to climate change, but as a worldmaking process. Abram, Horsfall, and Crossland (2020) contend, though, that only focusing on decarbonization obscures a choice between different energy pathways, while Sovacool et al. (2019) caution that decarbonization, although bringing net social benefits, can also exacerbate social and economic vulnerabilities. Drawing on case studies from France, Germany, Ghana, and the Democratic Republic of the Congo, Sovacool et al. (2021) trace how decarbonization pathways are linked to negative impacts within specific communities and call for greater policy attention to be given to addressing such vulnerabilities, while research by Lansing (2012) in Costa Rica argues that strategies for carbon offsets have a performative aspect to them that is characterized by uneven power relations. Some of the concerns expressed by people in Flintshire about the decarbonization pipeline were feelings that the HyNet North West project would not benefit many in northeast Wales. Jobs, it is claimed, will be generated in Cheshire in the carbon capture process as well as in the hydrogen plant, but many people had questions about what jobs would be created in Flintshire.

To protect the atmosphere – and to ensure the integrity of planetary boundaries – decarbonization (and hydrogen) projects are presented by their proponents, such as Hynet North West, in a way that tell us that we must look to the underground as a site that is necessary for worldmaking (cf. Kearnes and Rikhards ibid.). However, while this technological deployment of a pipeline as one element of a decarbonization assemblage is celebrated for how it will re-make a region and beyond (cf. Devine-Wright 2022), the local responses to it so far reveal anxieties that suggest many people who live in the region – and who are engaged in place-making – have concerns and worries over the impacts on everyday life, on communities, on health, and on local environments. This may have much to do with the way the project has been promoted and communicated, and with the difficulty of getting the right kind of information many feel they need. It may also reveal something about how climate change is not necessarily an everyday concern. Regardless, these local responses, so far at least, appear to be indicative of more immediate preoccupations than a widespread support for the stated ambitions of economic prosperity, a net-zero future, and the solutions to climate change the project promises it will realize.

Notes

1 See: https://www.gov.uk/government/publications/the-ten-point-plan-for-a-green-industrial-revolution and https://www.gov.uk/government/publications/energy-white-paper-powering-our-net-zero-future (both accessed 26 April 2022).
2 San Francisco's Climate Action Plan 2021: Available at https://www.sfcta.org/blogs/san-francis co-climate-action-plan-roadmap-net-zero-emissions.
3 On its website, Airbus states that "Today, we know our love of air travel also comes at a cost: the aviation industry represents approximately 2.5% of global human-induced CO_2 emissions. But aviation is not the problem. Emissions are the problem." https://www.airbus.com/en/sustainability/respecting-the-planet/decarbonisation (accessed 26 July 2021).
4 HyNet North West, https://hynet.co.uk/ (accessed 26 April 2022)
5 Press release, "28 organisations commit to switching to UK-produced low carbon hydrogen from HyNet" https://hynet.co.uk/28-organizations-commit-to-switching-to-uk-produced-low-carbon-hy drogen-from-hynet/ (accessed 22 April 2022).

Acknowledgement

The early research on which this chapter is based was funded by the Henry Marshall Tory Chair research program in the Department of Anthropology, University of Alberta.

References

Abram, Simone, Alton Horsfall, and Andrew Crossland. 2020. "'Decarbonisation' may be the wrong goal for energy – here's why." *The Conversation*October 28, 2020, https://theconversation.com/decarbonisation-may-be-the-wrong-goal-for-energy-heres-why-148388.

Bandilla, Karl W. 2020. "Carbon capture and storage." In Trevor M.Letcher (ed.) *Future Energy: Improved, sustainable and clean options for our planet*. Amsterdam: Elsevier, pp. 669–692.

Barker, Andrew, Héléne Blake, Filipo MariaD'Arcangelo, and Patrick Lenain. 2022. *Towards Net Zero Emissions in Denmark*. OECD Economics Department Working Papers No. 1705. Paris: OECD.

Bennett, Jane. 2010. *Vibrant Matter: A political ecology of things*. Durham and London: Duke University Press.

Deutch, John. 2020. "Is net zero carbon 2050 possible?" *Joule* 4 (11): 2237–2240.

Devine-Wright, Patrick. 2022. "Decarbonisation of industrial clusters: a place-based research agenda." *Energy Research & Social Science* 91, 102725.

Caglayan, Dilara Gulcin, Nikolaus Weber, Heidi Heinrichs, Jochen Linßen, Martin Robinius, Peter A. Kukla and Detlef Stolten. 2020. "Technical potential of salt caverns for hydrogen storage in Europe." *International Journal of Hydrogen Energy* 45 (1): 6793–6805.

Günel, Gökçe. 2016. "What is carbon dioxide? When is carbon dioxide?" *PoLAR: Political and Legal Anthropology Review* 39 (1): 33–45.

IEA. 2021. *Net Zero by 2050: A roadmap for the global energy sector*. Paris: International Energy Agency.

Kearnes, Matthew and Lauren Rikhards. 2017. "Earthly graves for environmental futures: techno-burial practices." *Futures* 92: 48–58.

Kuletz, Valerie. 1998. *The Tainted Desert: Environmental and social ruin in the American West*. London and New York: Routledge.

Lansing, David M. 2012. "Performing carbon's materiality: the production of carbon offsets and the framing of exchange." *Environment and Planning A: Economy and Space* 44: 204–220.

Leach, Melissa and Ian Scoones (eds.). 2015. *Carbon Conflicts and Forest Landscapes in Africa*. London and New York: Routledge.

Lyons, Kristen and Peter Westoby. 2014. "Carbon colonialism and the new land grab: plantation forestry in Uganda and its livelihood impacts." *Journal of Rural Studies* 36: 13–21.

Marker, Margaret E. 1967. "The Dee Estuary: its progressive silting and salt marsh development." *Transactions of the Institute of British Geographers* 41: 55–71.

Meier, Lars. 2012. "Encounters with haunted industrial workplaces and emotions of loss: class-related senses of place within the memories of metalworkers." *Cultural Geographies* 20 (4): 467–483.

NEA. 2019. *The Costs of Decarbonisation: System costs with high shares of nuclear and renewables*. Paris: OECD Publishinghttps://doi.org/10.1787/9789264312180-en.

Nuttall, Mark. 2020. "Lead mining, conservation and heritage: shaping a mountain in Northeast Wales." *Humanities* 9 (3): 70; https://doi.org/10.3390/h9030070.

Nuttall, Mark. 2021. "Visualising the subterranean: tunnels and flows beneath a Welsh lead mining landscape." In Marko Krevs (ed.) *Hidden Geographies*. Cham: Springer, pp. 193–213.

Paladino, Stephanie and Shirley J. Fiske (eds.). 2017. *The Carbon Fix: Forest carbon, social justice, and environmental governance*. New York and London: Routledge.

Pasek, Anna. 2021. "Carbon vitalism: life and the body in climate denial." *Environmental Humanities* 13 (1): 1–20. https://doi.org/10.1215/22011919-8867175.

Portarapillo, Maria and Almerinda Di Benedetto. 2021. "Risk assessment of the large-scale hydrogen storage in salt caverns." *Energies* 14, 2856. https://doi.org/10.3390/en14102856.

Raven, Paul Graham and Johannes Stripple. 2021. "Touring the carbon ruins: towards an ethics of speculative decarbonisation." *Global Discourse* 11 (1–2):221–240.

Rosenow, Jan. 2022. "Is heating homes with hydrogen all but a pipe dream? An evidence review." *Joule* 6 (10): 2225–2228.

Sovacool, Benjamin K., Mari Martiskainen, Andrew Hook, and Lucy Bell. 2019. "Decarbonisation and its discontents: a critical energy justice perspective on four low-carbon transitions." *Climatic Change* 155: 581–619. https://doi.org/10.1007/s10584-019-02521-7.

Sovacool, Benjamin K., Bruno Turnheim, Andrew Hook, Andrea Brock and Mari Martiskainen. 2021. "Dispossessed by decarbonisation: reducing vulnerability, injustice, and inequality in the lived experience of low-carbon pathways." *World Development* 137https://doi.org/10.1016/j.worlddev.2020.105116.

Starosielski, Nicole. 2015. *The Undersea Network: Sign, storage, transmission*. Durham, NC and London: Duke University Press.

Stephenson, Michael. 2018. *Energy and Climate Change: An introduction to geological controls, interventions and mitigations*. Amsterdam: Elsevier.

Stobart, Jon. 2004. *The First Industrial Region: North-West England c. 1700–60*. Manchester: Manchester University Press.

Stripple, Johannes and Harriet Bulkeley. 2019. "Towards a material politics of socio-technical transitions: navigating decarbonisation pathways in Malmö." *Political Geography* 72: 52–63.

Urry, John. 2013. "A low carbon economy and society." *Philosophical Transactions of the Royal Society A* 371: 20110566. http://dx.doi.org/10.1098/rsta.2011.0566.

Whitington, Jerome. 2016a "Carbon. Theorizing the contemporary." *Fieldsights*, April 6. https://culanth.org/fieldsights/carbon.

Whitington, Jerome. 2016b. "Carbon as a metric of the human." *PoLAR: Political and Legal Anthropology Review* 39 (1): 46–63.

WIMD. 2019. *Welsh Index of Multiple Deprivation (WIMD) Results Report*. Cardiff: Statistics for Wales, Welsh Government.

Zhao, Xin, Xiaowei Ma, Boyang Chen, Yuping Shang, and Malin Song. 2022. "Challenges toward carbon neutrality in China: strategies and countermeasures." *Resources Conservation and Recycling* 176, 105959https://doi.org/10.1016/j.resconrec.2021.105959.

18

REPRESENTATION AND LUCK

Reflections on Climate and Collaboration in Shishmaref, Alaska

Dennis Davis and Elizabeth Marino

Introduction of Authors and Why we take Pictures and Write

This chapter is about collaboration, representation, and what has risen to the surface as meaningful and critical in the wake of living with, and studying, climate change in Shishmaref, Alaska. Dennis Davis is an Iñupiat photographer, videographer, and 26-year resident of Shishmaref. He was born and raised up the coast in Kotzebue, Alaska, and his family has deep roots in Shishmaref. Elizabeth Marino is a white, non-Indigenous anthropologist trained at the University of Alaska Fairbanks, who has been working (off and on) in Shishmaref, Alaska since the early 2000s. Both authors have created images, words, and presentations that show how Shishmaref has been affected by climate change, how the community is responding, and how both colonial histories and the lack of contemporary funding and investment by state and federal governments creates risk.

This chapter focuses on how community representation matters; and how understanding community needs and perspectives is a central necessity of combatting climate change. We also believe that lessons learned and wisdom found in Shishmaref are applicable and meaningful for the rest of the world in our collective struggle to grapple with the outcomes of a changing climate and structural inequities. There is some controversy in saying this – Indigenous wisdom has long been simplified, romanticized, and extracted for the commodification and benefit of others. Our work is primarily dedicated to the ongoing strength, survival, and sovereignty of *Kigiqtamiut* people. We likewise believe that the cultural insights of elders, and subsistence practices found in Shishmaref, are a fiercely insightful example of sustainable and respectful human/non-human relationships and can compel non-*Kigiqtamiut* people towards self-introspection, material reckoning, and sustainable living. The main points of this chapter are: 1) that changes due to anthropocentric climate change are happening at a rapid rate in Shishmaref and are observed by residents and scientists alike; 2) that many journalists, filmmakers, and researchers have written about climate change in Shishmaref, often focusing on the narrative of a harsh environment harming Indigenous, Arctic peoples;

DOI: 10.4324/9781003242499-22

3) and that Iñupiat philosophical concepts that have arisen in our work, such as "luck" and "beauty" are important starting points for understanding how to move forward with climate change solutions, and more pluralistic discourses.

Methods

All photographs and their captions in this photo essay are the work of Dennis Davis. These photographs are part of an exhibition called "Our Knowledge is Power," a collective exhibit from Dennis and artist and curator Chantel Lady Dolphin Cormadel. It is hosted online by the Jean Charles Choctaw Nation of coastal Louisiana and featured here (http://www.isledejeancharles.com/museum-exhibit). This chapter was primarily drafted by Elizabeth Marino. Dennis and Elizabeth have been in conversation for over three years, working together on a grant from the National Science Foundation (NSF). As part of this work, Dennis and Elizabeth have given many collaborative presentations about Shishmaref, including about Dennis's photographs and the reasons Dennis is taking photos and talking to outsiders about Shishmaref. Some of these collaborative conversations have been recorded. For this chapter, Elizabeth has rendered these conversations into text. Dennis has reviewed the chapter, made changes and comments, and then the entire chapter was edited and submitted for publication. The project has been approved by the Shishmaref IRA, the City of Shishmaref, the Shishmaref Native Corporation, and the Elders' Council – but this chapter has only been vetted by the authors. A longer publication which includes interviews by elders and community members in Shishmaref is forthcoming.

Climate Change in Shishmaref

Shishmaref, Alaska is a 600-person village on the western coast of Alaska. The community is predominantly *Iñupiat*, a word that translates into *Inu* meaning person; and the clause *'piat'* which loosely translates into 'real' with the 't' marking 3 or more plural. Shishmaref has traditionally been called *Kigiqtaq*, or island, in Iñupiat. The community is now mostly comprised of families whose ancestors lived up and down the coast, moving between staging seal mammal hunts on a stretch of barrier sand islands, and then going slightly inland for river fishing, land mammal hunting, and berry and plant gathering. These seasonal migrations of people, animals, and land use areas were a thoughtful and adaptive economic and social system that was capable of withstanding changes in ecology and coastal dynamics. Colonial intrusion began in the region at the end of the nineteenth and beginning of the twentieth centuries. A rapid combination of development, forced schooling policies, the 1918 influenza pandemic, and other forms of violence transitioned the community. Today, most families that Elizabeth knows from Shishmaref and Dennis is related to and knows from Shishmaref, live year-round in the village. However, most people continue travel over the ice in the spring, and over the landscape via rivers in the summer, in order to practice subsistence and put food away for the winter.

The Arctic has experienced climate change at a higher rate than the rest of the globe as has long been recorded (ACIA 2004). These regional changes have local effects. They include increased storminess and windiness, later freezing of ocean ice, earlier breakup, rain in late

FIGURE 18.1 Breakup: May 28, 2016. I took this picture during breakup of the ocean ice, when I was trying to find a trail for people to go out birding. They were going across the channel. With the drone I can see where all the rotten ice is and make and find a better trail for them. It's the same thing for when they go out *ugruk* (bearded seal) hunting, I can make the best trail for them, going out. (Dennis Davis)

winter and early spring, and flooding (ACIA 2004; Dennis Davis experiential knowledge). Ongoing flooding, especially since the 1970s has made *Kigiqtamiut* people consider relocation as an adaptation strategy, if the island's integrity becomes compromised and sea walls and other revetments are not able to protect it against significant erosion. This is a difficult decision – as seal and other sea mammal hunts are staged from the island and moving inland means a significant increase in the cost and logistics of these hunts; and possible complications with the preservation of foods because of different winds and temperatures further inland.

Representation and Ventriloquism in Shishmaref

Shishmaref has been featured in over a hundred news articles, news segments on television, national and international documentary films, and has been the subject of multiple research projects. Dennis believes that about half of these representations have been done by good people with good intentions; and that the outcomes are mostly positive. There is a strong sense among some people in Shishmaref that after many years (1970s–2000s) of trying to get attention and funding to the community for disaster relief and sea wall protection, that getting the word out about Shishmaref and climate change is important. Journalists, documentary films, and research can be successful in doing this. Among our colleagues, friends, and family in Shishmaref there is also the observation that people who cover climate change in Shishmaref are doing so to make money, and do not care enough about the community.

FIGURE 18.2 *Make America Native Again.* I was actually doing a little photo shoot – what better kid to use than your own? I liked that I caught my son in mid-air. Did you notice the hats? They say *Make America Native Again* – the hat bill and beanie. This one shirt says, ban the books – when Portugal. The Man stood up for the kids in Wasilla. The other one is Austin City Limits – the first time PTM played Austin City Limits. PTM is from Alaska and they are friends of mine. (Dennis Davis)

In approximately half of journalists' stories, according to our friends and colleagues, there can also be more problematic types of misrepresentation. Journalists can use Shishmaref as a foil – a way to tell a story they already had written and already wanted to tell before ever speaking to a Shishmaref community-member. This is a kind of ventriloquism, a phenomenon that Carol Farbotko and Heather Lazrus (2012) have written about in relationship to climate change and Tuvalu. Ventriloquism in this context is the use of an emotionally salient story by a person of greater privilege, to convey the thoughts and belief structures of the privileged person under the guise of a more emotionally salient person or community, often someone rhetorically constructed as "victim." Farbotko and Lazrus (2012) in particular point to ways in which "immanent climate refugees" are dispatched by western news outlets as a way to "present a particular (western) 'crisis of nature'" that speaks much more to the west's anxiety than to the lived experiences, philosophical position, or adaptive strategies of the communities being covered.

This type of representation ruptures any real collaboration between the outside journalist, filmmaker, or researcher with individuals in Shishmaref. In the case of Indigenous communities these representations can be extractive. What is the line between disaster voyeurism and care? In this case, is climate suffering a colonial extraction? Research-based, and journalist-based ventriloquism around issues of climate and inequity is pervasive, and simplifies the stories, histories, and needs of people on the ground. Participating in theoretical trends in anthropology, or creating clickable headlines in newspapers, can all be powerful incentives for researchers and journalists to put their own words and ideologies into the mouths of frontline community members; and the stories they tell about Shishmaref. Elizabeth remembers a time when, being interviewed about her work, a journalist demanded: "just tell me if 'they' are climate refugees or not," referring to community members in Shishmaref.

Is it ever appropriate for outsiders to tell Shishmaref stories? In the early days of Elizabeth's work, a government report came out that claimed that extreme erosion in rural Alaskan communities was a difficult problem to solve because these communities were "easy to ignore." Attracting the attention of journalists is one way community members in Shishmaref have wrestled attention from institutions that found them "easy to ignore." Social science analysis has helped publicly describe the systematic and historical mechanisms that cause climate change impacts to be inequitably distributed. However, most of this work (social science research and journalism) is built from listening to, collecting, and synthesizing the experiences and stories of others. How does anyone do this work, and recognize diverse positionalities, without replicating the ventriloquism trap?

Beauty Comes First

One thing Dennis, Elizabeth, and our collaborators have discussed is that when outsiders talk about Shishmaref, or other communities that are disproportionately suffering under climate impacts, the images used and evoked are almost always negative. Julian Rebotier has written about how the power of identifying a place as risky is a power of naming (Rebotier 2012), of isolating the character of a place to a discreet set of identities. Places

FIGURE 18.3 *Nigiitchiak* (Rainbow). This photo is awesome because you've got the rainbow, but you've got all the racks with meat (*ugruk*, bearded seal). It's not a pot of gold, but it's a pot of food. That's the way I was looking at it, you're not getting gold, but you're getting food for the winter. It's food for the future; and I'd rather have food than gold. The picture is exactly the way it was – it was perfect because you can see it's dark on one side and light on one side. Taste the rainbow, literally. (Dennis Davis)

like Shishmaref, and Isle de Jean Charles, have borne the burden of narrativizing and "humanizing" climate change; of "making climate change real" as a way of garnering increased political and public interest in climate change mitigation and adaptation policy. In doing so, the "naming" of Shishmaref can focus on the negative – the flooding, the isolation of extremely rural places, even of cultures that have been historically harmed. When our collaborative research group got together to talk about an art exhibit focused on climate change in Shishmaref and Isle de Jean Charles, produced and curated by community members, what first rose to the top was notions of "beauty." Our first of five themes in the exhibit is beauty; and when we talk about the islands, both in Louisiana and in Alaska, beauty is always part of the conversation.

Closely tied to the theme of beauty, is the theme of knowledge and power. In many talks over the last two years, Dennis has discussed elders as the center of power and knowing because of their ability to survive *anything*. There have been many critiques of resilience in the social sciences (Barrios 2016), ones that Elizabeth feels are necessary and right. But when Dennis talks about survival as the culmination of knowledge and power, he ascribes a material and relational redefining of resilience. One outcome of this knowledge and power, as the image above suggests, is a creation of beauty. Identifying beauty as a method of getting to representational justice, material resilience, and right relations with the more than human world is something Elizabeth has thought deeply about since working with Dennis and encountering his art and photography.

Luck as Climate Change and Representational Solutions

"Luck" is a word that is powerful and infinitely complex in Shishmaref. Although it will not be fully described or conveyed here, it is a structuring and growing part of our understanding of moral action. Hopefully the concept will continue to be theorized and incorporated into ongoing philosophical conversations by Iñupiat philosophers and thinkers for hundreds of years to come. In some cases, "luck" is used to convey the inevitable "out-of-one's-hands- ness" about the world and future. Talking about the future as predictable, measurable, or certain can be both foolish and dangerous. Outlining expectations for the future renders one blind to the many agentive and powerful forces that exist on their own and outside of human control. To have had luck in hunting is to have been ready, to have shown respect to the animal, to have been ethically worthy, and to have had the animal act in a way that allowed you to hunt. To have luck is to be responsible, respectful, worthy, practiced, and trained – but ultimately not in control.

This idea of having luck to address climate change, Elizabeth believes, is deeply unsettling to many people, including herself. It seems to displace responsibility for one's actions into the hazy and depoliticized conception of fate that exists within many western traditions. What Elizabeth has gradually come to realize is how responsibility and preparedness are internalized within the Iñupiat concept of luck, as it is used in Shishmaref. To have prepared and be on a precipice of unknowing, she would now argue, is an ultimate expression of both responsibility and humility, which may then produce the necessary psychological and material conditions for preparing for and mitigating climate change.

Luck is a moral condition that has changed the structure of our research collaborative, a shifting group of front line community members, researchers, and law experts who look for ways to bring justice to story-telling, policy, and science. Dennis and Elizabeth

FIGURE 18.4 *Respect.* This is on a musk ox hunt; and my son is just paying his respects to the musk ox. I thought that was an awesome shot. He's thanking the musk ox, just like me. I thank every animal after I get them. I thank them for feeding my family. It's the only way to do it. We had to haul this back a quarter mile to the boat, and that really sucked! We butchered this one right there and hauled it out. It was a big old bull, and you really don't want to get a musk ox at the opening of the season. You want to get a musk ox in the winter time. In the spring they taste like that old ladies' perfume – musky old lady's perfume. My grandma used to wear this perfume – you can smell it, you can taste it. (Dennis Davis)

are part of, and co-founders of, this group. Whether our collaborations work, whether we are all available on any given zoom meeting, whether we gather in a mindset that allows us to be creative or distracted, whether we replicate or subvert racialized and hegemonic inequities in our collaborations – some of these things are out of our control. When a storm disrupts internet service, when friends and family pass away, when IRB wants to "make sure" a tribally appointed collaborator meets their standards of expert – these affect our project and we do not always have control over them. To say in particular that we need luck for equity feels earth-shatteringly precarious; but it has also been true. If we are truly committed to equity, racial justice, and tribal sovereignty, then this realization should make us more prepared to seize upon (and not postpone) moments when we can act to forward these fundamental beliefs. This realization makes us all the *more* responsible if it *is* within our grasp to subvert historical and racialized power dynamics and we fail to do it. This project has been made and remade many times over – in part because we recognize the shifting nature of the world around us. It also makes us patient for things coming in their right time. This is largely antithetical to funded scientific projects which are often institutionally conceived of as linear, with annual goals and budgetary timelines; but we have been the opposite of lazy. We have produced the unexpected. This has been partially due to situations out of our control, and partially due to our readiness to act in right relations, with the places and opportunities in which we find ourselves. We do not know ultimately everything that is to come from this project, but are preparing ourselves and working on building robust knowledge sets and relationships so that we will hopefully survive whatever we encounter ahead, and that what we produce will be beautiful.

The concepts of beauty and luck give us some direction in how to envision representational politics as well. If justice within the academy and within journalistic institutions is growing, then we should expect the emergence of radically divergent and pluralistic sets of anthropological theory. We should expect unusual journalism, in both form and content. We should have the humility to not pre-suppose. Dennis and Elizabeth are committed to "getting the word out" about what is happening in Shishmaref with climate change. We see this as a critical "clap back" to the measurable violence and neglect that has happened and continues to happen in rural Alaska under the colonial state. We are also willing to accept that we cannot tell what will happen next, or even if our efforts are in vain. Instead of certainty, we will keep doing our best, and, with luck, we will enjoy the ride.

Note: All photographs in this essay remain copyrighted to Dennis Davis, not the editors or publishers of this book and cannot be reprinted without permission by the artist.

References

ACIA (Arctic Climate Impact Assessment). 2004. "Impacts of a warming Arctic: Arctic Climate Impact Assessment". https://acia.amap.no/.

Barrios, Roberto. 2016. "Resilience: a commentary from the vantage point of anthropology." *Annals of Anthropological Practice* 40 (1): 28–38.

Farbotko, Carol and Heather Lazrus. 2012. "The first climate refugees? Contesting global narratives of climate change in Tuvalu." *Global Environmental Change* 22 (2): 382–390.

Rebotier, Julien. 2012. "Vulnerability conditions and risk representations in Latin-America: framing the territorializing urban risk." *Global Environmental Change* 22 (2): 391–398.

19

AGRICULTURAL INTENSIFICATION IN NORTHERN BURKINA FASO

Smallholder Adaptation to Climate Change

Colin Thor West and Carla Roncoli

To most outsiders, the northern Central Plateau region of Burkina Faso looks degraded. There are widespread gullies, vast areas of bare soil, and fields filled with dead trees. Scholars of Sahelian West Africa have long considered this area to be a classic example of desertification. During the severe Sahelian drought of 1968–72, the northern Central Plateau figured prominently in the formulation of desertification as a scientific concept. In fact, a 1980 report by the Sahel Club and Permanent Interstate Committee for Drought Control in the Sahel (CILSS) specifically noted the following:

> Rainfed agriculture continues to be largely "extensive and traditional" and features a particularly unequal distribution of the population (overpopulation in the Senegalese Peanut Basin, the Mossi Plateau…[Central Plateau] and a general stagnation of farming and soil productivity…), increasingly lands are becoming overexploited and degraded. *The Sahel has started to consume its land capital – seriously compromising its future.*
> (BAN 1980 20578 – *translated from the French by the author; italics appear in original*)

In more recent years, scientific understandings of desertification on the northern Central Plateau have shifted and the region is now strongly associated with environmental restoration and rehabilitation (Cherlet et al. 2018). Households have widely adopted improved soil and water conservation (SWC) measures that have transformed their degraded landscapes (Reij et al. 2005). This chapter combines local accounts of environmental change with geographic data to compare the adoption of SWC in two study areas. In terms of the above quote, agriculture on the northern Central Plateau is now decidedly "intensive," but still "traditional" and large areas are no longer "degraded," but now "rehabilitated." This process of intensification, however, varies geographically and has produced different environmental outcomes. Notably, extensive SWC interventions in the Commune of Kongoussi have produced positive regional patterns of vegetation productivity (i.e., "greening"). In the other study area, the northern Commune of Boulsa, the adoption of SWC is not widespread, vegetation trends are not positive, and, in fact, some

DOI: 10.4324/9781003242499-23

areas exhibit negative vegetation trends (i.e., "browning"). These differences are due to variations in the amounts of institutional support for environmental development.

Research Context

We have both conducted climate change research in the northern Central Plateau region for decades. Our ethnographic fieldwork has been mostly intermittent and short-term (with the exception of twelve months of dissertation research by Colin Thor West in 2004). We have worked primarily in Mossi rural communities. West has focused in the Commune of Kongoussi in the Province of Bam and Carla Roncoli worked in the Commune of Boulsa in the Province of Namentenga (Figure 19.1). Roncoli established field sites in 1997 as part of an interdisciplinary National Oceanic and Atmospheric Administration (NOAA) project on the potential use of seasonal climate forecasts for improved agricultural decision-making (Roncoli et al. 2001). She and her host-country collaborators documented the ways in which households adapt to climate variability (Roncoli et al. 1999). Building on this scholarship, West selected Kongoussi because unlike Boulsa, it was one of the epicenters of SWC development projects on the northern Central Plateau.

This chapter integrates our ethnographic accounts of environmental change and adaptation with longitudinal geographic data on precipitation, land-use/land-cover (LULC) change, and regional vegetation trends. The analysis is comparative and explores how the process of agricultural intensification differs between study areas and what effects this difference has had on regional patterns of vegetation productivity.

The Northern Central Plateau

The Central Plateau is an elevated plain that encompasses nearly one-third of Burkina Faso. Mossi are the dominant ethnolinguistic group in terms of population and political

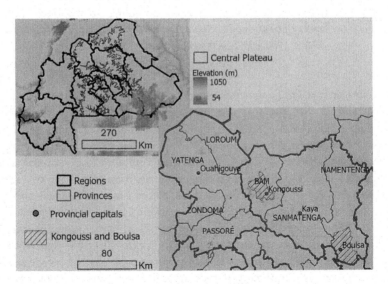

FIGURE 19.1 Burkina Faso (top-left) and northern Central Plateau (bottom-right).

organization. The plateau formed the core of five Mossi kingdoms and Mossi traditional chiefs exert political authority alongside state structures. In fact, the Central Plateau is often referred to as the "Mossi Plateau" (see quote above) for exactly these reasons (see Izard 1985). The northern Central Plateau from roughly 13° N to 15° N is considered the most vulnerable area of Burkina Faso, suffers from chronic seasonal food insecurity, and has historically been the site of famines. For these reasons, it has been a distinct region within the country for research and for SWC interventions (Reij and Thiombiano 2003).

Droughts, Desiccation, and Desertification

For decades the West African Sahel has figured prominently in climate change research. The Sahel is a wide semi-arid biogeographic region usually defined by the 200 mm and 700 mm rainfall isohyets. Between 1968 and 1972, it was struck by a severe and prolonged drought. Decreased rainfall destroyed crops, devastated herds, and caused widespread famines (Franke and Chasin 1980). Meteorologist Jules Charney coined the term "desertification" in 1975 to refer to the process by which human land-use practices (extensive agriculture, deforestation, and overgrazing) removed vegetative cover, which increased surface albedo and decreased regional rainfall in a vicious biophysical feedback whereby the "desert feeds back upon itself" (Charney 1975: 193). Concerned world leaders convened at the first United Nations Conference on Desertification (UNCOD) in Nairobi, Kenya in 1977 that eventually led to the United Nations Convention to Combat Desertification (UNCCD) ratified in 1994 (Behnke and Mortimore 2016). The UNCCD catalyzed many large-scale development projects in the northern Central Plateau discussed in greater detail below.

Severe and prolonged droughts re-occurred in 1982–1985. With additional meteorological data, scientists concluded that the region underwent a 30-year period of decreased annual precipitation, which came to be known as "Sahelian desiccation" (Nicholson 2001). Climatologist Mike Hulme stated, "The African Sahel provides the most dramatic example of multi-decadal climate variability that has been quantitatively and directly measured" (Hulme 2001: 19). Between 1970 and 2000 climate fundamentally changed for people, animals, and plants in the Sahel. Climatologists attribute this long-term drying trend to global climate change. Global warming altered ocean sea surface temperatures that disrupted regional rainfall patterns. Conditions were dryer, droughts occurred more frequently, and these droughts were both more severe and prolonged. Contemporary landscapes and livelihoods need to be understood as a response to desiccation and droughts.

The chart below shows departures from the 1991–2020 mean annual precipitation for the Center-North Region of Burkina Faso, which encompasses both study areas. The chart shows the extreme droughts of the 1970s and 1980s and desiccation is also evident from 1970 through 2002. Figure 19.2 also indicates a "rainfall recovery" of increased precipitation from 2002 through the present, which is recognized by climatologists. These scientists note, however, that this is total "annual" rainfall but the distribution of precipitation during the rainy season continues to be highly variable. Though desiccation has "ended" in the Sahel, climate change persists in the form of highly erratic rainfall and particularly long dry periods during the rainy season.

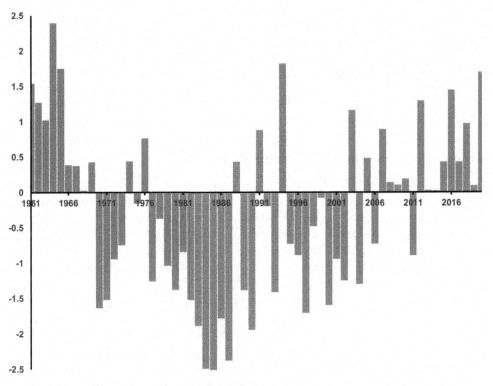

FIGURE 19.2 Departures from 1991–2020 mean Annual Precipitation for Center-North Region, BF.
Source: World Bank Climate Change Knowledge Portal

Residents remember these droughts and sense that their climate changed for an entire generation (West et al. 2008). Climate change also had an effect on the landscape. When talking about droughts in the 1970s, older Mossi rural producers state that for three years, the lack of rainfall severely affected vegetation. As one elder told us, "People couldn't even gather the wild grasses they use to construct *greniers* (Fr. – granaries). Erosion began to occur and gullies expanded. In fact, trees died and fell into the gulches!" (kon_03_030812).[1] Another older male stated that lakes dried up completely at this time; "You could walk across the entire lake because there was no water" (kon_08_070812). Droughts in the 1980s were also severe. For several years "crops failed completely. Not even the Government had grain to distribute" (kon_08_070812). Roncoli documented how residents of Boulsa used a broad suite of local indicators to predict the rainy season. This included insect behavior, flowering plants, and other environmental phenomena (Roncoli et al. 2002). Regional desiccation altered rainfall patterns and people lost confidence in their ability to read the rains.

Households on the northern Central Plateau responded to droughts, desiccation, and desertification by engaging in several different types of adaptation. Some migrated away from the region. Others stayed and initiated a process of agricultural intensification. These efforts have transformed many parts of the northern Central Plateau. The adoption of SWC measures has been fundamental to these adaptations but varies between the two study areas.

Soil and Water Conservation (SWC)

The Sahelian droughts and attendant famines attracted international scientific attention and foreign development assistance. Because the northern Central Plateau was well known among scholars as a hot spot for desertification, it became targeted for several environmental rehabilitation projects in the mid-1970s (Marchal 1983). Development agencies initiated widespread, intensive soil and water conservation projects across parts of the northern Central Plateau in the mid-1980s (Reij et al. 2005). According to an International Fund for Agricultural Development (IFAD) report, 25 to 50 percent of all agricultural land in the Commune of Kongoussi has been treated with SWC (2004: XV). In Boulsa, however, this was less than 5 percent. We draw on spatial environmental data to understand the effects of low SWC adoption in Boulsa and how this affected regional vegetation trends.

With funding from UNCCD programs, non-governmental organizations (NGOs) developed the "lines of stone," or contour stone bunds, which are locally referred to as "*diguettes*" (Atampugre 1993). Diguettes consist of long low rock barriers that lie parallel to one another and follow the contours of agricultural fields. Diguettes create a network of low walls that slow the passage of water when rain falls. This permits rain to percolate deeper into the soils, which then retain this humidity longer. Thus, sheet erosion is reduced and soil conserved.

In the 1980s, a French development volunteer encouraged residents of Rissiam, which lies 5 km west of Kongoussi in a steep valley, to construct a rock dam across an expanding gully (Reij, et al. 2005: 648). PATECORE improved this technique and established a new method of soil and water conservation. These dams are referred to as "level permeable rockdams" because they allow some water to flow through after rainstorms but trap much of the sediment and organic matter.

The Government of Burkina Faso partnered with international NGOs to promote SWC and especially diguettes and level permeable rockdams in select administrative regions or communes throughout the northern Central Plateau. Kongoussi was one of these select communes while Boulsa was not (IFAD 2004). The largest and most prominent of these was the Central Plateau Land Improvement and Resource Conservation Project (PATECORE) based in Kongoussi. Funded by the German Corporation for Technical Cooperation (GTZ), PATECORE provided technical and logistical assistance through village self-help committees, or *grouppements* (Fr.). Households within individual communities would collectively form a grouppement and then receive training from PATECORE. PATECORE provided trucks for transporting large quantities of rock from surrounding hills to village fields. Members of each village grouppement first filled the trucks with rock and then constructed diguettes or dams once the rocks were delivered.

Diguettes and level permeable rockdams improve soils and conserve water. They also promote the spontaneous regeneration of native trees, grasses, and shrubs. As rain falls, organic matter such as leaves, bark, and especially seeds from surrounding plants become trapped. Since soils are now stabilized, native plants flourish along contour stone bunds and level permeable dams. These two types of soil and water conservation interventions have helped farmers not only adapt to desiccation, but also promoted biodiversity.

Zaï are a third type of SWC measure. Zaï consist of shallow planting pits that are dug during the dry season. Farmers leave a low berm on the downslope side of each pit. Once the rains start, they plant the hole with sorghum or millet seed, add a small amount of compost, and cover it with soil. The shallow pit allows rain to collect and remain to decrease runoff. Compost adds organic matter and allows germinated seeds to withstand dry periods. By adding more and more zaï planting pits every year, they can slowly rehabilitate even the most degraded *zipellé* soils (Mooré – "bare soil"). A local agricultural extension agent in Kongoussi recounted the following:

> Zaï allow people to cultivate in zipellé soils which are very degraded. It also permits someone to conserve their compost or manure. With time, it rehabilitates the soil to the point where you can farm it like any other field. However, it means going out in the dry season and digging the holes which is very labor intensive.

> ...there was one farmer who dug zaï, and then planted them with sorghum immediately following the first light rains in May, the mango rains. Everyone thought it was crazy. But, it worked and he started eating and harvesting it when everyone else was struggling.
> *(kon_01_080104)*

Spatial Comparison between Kongoussi and Northern Boulsa

As noted above in the 2004 IFAD report, SWC is dramatically more prevalent in Kongoussi than Boulsa. This is because there has been much more institutional support from the Government of Burkina and NGOs. In his work, West has mapped the extent of dam and diguette construction using high-resolution satellite imagery for select areas in Kongoussi. They are extensive throughout the commune. Based on intensive fieldwork in three study sites (Sakou, Kouka, and Loulouka) West and his students conservatively estimate that 500 to 1000 hectares of agricultural land has been treated with SWC for each (West et al. 2020: 17).

Roncoli and her colleagues conducted initial fieldwork in the village of Bonam in the northern half of the Commune of Boulsa in 1997 and 1998. Although they did not map SWC investments, they documented that Mossi farmers were experimenting with diguettes and zaï (Roncoli et al. 1999). The authors noted that some attempts to use zaï had failed because rural producers did not add adequate amounts of compost or improperly buried seeds with soils rich in clay that hardened after the rains (ibid, 37). Participants in Bonam reported that they constructed contour stone bunds in only upland fields or sandy soils where they plant sorghum (ibid., 37). In their project reports and articles, Roncoli and her colleagues frequently pointed out that the adoption of SWC by Bonam households was sharply constrained by access to household labor and technical assistance (ibid., 2001). In contrast, PATECORE provided massive technical assistance and training while village grouppements provided collective labor for constructing dams and diguettes.

Over twenty years after Roncoli's fieldwork in Bonam, West used Google Earth to identify the extent of SWC investments in and around Bonam using techniques similar to those used in Kongoussi (see West et al. 2020). Only a limited area around a low plateau in the southern part of the village appeared to be definitively treated with diguettes – i.e., clear parallel lines of stone were visible. There was widespread visual evidence of extensive stone barriers that appeared to form boundaries of individual fields throughout the village. Whether these were deliberate SWC measures or merely boundary markers, however, remains ambiguous. There was no evidence of level permeable rockdams and individual zaï holes are too small to be detected in high-resolution satellite imagery.

Analysis of Spatial Environmental Data

Through a collaborative partnership, the Institut Géographique du Burkina (IGB) provided West with the Base Nationale des Données Topographiques (National Topographic Database – BNDT) that includes administrative, road, hydrological, and other spatial data (IGB 2014). These layers can be analyzed and visualized using geographic information system (GIS) software. In partnership with the United States Geological Survey (USGS) the Comité Permanent Inter-états de Lutte contre la Sécheresse dans le Sahel (CILSS) completed a detailed analysis of land-use/land-cover (LULC) trends for West Africa (CILSS 2016). These GIS data are publicly available at: https://eros.usgs.gov/westafrica/data-downloads. The CILSS-USGS data maps LULC for West Africa based on the classification of satellite imagery for three distinct time periods: 1975, 2000 and 2013. The spatial resolution of the data is 2 km X 2 km. West and his colleague Dr. Aaron Moody have used a time series of satellite imagery and rainfall data to identify areas of increasing (greening) and decreasing (browning) vegetation productivity for Burkina Faso (West et al. 2017). Here, we combine these datasets to compare environmental trends in the Commune of Kongoussi and the northern Commune of Boulsa to complement our ethnographic fieldwork.

West's fieldwork in Kongoussi took place primarily in the villages of Sakou, Kouka, and Loulouka (Figure 19.3 – left panel). Roncoli and her colleagues conducted most of their fieldwork in the village of Bonam in northern Boulsa (Figure 19.3 – right). Kongoussi lies within a region of volcanic hills and plateaus that form valleys in the southeast

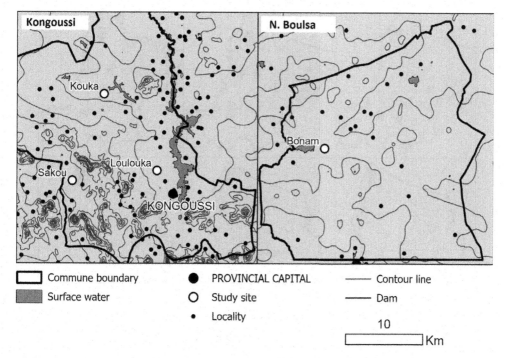

FIGURE 19.3 Commune of Kongoussi (left) and the Northern Commune of Boulsa (right) with study sites.
Source: IGB BNDT, 2014.

and broad plains to the north. The country's largest natural lake, Lake Bam lies along the eastern border near the provincial capital Kongoussi. Northern Boulsa consists entirely of a long, low plain with little topographic relief or surface water. This means Kongoussi is much more susceptible to erosion and land degradation is much more evident. Kongoussi has a population density of approximately 100 persons/km^2 and Boulsa is much lower at 60 persons/km^2. Figure 19.3 strongly suggests that Kongoussi's population is more dense and concentrated because localities are more numerous and are located in close proximity to one another. Villages are fewer and more dispersed in northern Boulsa.

We combined the spatial data from the IGB BNDT with the CILSS-USGS LULC data to analyze trends in land-use/land-cover for three distinct periods: 1975, 2000, and 2013 (Figure 19.4). The dataset features many different classes such as agriculture, irrigated agriculture, steppe, savanna, etc. For simplicity, we combined two or more similar classes so that their spatial distribution could be more easily visualized. Thus, we combined the following: 1) agriculture and irrigated agriculture into "Agriculture"; 2) steppe and savanna into "Steppe/savanna"; 3) water, wetland, rock, and urban into "Rock, urban, water"; and 4) bare soil as its own category. Bare soil is locally referred to as "*zipellé*" in *Mooré*, the Mossi language. It consists of degraded and crusted soils where nothing grows. The presence and extent of zipellé soils indicates severe land degradation and these areas are frequently targeted for SWC treatment to bring them back into

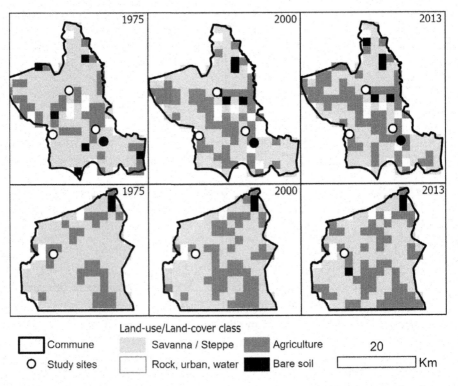

FIGURE 19.4 Maps of land-use/land-cover (LULC) – Kongoussi (top) and N. Boulsa (bottom), 1975, 2000, and 2013.
Source: CILSS 2016.

agricultural production. Because these data are a time series, we can detect both spatial and temporal trends in LULC change for Kongoussi and northern Boulsa. Moreover, we expect these changes to differ between the two communes.

Standard GIS procedures produced the maps above for Kongoussi and northern Boulsa. They show that steppe/savanna (light gray) was the dominant land cover class in 1975, but that agriculture (darker gray) replaced these step/savanna landscapes over time. Both Kongoussi and northern Boulsa featured some bare soil (black) in 1975, but there were only a few scattered areas of this class. The maps clearly show how agriculture increased between both the 1975 to 2000 and 2000 to 2013 time periods and how steppe/ savanna decreased. It is more difficult, however, to quantify these changes in the maps.

Again using standard GIS procedures (see West et al. 2017), we calculated the percent of each class for every time period within the boundaries of the two communes. This produced the two charts below (Figure 19.5 and Figure 19.6).

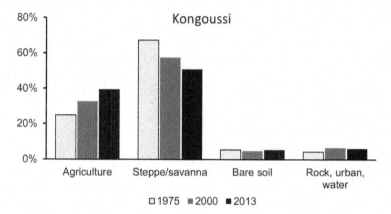

FIGURE 19.5 Kongoussi LULC change – 1975, 2000, 2013.
Source: CILSS 2016.

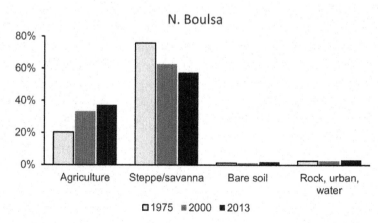

FIGURE 19.6 N. Boulsa LULC change – 1975, 2000, 2013.
Source: CILSS 2016.

These two charts indicate that indeed agriculture has increased from roughly 20 percent of the area in 1975 to about 40 percent in 2013 in both study areas. This increase has come mostly at the expense of steppe/savanna, which has decreased from around 70 percent to roughly 50 percent of the land in both over the same time period. Bare soil does not represent a large percentage of the total area in either commune – 5 percent in Kongoussi and 1–2 percent in northern Boulsa. There is no change in bare soil over time for Kongoussi and just a 1 percent increase in northern Boulsa between 1975 and 2013. Agricultural expansion in both study sites, however, has slowed in recent decades – increasing by just 4 to 6 percent. This provides evidence that farmers are no longer clearing steppe/savanna, but intensifying existing agricultural fields. Overall, LULC conditions and trends are remarkably similar in both study areas. But, what are the consequences of this intensification where one commune has intensified through SWC and the other has not?

Several scholars have identified the northern Central Plateau as a distinct area of "greening" within a larger regional pattern of greening throughout the Sahel (Herrmann et al. 2005). Analyses of satellite imagery suggest that many parts of the Sahel exhibit distinctly positive trends in green vegetation that cannot be explained by precipitation alone. West and his colleagues (2017) performed a similar analysis of vegetation and rainfall trends for Burkina Faso using a time series of satellite data during 1983–2009. This dataset was used to assess greening in Kongoussi and northern Boulsa. The results of this analysis appear in Figure 19.7.

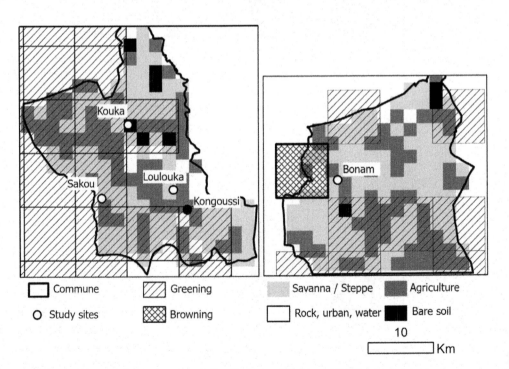

FIGURE 19.7 Greening/browning trends for Kongoussi (left) and N. Boulsa (right). Source: West et al. 2017.

The map indicates a large and spatially coherent region of greening throughout Kongoussi. This occurs in agricultural areas with extensive SWC investments. The map above complements West's ethnographic fieldwork in the study area. The two study sites in the north and west (Sakou and Kouka) are villages where communities have treated large areas with diguettes, dams, and zaï. In the eastern study site of Loulouka, there has been much less SWC activity. The greening in northern Boulsa is not as extensive or spatially coherent. Instead, the pattern is patchy. Moreover, there is a single region of browning, which indicates negative green vegetation productivity – or, more simply, degradation (see West et al. 2017). This browning is adjacent to Bonam and lies immediately to the west of it. The study site of Bonam itself is not located in an area of greening. Thus, there is extensive greening in Kongoussi and especially in areas treated with SWC. Greening in northern Boulsa is less extensive and patchy. It appears that the small local SWC investments in Bonam have not had a larger regional effect on vegetation trends. In fact, these analyses indicate areas adjacent to Bonam are actually degrading.

Conclusion

Just as the contemporary northern Central Plateau looks degraded to outsiders, its contemporary inhabitants see a landscape that has been transformed through decades of hard work. Many of the gullies have stopped expanding and are now filled in. Bare soils have been reclaimed and converted to fertile fields. The "dead trees" in these fields are actually very much alive and indicate increased soil fertility and biodiversity. This transformation is due to the adoption of soil and water conservation measures by Mossi rural producers. Long networks of level permeable rockdams have halted gullies and allowed farmers to re-establish fields in these valley floors. Abandoned zipellé soils have been treated with diguettes and zaï, which now allow millet and sorghum to grow and produce grain even if rains fail. Combined, these different types of SWC measures have slowed erosion and allowed native trees, grasses, and shrubs to germinate and reproduce in soils that are now stabilized. The "dead trees" that appear in these treated fields are very much alive. In fact they are called "*zaanga*" in Mooré and are the famous "apple-ring acacia" (or "*faidherbia*" in French – *Faidherbia albida*). Unlike other Sahelian trees, they lose their leaves at the beginning of the rainy season, which makes them appear "dead" when all the surrounding crops, trees, and grasses are green from the rains. These dried leaves add organic matter when crops need it most. Zaanga are also leguminous and increase nitrogen in surrounding soils. Their root system consists of a single deep tap root, which means they do not compete with adjacent millet or sorghum for water during the growing season and further stabilize soils. They provide nutritious green leaves and rich seed pods as animal fodder during the dry season when many other trees are bare. Mossi farmers in Kongoussi state that this unique and invaluable tree had almost disappeared until SWC and better management helped it re-establish.

Agriculture throughout the northern Central Plateau is no longer extensive, but definitively intensive. In Kongoussi, this process of agricultural intensification took place alongside widespread adoption of SWC, which was assisted by long-term and massive institutional support by the government and NGOs. In northern Boulsa, on the other hand, agricultural intensification also occured among Mossi rural producers but this was not accompanied by the same level of SWC activity. This has produced different environmental outcomes. In Kongoussi, households have constructed diguettes and dams throughout their entire village *terroir* ("territory" in French) and this adoption of SWC has been reproduced among contiguous villages producing a landscape-level effect of positive vegetation trends. Higher soil fertility, decreased erosion, and increased tree cover have contributed to a regional pattern of overall greening in Kongoussi. This is not the case in northern Boulsa. Agricultural intensification without soil and water conservation has not led to widespread greening and, in fact, there are areas where vegetation trends are negative, which indicates browning and degradation.

Overall, this chapter underscores the value of integrating long-term and fine-grained ethnographic data with coarser spatial environmental data to understand how climate change and household adaptations dynamically interact to produce different ecological patterns of both degradation and rehabilitation. Climate fundamentally changed in the northern Central Plateau – there was a 30-year drought during a period of overall desiccation. Though rainfall appears to have recovered in recent years (see Figure 19.2), climate change is ongoing in the form of enhanced precipitation variability and especially frequent and long dry periods within the rainy season. Households in the region have adapted using SWC. Our chapter also shows the importance of conducting comparative research. We argue that the success of these SWC investments in Kongoussi provide important lessons for promoting this distinct form of agricultural intensification in northern Boulsa and other parts of the country. Combining our insights from fieldwork conducted in different places at different points in time, we conclude that promoting soil and water conservation alone is not sufficient. It has to be done with long-term investment and massive technical assistance to have an impact. In short, adaptation without strong institutional support from governments and development organizations is likely to have no lasting beneficial effect on households or landscapes.

Note

1 This designation preserves participant anonymity but allows the authors to cross reference the individual with their transcript and household survey in a de-identified database.

References

Atampugre, Nick. 1993. *Behind the Lines of Stone: The social impact of a soil and water conservation project in the Sahel*. Oxford: Oxfam Publications.

BAN. 1980. "Modalités révisées de la Strategie de lutte contre la sécheresse et de développement dans le Sahel." *Bulletin de l'Afrique Noire* 1071: 20577–20578.

Behnke, Roy H., and Michael Mortimore. 2016. "Introduction: the end of desertification?" In Roy H. Behnke and Michael Mortimore (eds.) *The End of Desertification: Disputing environmental change in the drylands*. Heidelberg: Springer-Verlag, pp. 1–34.

Charney, Jules G. 1975. "Dynamics of deserts and drought in the Sahel." *Quarterly Journal of the Royal Meteorological Society* 101: 193–202.

Cherlet, Michael, Charles Hutchinson, James Reynolds, J. Hill, Stefan Sommer, and Graham von Maltitz (eds.) 2018. *World Atlas of Desertification*. Luxembourg: Publication Office of the European Union.

Comité permanent inter-états de lutte contre la sécheresse dans le Sahel (CILSS). 2016. *Landscapes of West Africa: A window on a changing world*. Garretson, SD: US Geological Survey.

Franke, Richard W., and Barbara H. Chasin. 1980. *Seeds of Famine: Ecological destruction and the development dilemma in the West African Sahel*. Montclair, NJ: Allanheld, Osmun and Co.

Herrmann, Stefanie M., Assaf Anyamba, and Compton J. Tucker. 2005. "Recent trends in vegetation dynamics in the African Sahel and their relationship to climate. *Global Environmental Change* 15 (15): 394–404.

Hulme, Mike. 2001. "Climatic perspectives on Sahelian desiccation: 1973–1998." *Global Environmental Change* 11 (1): 19–29.

Institut Géographique du Burkina (IGB). 2014. *Projet de Cartographie Topographique Numérique au Burkina Faso.* Ouagadougou, BF: IGB.

International Fund for Agricultural Development (IFAD). 2004. *Rapport d'Evaluation Intermédiaire de Programme Spécial Conservation des Eaux et des Sols - Agroforesterie (Ps CES/AgGF) du Burkina Faso.* Ouagadougou, BF: IFAD.

Izard, Michel. 1985. *Gens du Pouvoir, Gens de la Terre.* Cambridge: Cambridge University Press.

Marchal, Jean-Yves. 1983. *Yatenga Nord Haute Volta: La dynamique d'un espace rural Soudano-Sahelian.* Paris: Office de la Recherche Scientifique et Technique Outre-Mer.

Nicholson, Sharon E. 2001. "Climatic and environmental change in Africa during the last two centuries." *Climate Research* 17 (2): 123–144.

Reij, Chris, Gray Tappan, and Adema Belemvire. 2005. "Changing land management practices and vegetation on the Central Plateau of Burkina Faso (1968–2002)." *Journal of Arid Environments* 63 (3): 642–659.

Reij, Chris and Taladia Thiombiano. 2003. "Développement rural et environnement au Burkina Faso: la réhabilitation de la capacité productive des terroirs sur la partie Nord du Plateau Central entre 1980 et 2001." 82. Amsterdam: Vrije Universite.

Roncoli, Carla, Abdou-Salam Bahadio, and Salifo Daniel Boena. 1999. *The Role of Rainfall Information in Farmers' Decisions: Ethnographic research in the Mossi Plateau (Namentenga Province).* 94. Athens, GA: University of Georgia.

Roncoli, Carla, Keith Ingram, and Paul Kirshen. 2001. "The costs and risks of coping with drought: livelihoood impacts and farmers' responses in Burkina Faso." *Climate Research* 19 (2): 119–132.

Roncoli, Carla, Keith Ingram, and Paul H. Kirshen. 2002. "Reading the rains: local knowledge and rainfall forecasting in Burkina Faso." *Society and Natural Resources* 15 (5): 409–427.

West, Colin Thor, Sarah Benecky, Cassandra Karlsson, Isabella Reiss, and Aaron Moody. 2020. "Bottom-up perspectives on the re-greening of the Sahel: an evaluation of the spatial relationship between soil and water conservation (SWC) and tree-cover in Burkina Faso." *Land* 9: 208.

West, Colin Thor, Aaaron Moody, Elisabeth Kago Nébié, and Oumar Sanon. 2017. "Ground-truthing Sahelian greening: ethnographic and spatial evidence from Burkina Faso." *Human Ecology* 45 (1): 89–101.

West, Colin Thor, Carla Roncoli, and Frédéric Ouattara. 2008. "Local perceptions and regional climate trends on the Central Plateau of Burkina Faso." *Land Degradation and Development* 19 (3): 289–304.

20

ANTHROPOLOGICAL CONTRIBUTIONS TO IPCC ASSESSMENT WORK

Pamela McElwee

Introduction

Over the past 30 years the Intergovernmental Panel on Climate Change (IPCC) has issued increasingly dire assessments on the causes, consequences, and potential solutions to climate change. The first IPCC assessment reports that began in the 1990s primarily drew from physical and biological sciences and only occasionally featured anthropologists as authors or engaged with anthropological literatures. However, more recently, an increasing number of anthropologists are helping to write IPCC reports as lead authors.[1] As a result, recent reports have drawn more extensively on the works of anthropology scholars, helping to highlight important issues such as definitions of vulnerability, how Indigenous knowledge systems understand and adapt to climate change, and cultural constraints to adaptation, among other topics.

Additionally, anthropologists and other scholars of science and technology studies are increasingly turning their ethnographic gaze to understand the workings of the IPCC and other science-policy assessment bodies as institutions (Tollefson 2013). Such studies have been focused on both the contents of report outcomes and the process by which they are generated, particularly with regards to how epistemic authority is produced (Oppenheimer et al. 2019). Some anthropologists have provided an insider's view through participant-observation of how climate scientists grapple with questions of authority and consensus (McElwee 2020). Others have approached the IPCC as outside observers, documenting the practices by which knowledge is produced, risks are assessed, and outcomes are communicated to the public (Vardy et al. 2017). By examining the IPCC, anthropologists are also helping to identify how and why climate assessment reports and specific types of communication strategies resonate with activists, policymakers, and other audiences (Fiske et al. 2018).

Anthropologists and the IPCC

The IPCC was established in 1988 by the World Meteorological Organization (WMO) and the United Nations Environment Programme (UNEP) with a mandate to regularly

DOI: 10.4324/9781003242499-24

assess climate change based on the most recent and best available science. The IPCC is structured as a consensus body of 195 governments, which sets priorities and approves assessment documents written by scientist authors (Vardy et al. 2017). There are three key working groups within IPCC, each of which has a different mandate. Working Group 1 (WG1) issues regular assessments of the physical science basis of climate change; Working Group 2 (WG2) examines impacts, adaptation, and vulnerability to climate change; and Working Group 3 (WG3) is charged with mitigation options to reduce the drivers of climate change, namely anthropogenic greenhouse gas emissions (Fløttum et al. 2016). These reports are often timed for and used by governments who negotiate policy responses to climate change through the UN Framework Convention on Climate Change (UNFCCC), the preeminent global environmental agreement dealing with anthropogenic climate change. The IPCC is under the explicit mandate to provide policy-relevant assessments, not policy-prescriptive ones, a writing approach that is often challenging for lead-author scholars. However, this line between the two is often somewhat blurry (Hulme and Mahony 2010).

The IPCC works through multi-year cycles, and as of 2023 has concluded the Sixth Assessment Report cycle (AR6) which saw the publication of the three working group reports and a synthesis report across the entire cycle's products. Special reports that are requested by member governments on particular topics are also produced, and the AR6 cycle has generated three such reports, including *Global Warming of 1.5°C* (also known as SR15) from 2018 and both the *Special Report on Climate Change and Land* (known as SRCCL) and the *Special Report on the Ocean and Cryosphere in a Changing Climate* (SROCC) finished in 2019. Assessment reports are produced by hundreds of volunteer authors nominated by member governments and observer organizations, and then selected by the IPCC bureau, with the intent to achieve a balance of disciplinary expertise, age, gender, and nationality. Selected authors then work on assigned chapters with a team of other scientists, who meet regularly in lead author meetings to produce several rounds of draft reports, each one of which is open to public and governmental comment. The authors aim to summarize the state of knowledge, rather than producing new data or outcomes themselves, which is why these reports are labelled as "assessments."

Although social scientists are increasingly in demand as lead authors, economics is the most common social science discipline as reflected in author background and literature assessed. The tendency of economics to engage in policy-relevant, predictive, and quantitative work has been one major reason why it has been emphasized in IPCC reports, particularly in the modelling of future impacts and responses (Roscoe 2016). Recent calls for IPCC to increase epistemic diversity by including more qualitative social science and humanities, as well as authors who are Indigenous or who work with Indigenous knowledge, have resulted in more attention to the role that anthropology and anthropologists might play within the IPCC (Ford et al. 2012; Beck and Mahony 2018). Anthropologists have been authors on many of the recent reports in the AR6 cycle, but have not been represented in great numbers. For example, only two out of 84 total authors were anthropologists on the SRCCL report (myself and John Morton from the University of Greenwich) despite that the report was about how land use both drives and is impacted by climate change, a topic with which anthropologists have extensive experience. Similarly, only two anthropologists (Ben Orlove and Susan Crate) served on the SROCC report on oceans and the cryosphere. Within the regular working group reports, anthropologists have primarily been included as authors in WG2, which focuses on impacts and vulnerabilities, but generally excluded from the other two working groups on the state of climate science and on mitigation options. One possible reason for the low participation of anthropologists has likely been perceptions among other scientists that our work is anecdotal and not rigorous or generalizable (Obermeister 2017).

Other disparities plague the IPCC process. Many have called for increased geographic diversity in the IPCC lead author selection as well as interdisciplinarity, as report teams have in the past been dominated by physical and biological scientists from the Global North (Corbera et al. 2016; Yamineva 2017). (The SRCCL special report was the first IPCC report to have a majority of scientists from developing countries.) There has been concern that a lack of balance in including Global South authors has led to less attention to justice and equity issues within the reports themselves (Chakraborty and Sherpa 2021). Women have also tended to make up a smaller percentage of authors even though gender balance is supposed to be taken into account in selection of author teams: just 5 per cent of authors were women in the first report in 1990, rising to one-third by the AR6 cycle (Gay-Antaki and Liverman 2018). The IPCC established a Task Group on Gender in 2018 to address these disparities, and the group issued a report in 2019 showing that there were several barriers and biases that prevented deeper and more systematic engagement of women in IPCC processes. These included the general smaller numbers of women researchers working in the earth sciences; lack of access to funding and recognition on par with men; and competing demands such as childcare or heavier teaching and service loads that make additional volunteer work with IPCC difficult. Eleven per cent of authors surveyed by the Task Force also reported observing or experiencing sexual harassment as part of IPCC work (Liverman et al. 2022).

Co-production of Knowledge in the IPCC

IPCC reports are an example of scientific co-production at work: the idea that science is as much the product of politics as of objective research, and that action and knowledge combine in the creation and uptake of scientific concepts (Miller and Wyborn 2020). For example, during several rounds of government and public review of draft reports, as well as approval at the final plenary, government representatives reflect on the words scientists have written, often inserting their own ideas and changes, while scientists at the meeting consult as to whether government assertions are scientifically defensible and useful (Vardy et al. 2017). These push and pull negotiations range from basic, as when scientists simply clarify why some conclusions are drawn and written the way they are, to antagonistic, as some controversial comments or topics cause report approval sessions to go late into the night or to miss final deadlines. For example, at the SRCCL plenary, the Brazilian delegation right off the bat expressed concern over the language in the report around biofuels, particularly the conclusion that production at large scales could have negative impacts on food security and biodiversity. The balance between listening to government concerns and defending words already written, as well as representing and arguing for the strength of the knowledge base in assessments, often proves challenging for authors (Tschakert 2015).

The line-by-line editing of summaries for policymakers that takes place at plenary approval sessions reflects the form and mandate of the IPCC to achieve consensus (Figure 20.1); any government may object to a word or sentence but is expected to negotiate and come to

FIGURE 20.1 Working through SRCCL report text at IPCC plenary in Geneva, August 2019 (author second from right). Photo by Valérie Masson-Delmotte.

agreement on alternatives. Some have suggested that this focus on consensus reflects post-normal science, where political consensus is one of the only ways to tackle "wicked" problems like climate change (Hoppe and Rödder 2019). Others see consensus as an inappropriate response to the complexity of climate change, and an attempt to provide a narrow framing on a topic that should allow for multiple and competing interpretations (Berg and Lidskog 2018). In terms of the communication outcomes of consensus statements, while some scholars and participants believe the consensus process produces sharper messaging and clear policy-relevant science due to the key participation of government delegates, others believe that this "negotiation" of facts is at best producing bland, non-controversial statements or at worst is politicizing science (Beck and Mahony 2018, Pearce et al. 2018).

The communication of complexity and uncertainty are additional key challenges for IPCC reports (O'Reilly et al. 2011). Uncertainty around certain processes or future outcomes are supposed to be expressed in what is called "calibrated language," such as the use of terms like "very likely" or "unlikely" which have specific probabilities assigned to each. Yet how these terms are understood and used by authors is often subjective and uneven throughout the different reports (Janzwood 2020), while nonetheless these subjective expert knowledges often are presented as authoritative and rigid assessments of risk (Mahony 2015). Complexity is also manifested in the inability of single scholars or disciplines to be able to understand all aspects of the physical climate system as well as the need for models to predict future pathways. Complexity is also clear in the inherent unpredictability of much human behavior, a topic about which anthropologists have considerable expertise. Tensions over what methods and approaches are most effective in predicting human actions have become particularly relevant when trying to assemble future scenarios that rely on understanding decision-making ten, twenty or even fifty years in the future. Many decisions related to climate mitigation policy rely on individual choices (such as flying less or shifting to electric vehicles) which are hard to model, while large scale measures like geoengineering can be included in the models with more ease (Ackerman and Munitz 2016; Vardy et al. 2017). This has led to concerns that IPCC reports overemphasize certain solutions (such as carbon dioxide removal) and under-emphasize other outcomes (such as individuals choosing to curb their energy demand or increase their adaptive capacity) (Larkin et al. 2018)

Those who have engaged in studies of the IPCC's processes have asserted that much of what the organization does is boundary work (Beck and Mahony 2018). By this, scholars mean that "boundary" organizations like IPCC take on the task of policing what are acceptable bounds between science and politics and what knowledge is legitimate and what is not. Some have suggested that such boundary work can lead to increased separation of science and society, while other scholars believe that boundary organizations play a key role in modulating these two sides (Clark et al. 2016). Ultimately, boundary work is about the process of establishing epistemic authority. While a traditional linear model of science expertise suggests that science be walled off from political and social processes and be presented to decision-makers as an objective assessment of knowledge, scholars working in the field of science and technology studies have emphasized the concept of post-normal science as one IPCC ought to take more account of (Sluijs 2012). In this they suggest that when certainty cannot be known and stakes are high, alternative models of decision-making for science should be pursued (Funtowicz and Ravetz 1993). For example, some have called for the IPCC to include not just "speaking for" climate science but also "listening to" different communities' experiences and alternative knowledge systems (Dudman and Wit 2021). Other have suggested that better integration of social and natural sciences or a wider range of actors in IPCC work would help the IPCC rethink the role of science in providing solutions (Pryck and Wanneau 2017).

Role of Indigenous Knowledge Systems

There have also been calls for greater inclusion of Indigenous knowledge and local knowledge in IPCC assessments and to seek opportunities to collaborate and connect these knowledge systems resulting in co-produced outcomes. Reasons for including these knowledge systems have stemmed from the need for more comprehensive data on climate impacts, particularly in remote areas, and as a mode for inclusion, participation, and respect for Indigenous peoples in global institutions (Makondo and Thomas 2018; Pet-zold et al. 2020). Many anthropologists have been at the forefront of engaging Indigenous voices and knowledge in climate assessment work (Chisolm Hatfield et al. 2018; Maldonado and Lazrus 2019).

Yet there are also concerns about the challenges and efficacy of including Indigenous knowledge and local knowledge in science assessments like IPCC, given that both Indigenous knowledge and science are distinct types of knowledge systems, which are often asymmetrical in terms of power and can thus be incommensurable (Hill et al. 2020). Some of the IPCC's formal rules of procedure, such as restricting sources to peer-reviewed literature, has limited engagement with other knowledge systems in the past. Practical challenges of how Indigenous knowledge and local knowledge is passed on and recorded (often oral rather than written) have also made it difficult to incorporate

Indigenous knowledge and local knowledge into IPCC reports (Ford et al. 2016). Experience from other science assessments highlights that successfully bringing Indigenous knowledge and local knowledge into assessment processes and policy arenas requires an approach that facilitates recognition of different knowledge systems through understanding the mechanisms and contexts in which the knowledge is embedded (McElwee et al. 2020).

Although other ways of knowing, referred to as traditional knowledge, local knowledge, traditional ecological knowledge, and other terms, were mentioned here and there in previous IPCC reports, SROCC was the first IPCC report to specifically define and frame Indigenous knowledge and local knowledge (IPCC 2019a). SROCC described Indigenous knowledge as: "the understandings, skills, and philosophies developed by societies with long histories of interaction with their natural surroundings. It is passed on from generation to generation, flexible, and adaptive in changing conditions (Abram et al. 2019: 102). Furthermore, that local knowledge is "what non-Indigenous communities, both rural and urban use on a daily and lifelong basis. It is multi-generational, embedded in community practices and culture, and adaptive to changing conditions" (ibid).

The SRCCL report also paid particular attention to both Indigenous knowledge and local knowledge in specific sections (IPCC 2019b: 384, 514, and 746). The testament to the work in framing and substantiating Indigenous knowledge and local knowledge in these special reports is the number of citations found in the AR6 to Indigenous knowledge and local knowledge as compared to pre-SROCC/SRCCL. The AR6 report cycle tackled these challenges by explicitly noting "the value of diverse forms of knowledge such as scientific, as well as Indigenous knowledge and local knowledge, in understanding and evaluating climate adaptation processes and actions to reduce risks from human-induced climate change" (IPCC 2022: 5). The SPM of WG2 notes in multiple places that Indigenous knowledge has important roles to play in planning for adaption and climate resilient development, with the topic especially emphasized in chapters on water, food, and a cross-chapter box "The Role of Indigenous Knowledge and Local Knowledge in Understanding and Adapting to Climate Change."

Influence of Anthropologists on IPCC Concepts

In the AR6 cycle, anthropological literature is cited the most in the WG2 report, where twelve chapters and three cross-chapter papers (CCP) include literature from key anthropological journals in their references. Particularly in discussions on "Perceiving Climate Risk and Human Responses" in chapter 1, anthropological literature is used explicitly to frame ways of thinking about these problems. Anthropologists also served as either lead or contributing authors on several chapters of the WG2 report.

However, in the WG3 report on mitigation options, only chapter 10 includes one anthropology citation, indicating far less influence in this working group. Despite the fact that anthropologists have been working on key issues related to mitigation, such as cultural influences on energy use (Love and Isenhour 2016; Smith and High 2017), the politics of energy extractive industries (de Rijke 2013; Espig and de Rijke 2018), and inequitable geographies of risk from energy generation (Masco 2006; Strauss et al. 2013), they remain underutilized in WG3 assessments as both lead authors and sources of citable knowledge. The same is also true of WG1, to which almost no social scientists contribute.

Anthropologists have influenced key concepts and approaches within the WG2 reports, particularly around scalar concerns, the role of culture, and definitions of vulnerability and adaptation (Oliver-Smith 2016). For example, the global focus and mandate of IPCC can overshadow interest in local impacts and responses, given the tendency towards "standardization, aggregation and simplification" at global scales (Livingston et al. 2018). Anthropologists have brought a wealth of regionally and locally specific data to underpin some of the headline global numbers, as the unevenness of risks cannot be well represented by a simple degree of temperature change or a general schematic diagram of vulnerability (Liverman 2009; Orlove et al. 2014). There are a wide range of local impacts identified by anthropologists and cited in the most recent assessment, including local perceptions of environmental change (Crate and Nuttall 2009, 2016), intersections between climate and pandemics (Stammler and Ivanova 2020), and how grief can shape responses to climate impacts (Kent and Brondo 2020). Anthropologists have also influenced how the concept of culture is treated. Distinguishing culture as something that is static and threatened by climate change was emblematic of early IPCC reports (Matus et al. 2021), while more recent work has emphasized the dynamic and intersectional nature of culture in shaping responses to climate, such as through adaptation pathways (Marks et al. 2022).

The concept of vulnerability has been refined and improved through the contributions of anthropologists as well. Much of the early literature on defining climate vulnerability came from human geographers, particularly those working around the idea of Amartya Sen's capabilities framework (Adger et al. 2005). The notions of vulnerability as a function of exposure, sensitivity, and adaptive capacity were enshrined in IPCC reports, and this framing remains a common approach. Yet discomfort that this simplistic definition can "flatten" people's lived experiences of harm and damage has spurred anthropologists to more critical discussions (Marino and Faas 2020). For example, definitions of vulnerability that have focused more on access to resources, governance, and structural violence have emerged as a counterpoint (Thomas et al. 2019) and anthropologists have been at the forefront of asserting that key factors like colonialism or resource extraction play important roles in shaping such vulnerability (Cameron 2012). Yet IPCC reports have often shied away from acknowledging these structural constraints as they are not considered direct climate-related drivers (Schipper et al. 2021).

Adaptation has also been critiqued for how it is presented in IPCC reports (Morchain 2018; Dilling et al. 2019). For example, in the previous assessment cycle, the WG2 report was criticized as it "focused largely on observed, projected, and transboundary climate impacts in small islands, failing to delve into some of the human, social and policy dimensions of adaptation in these complex geographies" (Robinson 2020). Many anthropologists have pointed out that local ways of knowing and adapting that do not fit into standard narratives of adaptation within IPCC reports may be experienced as "less real" (Rudiak-Gould 2014a). There has been ambivalence on the part of many anthropologists to embrace terms used by IPCC reports like "resilience," noting that limited visions of the concept often ignore emotional and spiritual relations with nature and others (Shah et al. 2017). Anthropologists have also contributed to the growing literature on the politics of adaptation, which has focused on the need to understand power, authority, knowledge, and subjectivity, which shape everything from funding to participation in adaptation (Eriksen et al. 2015; Nightingale 2017). For example, adaptation projects often impose local costs or can lead to maladaptation, which is why they may be unsupported or protested by local actors (Dewan 2021).

Gaps in IPCC Work

One area ripe for more contributions from anthropology in the IPCC is in the WG3 reports on understanding the cultural and economic drivers of climate change, such as energy use and consumption, and the ways in which socio-cultural experiences and understandings shape mitigation responses (Smith and High 2017; Jorgenson et al. 2019). For example, work by other disciplines (namely engineering and economics) on future energy transitions reflects a great deal of technological optimism, and like studies of vulnerability, tends to neglect consideration of equity and justice. Anthropological researchers have engaged in trying to understand why, despite education and other policy campaigns, consumption emissions continue to rise, and what structural barriers people face in mitigating emissions (Love and Isenhour 2016; Johnson 2019). Anthropologists have also been skeptical of mitigation policies like neoliberal market-based cap and trade or carbon taxes for prioritizing large-scale capital investments and devolving to individuals responsibility for what are structural problems (Whitington 2016; Wilk 2016).

Another area of IPCC work where anthropologists are underrepresented is in the modelling that often underpins studies of both future impacts and mitigation responses (Roscoe 2014, 2016). These integrated assessment models (IAMs) are used to represent what future climates and societies can look like and what kind of pathways will lead toward desired end states. IAMs are often used in conjunction with what are known as shared socio-economic pathways (SSPs), which were developed over the last decade to provide plausible narratives of future development and population outcomes (O'Neill et al. 2017). There are currently five main SSPs in use by IPCC and the modelling community, ranging from SSP1, a high sustainability scenario, to SSP 5, a fossil-fueled development scenario. These SSPs are not predictions about the future but are more like narratives about how the future might unfold, not dissimilar to climate science fiction books (Nikoleris et al. 2017).

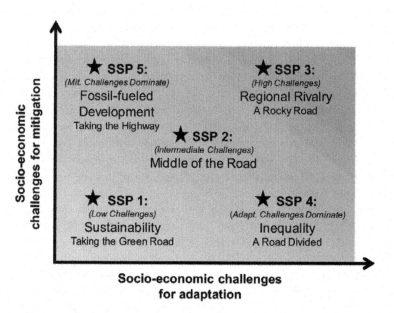

FIGURE 20.2 Shared Socio-Economic Pathways (SSPs) in use by IPCC.
Source: O'Neill et al. 2017.

The SSP scenarios rely on certain assumptions, often rooted in past trends and experience, across variables in six broad categories: demographics, human development, economy and lifestyle, policies and institutions (excluding climate policies), technology, and environment and natural resources. Anthropologists were not strongly involved in developing the SSPs and might have chosen different categories of variables to represent likely futures or how use of stories and alternative narrative methods might compare with the SSPs. Further, as noted previously, there are significant challenges to incorporating uncertainty around human responses in such long-term foresight analysis, with little attention to human capacity to change.

Overall, both the SSPs in specific and the IAMs in general suffer from a "black box" problem in that the specialized expert knowledge to create these models and scenarios is opaque to many (Robertson 2021). Even though IAMs are designed to help understand risk and take action to avert it, they are not able to provide a good model for either vulnerability or responses to increasing harm (Markandya et al. 2019). For example, rising income in most IAMs is taken as a proxy for increases in adaptive capacity, while in fact anthropologists have long asserted that people's ability to adapt successfully depends on much more than their aggregate income (Thomas et al. 2019). The climate policies that most anthropologists are interested in range across state, local, and individual responses for mitigation, as well as both collective and individual action for adaptation, but the IAMs cannot model these with much detail, nor assess such intangibles as institutional power (Moore et al. 2022). New generations of models of social behavior and climate are being suggested, although anthropology's aversion to prediction may make our participation in these more limited than other disciplines (Beckage et al. 2020).

The Anthropology of Knowledge Uptake

A final important role for anthropology has been to document how assessment reports like those of the IPCC and other science-policy bodies are read, understood, and used by different communities. For example, anthropologists have been at the forefront of the field of "reception studies" – that is, how reports and other forms of science travel out in the world and influence people's indirect perceptions of how climate is changing (Rudiak-Gould 2014b; Schnegg et al. 2021; Wit and Haines 2022). Such studies can help the IPCC understand how reports influence perceptions and actions on the ground. For example, framings of the climate problem from IPCC reports are often taken up by the wider public in ways that may not be intended by scientists, such as the framings of risk that were presented from the 1.5 degrees report and which led to much discussion about the short amount of time left to tackle climate change before it was "too late" (Livingston and Rummukainen 2020).

The current gap between knowledge and action on climate often appears overwhelming (Knutti 2019), such that some have suggested that scientists ought not to participate in the IPCC process anymore since it is not more knowledge that is needed but more political action (Glavovic et al. 2022). Anthropologists have important roles to play in exploring this action gap through our research, as well as taking on roles as activists for climate policy ourselves (O'Reilly et al. 2020). For example, anthropologists have studied how youth movements and climate strikes have rapidly expanded in Europe spurred by climate assessment work (von Storch et al. 2021) while others have shown how storytelling can increase the salience of activism (Vaughn 2021). Anthropologists have also documented their own roles in climate action and justice movements (Baer 2021) or worked with communities to envision alternative energy futures (Willow 2021).

Conclusions

Through work as authors on IPCC reports, and through publications that are picked up and reviewed by the assessment process, anthropologists have become more engaged with the IPCC over time, but there is still much more to be done. Scholars in subfields of anthropology, such as archeologists, are being encouraged to understand and become more engaged with IPCC reports to fill in our gaps on how past human behavior can help us understand future possibilities (Jackson et al. 2018; Kohler and Rockman 2020). Anthropology's strengths in documenting the important roles of memory, narrative, and emotion regarding interactions between people, landscapes, and climate and how cultural values are impacted by changing climates, including community, identity and sense of place, remain necessary for contextualizing the physical impact of climate change on human communities (Barnes et al. 2013). There are also calls for the IPCC to engage more with the telling of stories and plural perspectives, as well as qualitative examinations of human behavior (Bloomfield and Manktelow 2021; Schipper et al. 2021). Linking understanding of climate changes as outlined in IPCC reports to how they are received by different audiences, given varying perceptions of risk or the emotive appeal of stories and framings of responsibility, can potentially help anthropologists and activists work together to spur yet more climate engagement. All of these are strengths of anthropology as a discipline and foretell even more important roles for us in the future in the IPCC.

Note

1 I am one such anthropologist: for three years I served as a lead author for the Special Report on Climate Change and Land, joining more than 80 other authors from around the world. I participated both in the writing of the main report, where I was a contributor to Chapter 6, "Interlinkages between Desertification, Land Degradation, Food Security and GHG Fluxes: Synergies, Trade-offs and Integrated Response Options" as well as the Summary for Policymakers (SPM), the abbreviated summation of the entire report that must be approved by consensus of all member states.

References

Abram, Nerilie, Jean-Pierre Gattuso, Anjal Prakash, Lijing Cheng, María Paz Chidichimo, Susan Crate, Hiroyuki Enomoto, et al. "Framing and context of the report." In *IPCC Special Report on the Ocean and Cryosphere in a Changing Climate* [Pörtner, Hans-Otto, Debra C. Roberts, Valérie Masson-Delmotte, Panmao Zhai, Melinda Tignor, Elvira Poloczanska, Katja Mintenbeck et al. (eds.)] Cambridge University Press (2019).

Ackerman, Frank and Charles Munitz. "A critique of climate damage modelling: carbon fertilization, adaptation, and the limits of FUND." *Energy Research & Social Science* 12 (2016): 62–67.

Adger, W. Neil, Nigel W. Arnell, and Emma L. Tompkins. "Adapting to climate change: perspectives across scales." *Global Environmental Change* 15, no. 2 (2005): 75–76.

Baer, Hans A. "Efforts to update the climate emergency framework: from Australia to the world and back to Australia." *Practicing Anthropology* 43, no. 1 (2021): 6–10.

Barnes, Jessica, Michael Dove, Myanna Lahsen, Andrew Mathews, Pamela McElwee, Roderick McIntosh, Frances Moore, et al. "Contribution of anthropology to the study of climate change." *Nature Climate Change* 3, no. 6 (2013): 541–544.

Beck, Silke and Martin Mahony. "The IPCC and the new map of science and politics." *Wiley Interdisciplinary Reviews: Climate Change* 9, no. 6 (2018): e547.

Beckage, Brian, Katherine Lacasse, Jonathan M. Winter, Louis J. Gross, Nina Fefferman, Forrest M. Hoffman, Sara S. Metcalf, et al. "The Earth has humans, so why don't our climate models?" *Climatic Change* 163 (2020): 181–188.

Berg, Monika and Rolf Lidskog. "Pathways to deliberative capacity: the role of the IPCC." *Climatic Change* 148, no. 1–2 (2018): 11–24.

Bloomfield, Emma Frances and Chris Manktelow. "Climate communication and storytelling." *Climatic Change* 167, no. 3–4 (2021): 34.

Cameron, Emilie S. "Securing Indigenous politics: a critique of the vulnerability and adaptation approach to the human dimensions of climate change in the Canadian Arctic." *Global Environmental Change* 22, no. 1 (2012): 103–114.

Chakraborty, Ritodhi and Pasang Yangjee Sherpa. "From climate adaptation to climate justice: critical reflections on the IPCC and Himalayan climate knowledges." *Climatic Change* 167, no. 3–4 (2021): 49.

Chisholm Hatfield, Samantha, Elizabeth Marino, Kyle Powys Whyte, Kathie D. Dello, and Philip W. Mote. "Indian time: time, seasonality, and culture in traditional ecological knowledge of climate change." *Ecological Processes* 7, no. 1 (2018): 1–11.

Clark, William C., Thomas P. Tomich, Meine Van Noordwijk, DavidGuston, DeliaCatacutan, Nancy M.Dickson, and Elizabeth McNie. "Boundary work for sustainable development: natural resource management at the Consultative Group on International Agricultural Research (CGIAR)." *Proceedings of the National Academy of Sciences* 113, no. 17 (2016): 4615–4622.

Corbera, Esteve, Laura Calvet-Mir, Hannah Hughes, and Matthew Paterson. "Patterns of authorship in the IPCC Working Group III report." *Nature Climate Change* 6, no. 1 (2016): 94–99.

Crate, Susan A. and Mark Nuttall, eds. *Anthropology and Climate Change: From encounters to actions*. Routledge, 2009.

Crate, Susan A. and Mark Nuttall. *Anthropology and Climate Change: From actions to transformations*. Routledge, 2016.

De Rijke, Kim. "Hydraulically fractured: unconventional gas and anthropology." (Respond to this article at http://www. therai. org. uk/at/debate) *Anthropology Today* 29, no. 2 (2013): 13–17.

Dewan, Camelia. *Misreading the Bengal Delta: Climate change, development, and livelihoods in coastal Bangladesh*. University of Washington Press, 2021.

Dilling, Lisa, Anjal Prakash, Zinta Zommers, Farid Ahmad, Nuvodita Singh, Sara de Wit, Johanna Nalau, Meaghan Daly, and Kerry Bowman. "Is adaptation success a flawed concept?" *Nature Climate Change* 9, no. 8 (2019): 572–574.

Dudman, Karl and Sara de Wit. "An IPCC that listens: introducing reciprocity to climate change communication." *Climatic Change* 168, no. 1–2 (2021): 2.

Eriksen, Siri H., Andrea J. Nightingale, and Hallie Eakin. "Reframing adaptation: the political nature of climate change adaptation." *Global Environmental Change* 35 (2015): 523–533.

Espig, Martin and Kim de Rijke. "Energy, anthropology and ethnography: on the challenges of studying unconventional gas developments in Australia." *Energy Research & Social Science* 45 (2018): 214–223.

Fiske, Shirley, Susie Crate, Naveeda Khan, Julie Raymond, and Jessica O'Reilly. "AAA Goes to the Conference of the Parties." *Anthropology News* 59, no. 3 (2018): e130–e131.

Fløttum, Kjersti, Des Gasper, and Asuncion LeraSt Clair. "Synthesizing a policy-relevant perspective from the three IPCC 'Worlds' – a comparison of topics and frames in the SPMs of the Fifth Assessment Report." *Global Environmental Change* 38 (2016): 118–129.

Ford, James D., Laura Cameron, Jennifer Rubis, Michelle Maillet, Douglas Nakashima, Ashlee Cunsolo Willox, and Tristan Pearce. "Including Indigenous knowledge and experience in IPCC assessment reports." *Nature Climate Change* 6, no. 4 (2016): 349–353.

Ford, James D., Will Vanderbilt, and Lea Berrang-Ford. "Authorship in IPCC AR5 and its implications for content: climate change and Indigenous populations in WGII." *Climatic change* 113 (2012): 201–213.

Funtowicz, Silvio O., and Jerome R. Ravetz. "Science for the post-normal age." *Futures* 25, no. 7 (1993): 739–755.

Gay-Antaki, Miriam and Diana Liverman. "Climate for women in climate science: women scientists and the Intergovernmental Panel on Climate Change." *Proceedings of the National Academy of Sciences* 115, no. 9 (2018): 2060–2065.

Glavovic, Bruce C., Timothy F. Smith, and Iain White. "The tragedy of climate change science." *Climate and Development* 14, no. 9 (2022): 829–833.

Hill, Rosemary, Çiğdem Adem, Wilfred V. Alangui, Zsolt Molnár, Yildiz Aumeeruddy-Thomas, Peter Bridgewater, Maria Tengö et al. "Working with Indigenous, local and scientific knowledge in assessments of nature and nature's linkages with people." *Current Opinion in Environmental Sustainability* 43 (2020): 8–20.

Hoppe, Imke, and Simone Rödder. "Speaking with one voice for climate science – climate researchers' opinion on the consensus policy of the IPCC." *Journal of Science Communication* 18, no. 3 (2019): A04.

Hulme, Mike, and Martin Mahony. "Climate change: what do we know about the IPCC?" *Progress in Physical Geography* 34, no. 5 (2010): 705–718.

IPCC. *IPCC Special Report on the Ocean and Cryosphere in a Changing Climate* [Hans-Otto Pörtner, Debra C. Roberts, Valérie Masson-Delmotte, Panmao Zhai, Melinda Tignor, Elvira Poloczanska, Katja Mintenbeck et al. (eds.)]. Cambridge University Press (2019a).

IPCC. *Climate Change and Land: An IPCC special report on climate change, desertification, land degradation, sustainable land management, food security, and greenhouse gas fluxes in terrestrial ecosystems* [Priyadarshi R. Shukla, Jim Skea, E. Calvo Buendia, Valérie Masson-Delmotte, Hans Otto Pörtner, D.C. Roberts, Panmao Zhai, et al. (eds.)]. Cambridge University Press (2019b)

IPCC. *Climate Change 2022: Impacts, adaptation and vulnerability.* Working Group 2 Contribution to the Sixth Assessment Report of the Intergovernmental Panel on Climate Change, 2022.

Jackson, Rowan C., Andrew J. Dugmore, and Felix Riede. "Rediscovering lessons of adaptation from the past." *Global Environmental Change* 52 (2018): 58–65.

Janzwood, Scott. "Confident, likely, or both? The implementation of the uncertainty language framework in IPCC special reports." *Climatic Change* 162, no. 3 (2020): 1655–1675.

Johnson, Charlotte. "Anthropology and energy policy." In Ozawa, Marc, Jonathan Chaplin, Michael Pollitt, David Reiner, and Paul Warde (eds), *In Search of Good Energy Policy.* Cambridge University Press, (2019): 69–75.

Jorgenson, Andrew K., Shirley Fiske, Klaus Hubacek, Jia Li, Tom McGovern, Torben Rick, Juliet B. Schor, William Solecki, Richard York, and Ariela Zycherman. "Social science perspectives on drivers of and responses to global climate change." *Wiley Interdisciplinary Reviews: Climate Change* 10, no. 1 (2019): e554.

Kent, Suzanne and Keri Vacanti Brondo. "'Years ago the crabs was so plenty': anthropology's role in ecological grieving and conservation work." *Culture, Agriculture, Food and Environment* 42, no. 1 (2020): 16–24.

Knutti, Reto. "Closing the knowledge-action gap in climate change." *One Earth* 1, no. 1 (2019): 21–23.

Kohler, Timothy A. and Marcy Rockman. "The IPCC: a primer for archaeologists." *American Antiquity* 85, no. 4 (2020): 627–651.

Larkin, Alice, Jaise Kuriakose, Maria Sharmina, and Kevin Anderson. "What if negative emission technologies fail at scale? Implications of the Paris Agreement for big emitting nations." *Climate policy* 18, no. 6 (2018): 690–714.

Liverman, Diana M. "Conventions of climate change: constructions of danger and the dispossession of the atmosphere." *Journal of Historical Geography* 35, no. 2 (2009): 279–296.

Liverman, Diana, Nicolena von Hedemann, PatriciaNying'uro, MarkkuRummukainen, Kerstin-Stendahl, MiriamGay-Antaki, MarliesCraig et al. "Survey of gender bias in the IPCC." *Nature* 602, no. 7895 (2022): 30–32.

Livingston, Jasmine E., Eva Lövbrand, and Johanna Alkan Olsson. "From climates multiple to climate singular: maintaining policy-relevance in the IPCC synthesis report." *Environmental Science & Policy* 90 (2018): 83–90.

Livingston, Jasmine E. and Markku Rummukainen. "Taking science by surprise: the knowledge politics of the IPCC Special Report on 1.5 degrees." *Environmental Science & Policy* 112 (2020): 10–16.

Love, Thomas and Cindy Isenhour. "Energy and economy: recognizing high-energy modernity as a historical period." *Economic Anthropology* 3, no. 1 (2016): 6–16.

Mahony, Martin. "Climate change and the geographies of objectivity: the case of the IPCC's burning embers diagram." *Transactions of the Institute of British Geographers* 40, no. 2 (2015): 153–167.

Makondo, Cuthbert Casey and David S.G. Thomas. "Climate change adaptation: linking Indigenous knowledge with western science for effective adaptation." *Environmental Science & Policy* 88 (2018): 83–91.

Maldonado, Julie and Heather Lazrus. "A story of "rising voices" and intercultural collaboration." *Practicing Anthropology* 41, no. 3 (2019): 34–37.

Marino, Elizabeth K., and Albert J. Faas. "Is vulnerability an outdated concept? After subjects and spaces." *Annals of Anthropological Practice* 44, no. 1 (2020): 33–46.

Markandya, Anil, Enrica De Cian, Laurent Drouet, Josué M. Polanco-Martínez, and Francesco Bosello. "Building risk into the mitigation/adaptation decisions simulated by integrated assessment models." *Environmental and Resource Economics* 74 (2019): 1687–1721.

Marks, Danny, Mucahid Mustafa Bayrak, Selim Jahangir, David Henig, and Ajay Bailey. "Towards a cultural lens for adaptation pathways to climate change." *Regional Environmental Change* 22, no. 1 (2022): 22.

Masco, Joseph. *The nuclear borderlands: The Manhattan project in post-cold war New Mexico.* Princeton University Press, 2006.

Matus, Claudia, Pascale Bussenius, Pablo Herraz, Valentina Riberi, and Manuel Prieto. "Nature is for trees, culture is for humans: a critical reading of the IPCC report." *Sustainability* 13, no. 21 (2021): 11903.

McElwee, Pamela D. "The social lives of climate reports." *Anthropology News* April (2020): 11–15.

McElwee, Pamela D., Álvaro Fernández-Llamazares, Yildiz Aumeeruddy-Thomas, Dániel Babai, Peter Bates, Kathleen Galvin, Maximilien Guèze, et al. "Working with Indigenous and local knowledge (ILK) in large-scale ecological assessments: reviewing the experience of the IPBES Global Assessment." *Journal of Applied Ecology* 57, no. 9 (2020): 1666–1676.

Miller, Clark A., and Carina Wyborn. "Co-production in global sustainability: histories and theories." *Environmental Science & Policy* 113 (2020): 88–95.

Moore, Frances C., Katherine Lacasse, Katharine J. Mach, Yoon Ah Shin, Louis J. Gross, and Brian Beckage. "Determinants of emissions pathways in the coupled climate–social system." *Nature* 603, no. 7899 (2022): 103–111.

Morchain, Daniel. "Rethinking the framing of climate change adaptation: Knowledge, power, and politics." In Klepp, Silja and Libertad Chavez-Rodriguez (eds), *A Critical Approach to Climate Change Adaptation: Discourses, policies and practices.* Routledge (2018): 77–96.

Nikoleris, Alexandra, Johannes Stripple, and Paul Tenngart. "Narrating climate futures: shared socioeconomic pathways and literary fiction." *Climatic Change* 143 (2017): 307–319.

Nightingale, Andrea J. "Power and politics in climate change adaptation efforts: struggles over authority and recognition in the context of political instability." *Geoforum* 84 (2017): 11–20.

Obermeister, Noam. "From dichotomy to duality: addressing interdisciplinary epistemological barriers to inclusive knowledge governance in global environmental assessments." *Environmental Science & Policy* 68 (2017): 80–86.

Oliver-Smith, Anthony. "The concepts of adaptation, vulnerability, and resilience in the anthropology of climate change: considering the case of displacement and migration." In Crate, Susan A. and Mark Nuttall (eds), *Anthropology and Climate Change.* Routledge (2016): 58–85.

O'Neill, Brian C., Elmar Kriegler, Kristie L. Ebi, Eric Kemp-Benedict, Keywan Riahi, Dale S. Rothman, Bas J. Van Ruijven et al. "The roads ahead: narratives for shared socio-economic pathways describing world futures in the 21st century." *Global Environmental Change* 42 (2017): 169–180.

Oppenheimer, Michael, Naomi Oreskes, Dale Jamieson, Keynyn Brysse, Jessica O'Reilly, Matthew Shindell, and Milena Wazeck. *Discerning Experts: The practices of scientific assessment for environmental policy.* University of Chicago Press, 2019.

O'Reilly, Jessica, Keynyn Brysse, Michael Oppenheimer, and Naomi Oreskes. "Characterizing uncertainty in expert assessments: ozone depletion and the West Antarctic Ice Sheet." *Wiley Interdisciplinary Reviews: Climate Change* 2, no. 5 (2011): 728–743.

O'Reilly, Jessica, Cindy Isenhour, Pamela McElwee, and Ben Orlove. "Climate change: expanding anthropological possibilities." *Annual Review of Anthropology* 49 (2020): 13–29.

Orlove, Ben, Heather Lazrus, Grete K. Hovelsrud, and Alessandra Giannini. "Recognitions and responsibilities: on the origins and consequences of the uneven attention to climate change around the world." *Current Anthropology* 55, no. 3 (2014): 249–275.

Pearce, Warren, Martin Mahony, and Sujatha Raman. "Science advice for global challenges: learning from trade-offs in the IPCC." *Environmental Science & Policy* 80 (2018): 125–131.

Petzold, Jan, Nadine Andrews, James D. Ford, Christopher Hedemann, and Julio C. Postigo. "Indigenous knowledge on climate change adaptation: a global evidence map of academic literature." *Environmental Research Letters* 15, no. 11 (2020): 113007.

De Pryck, Kari and Krystel Wanneau. "(Anti)-boundary work in global environmental change research and assessment." *Environmental science & policy* 77 (2017): 203–210.

Robertson, Simon. "Transparency, trust, and integrated assessment models: an ethical consideration for the Intergovernmental Panel on Climate Change." *Wiley Interdisciplinary Reviews: Climate Change* 12, no. 1 (2021): e679.

Robinson, Stacy-Ann. "Climate change adaptation in SIDS: a systematic review of the literature pre and post the IPCC Fifth Assessment Report." *Wiley Interdisciplinary Reviews: Climate Change* 11, no. 4 (2020): e653.

Roscoe, Paul. "A changing climate for anthropological and archaeological research? Improving the climate-change models." *American Anthropologist* 116, no. 3 (2014): 535–548.

Roscoe, Paul. "Method, measurement, and management in IPCC climate modeling." *Human Ecology* 44, no. 6 (2016): 655–664.

Rudiak-Gould, Peter. "Climate change and accusation: global warming and local blame in a small island state." *Current Anthropology* 55, no. 4 (2014a): 365–386.

Rudiak-Gould, Peter. "Progress, decline, and the public uptake of climate science." *Public Understanding of Science* 23, no. 2 (2014b): 142–156.

Schipper, E. Lisa F., Navroz K. Dubash, and Yacob Mulugetta. "Climate change research and the search for solutions: rethinking interdisciplinarity." *Climatic Change* 168, no. 3–4 (2021): 18.

Schnegg, Michael, Coral Iris O'Brian, and Inga Janina Sievert. "It's our fault: a global comparison of different ways of explaining climate change." *Human Ecology* 49 (2021): 327–339.

Shah, Sameer H., Leonora C. Angeles, and Leila M. Harris. "Worlding the intangibility of resilience: the case of rice farmers and water-related risk in the Philippines." *World Development* 98 (2017): 400–412.

Van der Sluijs, Jeroen P. "Uncertainty and dissent in climate risk assessment: a post-normal perspective." *Nature and Culture* 7, no. 2 (2012): 174–195.

Smith, Jessica, and Mette M. High. "Exploring the anthropology of energy: ethnography, energy and ethics." *Energy Research & Social Science* 30 (2017): 1–6.

Stammler, Florian M. and Aytalina Ivanova. "From spirits to conspiracy? Nomadic perceptions of climate change, pandemics and disease." *Anthropology Today* 36, no. 4 (2020): 8–12.

Strauss, Sarah, Stephanie Rupp, and Thomas Love. *Cultures of Energy: Power, practices, technologies.* Routledge, 2013.

Thomas, Kimberley, R. Dean Hardy, Heather Lazrus, Michael Mendez, Ben Orlove, Isabel Rivera-Collazo, J. Timmons Roberts, Marcy Rockman, Benjamin P. Warner, and Robert Winthrop.

"Explaining differential vulnerability to climate change: a social science review." *Wiley Interdisciplinary Reviews: Climate Change* 10, no. 2 (2019): e565.

Tollefson, Jeff. "Study aims to put IPCC under a lens." *Nature* 502, no. 7471 (2013): 281–281.

Tschakert, Petra. "1.5 C or 2 C: a conduit's view from the science-policy interface at COP20 in Lima, Peru." *Climate Change Responses* 2 (2015): 1–11.

Vardy, Mark, Michael Oppenheimer, Navroz K. Dubash, Jessica O'Reilly, and Dale Jamieson. "The intergovernmental panel on climate change: challenges and opportunities." *Annual Review of Environment and Resources* 42 (2017): 55–75.

Vaughn, Sarah E. "The aesthetics and multiple origin stories of climate activism." *Social Anthropology/Anthropologie sociale* (2021): 213–215.

Von Storch, Lilian, Lukas Ley, and Jing Sun. "New climate change activism: before and after the Covid-19 pandemic." *Social Anthropology* 29, no. 1 (2021): 205.

Whitington, Jerome. "What does climate change demand of anthropology?" *PoLAR Political and Legal Anthropology Review* 39 (2016): 7–15.

Wilk, Richard. "Is a sustainable consumer culture possible?" In Susan Crate and Mark Nuttall (eds). *Anthropology and Climate Change: From actions to transformations*. Routledge (2016): 301–319.

Willow, Anna J. "The world we (re) build: an ethnography of the future." *Anthropology and Humanism* 46, no. 1 (2021): 4–20.

de Wit, Sara and Sophie Haines. "Climate change reception studies in anthropology." *Wiley Interdisciplinary Reviews: Climate Change* 13, no. 1 (2022): e742.

Yamineva, Yulia. "Lessons from the Intergovernmental Panel on Climate Change on inclusiveness across geographies and stakeholders." *Environmental Science & Policy* 77 (2017): 244–251.

21

NEGOTIATING SCIENCE AND POLICY IN INTERNATIONAL CLIMATE ASSESSMENTS

Jessica O'Reilly

Introduction

The practice of science is meant to understand the world through observation, conveying facts of nature through an objective lens. Scientists understand that their work, as a human endeavor, is biased, but are trained and usually careful to minimize those biases. However, when we pan out from observing a researcher observing a natural phenomenon, it quickly becomes apparent that the practice of natural history emerges from a particular time and space (exploratory and colonizing Europe). This history – from which western science emerges – continues to shape modern technoscience, including global climate science, today. We can see it when we track where the powerful research universities are situated, where science funding comes from, and who has access to training, technology, publications, and research networks.

Contemporary scientific practice interacts with global politics not only in its historical origins, but as scientists provide policy advice to decision makers. The "assessment economy" has seemingly taken on a life of its own, as massive, multiyear, professionalized subnational, national, and intergovernmental assessments are written by experts and taken up by policymakers (Oppenheimer et al. 2017). When scientists and their work show up in diplomatic spaces, anthropologists can observe the rough edges where climate science and policy meet. Sometimes called a boundary, other times an interface, these powerful epistemic and discursive zones can help us learn about what is at stake in the translations between science and policy. This chapter, using ethnographic observations and reports from meetings of the Intergovernmental Panel on Climate Change (IPCC), the Antarctic Treaty, and the United Nations Framework Convention on Climate Change (UNFCCC), analyzes the key tactics that scientists, diplomats, and technocrats use – be they framings, ethical or ideological interventions, or strategies for stalling or accelerating progress.

These tactics – tools in a meeting that help shift conversations and decisions in specific directions – are deployed to consolidate or to challenge power dynamics, including the longstanding dynamics of western science. Such challenges are particularly important as technoscientific advances brought about the machines and energy systems that rely on the

DOI: 10.4324/9781003242499-25

combustion of fossil fuels and contributed not only to anthropogenic climate change but also the continuation of historical inequalities among nations. When these nations meet – those most responsible for anthropogenic climate change, those most vulnerable to climate impacts, and those trying to develop as the polluting industrialized nations pull up the ladder behind them – discussions over scientific knowledge become, necessarily, tangled up with global climate politics. By considering science and policy spaces as sites of cultural production, this chapter analyzes a case study of how powerful developing countries intervene in substantial and tactical ways to work to shift, or at least underscore, the uneven epistemic and political terrains that are often erased in calls for a unified, global climate policy.

Scientific and Diplomatic Spaces as Sites of Cultural Production

Understanding the interfaces between science and policy ethnographically requires fieldwork into these spaces where knowledge and policy documents are produced. Anthropologists of science, including climate science, conduct research in labs and at fieldsites, observing the practices of scientific knowledge production. Ethnographic observations can illuminate some of the informal, under-described parts of scientific practice. While media reporting about scientists may focus on heroic narratives and discovery, ethnographic description brings into focus the mundane, almost intuitive, details of scientific life, such as genetics (Tamarkin 2020), soil sampling (Latour 1999), or ice coring (Salazar 2018). Analyses of scientific practice and uptake help us understand how facts and concepts are created, travel, and gain meaning in the world. The establishment and mobilization of climate science as a set of agreed-upon knowledge is a cultural practice as much as an epistemological one.

The anthropology of policy is a different knowledge domain, both in terms of fieldsites and practices, but also has a different anthropological subculture. The anthropologists of science and those of policy are different crews at the annual meetings of the American Anthropological Association, for instance. Though there is some overlap (for examples: Barnes et al. 2013; Greenhalgh 2008; Jasanoff 1990), it is not extensive. Ethnographic policy spaces pull from a long tradition in political anthropology (Shore and Wright 1997; Tate 2020). In the context of climate change, climate policy spaces occur across all scales of governance, from city councils in rural Alaska (Marino 2015) to Laotian hydropower projects (Whitington 2019) to international meetings (Khan forthcoming). For the purposes of this chapter, I consider international climate spaces as one, but not the only, site where climate policy is negotiated and articulates with climate science.

Crafting policy is a highly expert skill, one that requires policymakers to make judgements, consider and use evidence, balance (or not) the needs and desires of multiple factions, rightsholders, or interest groups – and also find all the words that can satisfy these sociocultural requirements. This work, like field sciences, occurs daily in offices (or laboratories), and then culminates in "field excursions" to negotiating spaces. At international meetings, there are formal rules of procedure and just as importantly, informal techniques that can smooth the way to agreement.

This chapter analyzes the cultural production of knowledge through negotiating tactics at three different international meetings. The Antarctic Treaty meetings are political meetings of all Antarctic Treaty Consultative Parties: these are intimate meetings with few observers and little media scrutiny. Conversely, the United Nations Framework

Convention on Climate Change (UNFCCC) is a massive political meeting, verging on a spectacle, of up to 40,000 negotiators and observers working on implementing the Paris Agreement. These meetings – called the Conference of Parties (COP) – receive intense media and scholarly attention. The final set of meetings – and the focus of analysis for this chapter – is the Intergovernmental Panel on Climate Change (IPCC). These "approval plenary" meetings I describe below are the moments where the climate assessment reports, written by an international team of scientist-authors, are approved by governments. IPCC reports are scientific documents that are finalized with a political seal of approval in the Summary for Policy Makers. Therefore, these meetings are particularly salient performances of science policy interactions.

The meetings described below are convened regularly in spaces around the world. The location matters but usually to an incremental extent – for example, you must pack your suitcase differently for a meeting in Scotland compared to a gathering in Egypt. In each place you will eat different food. Whatever the location, though, in all these diplomatic spaces there are meeting rooms with elevated plenary stages and an array of desks with microphones for the participants. There are smaller rooms with slightly more casual seating arrangements for side meetings in which smaller, more conversational work on the stickier issues is done. And there are spaces and times for breaks and receptions, which mark the pause of formal work but also sustain the conversation and relationships necessary to resume it.

Decisions taken in international meetings are agreed upon usually by consensus, but the meaning of consensus can vary. In the Antarctic Treaty System, consensus agreement indicates that there is no disagreement from any state in the decision. In the UNFCCC, consensus is achieved through a more complex balancing of the final text, with tradeoffs and elements of disagreement included. When that final decision is gaveled down – formally finalized – parties can note matters they do not agree with but point to the "wins" in the text that balance it out. That balance is the aim of accord in climate meetings matters for how the science is agreed upon as well.

In the IPCC report approval plenaries, the IPCC leadership and state delegates must agree on the SPM text, line-by-line. The effort put forth to reach strong consensus is considerable, but there are off ramps for intransigence beyond simply deleting dissensus text. Disagreements are often articulated in footnotes as a compromise, and there exists a formal "nuclear option" for recording a state's disagreement with the scientific findings.

Even though international meetings operate under the assumption of one-state-one-vote, which is an egalitarian, diplomatic stance, there are states, through their delegates, exercising various forms of geopolitical power. Alliances of interests and more formal voting blocs are immediately apparent when observing meetings, as are silent state delegations and their counterparts – vigorous, vociferous delegations that take up much of the discursive space and time of the meeting. This does not always map neatly onto conventional notions of geopolitical power, as explained below.

Negotiations at meetings take diverse forms. Ahead of the meetings proper, there are bilateral and multilateral preparatory meetings to form positions and alliances. There are similar side meetings at the events themselves, from formal bloc and bilateral meetings to the informal conversations that occur at meals, coffee breaks, and in corners and hallways. The plenary meetings, with flags raised, interpretation, formal orders of procedure, and diplomatic decorum, are the icing on a cake baked well in advance and in less public and formal settings. The sidelining of much of the negotiation process is not a surprising additional feature but it is the process itself. However, much of this traditional negotiating practice was erased with the Covid-19 pandemic and the move to Zoom. The online format removed some of the sideline conversations entirely; others took frontstage in plenary meetings. For the meetings described below, the IPCC was convened on Zoom while the others are in-person meetings; these modalities affected my observations as well as the negotiating choices delegates made.

Ethnographically, we can think of meetings as sites of knowledge production, sites of political negotiation, a formalized space where matters are considered among groups of people. Under these temporary conditions, we see the interfaces of science and policy – and other concerns that articulate with climate change – enacted.

Negotiating Tactics at the Intergovernmental Panel on Climate Change

The Intergovernmental Panel on Climate Change (IPCC) is an organization founded by the United Nations Environment Programme (UNEP) and the World Meteorological Organization (WMO) in 1988, to produce assessments of global knowledge about climate change. Governments on the panel (almost all states on the planet are represented) nominate authors from their countries, and approve outlines, and, after the authors write their reports over the course of several years, approve the Summary for Policy Makers (SPM) and adopt the underlying report. So, while the authors – mostly academics – write the content, the final SPM undergoes political scrutiny, line-by-line, in a rigorous approval plenary session.

In the days of the approval plenary, politics and science mix. There is careful boundary work – the IPCC is not going to alter its science for diplomats, but the science can be phrased in ways that are more clear and apparently neutral. Authors are expected to write up the science so that it is "policy-relevant but not policy-prescriptive." The science can also be rephrased, packaged, and communicated in ways that make it more politically palatable – and therefore approvable – for governments.

As the plenary moves through the text of the SPM, IPCC leaders collect questions from the delegates and IPCC authors respond. Many of these questions are about making the language clearer – though clarity and obfuscation are both subjective, negotiated categories – or asking questions about complex or new science. Some of the questions veer towards ensuring that climate knowledge about particular countries, regions, or ecosystems is well represented in the SPM. As most decision makers will not read the 400-page full reports, the SPM, as a concise summary, is the most-read and referenced document. If environment ministers want to encourage their governments to take climate action, having climate impacts, like drought, specifically tied to their region in the SPM, helps their case. In addition, scientific research continues its longstanding bias towards the Global North, leaving data gaps and research blind spots in areas and societies that are particularly climate vulnerable, ecologically, socioeconomically, and politically.

Other questions are more politically loaded and difficult to solve at the approval plenary. Some countries' entire economic system is built around the fossil fuel industry. Their state interest, then, is to slow the sense of urgency to delay action or give their economy time to transition away from fossil fuels. Other countries, like the United States, bear the historical responsibility of greenhouse gas emissions that cause climate change – to their economic advantage. Those states often advocate for a climate policy discourse of shared responsibility – the idea that we are all on the planet together, so that we must all work together to solve the problem. Unifying and idealistic, this approach also shrugs off the notion that states who have historically emitted the most should shoulder a proportionately high burden in paying for transitioning to renewable energy globally, as well as the damages incurred by climate impacts. For example, at the 2021 WGI approval plenary, an Indian delegate succinctly objected to one word: "with regard to the figure's heading stating that 'every tonne of CO_2 we put in the atmosphere adds to global warming,' INDIA called for the deletion of the 'we.'" (IISD 2021: 23). This intervention can be read doubly, as a line edit or as an ethical statement, objecting to the idea that all of humanity shoulders an equal blame for carbon emissions.

The Indian delegation is particularly attuned to climate equity and justice issues and will champion them, sometimes to an exhausting degree. While not the only delegation to express concern and interest in climate justice, the Indian delegation took up the most "air time" in the approval plenary on this topic, for two reasons.

One reason is a specific person on the delegation. Thiagarjan Jayaraman can craft a speech. He is a physicist by training, but with an education and career that has combined science with the Indian tradition of scholars being involved in the work of nation building (Anderson 2010). When I first began hearing his philosophical style of intervention, I looked him up. He is, in short, "one of us," a scholar of science and technology studies, using the analytical tools of our field to intervene on climate politics at the highest level. Following a long career at the Tata Institute of Social Science, he is now a Senior Fellow of Climate Change at the M.S. Swaminathan Research Foundation. This foundation, in the fall of 2021, launched a website and data tracker called the Climate Equity Monitor (climateequitymonitor.in).

The website encapsulates Professor Jayaraman's ideology in graphical form. The landing page features a world map. On the map, you can toggle between "Annex I" and "non-Annex I" countries. This refers to the original United Nations Framework Convention on Climate Change (UNFCCC 1992). Annex I countries are those that, in 1992, were developed countries or were economies-in-transition: moving towards a market economy. Non-Annex I, then are all other countries, the 1992 developing world. The 2015 Paris Agreement, the current UNFCCC accord, does not dissolve this bifurcation but takes significant steps to blurring these two categories. The United States (then represented by the Obama administration) insisted on an "all hands on deck" approach to the Paris Agreement's next generation of climate policy, where every state has responsibilities to work to lower carbon emissions as quickly as possible for that nation.

This is an easy position for powerful, rich countries to take in relation to the converse, by which states that have caused the most carbon dioxide pollution are those most responsible for causing the problem. Calculating emissions becomes an ethical act in which responsibility is distributed. *Current emissions* show a snapshot of the present by country view, showing how much greenhouse gas emissions each state – the entity through which emissions are considered under the Paris Agreement – is emitting. This calculus positions China as the world's top emitter, followed by the US, then India. These countries have different trajectories, however, so China and India may choose to emphasize a different method of calculation. *Per capita emissions*, given the large populations of China and India, brings consumption into focus: people in the United States live much more carbon intensive lives. Alternately, *historical emissions* frame the responsibility over time. Calculating emissions in this manner quickly shows the industrial advantage of the West over the past century, with opportunities to gain wealth and higher standards of living, fueled by combustion of fossil fuels.

The second reason is India – and by this I mean representatives authorized to speak on behalf of the Indian government – has a tradition of interventions on behalf of blocs of non-western countries. These can be described as developing countries, which points to economic status along with some other standard-of-living indicators, or G-77 and China, a UN bloc, or the non-aligned states, which is a political position that emerges from the Cold War – these are the states that choose not to pick a side. As a powerful developing country, Indian interventions often provide direct challenges to developed countries and their hegemonic positions.

As an anthropologist of science and policy, I have observed these interventions mostly at this interface. India has nuclear weapons, the development of which is partially about demonstrating technological power in a postcolonial context (Abraham 1998). In my Antarctic research, India's postcolonial framing of scientific research and international power caused controversy. India, a newcomer to the Cold War-era Antarctic Treaty, had to demonstrate and maintain a "scientific presence" in the Antarctic for membership. Traditionally, such presence was demonstrated through the establishment of a national research station. Their first station, Dakshin Gangotri, was established in the 1983–1984 season but was poorly positioned; it quickly became buried under ice and snow and was decommissioned by the end of the decade. The second station, Maitri began construction in 1984 and was completed in 1989 to replace Dakshin Gangotri. Maitri was the sole Indian station until the Republic of India decided to building a new base in the Larsemann Hills.

Decisions are made through absolute consensus in the Antarctic Treaty System. India needed to follow a chain of environmental planning procedures through the system, starting with the Committee for Environmental Protection. The announcement, at the 2006 Antarctic Treaty meeting in Edinburgh, went poorly, as India tacked on their plans following a presentation by Australia, China, Russia, and Romania on a planned Antarctic Specially Managed Area in the region. Those parties already had research stations there, and India wanted their new research station to be built in the centre of their mapped protected area. The Indian delegate explained their reasons for that specific location as religious and geological: that site was where India and Antarctica were connected 600 million years ago, as part of the Gondwana supercontinent. The new India base was to be built near the ancient riverbed of the Godavari River, a sacred river which still flows on the Indian subcontinent.

That meeting was the first international, diplomatic event I had observed as an anthropologist, and I was transfixed by this controversy. The delegates opposed to the Indian plan were so angry! In conversations, interviews, and media stories, these delegates indicated that the Indian delegates were not following the conventions of the Treaty system, suggesting that they didn't understand "the process," with one person even mentioning to me that the Indians didn't understand English (not true, of course, as English is an official language of the former British colony).

What followed was a couple of years of negotiations between India and some other delegations, namely, those already with stations in the Larsemann Hills. I admired India's strategy at causing a disruption in the polite, often dull, Antarctic Treaty Meetings and to bring some of the historical political alignments of the institution into daylight. By the following year, India had been invited to join the Antarctic Specially Managed Area management team. They proceeded with their plans to build a base, even as they continued to be called out for evading the agreed-upon environment impact assessment process, as they installed temporary "melon" huts at the site in the 2006–2007 summer season. With the advice of their Antarctic colleagues, they shifted their nationalist rationale for building in the Larsemann Hills to a scientific discourse, rendering the plan acceptable in Antarctic diplomacy (O'Reilly 2017). In short, the Indian station Bharati was built in 2012 and the delegation provided a master class in wielding power from below in diplomatic settings.

At the IPCC approval plenaries, the Indian delegation elaborated on this tradition, in higher stakes circumstances and with higher visibility. Other IPCC member delegates align with India, with Saudi Arabian delegates being the most vocally aligned, and with the favor returned in the other direction. The Chinese delegates were quite quiet at the IPCC approval plenaries in comparison but would also join in, with Brazil and South Africa also sometimes in alignment. But over the duration of the three Working Group approval plenaries (in July 2021, February 2022, and March 2022), the Indian delegation led the charge on calling for inclusion of historical responsibility of carbon emissions, differentiation in economic development, and questioning the assumptions and biases in the depiction of IPCC knowledge.

Delegates performed the taking of time as a tactic. They called for breaks, a five-minute pause halfway between each three-hour work session. They refused to continue work after the three hours, citing limitations of delegate size, the need for breaks, or the lack of interpretation. They objected to adding extra sessions (though the IPCC leadership overrode these objections as all of the meetings began to run over time). And some delegates' interventions took up meeting time in a way that no other individual's remarks did. These interventions were presented with an explanatory, conceptual oratorical style more in line with academia – not the technocratic efficiency of a diplomat. The taking of time can be seen more than a style of speech, however, but as a means for exercising power in a meeting. Indeed, the time delegates took could (and delegates noted did) take time from other perspectives being expressed, other concerns being addressed.

Another tactic involved procedural delays. As these meetings were the first approval plenaries conducted on Zoom, a new set of guidelines for the conduct of online meetings was agreed upon. These new guidelines led to confusion about process which in turn seemed to become another opportunity to run out the clock on discussing report content. From clarification questions about process to declarations of "point of order!" to questioning, or even refusing, any activity that seemed to contradict typical IPCC procedures, conversations about process also resulted in running out the clock.

Delegates also attempted to saturate the discursive space of the meeting with their core concerns, globally throughout the text. Every national delegation arrives to a meeting with specific goals, worked through in advance with their government agencies and their delegates. Members may have a red line – like certain depictions of solar radiation management – that cannot be crossed, and delegations are usually respectful and understanding of these diplomatic limits, though there may be robust conversation about these topics.

While the insertion of values and concerns is part of the mundane editing of report text, some delegations sought to saturate the text with their concerns. I could not discern if this tactic was meant to restructure the narrative of the text with an additional through-line of, say, climate justice, or unabated emissions – or if the delegates working on this were simply trying to add their concern in wherever and see where it might stick. Nonetheless, the relentless work towards trying to include a concept, even if already covered elsewhere in the text, had the effect of stalling steady progress towards approval.

Ultimately, gumming up the time and discursive space of the planned meeting required a lengthening and hastening of approval in the final days and hours. Sometimes this meant that a figure or a paragraph that was controversial but might have eventually received full support with some more revision, had to be dropped. Following Parkinson's Law – that work expands to fill the time allotted to it – the time and space had to be filled somehow, and specific delegations took it upon themselves to do so, with necessary but difficult to ascertain subtractions following.

These tactics are used by delegates who occupy a specific stratum of geopolitical power. These are not tactics frequently used by western states – those members, and their views on the science have already been incorporated into the text, anticipated by the authors. Their views are hegemonic in the IPCC and only are rarely challenged. Their remarks, then, can be framed as modest questions of clarification. Their epistemological framing is the frame of the report.

These are also not tactics typically used by the most climate vulnerable and least politically powerful states. Small island states, for example, often worked in blocs, to preserve and emphasize science directly related to their futures. A key concern was the preservation of 1.5°C as a unit of analysis, even when limiting global warming to that threshold was unlikely or understudied. These members were adept at presenting their concerns, with a strong ethical valance, and were usually broadly supported by developed countries.

Instead, the interventions above are the domain of powerful developing country interventions. Their objections are often in contrast to hegemonic western framings of knowledge and depictions of the past and future that skim over the unequal trajectories countries are on, due to events set in motion well before the industrial revolution. Their interventions are longer and more complex, as their views are not always already comprehensively enfolded into the text, nor might their review comments ahead of the meeting have been taken into account. To counter this, they exert their authority in the space of the meeting.

The interventions the delegations above are requesting are complex: part of the complication is that addressing them cannot usually be completed with a quick edit or re-wording by the IPCC authors. The issues – distributive justice, equity, and differentiation – all get glossed over as a list of values in the IPCC report, but the explicit detail of how to achieve these fails to show up in the Summary for Policy Makers. The knowledge is there; you can find it in the underlying chapters of the IPCC report, which are adopted by affirmation at the IPCC plenaries, instead of undergoing the line-by-line governmental scrutiny of the SPM. But the knowledge – and it is messy, politically difficult, and complex knowledge, requiring critical rethinking of some of the longstanding arrangements we have made – cannot make it through the gauntlet of politics into the totalizing, difference-erasing, message-to-the-world SPM text. Nonetheless, the delegates concerned about this use tactics ranging from direct interventions on the subjects to more indirect but still effective-enough actions like stalling, repeating, and exerting power over the meeting's time and discursive space.

The IPCC reports, once approved, become the scientific basic for climate policy decisions across various levels of governance. The reports and the institution become signifiers of scientific consensus, lending decisions scientific credibility. This extends to people involved with the IPCC. IPCC vice chairs, co-chairs and authors, for example, are invited to speak at UNFCCC meetings, in high profile plenary events. These events, in which national delegates ask questions or make statements of support (or not) signal a high-level handing off of knowledge from scientists to policymakers.

The boundary, however neatly performed, is not crisp and clear. For example, at the UNFCCC's COP26 in Glasgow, which was held from October 31 to November 13, 2021, the COP organizers provided several opportunities for the WGI leadership and authors to present their report, which had been approved three months prior. One of the events was a two-part series called the Structured Expert Dialogue, consisting of science presentations and then question-and-answer sessions between the scientists and the government delegates. The IPCC report authors were front-and-center, though representatives of other major organizations, such as Rodolfo Lacy of the OECD – representing "free market" democracies, along with Meena Raman representing the Third World Network – were also present on the stage. Delegates sat in the audience behind placards indicating their nation's name, and when questions began, stood in front of microphones facing the stage.

Professor Jayaraman walked up to a microphone and continued his points from the IPCC plenary. I am happy to see him in person after listening to him on Zoom for two long weeks. He seemed animated, perhaps frustrated, and referenced a point that the Third World Network had just made ahead of him about the historical responsibility of developed nations for the fact that more than 80% of the carbon budget to reach 1.5°C has already been spent. Jayaraman noted that the Structured Expert Dialogue is not meant to just be a technical exercize to review the results of the IPCC. He got to the point with his questions, though they were delivered in his characteristic multi-faceted, philosophical, oratorial style: what is the total of OECD cumulative emissions, what proportion does it represent of historical cumulative emissions? What are the cumulative emissions of Nationally Determined Contributions and pledges of all OECD countries, aggregated?

His direct questions indirectly asked the experts on stage to address a gap different than the one presented in the annual UNEP "Emissions gap report" between global actions and pledges to reduce carbon emissions, actual reductions, and the remaining carbon budget to various temperature thresholds. Jayaraman's gap would show the difference between historical, cumulative emissions of wealthy developed states and their actions and pledges to address their emissions that got them to that status.

After taking some more questions, the OECD expert, Mr. Lacy, answered Jayaraman's questions. Lacy said that he would be happy to report back to India with more granular data, but noted the point about providing more historical data. Governments are not providing that information, Lacy said, it is scientists doing that work. In this instance, the tension between what is apparent and what is invisible is reversed: here, the accounting for historical emissions is relegated to scientific research and not government accounting. In the IPCC approval plenaries it is the opposite. In that moment, the zone of interaction between science and politics feels like a black hole, an opportunity to continuously shift responsibility between the two domains. If that is also a tactic, then the recurring, multi-institutional insistence by some delegates to foreground these responsibilities at every turn is necessary.

Conclusion

Boundary work that delineates the practice of science from other human activities is a longstanding object of study (Gieryn 1983). Contemporary environmental politics, including those addressing climate change, challenge this notion of boundary work (de Pryck and Wanneau 2017). Leaders and authors of scientific assessment reports like those of the IPCC seek policy relevance, involvement as information providers to decision makers, and participate in political negotiations.

The increased formalization of people and organizations working in science/policy boundary spaces has led to an "assessment economy" and in turn, assessment subcultures. Anthropological research can help us understand how these subcultures are formed, work, and change, instead of taking them as a neutral given for translating scientific knowledge into political action. Ethnographic engagement with these people and events lends insight into the values, tactics, and sets of knowledge that lead to decisions on critical issues. In international diplomacy, as well as at smaller scales of decision making, scientific knowledge for policy is produced by people with multiple interests and skills.

Moments where experts in science and diplomacy interact provide opportunities for ethnographic observation and analysis of this complex interface between these domains. Additionally, there are people who are experts at working along the edges of this interface, helping to communicate science in more policy-relevant or politically-palatable styles. Relevance and palatability are not universal signifiers, however, and conflicts show up in moments when the understandings of climate change, its implications, and its solutions are negotiated. The meeting tactics above help delegates maneuver in this complex space and can help directly and indirectly challenge entrenched structures of power. By studying the knowledge communities and practices which form competing ideas around climate concerns, anthropology can contribute to understandings of the problems of and solutions to climate change.

References

Abraham, Itty. 1998. *The Making of the Indian Atomic Bomb: Science, secrecy and the postcolonial state*. Zed Books.

Anderson, Robert S. 2010. *Nucleus and Nation*. University of Chicago Press.

Barnes, Jessica, Michael Dove, Myanna Lahsen, Andrew Mathews, Pamela McElwee, Roderick McIntosh, Frances Moore, Jessica O'Reilly, Benjamin Orlove, Rajindra Puri, Harvey Weiss, and Karina Yager. 2013. "Contribution of anthropology to the study of climate change." *Nature Climate Change* 3 (6): 541–544.

De Pryck, Kari and Krystel Wanneau. 2017. "(Anti)-boundary work in global environmental change research and assessment." *Environmental Science & Policy* 77: 203–210.

Gieryn, Thomas F. 1983. "Boundary-work and the demarcation of science from non-science: strains and interests in professional ideologies of scientists." *American Sociological Review* 48 (6): 781–795.

Greenhalgh, Susan. 2008. *Just One child: Science and policy in Deng's China*. University of California Press.

IISD. 2021. "Summary of the 54th Session of the Intergovernmental Panel on Climate Change and the 14th Session of Working Group I: 26 July–August 6 2021." *Earth Negotiations Bulletin* 12 (781): 1–27.

Jasanoff, Sheila. 1990. *The Fifth Branch: Science advisers as policymakers*. Cambridge, Mass.: Harvard University Press.

Kahn, Naveeda. 2023. *In Quest of a Shared Planet: Negotiating climate from the Global South*. New York: Fordham University Press.

Latour, Bruno. 1999. *Pandora's Hope: Essays on the reality of science studies*. Cambridge, Mass.: Harvard University Press.

Marino, Elizabeth. 2015. *Fierce Climate, Sacred ground: An ethnography of climate change in Shishmaref, Alaska*. Fairbanks: University of Alaska Press.

Oppenheimer, Michael, Naomi Oreskes, Dale Jamieson, Keynyn Brysse, Jessica O'Reilly, Matthew Shindell, and Milena Wazeck. 2019. *Discerning Experts: The practices of scientific assessment for environmental policy*. Chicago: University of Chicago Press.

O'Reilly, Jessica. 2017. *The Technocratic Antarctic: An ethnography of scientific expertise and environmental governance*. Ithaca, NY: Cornell University Press.

Salazar, Juan Francisco. 2018. "Ice cores as temporal probes." *Journal of Contemporary Archaeology* 5 (1): 32–43.

Shore, Cris and Susan Wright S. 1997. *Anthropology of Policy: Perspectives on governance and power*. London and New York: Routledge.

Tamarkin, Noah. 2020. *Genetic Afterlives*. Durham, NC: Duke University Press.

Tate, Winifred. 2020. "Anthropology of policy: tensions, temporalities, possibilities." *Annual Review of Anthropology* 49: 83–99.

UNFCCC. 1992. *United Nations Framework Convention on Climate Change*. New York: United Nations.

Whitington, Jerome. 2019. *Anthropogenic Rivers: The production of uncertainty in Lao hydropower*. Ithaca, NY: Cornell University Press.

22

FROM "LONE RANGER" TO TEAM PLAYER

The Role of Anthropology in Training a New Generation of Climate Adaptation Professionals

Sarah Strauss and Courtney Kurlanska

Introduction

Since the release of the latest IPCC reports (AR6-WGII, 2022 and AR6-WGIII, 2022), it has become clear that the world has not yet moved away from "business as usual" approaches. However, the work of climate change mitigation to reduce greenhouse gas emissions, along with adaptation to the multifaceted transitions of transforming climates, shifting energyscapes (Strauss, Rupp and Love 2013), and decolonizing cultures and political economies, is finally starting to take place at the different scales and scopes that are needed for lasting impacts. Both AR6 reports also highlight the emergence of increasingly diverse actors and strategies, from local to regional contexts, and the parallel efforts to integrate our work on mitigation, adaptation, and development (e.g., Sustainable Development Goals – SDGs) in ways that are synergistic rather than redundant or even antagonistic.

As documented in the three editions of this volume and elsewhere, the anthropology of climate change itself has grown and shifted in many ways. With *Weather, Climate, Culture* (2003), Sarah Strauss and Ben Orlove began to define a set of scales (days, years, generations) and to integrate these temporal aspects across material and symbolic concerns, while documenting the language of weather, seasons, and climate across cultures, considering how our descriptions relate to our understandings as well as our practices. The majority (but by no means all, cf. Roncoli et al. 2003) of the work included in Strauss and Orlove (2003) and also in Crate and Nuttall (2009, 2016) was written in the usual anthropological context of the lone anthropologist, whether operating in an "applied" or more theoretical context, witnessing and experiencing and learning through participant observation, archival research, or archaeological methods. As we have moved through the decades, anthropology has changed, becoming more collaborative as well as multi-sited, and bringing our four-field intradisciplinary holism into more direct application as part of transdisciplinary teams. We recognize the need for engaging and connecting many ways of knowing, and for developing approaches that not only welcome, but require, a collective engagement with the challenges we face in addressing the reality of a

DOI: 10.4324/9781003242499-26

changing climate and all that this implies at more fine-grained scales. This chapter, moving from Strauss's earlier contributions (Crate and Nuttall 2009, 2016) as "lone ethnographer" (Galman 2018) presenting ethnographic work from Leukerbad, Switzerland, has shifted to a collaborative effort with Courtney Kurlanska to present ways that the theory and practice of cultural anthropology can provide grounding for a transdisciplinary approach to training a new cadre of community climate adaptation practitioners.

In this chapter we explore how anthropology can support the training of graduate students for careers in community climate adaptation. With our holistic approach and emphasis on local community context, anthropologists are well placed to work with engineers and other experts to train the new generation of climate adaptation professionals to help meet local needs and provide innovative strategies for adapting to a changing climate. Worcester Polytechnic Institute (WPI), where we both work, has recently built a new transdisciplinary master's program that puts ethnographic methods at the center of a novel team-research-based strategy to address the multifaceted and complex problems associated with climate change. No single discipline or area of expertise is, of course, sufficient to address this global challenge (Brondizio 2016). Drawing on a place-based and problem-centered approach, the Community Climate Adaptation degree program offers students from a range of different backgrounds a way forward to collaborate effectively with community members, sociocultural practitioners, physical and environmental scientists, engineers, and policymakers in support of effective local adaptation practices. In this way, among others, the contributions of anthropology to the field of climate change adaptation can perhaps live up to Kirsten Hastrup's call to "acknowledge people's powers of theorizing, anticipating, and acting and to meet a future, where all humans are seen as potential contributors to sustainable solutions" (Hastrup 2016: 53).

We first provide background for ourselves, and how we have come to think about anthropology's role in a broader community of adaptation practice. We then discuss the emergence of the new field of community climate adaptation, followed by the development of the new graduate program at WPI in relation to our own training and that of our colleagues.

Community Climate Adaptation: Coming to Terms with a New Field

Anthropology is in many ways a discipline of dilettantes, of people whose experiences with multiple other fields converge into a space of practice that admits a broader range of theoretical and methodological approaches than many more "traditional" social science disciplines (like economics and psychology) generally permit. In our own cases, we brought degrees in journalism and urban studies (Kurlanska), public health and comparative religion (Strauss), to our work in anthropology. Through our work experiences at various institutions from western public land grant to eastern private technical schools, we have had opportunities to collaborate across multiple disciplines and settings and find that these different threads continue to have relevance for our teaching and research on community climate adaptation. It is clear that the substantive body of work done by the editors and contributors to this volume, among many others (*inter alia* Rayner and Malone 1998; Strauss and Orlove 2003; Crate 2011; Crate and Nuttall 2009, 2016; Lazrus et al. 2022; Barnes and Dove 2015; Fiske et al. 2014; Hastrup 2016; O'Reilly et al. 2020; Eriksen 2021; Vaughn 2022), has created a strong foundation upon which a new generation is building a more engaged anthropology of climate action; for example, we have now seen formation of a new Climate Change interest group (2021) within the American Anthropological Association. From this body of work, developed over the thirty years since the Rio Summit, we know that anthropology has a substantial role to play in addressing climate change; the best chance we have for successful adaptation is to ensure continuing collaboration across academic disciplines and global cultures; public and private sectors; professional practitioners and householders; old and young of every gender; and engagement with the non-human world with respect as well as urgency.

In order to help us move forward together, we need a cadre of adaptation professionals whose purpose is to collaborate with and support communities in these inevitable transitions. This effort can be seen as similar to the development of public health as a new professional field (Moser et al. 2017). As a response to the challenges faced by an increasingly urbanizing population and the need for attention to social services and health management at the community scale (Tulchinsky and Varavikova 2014), the field of public health began to blossom in the mid-nineteenth century. The requirements for that profession, as with this new field of climate adaptation, reflected the emergent needs of the times for ensuring community-scale resilience to problems that in many cases had always existed, but whose severity and impact for human populations had intensified with the increasing challenges of urbanization, population increases, technological innovation, and nationalism. When human populations were small and scattered, the difficulty of adapting to a changing planet was managed by two basic strategies, loosely understood as culture and mobility. People moved across landscapes following resources and favorable climates, and for a very long time, were not hampered in doing so by national borders and political considerations. Given the current political and economic climate, mobility options are severely limited, dictating a greater reliance on our cultural innovations.

With this understanding of adaptation as our primary cultural strategy for dealing with climatic changes, and more specifically, following the principles adopted by the American Society of Adaptation Professionals, we acknowledge that:

- Climate change is a real and serious danger to all sectors and systems. Its root causes must be addressed.
- Adaptation and resilience build stronger, more prepared regions, ecosystems, communities, economies, neighborhoods, and households.
- Adaptation and resilience must serve the interests and health of the natural world, both because of its intrinsic value and because these interests also serve those of human health, security, and overall well-being.
- Adaptive decision-making, creativity, innovation, and transformative problem solving are essential to address new and changing climate conditions.
- Individuals and communities on the frontlines of climate change hold expertise and resilience that must be centered in adaptation processes and decisions.
- Science is a critical foundation for our climate adaptation knowledge.
- Grave injustices of the past, which have been allowed to perpetuate today, have created an unjust and inequitable society. Climate change exacerbates these inequities, as those who are the least responsible for climate change are often the most impacted.

(ASAP 2022a)

As these principles suggest, we humans have always had our cultures to deploy: innovative abilities to learn, share, and transform our material worlds and ideas in service of subsistence needs as well as performance of aesthetic and ethical values. Now more than ever, a diverse range of cultural strategies needs to be considered in order to successfully navigate the challenges presented by global climate change (cf. Lazrus et al. 2022).

Worcester Polytechnic Institute has therefore developed a graduate program in Community Climate Adaptation that builds on these values, beliefs, and practices – many of which are also expressed in the *Statement on Humanity and Climate Change* (AAA 2015) that emerged from the report of the American Anthropological Association's Task Force on Global Environmental Change, *Changing the Atmosphere* (Fiske et al. 2014). In this chapter, we explore the ways that an anthropological perspective can enhance and integrate transdisciplinary training in the new field of community climate adaptation, providing a model for future efforts in this arena.

The Value of an Anthropological Approach in a Transdisciplinary Endeavor

As our human demands on the world's resources have grown, the interactive implications of our simultaneous depletion of our resources, along with innovative recombination and processing of these same resources (sometimes with unknowable side-effects), has boxed us into unsustainable lifeways that are also restricted geographically based on territorial claims (cf. Peterson and Maldonado 2016). So, we cannot easily move far to escape new climatic conditions, and the resources needed to survive in the places where we have landed are likewise limited or contaminated. We have, in other words, found ourselves in the geological epoch of the Anthropocene, and our actions have become the primary drivers for change on this finite planet. With this transformative turn, we have seen over the past 30 years the development of an international-scale response to the climatic changes we have identified, the Intergovernmental Panel on Climate Change (IPCC), and then a cascade of national, state, and local level policy initiatives (C2ES 2022; and see Odell 2023); to address targets determined as sufficient to minimize the impacts of the shifts we have set in motion. While climate change is a global problem, it is experienced in particular ways in specific places, and these local experiences must be understood in order to respond effectively to support any given community at any given time. The field of anthropology, with its intradisciplinary four-field approach to making sense of humanity over time and across regions, is uniquely primed to contribute to our understanding of climate adaptation needs in the Anthropocene. But it is not sufficient.

Climate change is a complex problem, and to deal with the challenges of addressing issues associated with climate change, collaborative, transdisciplinary approaches are needed. In the realm of climate change policy and debate, economists and scientists tend to be the most influential voices (Baer and Singer 2018; Krauss 2015). To find long-term strategies for complex global issues like climate change, a multitude of voices need to enter the discussion. This includes not only academics from the social sciences and humanities, but also community members, NGOs, and other collaborators across many professions (Baer and Singer 2018). In this transdisciplinary, collaborative approach to addressing complex problems, anthropologists are particularly well placed to contribute to three key areas: knowledge production; addressing issues of vulnerability, resilience, and social justice; and transcending the local to move towards theoretical discussions of interconnection (O'Reilly et al. 2020; Baer and Singer 2018; Krauss 2015; Hastrup 2013).

O'Reilly et al. highlight how understanding knowledge production also advances our ability to engage with these other factors; they argue that "Anthropological research can show how people adapt to rapidly changing environments and point out diverse notions of value and knowledge that can help us understand and respond to the climate crisis in more just and effective ways" (2020: 23). This allows us to question who the experts are, why they are considered experts, and who is excluded from this category. Drawing on local-level community examples helps to highlight that local knowledge can be just as, if not more valuable than "expert" knowledge that is not grounded in the local context. This supports the critique by Baer and Singer (2018), who argue that traditional analyses of causes and solutions to climate change don't typically discuss structures of power and social inequality and, as a result, do not provide an accurate assessment of the issue. Anthropology plays a critical role in helping bring these less-dominant voices and ways of seeing the world to the forefront to work in collaboration with those creating and implementing policy. When these voices are heard, it sets the stage for an open dialogue about knowledge production and collaboration and makes possible the needed shift in perspective that can bring issues such as climate change back into democracy (Krauss 2015). This is taken a step further when anthropologists adopt an engaged praxis orientation, merging theory with social action to focus on and engage with issues of equity, justice, and participatory democracy.

The examination of global problems and their local implications through environmental, economic, political, and social aspects lays the foundation for the discipline's ability to address vulnerability, resilience, and social justice (Hastrup 2013). While the understanding that local knowledge production is often devalued is one component of this, it is important to examine how global climate change unevenly impacts populations around the world. Anthropology and ethnography provide a window into how different communities engage with their environment (Baer and Singer 2018) and how the policies and programs meant to mitigate and adapt to these challenges impact different places in different ways, often exacerbating already existing inequalities (Markkanen and Anger-Kraavi 2019). As noted above, however, ethnographic methods also provide the opportunity to examine how communities respond to these policies differently and how this uneven implementation can lead to new and innovative strategies for addressing complex problems or act as the impetus for local organizing and political action (Ersoy and van Bueren 2020).

What may be anthropology's most valuable contribution, however, is its holistic, collaborative approach and its ability to broaden the discussion on critical issues like climate change, opening possibilities for diverse solutions and transformative futures (Baer and Singer 2018; O'Reilly et al. 2020). As Hastrup (2013) argues, for anthropology to reach this transformative capacity, it needs to rescale the concept of holism and work to transcend the local, focusing on the connections between places, times, and different types of knowledge. With this as a guiding principle, the discipline can offer theoretical suggestions for large-scale global issues (Hastrup 2013; Baer and Singer 2018). Enhanced by a collaborative approach to framing problems, society can begin to see things in new and important ways (Krauss 2015) that have the potential for long-term transformative change.

"*Lehr und Kunst*": Project-Based Learning and Community Collaboration

To move towards this transformative, collaborative vision, we need to reimagine how professionals, experts, and community members engage with and work to address global issues like climate change in local contexts. WPI's innovative engineering program, honored by the National Academy of Engineers with the 2016 Bernard M. Gordon Prize for Innovation in Engineering and Technology Education, emerged as a response to following this unorthodox path for over fifty years, with an undergraduate degree requirement that encapsulates the motto of *"Lehr und Kunst"* or theory and practice. This degree requirement, called the Interactive Qualifying Project (IQP), completed over two seven-week terms, is based on three core pillars: project-based learning, interdisciplinarity, and local community involvement. We have used the IQP model to develop a deeper and more comparative framework for the Community Climate Adaptation (CCA) graduate program, and so will preface our description of CCA with an explanation of this undergraduate model.

The fundamental goal of the IQP is for students to recognize and engage with the intersection of science and society (Elmes and Loiacono 2009). This is accomplished through a unique combination of team-based research and community partnerships. Students work as part of an interdisciplinary team to complete a project that is sponsored and overseen by a community organization. WPI's Global Projects Program (GPP) runs more than 40 project centers located around the globe, and these faculty-directed centers support the IQP program as well as a number of other programs for undergraduates and graduate students, including CCA. Center directors work in close collaboration with local organizations such as NGOs, schools, small businesses, and government organizations to identify projects where students can support these organizations and assist them in developing strategies to meet the organization's needs. For the IQP, students travel for seven weeks to work full-time, on-location with a local organization, two faculty advisors, and team members to address the challenge presented by their local sponsor. Given the range of needs presented globally, these projects differ dramatically from location to location and from sponsor to sponsor. Students have worked on projects that range from specific technical issues, such as revamping a medical filing system in Armenia, to documenting the local impacts of climate change in New Zealand.

In preparation for this project work, students take a seven-week course in Social Science Research Methods, which is taught primarily by faculty in the Department of Integrative and Global Studies (DIGS); the disciplinary expertise of DIGS faculty includes about a dozen with Anthropology and Cultural Geography (mostly in the Clark University/Boasian tradition) backgrounds, another dozen with interdisciplinary Environmental, Urban, and Policy Studies training, and the remaining half-dozen ranging from law to philosophy, ecology, and education. Place-based qualitative field research experience in both academic, governmental, and non-profit contexts dominate the methodological expertise, though many other skill sets are present in the department. During the research methods course, the students work in pre-set teams (determined by interest surveys) to research the problem they have been tasked to address, explore relevant contextual information, and are introduced to the fundamentals of qualitative research methods. It is important to note that this program is a central and required component of the curriculum at a STEM school, where nearly all the student body is majoring in engineering or a basic science; in fact, it is considered to be the "flagship" program of the school and the reason why many students choose this school over other options. While the students are well versed in quantitative data collection and analysis, the concept of qualitative data and its importance to the successful outcomes of project work is often a difficult sell to students (and some faculty). In addition to the course instructor, the school invests in sending two project advisors with the teams to their Project Center. The advisors meet with each team of students on a weekly basis in the term prior to the fieldwork experience, and at least twice a week during the field term, in addition to class or other group sessions.

In addition to qualitative methods, the research course also emphasizes teamwork and communication. Students are assigned a series of individual and team-based tasks to help develop an appreciation for how different perspectives, beliefs, experiences, and backgrounds can contribute to the overall project (Pfeifer and Stoddard 2019). These exercises also help identify and address potential areas of conflict, including differing expectations around experience, gender, identity, and outcomes (Morse 2019; Stoddard and Pfeifer 2018). Strategies such as alternating team roles of leader and note-taker, for example, help prevent teams from falling into detrimental patterns of behavior. In addition, creating a team contract helps get all team members on the same page concerning workload, contribution, and expected outcomes, while a writing and revision plan helps teams organize and adjust workload as the course progresses (Wolfe 2010). Communication and professionalism are also emphasized in weekly meetings with their advisors to help students develop the skills needed to successfully engage with their community sponsors while at the fieldwork site.

From an anthropological perspective, there are some areas for improvement within the GPP. While the IQP has a learning outcome related to culture "Demonstrate an understanding of the project's technical, social and humanistic context" (WPI), there is no specific or dedicated space for students to learn about the social or cultural context of the project center and the place where they will be working. The seven-week prep term focusing on creating a research proposal is centered on the "problem" they are addressing. While relevant contextual information is expected to be included, the course itself does not specifically address the cultural context. Any preparation related to the local culture, worldviews, or social interactions is up to the project center director, instructor, or project advisors to provide, as most center directors are not trained in cultural competency, and this type of additional work is uncompensated; it is rarely addressed. This lack of cultural sensitivity manifests itself in various ways, from students and faculty unaware of local practices and customs to the expectation that English will be spoken as the default language when interacting with the local population. While some centers require baseline foreign language expertise, this is not always the case, and the linguistic skills of the students can vary widely. At the same time, we have both advised in the same project center (Monteverde, Costa Rica), and have found that our anthropological expertise and approach has helped not only to prepare students more effectively for their project work, but also to provide an opportunity to conduct participant-observation ourselves, over a period of years, utilizing our relationships as student advisors to further understand the local project sponsors and their organizations, as a way in to community sustainable development goals (Kurlanska and Strauss, in preparation).

At its core, the CCA program builds on the foundations of the IQP with its emphasis on interdisciplinarity, community engagement, and the global project centers. In reimagining the vision for a graduate program, it became clear that the fundamentals, qualitative research, contextualization, and teamwork needed to be augmented with a greater focus on transdisciplinary, community-based, and action-oriented research for students in the Master's Program. The graduate equivalent of the research methods does this by placing a greater emphasis on the location and context of the adaptation strategies; this is a natural outcome of emphasizing community and action-oriented research. One reason for this is the comparative context that is at the core of the CCA program, with student teams expected to compare how similar issues are addressed in different locations. When student teams return to campus after their research semester, they are then required to participate in a capstone seminar, in which they compare the work done at the different project centers, thus strengthening the comparative framing and highlighting the important role of context in addressing the challenges at the local level. Climate change is a global problem, but it can only be understood and addressed effectively at the local level if we are attentive to the need to "straddle the gap between the particular and the universal" (Hastrup 2016: 54).

Learning Outcomes and Program Elements for the CCA Graduate Program

We developed the CCA graduate program as a joint endeavor of the Department of Integrative & Global Studies and the Department of Civil, Environmental, and Architectural Engineering; to do this effectively, we considered both the needs and requests of faculty, local project sponsors, and the growing community of climate adaptation professionals. WPI's project-based undergraduate curriculum provided an excellent foundation, but it needed more depth and interdisciplinary skill development. We decided that the framework for the program should be fit within three semesters, beginning with a theoretical grounding in concepts of adaptation, community, and social/environmental justice. We require coursework in climate science and human dimensions of climate change, as well as methods that span project management, environmental planning, and qualitative skill sets. Students can join the program from a variety of disciplinary backgrounds, and are assigned to a team, as described above for the undergraduates in the IQP projects.

For the CCA program, we have committed to maintaining at least one project local to our institution in the northeast USA, but also to having options for work at one of the international project centers. Optimally, when the program is at capacity, we would have 4–6 teams of 2–4 students in each cohort, allowing the teams to develop strong depth expertise in a particular community, while ensuring that they have time to engage with the other teams in both methods courses and the capstone seminar to provide a strong comparative framework for supporting their understanding of the many different considerations – cultural, historical, geographic, etc. – that comprise appropriate adaptation strategies for any given community at a particular moment in time. The framework (Figure 22.1) clarifies the structure of the program and the assorted elements that are integrated across the three semesters.

Given that there is already a project and place-based learning framework established at the undergraduate level, the CCA graduate program builds on this existing structure, both physically (i.e., project center locations) and from a pedagogical perspective; we recognize that this structure would not be possible without the collaboration of the faculty project center directors, who build and maintain the networks of project sponsors in each locale. Identifying how the graduate program is essentially a directed outgrowth and amplification of the undergraduate GPP helps to create buy-in and integration of faculty who organize the project

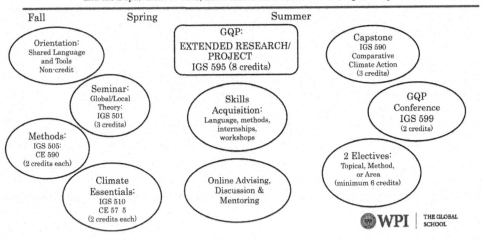

FIGURE 22.1 CCA Program Elements.

centers but may not be directly involved with the graduate program. As Table 22.1 shows, the graduate program goes beyond theory and practice to promote action.

The graduate program takes a more targeted approach to the generalized learning outcomes for the IQP and focuses on the specific challenges associated with climate change adaptation, with a focus on community engagement and the development of research projects that are initiated by local sponsoring organizations or governments. Students who have completed an IQP through the WPI BS/MS option will recognize the structure and continuity of the program but may struggle with some of the ways in which the program diverges from their experiences as an undergraduate. For students coming into the program from other backgrounds, the program components that emphasize teamwork and a transdisciplinary approach may be a bit jarring, but this strategy reinforces the importance of a holistic approach and highlights the need for an integrated and collaborative framework for addressing climate adaptation challenges.

Critical Elements for an Emerging Field

In addition to the coursework and research requirements, there are several critical pedagogical elements that comprise the CCA graduate program. During the first semester, students complete an orientation program (a total of 8–10 hours throughout the semester) that includes both opportunities to get to know each other and the faculty and share the varied experiences that they bring to the program, as well as simulations for cross-cultural understanding, community planning/problem-solving, and conversations about shared vocabulary, ethics, and transdisciplinary/public-facing communications more generally. A seminar series sponsored by the Department of Integrative and Global Studies, entitled *Collaboration for a Better World*, and other ongoing Global School events

TABLE 22.1 IQP and CCA comparison.

IQP Learning Objective	Graduate Program Interpretation
Develop Contextual Understanding	
Demonstrate an understanding of the project's technical, social, and humanistic context.	Characterize the ways that climate change and associated uncertainties impact food, energy, water, and social-ecological systems in specific localities.
Critically identify, utilize, and properly cite information sources and integrate information from multiple sources to identify appropriate approaches to addressing the project goals.	Analyze the local challenges of adapting to climate change, including the ways that transition to a low-carbon economy influences global and regional development.
Demonstrate an awareness of the ethical dimensions of their project work.	Demonstrate an ability to develop, implement, and monitor alternative solutions to climate adaptation that incorporate sociocultural, technical, economic, and ethical dimensions, as well as an appreciation for public-private collaboration and a multilevel governance approach.
Approach to the Issue	
Define clear, achievable goals and objectives for the project.	Promote an approach to transformative change that employs a community-based relational perspective as well as an understanding of technical feasibility to identify shared visions, values, ideas, and actions around adaptation and resilience.
Analyze and synthesize results from social, ethical, humanistic, technical, or other perspectives as appropriate.	
Select and implement a sound approach to solving an interdisciplinary problem.	Plan and design sustainable, low carbon, adaptive, resilient community-based solutions to problems associated with climate impacts and the built environment.
Demonstrate Professionalism and Outreach	
Maintain effective working relationships within the project team and with the project advisor(s), recognizing and resolving problems that may arise.	Lead diverse groups of people in defining a shared adaptation action agenda, including agreed measures of progress and success, while opening minds with novel ideas about building adaptation and resilience solutions.
Demonstrate the ability to write clearly, critically, and persuasively	This is demonstrated throughout the program but is culminated with the completion of the CCA thesis.
Demonstrate strong oral communication skills, using appropriate, effective visual aids.	Participate in CCA related conference.

(Forum on SDG themes, workshops, panel discussions, film series, informal discussion sessions) are also required for all graduate students.

WPI is also an institutional member of the American Society of Adaptation Professionals (ASAP), the US professional organization for this emergent field. All of the students receive membership in this organization while they are enrolled, and during the research semester, they have the opportunity to participate in a professional mentoring program through ASAP. Through this program, the students are paired with a professional in their area of interest (e.g., water management; regenerative agriculture; sustainable infrastructure; urban planning; etc.), to learn more about job opportunities in the field and other applications of their coursework and research activities. Excellent materials developed by ASAP, including a glossary, professional code of ethics, and knowledge/competency framework, are also introduced in the orientation program and integrated into core curriculum syllabi (see above and ASAP 2022b). We are also developing summer opportunities that would include an annual climate communications workshop with partner institutions, and mentoring opportunities with K-12 and community programs. As the program is only in its second year, we are still adjusting program elements and opportunities.

Specific team research projects for CCA student thesis/GQP (graduate qualifying project) work include vulnerability assessments and integrated land use planning for climate adaptation and sustainability in marginalized communities within the Springfield, Worcester, or Boston, MA metro regions, as well as in rural areas connected to these urban centers; development of community resilience centers in abandoned schools across Puerto Rico, for emergency response to hurricanes as well as everyday power and water management needs; climate impact assessment and circular economy resource recovery (e.g., recyclable materials, biogas, compost, or reclaimed wastewater) for a community waste management center in Costa Rica. As CCA faculty obtain grant funding for specific adaptation research, we are also able to bring more students into these arenas; these include participation in the newest NOAA-CAP/RISA in the Caribbean region, as well as NSF funding of regional network development projects focused on climate adaptation.

All of these projects begin with a sponsoring organization (NGO, municipality, educational institution; commercial enterprise) in the local community, proposing a project that they would like assistance with starting, or in some cases, completing, and then continued team development of the project proposal (including IRB review), conduct of the background (first semester) and field research (second semester), with weekly meetings of the full team, sponsors, and academic project advisors throughout the process. In the final semester of the degree program, students present a team thesis defense and complete the written thesis requirement. The "team thesis" represents a unique and extended embodiment of the collaborative process that the CCA program hopes to instill in its students, and demonstrates a commitment to the kind of engaged, community-grounded and policy-relevant research that defines the move from "lone ranger" thesis programs to "team player" outcomes as we build the community climate adaptation professionals that the world needs.

Although the CCA program was only launched in 2021, we are beginning to see positive responses from both the US climate adaptation community, which is growing at a rapid pace, and sees a great need for workforce development to support local efforts, and, on the recruiting end, international Fulbright students seeking training in this emergent field. Indeed, the majority of students currently in or expressing interest in the CCA program are either international or from marginalized communities in the US. We hope to be able to offer "stackable" certificates to support more flexible graduate program enrollment structures as we move forward and see great opportunities to follow Margaret Mead's (Kellogg and Mead 1980) lead in applying anthropological and other humanistic disciplines to addressing our anthropogenic climate challenges that require far more human responses than technological strategies alone can solve.

References

AAA. 2015. "Statement on humanity and climate change." https://s3.amazonaws.com/rdcms-aaa/files/production/public/FileDownloads/pdfs/cmtes/commissions/CCTF/upload/AAA-Statement-on-Humanity-and-Climate-Change.pdf.

ASAP. 2022a. "About." Accessed November 1, 2022. https://adaptationprofessionals.org/about/#mission-and-history.

ASAP. 2022b. "Resources." Accessed November 1, 2022. https://adaptationprofessionals.org/join-us/resource/.

Baer, Hans and Merrill Singer. 2018. *The Anthropology of Climate Change: An integrated critical perspective* (2nd edition). Boca Raton, FL: Routledge.

Barnes, Jessica and Michael Dove, eds. 2015. *Climate Cultures.* New Haven: Yale University Press.

Brondizio, Eduardo. 2016. "Entangled futures: anthropology's engagement with global change research." In Susan Crate and Mark Nuttall eds. *Anthropology and Climate Change: From actions to transformations* (2nd edition), pp. 121–137. New York: Routledge.

C2ES. 2022. *US State Climate Action Plans.* Accessed November 1, 2022. https://www.c2es.org/document/climate-action-plans/.

Crate, Susan. 2011. "Climate and culture: anthropology in the era of contemporary climate change." *Ann. Rev. Anthropology* 40: 175–194.

Crate, Susan and Mark Nutall 2009 eds. *Anthropology and Climate Change: From encounters to actions.* Walnut Creek, CA: Left Coast Press.

Crate, Susan and Mark Nutall eds. 2016. *Anthropology and Climate Change: From actions to transformations* 2nd edition. New York: Routledge.

Elmes, Michael and Elanor Loiacono. 2009. "Project-based service-learning for an unscripted world: the WPI IQP experience." *International Journal of Organizational Analysis* 17 (1): 23–39 doi:10.1108/19348830910948887.

Eriksen, Thomas Hylland. 2021. "Climate change." In Felix Stein ed. *The Cambridge Encyclopedia of Anthropology.* http://doi.org/10.29164/21climatechange.

Ersoy, Aksel and Elen van Bueren. 2020. "Challenges of urban living labs towards the future of local innovation." *Urban Planning* 5 (4): 89–100. doi:10.17645/up.v5i4.3226.

Fiske, Shirley, Susan Crate, Carole Crumley, Kathleen Galvin, Heather Lazrus, Lisa Lucero, Anthony Oliver-Smith, Ben Orlove, Sarah Strauss, and Richard Wilk. 2014. *Changing the Atmosphere: Anthropology and climate change.* Final report of the AAA Global Climate Change Task Force, 137 pp. December 2014. Arlington, VA: American Anthropological Association.

Galman, Sally. 2018. *Shane the Lone Ethnographer: A beginner's guide to ethnography.* 2nd ed. Walnut Creek, CA: Rowman & Littlefield.

Hastrup, Kirsten. 2013. "Anthropological contributions to the study of climate: past, present, future." *WIREs Clim Change.* 4: 269–281. doi:10.1002/wcc.219.

Hastrup, Kirsten. 2016. "Climate knowledge: assemblage, anticipation, action." In Susan Crate and Mark Nuttall eds. *Anthropology and Climate Change: From actions to transformations* (2nd edition), pp. 35–57. New York: Routledge.

IPCC. 2022. *Climate Change 2022: Impacts, adaptation, and vulnerability.* Contribution of Working Group II to the Sixth Assessment Report of the Intergovernmental Panel on Climate Change [H.-O. Pörtner, D.C. Roberts, M. Tignor, E.S. Poloczanska, K. Mintenbeck, A. Alegría, M. Craig, S. Langsdorf, S. Löschke, V. Möller, A. Okem, B. Rama (eds.)]. Cambridge University Press. In Press.

IPCC. 2022. *Climate Change 2022: Mitigation of climate change.* Contribution of Working Group III to the Sixth Assessment Report of the Intergovernmental Panel on Climate Change [P.R. Shukla, J. Skea, R. Slade, A. Al Khourdajie, R. van Diemen, D. McCollum, M. Pathak, S. Some, P. Vyas, R. Fradera, M. Belkacemi, A. Hasija, G. Lisboa, S. Luz, J. Malley, (eds.)]. Cambridge University Press, Cambridge, UK and New York, NY. doi:10.1017/9781009157926.

Kellogg, William and Margaret Mead eds. 1980. *The Atmosphere: Endangered and endangering.* London: Castle Hill Publishing, Ltd.

Krauss, Werner. 2015. "Anthropology in the anthropocene: sustainable development, climate change and interdisciplinary research." In H. Greshke, J. Tischler eds. *Grounding Global Climate Change.* Springer Science+Business Media Dordrecht. doi:10.1007/978-94-017-9322-3.

Kurlanska, Courtney and Sarah Strauss. n.d. *The Intersection of the Social and Solidarity Economy, Covid-19, and Sustainable Development in Monteverde, Costa Rica.* Manuscript in preparation.

Lazrus, Heather, Julie Maldonado, Paulette Blanchard, M. Kalani Souza, Bill Thomas, and Daniel Wildcat. 2022. "Culture change to address climate change: collaborations with Indigenous and Earth sciences for more just, equitable, and sustainable responses to our climate crisis." *PLOS Clim* 1 (2): e0000005. https://doi.org/10.1371/journal.pclm.0000005.

Markkanen, Sanna and Annela Anger-Kraavi. 2019. "Social impacts of climate change mitigation policies and their implications for inequality." *Climate Policy*, 19, (7): 827–844, doi:10.1080/14693062.2019.1596873.

Morse, Charlie. 2019. "Managing team dynamics and conflict on student project teams." In Kristin Wobbe and Elisabeth Stoddard, eds. *Project-Based Learning in the First Year: Beyond all expectations*, pp. 264–279. Virginia: Stylus Publishing.

Moser, Susanne, Joyce Coffee, and Aleka Seville. 2017. *Rising to the Challenge, Together: A review and critical assessment of the state of the US climate adaptation field.* Report Prepared for the Kresge Foundation. Troy, MI: The Kresge Foundation.

Odell, John. 2023. "Sustainability & resilience." City of Worcester. https://www.worcesterma.gov/sustainability-resilience.

O'Reilly, Jessica, Cindy Isenhour, Pamela McElwee, and Ben Orlove. 2020. "Climate change: expanding anthropological possibilities." *Annual Review of Anthropology* 49: 13–29. https://doi.org/10.1146/annurev-anthro-010220-043113.

Peterson, Kristina and Julie Maldonado. 2016. "When adaptation is not enough: between the 'now and then of community-led resettlement'." In Susan Crate and Mark Nuttall, eds. *Anthropology and Climate Change: From actions to transformations* (2nd edition), pp. 336–535. New York: Routledge.

Pfeifer, Geoff and Elisabeth Stoddard. 2019. "Equitable and effective student teams." In Kristin Wobbe and Elisabeth Stoddard, eds. *Project-Based Learning in the First Year: Beyond all expectations*, pp. 264–279. Sterling, VA: Stylus Publishing.

Roncoli, Carla, Keith Ingram, Christine Jost, and Paul Kirshen. 2003. "Meteorological meanings: farmers' interpretations of seasonal rainfall forecasts in Burkina Faso." In Strauss and Orlove, eds. *Weather, Climate, Culture*, pp.181–200. Oxford: Berg Books, Ltd.

Rayner, Steve and Elizabeth Malone. 1998. *Human Choice and Climate Change.* Washington: Battelle.

Stoddard, Elisabeth and Geoff Pfeifer. 2018. "Working towards more equitable team dynamics: mapping student assets to minimize stereotyping and task assignment bias." *American Society for Engineering Education.* The Collaborative Network for Engineering and Computing Diversity Conference: Crystal City, Virginia.

Strauss, Sarah and Ben Orlove eds. 2003. *Weather, Climate, Culture.* Oxford: Berg Books, Ltd.

Strauss, Sarah, Stephanie Rupp, and Thomas Love eds. 2013. *Cultures of Energy: Power, practices, technologies.* New York: Routledge.

Tulchinsky, Theodore and Elena Varavikova. 2014. "A history of public health." In Theodore Tulchinsky and Elena Varavikova eds. *The New Public Health*, pp. 1–42, (3rd edition). Academic Press, https://doi.org/10.1016/B978-0-12-415766-8.00001-X.

Vaughn, Sarah. 2022. *Engineering Vulnerability: In pursuit of climate adaptation.* Durham: Duke University Press.

Wolfe, Joanna. 2010. *Team Writing: A guide to working in groups.* Boston: Bedford/St. Martin's.

WPI. 2023. *Interactive Qualifying Project Learning Outcomes.* Accessed February 28, 2023. https://www.wpi.edu/academics/undergraduate/interactive-qualifying-project/outcomes.

23

CLIMATE COUNTER-HEGEMONY

Crafting an Anthropological Climate Politics Through Student–Faculty Collaborations in the Classroom and on the Streets

Brian J. Burke, Sydney Blume, and Michael Z. Weiss

Introduction: World Breaking, Worldmaking

On October 8, 2018, our world broke. In truth, the world had been broken for some time, and we had already dedicated ourselves to teaching, studying, researching, and acting on the dehumanizing socioeconomic and cultural systems that fuel the violence of climate devastation. But October 8 brought something new. The stark desperation of the *IPCC Special Report on Warming of 1.5°C* forced the world's brokenness fully into our souls. Loss became palpable in a new way. Not just the loss of lives, human and non-human. Not just the unconcerned taking of those lives. But clarity that we had, in fact, already lost the fight against climate change. And with that, a certainty that all we could do was fight harder.

Echoing Naomi Klein's argument that climate change "changes everything," the IPCC wrote that limiting global warming to 1.5 degrees "would require rapid, far-reaching, and unprecedented changes in all aspects of society." We needed to engage in new projects of worldmaking, right here, right now, and everywhere. The most strategic here and now for us was Appalachian State University, where Michael was a student, Sydney was an alumnus and staff person, and Brian was a professor.

Appalachian State (or, more commonly, App State) seemed like an auspicious environment for climate advocacy. The 20,000-student public university had a reputation and government mandate for sustainability, defined its mission around "building healthy, just, and sustainable communities," had a small but active Office of Sustainability, and a student-funded and student-run renewable energy program. With strong research and teaching in sustainable technology, sustainable development, planning, and sustainable business, App had the potential to test and model just sustainability for our entire state. And it was located in the climate-friendly mountain town of Boone, NC, the first municipality in the country to formally petition a state to adopt 100% renewable energy. Yet there was a curious inertia at the university. The university's 2010 climate action plan, which set a carbon neutrality goal of 2050, was almost entirely unimplemented, we were not complying with state requirements to develop a social and environmental purchasing

DOI: 10.4324/9781003242499-27

plan or hire an energy manager, and most of the discourse about sustainability was focused on litter clean-ups, voluntary behavioral changes, building upgrades, and voluntary carbon offsets for commuters. This individualistic and technocratic approach left huge swathes of our carbon emissions off the table.

Spurred on by the IPCC report, Brian's colleagues in the Department of Sustainable Development issued a call to action, asking the university community to come together on October 15 to imagine how we could become a national and global leader in just climate responses. To our surprise, nearly 200 faculty, students, and community members showed up to the event. We packed ourselves into a 130-person room to hear three lightning talks about the IPCC report and climate catastrophe, and then divided into more than a dozen brainstorming teams spread across the student union. The brainstorming groups brought together students, staff, faculty, and community members in unprecedented conversations, generating proposals that ranged from small "fixes" to radical overhauls. The energy was incredible; the movement had begun. But now we had to organize it. How could we use the urgency and this new breadth of interest and agency to build more ambitious programs atop the foundation already laid by the institution and past advocates? How could we harness this new people power to advance real change?

We thus began to make our world anew. The October 15 summit unleashed the desire to eliminate our university emissions, but we wanted to go beyond mere institutional reform. The IPCC called for worldmaking, for transforming the institutional cultures and decision-making structures that made App's emissions seem tolerable and inevitable in the first place, and for creating alternative socio-political and economic structures that would allow new ways of being together in justice and sustainability. We quickly planned follow-up meetings to show participants that we would move from talk to action, and by November working groups had developed a clear list of goals to be vetted by the "general assembly" of all community members committed to urgent action. Our goals included ambitious timelines for carbon neutrality, increased transparency and leadership by a climate advisory board composed of diverse university and community stakeholders, internal carbon pricing, a 100% renewable energy purchasing plan, and hiring of several university positions to carry forth these tasks. (We later added more specificity to demands for a "just approach," including specific language about economic redistribution to historically marginalized and climate vulnerable populations.)

Inspired by concepts of prefiguration, we also sought to craft a different style of politics that would allow our community to begin building skills and sensibilities for a just climate-changed future. Sydney and Dustin Hicks, another student organizer, explained this in an email to all participants:

> As we are gearing up to establish the ASU Climate Action Movement, we have a distinct opportunity for re-creation, to form an organizing system that is consistent with our goals of system resiliency and sustainability. We can create an organizing system that is a model for transformative politics; one that prevents the concentration and abuse of power, promotes social engagement, and is highly adaptable to changing community needs. We want to propose such a potential structure [drawing on lessons from the Zapatistas and the Haudenosaunee and Oromo people]. This system is designed not to create leaders, but to organize the collective for efficient grassroots action.

Sydney, Dustin, and others used insights from feminism, anarchism, decolonial theory, and environmental justice movements to design an unofficial organization – the Appalachian Climate Action Collaborative (ClimAct) – according to principles of direct democratic engagement and distributed power, and with a justice-centered approach to environmentalism. Within our first year we passed unanimous bills in the student and faculty senate that led to small policy changes, including hiring a university energy manager, committing to reinvest profits from energy efficiency measures back into sustainability efforts, and reviving an advisory sustainability working group. Yet, even while working in these modest campaigns in student and faculty government, activists were consistently hindered by the internal and external conditions that shore up complacency and make a climate-destroying university hegemonic.

We expected some of this resistance – after all, we understood that institutions tend to function conservatively, and we were aware that our state universities' dominant logic was cost saving and revenue generation via growth rather than mission-driven and values-based leadership – and we were preparing for it. For example, Greg Reck, an Appalachian State anthropologist with previous activist experience, noted in November 2018:

> Let us be realistic. If we present the "necessities" of transformation of ASU in order to meet the emergency of the IPCC report, we will meet resistance. We need to be prepared for that resistance.... In order to be prepared for resistance, we need a plan for the escalation of action based on the desire to achieve our stated goals. If it turns out we don't need to escalate, all the better. But I'd place my money (if I had any) that we will need to. At best, we can expect the administration to respond by tasking the Office of Sustainability or some appointed task force with studying the issues and responding with realistic, pragmatic initiatives. While this response might be necessary, it is not sufficient.

While some organizers reserved hope for success via institutional channels, we all knew we had to prepare ourselves to act outside of these processes. A few days earlier Brian had scheduled a training with an expert in nonviolent direct action so we could begin building our skills and strategy in case escalation was necessary. Yet it was no easy task to confront the full range of cultural, material, and institutional dynamics that defined our climate-destroying hegemony.

Over the past four years (at the time of this writing), students and a handful of faculty and community members have worked hard to build ClimAct, work existing institutional channels to their limits, and then mount pressure campaigns to demand action beyond the "win–wins" that fit the logics of university administrations in an extractive economy. This work required activists to confront, subvert, and develop alternatives to the constrained "common sense" worldviews that underpin the "business-as-usual" that drives climate destruction. In this chapter, we review theories of hegemony and change that underpin our work, examine the internal and external resistance we have faced, and describe several tactics we've used to make student-faculty-community organizing successful in terms of both reducing carbon emissions and generating a new worldview centered on citizen agency, the publicness of public institutions, and the imbrication of climate and other forms of justice and well-being. To be clear, our work is unfinished and we can offer no certain recipe for change. However, we hope that theorizing this work will enable other academic anthropologists (and student activists) to adapt our work to their own contexts, advancing counter-hegemonic climate justice praxis.

Hegemony and the Common Sense of an Extractive University

As we deepened our analysis from carbon emissions to the governance systems that permit climate devastation and then to the broader worldviews and structures that undergird those, we began to ask new questions about the world we could build. Could we make a world in which an unsustainable university is inconceivable and impossible? One in which it would be an unthinkable betrayal for a university to continue business-as-usual while violating planetary boundaries, or the dignity of students, faculty, and staff of color, or the well-being of long-term locals? What worldviews and power structures would such a world need? The Just Transition framework provided one guide for our work. It offers a utopian vision and theory of change developed by frontline communities and environmental justice movement leaders and represented by Movement Generation and the Climate Justice Alliance's Our Power Campaign (Figure 23.1).

For us, three features of the framework are especially important. First, it de-silos climate change by emphasizing that climate change is rooted in the very same extractive worldviews and structures that underpin systemic racism, sexism, classism, colonialism, and militarism, among other major oppressive systems. This immediately shifts environmentalism from a niche realm focused on ecosystems, energy use, and carbon accounting to a foundational pillar for advancing justice in the twenty-first century. Second, the Just Transition framework provides a values-based vision of where we are going: toward a living economy governed democratically in order to achieve ecological regeneration and social well-being through cooperation, caring, and sacredness. Similarly, it provides a clear vision of what we are against. Finally, the Just Transition framework highlights five key tactics: stop the bad, build the new, divest from their power, invest in

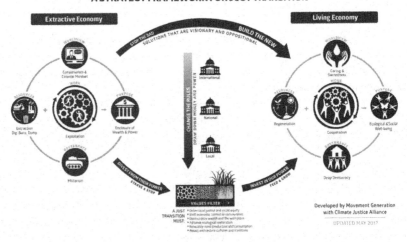

A STRATEGY FRAMEWORK FOR JUST TRANSITION

FIGURE 23.1 This diagram, illustrating a Just Transition, is used to orient new members of the organization, guide strategy discussions, and frame the organization's work to the public. View the full image at movementgeneration.org/justtransition/.

Source: Movement Generation Justice & Ecology Project and the Climate Justice Alliance Our Power Campaign.

our power, and change the rules to level and eventually invert the playing field. Borrowing from the Climate Justice Alliance, we would add "change the story" as a sixth essential strategy. Just Transition deepened and broadened our climate justice activism and encouraged a "fight and build" approach (Akuno 2017; Dixon 2014) that combines traditional activist tactics with less conventional worldmaking practices that, together, are meant to shift climate "solutions" from the techno-optimism and symbolic activism common on college campuses and in liberal discourse to radical and strategic material-institutional-cultural activism and movement building. Ultimately, we hope to build positive feedbacks between the cultural work of changing the story and the "propaganda of the deed" accomplished through fighting and building (see Lakey 2012).

Unfortunately, no organizing model, however good, will work if there's not a window of opportunity for change. In 2018 – and even more so today – the political and material conditions at App State seemed favorable to a climate justice movement that would increase the power and ambitions of the Office of Sustainability. There was clearly a climate need: the university was on a trajectory to continue contributing to climate change until at least 2115, sixty-five years after the 2050 goal set by the IPCC, App State, and now the University of North Carolina System (ClimAct 2020a).[1,2] More broadly, faculty were stirred up by increasingly authoritarian governance styles that seemed to prioritize student "customer" experience over learning and knowledge generation, and students were concerned about their own struggles with food insecurity, inadequate mental health services, the high cost of housing, racism, and the more general challenges of being a twenty-something in late capitalism. As if these internal critiques were not enough, many in the broader High Country community experienced the university as yet another invader taking over Appalachian land and lifeways and sucking wealth out of the mountains. The university's focus on growth despite community objections was contributing to housing and employment crises in some of North Carolina's poorest and most unequal counties, making it increasingly difficult for local youth to build a life in their home places. Despite "objective conditions" that might theoretically favor dissent, the App community was not rising up.

This brings us to our main topic in this chapter: the dynamics of hegemony.[3] Sustaining the movement's momentum has required continual confrontation with subjectivities, institutions, cultures, and material environments that disempower, marginalize, dull, and pacify would-be change-makers (students, faculty, and local residents alike). As Linger (1993) noted, people come to expect and accept certain power dynamics, including their own powerlessness. Importantly, there is not only a *sense* that we are less powerful: the Tayloristic norms and incentive structure of K-12 education nudge students from curiosity and agency to followership (Au 2011; Stoller 2015); the rules of institutional governance actually make faculty members' voices irrelevant; state laws and governing practices limit community members' ability to contain the university they "host"; student activism is increasingly criminalized; and economic precarity militates against dedicated efforts to change any of this. Beyond this, as student organizer Sarah Sandreuter said, we face "the dissonance of fighting the university we're paying thousands of dollars to attend and doing unpaid but necessary work for them that we shouldn't have to be doing." Thus, for us, as for Italian activist-intellectual Antonio Gramsci (2000), counter-hegemony needs to be cultivated through a broad range of cultural and material work that fundamentally changes what people expect, what they accept, and the resources they can mobilize to use their power.

So what exactly are the material, cultural, and institutional conditions that generate consent to a climate-destroying, extractive, and undemocratic university, even among people who believe that anthropogenic climate change must be stopped, including students who chose the university for its sustainability reputation and staff whose job is to pursue sustainability? Effective greenwashing is clearly important. However, the full complexity of inaction goes beyond deceitful marketing. Following Gramsci, we believe that inaction has much more to do with people's "common sense" views of self and society – "those heterogeneous beliefs people arrive at not through conscious reflection, but encounter as already existing, self-evident truths" (Gramsci 2000; Crehan 2016: 1). People use this common sense to understand our climate-destroying university and the range of possible responses. Norgaard (2011) makes a similar argument about climate inaction, suggesting that *inactive believers* may be a bigger and more interesting problem than denialists. She demonstrates that norms regarding appropriate emotion, attention, and conversation can lead communities to a "double life" of "implicatory denial," in which people know that climate change is real and threatening but deny the moral and political implications that follow from this. To cultivate a counter-hegemonic movement, we needed to burst through this implicatory denial by combatting the various ways that complacency, consent, and coercion were being created.

In Table 23.1, we highlight sentiments encountered in our activism that demonstrate key elements of the "common sense" at our extractive university. In addition to these cognitive and linguistic components of hegemony, the actual design of the university also enables material coercion. Governing structures such as the student and faculty senate are symbolic at best (passed bills are no more than "recommendations"). Bureaucratic hoops around proper decorum and the precarity of some academic jobs create an unwillingness to ruffle feathers or divert from pre-existing plans. Closed meetings prevent transparency around budgets, energy use, and contracts. Even once critical information is obtained, opaque decision-making structures make the process of influencing decisions even more challenging. Furthermore, the logic of cost–benefit analysis underpins decision making and displaces other values.

The material dynamics of hegemony go beyond the university walls as well. Perhaps the most significant are the simple economic coercion of time and money. It is challenging for students and faculty to take action or even become aware of issues because faculty face reduced salaries and increasing job responsibilities, while students face tuition expenses, elevated costs of living (due largely to the university's decision to grow beyond our town's ability to absorb new residents), and heavy course-load requirements. Meanwhile, the administrators formally authorized to maintain business as usual (including sustainability as usual) within the extractive university are able to do so for pay during their usual work hours. These challenges are more than just personal struggles; they impede meaningful engagement by depriving those outside of positions of power of a voice, the security to speak out, the information needed to take a stand, and the time to do so.

Further, these material structures solidify cultural aspects of hegemony. The inability to make an impact through formal channels supports feelings of powerlessness. The power and unaccountability of unelected individuals such as the Chancellor, Board of Trustees, and Board of Governors encourages a strategy of either appealing to those in power using their language or their values, or giving up. These real limits on people

TABLE 23.1 Hegemony and the language of consent.[4]

First reactions say a lot. Below are some of the most common responses to our proposals for just climate action at App State. We hope this list – which illustrates some of the beliefs and linguistic strategies that support a climate-destroying hegemony – may serve as red flags for other activists. Interestingly, they have come from supporters and opponents alike.

1. *Do believe the hype.* "But App is already doing so much." "Is it really that bad?" "If you read our 2010 climate action plan you'll see that this proposal is already there." "Well, we've already committed to neutrality by 2050. That's a state requirement."

2. *Deflection and general cynicism.* "Is anybody else really much better?" "But is that even possible?" "Well of course the Chancellor won't do this – she's full of shit." "Let's table this until next fall [because delaying doesn't matter that much anyway since we have so little impact]." "Whatever. The university is a lost cause."

3. *"Implicatory denial"* and incrementalism. "This isn't how change works. You have to move these people along slowly by finding the places where sustainability will save them money and achieve their goals." "Critiquing and demanding will get you nowhere." "The problem with target dates is that people then yell and scream if you don't achieve them."

4. *Prioritizing finances above biospheric integrity.* "But can we afford that?"

5. *Learned helplessness.* "I mean, that's what the institution is going to do." "Of course I don't like paying so many fees for athletics and so little for sustainability, but what can I do?" "I'm just trying to get my degree and get out of here."

6. *Accepting the obstacles.* "But the budget rules don't allow us to do that." "The state says we can't take that into account." "You need to talk with ___ about how the budget works." "Students are never going to accept that."

7. *Personalizing the problem.* "[That administrator's] heart is in the right place and he's doing what he can." "Critiquing the institution just hurts people's feelings." "It would be great if we could get people to stop eating meat and to buy electric cars but we're a long way from that." "Unless faculty are willing to give up travel, we're not going to get there."

8. *Assuming experts know best (and the public/activists are naive).* "We already have all of the experts in the room figuring out how to maximize our energy efficiencies." "We've tried to involve others but then you have to start every meeting with an hour of getting everyone up to speed and getting them on the page that we want them to be on." "But what do you really want in practice?" "You should go talk with ___ about how the budget works." "You know, those kids *actually* had some interesting ideas."

9. *False trade-offs.* "The revenue from New River Light and Power [our university-owned utility] goes toward scholarships, so if we make changes then we won't be able to support low-income students."

power within the university amplify, we believe, Norgaard's "implicatory denial." Without clear pathways for making change, many people are left with no vision of how they even could honor their climate responsibilities.

Additionally, we have found that the hegemony of the extractive university is undergirded by a common sense that separates climate change from other issues, that presumes that "the little people" are generally powerless over the "larger forces" and institutions of the world, that provides few tools for thinking about the commons and public goods, and that radically constricts people's vision of possibility through appeals to pragmatism, finances, political will, or the immovability of similar obstacles. We have been particularly troubled that trustees, administrators, and the broader public often fail to conceptualize the university as a genuinely *public* institution, a stance that absolves them of the duties of community membership and public service. Many friends and colleagues at App State seem to have fallen prey to what Lukes called "the supreme and most insidious exercise of power":

> to prevent people... from having grievances by shaping their perceptions, cognitions and preferences in such a way that they accept their role in the existing order of things, either because they can see or imagine no alternative to it, or because they see it as natural and unchangeable.
>
> *(1974: 24).*

Climate Counter-Hegemony: Tactics and Experiences

If our analysis is correct, then ClimAct needs to fight the coercion and consent that reproduce hegemony and simultaneously create new institutional processes, material conditions, and a common sense that can establish and sustain a just transition. Our material goals have coalesced around demanding a multi-stakeholder committee on the Board of Trustees, transparency of all climate data progress, and rapid decarbonization of the university through a robust community engagement process that benefits historically marginalized communities. We have also aimed to practice democracy internally via general assembly meetings, community town halls, and non-hierarchical approaches to leadership, though admittedly it has been difficult to fully realize our hopes in this regard. These material shifts require cultural change as well. In the words of the Climate Justice Alliance, part of our responsibility is to "change the stories that normalize unjust power structures" so we can "make fundamental change imaginable," and then to build the skills, desires, and alliances necessary to achieve that change.[5] We aim to support cultural changes by building a community that consistently reinforces the notion that people-led structural change is necessary, possible, and alluring.

In this section, we describe four key tactics for empowering our community: 1) building skills and subjectivities for climate movement work and alternative worldmaking by engaging students as knowledge-producers, world-builders, and actively engaged citizens within the university and beyond; 2) reframing the university by revealing a leadership crisis and the status quo's fundamental inability to resolve climate justice problems; 3) broadening political imaginations and creativity in problem-solving and modeling new institutions; and 4) overcoming material constraints to engagement. The first two tactics are meant to change the power relations that our community expects and accepts by increasing students' belief in the possibility and necessity of "our power." The third and fourth tactics are meant to unleash our political imaginations by reorienting our understanding of constraints and the role of our university as a public commons.

Tactic 1: Building Skills, Subjectivities, and On-Ramps for Climate Movement Work

Since the start of our movement in the fall of 2018, building climate movement skills, shifting subjectivities, and creating opportunities for action has been a broad effort through developing focused courses, integrating key lessons or projects into existing classes, facilitating workshops, and perhaps most importantly, building a movement from scratch. In Spring 2019, we were all involved in a course called "Climate Action at

Appalachian State" – Brian as professor, Sydney as unofficial TA, and Michael as student. Sydney and Brian designed the course to build students' sense of agency and empowerment, to engage them in a budding climate movement, and to develop organizing and activist-research skills. Specifically, the course focused on developing student expertise in the university's carbon emissions accounting (especially sectors of emissions that were unclear, unmeasured, or intentionally obfuscated), studying carbon mitigation efforts successfully pursued elsewhere, and demonstrating that broad-scale mitigation is both possible and desirable.

Shaping student subjectivities required us to engage with students as whole people in a learning environment. Per our syllabus, our class sessions were designed to address "the head, the heart, the hands, and the whole," so we would develop tools to think, feel, organize, and collectively embody climate solutions. In addressing the head, we needed to first amplify students' identities as knowledge-producers and citizen-activists. We invited them to discard the disempowering components of conventional student subjectivities, such as passive acceptance of professors' learning goals and curricular design, submission to others' evaluative norms, and other components of the "empty vessel" or "deficit" model of education by inviting constant student direction. Having two recent graduates join Brian in course design and instruction was one way of blurring conventional hierarchies. Another was to build much of the course around team projects through which learners would gain more topical expertise than the professor-facilitator and contribute to a course project that went beyond the boundaries of a class.

We also re-valorized the affective aspects of climate action through engaging hearts, emotions, and values in our work. On the second day of class, Brian was intentionally absent, leaving the students and TAs to set the tone for the class, entitled "Doom, Gloom, and other Facts." The latest IPCC and National Climate Assessment reports provided a common understanding of the immensity of the crisis at hand, but class discussion focused on people's personal experiences and feelings of living in a crisis-stricken world. Many students were shy to speak up at first or to speak emotionally and not intellectually in a classroom, but before long the blackboard was filled with their contributions (Figure 23.2). This space also facilitated a sort of student-to-student knowledge exchange; for example, students shared the ways that they framed the crisis to enable motivation and the ways they communicated about climate change with skeptics. We used this exercise as a way to create a sense of commonality within the class, to validate these feelings and experiences as key to understanding our climate context and shaping a way forward, and stoking a fire to be directed towards action. Restricting climate conversations to facts and ideas misses a key part of why the climate crisis is so disturbing and a whole sphere of human knowing. As Luhrmann (2006) wrote, emotions are "our most basic moral reactions" and a guide to the values and norms that we hold dear, often even in non-cognized ways. Bringing emotions (and emotional knowledge) into the conversation from the beginning helped us study what matters (what we were grieving) and avoid cognitive dissonance – if the crisis were as life-altering as we think it is, we would likely be having a visceral response; if we don't react viscerally, could it really be so bad?

Beyond the head and the heart, we also wanted to use institutional ethnography to reconfigure students' understanding of the conditions of possibility and constraints on change, and to build their skills for systems analysis and creative problem solving, developing a whole host of research-activist skills. Student action teams examined different sectors of the university, researched other institutions' climate efforts, interviewed key

FIGURE 23.2 Emotions fill the room and the chalkboard as students explain how feelings underpin their action and inaction on climate change.
Source: Sydney Blume.

stakeholders and decision makers on campus, and investigated how the university was operating so they could determine what systems, relationships, beliefs, and cultures were underlying action and inaction. We encouraged an ethnographic approach that paired interviews with participant-observation at meetings and during day-to-day operations. This allowed students to interrogate not only *what* was said by administrators and decision makers, but how they said it, what they avoided, what they did, and how they interacted with colleagues. The students who succeeded in this more ethnographic approach generated keen insights into institutional barriers and opportunities like the need for more democratic governance in the campus dining board, a revision of the aesthetic goals on campus, and lobbying the state government to permit longer-term return on investment calculations that would make possible more intrinsically sustainable university facilities. These approaches to institutional climate action, while deemed "unfeasible" by the sustainability professionals on campus, were based on a holistic understanding of the climate crisis and its disproportionate impacts, theories of system intervention, case studies that demonstrated similar tactics, discussion on feasibility and appropriateness, interviews, participant observations, and other data.

The process revealed to students that they actually were able to develop achievable and potentially impactful solutions – and more importantly, that the experts and professionals of the university were perhaps too entrenched in the cultural hegemony of cost-effectiveness, decorum, and otherwise business-as-usual. While these decision makers were blinded by hegemony to alternative logics and creativity, the students were not. For many, this was extremely frustrating, yet it also demonstrated the importance of other class lessons around building political movements and political will.

We aimed to introduce students to concrete tools necessary for building political will, such as the stages of a movement and its associated actions from Bill Moyer's Movement Action Plan,[6] power mapping, and the spectrum of allies. Just as institutional ethnography was meant to make institutional change local and concrete, these tools were meant to open up the black box of activism and make it tangible and learnable. In concert with these tools in the classroom, we created clear on-ramps for students to apply their new skills by participating in protests, meetings, and events with the Climate Action Collaborative throughout the semester. When students joined ClimAct, they joined action teams to plan events, do outreach, or engage with institutional efforts, and they engaged in peer-to-peer education and activist trainings. Shifting from classroom strategizing, which can feel hypothetical, to movement strategizing further advanced their learning. Combining the lessons and theories that were learned in classes and workshops with actual organizing, students were able to implement this knowledge in conversation with their community. For many, this praxis provided nuance and grounded the lessons in reality for a more embodied understanding.

All classes are, potentially, powerful cognitive and emotional experiences. Many anthropologists are already designing their classes with those impacts in mind. However, we think faculty might do more to use classes in the service of – and as an on-ramp to – movements by cultivating a sense of power and possibility and by designing coursework to serve activists and implicate students in ongoing activism. Through our class, students developed strong arguments that ambitious climate action is possible and oftentimes offers a multitude of benefits. One shared a common sentiment in a survey two years later: "participating in the Climate Action Collaborative and the Climate Action class helped me believe that change is possible, and that I could be a part of making things change." Another wrote, "We were not only taught about the issues we are facing but were given the tools to participate directly, which empowered us to keep working for change after we left App State." Interestingly, while coursework and conversations introduced new frameworks for students to understand their context, it was the interviews, research, and imagination of students that allowed them to come to a new understanding of their own collective power and a conceptualization of a better university. Then practicing these new understandings *through participating in ClimAct* helped students actually realize their collective power to initiate the changes they had researched and envisioned.

The Climate Action class, of course, was just one example of the ways faculty and students are transforming subjectivities and skill sets. Other courses such as "Practicum in Resilience" (Reed), "All We Can Save" (Blume, Nesbitt, and England), and "Applications of Sustainable Development" (Burke) have also centered on developing holistic perspectives of the climate crisis, organizing and movement-building skills, and deep engagement with one's place in the collective work of climate justice. Cross-course projects such as the university's Climate Stories Collaborative (England et al. 2019) also engage students in finding their voices within the climate conversation. But again, perhaps the most critical education came through connecting classroom learning with action in the streets.

Tactic 2: Unveiling the Inevitable Failure of University Leadership

Prompted largely by our activism, the university's Office of Sustainability (OoS) began developing a new "Climate Action Plan" (the AppCAP) in summer 2019. Although ClimAct was skeptical about the process and potential of the AppCAP – in part because the

OoS director had actively hindered our efforts to pass a faculty senate bill for climate neutrality – we decided it was critical to engage earnestly both to see how much progress we could make internally and to ensure we would later be perceived as legitimate contributors who had pursued all possible institutional routes for change.

Perhaps not surprisingly, the AppCAP's process mimicked the weak forms of public participation that we see in many environmental consultation processes. Meetings were never announced to the public, only known "experts" and ClimAct representatives were invited, and there were no agendas, minutes, or other provisions for meaningful participation by people who could not make the business day/school day meeting schedules. Student members of ClimAct quickly encountered uncompromising resistance to their input and outright belittlement, particularly when they attempted to shift conversations beyond solutions that they saw as technocratic, limited, and inequitable. One ClimAct member reflected on those meetings:

> There were a couple different meetings where I would cry during or after the meeting, just because they were so frustrating. The things they said [about who they wanted in the room and what knowledge they valued] made me keep my mouth closed. When you're basically told that expert opinions are prioritized and you have very little technical knowledge, it was hard to be able to speak up just because of my personal confidence. [The experts] have a lot of knowledge about how change works at the university. But speaking with them about how to make change at the university becomes difficult because they are tasked with upholding the status quo; just to keep things going at the university.

The format and tenor of these meetings made the real benefits of participation – that students and others might introduce novel solutions by thinking beyond the technical realm – an impossibility.

Ultimately, we learned that the administrators tasked with climate and energy policy did not just have different goals or interests (such as protection of the university's reputation or finances). They actually lived in a different world. We were negotiating ontological differences. The defining feature of the administrators' world was the existence of the university. It must continue to exist because it had always existed, so the proper way to think about climate action was to start from where the university was in 2018 and ask which next steps were most efficient and feasible. Justice was then a "filter" to be applied later. From this perspective, institutional rules and norms were hard barriers that defined what was possible and impossible.

The defining feature of our world, on the other hand, was the climate justice emergency. In the wake of our world-breaking, that was what was really real. The university was a mere human construct. Our thoughts on climate action thus began from the question "where does the planet need us to be" and asked what could get us there most effectively. The university's existence – or its existence in its present form – was not guaranteed because we assumed that any university that could not operate within planetary boundaries should not exist. For us, justice was also a starting point. Racism, economic exploitation, and manufactured vulnerability were as real as climate change, so any action on climate should proactively advance justice by shifting resources, advantages, and influence to historically marginalized groups. Institutional rules and norms were precisely what needed to be transformed in order to make possible what we believe is necessary.

Engaging in the AppCAP was powerful precisely because it revealed that university leaders could not contribute to meaningful and just climate action *even when they sincerely wanted to*. The world they lived in, and their resulting conception of climate action, was exclusionary, unjust, and adherent to the status quo over any other factors. Thus, while our classes and activism suggested that radical change was possible, this experience illustrated that a fundamentally different system of governance was *necessary*. After several months of engagement, ClimAct decided to depart from and publicly denounce the AppCAP and the planning process, writing:

> ClimAct cannot in good conscience continue to participate in a climate action planning process that is so limited by improper funding and a lack of power, ignores the scientific consensus, deprioritizes justice, fails to achieve broad participation, and accepts it as inevitable that Appalachian will continue to exceed our planetary boundaries for decades to come.
>
> *(ClimAct 2020b)*

Stepping out of the AppCAP process compelled ClimAct to shift to tactics that went beyond institutional advocacy to more profound worldbuilding. As ClimAct member Hannah Cullen wrote:

> Seeing how impossible it has been to enact change within the systems of change provided by the institution has furthered my belief that we cannot work within the system to make change, especially… if the institution is unwilling and unwanting to do this. The system is designed to be destructive and unjust, [so] the system must be transformed to improve wellbeing and the environment.

It was clear that a new fundamental logic would need to take hold, and that this would not occur through a process of asking nicely. It would likely require that we devise tactics to "stop the bad" while we "build the new" in the spaces we could control.

Tactic 3: Imagining a Climate-Just University and Building New Institutions

ClimAct's commitment to worldbuilding and counter-hegemony is reflected in our vision statement: "We envision a world where anthropogenic climate change *could not happen*" [emphasis added]. Moving forward on world-building required that we use our movement to create new institutions that *can* support just and effective governance and that can block the unjust and ineffective half-measures we had seen in the AppCAP. But to create these, we needed a continual practice of envisioning, imagining, and learning from inspired sources in our community.

In the winter of 2019, we facilitated visioning exercises in which people described what a utopian world might look like to them. To us, this was an important step in connecting to our community and to each other not simply around our "no" (to fossil fuels, climate change, extraction, hierarchy, systems of supremacy), but also around our "yeses" (like transparent and democratic decision making, good public transportation, food forests, alternative justice systems, and policies guided by community rather than market needs). With some coaxing, even community members as young as five years old shared their visions for flowers around town so the bees would have more food and fruit trees in the playgrounds so kids could have snacks. In this visioning work, it has been helpful to stoke the imagination with inspiring examples, including speculative fiction, literature from the Zapatistas and the Leap Manifesto, and essays from *All We Can Save*, which addresses the need to infuse the climate movement with feminine and feminist leadership.

Imagining beyond the realm of what is immediately politically feasible, though rare, is important, especially when done with others. Without these moments, it would be easier for students to be convinced of the narrow visions projected by those in power. Without a powerful vision of a world where climate change could not happen, technocratic solutions might appear as worthwhile pursuits. Yet, with inspiring visions, students are motivated to fight against the unambitious and conventional "solutions" of climate action to pursue large-scale shifts in our world. As one former leader noted:

> Change is often hard to feel confident about, especially in climate work. It can be tiring and not always rewarding work, but what I learned from these experiences is... how change is manifested. Throughout this work it pushes individuals and collectives to challenge themselves every step of the way because we realize the sacredness and significance of doing this work. It shows me it is not as much as moving the meter of CO_2 emissions but instead cultivating the world you want to see to prepare for inevitable change. Through hard work, lots of learning and unlearning, I have started to understand that power is not institutions and administrators, power is working towards a world that delegitimizes hierarchy and control.

This points to a second benefit of visioning: it leads us to the actual governing systems and relations necessary for counter-hegemony. It reveals what might replace the types of top-down or market-based decision making and shallow participation we had encountered in the AppCAP. Drawing from a politics of prefiguration, it was important for us to model the kind of organizing and governing that we demanded and worked towards at higher levels.

From our earliest days, we attempted to practice non-hierarchical leadership within our organization. It manifested at many levels, from group working agreements and ways of facilitating small meetings to the way we engaged the broader movement in collective decision making through online polls and general assemblies. We wanted to model an alternative to top-down and unelected decision making. In our earliest iteration of organization, we also sought to be leaderless, by instead attempting to have a cycling group of coordinators that did not take on power, but helped maintain the broad picture of actions, strategy, and goal. However, within the first half year of this attempt, we both realized and received feedback that this was not working as planned. Those who were able to (and had the time privilege to) put in more work were taking on the bulk of coordinating, strategizing, and day-to-day decision making. We did have leaders, we just weren't recognizing them as such because of our goal of being non-hierarchical. From this, we adapted our model to recognize leaders and also be transparent about the kinds of major decisions that we would deliberate on as a large group and the sorts of activities that any member could comfortably take on without prior approval. Even with our relative failure at non-hierarchical organization at first, we were able to adapt to the changing size, needs, efforts, and commitment of our movement. Over the years, newer leaders have continued to adjust our approach for making decisions, seeking help, and sharing updates so that ClimAct gets closer and closer to a real practice of non-hierarchy, adaptability, and transparent communication. We believe this is essential as we push for democratic and transparent institutions and communities capable of advancing climate justice in the context of crisis.

In pursuing climate justice, ClimAct's work has been marked by a tension between building new institutions and transforming our existing institutions. Calling back to the challenges of hegemony, it can be challenging to imagine our institutions operating ethically and democratically because they have been designed to be opaque, hierarchical, and financially oriented. Further, since the efforts of making them at least *more* democratic or transparent are uphill battles, many activists have decided it is not worth the effort. While building new institutions comes with its own challenges of generating buy-in, establishing a sense of legitimacy, and staying true to values in structure, this avenue has often seemed more compelling, inspiring, and less grueling than the frustrating and sometimes tear-filled slog of working within existing institutions. ClimAct has sought to pursue both avenues, and use the combined effort synergistically.

Addressing existing institutions, ClimAct moved on from the AppCap process to target the Board of Trustees rather than the Office of Sustainability and Chancellor, especially highlighting the anti-democratic nature of decision making and the university's failure to serve North Carolinians. Tapping into commonly held values of fairness, democracy, and the responsibility of public officials, as well as concerns about the health and economic well-being of the local community and "misspent tax-dollars," we used this campaign to broaden the conversation beyond "environmentalism" in a way that would build bridges to other organizations in the area. In a demonstration on the day of the International Climate Strike of 2021, ClimAct members led protesters to the lobby outside of the trustees' meeting for an open mic. Taking the stage, one participant asked, "why is it that *they* can sit in that room and make decisions about *our* lives, while we aren't even allowed in" (paraphrased). This protest and its framing helped build new expectations about ourselves as a community capable of and entitled to democratic self-governance. While the escalation continued, ClimAct also organized to create new institutions for community governance by establishing a people's assembly.

Inspired by the People's Assemblies in Jackson, MS (Akuno 2017), our people's assembly examined how we might bring the ownership and governance of regional energy directly into the people's hands. Student organizers began the Zoom-based assembly by summarizing the issues and frustrations expressed at a recent energy summit organized by Appalachian Voices, ClimAct, and Sunrise Boone, including policies that made renewable energy unaffordable, a lack of weatherization initiatives, and high costs of energy for low-income households. Highlighting the reality that this was not acceptable, we then expanded the realm of possibility by providing examples of energy justice initiatives across the US through which residents are taking control of their energy, saving money, and reducing environmental impacts in ways that combat inequity. After a bit of discussion, the 50 participants divided into groups to decide which energy justice initiatives they wanted to pursue. At the end of the event, thirteen volunteers formed action teams to flesh out these initiatives and return recommendations to the full assembly. We analyzed notes from the conversation, using community sentiment to guide our goals and strategies. For several weeks, the action teams met to conduct research on similar initiatives, meet with local policy experts and staff from the electric utilities, and to develop long-term strategies.

The People's Assembly was our first foray into direct action to build our own counter-institutions for self-governance – not just a sense of power, but actual ownership, policy change, and governing systems. Attempted during the Covid-19 pandemic during a time of low organizational capacity, the efforts eventually failed, but the lessons stayed with us. It is a process that we have repeated with community town halls related to university growth and by supporting public fora on housing insecurity, both of which we hope are leading to longer-term action to build community-owned institutions for direct service provision and empowerment.

Tactic 4: Addressing Material Constraints to Activism

A final tactic that we deem important has been to reduce the material constraints that activists face. We have used classes, internships, and independent studies to help students (and sometimes faculty) "double-count" their activism and thus dedicate more time to it. We have found scholarship funding so several lower-income students could dedicate their time to activism rather than summer jobs. We have advertised other paid community organizer positions so students could earn a living while building movement skills, rather than engaging in more traditional service work. And we have also tried to use potlucks and other forms of mutual aid to reduce people's everyday burdens.

These efforts have sustained ClimAct across four years and multiple leadership changes. For example, funding four students during our first summer was probably essential for maintaining momentum into year two, and Michael's use of independent studies allowed him to dedicate time to the organization during a period of low participation. However, our work on the material constraints on activism has never been perfect. Several of our student leaders – and virtually all faculty participants – have burned out or bailed out in response to the difficulty of integrating activism with other life demands. As a result, more-privileged students tend to show up the most, imbuing them with expertise, skills, and confidence that propels them into leadership positions. Thus hierarchies of the dominant culture are replicated within our organization even as we fight against them.

Since 2020, ClimAct has dedicated less effort to building material resources for activism. This is partly due to pandemic-related disruptions, partly due to Brian taking a more distanced role, and partly because new student leaders have been less proactive in seeking to combine ClimAct and other work. However, we may need to take this up again. The financial and time constraints on activism are big, and they are increasing thanks to the effects of university growth on local housing costs and job markets. It seems unlikely that we will build the resources to address these material constraints in a widespread way, but we may be able to make enough of a difference to sustain momentum through lulls and leadership changes.

Lessons for the Roads Ahead

George Lakey argues that any enduring revolution requires, first and foremost, cultural preparation. People must "chang[e] the way they look at themselves" and "also their image of the system" (2012: 72, 74). In our climate justice activism at Appalachian State

University – where we seek to revolutionize the university and broader community through serious and creative engagement in a just transition – we have found common sense views of ourselves and our society to be major impediments. They demobilize the masses, foster consent for undemocratic and oppressive decision-making, and frequently constrain activist (i.e., our own) creativity and effectiveness. In many ways, power and inaction at the university is a microcosm of larger hegemonic structures – national governments, intergovernmental development agencies, global economies, and the UNFCCC Conference of Parties (better known as the COPs).

In this chapter, we've discussed four of our main strategies for supporting cultural preparation for a just transition: using coursework and formal trainings to build new subjectivities and skills for a sense of empowerment; revealing the inability to address vital concerns through conventional institutional approaches; building new imaginations of self-governed climate justice and institutions that (attempt to) embody those visions; and reducing the material challenges that constrain activist engagement. Through these efforts we are striving to create a new common sense – what Gramsci would call a "good sense" – that makes climate justice and inclusive, democratic, and values-based governance into taken-for-granted expectations in our community. Only then will it be a true outrage for our university to continue operating despite violating planetary boundaries, systematically violating the dignity of students, faculty, and staff of color, exploiting and harming locals, or nonconsensually endangering faculty and staff during a pandemic.

Only four years in, our work is just beginning to bear fruit, though we do see promising signs of a deeper sense of empowerment and critical consciousness within our community and evidence that these gains are being "inherited" as student-activists graduate and new leaders take the helm. Still, we have far to go. Recognizing that our business is unfinished and our perspectives extremely partial, we would like to offer some reflections on what we might have done differently and what we might do next to broaden and deepen our counter-hegemonic cultural work.

First, we would like to build easier bridges to radicalism. Internally, this means making it easier for people to find their place without resorting to traditional leadership. Our initial plan for a non-hierarchical (leaderless/leaderful) organization may have been counter-hegemonic, but that also made it unfamiliar and challenging for participants. This was perhaps especially true for less privileged participants, who had less time to navigate an unknown organizational style, carve out their own spaces, and take risks. We need to develop processes and a language to welcome people in as followers if that's where they are, to offer them a pathway to leadership, and to convey the value of blurring that distinction.

Second, it might be productive to develop stronger languages and practices around new subjectivities and a new common sense. Leveraging Norgaard's insights, can we establish new norms for emotion and communication that normalize caring, action, and engagement? And following Gramsci and Foucault, can we develop metrics or standards of evaluation (for ourselves and the institution) that help us appreciate the impact of small victories while also naturalizing values of democracy, climate reality, and proactive justice? Our previous community-building work (including frequent potlucks, volunteer days, and mutual aid events) clearly built a community of peer influencers, but we can strategize more effectively about how to take advantage of this and how to ensure it rejuvenates people and advances the work rather than becoming yet another thing to plan.

Third, we have learned that "propaganda of the deed" and our efforts at direct action need to work well or they risk reinforcing hegemonic understandings of power and effectiveness. Our people's assembly action teams fizzled out after a couple of months as volunteers lost momentum, as did an effort to do covid-related mutual aid within the structure of a class. In both instances, the cultural and material barriers to sustained engagement were higher than we anticipated. As we move forward on future direct action organizing – whether to fight or build – we need to be more strategic about the resources we need to sustain activism.

Finally, we hope to engage in more collaborative projects that illustrate the just transition and build alliances through the practical de-siloing of climate change. By walking side-by-side with local housing justice, migrant justice, and food justice advocates, we hope to identify climate justice synergies and shared critiques. With enough of our community united in a commitment to a climate just future, perhaps we really can erode hegemonic power and build ours.

Ultimately, your path will be different from ours. We hope, however, that this chapter plants some seeds about how you may leverage your positionality as students and faculty to nurture truly counter-hegemonic climate movements that can "change everything" and in which the power, agency, and imaginative striving of student-citizens become our new common sense.

A Note of Gratitude

Throughout the text, we reference the work of ClimAct, which is nothing but the collective power of its members. We owe gratitude to the many people who have made ClimAct since 2018; those that dedicated years to organizing, those that have joined in for any amount of time, and those that simply mingled their shouts with ours for a day. We are also thankful to those who organize with ClimAct presently and those who will carry on the work in the years to come. We are especially grateful to those ClimActors that provided such extensive and thoughtful comments on this chapter; we continue to celebrate this divine act of thinking together and making each other better.

Notes

1 The University of North Carolina System is composed of seventeen state-funded universities in North Carolina and governed by one Board of Governors.
2 The university's progress toward true carbon neutrality is far worse than these official numbers suggest. Like most universities, App State ignores a wide range of greenhouse gas emissions, including those related to food, most waste and wastewater, the embodied carbon of all of our buildings, the carbon footprint of all university purchases, the full carbon footprint of the extraction, processing, and delivery of fuels, and the impact of university investments. The full carbon footprint is likely 1.6–3.2 times greater than what the university is counting, even without including the university-owned electric utility (ClimAct 2020a).
3 We do not pretend to offer a complete analysis of hegemony here, but highlight several components of hegemonic struggle that we think are especially relevant for climate justice activism at App State and other universities. Some are directly related to climate hegemony, and others are more focused on the common sense of leadership, followership, and public institution.
4 This table's title derives from Roseberry's (1994) article; Public Enemy (1988) inspired language on "the hype."

5 CJA also argues that changing the story involves helping other movements "see the climate crisis as a key driver of structural change in the 21st century and therefore a critical opening towards building a new economic system." This de-siloing of climate change and the construction of multiracial alliances that uplift communities of color are two shortcomings of our work so far, despite our efforts to advance them through our stories, goals, and outreach.

6 The Movement Action Plan identifies stages of social movement progress and helps activists discern where they are and what strategies and tactics will move them forward.

References

Akuno, Kali (for the New Afrikan People's Organization and Malcom X Grassroots Movement). 2017. "People's Assembly overview: The Jackson People's Assembly model." In *Jackson Rising: The struggle for economic democracy and Black self-determination in Jackson, Mississippi.* Edited by Cooperation Jackson (Kali Akuno, Sacajawea Hall, and Brandon King) and Ajamu Nangwaya, pp. 87–98. Québec: Daraja Press.

Au, Wayne. 2011. "Teaching under the new Taylorism: high-stakes testing and the standardization of the 21st century curriculum." *Journal of Curriculum Studies* 43 (1): 25–45. https://doi.org/10.1080/00220272.2010.521261.

Climate Action Collaborative (ClimAct). 2020a. *The Just Climate Action Plan for Appalachian State.* Boone, NC: Climate Action Collaborative. https://appclimact.wixsite.com/climateaction/just-climate-action-plan.

Climate Action Collaborative (ClimAct). 2020b. *Letter to the Chancellor,* Office of Sustainability, Faculty Senate, and Student Government Association. Sept 15, 2020.

Crehan, Kate. 2016. *Gramsci's Common Sense: Inequality and its narratives.* Durham, NC:Duke University Press.

Dixon, Chris. 2014. *Another Politics: Talking across today's transformative movements.* Berkeley: University of California Press.

England, Laura, Jennie Carlisle, Rebecca Witter, Derek Davidson, Lynette Holman and Dana Powell. 2019. "Storying climate change at Appalachian State University." *Practicing Anthropology* 41 (3): 21–26.

Gramsci, Antonio. David Forgacs (ed.). 2000. *The Antonio Gramsci Reader: Selected writings 1916–1934.* New York: NYU Press.

Intergovernmental Panel on Climate Change (IPCC). 2018. *Global Warming of 1.5°C.* An IPCC Special Report on the impacts of global warming of 1.5°C above pre-industrial levels and related global greenhouse gas emission pathways, in the context of strengthening the global response to the threat of climate change, sustainable development, and efforts to eradicate poverty. Edited by Masson-Delmotte, V., P. Zhai, H.-O. Pörtner, D. Roberts, J. Skea, P.R. Shukla, A. Pirani, W. Moufouma-Okia, C. Péan, R. Pidcock, S. Connors, J.B.R. Matthews, Y. Chen, X. Zhou, M.I. Gomis, E. Lonnoy, T. Maycock, M. Tignor, and T. Waterfield. https://www.ipcc.ch/site/assets/uploads/sites/2/2019/06/SR15_Full_Report_High_Res.pdf.

Klein, Naomi. 2015. *This Changes Everything: Capitalism versus the climate.* New York: Simon & Schuster.

Lakey, George. 2012. *Toward a Living Revolution: A five-stage framework for creating radical social change.* Eugene, OR: Wipf & Stock.

Linger, Daniel T. 1993. "The hegemony of discontent." *American Ethnologist* 20: 3–24.

Luhrmann, Tanya M. 2006. "Subjectivity." *Anthropological Theory* 6 (3): 345–361. https://doi.org/10.1177/1463499606066892.

Lukes, Stephen. 1974. *Power: A radical view.* New York: Macmillan.

Movement Generation Justice & Ecology Project. 2016. *From Banks and Tanks to Cooperation and Caring.* Berkeley, CA. https://movementgeneration.org/wp-content/uploads/2016/11/JT_booklet_English_SPREADs_web.pdf.

Norgaard, Kari Marie. 2011. *Living in Denial: Climate change, emotions, and everyday life*. Cambridge, MA: MIT Press.

Public Enemy. 1988. "Don't believe the hype." On the album *It Takes a Nation of Millions to Hold us Back*. Written by Eric Sadler, Hank Shocklee, Chuck D., and Flavor Flav. Produced by Chuck D. and Hank Shocklee. Def Jam Recordings.

Roseberry, William. 1994. "Hegemony and the language of contention." In *Everyday Forms of State Formation: Revolution and the negotiation of rule in modern Mexico*, eds. Gilbert M. Joseph and Daniel Nugent, pp. 355–366. Durham, NC: Duke University Press.

Stoller, Aaron. 2015. "Taylorism and the logic of learning outcomes." *Journal of Curriculum Studies* 47 (3): 317–333.

24

CAIYUGLUKU

Pulling from Within to Meet the Challenges in a Rapidly Changing Arctic

Fred Phillip, Raychelle Aluaq Daniel, Jonella Ququngaq Larson, Anne Stevens Henshaw, and Erin Dougherty Lynch

Introduction

The Yup'ik drum song *Caiyugluku*, meaning "To Pull", has become a touchstone for Pamyua, a contemporary dance and vocal group whose perfomances showcase Indigenous knowledge and history. The lyrics, sung in Yup'ik, are about looking for ground squirrels while on a hunt, but are also understood as a prayer for strength. *Caiyugluku* is especially relevant for understanding how Yup'ik in Alaska conceptualize the challenges they face – whether from climate, colonialism, or other societal stressors. It describes problem-solving by drawing on one's mental and physical strength, or from the strength of Indigenous culture. This chapter reframes the climate crisis as a *aaqsunarqelriitin* (crisis) in the frameworks and systems of institutions and organizations that lack the deep values-based relationships that lie at the center of Indigenous ways of knowing and being. As they face the challenge of climate change, Yup'ik communities seek to build genuine trust and understanding – prerequisites for governance and management regimes rooted in *ciungani atullruaqa* (peoples' lived experience) and that embrace multiple ways of knowing and being in a rapidly changing world. We explore efforts underway to rebuild, repair and renew those relationships in ways that exercise localized cultural values and governance with allied organizations and institutions.

In sharing our perspectives, we bring in both our lived experience from the Northern Bering Sea region and also draw on our first-hand knowledge from the fields of philanthropy, research, conservation and law in building more equitable spaces that include Indigenous Peoples. Jonella Larson is St. Lawrence Island Yupik with extended family ties in Savoonga. Raychelle Aluaq Daniel is Yup'ik and grew up in Tuntutuliak. Anne Henshaw is an anthropologist by training and has spent the last 15 years working in private philanthropy building relationships and supporting Indigenous-led organizations in the Arctic. Fred Phillip is the former Tribal Council President of the Native Village of Kwigillingok and is the Chair of the Bering Sea Elders Group. Erin Dougherty Lynch is the Managing Attorney of the Alaska Office of the Native American Rights Fund.

The Yup'ik terms referenced throughout this chapter are drawn from both our personal use of Yup'ik and St. Lawrence Island Yupik in use by Indigenous friends and colleagues and also

DOI: 10.4324/9781003242499-28

from a recent glossary of terms translated by 14 language experts from the Bering Strait region, compiled by Brenden and Julie Raymond-Yakoubian (Aluska et al. 2022). We recognize that terminology is not uniformly shared across linguistically similar peoples and that there are differences in spelling and meaning depending on the relationship that a family, clan, village, or cluster might have with lands and waters. We also recognize the majority of the terms we have highlighted are general Yup'ik terms and that there are many more descriptive and complex terms related to "sharing," "respect," and "responsibility" based on the above. Additionally, we center the scholarly work, experience, and knowledge from Indigenous Peoples contributing from different sectors of society to prioritize Indigenous ways of knowing and being and welcome correction and response to any errors we have made in spelling or meaning of terms.

Setting the Context

Central to the Yup'ik worldview is that people are considered part of an interconnected system (*nunaput ellaput-llu elluatun eglertut*) and not separate from it. These connections were best expressed by Harry Lincoln, a Yup'ik elder (*tegneq*) in relation to the ocean he called home:

> Imarpik. In my Yup'ik language, this means the big water, the ocean. This is the Bering Sea. It is where our stories come from and how we have survived since time immemorial. Almost everything our bodies need comes from the ocean – seal, whale, walrus, birds, fish and shellfish species. These are traditional foods, and are a foundation of our village economies. To us, the northern Bering and strait region is a special place, a whole ecosystem driven by the rhythm of sea ice forming in the fall and retreating in the spring. Each part is connected to all other parts, and our long human history here accounts for the large territory Yup'ik and Inupiat peoples use for hunting and fishing. Here, every spring and fall, one of the Earth's great migrations occurs. We wait for it and prepare for it – walrus, whales, seals, and millions of birds and shellfish species – all moving past islands and along the coast. St. Lawrence Islanders call this Katawhsaqa, or "pouring out," because of the great abundance and movement of the animals. In Central Yup'ik, it is called Utarrluten, meaning "moving to another place."
>
> *(Lincoln 2016)*

Systems like those described above include aspects of the environment (*ella*) and all it encompasses, time, and how humans interact with these elements. This holistic view extends not only to spirituality, but to the values surrounding health and wellness. The system also could be described as "a way of life" or "subsistence practices" using various English terminologies. This way of life or *yuuyaraq* holds the foundation or framework for Yup'ik and is central to Elder teachings such as those shared by Dr. Chief Kangrilnguq Paul John and Peter Paniguaq Jacobs (e.g., see John-Shields 2018). This Yup'ik philosophy brings together values, customs, Indigenous knowledge, skills, practices, and spirituality.

Such ways of knowing and relating to all living beings continue to be passed down and embraced by generations who have followed – including a group of forty next generation Indigenous leaders who gathered in Anchorage in January 2020 eager to shape the future of their communities – and the globe. The convening was called "Our seas are rising and so are we" to reflect a growing trend in climate advocacy, research, and conservation where the next generation brings an awareness of the power, agency, and responsibility they hold for themselves, their communities, and the planet – building on the generational values, experience, practical knowledge, and wisdom that make them who they are.

Much of this energy and enthusiasm is born from deep frustration and historical trauma since colonial structures took hold in the Arctic, including Alaska, centuries ago. These structures are defined not only by *all'am yuum alerquun* (someone else's laws) in which Indigenous communities currently have to navigate but also the economic and education systems that still dominate the Arctic today. The imprint of the colonial legacy has been devastating, often requiring people to cope with multiple and often compounding stressors including high rates of suicide, social inequality, poverty, dwindling access to natural resources, inadequate housing and health care, substance abuse, unsafe drinking water, low educational attainment, food insecurity, and most recently a global pandemic. As Huntington et al. (2019: 1218) rightly point out, "focusing on climate change as the only or the primary threat misses much that is more pressing and worrisome. The amount of attention given singularly to climate change in and of itself, as opposed to climate in the context of numerous other risks, can even distract from what matters to Arctic communities."

It is against this backdrop that the next generation of leaders are interrogating and dismantling systems while reclaiming their values within institutions to protect their futures. Key to their approach is refocusing and reframing the way research, conservation, and climate solutions are carried out and supported. Increasingly Indigenous-led research and conservation models question the burdens historically placed on Indigenous Peoples by academic researchers and environmental groups that devalue Indigenous knowledge and stewardship practices while perpetuating power asymmetries and structural inequities designed to advance western governance, management, and knowledge systems (Bennett et al. 2021). What has resulted over time is deep seated mistrust and frustration over policies and practices not rooted in place or long-standing cultural values; in essence, a crisis in relationships. Or, as Kyle Whyte (2021) has argued in an analysis of discordant concepts of time related to climate change, a breakdown of kinship relations rooted in shared responsibility.

While such breakdowns stem from a range of root causes from colonialism to capitalism they continue to perpetuate structural inequities that disproportionately impact Indigenous Peoples across the globe. Meredith McCoy[2] and her colleagues at the Center for Humans and Nature call for the urgent need to shift our relational practices to address the threats to the lands and waters that sustain Indigenous communities, a return of governance to Indigenous territories, and a revitalization of Indigenous educational practices that prioritize preparing the next generation of Indigenous leaders to tend to the land, community, and one another. Indigenous approaches to climate change mitigation and adaptation go hand-in-hand with rethinking governance and re-asserting the role of Indigenous peoples to steward the lands and resources within their cultural homelands. This allows for transformative emergent opportunities and for greater tribal self-determination. If the solutions for climate and social challenges continue to be made from external sources, opportunities for Indigenous Peoples in Alaska and around the globe will remain limited.

With the racial reckoning associated with the murder of George Floyd, there has been a growing recognition of the importance of advancing social equity and justice across all aspects of society. Western-trained researchers, conservationists, and climate change activists and advocates are starting to recognize that *yupiit elisngalriit ayuquciat* (Indigenous knowledge) and values have key roles to play in protecting biodiversity, addressing the climate crisis, and for advancing knowledge and solutions that meet immediate local needs of Indigenous Peoples.

This is not just in the Arctic but globally (Gadamus et al. 2015; Ellis et al. 2021). The call for the "re-indigenization of principles" has been at the heart of a new era governing how we steward and govern rich biodiverse *nunaq* (land) and *imarpig* (ocean) in the midst of rapid change (M'sɨt No'kmaq et al. 2020).

Herein, we provide examples of how such relationships are taking root within new and existing organizational and management initiatives centered on the Yup'ik concept of *Auluk* (taking care of lands and waters). We begin with an exploration into relationality and its connection with broader Indigenous values of reciprocity, respect, and responsibility within Yup'ik and Yupik worldviews. We then present two case studies that demonstrate how Yup'ik and Yupik peoples are centering relationships in decision-making within new and existing governance structures that strengthen relationality and resilience through connection to community, place, and language.

Centering Yup'ik and St. Lawrence Island Yupik Relational Values

To understand the importance of relationality, we share a quote from Vera Metcalf, a longtime advocate and Yupik elder from St. Lawrence Island, as it centers many of the core values of what it means to be in "right relationship" with each other and all living beings:

> Only by cherishing the blessing of a harvested walrus (or whale, or seal) are we worthy of continued successful hunting. Even our thoughts while accepting the gift offered to us must be proper and respectful, because they reflect how well we care for and conserve what is given. We give thanks. The cultural practice of humbly sharing our harvest is an expression of this understanding. While it is beyond translation, this profoundest Indigenous Knowledge and way-of-knowing in my language is Esla.... . So while the natural world is acting strangely and the traditional rhythms of our lives are unsettled, the Arctic will always be our home, eternal and sacred. It seems that we now are struggling with our land and waters and are not in balance with them, as before; but our communities will continue adapting and will rely on our Indigenous Knowledge to maintain our relationship properly with our world.
>
> *(Metcalf 2021: 427)*

Such sentiments are echoed across the Indigenous cultures globally that recognize receiving resources as a privilege with concurrent reciprocal responsibilities (Kealiikanakaoleohailiani and Giardina 2016). For the purposes of this chapter, relationality centers on three Yup'ik and Yupik interrelated values underpinning their holistic understanding of *Yuuyaraq* (way of life) and the greater powers of *Ellam Yua* (the spirit or person of the universe) (Ellam Yua et. al. 2022; Ayunerak et al. 2014).

Aruqulluki *(Sharing)*

Sharing what you have will bring you abundance and plenty. For one word, there are many different aspects showing the depth of what it means to share. For example, in Jacobson (1984) sharing definitions originate from different contexts within the practice occurs. As translated it is *nengi*; to share a catch *aruqe-*, *kuyagtar-*; to share food with *naruyake-*; to share with *avgute-*; to distribute ~s after a hunt *pitar-, tulimite-, uqicetaar-*; have enough to ~ *vegvingqerr-*; not want to ~ *kiimurrsug*.

Takaq *(Respect)*

Respect one another as everyone has something they can share. The concept of respect is applied across the human, non-human and the spiritual realms. Because of this, there are multiple values that relate to showing respect and the responsibility that comes along with knowing how to be respectful. Elders have shared, "never look down on people if they disagree with you. You should also never look up to people with envy. Instead, when we are faced with a challenge or opportunity is when we should look to people to help create the best solution and way forward."

Aulukluki *(Responsibility)*

Responsibility means understanding, caring for and nurturing your relationships. As a person, you hold different types of responsibility across time (past and future ancestors), dimensions (spirituality), systems (natural and built environment). It is within the values of *yuuyaraq* that contain the instructions for living life and understanding how to carry out your responsibilities. Many of these values are rooted in ways Yup'ik pass knowledge on to younger generations which differ substantively from western-oriented educational practices. Traditionally, Yup'ik ways of learning are connected to a holistic approach guided by relationships and values.

While many of these values are passed down informally from one generation to the next, they are becoming more formalized through progressive education such as the Ayaprun Elitnaurvik Yup'ik Immersion School in Bethel, Alaska. The school explicitly takes a Yup'ik values-based approach to education in formative years in children with strong underlying values of relationality. The mission of the school is to:

> *Ayaprun Elitnaurvigmi elluarrluta Yugtun qaneryaram tunginun elitnauriciqukut: ellaturivkarluki, taikanivkarluki Yugtun piciryaraput, qaneryaraput, yuuyarput-llu.*

> We, the community of Ayaprun Elitnaurvik, will strive to provide a high quality Yugtun immersion education: empowering our diverse students by strengthening their knowledge, use, and understanding of Yup'ik core values, language, and culture.

The school was established with values surrounding the responsibility to understand and know the world through the Yup'ik language and to foster values of mutual respect. Further embedded in this view is that the Yup'ik language provides insight into the worldview and a deeper understanding of culture. Agatha John-Shields (2018) talks about becoming aware (*Ellangeq*) and the role that education plays in a deepening understanding that shapes who you are as a person throughout life. An important part of that understanding includes the close association with family and community. Parents and community are critical in the curriculum of Ayaprun. Learning is hands-on and includes the learning of anatomy of fish and seals, to cutting fish, preparing traditional foods and celebrating through *yuraq* (dance).

It is within this context of a value-based knowledge system and a changing climate, that we explore how Yup'ik communities are working within existing structures while creating new models of decision-making and governance that are grounded in *aruqulluki, takaq*, and *aulukluki*. As we find it is not only important to adapt and change to physical environmental impacts but to be adaptable to relationship models that build on these concepts of shared values, respect and responsibility.

The Bering Sea Elders Group (BSEG)

Knowledge is highly prized in Yup'ik communities. Yup'ik value the holders of that knowledge, recognize the need for those holders of the knowledge, and understand their responsibility to share that knowledge. It may have been implied, but these are not mutually exclusive. The responsibilities of these knowledge holders, while they may differ over time, is upon every Yup'ik person because all will play some role over the course of their lifetimes. These responsibilities are best expressed through *Caiyugluku* (the need to pull from the strength within) to meet the challenges Yup'ik communities face today.

To illustrate, we highlight the work of the Bering Sea Elders Group (BSEG) as an example of how Yup'ik values are reflected in broader Indigenous efforts to influence policy. Yup'ik Elders are recognized for their living knowledge carried across time to today and deepening understanding of *Ellangeq* comes from not only knowing values but practicing them in everyday life as is clearly stated in the mission statement of the organization:

> The knowledge of the elders about how to live with the ocean and the land was given to us by our ancestors with instructions not to keep it for ourselves, but to pass it on to our children so that they may continue to prosper and continue our way of being.
> *(Bering Sea Elders Group, Resolution Expressing Our Mission, November 3 2011)*

BSEG is an organization of 38 Tribes from the Kuskokwim Bay to the Bering Strait. BSEG member Tribes represent Yup'ik, Cup'ik, St. Lawrence Island Yupik, and Inupiaq people. Each appoints an Elder Representative to serve on the BSEG Elders Board. BSEG's mission is to:

> [S]peak and work together as one voice to protect and respect our traditional ways of life, the ocean web of life that supports the resources we rely on, and our children's future. As Elders, we are messengers to our children, our tribal councils, and the people who make decisions that affect our marine resources, ecosystem, and ways of life.

BSEG initially formed in response to tribal concerns about the large commercial bottom trawl fisheries in Kuskokwim Bay and the possible expansion into the Northern Bering Sea Research Area, an area established by the North Pacific Fisheries Management Council (NPFMC). For over a decade, BSEG has understood the importance of working in coalition, and has worked closely with Bering Sea tribal partners including the Association of Village Council Presidents, Kawerak, Inc., and the Aleut Community of St. Paul Island.

One of BSEG's first projects was *The Northern Bering Sea: Our Way of Life*[3], a detailed mapping project showing species and habitats critical to supporting the ways of life for communities along the Bering Sea. The maps were used as a basis for advocating for protection of these areas, including advocacy on specific issues before the NPFMC, and for pushing for a stronger role for tribal governments in federal decision-making processes that affect the Bering Sea.

The full BSEG Elders Board meets annually for a multi-day summit at which Elder Representatives discuss changes that they are witnessing in the Bering Sea. The format and structure of the summits provide an open, equitable space that centers individual knowledge systems and Elder knowledge holders; the room is arranged so that there is no lead dictating the agenda, there is no firm time limit on conversation, and simultaneous translation is available so that Yup'ik, Cup'ik, St. Lawrence Island Yupik, and Inupiaq Elder Representatives can understand each other's perspective. At the Summits, the 38 Elder Representatives collectively draft and pass resolutions which guide the work of the organization. Resolutions have focused on food security, changes to federal management structures, the importance of incorporating and treating as equal Indigenous knowledge into federal management decisions, and tribal self-determination over the management of natural resources. Many of BSEG's resolutions begin by recognizing that the Bering Sea is an integral part of the Elder Representatives' identities as Yup'ik, Cup'ik, St. Lawrence Island Yupik, and Inupiat Peoples, and that the water is as important to them as the land.

These resolutions were the basis for BSEG's work with coalition partners to advocate for greater protections for the Northern Bering Sea. This advocacy paid off on December 9, 2016, when President Obama signed an executive order creating the 112,300 square mile Northern Bering Sea Climate Resilience Area. The Executive Order provides a pathway for Alaska Tribes to exercise their self-determination and a greater role in decision-making over the northern Bering Sea and Bering Strait region. This is the first time a President has required that Indigenous knowledge and expertise be applied to federal management decisions, answering a decades-long drum beat of Native Peoples. While the designation was rescinded by President Trump in April 2017, President Biden reinstated the Northern Bering Sea Climate Resilience Area in January 2021 on his first day in office. BSEG and its partners the Association of Village Council Presidents (AVCP), Kawerak, and the Aleut Community of St. Paul Island have continued their coalition efforts to now implement the Executive Order.

BSEG's approach has been and continues to be grounded in *aruqulluki, takaq,* and *aulukluki,* and the organization provides a space for tribally appointed Elder Representatives to use their wisdom and traditional values and knowledge of how to live on the land and ocean to protect and manage the resources of the Bering Sea. As their founding vision for the Bering Sea states:

> The teaching of our ancestors was based on respect for what the ocean provides. Respectful actions are rewarded by hunting success; disrespectful actions have negative consequences. We were taught never to waste what the Creator has given us, to share our food with the community and to listen to our Elders because they acquired wisdom over a long life and sharp observation. Today, while technology has changed, our traditional values and our hunting, fishing, and gathering ways of life, remain the foundation of our culture. Respect for the natural world and caring for our natural resources are necessary for our people to continue thriving off the ocean and land and providing for our children's inheritance.[4]

Discussion

Throughout this chapter, we have described how values are central to understanding how Yup'ik communities think about the myriad of societal and environmental changes happening around them. Many of these values are best expressed through the power of relationships similar to what Daniel Wildcat, a Yuchi member of the Muscogee Nation of Oklahoma, describes from his worldview:

> Can you imagine a world where nature is understood as full of relatives not resources, where inalienable rights are balanced with inalienable responsibilities and where wealth itself is measured not by resources, ownership and control but by the number of good relationships we maintain in the complex and diverse life systems of this blue green planet? I can."
>
> *(Wildcat 2013: 515)*

These values are important not simply as an abstract philosophy but are fundamental to how Yup'ik communities and other Indigenous Peoples across the Arctic connect their knowledge systems, climate solutions, and decision-making practices in relation to the environment and the climate crisis. As the climate crisis only worsens, Indigenous Peoples will continue to face basic human rights issues around climate-forced displacement, food insecurity, basic community infrastructure, and changes associated with a rapidly changing ecosystem.[5] Centering values, relationality, and Indigenous knowledge in decision-making processes, including how resources are allocated, is critical to driving durable solutions that meet community needs over the long term. Putting these values into practice is what gives meaning to *Caiyugluku* – the need to pull from values within is what provides the inner strength to face what can appear to be insurmountable and complex challenges.

Pulling from within also means ensuring that we are carrying forward the values connecting relationality whether in existing structures and processes or by creating new systems built on relationality frameworks. Both need to happen simultaneously; however, often such initiatives are occurring in siloed and compartmentalized sectors that lead to the "measurement of resources" Daniel Wildcat describes as a modern challenge. The inclusion of both Elders and youth is critical for meeting this challenge and bridging silos. Ayaprun Elitnaurvik and BSEG recognize the values of relationality we highlighted in this chapter which show the kind of complexity and diversity that would benefit "resource management."

A persistent challenge is the dichotomy between Indigenous knowledge and western science. Indigenous knowledge should not be thought of as uniform; rather, Indigenous knowledges represent many diverse ways of knowing. Indigenous knowledges are valid knowledge systems, each of which is unique. Indigenous knowledge is not only connected in a holistic worldview – it is living body of knowledge that is a part of and cannot be separated from the people who steward lands and waters. In this rapidly changing climate, the importance of basing decisions on our best knowledge is even more critical in making decisions about lands and waters – Indigenous People and their ways of knowing must be part of the process (Daniel et al. 2022).

Strengthening partnerships with Indigenous Peoples includes supporting their sovereign right to make decisions and inform and create policy on behalf of their peoples and homelands. For too long, Alaska's Indigenous Peoples have had to react and respond to policies and laws that diminish their decision-making power as it relates to protecting core values and their identity. Inverting this process and ensuring decision-making responsibility is in the hands of Indigenous Peoples in turn recognizes the sovereignty of the lands, waters, ecosystems, and all living beings.

A promising practice that provides a framework based on relations for equitably bringing together different ways of knowing and science (coming from a "western" worldview) is the "Co-production of Knowledge" approach (Ellam Yua et al. 2022). The elements of a Co-production of Knowledge approach form the foundation for equity. These elements described in Ellam Yua et al. (2022) include relationships, empowerment, capacity, means and ability, practice being deliberate and intentional, ethics, decolonization, sovereignty, and trust and respect. The framework itself is set in a relational space, recognizing that multiple elements need to be considered simultaneously when undertaking a (research, policy, or co-management) process that equitably includes Indigenous knowledges. A Co-production of Knowledge approach provides that roadmap for how to include people in a meaningful way in the process. In addition to the means of knowledge production, the role of public and private sector funding is also critical to ensuring more inclusive models of governance and decision-making as Indigenous Peoples navigate a new and changing Arctic.

Within philanthropy, direct grant making to progressive, Indigenous-led, non-profit organizations advocating for themselves and their priorities provides an important avenue to ensure adequate resourcing (Henshaw 2013). There is also a host of new initiatives that revolve around more participatory approaches to grant making itself whereby Indigenous Peoples themselves decide on how and where resources should be directed (Scott-Enns 2020; Angarova 2020; Meyer et al. 2021). The Arctic Indigenous Fund is one example of how philanthropic initiatives are being designed to shift power, advance decolonization, and to recognize that Arctic Indigenous Peoples themselves are best positioned to make funding decisions. The Fund is directed by a set of advisors from Inuit, Northern Dene, and Sámi communities who oversee the grantmaking. As one of the original advisors Dewey Kk'ołeyo Putyuk Hoffman notes the Advisors "rely on broad-based Indigenous approaches to this work, each with their own distinct beliefs, cultural practices, and communication styles. We acknowledge the interwoven history that includes interests that actively work to destroy Indigenous ways of life, those who actively uplift the dignity and honor of Indigenous lifeways, and others somewhere else along the spectrum. This requires an ongoing constant process of filtering things out based upon our individual *and* collective value system and beliefs. We can apply teachings from one set of experiences to another and begin to uphold a holistic worldview."[6] The Arctic Indigenous Fund and Indigenous led funds that are starting to flourish globally reflect how Indigenous Peoples are centering values in decision-making to better meet the current needs and priorities of communities so they thrive into the future.

In another example of progressive philanthropy, the Alaska Venture Fund (AVF) is working on methods to capture, communicate, and elevate the narratives of Indigenous leaders in Alaska who are working to protect and sustain cultural values amid complex challenges, including climate change and social injustice. The emergent approaches create opportunities for people to document and communicate information that is culturally appropriate, contribute to equitable conversations and understandings of Indigenous ideologies and strategies, and ultimately increase the financial support for those who are working toward a just and sustainable Alaska. These efforts are core to the Alaska Venture Fund.

AVF recognizes that Alaskans are at the front lines of the climate crisis and are experiencing accelerating impacts with every season. To effectively address and counter the negative impacts of climate change, it is imperative for human societies to rethink their relationship with the planet. One approach AVF takes is through the cultural lenses of Indigenous Peoples. A part of this process recognizes the validity of Indigenous knowledge systems and the profound values these systems uphold when it comes to cultural understandings of how to live in relationship with the land, waters, and environment. Another part of the process is for humanity to fully understand the impact western policies and imposed systems have had, and in some cases continue to have, in diminishing Indigenous Peoples' ability to fully exercise and sustain their fundamental values. Society must find radically creative ways to support the new and emergent systemic approaches that are created, designed, and implemented by Indigenous leaders. Doing so will help them maximize opportunities they need to reclaim, strengthen, and share their knowledge and rebuild communities.

AVF works to develop partnerships across sectors and issues while amplifying diverse voices, cultures, and talent to benefit everyone through the values of collaboration, equity and inclusion, innovation, insight, and integrity.

Conclusion

> Pulling from within / pulling from within
> My people I come to you
> Are you looking for ground squirrels?

Yup'ik elder Marie Meade learned *Caiyuguluk* from Chuna McIntyre, the Yupik culture bearer from Eek, who founded the dance troupe Numamta. According to Meade (as cited by Christianson 2012: 1), "the first line describes the muscular strength and internal discipline required to live off the land and provide for a village." It emphasizes how the intersection of sharing, understanding your responsibility to community may be manifested. She goes on to say that "the second line may be interpreted as a promise that the land will provide." We believe it further speaks towards the importance of knowledge about relationality and your role in the value of responsibility therein. She continues on to say that "the third line can be baffling – it places the smallest of land mammals as something to be sought after. Meade, when asked about the ground squirrel, said there are no small animals. "They're all big to me. They're all big and they're all important," she said. "The song is a prayer for survival and for sustenance and you rely on all that is available." Understanding nuances or what might not be apparent shows the importance of Elder wisdom; and the BSEG example shows how modern policy solutions can benefit from this knowledge. Yup'ik continue to rely on "all that is available" to meet the challenges of their present-day circumstances through building on their long-standing values in new ways. It is what provides strength in working as a collective in the best interests of communities today and for future generations.

Notes

1 Christianson, Scott (October 18, 2012). Anchorage Press Article on new CD. https://tribalfunk. wordpress.com/category/pamyua/
2 McCoy, Meredith, Emma Elliott-Groves, Leilani Sabzalian, Megan Bang. 2020. *Restoring Indigenous Systems of Relationality*. Liberty Illinois: Center for Humans and Nature. https://huma nsandnature.org/restoring-indigenous-systems-of-relationality/
3 Bering Sea Elders Group. 2011. The Northern Bering Sea: Our Way of Life. Available at https:// eloka-arctic.org/
4 Bering Sea Elders Group, Resolution Expressing Our Mission, November 3, 2011. https://bering seaelders.org/about-us/
5 M. Bahnke, V. Korthuis, A. Philemonoff, M. Johnson, Letter to "Navigating the New Arctic Program, National Science Foundation," March 19, 2020; https://kawerak.org/download/naviga ting-the-new-arctic-program-comment-letter/.
6 Dewey Kk'oḽeyo Putyuk Hoffman, Arctic Indigenous Fund Invests in Movement Making Across the Circumpolar North, March 2020. International Funders for Indigenous Peoples.

References

Ayunerak, P., Alstrom, D., Moses, C., Charlie , J. Sr., and Rasmus, S.M. 2014. "Yup'ik culture and context in Southwest Alaska: community member perspectives of tradition, social change, and prevention." *American Journal of Community Psychology* 54 (1–2): 91–99.

Aluska, Minnie, Rebecca Atchak, Esther Bourdon, Charlie Fitka, Jr., Megan Sigvanna Topkok, Morris Nashoanak, Sr. Arlene Waghiyi, Joseph Washington, Bernadette Yaayuk Alvanna-Stimpfle, Sylvester Ayek, Josephine Bourdon, Larry Kaplan, George Noongwook, John Waghiyi, Jr. 2022. *Four Language Glossary: Inupiaq, St. Lawrence Island Yupik, Yup'ik, and English Terms for research, science and policy*. Compiled and edited by Brenden Raymond-Yakoubian and Julie Raymond-Yakoubian. Nome, Alaska: Kawerak Inc.

Angarova, G. Daisee Francour and Lourdes Ingas. 2020. "Indigenizing philanthropy: Indigenous-led funds." *Cultural Survival Quarterly*March.

Bennett, N.J., Katz, L., Yadao-Evans, W., Ahmadia, G.N., Atkinson, S., Ban, N.C., Dawson, N.M., de Vos, A., Fitzpatrick, J., Gill, D., Imirizaldu, M., Lewis, N., Mangubhai, S., Meth, L., Muhl, E.-K., Obura, D., Spalding, A.K., Villagomez, A., Wagner, D., White, A., and Wilhelm, A. 2021. Advancing social equity in and through marine conservation. *Frontiers in Marine Science*, 8: 711538.

Bering Sea Elders Group. 2011. *The Northern Bering Sea: Our way of life*. Available at https://eloka -arctic.org/.

Daniel, Raychelle Aluaq, T. 'Aulani Wilhelm, HaleyCase-Scott, GretchenGoldman, and Larry Hinzman. 2022. *What is "Indigenous Knowledge" and Why Does it matter? Integrating ancestral wisdom and approaches into federal decision-making*. Office of Science and Technology, White House. Decemberhttps://www.whitehouse.gov/ostp/news-updates/2022/12/02/what-is-indigenous-knowledge-and-wh y-does-it-matter-integrating-ancestral-wisdom-and-approaches-into-federal-decision-making/.

Ellam Yua, J.Raymond-Yakoubian, R. Aluaq, Daniel, and C. Behe. 2022. "A framework for co-production of knowledge in the context of Arctic research." *Ecology and Society* 27 (1): 34.

Ellis, Erle C., Nicolas Gauthier, Kees Klein Goldewijk, Rebecca Bliege Bird, Nicole Boivin, Sandra Díaz, Dorian Q. Fuller, Jacquelyn L. Gill, Jed O. Kaplan, Naomi Kingston, Harvey Locke, Crystal N.H. McMichael, Darren Ranco, Torben C. Rick, M. Rebecca Shaw, Lucas Stephens, Jens-Christian Svenning, James E.M. Watson. 2021. People have shaped most of terrestrial nature for at least 12,000 years. *Proceedings of the National Academy of Sciences* 118 (17): 1–8.

Gadamus, Lily, Julie Raymond-Yakoubian, Roy Ashenfelter, Austin Ahmasuk, Vera Metcalf, GeorgeNoongwook. 2015. Building an Indigenous evidence-base for tribally-led habitat conservation policies. *Marine Policy* 62: 116–124.

Henshaw, A. 2013. Fostering resilience in a changing sea ice context: a grant maker's perspective. *Polar Geography* 36 (1–2): 126–141.

Huntington, Henry, Mark Carey, Charlene Apok, Bruce C. Forbes, Shari Fox, Lene K. Holm, Aitalina Ivanova, Jacob Jaypoody, George Noongwook, and Florian Stammler. 2019. Climate change in context: putting people first in the Arctic. *Regional Environmental Change* 19: 1217–1223.

Jacobson, Steven A. 1984. *Yup'ik Eskimo Dictionary*. Fairbanks: Alaska Native Language Center, University of Alaska.

John-Shields, A. 2018. *Tangerqengiaraucaraq (Being Present)*. Ph.D. Applied Linguistics, University of Alaska Fairbanks, August 2018.

Lincoln, Harry. 2016. Elders thank Obama for Bering Sea designation. *Anchorage Daily News*. December 11.

Kealiikanakaoleohailiani, K. and Giardina, C.P. 2016. Embracing the sacred: an Indigenous framework for tomorrow's sustainability science. *Sustainability Science* 11 (1): 57–67.

Metcalf, Vera. 2021. Nangaghneghput – our way of life. *Frontiers in Ecology and the Environment* 19 (8): 427.

Meyer, M., Goering, E., Hopkins, K., Hyde, C., Mattocks, N., and Denlinger, J. 2021. "Walking the talk in participatory philanthropy." *The Foundation Review*, 13 (2).

M'sɨt No'kmaq, Albert Marshall, Karen F. Beazley, Jessica Hum, shalan joudry, Anastasia Papadopoulos, Sherry Pictou, Janet Rabesca, Lisa Young, and Melanie Zurba. 2021. "Awakening the sleeping giant: re-Indigenization principles for transforming biodiversity conservation in Canada and beyond." *FACETS* 6: 839–869.

Scott-Enns, I. 2020. *Indigenous Ways of Giving + Sharing: Indigenous-led funds landscape scan report*. San Francisco: International Funders for Indigenous Peoples.

Whyte, Kyle. 2021. "Time as kinship." *The Cambridge Companion to Environmental Humanities*, edited by Jeffrey Cohen and Stephanie Foote. Cambridge: Cambridge University Press.

Wildcat, D.R. 2013. Introduction: climate change and Indigenous Peoples of the USA. *Climate Change* 120 (3): 509–515.

25

CULTURE AND HERITAGE IN CLIMATE CONVERSATIONS

Reflections on Connecting Culture, Heritage, and Climate Change

William P. Megarry, Hana Morel, Sarah Forgesson, and Eduardo S. Brondizio

Introduction

Cultural heritage is a key asset for climate change science, adaptation, and mitigation. It is also an enabler to building resilience and for climate action. There is an urgent and time-sensitive need to better realise this value within the wider climate science community. From traditional land and water management practices to sustainable low-carbon materials and transitions, cultural heritage remains largely absent from major climate change reportage and is an underutilised resource in climate understanding and action. In recent years there have been increased efforts from the heritage sector to engage more meaningfully with climate change. This has included studies into loss and damage and vulnerability under the heading of non-economic losses. However, the immense value of cultural heritage as a driver and resource for climate action remains under-appreciated. This is especially the case in assessment reports from the Intergovernmental Panel on Climate Change (IPCC), which summarise and synthesise the state-of-the-art in climate research to produce policy relevant but not policy prescriptive guidance for state parties and other actors.

This absence was the catalyst for the Connecting Culture, Heritage, and Climate Change project, a collaboration between the Intergovernmental Panel on Climate Change (IPCC), the International Council on Monuments and Sites (ICOMOS), and the United Nations Educational, Scientific, and Cultural Organization (UNESCO). This chapter explores efforts from researchers and practitioners in the cultural heritage sector to engage more meaningfully in this synthesis process; specifically, it will present the vision, methodology and reflections from the project, which brought together over 100 international researchers and practitioners from diverse knowledge systems (scientific, practitioner, Indigenous and local) to explore the contributions of culture and heritage to understanding and responding to climate change. It involved a series of activities including workshops, three White Papers, and the first International Co-sponsored Meeting on Culture, Heritage, and Climate Change (ICSM CHC), which together contributed targeted policy recommendations, and a global research and action agenda report.[1]

DOI: 10.4324/9781003242499-29

These outputs represent a convergence of disciplines and practices over a two-year process, which included collaborative and inclusive methods for the selection of participants, the selection and commissioning of a diverse group of White Paper authors, the delivery of discussion-based meetings and webinars, the creation of a private web portal to stimulate discussions, and the sharing of existing and emerging research aligned to the key project themes.[2] The effort highlighted the potential of heritage and cultural practices to act as a bridge between different ways of knowing, to embody inherited knowledge accumulated over generations, and to serve as entry points for climate action. Building such a bridge requires acknowledging, respecting, and implementing a plurality of knowledge systems inherent in culture, heritage, and creative practices. This includes reaching beyond established academic processes and outputs, which are often exclusionary, to explore place and people-centred experiences and approaches. After providing background, history, and developments to date, we conclude with an overview of selected key messages from an international meeting, which represented the culmination of the project and illustrated this inclusive approach.

The Need for a Broader Conversation on Culture, Heritage, and Climate Change

Conversations about climate change and heritage normally focus on impacts to iconic or well-known sites. This includes discussions about the risk to and vulnerability of both cultural and natural UNESCO World Heritage sites (for examples, see Perry 2011; Vousdoukas et al. 2022; Simpson et al. 2022). Conversely, the contributions of culture and heritage to understanding and responding to climate change have received less attention or are primarily noted due to their absence from discussions (ICOMOS 2019). Of particular concern is the paucity of reference to culture, heritage, and non-scientific knowledge systems in global (ex. IPCC) and/or national climate change assessments (Morel 2018), which provide periodic summaries of the state-of-the-art on biophysical, social, and policy dimensions of climate change. Gaps in these reports reflect the unequal global distribution of and funding towards published research, technical reports, and policy responses. This inequality is further exacerbated by the exclusion of "grey literature" and other forms of knowledge, which contributes to further pushing diverse knowledge systems, intrinsic to culture and heritage, to the margins of the conversation (Schlingmann et al. 2021; Simpson et al. 2022). Exclusion from such conversations further distances already marginalised yet diverse actors and communities from decision-making and climate change planning and action. Awareness of these gaps have further contributed to growing calls for international attention to culture, heritage, and climate change. For example, in 2016, at its 40th session (Istanbul/UNESCO 2016), the UNESCO World Heritage Committee recommended greater collaboration and engagement from heritage organisations with other organisations working on climate change, in particular the UNFCCC and IPCC, to respond to the threats from climate change on World Heritage properties.

A proposal for a co-sponsored effort to address culture and heritage knowledge and action gaps in global climate science and climate change thinking, and to advance the contributions of culture and heritage to climate change mitigation and adaptation, was initially presented by ICOMOS to the IPCC Working Group chairs in June 2020. This had three overarching goals:

1. Take stock of the state of knowledge regarding connections of culture and heritage with anthropogenic climate change.
2. Establish a baseline of reference regarding the nature, depth of, and gaps in knowledge regarding these connections.
3. Build new conversations and collaborations between the broad fields of culture, heritage, and climate change that will support future research and action in climate science, adaptation, and mitigation.

These themes and their interdependencies can be visually represented by Figure 25.1:

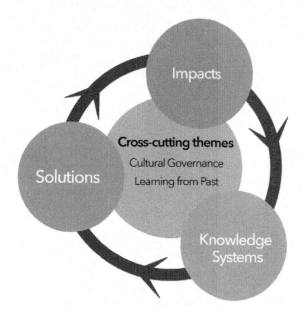

FIGURE 25.1 Themes and objectives guiding a joint effort on culture, heritage, and climate change (figure by the authors).

Two cross-cutting themes were also included in the original concept. On the one hand, the role of heritage governance and the capacity to learn from the past, and, on the other hand, the exploration of relevant concerns such as ownership, the management and framing of heritage, and ways of overcoming nature–culture dualism. This proposal was accepted and then endorsed by the IPCC Executive Committee. In July 2020, UNESCO confirmed their involvement as co-sponsors while the International Union for the Conservation of Nature (IUCN) and Local Governments for Sustainability (ICLEI) joined the project as partners. The management of the project was led by ICOMOS.[2]

Participation and Inclusion to Expand the Conversation

The need to expand the conversation on culture, heritage, and climate change, herein CHC, became apparent during the process reported here. An international call for participation in the CHC effort drew more than 300 nominations from a wide range of backgrounds and expertise.[3] The disciplinary, geographical, and gender distribution of contributors encapsulates the multi-dimensional nature of the topic (Figure 25.2) and brought an enriched perspective and regional experiences to the conversation. The entire project process was designed to maximise opportunities for inclusion and discussion through regular communication and included webinars and a project website which facilitated further sharing. Nevertheless, there remained major gaps in representation from Latin America, Africa, Eastern Europe, and Southeast Asia.

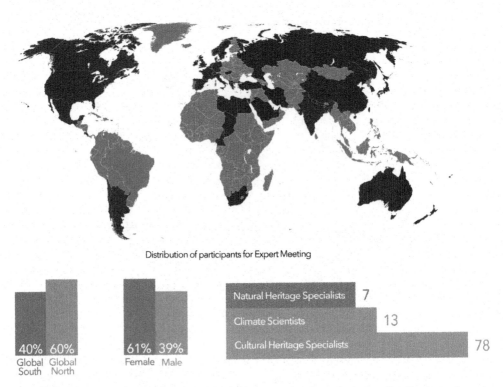

FIGURE 25.2 Infographic showing disciplinary, geographical, and gender distribution of participants (figure by the authors).

The CHC process is outlined in Figure 25.3 below. Each decision of the project, including delivery of activities and outcomes, was discussed in depth with the co-sponsor chairs and the Scientific Steering Committee. At later stages, participants also played a critical role in the direction of the themes and messaging advocated more widely in subsequent reports and recommendations. The project followed a meticulous and time-consuming reflexive process, which helped revisit and relearn language, concepts and approaches that might implicitly be exclusionary, insensitive, or socio-politically loaded. One such term changed throughout the project was "integration of knowledge systems," which overlooks questions of ownership and governance across communities. This term was revised to "collaboration" to allow joint efforts without loss of autonomy (Orlove et al. 2022).

Key project themes are presented in Table 25.1 below, which also includes additional topics to frame conversations that were inspired by the White Papers. These three White Papers explored the three key overarching questions (themes) and cross-cutting issues:

Thematic Development	White Papers	Webinars and Website	International Meeting	Research and Recommendations
Developed in the application phase and presented to the IPCC, **three overarching questions** and **two cross-cutting issues** formed the thematic foundation for the Project.	Commissioned from groups of international experts from a wide range of backgrounds, **White Papers** explored the three key themes in preparation for future discussions and the international meeting.	Held in advance of the meeting, **Webinars** created a space for White Paper authors to receive feedback from meeting participants while the **Website** facilitated discussion, sharing work and helped to build community	Over 100 participants from a diverse range of backgrounds joined an **International Meeting** to discuss Project themes and questions, building on themes from the White Papers and discussions from the Website	Built from projects discussions and identified knowledge and action gaps, **key messages and recommendations** were published to stimulate awareness and further action on CHC.

Regular and ongoing communications between SSC and CHC meeting participants

FIGURE 25.3 Key steps in the project (figure by the authors).

TABLE 25.1 Key themes and topics guiding the CHC project.

Theme	*Systemic connections of culture, heritage, and climate change*	*Loss, damage, and adaptation for culture and heritage*	*Culture and heritage in transformative change and alternative sustainable futures*
Topic 1	Knowledge systems, power, and interpretation of climate change	Collective understanding of uncertainty	Climate justice
Topic 2	New conditions, new knowledge	Identifying common factors for vulnerability and resilience	Impacts and capacity building
Topic 3	Challenges and opportunities of integrating knowledge systems	Impacts, power, and interpretations of climate change	The power of heritage in climate thinking

Intangible cultural heritage, diverse knowledge systems and climate change (Orlove et al. 2022); Impacts, vulnerability, and understanding risks of climate change for culture and heritage (Simpson et al. 2022); The role of cultural and natural heritage for climate action (Shepherd et al. 2022). The White Papers were used to guide and inform readers about the complex issues and concerns raised from their focus, tease out provocations on each theme, and act as providers of focal points. They also took stock of the existing state of knowledge regarding connections of culture and heritage with anthropogenic climate change and created a baseline reference to assess the nature, depth, and gaps in the existing understanding of CHC.

An inclusive framing was critical for CHC conversations to be successful, ensuring "holistic and inclusive understanding of culture, heritage, and climate change" and including as equally valuable "voices representing diverse knowledge systems and practical experiences" (Morel et al. 2022). For example, the development of the White Papers involved co-chairs, the Scientific Steering Committee, and participants at all stages via webinars, authors' workshops, and peer review drafts before completion. A dedicated public and private-facing website, with an embedded networking/chat function and file upload capacity, was created and open to all participants to support collaboration proactively. The public-facing page hosted three separate panel discussions open to all members of the public, and provided project information, and relevant links to project outcomes. In the restricted-access pages, participants have access to participant biographies, were able to share resources and have access to those who shared posters and videos based on their work. This process led to the identification of case studies from around the world and across disciplines. As such, the webpage served two purposes: firstly, it helped to share resources in a consistent way and build a sense of community prior to a final five-day meeting; secondly, it acted as a repository for key resources and project memory of discussions. The meeting itself was again based on a collaborative and "all voices equal" approach: over five days, 15 sessions were hosted in which each participant was given a series of talking points and provocations to discuss with other participants in break-out rooms. Intentionally, there were no designated presentations, talks, nor chairs. Each group was left to discuss as loosely or in-depth as they liked over the course of 1 hour; all discussions were recorded.

Building Capacity Through Meaningful Recognition and Validation Across Knowledge Systems and Experiences

As valuable as the project's high-impact outcomes, the inclusive and participatory approach and inclusion of diverse voices in its design, planning, delivery, and outputs provided important lessons for future engagements and transdisciplinary collaborations. While this type of engagement may be familiar to those who have long worked across communities in a meaningful and respectful way, such approaches are still developing in international efforts around climate change. This collaborative process led to the development of 43 key messages, 13 case studies and action items outlined in detail in the Global Research and Action Agenda on Culture, Heritage and Climate Change (GRAA) (Morel et al. 2022). Below, we highlight key research themes from the project and two areas where action could help enhance collaboration and problem-oriented research and action bridging culture, heritage, and climate change.

Underlying Issues in Culture, Heritage, and Climate Change

Themes outlined in Table 25.1 were informed, developed, and addressed throughout the project and are reflected in outcomes from both the IPCC recommendations and as key messages in the GRAA, which were targeted at a broad range of readers from heritage and climate science. Specific examples illustrated the need for scientists and researchers in the social and natural sciences to proactively work with Indigenous Peoples and local communities. These engagements should be grounded, at all stages, in co-production approaches that acknowledge the equal value of place-based knowledge and practices to scientific approaches. This is a difficult and challenging enterprise that requires rethinking collaborations at different stages of the research process from project conception to the diffusion of project outputs. These collaborations should start with the premise that each makes valuable contributions to addressing climate change and emerging problems. These problems may include better place-based understandings of loss and damage, culture, and heritage-informed adaptation strategies or mitigation strategies; specifically, the role of

Indigenous knowledge and local knowledge in sustainable ecosystem management. Crucially, collaborations must focus on both promoting synergies but also identifying and negotiating trade-offs.

Other recommendations included supporting efforts for aligning different research methodologies including forms of monitoring, observing, and interpreting data. Engagement between disciplines and between knowledge systems should not include the assimilation of one into another but an equitable collaboration based on mutual respect where the value of all approaches are respected and acknowledged. There is a need to acknowledge that robust evidence regarding climate change impact and responses to these come in different forms and are complementary in deliberative processes surrounding climate action decision-making.

While Progress is Apparent, Continuing Efforts are Needed for Working Together Across Disciplines and Knowledge Systems

Although there is broader recognition that culture and heritage play an indispensable role as enablers of transformative climate action and climate-resilient sustainable development, knowledge gaps remain significant across sectors and regions. These gaps are particularly acute when it comes to national, sub-national, and local decision-makers and/or researchers from established institutions recognising local and Indigenous knowledge systems as valuable contributions to understanding and addressing climate change. Systemic problems continue to reinforce inequalities and inequities, reflected in a lack of sufficient collaborative research based on ethical co-design and co-production. The CHC project stresses the need for clear guidelines to increase ethical collaboration across holders or communities of diverse knowledge systems, with a focus on ensuring that data and resources are not appropriated or represented without consent, but also that the collaboration benefits all parties. By empowering and funding local and Indigenous knowledge holders to devise and direct research projects and lead in dissemination activities, the cultural heritage sector can contribute to and address existing gaps in future reportage. This should be complemented by clear guidelines to research, policy, and practice organisations to increase ethical engagement across diverse knowledge systems, including the inclusion of alternate outputs including narration and storytelling as forms of evidence.

Those working to produce, synthesise and disseminate knowledge must make efforts to move beyond existing biases and prejudices, including specific and limited interpretations of what can be used as evidence. For example, many traditional communities have long observed and monitored natural cycles and interconnections across habitats that may be invaluable for understanding significant changes due to anthropogenic climate change (Brondizio et al. 2021). Thus, guidelines are of particular importance to bridge the existing gap between communities (scientific/research, local, Indigenous Peoples) engaged in climate action and other organisations, such as public bodies and institutions responsible for synthesising research, setting agendas and funding opportunities, and making policy-based decisions. Knowledge can be coded and shared in different ways and so these guidelines must support and recognise diverse forms of evidence as equally valuable and robust, including oral histories, narration, and storytelling passed down through various forms of tangible and intangible culture and heritage.

The Need to Embed the Heritage Sector into Climate Change Decision-Making

Culture and heritage are too often overlooked, and unrecognised, in climate change decision-making and planning. Cultural heritage has much to contribute to existing and emerging climate change conversations, including the use and reconstruction of past dynamics such as land and sea-scape management, the use of local materials and traditional skills and knowledge in the built environment, ways of life and acute understandings of ecosystems, and patterns relating to the long-term history of consumption and production (McElwee et al. 2020). Yet, those involved with the culture and heritage sector rarely are included or involved in climate change planning and significant decisions. This is particularly the case with local communities and Indigenous Peoples whose own life experiences, observations, monitoring, and assessments are discounted as irrelevant or excluded from dominant systems in place that enforce scientific reporting standards. Cultural knowledge and heritage are powerful assets for those engaged in climate action and cultural practitioners need a seat at that table. Key to this is engaging in transdisciplinary research and activities with diverse partners, working across sectors to engage with key climate and global issues including sustainability, adaptation planning, biodiversity, and mitigation strategies. This might include addressing topics like migration and mobility, agriculture, or retrofitting historic buildings. These engagements will yield benefits but they will also involve trade-offs. For example, tensions can exist between carbon mitigation strategies and landscape preservation or between adaptation planning, infrastructure building, and conservation. While undoubtedly challenging, these tensions should not become roadblocks for potentially transformative collaborations.

Final Remarks

The preceding action areas cannot be addressed without a fundamental rethink of how climate adaptation and mitigation research is funded. Those involved in the CHC process described here noted that existing funding systems perpetuate traditional inequalities by prioritising approaches and solutions to climate change driven by the agenda of wealthier countries and interest groups. Reforming this dynamic will involve devising new funding models to progressively reverse the current geographical biases in research leadership and agendas while also promoting academic partnership with non-academic stakeholders of diverse backgrounds.

The CHC project put forward a process for engaging and working across knowledge systems and disciplines for climate action, which can be further developed and refined. In fact, several of the key messages and action areas identified are intended to promote the continuation of this dynamic. It must be inclusive, respectful, and equitable drawing from a far wider range of knowledge than currently utilised and respecting an equal plurality of scientific, local, and Indigenous knowledge systems. This will not always be simple or straightforward. All parties must not only embrace synergies but accept that trade-offs are inevitable and be willing to compromise. This will bring more people to the table and add much needed diversity to decision-making processes. Central to this is the message that culture is not only valuable in climate action but is an essential and long overlooked component to engaging in impactful climate action.

Notes

1 For more information about the international meeting and access to the report and three White Papers, please see: https://www.cultureclimatemeeting.org
2 The development of the project's core concept and proposal was led by a Project Manager and Scientific Coordinator. A Scientific Steering Committee (SSC) was composed of experts from culture, cultural heritage, biodiversity, natural heritage, climate science, and cities and was charged with supporting the organisation of the Co-Sponsored Meeting. This included the selection of participants, the reviewing of documents and papers prepared for the meeting, chairing meeting sessions and authoring meeting outputs and recommendations. The SSC was led by three co-chairs from ICOMOS, UNESCO, and the IPCC.
3 Nominations were requested from SSC members and their organisations, IPCC national focal points via the IPCC Secretariat and UNESCO member states.

Acknowledgements

This project was possible with contributions from additional members of the project not included here as authors. We would like to thank the following: Organising Committee (Andrew Potts, Marie-Laure Lavenir, Angelique Ploteau (ICOMOS); Dorine Dubois, Maria Gropa, Sara García de Ugarte (UNESCO); and Melinda Tignor (IPCC)); the ICSM Co-Chairs (Debra Roberts, IPCC; Metchild Rössler, UNESCO (07/2019–08/2021); Jyoti Hosagrahar, UNESCO; Marcy Rockman (ICOMOS Co-Chair, Scientific Coordinator (07/2019–08/2021)); the Scientific Steering Committee (Yunus Arikan, May Cassar, Jyoti Hosagrahar, Rohit Jigyasu, Valérie Masson-Delmotte, Greg Flato, Hindou Oumarous Ibrahim, Hans-O. Poertner, Debra Roberts, Sandeep Sengupta, Pasang Dolma Sherpa, Richard Veillon). We would also like to thank the lead authors and contributing authors of all three White Papers.

This project was funded by the Deutsche Bundesstiftung Umwelt (DBU) with additional support from Schweizerische Eidgenossenschaft and China Cultural Heritage. Special thanks are due to Constanze Fuhrmann and Oliver Martin in this capacity.

References

Brondizio, Eduardo S., Yildiz Aumeeruddy-Thomas, Peter Bates, Joji Carino, Álvaro Fernández-Llamazares, Maurizio Farhan Ferrari, Kathleen Galvin, Victoria Reyes-García, Pamela McElwee, Zsolt Molnár, Aibek Samakov, Uttam Babu Shrestha. 2021. Locally based, regionally manifested, and globally relevant: Indigenous and local knowledge, values, and practices for nature. *Annual Review of Environment and Resources* 46: 481–509.
ICOMOS Climate Change and Cultural Heritage Working Group. 2019. *The Future of Our Pasts: Engaging cultural heritage in climate action Outline of Climate Change and Cultural Heritage.* Technical Report. International Council on Monuments and Sites – ICOMOS: ICOMOS Paris.
McElwee, Pamela, Álvaro Fernández-Llamazares, Yildiz Aumeeruddy-Thomas, Dániel Babai, Peter Bates, Kathleen Galvin, Maximilien Guèze, Jianguo Liu, Zsolt Molnár, Hien T. Ngo, Victoria Reyes-García, Rinku Roy Chowdhury, Aibek Samakov, Uttam Babu Shrestha, Sandra Díaz, Eduardo S. Brondizio. 2020. Integrating Indigenous and local knowledge (ILK) into large-scale ecological assessments: the experience of the IPBES global assessment. *Journal of Applied Ecology* 57 (9): 1666–1676.
Morel, Hana. 2018. *Exploring Heritage in IPCC Documents.* Available at: https://heritage-research. org/app/uploads/2018/11/Exploring-Heritage-in-IPPC-Documents-2018.pdf Accessed in March 2023.
Morel, Hana, William Megarry, Andrew Potts, Jyoti Hosagrahar, Debra Roberts, Yunus Arikan, Eduardo Brondizio, et al. 2022. *Global Research and Action Agenda on Culture, Heritage and*

Climate Change. Charenton-le-Pont, France and Paris, France: ICOMOS & ISCM CHC. https://openarchive.icomos.org/id/eprint/2716/.

Orlove, Ben, Neil Dawson, Pasang Sherpa, Ibidun Adelekan, Wilfredo Alangui, RosarioCarmona, Deborah Coen, et al. 2022. *ICSM CHC White Paper I: Intangible cultural heritage, diverse knowledge systems and climate change. Contribution of Knowledge Systems Group I to the International Co-Sponsored Meeting on Culture, Heritage and Climate Change.* Charenton-le-Pont, France and Paris, France: ICOMOS & ISCM CHC. https://openarchive.icomos.org/id/eprint/2717/.

Perry, J. 2011. World Heritage hot spots: a global model identifies the 16 natural heritage properties on the World Heritage List most at risk from climate change. *International Journal of Heritage Studies* 17(5): 426–441.

Schlingmann, Anna, Sonia Graham, Petra Benyei, Esteve Corbera, Irene Martinez Sanesteban, Andrea Marelle, Ramin Soleymani-Fard, Victoria Reyes-García. 2021. Global patterns of adaptation to climate change by Indigenous Peoples and local communities. a systematic review. *Current Opinion in Environmental Sustainability* 51: 55–64. https://doi.org/DOI:10.1016/j.cosust.2021.03.002

Shepherd, Nick, Joshua Benjamin Cohen, William Carmen, Moses Chundu, Christian Ernsten, Oscar Guevara, Franziska Haas, et al. 2022. *ICSM CHC White Paper III: The role of cultural and natural heritage for climate action: Contribution of Impacts Group III to the International Co-Sponsored Meeting on Culture, Heritage and Climate Change.* Charenton-le-Pont, France and Paris, France: ICOMOS & ISCM CHC. https://openarchive.icomos.org/id/eprint/2719/.

Simpson, Nicholas P., Scott Allan Orr, Salma Sabour, Joanne Clarke, Maya Ishizawa, R. Michael Feener, Christopher Ballard, et al. 2022. *ICSM CHC White Paper II: Impacts, vulnerability, and understanding risks of climate change for culture and heritage: contribution of Impacts Group II to the International Co-Sponsored Meeting on Culture, Heritage and Climate Change.* Charenton-le-Pont, France and Paris, France: ICOMOS & ISCM CHC. https://openarchive.icomos.org/id/eprint/2718/.

Vousdoukas, M.I., Clarke, J., Ranasinghe, R., Reimann, L., Khalaf, N., Duong, T.M., Ouweneel, B., Sabour, S., Iles, C.E., Trisos, C.H. and Feyen, L. 2022. African heritage sites threatened as sea-level rise accelerates. *Nature Climate Change* 12(3): 256–262.

EPILOGUE

Susan A. Crate and Mark Nuttall

Climate change forces us to recognize and acknowledge how human activity has transformed and shaped the Earth. However, it is not as simple as a cause and an effect. The complexity of how a warming atmosphere comes into our planetary system, with all its multiple atmospheric, hydrological, chemical, and biological interactions, feedback loops, ripple effects, and thresholds can overwhelm even the most seasoned scientist. Most of us now experience the effects climate change is having – especially as they may be evident in extreme weather events – in real time and in a known place. As Jessica O'Reilly and colleagues write, while the climate change crisis is existentially urgent, it is also a conceptually abstract problem that "stretches the bounds of knowable facts, yet it is grounded in the material realities of melting ice, burning forests, and people fleeing rising seas" (O'Reilly et al. 2020: 14). Getting a grip on the reality of climate change requires us to ponder the nature of human social and economic life, to reflect deeply on how we live on, act towards, and engage with the Earth, and think about not just our future on the planet but also the future of all beings we share the Earth with.

Anthropologists have critical roles to play in understanding such transformations, their impacts, how we respond, how we engage in worldmaking practices, and how we imagine ourselves in the future. Furthermore, because humans drive climate change, anthropology has to do double duty by going deeper in analyzing the forces that compel over-consumption, affluence, technological myopia and the many forms of discrimination and inequality. Climate change and human influences on the biosphere challenge the theoretical and methodological assumptions of anthropological practice and the ethnographic settings and field sites in which anthropologists carry out their research. However the exigency of the climate crisis leaves little time to ponder our approach and quickens our attention towards urgent action.

For more than a decade, especially in the years leading up to IPCC Fifth Assessment Report in 2014, which was key to the deliberations which led to the Paris Agreement, the scientific evidence that humans have been altering the Earth's climate appeared irrefutable. However, scientists restrained their concern about the dramatic nature of change due to both the uncertainty in climate models and the cautious nature of scientific assessment overall, as well as the expectation that scientists should offer policy relevant but

DOI: 10.4324/9781003242499-30

not policy prescriptive statements. We both know this from our own participation in climate assessments. But scientific studies – and regional and global assessments – have continued to point out that the world's climate is not only changing, evidenced in the increasing prevalence of extreme weather events globally, and environmental disasters such as the devastating and seemingly relentless wildfires in Canada, the United States, and several southern European countries in 2023, but that climate systems and some ecosystems are approaching thresholds and tipping points of irreversible change. More recent IPCC reports assert with higher confidence, and greater certainty, that human-induced greenhouse gas emissions have caused the global warming our planet is experiencing. The historic global agreement in Paris in 2015 to reduce carbon emissions was hailed as a breakthrough for climate policy. Yet, many scientists and climate activists consider that it is too little too late and describe climate change as an existential crisis that requires us not only to understand the relationship between society and nature, but to rethink it.

The narrative of tipping points describes an uncertain future characterized by dramatic environmental and societal shifts with their multiple and far-reaching impacts (Lenton 2011). Furthermore, theorists of the planetary boundaries framework have argued that climate change and biosphere integrity – two core boundaries – have the potential to drive the Earth system into a new state if they are persistently, substantially, and significantly transgressed (Steffen et al. 2015). Imagining a dystopian future when sea-level rise has made cities like Kolkata, Bangkok, and New York uninhabitable, Amitav Ghosh has written that people will look back on our current era and possibly regard it as the time of the Great Derangement, when people failed to recognize the realities of their plight (Ghosh 2016). The politics of climate change may be preoccupied with mitigation and adaptation and on reducing greenhouse gas emissions, but as a statement by the American Anthropological Association (AAA) has put it, "focusing solely on reducing carbon emissions will not be sufficient to address climate change. That approach will not address the systemic causes. Climate change is rooted in social institutions and cultural habits. Real solutions will require knowledge and insight from the social sciences and humanities, not only from the natural sciences. Climate change is not a natural problem, it is a human problem." This statement on "Humanity and Climate Change" was based on the final report produced by the AAA Global Climate Change Task Force (Fiske et al. 2014).

Almost ten years later, the IPCC's AR6 synthesis report has re-stated that the urgency of the climate crisis requires us to negotiate and implement policy solutions and develop technologies for adaptation and mitigation and renewable energy. This makes demands on us for societal and cultural transformations, and to question economic systems, so that we can deal with the effects and the consequences, and forge ways of living sustainably within the limits of planetary boundaries. We restate the words of Anita Girvan, which we quoted in the Introduction to this volume: "climate change challenges us to imagine the worlds we would like to inhabit through creative forward thinking" (Girvan 2017: 1052). Ghosh draws attention to how we must think about, and confront the unthinkable. The problem, as he puts it succinctly, is that

> one of the reasons why climate change is a "wicked" problem as opposed to a "normal" problem is that the time horizon in which effective action can be taken is very narrow: every year that passes without a drastic reduction in global emissions makes catastrophe more certain.
>
> *(ibid.: 160)*

One important shift in both climate policy discussions and in climate science that has been more noticeable over the last few years is a move away from thinking only about adaptation and mitigation and to imagining ways for climate restoration. This is often framed in the language of techno-fixes as answers to how global emissions can be reduced. This is not to say that adaptation and mitigation have been abandoned as "solutions," but to point to how technical modification and manipulation is increasingly spoken about as a way to "restore" ecosystems damaged by climate change as well as to protect planetary boundaries. One example that is proposed is restoring the reflectivity of Arctic sea ice (Field et al. 2018). Arctic sea ice cover is diminishing at an accelerated rate and the loss of ice increases radiative forcing and contributes to global warming. There has been serious investment in laboratory and field-based experimentation to enable scientists to model and assess the prospects of techniques that could increase multiyear ice. Suggestions for how this would happen involve, for example, the utilization of floating materials, ranging from granular powders and glass microspheres. But is this form of geoengineering a way forward? Or does it just miss the point about dealing with the systemic issues that have led to the loss of sea ice in the first place?

In reflecting on how we may want to rethink our relationships with the environment and the non-human entities that constitute it, Utah-based writer Terry Tempest Williams draws attention to the gradual disappearance of Great Salt Lake, an ecological catastrophe many people cannot grasp. It is, she says, "a chronicle of death foretold." The demise of Great Salt Lake began with the diversion of water for agricultural, industrial, and municipal use. It continued with the contamination of the remaining waters with agricultural runoff, industrial waste and other issues that have rendered a host of toxic pollutants in the lake's sediment to include arsenic, cadmium, mercury, nickel, chromium, lead, and organic contaminants. These not only poison what life is left that depends upon the lake but, as it shrinks, the dust from the dried lake areas that have emerged from where there was once water creates toxic clouds threatening animals, plants, and humans in their path. Williams calls for the renunciation of the overexploitation of the lake and a reassessment of humans' relationship to her:

> If we can shift our view of Great Salt Lake from a lake to be avoided to a lake we cherish; from a body of wasted water to an ancient body of wisdom; not to exploit, dam, and dike, but to honor and respect as a sovereign body, our relationship and actions toward the lake will be transformative.
>
> *(Williams 2023)*

We are also at the point in this existential crisis where, then, to paraphrase Holly Buck (2019), we need we consider the kind of future we do *not* want. She says that a future that perhaps we don't want to be in is one which has been shaped by solar geoengineering as a solution to climate change that has made no difference in terms of systemic change. Buck suggests that while "it sounds like complete lunacy to intentionally mess with something as fundamental as incoming solar radiation" (ibid.: 3), it is not a "straightforwardly irrational idea" and becomes normalized:

> because human activity is already messing with the balance of radiation through both greenhouse gas emissions (warming) and emitting particulate matter from industry

and vehicles (cooling), it doesn't sound as absurd to entertain the idea that another tweak might not be that significant – especially if the counterfactual scenario is extreme climate suffering.

(ibid.: 4)

The question is, she asks,

are we at the point – let's call it "the shift" – where it is worth talking about more radical or extreme measures – such as removing carbon from the atmosphere, leaving oil in the ground, social and cultural change, radical adaptation, or even solar geoengineering?

(ibid.)

What kinds of interventions, manipulations, and worldmaking practices become essential, then for the envisioning of desirable futures?

Anthropology has long had a concern with understanding practices of weather modification in different social and cultural settings. Rainmaking practices, for example, are evident in a number of societies and often involve ritual intervention that are based upon a culture's specific worldview and cosmology. On a larger scale, though, state-sponsored attempts to influence precipitation processes through technical intervention have a shorter history but a relatively long lineage. One example is cloud seeding, a technique whereby dry ice and iodide are introduced into moist clouds of relatively low temperature. Although cloud seeding is considered positively, being used to increase or alter precipitation in periods of drought and floods respectively, to disperse fog at airports and to weaken hurricanes or change their direction, its use remains controversial. For instance, the US military used cloud seeding during the Vietnam war – Operation Popeye, as it was known, which attempted to increase rainfall to slow Vietnamese military truck movements.

However, geoengineering involves a range of initiatives that aim at the deliberate large-scale manipulation of the planetary environment, such as the alteration of planetary albedo, the reduction of ocean acidification, or the management of carbon (Keith 2000). And, as the above example shows, the restoration of sea ice. These represent considerable differences in scale and provoke controversies and debates about the social and political acceptability, as well as the moral, inequitable, and violent dimensions, of altering the weather and even re-setting the climate, or controlling it as we would use a thermostat in a building.

Our volume, as the two volumes before it, strives to showcase the range of tools and approaches that anthropology can offer to contribute to the amelioration of the existential climate crisis. As with adaptive capacity and resilience, worldmaking depends on the strength of culture, of human–environment relations, cohesiveness of community, identity, and of strong social relationships. Worldmaking is also about decision-making processes at various levels and scales – from the ways individuals, households, and communities think about, devise, select, and enact adaptive responses to climate change, to the broader international processes and institutional contexts that shape those local decisions. We recognize, however, based upon our training in understanding human nature and cultural differences, that there are as many responses to be made as there are communities within cultures on the planet. The experience of climate change, the exposure to its negative impacts or the abilities of communities to seize the opportunities it may bring, depends on where people are socially, culturally, economically, and geographically but also on how they are positioned in terms of institutional, political and legal contexts.

This is not about a colonial academic exercise where the experts come in to save the day and decide what is best for those on the ground. It is a call to meet communities where they are, to allow their full participation and leadership to forge a way forward and to make a world that works for them into a future that they choose. It is about facilitating change that engages all relevant rightsholders, knowledge systems, and disciplinary approaches. But we must also take responsibility for perpetuating anthropological tools and methods for investigating and countering the human drivers of climate change. As George Monbiot (2017) explains, those of us in western consumption societies have been seduced by individualism and competition to the extent that we have lost our true capacities for altruism and reciprocity. We need to identify and recognize these and other systemic reasons for the climate crisis we are facing. Monbiot urges us to develop a "politics of belonging" which will bring us back to our origins as social animals who share, care, and are stewards to each other and all beings. This is the same view urged by Terry Tempest Williams in her plea for reassessing our relationships to the places around us and in which we dwell. And it is in the same spirit that we put forth this work of multiple and diverse academic and practitioner anthropologists to contribute towards the global efforts of transformation and worldmaking.

References

Buck, Holly Jean. 2019. *After Engineering: Climate tragedy, repair, and restoration.* London: Verso Books.

Field, L., D. Ivanova, S. Bhattacharyya, V. Mlaker, A. Scholz, R. Decca, A. Manzara, D. Johnson, E. Christodoulu, P. Walter, and K. Katuri. 2018. "Increasing sea ice albedo using localized reversible geoengineering." *Earth's Future* 6 (6): 882–901.

Fiske, S.J., S.A. Crate, C.L. Crumley, K. Galvin, H. Lazrus, L. Lucero, A. Oliver-Smith, B. Orlove, S. Strauss, and R. Wilk. 2014. *Changing the Atmosphere. Anthropology and climate change.* Final report of the AAA Global Climate Change Task Force, December 2014. Arlington, VA: American Anthropological Association.

Ghosh, Amitav. 2016. *The Great Derangement: Climate change and the unimaginable.* Chicago: Chicago University Press.

Girvan, Anita. 2017. "Trickster carbon: stories, science, and postcolonial interventions for climate justice." *Journal of Political Ecology* 24 (1): 1038–1054.

Keith, David. W. 2000. "Geoengineering the climate: history and prospect." *Annual Review of Energy and the Environment* 25: 245–284.

Lenton, Timothy M. 2011. "Early warning of climate tipping points." *Nature Climate Change* 1 (4): 201–209.

Monbiot, George. 2017. *Out of the Wreckage: A new politics for an age of crisis.* London: Verso Books.

O'Reilly, Jessica, Cindy Isenhour, Pamela McElwee and Ben Orlove. 2020. "Climate change: expanding anthropological possibilities." *Annual Review of Anthropology* 49: 13–29.

Steffen, W., K. Richardson, J. Rockström, S.E. Cornell, I. Fetzer, E.M. Bennett, R. Biggs, S.R. Carpenter, W. De Vries, C.A. De Wit, and C. Folke. 2015. "Planetary boundaries: guiding human development on a changing planet." *Science* 347 (6223): 1259855.

Williams, Terry Tempest. 2023. "I am haunted at what I have seen at Great Salt Lake." Opinion piece, with photographs by Fazal Sheikh. *New York Times*, March 25, 2023. https://www.nytimes.com/2023/03/25/opinion/great-salt-lake-drought-utah-climate-change.html?searchResultPosition=1.

INDEX

Please note that page references to Figures will be in **bold**, while references to Tables are in *italics*. Footnotes will be denoted by the letter 'n' and Note number following the page number.

Taylor & Francis Group
an **informa** business

Taylor & Francis eBooks

www.taylorfrancis.com

A single destination for eBooks from Taylor & Francis
with increased functionality and an improved user
experience to meet the needs of our customers.

90,000+ eBooks of award-winning academic content in
Humanities, Social Science, Science, Technology, Engineering,
and Medical written by a global network of editors and authors.

TAYLOR & FRANCIS EBOOKS OFFERS:

A streamlined
experience for
our library
customers

A single point
of discovery
for all of our
eBook content

Improved
search and
discovery of
content at both
book and
chapter level

REQUEST A FREE TRIAL
support@taylorfrancis.com

 Routledge
Taylor & Francis Group

 CRC Press
Taylor & Francis Group